For Private Circulation only.

List of British Officers taken prisoner in the various Theatres of War between August, 1914, and November, 1918.

Compiled from Records kept by Messrs. COX & Co.'s Enquiry Office, at Harrington House, Craig's Court, Charing Cross, London, S.W. 1.

The Naval & Military Press Ltd

Published by

The Naval & Military Press Ltd
Unit 5 Riverside, Brambleside
Bellbrook Industrial Estate
Uckfield, East Sussex
TN22 1QQ England

Tel: +44 (0)1825 749494

www.naval-military-press.com
www.nmarchive.com

In reprinting in facsimile from the original, any imperfections are inevitably reproduced and the quality may fall short of modern type and cartographic standards.

CONTENTS.

	PAGE.
CONTENTS	3
PREFATORY NOTE	5
AEGEAN GROUP	187
ARGYLL AND SUTHERLAND HIGHLANDERS	112
ARMY CHAPLAINS DEPARTMENT	135
ARMY CYCLISTS CORPS	116
AUSTRALIAN FORCE	136
BALKAN FORCE	187
BEDFORDSHIRE REGIMENT	45
BLACK WATCH	73
BORDER REGIMENT	68
CAMBRIDGESHIRE REGIMENT	126
CAMERON HIGHLANDERS	107
CAMERONIANS (SCOTTISH RIFLES)	59
CANADIAN FORCE	138
CHESHIRE REGIMENT	54
COLDSTREAM GUARDS	18
CONNAUGHT RANGERS	111
DARDANELLES	178
DEVONSHIRE REGIMENT	36
DORSETSHIRE REGIMENT	71
DRAGOONS	8
DRAGOON GUARDS	8
DUKE OF CORNWALL'S LIGHT INFANTRY	66
DURHAM LIGHT INFANTRY	99
EAST AFRICA	189
EASTERN THEATRE OF WAR	178
EAST KENT REGIMENT (BUFFS)	22
EAST LANCASHIRE REGIMENT	63
EAST SURREY REGIMENT	65
EAST YORKSHIRE REGIMENT	43
ESSEX REGIMENT	75
GLOUCESTER REGIMENT	61
GRENADIER GUARDS	17
GORDON HIGHLANDERS	105
HAMPSHIRE REGIMENT	69
HEREFORDSHIRE REGIMENT	131
HERTFORDSHIRE REGIMENT	131
HIGHLAND LIGHT INFANTRY	103
HOUSEHOLD BATTALION	8
HOUSEHOLD BRIGADE (CAVALRY)	8
HUSSARS	9
INDIAN ARMY	143
IRISH GUARDS	18
KING EDWARD'S HORSE	9
KING'S LIVERPOOL REGIMENT	31
KING'S OWN ROYAL LANCASTER REGIMENT	23
KING'S OWN SCOTTISH BORDERERS	58
KING'S OWN YORKSHIRE LIGHT INFANTRY	85
KING'S ROYAL RIFLE CORPS	90
KING'S SHROPSHIRE LIGHT INFANTRY	86
KUT GARRISON	182
LANCASHIRE FUSILIERS	50
LANCERS	9
LEICESTERSHIRE REGIMENT	45
LEINSTER REGIMENT	112
LINCOLNSHIRE REGIMENT	35
LONDON REGIMENT	126
LOYAL NORTH LANCS.	79

	PAGE.
MACHINE GUN CORPS	116
MANCHESTER REGIMENT	94
MESOPOTAMIA	180
MIDDLESEX REGIMENT	87
MONMOUTHSHIRE REGIMENT	126
M.O.R.C.—U.S.A.	135
NEWFOUNDLAND REGIMENT	141
NEW ZEALAND FORCE	141
NORFOLK REGIMENT	34
NORTHAMPTONSHIRE REGIMENT	81
NORTH STAFFORDSHIRE REGIMENT	97
NORTHUMBERLAND FUSILIERS	24
OXFORDSHIRE AND BUCKINGHAMSHIRE LIGHT INFANTRY	75
PALESTINE	178
PERSIAN GULF	180
RIFLE BRIGADE	114
ROYAL AIR FORCE	146
ROYAL ARMY MEDICAL CORPS	131
ROYAL ARMY SERVICE CORPS	131
ROYAL BERKSHIRE REGIMENT	82
ROYAL DUBLIN FUSILIERS	113
ROYAL ENGINEERS	16
ROYAL FIELD ARTILLERY	10
ROYAL FUSILIERS	30
ROYAL GARRISON ARTILLERY	15
ROYAL GUERNSEY LIGHT INFANTRY	135
ROYAL INNISKILLEN FUSILIERS	59
ROYAL IRISH FUSILIERS	110
ROYAL IRISH REGIMENT	47
ROYAL IRISH RIFLES	108
ROYAL MUNSTER FUSILIERS	113
ROYAL NAVAL AIR SERVICE	176
ROYAL NAVAL DIVISION	143
ROYAL SCOTS	19
ROYAL SCOTS FUSILIERS	53
ROYAL SUSSEX REGIMENT	69
ROYAL WARWICKSHIRE REGIMENT	28
ROYAL WELSH FUSILIERS	56
ROYAL WEST KENT REGIMENT	83
ROYAL WEST SURREY REGIMENT (QUEEN'S)	21
SCOTS GUARDS	18
SEAFORTH HIGHLANDERS	104
SHERWOOD FORESTERS (NOTTS AND DERBY)	77
SOMERSET LIGHT INFANTRY	38
SOUTH AFRICAN FORCE	141
SOUTH LANCASHIRE REGIMENT	71
SOUTH STAFFORDSHIRE REGIMENT	70
SOUTH WALES BORDERERS	57
STAFF	7
SUFFOLK REGIMENT	37
TANK CORPS	124
WELSH REGIMENT	72
WEST AFRICAN FORCE	189
WEST RIDING REGIMENT (DUKE OF WELLINGTON'S)	67
WEST YORKSHIRE REGIMENT	39
WILTSHIRE REGIMENT	93
WORCESTERSHIRE REGIMENT	62
YEOMANRY	10
YORKSHIRE REGIMENT	48
YORK AND LANCASTER REGIMENT	98

ALPHABETICAL INDEX TO NAMES AT END OF BOOK.

PREFATORY NOTE.

MESSRS. COX & Co.'s Enquiry Office was opened in September, 1914, in a small room lent by Lord Harrington in his house adjoining the Bank in Craig's Court.

It was instituted for the purpose of giving general advice and information regarding the wounded to the relatives of officers of the original Expeditionary Force

In consequence of the unparalleled strain placed on the Casualty Department at the War Office, and of the conditions existing in France at the beginning of the War, Messrs. COX & Co.'s organization was found to be of considerable benefit in obtaining fuller details of individual cases and also in conveying messages to and from wounded officers still in hospital in France.

A system was also built up of obtaining all available information regarding officers reported "missing"; and this gradually came to be the principal work of the Enquiry Office, who had the great pleasure of being able to give, in a very large number of cases, the first news of the safety of missing officers.

This information was obtained in various ways, but chiefly by means of the fact that a missing officer's cheque was often the first intimation of his being a Prisoner of War, and that all cheques cashed by officer prisoners in Germany passed through the hands of Messrs. COX & Co. Careful records were kept from the beginning, drawn from official and other sources, of all Prisoners of War, and it is from these records that the following list is compiled. As the Army grew, so did the work of the Enquiry Office, and, early in 1915, Lord Harrington kindly allowed Messrs. COX & Co. the use of his large Music Room at Harrington House, and in these two rooms the work was carried on until the end.

The organization was extended, as necessity arose, to every theatre of War in which British or Colonial Troops were engaged, and through Messrs. COX & Co.'s representatives in all parts of the world, information could be had, which in many cases would have been otherwise unobtainable.

Between September 8th, 1914, and February 1st, 1919, the Enquiry Office was never closed to the public for a single day.

JUNE, 1919.

List of British Officers taken prisoner in the various Theatres of War between August, 1914, and November, 1918.

(1) WESTERN THEATRE OF OPERATIONS.

STAFF.

Name.		Missing.	Interned.	Rapatriated.
H. G. ROBERTSON.	*Staff Surgeon.*	30/10/14		1/7/15
Lieut. C. J. GAGE-BROWN	*Interpreter att. 1st Life Guards.*	6/11/14	Holland 24/2/18	22/1/19
Lieut. H. MARTIN.	*Intelligence Corps.*	–/14	Holland 6/2/18	23/ 9/18
Lieut. F. H. BEVAN.	*Intelligence Corps.*	–/14	Holland 6/2/18	23/10/18
Lieut. T. BREEN.	*Intelligence Corps.*	–/14		
Lieut. H. LE GRAND	*Intelligence Corps.*	–/15	Switzerland 30/5/16	23/12/18
Brig.-Gen. C. D. BRUCE.	*27th Infantry Bde.*	26/9/15	Holland 19/4/18	–/ 4/19
Capt. P. ROSE.	*63rd Infantry Bde.*	–/15		9/12/16
Lt.-Col. Hon. H. NAPIER	*General Staff.*	–/16		
Brig.-Gen. H. S. L. RAVENSHAW.		4/12/17		18/12/18
Capt. F. H. D. VICKERMAN.		4/12/16		14/12/18
Capt. J. BROADWOOD.	*35th Infantry Bde.*	30/11/17		29/11/18
Capt. F. B. RYAN.	*R.A.M.C. att. R.E. H.Q.*	30/11/17		23/ 2/18
Capt. G. PEIRSON.	*48th Infantry Bde.*	–/3/17		23/ 2/18
Brig.-Gen. V. T. BAILEY.	*142nd Infantry Bde.*	23/3/18		30/12/18
Brig.-Gen. F. S. DAWSON.	*S. Africans att. H.Q.*	24/3/18		30/12/18
Capt. R. BEVERLEY.	*S. Africans att. H.Q.*	24/3/18		25/12/18
2/Lieut. E. A. F. BATTY.	*Intelligence att. 41st Infantry Bde.*	24/3/18		25/12/18
Lt.-Col. C. O. PLACE	*36th Infantry Division*	26/3/18		8/12/18
Brig.-Gen. E. H. BELLINGHAM.	*118th Infantry Bde.*	28/3/18		–/12/18
Bde.-Major F. H. GUNNER.	*39th Division.*	28/3/18		31/12/18
Major P. C. VELLACOTT.	*23rd Infantry Bde.*	28/3/18		31/12/18
Capt. J. P. CUTHBERT.	*42nd Infantry Bde.*	4/4/18		25/12/18
Brig.-Gen. J. K. DICK CUNYNGHAN	*152nd Infantry Bde.*	12/4/18		13/12/18
Capt. H. P. M. BERNEY FICKLIN.	*152nd Infantry Bde.*	12/4/18		3/12/18
Capt. W. DRUMMOND.	*152nd Infantry Bde.*	12/4/18		2/12/18
2/Lieut. F. E. FAIRBANK	*H.Q.*	25/4/18		1/12/18
Brig.-Gen. H. REES.	*50th Division.*	27/5/18		–/12/18
Capt. A. S. WIMBLE.	*24th Infantry Bde.*	27/5/18		25/12/18
Capt. C. JENNINGS.	*7th Infantry Bde.*	27/5/18		6/12/18
2/Lieut. R. M. RUSTON.	*R.F.A. att. Divisional H.Q.*	4/6/18		16/12/18
Lieut. J. L. OUTRAN	*Interpreter*	–/18		1/12/18
Brig.-Gen. C. E. BRADLEY		–/16	Holland	24/2/18
2/Lieut. J. A. THIN	*5th Corps Cavalry*	22/3/17		14/12/18

1st LIFE GUARDS.

Name.	Missing.		Interned.	Repatriated.
Lieut. C. J. GAGE-BROWN.	6/11/14	Holland	24/2/18	22/1/19

2nd LIFE GUARDS.

Capt. H. C. S. ASHTON.	19/10/14	Holland	6/2/18	18/11/18
Lieut. K. R. PALMER.	19/10/14	Holland	6/2/18	18/11/18

ROYAL HORSE GUARDS.

Lieut. A. J. CAMPBELL.				19/12/18

HOUSEHOLD BATTALION.

2/Lt. B. M. GREENHILL.	3/5/17			4/12/18

DRAGOONS.

1st (Royal).

Capt. H. JUMP.	30/12/14	Switzerland	9/12/17	9/12/18

2nd (Scots Greys).

Capt. H. ESTCOURT.	4/12/15	Switzerland	5/12/17	23/12/18

6th (Inniskilling).

2/Lt. A. M. NIALL.	1/12/17			31/12/18
Lieut. F. K. PRIDEAUX-BRUNE.	23/3/18			12/10/18

DRAGOON GUARDS.

4th (Royal Irish).

*Capt. A. Fitz. G. RAMSAY.	11/9/14	Holland	24/2/18	
Capt. Sir A. HICKMAN.	11/9/14	Holland	29/12/17	17/11/18
Lieut. O. SANDERSON.	11/9/14	Switzerland	9/12/17	24/3/18
Capt. H. GURNEY.				–/12/18

5th (Princess Charlotte of Wales's).

Lieut. M. B. BURROWS.	2/9/14	Holland	6/2/18	18/11/18

6th (Carabiniers).

Lieut. R. H. H. JONES.	10–11/10/18			18/11/18

7th (Princess Royal's).

Capt. J. MONTGOMERY.	24/8/14	Holland	5/1/18	22/11/18

*Attached from 22nd Indian Cavalry.

HUSSARS.

4th (Queen's Own).

Name.	Missing.		Interned.	Repatriated.
Lieut. D. BIBBY.	16/9/14	Holland	29/12/17	22/11/18
Lieut. B. B. FAULKNER.	17/10/14	Holland	6/2/18	22/11/18

7th (Queen's Own).

Major P. L. E. WALKER.	27/10/18			10/1/19

8th (King's Royal Irish).

Capt. P. S. ALEXANDER.	22/3/18			28/11/18
2/Lt. J. P. ROBINSON.	22/3/18			–/11/18

11th (Prince Albert's Own).

Lieut. H. E. TALBOT.	19/10/14	Switzerland	19/12/16	–/12/17
Lieut. W. H. JAGGERS.	21/3/18			–/11/18

15th (The King's).

Lieut. J. C. ROGERSON.	10/9/14	Holland	6/2/18	16/11/18
2/Lt. W. J. PICKERING.	21/3/18			11/12/18
Capt. J. GODMAN.	22/3/18			14/12/18
Lieut. W. J. M. LOWE.	22/3/18			

18th (Queen Mary's Own).

Lieut. G. FIRTH.	20/10/14	Holland	6/2/18	18/11/18

19th (Queen Alexandra's Own Royal).

Lieut. W. G. HORNE.	3/9/14	Holland	5/1/18	22/11/18
Lieut. Sir C. W. CAYZER.	8/10/18			–/12/18
Lieut. J. S. COCKBURN.	8/10/18			13/12/18

20th.

Lieut. J. T. UPTON.	10/9/14	Holland	6/2/18	18/11/18

LANCERS.

5th (Royal Irish).

Capt. Hon. I. J. L. HAY.		Holland	5/1/18	18/11/18
Capt. J. A. T. RICE.	26/3/18	(Died 14/4/18 at Cugny).		

9th (Queen's Royal).

Lieut. R. G. PEEK.	29/8/14			13/9/17
Lieut. C. W. NORMAN.	30/10/14	Holland	24/2/18	24/11/18
Lieut. F. S. CROSSLEY.	30/11/14	Holland	6/2/18	23/10/18
Lieut. E. JOICEY.	21/11/17			25/12/18
Lieut. S. G. BROCKWELL.	9/8/18			13/12/18

12th (Prince of Wales's Royal).

Major P. J. BAILEY.	11/9/14	Switzerland	9/12/17	6/12/18
Lieut. R. L. MOORE.	12/9/14	Switzerland	12/8/16	–/9/17

16th (The Queen's).

Capt. G. E. BELLVILLE.	11/9/14	Switzerland	12/8/16	11/9/17
Lieut. J. J. RYAN.	21/2/15	Holland	1/3/18	23/10/18

21st (Empress of India's).

Capt. G. N. REYNOLDS.	30/10/14	Holland	24/2/18	4/1/19
Capt. Hon. B. F. R. ROBERTSON.	30/10/14	Switzerland	30/5/16	17/9/17

KING EDWARD'S HORSE.

2/Lt. J. F. BRAKELL.	31/7/17			23/12/18
Lieut. D. G. LAURENSON.	9/4/18			13/12/18
Lieut. R. O'HALLORAN-GILES.	9/4/18	(Died)		
Lieut. Ian STEIN.	9/4/18			10/12/18

YEOMANRY.

Buckinghamshire.

Name.	Missing.	Interned.	Repatriated.
Major C. E. G. GOETZ.			23/12/18

Derbyshire.

Major W. WILSON.	27/3/18		29/11/18

Essex.

†Lieut. G. MORGAN.	28/4/18		–/12/18

Northumberland (Hussars).

Lieut. I. A. PATTERSON.	22/8/18		–/12/18

ROYAL FIELD ARTILLERY.

Name	Missing	Interned		Repatriated
Capt. I. L. SMYTHE.				–/11/18
2/Lt. R. F. GORE-BROWN.		Switzerland	9/12/17	24/3/18
Lieut. D. HILL.		Switzerland	30/5/16	14/9/17
Capt. C. J. F LEECH.	–/8/14	Holland	22/1/18	12/2/19
Capt. P. LYSTER.	24/8/14	Holland	29/12/17	23/9/18
Lt.-Col. C. STEVENS.	27/8/14	Switzerland	9/12/17	9/12/18
Major A. C. R. NUTT.	27/8/14	Switzerland	27/12/17	23/12/18
Major R. E. BIRLEY.	5/9/14	Switzerland	30/5/16	14/9/17
Major A. R. BAYLY.	10/9/14	Switzerland	9/12/17	–/2/19
Lieut. A. STEWART-COX.	10/9/14	Holland	22/1/18	4/10/18
Lieut. E. A. SPENCER.	10/9/14	Holland	5/1/18	18/11/18
2/Lt. R. W. McLEOD.	10/9/14	Holland	6/2/18	18/11/18
Lieut. J. STANFORD.	10/9/14	Holland	5/1/18	14/11/18
Lieut. J. E. YOUNGER.	10/9/14	Holland	5/1/18	18/11/18
Major G. H. F. TAILYOUR.	10/9/14	Holland	5/1/18	23/10/18
Major E. H. JONES.	10/9/14	Switzerland	12/8/16	14/9/17
Lieut. E. L. ARMITAGE.	26/9/14	Holland	5/1/18	17/11/18
Lieut. Michael ABRAHAM.	11/11/14	Switzerland	12/8/16	14/6/18
2/Lt. H. C. HINWOOD.	15/3/15	Switzerland	27/12/17	24/3/18
Lieut. A. COULSON.	9/5/15	Holland	23/3/18	18/11/18
Lieut. J. A. DONNELLY.	10/5/15			1/1/19
Capt. F. H. PRICHARD.	2/6/15	Holland	–/6/15	2/6/15
Lieut. K. W. POWER.	26/9/15	Holland	10/4/18	18/11/18
2/Lt. F. W. LONG.	4/6/16	(Died 28/6/16).		
2/Lt. H. F. DENHAM-SMITH.	18/11/16	Switzerland	27/12/17	24/3/18
Capt. A T. SLOAN.	25/2/17			12/11/18
*Lieut. B. P. LUSCOMBE.	10/7/17			14/12/18
2/Lt. C. L. NICHOLS.	10/7/17			17/12/18
2/Lt. H. TOWNSEND.	10/7/17			14/12/18
2/Lt. H. G. E. DURNFORD.	5/8/17			9/11/18
Capt. C. B. DARLEY.	30/11/17			14/12/18
*Lieut. L. GOLDSTEIN.	30/11/17			18/12/18
Lieut. H. MAYNARD.	30/11/17			3/12/18
*Lieut. J. G. LOMAX.	30/11/17			29/11/18
2/Lt. J. R. ANNANDALE.	30/11/17			17/12/18
*2/Lt. R. H. GRIBBLE.	30/11/17			17/12/18
2/Lt. K. S. PATTERSON.	30/11/17	(Died 6/12/17).		
2/Lt. H. J. WINDER.	1/12/17			27/11/18
Capt E. C. HAGEN.	1/12/17			25/12/18

* Attached T.M.B.   † Attached Divisional Artillery.

ROYAL FIELD ARTILLERY—continued.

Name.	Missing.	Interned.	Repatriated.
Lieut. H. S. ANDERSON.	16/1/18		14/12/18
Major W. R. CUNLIFFE.	-/3/18		19/1/19
Capt. W. V. DAWSON.	-/3/18		29/11/19
†Lieut. R. MacARTHUR.	-/3/18		1/1/19
2/Lt. F. G. J. RASMUSSON.	-/3/18		29/11/18
2/Lt. T. STUART.	-/3/18		1/12/18
2/Lt. Pat GORDON.	-/3/18		-/12/18
2/Lt. G. G. R. PATON.	20/3/18		28/11/18
Major A. F. M. RIECKE.	21/3/18		6/12/18
Major E. T. DOBBIE.	21/3/18		14/12/18
Major Cleveland KEYES.	21/3/18	(Died 24/3/18).	
Major R. H. FARREN.	21/3/18		18/12/18
Major R. V. MAUDSLAY.	21/3/18		17/12/18
*Capt. R. E. GUDGEON.	21/3/18	(Died 2/4/18 at Stendal).	
*Capt. A. D. BOLLAM.	21/3/18		4/12/18
*Capt. J. W. WHITAKER.	21/3/18		18/12/18
*Lieut. C. A. FELL.	21/3/18		2/12/18
*Lieut. Wm. HORSFIELD.	21/3/18		14/12/18
*Lieut. R. M. HAMMOND.	21/3/18	(Died 20/5/18 at Hoilbronn).	
*Lieut. B. D. M. BREWER.	21/3/18		11/12/18
*Lieut. E. C. ROSE.	21/3/18		17/12/18
*Lieut. T. K. MEIKLE.	21/3/18		1/12/18
Lieut. J. M. COUPER.	21/3/18	(Died 4/4/18 at Friedrichsfeld).	
Lieut. W. H. F. BIRD.	21/3/18		29/11/18
Lieut. F. A. HODGES.	21/3/18		5/1/19
Lieut. W. H. CROWDER.	21/3/18		19/12/18
Lieut T. A. B. COPESTAKE.	21/3/18		8/12/18
Lieut. E. T. SCOTT.	21/3/18		18/12/18
Lieut. Hugh G. LE RAY.	21/3/18		14/12/18
Lieut. H. R. Dale HARRIS.	21/3/18		6/12/18
‡Lieut. N. E. TYNDALE-BISCOE.	21/3/18		10/12/18
Lieut. P. H. GIBBONS.	21/3/18		28/11/18
Lieut. L. HANNAN.	21/3/18		18/12/18
Lieut. E. N. GODFREY.	21/3/18		17/12/18
‡2/Lt. G. D. CASTELLI.	21/3/18		25/12/18
2/Lt. G. K. STANLEY.	21/3/18		14/12/18
2/Lt. J. HOLLIDAY.	21/3/18		18/12/18
2/Lt. G. GREENWOOD	21/3/18		13/12/18
2/Lt. Robert HALL.	21/3/18		1/12/18
2/Lt. T W. W. GOODRIDGE.	21/3/18		14/12/18
2/Lt. E. GOSMORE.	21/3/18		4/12/18
2/Lt. J. HUTCHISON.	21/3/18		8/12/18
2/Lt. R. HOWL.	21/3/18		11/12/18
2/Lt. R. F. TROWER.	21/3/18		18/12/18
Lieut. E. V. GOODMAN.	21/3/18		29/11/18
2/Lt. C. F. TOD.	21/3/18		11/12/18
2/Lt. R. C. MacKIE.	21/3/18		13/1/19
2/Lt. I. MEO.	21/3/18		11/12/18
2/Lt. W. G. MITCHELL.	21/3/18		11/12/18
2/Lt. D. de E. STRICKLAND.	21/3/19		-/12/18
2/Lt. J. L. SPITE.	21/3/18		11/12/18
2/Lt. S. W. BALL.	21/3/18		18/12/18
2/Lt. A. TRUSLER.	21/3/18		11/12/18
2/Lt. H. SNODGRASS.	21/3/18		14/12/18

* Attached T.M.B.   † Attached from East Lancs.
‡ R.H.A.

ROYAL FIELD ARTILLERY—continued.

Name.	Missing.	Interned.	Repatriated.
2/Lt. J. A. BROWN.	21/3/18		12/12/18
2/Lt. D'A. J. LANGNER.	21/3/18		28/11/18
2/Lt. A. N. RAWES.	21/3/18		1/12/18
2/Lt. E. C. A RUNNELS-MOSS.	21/3/18	(*Died* 9/7/18 at Mainz).	
2/Lt. R. U. NUTTER.	21/3/18		2/12/18
2/Lt. R. G. W. NORRISH.	21/3/18		18/12/18
2/Lt. G. W. CARR.	21/3/18		29/11/18
2/Lt. J. H. DAVIES.	21/3/18		18/12/18
2/Lt. W. F. LONGDON.	21/3/18		11/12/18
2/Lt. R. E. R. LUFF.	21/3/18		2/12/18
2/Lt. F. B. JONES.	21/3/18		—/12/18
2/Lt. C. W. BROOKFIELD.	21/3/18		18/12/18
2/Lt. W. E. BOLTON.	21/3/18		18/12/18
2/Lt. H. A. BLUNDELL.	21/3/18		6/12/18
2/Lt. J. B. BENNETT.	21/3/18		5/1/19
2/Lt. J. S. WOOD.	21/3/18		—/12/18
2/Lt. E. B. WALLER.	21/3/18		18/12/18
2/Lt. D. WADDELL.	21/3/18		25/12/18
2/Lt. A. K. ROBERTS.	21/3/18		10/12/18
2/Lt. Hon. E. F. FRENCH.	21/3/18	(*Died* —/11/18 at Mainz).	
2/Lt. J. L. ELLIS.	21/3/18		28/11/18
2/Lt. J. R. EDWARDS.	21/3/18		14/12/18
2/Lt. J. DODDS.	21/3/18		29/11/18
2/Lt. T. H. DAVIES.	21/3/18		18/12/18
2/Lt. W. F. N. CHURCHILL.	21/3/18		14/12/18
2/Lt. E. S. PONT.	21/3/18		6/12/18
2/Lt. G. P. PITTAR.	21/3/18		11/12/18
2/Lt. G. H. PHILIP.	21/3/18		11/12/18
2/Lt. R. M. PATTERSON.	21/3/18		25/12/18
2/Lt. J. C. L. PARSONS.	21/3/18		11/12/18
2/Lt. E. G. PARFITT.	21/3/18		11/12/18
*2/Lt. J. H. YARDLEY.	21/3/18		18/12/18
*2/Lt. R. F. TODD.	21/3/18		14/12/18
*2/Lt. A. W. HUMPHREYS.	21/3/18		17/12/18
*2/Lt. B. L. WILKINSON.	21/3/18		28/1f/18
*2/Lt. J. H. GRAY.	21/3/18		5/1/19
2/Lt. W. G. DARNELL.	22/3/18		6/1/19
2/Lt. C. S. DAWNEY.	22/3/18		27/11/18
2/Lt. H. W. N. FANE.	22/3/18		28/11/18
2/Lt. R. G. M. JONES.	22/3/18		2/12/18
2/Lt. E. R. B. REYNOLDS.	22/3/18		3/1/19
2/Lt. W. MARLOW.	22/3/18		18/12/18
2/Lt. C. M. H. HICKS.	22/3/18		16/12/18
2/Lt. M. J. HARKER.	22/3/18		11/12/18
2/Lt. G. J. R. MacAULAY.	23/3/18		18/12/18
2/Lt. W. A. WILLIAMS.	23/3/18		17/12/18
2/Lt. F. W. LEWIS.	23/3/18		17/12/18
Lieut. R. REEVES.	25/3/18		14/12/18
†2/Lt. K. McBRYDE.	25/3/18		25/12/18
2/Lt. J. H. SWANN.	25/3/18		18/12/18
2/Lt. R. R. GREEN.	24–28/3/18		17/12/18
2/Lt. J. TODD.	27/3/18		31/12/18
Lieut. C. B. ROWE-EVANS.	28/3/18		17/12/18
Lieut. A. STROUDLEY.	28/3/18		—/1/19
2/Lt. D. S. D. NICHOLL.	28/3/18		25/12/18

* Attached T.M.B.   † Attached from A.S.C.

ROYAL FIELD ARTILLERY—continued.

Name.	Missing.	Interned.	Repatriated.
2/Lt. A. J. GOING.	28/3/18		25/12/18
2/Lt. J. R. HALL.	28/3/18		17/12/18
2/Lt. J. W. STONEMAN.	28/3/18		1/12/18
2/Lt. J. WILKIE.	28/3/18		17/12/18
2/Lt. W. H. PEARCE.	28/3/18	(*Died* 24/4/18 at Le Cateau).	
*2/Lt. A. M. URQUGART.	29/3/18		10/12/18
Capt. J. H. HUDSON.	4/4/18		1/1/19
Major J. N. RITCHIE.	9/4/18		17/12/18
Lieut. L. G. A. CUST.	9/4/18		1/12/18
Lieut. W. R. BOOTH.	9/4/18		29/11/18
Lieut. G. HULL.	9/4/18		3/12/18
2/Lt. H. S. THOMPSON.	9/4/18		18/12/18
*2/Lt. L. H. MAYNARD.	9/4/18		11/12/18
2/Lt. Andrew SALLEY.	9/4/18		14/1/19
2/Lt. F. McN. JACKSON.	9/4/18		1/12/18
*2/Lt. P. A. McEWEN.	9/4/18		5/12/18
2/Lt. J. R. WALKER.	9/4/18		29/11/18
2/Lt. E. McGEACHY.	9/4/18		29/11/18
Capt. W. J. BROOKS.	10/4/18		1/12/18
*Lieut. N. V. WATSON.	10/4/18		18/12/18
*2/Lt. W. E. GREEN.	10/4/18		25/12/18
Lieut. W. E. HUNTER.	11/4/18		8/12/18
Lt.-Col. F. FLEMING.	12/4/18		14/12/18
*2/Lt. T. R. SCOTT, M.C.	24/4/18		1/12/18
2/Lt. J. BRAILSFORD.	24/4/18		18/12/18
2/Lt. G. M. O. DAVY.	25/4/18		2/12/18
2/Lt. K. R. BLACKWELL.	25/4/18		29/11/18
Lieut. W. E. STRICKLAND.	26/4/18		-/12/18
2/Lt. George LORD.	26/4/18		18/12/18
Lieut. A. B. THOMSON.	10/5/18		-/12/18
2/Lt. H. R. WHITEMAN.	25/5/18		-/12/18
Major G. J. NANTES.	26/5/18		13/12/18
Major H. G. FISHER, D.S.O.	27–31/5/18		30/12/18
Capt. E. A. PALMER.	27–31/5/18		31/12/18
Lieut. E. H. THOMAS.	27–31/5/18		26/12/18
Lieut. D. C. OWEN.	27–31/5/18		31/12/18
*2/Lt. A. J. MACK.	27–31/5/18		23/10/18
*2/Lt. W. F. KEATING.	27–31/5/18		30/12/18
2/Lt. E. F. BRYAN.	27–31/5/18		2/1/19
2/Lt. M. de la P. BERESFORD.	27–31/5/18		31/12/18
2/Lt. K. HOLME-BARNETT.	27–31/5/18		30/12/18
2/Lt. M. C. HULLAH.	27–31/5/18		-/12/18
2/Lt. I. S. NICOL.	27–31/5/18		30/12/18
2/Lt. J. W. HART.	27–31/5/18		25/12/18
Colonel E. V. SARSON.	27/5/18		-/12/18
Lt.-Col. F. B. MOSS-BLUNDELL.	27/5/18		24/12/18
Major A. P. EVERSHED, M.C.	27/5/18		-/12/18
Major N. SOUTHERN.	27/5/18		31/12/18
Major G. CHAPMAM.	27/5/18		9/1/19
Major D. C. WILSOR, D.S.O.	27/5/18		-/1/19
Major Hon. G. BOSCAWEN.	27/5/18	(*Died* 7/6/18 at Liesse).	
Major W. H. H. HUTCHINSON.	27/5/18		21/12/18
Major W. GOLDING.	27/5/18		25/12/18
Capt. C. B. GOLDING, M.C.	27/5/18		31/12/18
Capt. J. E. HUMBERSTONE.	27/5/18		-/12/18

* Attached T.M.B.

ROYAL FIELD ARTILLERY—continued.

Name.	Missing.	Interned.	Repatriated.
Capt. L. F. STEMP.	27/5/18		14/12/18
Capt. B. K. BARTON.	27/5/18		30/12/18
Capt. E. DARLING, M.C.	27/5/18		31/12/18
Capt. A. L. CHANTRILL.	27/5/18		-/12/18
Lieut. C. O. FRANK.	27/5/18		22/1/19
Lieut. A. D. ROBERTS.	27/5/18		14/12/18
Lieut. G. E. PATTON.	27/5/18		-/12/18
Lieut. W. W. WHYTE.	27/5/18		-/12/18
Lieut. A. BOSTOCK.	27/5/18		-/12/18
Lieut. R. J. BARDSLEY.	27/5/18		-/12/18
Lieut. A. S. WITHERINGTON.	27/5/18		-/12/18
Lieut. J. MacLEOD.	27/5/18		14/12/18
Lieut. E. G. ATTENBOROUGH.	27/5/18		-/12/18
Lieut. C. M. HARVEY.	27/5/18		14/12/18
Lieut. H. R. HORNSBY.	27/5/18		31/12/18
Lieut. J. P. HUTCHINSON.	27/5/18		31/12/18
Lieut. T. M. GATHERAL.	27/5/18		31/12/18
Lieut. W. S. GALL.	27/5/18		13/12/18
Lieut. E. D. TUDHOPE.	27/5/18		30/12/18
2/Lt. D. H. THOMPSON.	27/5/18		-/1/19
2/Lt. K. M. GOODENOUGH.	27/5/18		25/12/18
2/Lt. C. E. HOLLIDAY.	27/5/18		25/12/18
2/Lt. F. J. HODDER.	27/5/18		25/12/18
2/Lt. W. GRAHAM.	27/5/18		13/12/18
2/Lt. G. W. PARKES.	27/5/18		30/12/18
2/Lt. A. O. STANDEN.	27/5/18		23/12/18
2/Lt. W. T. MERCER.	27/5/18		26/12/18
2/Lt. F. L. MAYNARD.	27/5/18		14/12/18
2/Lt. I. H. WHITE.	27/5/18		25/12/18
*2/Lt. W. E. WHITE.	27/5/18		-/12/18
2/Lt. R. WILSON.	27/5/18		26/12/18
2/Lt. H. W. ABEY.	27/5/18		-/12/18
2/Lt. H. BULLING.	27/5/18		30/12/18
2/Lt. W. JOYES.	27/5/18		-/12/18
2/Lt. E. J. CURPHEY.	27/5/18		2/1/19
2/Lt. B. V. CROAL.	27/5/18		25/12/18
2/Lt. D. H. COSTAR.	27/5/18		2/1/19
2/Lt. E. G. CLEMSON.	27/5/18		
2/Lt. W. E CLARKE	27/5/18		26/12/18
*2/Lt. E. H. B. CLARK.	27/5/18		31/12/18
2/Lt. C. W. CARTER.	27/5/18		13/12/18
2/Lt. S. R. K. REAKES.	27/5/18		31/12/18
2/Lt. A. H. PULLIN.	27/5/18		31/12/18
2/Lt. T. POWELL.	27/5/18		13/12/18
2/Lt. G. W. PARKES.	27/5/18		30/12/18
*Capt. S. R. C. PLIMSOLL.	29/5/18		11/12/18
2/Lt. R. M. RUSTON.	4/6/18		16/12/18
2/Lt. J. E. ELLIOTT.	2/9/18		8/12/18
2/Lt. J. A. SYKES.	2/9/18		8/12/18
2/Lt. J. C. D. SCARLETT.	6/9/18		13/12/18
2/Lt. A. H. P. WILKES.	10/10/18		15/12/18
2/Lt. H. R. VERNON.	24/10/18		27/11/18

* Attached T.M.B.

ROYAL GARRISON ARTILLERY.

Name.	Missing.	Interned.	Repatriated.
Capt. F. E. FRYER.	–/4/15	Holland –/4/15	–/8/18
2/Lt. A. W. PURNELL.	14/11/17	(*Died* –/11/17)	
Major H. WHITTINGHAM.	30/11/17	Holland 30/4/18	18/8/18
Lieut. A. H. FLINT.	30/11/17		3/12/18
Lieut. George SISSON.	30/11/17	(*Died* 20/12/17).	
Lieut. E. J. EDWARD.	30/11/17		2/12/18
2/Lt. H. L. H. FISHER.	30/11/17		2/12/18
2/Lt. O. J. B. COLE.	30/11/17		14/12/18
2/Lt. A. C. STIRLING.	30/11/17		18/12/18
2/Lt. F. E. S. JAMES.	30/11/17		5/12/18
2/Lt. P. S. GURNEY.	30/11/17		17/12/18
2/Lt. J. WOODS.	30/11/17		2/12/18
2/Lt. G. W. H. POTTER.	30/11/17		17/12/18
2/Lt. G. N. PHILLIPS.	30/11/17		17/12/18
2/Lt. J. A. BROWN.	30/11/17		–/12/18
Lieut. T. H. N. BATTLE.	21/3/18		25/12/18
Lieut. J. A. G. STUART.	21/3/18		14/12/18
2/Lt. A. FINLAYSON.	21/3/18		18/12/18
2/Lt. C. R. CHADWICK.	21/3/18		1/12/18
2/Lt. J. F. MacGREGOR.	21/3/18		4/12/18
2/Lt. A. E. CURTIS.	21/3/18		18/12/18
2/Lt. A. D. HEGGIE.	21/3/18		6/12/18
2/Lt. C. H. MAPP.	21/3/18		29/11/18
2/Lt. L. K. ROBINSON.	–/3/18		18/12/18
†Lieut. G. M. G. FARMER.	21/3/18		29/11/18
2/Lt. K. W. SAWREY.	21/3/18		29/11/18
2/Lt. J. L. CRAIG.	21/3/18		1/12/18
2/Lt. H. ALLSOP.	21/3/18		11/12/18
2/Lt. B. W. F. BRETON.	21/3/18		18/12/18
2/Lt. K. C. BOSWELL.	21/3/18		–/11/18
2/Lt. J. H. BENEDICTUS.	21/3/18		4/12/18
*2/Lt. D. WATKINS.	21/3/18		18/12/18
2/Lt. W. A. COCHRANE.	21/3/18		18/12/18
Lieut. R. A. LEE.	22/3/18		25/12/18
2/Lt. H. L. GUMMER.	22/3/18		8/12/18
2/Lt. W. M. HORSEMAN.	22/3/18		18/12/18
2/Lt. F. N. FLEMING.	28/3/18	(*Died* –/6/18 at Pforzheim).	
Capt. J. H. HUDSON.	4/4/18		1/1/19
Major A. M. STEPHEN.	9/4/18		–/12/18
Lieut. A. CAYLEY.	9/4/18		16/12/18
*Lieut. F. B. KIRBY.	9/4/18		17/12/18
2/Lt. G. C. VEYSEY.	9/4/18		30/11/18
2/Lt. F. GARNETT.	9/4/18		18/12/18
2/Lt. C. E. GATES.	9/4/18		29/11/18
2/Lt. G. F. GLENN.	9/4/18		29/11/18
2/Lt. P. N. GLEAVE.	9/4/18		29/11/18
2/Lt. R. P. M. BROWN.	9/4/18		1/12/18
2/Lt. S. ROGERS.	9/4/18		18/12/18
2/Lt. J. G. NOLAN.	10/4/18		25/12/18
2/Lt. A. G. HUTCHEON.	25/4/18		1/12/18
2/Lt. F. S. KILBURN.	25/4/18		–/12/18
Capt. F. H. WATTS.	27/5/18		28/12/18
‡Capt. H. R. FRENCH.	27/5/18		13/12/18
2/Lt. E. G. HOLMES.	27/5/18		–/12/18

* Attached T.M.B.   † Attached from A.S.C.
‡ Attached from 7th Dragoon Guards.

ROYAL GARRISON ARTILLERY—continued.

Name.	Missing.	Interned.	Repatriated.
2/Lt. S. J. LANGFORD.	27/5/18		-/12/18
2/Lt. W. J. G. STONE.	27/5/18		13/12/18
2/Lt. R. WILSON.	27/5/18		26/12/18
Capt. A. Scott RUSSELL.			16/11/18

ROYAL ENGINEERS.

Name.	Missing.	Interned.		Repatriated.
Lieut. O. BALFOUR.	25/8/14	Holland	5/1/18	
Capt. A. PARIS.		Switzerland	-/11/17	9/12/18
Lieut. R. C. WELLS.		Holland	6/2/18	18/11/18
2/Lt. C. ELLINGER.		Holland	30/4/18	18/11/18
Lieut. A. F. DAY.		Holland	29/12/17	21/1/19
Lieut. C. M. G. URE.	5/10/15	Holland	19/4/18	18/11/18
2/Lt. R. N. MONTGOMERY.	23/4/17			-/1/19
Capt. D. S. THORNE.	31/7/17			3/1/19
2/Lt. J. N. TINNISWOOD.	12/9/17			6/12/18
Lieut. F. G. HARNESS.	30/11/17			17/12/18
Lieut. A. F. NEAL.	30/11/17			27/11/18
Major A. F. G. RUSTON.	30/11/17			17/12/18
2/Lt. W. A. LOWE.	30/11/17			3/12/18
2/Lt. P. NEILL.	30/11/17			17/12/18
Capt. L. C. HALL.	30/11/17			3/12/18
Lieut. C. H. S. HAYGARTH.				-/12/18
Capt. C. J. R. GREENWOOD.				23/11/18
2/Lt. W. S. BEAUMONT.				17/12/18
Capt. W. LEGG.	-/3/18			25/12/18
Capt. C. LAYCOCK.	21/3/18			25/12/18
Lieut. W. HULSE.	21/3/18			29/11/18
Lieut. J. E. HENSHAW.	21/3/18			10/12/18
Lieut. G. BRANDON.	21/3/18			28/11/18
Lieut. W. DRAKE.	21/3/18			-/12/18
Lieut. G. P. H. WATSON.	21/3/18			30/12/18
2/Lt. J. B. LONGMUIR.	21/3/18			23/9/18
2/Lt. J. W. ENGLISH.	21/3/18			-/12/18
*2/Lt. A. L. HUSBAND.	21/3/18			29/11/18
2/Lt. R. A. MacDONALD.	21/3/18			18/12/18
Major E. L. V. DAKIN.	22/3/18			8/1/19
Capt. N. J. C. FARMER.	22/3/18			13/12/18
Lieut. E. C. MAXWELL.	22/3/18			30/12/18
Lieut. K. C. BARRELL.	22/3/18			29/11/18
Lieut. R. C. TOTTENHAM.	22/3/18			28/11/18
2/Lt. J. McCARTHY.	22/3/18			17/12/18
2/Lt. T. E. MORGAN.	22/3/18			13/12/18
2/Lt. C. K. ROYLANCE	22/3/18			2/12/18
Lieut. I. W. SMITH.	23/3/18			11/12/18
Lieut. R. L. GOLDSMITH.	23/3/18			29/11/18
Major W. F. BRUCE.	24/3/18			29/11/18
2/Lt. M. SWALES.	24/3/18			5/12/18
2/Lt. W. G. HOLE.	24/3/18			2/12/18
Lieut. J. LOGAN.	26/3/18			25/12/18
Lieut. E. L. PARKES.	26/3/18			18/12/18
2/Lt. P. M. HEPTINSTALL.	26/3/18			26/11/18
Lieut. R. E. WALSH.	27/3/18			29/11/18
2/Lt. Robert HARLAND.	28/3/18			18/12/18
2/Lt. John POPE.	28/3/18			2/1/19
Capt. E. M. BESLEY.	30/3/18			3/12/18

* Attached from Durham Light Infantry.

ROYAL ENGINEERS—continued.

Name.	Missing.	Interned.	Repatriated.
Lieut. C. A. BORASTON.	30/3/18		17/12/18
Lieut. G. I. SINCLAIR.	30/3/18		11/12/18
*2/Lt. W. F. WELSBY.	9/4/18		4/12/18
Capt. J. ELLMANN.	10/4/18		8/12/18
2/Lt. W. A. WILKEN.	11/4/18		4/12/18
2/Lt. S. C. MOSS.	11/4/18		–/12/18
2/Lt. John R. WALLACE.	11/4/18		29/11/18
2/Lt. A. H. TIBBOTTS.	12/4/18		6/12/18
2/Lt. A. K. ROBINSON.	12/4/18		11/12/18
Lieut. B. L. RIGDEN.	17/4/18		13/12/18
Lieut. B. E. REES.	18/4/18		18/12/18
Lieut. T. MARSLAND.	18/4/18		17/12/18
Major E. C. HILLMAN, M.C.	27/5/18		17/12/18
Major A. G. RAINSFORD-HANNAY.	27/5/18		–/12/18
Major John W. LLOYD.	27/5/18		19/1/19
Capt. Jack R. GRANT, M.C.	27/5/18		17/12/18
Capt. F. J. SLATTERY.	27/5/18		31/12/18
Lieut. H. J. HOGG.	27/5/18		31/1/19
Lieut. E. W. YOUNG.	27/5/18		31/12/18
Lieut. T. R. RUSSELL.	27/5/18		25/12/18
‡Lieut. D. V. L. CRADDOCK.	27/5/18		30/12/18
Lieut. R. H. REAY.	27/5/18		25/12/18
Lieut. P. BURR.	27/5/18		17/12/18
2/Lt. C. A. KENNEDY.	27/5/18		25/12/18
2/Lt. W. L. LAX.	27/5/18		13/12/18
2/Lt. Alan. ATKINSON.	27/5/18		–/12/18
2/Lt. H. F. SHARP.	27/5/18		–/12/18
2/Lt. R. H. WALMSLEY.	27/5/18		21/1/19
†2/Lt. P. H. WOODING.	27/5/18		13/12/18
2/Lt. W. F. GARDNER.	27/5/18		14/12/18
Lieut. R. G. GODSON.	28/5/18		11/12/18
2/Lt. A. H. FENNELL.	29/5/18		17/12/18
Lieut. N. D. McKAY.	6/8/18		10/1/19
Lieut. W. W. RUSSELL.	22/8/18		13/12/18
Lieut. T. DAVIES.	30/9/18		29/11/18

GRENADIER GUARDS.

1st Battalion.

Name	Missing	Interned		Repatriated
Lt.-Col. M. EARLE.	29/10/14	Switzerland	30/5/16	15/9/17
Lieut. C. G. GOSCHEN.	24/12/14			–/6/16
2/Lt. C. CRUTTENDEN.	25/8/18			13/12/18

3rd Battalion.

Name	Missing	Interned		Repatriated
Lieut. C. S. ROWLEY.	27/9/15	Holland	–/4/18	21/1/19

4th Battalion.

Name	Missing	Repatriated
Lieut. M. D. THOMAS.	12/4/18	18/12/18
Lieut. G. C. BURT.	13/4/18	18/12/18
Lieut. C. C. S. RODNEY.	13/4/18	1/12/18
Lieut. P. H. COX.	13/4/18	18/12/18
2/Lt. G. P. PHILIPS.	13/4/18	6/1/19

* Attached from King's Liverpool Regiment.

† Attached from Rifle Brigade.

‡ Attached from 9th Durhams.

COLDSTREAM GUARDS.

1st Battalion.

Name.	Missing.	Interned.		Repatriated.
Capt. E. CHRISTIE-MILLER.	3/11/14	Holland	24/2/18	12/1/19
Capt. J. E. GIBBS.	22/11/14	Holland	24/2/18	2/1/19
Lieut. R. J. WAVELL-PAXTON.	29/11/14	Holland	24/2/18	2/1/19
2/Lt. J. S. ALISON.	29/11/14	Holland	24/2/18	27/11/18
2/Lt. J. H. McNEILE.	22/12/14	Holland	1/3/18	18/11/18
*Capt. C. K. HUTCHISON.	25/1/15	Switzerland	–/11/17	23/12/18
2/Lt. H. N. CLIFTON.	25/1/15	(*Died* 1/2/15).		
2/Lt. O. STYLE.	26/9/15			22/11/18
Capt. G. H. SMITH.	16/10/18			

3rd Battalion.

Capt. Hon. R. O. D. KEPPEL.	26/8/14	Holland	5/1/18	18/11/18
Capt. J. A. C. WHITAKER.	13/4/18			18/12/18
Capt. R. P. ELWES.	13/4/18			1/12/18
Lieut. V. N. ROWSELL.	13/4/18			24/12/18
2/Lt. C. O. LEADBITTER.	13/4/18			13/12/18
2/Lt. W. A. MILLAR.	13/4/18			23/10/18
2/Lt. A. M. CARR.	13/4/18			30/11/18
2/Lt. J. ASHBY.	13/4/18			1/12/18

SCOTS GUARDS.

1st Battalion.

Major E. Y. VAN DER WEYER.	31/10/14	Holland	24/2/18	18/11/18
Capt. B. G. JOLLIFFE.	29/11/14	Switzerland	–/11/17	8/12/18
Lieut. R. FITZROY.	29/11/14	Holland	6/2/18	7/9/18
2/Lt. G. E. V. CRUTCHLEY.	25/1/15	Holland	1/3/18	18/11/18

2nd Battalion.

2/Lt. Lord GARLIES.	27/9/14	Switzerland	9/12/17	8/12/18
Lt.-Col. R. G. I. BOLTON.	27/10/14	Switzerland	9/12/17	6/12/18
Major Earl of STAIR.	27/10/14			13/9/17
Capt. C. V. FOX.	27/10/14		(Escaped)	–/7/17
Capt. Hon. J. COKE.	27/10/14	Holland	24/2/18	18/11/18
Lieut. E. B. TRAFFORD.	27/10/14	Holland	24/2/18	24/2/18
Lieut. R. STEUART-MENZIES.	27/10/14	Holland	24/2/18	7/9/18
Lieut. Lord G. GROSVENOR.	28/10/14	Holland	24/2/18	23/9/18
Capt. Sir F. L. FITZWYGRAM.	17/5/15	Holland	10/4/18	26/12/18

3rd Battalion.

Major A. C. MORRISON-BELL.	25/1/15	Switzerland	5/12/17	28/11/18

IRISH GUARDS.

2nd Battalion.

2/Lt. B. O'D. MANNING.	13/9/17		23/12/18
2/Lt. W. G. REA.	27/11/17		14/12/18
Lieut. M. R. FITZGERALD.	13/4/18	(*Died* 19/4/18).	

3rd Battalion.

Lord C. H. SETTRINGTON.	13/4/18		1/12/18

* Attached from Royal Scots.

ROYAL SCOTS.
1st and 2nd Battalions.

Name.	Missing.	Interned.		Repatriated.
Lt.-Col. H. McMICKING.	26/8/14	Switzerland	9/12/17	23/3/18
Major G. S. TWEEDIE.	3/9/14	Holland	29/12/17	Returned for Duty.
Capt. A. F. GRAHAM-WATSON.	10/9/14	Holland	22/1/18	18/11/18
Lieut. C. SCARISBRICK.	10/9/14	Holland	22/1/18	24/1/19
2/Lt. C. D. MAYO.	25/9/15	Holland	10/4/18	18/11/18
2/Lt. D. PEASE.	26/9/15			22/11/18
Capt. D. KININMONTH.	12/4/18			1/12/18
Capt. J. HENDERSON.	12/4/18			1/12/18
Lieut. A. ROBERTSON.	12/4/18			18/12/18
2/Lt. R. C. WILKIE.	12/4/18			13/12/18
2/Lt. R. MURCHISON.	12/4/18			18/12/18
2/Lt. A. E. W. McLACHLAN.	12/4/18			6/1/19
2/Lt. James TODD.	12/4/18			18/12/18

4th Battalion.

Name.	Missing.			Repatriated.
*2/Lt. F. B. MOFFATT.	21/3/18			29/11/18
2/Lt. G. R. FORRESTER.	23/3/18			29/11/18

7th Battalion.

Name.	Missing.			Repatriated.
Lieut. W. F. R. MACARTNEY.	21/9/18			–/11/18

8th Battalion.

Name.	Missing.			Repatriated.
Major J. A. TODD.	12/4/18			17/12/18
Capt. A. D. JONES.	12/4/18			17/12/18
Lieut. A. MUNRO.	12/4/18			–/12/18
2/Lt. A. M. WHITE.	12/4/18			–/12/18

9th Battalion.

Name.	Missing.	Interned.		Repatriated.
Lieut. N. MACDONALD.	16/6/15	Holland	10/4/18	22/1/19
2/Lt. D. WALLACE.	24/3/18	(*Died* 18/4/18 at Guise).		

11th Battalion.

Name.	Missing.	Interned.		Repatriated.
Lieut. G. L. BRANDER.	26/9/15	Holland	10/4/18	15/12/18
Lieut. H. C. MEIN.	21/3/18			30/12/18
2/Lt. W. L. DOUGLAS.	21/3/18			25/12/18
2/Lt. C. L. CHEYNE.	23/3/18	(*Died* 21/4/18 at Hammerstein).		
Lieut. J. J. MANN.	25/7/18			14/12/18

12th Battalion.

Name.	Missing.			Repatriated.
Capt. J. BROADWOOD.	30/11/17			29/11/18
2/Lt. T. G. NICHOLSON.	23/3/18			13/12/18
2/Lt. H. G. COLQUHOUN.	24/3/18			18/12/18
2/Lt. A. M. YOUNG.	25/3/18			29/11/18
Capt. G. S. P. McMEEKEN.	26/3/18	(doubtful).		
Lieut. G. MIDDLEMAS.	26/3/18			29/11/18
2/Lt. D. C. COCHRANE.	25/4/18			29/11/18
2/Lt. A. CROW.	25/4/18			6/12/18
Capt. H. E. SANDERSON.	26/4/18			2/12/18
Capt. W. R. DAWSON.	26/4/18			3/12/18
2/Lt. R. A. SCOTT.	26/4/18			29/11/18
2/Lt. J. MILLAR.	26/4/18			–/12/18
2/Lt. C. H. SUTHERLAND.	29/9/18			29/12/18
2/Lt. H. S. DRIVER.	1/10/18			26/12/18

* Attached T.M.B.

ROYAL SCOTS—continued.

13th Battalion.

Name.	Missing.	Interned.	Repatriated.
Lieut. G. N. DOBBIE.	1/8/17		17/12/18
2/Lt. W. T. LOW.	1/8/17		25/12/18
2/Lt. J. GIBSON.	1/8/17	Switzerland 27/12/17	7/12/18
2/Lt. J. S. AITKEN.	1/8/17		14/12/18
2/Lt. L. W. GUTHRIE.	22/3/18		25/12/18
Lieut. J. V. R. MITCHELL.	28/3/18		26/12/18
Lieut. A. A. FARQUHARSON.	28/3/18		18/12/18
2/Lt. J. HOBBS.	28/3/18		18/12/18
2/Lt. J. S. McGREGOR.	28/3/18		13/12/18
2/Lt. S. C. CUMMING	28/3/18		18/12/18
2/Lt. W. A. MATHIESON.	28/3/18		18/12/18

15th Battalion.

Name.	Missing.	Interned.	Repatriated.
Capt. L. S. ROBSON.	28/4/17		6/12/18
Lieut. J. D. FERGUSON.	28/4/17		17/12/18
2/Lt. J. R. FISHER.	28/4/17		31/12/18
2/Lt. M. WARREN.	28/4/17		6/12/18
2/Lt. G. A. STEWART.	28/4/17		7/1/18
2/Lt. J. E. V. CHUBB.	22/10/17		3/12/18
2/Lt. A. B. B. DOWIE.	21/3/18		—/12/18
Capt. W. MILNE.	22/3/18		18/12/18
Capt. S. J. BROWN.	22/3/18		17/12/18
Lieut. J. R. KINNES.	22/3/18		18/12/18
Lieut. A. T. McLAREN.	22/3/18		11/12/18
2/Lt. R. ANDREW.	22/3/18		18/12/18
2/Lt. J. R. L. SMITH.	22/3/18		11/12/18
2/Lt. J. MATHESON.	22/3/18		11/12/18
Capt. E. B. PALMER.	10/4/18		19/12/18
Capt. N. BIDDOLPH.	10/4/18		25/12/18
*Capt. E. B. NICHOLSON.	11/4/18		25/12/18

16th Battalion.

Name.	Missing.	Interned.	Repatriated.
Capt. A. WHYTE.	1/7/16	Switzerland 27/12/17	14/6/18
2/Lt. R. M. PRINGLE.	2/7/16	Holland 15/6/18	23/10/18
†2/Lt. C. W. WOOD.	20/7/16	Holland 15/6/18	21/1/19
Capt. Hon. M. C. H. BOWES-LYON.	28/4/17		29/11/18
2/Lt. W. D. HOWAT.	28/4/17		6/12/18
2/Lt. G. H. HENDERSON.	28/4/17	Switzerland 27/12/17	9/12/18
2/Lt. F. M. DUFF.	28/4/17		6/12/18
2/Lt. G. H. DALGETY.	28/4/17	Switzerland 27/12/17	9/12/18
Capt. R. B. EVANS.	22/10/17		27/11/18
Capt. C. J. LAMBERT.	22/3/18		28/11/18
Lieut. P. M. MacANDREW.	22/3/18		28/11/18
Major A. E. WARR.	9/4/18		28/11/18
2/Lt. A. ROBINSON.	9/4/18		1/12/18
2/Lt. H. TONATHY.	9/4/18		11/12/18
Capt. H. W. RAWSON.	10/4/18	(Died 22/4/18).	
2/Lt. W. LAWRIE.	10/4/18		25/12/18
2/Lt. W. C. MOLLOY.	11/4/18	(Died 10/5/18 at Ingolstadt).	

17th Battalion.

Name.	Missing.	Interned.	Repatriated.
2/Lt. A. I. GRANT.	30/9/18		28/11/18

* Attached T.M.B.   † Attached M.G.C.

ROYAL WEST SURREY REGIMENT.
1st and 2nd Battalions.

Name.	Missing.	Interned.		Repatriated.
Capt. H. F. H. MASTER.	25/10/14			13/9/17
Capt. E. de L. BARTON.	29/10/14	Holland	6/2/18	31/8/18
Capt. C. E. SOAMES.	29/10/14	Holland	24/2/18	18/11/18
Lieut. W. GREEN.	29/10/14	Holland	6/2/18	18/11/18
2/Lt. J. M. ROSE-TROUP.	29/10/14	Holland	24/2/18	18/11/18
Lieut. C. ELLIOT.	31/10/14	Holland	24/2/18	23/9/18
Capt. W. H. ALLEYNE.	7/11/14	Holland	24/2/18	18/8/18
2/Lt. C. J. ROUGHT.	18/12/14	Holland	24/2/18	18/11/18
2/Lt. E. A. WALMISLEY.	18/12/14			11/9/17
Capt. R. C. G. FOSTER.	14/3/17			14/12/18
2/Lt. C. R. SMITH.	14/3/17			30/12/18
Capt. F. S. BALL.	23/4/17	Holland	15/6/18	23/10/18
Capt. R. BRODHURST-HILL.	23/4/17			2/12/18
Capt. F. GODFREY.	23/4/17			30/12/18
2/Lt. O. V. BOTTON.	23/4/17			6/12/18
2/Lt. J. HOLLIDAY.	23/4/17			30/12/18
2/Lt. G. P. S. JACOB.	23/4/17			6/1/18
2/Lt. R. S. WALKER.	23/4/17			20/12/18
Lieut. W. F. CLENSHAW.	25/9/17			13/12/18
2/Lt. H. M. THOMPSON.	23/4/17			7/1/19

6th Battalion.

Name.	Missing.	Interned.	Repatriated.
Lieut. M. G. L. WALLICH.	3/7/16		15/12/18

7th Battalion.

Name.	Missing.	Interned.		Repatriated.
Capt. J. S. WALTER.	19/11/16	(Shot while escaping –/6/18).		
2/Lt. C. G. BROWN.	19/11/16	Holland	15/4/18	20/7/18
2/Lt. J. E. RUSSELL.	19/11/16	(*Died* 23/11/16).		
2/Lt. R. W. E. SHEATHER.	27/2/17			6/12/18
2/Lt. P. E. THORN.	27/2/17			27/11/18
2/Lt. H. W. VAUGHAN.	27/2/17			7/1/18
2/t. A. A. BROOKES.	21/3/18			18/12/18
2/Lt. A. OGDEN.	21/3/18			18/12/18
Capt. T. C. FILBY.	23/3/18			28/11/18
Lieut. W. R. COHEN.	23/3/18			28/11/18
Lieut. A. L. HAIG.	23/3/18			2/12/18
2/Lt. E. V. BATTEN.	23/3/18			18/12/18
2/Lt. A. F. A. HAY.	23/3/18			18/12/18
2/Lt. W. G. PHIPPS.	23/3/18			11/12/18

8th Battalion.

Name.	Missing.	Interned.		Repatriated.
Lieut. L. G. DUKE.	26/9/15			18/11/18
2/Lt. P. G. BURGESS.	26/9/15	(*Died* 13/10/15).		
2/Lt. C. P. BURNLEY.	19/3/16	Holland	30/4/18	18/11/18
2/Lt. J. E. DAY.	25/7/17			17/12/18
Capt. R. D. C. HIGHTON.	21/3/18			29/11/18
Lieut. C. W. H. P. WAUD.	21/3/18			28/11/18
Lieut. E. J. YOUNG.	21/3/18			28/12/18
2/Lt. C. J. DUGGINS.	21/3/18			28/11/18
2/Lt. P. E. MAY.	21/3/18			28/11/18
2/Lt. S. A. MARTIN.	21/3/18			29/11/18
2/Lt. A. C. NYE.	21/3/18			29/11/18
2/Lt. C. L. PIESSE.	21/3/18			17/12/18
2/Lt. W. P. TOMLEY.	21/3/18			28/11/18
2/Lt. D. C. EVANS.	22/3/18			28/11/18
*Capt. C. P. HAWARD.	9/8/18			17/12/18
Capt. A. E. WHEATLEY.	9/8/18			6/1/19

* Attached from Middlesex Regiment.

ROYAL WEST SURREY REGIMENT. continued.
10th Battalion.

Name.	Missing.	Interned.		Repatriated.
2/Lt. J. A. C. RECORD.	23/3/18			28/12/18
Lieut. J. Y. SCOTT.	24/3/18	(*Died* at Cassel 26/7/18).		
2/Lt. C. C. BRATTLE.	24/3/18			26/12/18
2/Lt. W. FENWICK.	24/3/18	(*Died* at Ohligs 5/4/18).		
2/Lt. H. S. PAYNE.	24/3/18			12/10/18

11th Battalion.

Name.	Missing.	Interned.	Repatriated.
†Colonel R. OTTER.	23/3/18		8/12/18
Capt. G. D. HENDERSON.	23/3/18		2/12/18
Lt. A. E. CLARET.	23/3/18		2/12/18
2/Lt. L. T. M. ALLEN.	23/3/18		13/12/18
2/Lt. R. S. BROWN.	23/3/18		25/12/18
2/Lt. E. W. SPENCER.	23/3/18		2/12/18

EAST KENT REGIMENT.
(Buffs).
1st and 2nd Battalions.

Name	Missing	Interned		Repatriated
Capt. H. E. WARD.	2/11/14			15/12/18
Lieut. A. L. D. RYDER.	16/2/15			18/12/18
2/Lt. E. F. D. STRETTELL.	16/2/15	Holland	2/3/18	25/12/18
2/Lt. E. W. P. HAYMAN.	16/2/15	Holland	6/2/18	4/10/18
Capt. F. W. TOMLINSON.	21/4/15	Switzerland	9/12/17	9/6/18
Lieut. L. H. SMITH.	21/4/15	Holland	23/3/18	31/8/18
Lieut. G. R. HOWE.	3/5/15	Holland	23/3/18	15/1/19
2/Lt. G. E. A. STEGGALL.	26/9/15	Holland	19/4/18	18/11/18
Capt. J. V. R. JACKSON.	30/9/15			13/9/17
2/Lt. T. F. HARRINGTON.	28/6/17			3/12/18
2/Lt. H. S. WOTTON.	21/3/18			4/12/18

(Buffs).
3rd Battalion.

Name	Missing	Interned		Repatriated
Capt. A. R. JACKSON.		Holland	24/2/18	7/9/18
*2/Lt. D. J. DAVISON.	21/3/18			17/12/18

6th Battalion.

Name	Missing	Interned		Repatriated
Lieut. A. E. GRANT.	3/5/17	Holland	30/4/18	18/8/18
2/Lt. E. A. KING.	3/5/17			6/12/18
Capt. L. P. CAUSTON.	30/11/17			2/1/19
Lieut. W. F. BEAVAN.	30/11/17			17/12/18
2/Lt. W. R. TAYLOR.	30/11/17			11/12/18
2/Lt. T. C. FILLERY.	30/11/17			8/12/18
2/Lt. A. E. W. SANDBACH.	30/11/17			19/5/18
2/Lt. W. T. STEVENS.	30/11/17			5/12/18

7th Battalion.

Name	Missing	Repatriated
2/Lt. N. G. BLAKE.	3/5/17	17/12/18
2/Lt. J. E. M. KNIGHT.	12/10/17	13/12/18
Capt. D. GRANT.	21/3/18	2/12/18
Capt. H. FINE.	21/3/18	18/12/18
Capt. W. E. CHANT.	21/3/18	2/12/18
Lieut. L. H. KENNETT.	21/3/18	18/12/18

† Attached from Norfolk Regiment.   * Attached T.M.B.

EAST KENT REGIMENT—continued.
7th Battalion—continued.

Name.	Missing.	Interned.		Repatriated.
Lieut. G. W. CAMERON.	21/3/18			29/11/18
2/Lt. H. F. DANA.	21/3/18			18/12/18
2/Lt. F. C. WINTER.	21/3/18			29/11/18
2/Lt. L. W. MARTIN.	21/3/18			18/12/18
2/Lt. S. A. HARVEY.	21/3/18			–/12/18
Capt. H. TUPPER.	5/8/18			24/12/18
Lieut. H. S. WATSON.	6/8/18			–/12/18
Lieut. R. H. PLUMB.	6/8/18			26/12/18
Lieut. J. W. BRYANT.	6/8/18			16/1/19
†2/Lt. A. G. BROWN.	6/8/18			29/11/18

8th Battalion.

Name.	Missing.	Interned.		Repatriated.
Major G. W. WARDEN.	26/9/15	Switzerland	9/12/17	24/3/18
Major D. F. ROBINSON.	26/9/15	Holland	10/4/18	1/11/18
Capt. F. W. WATSON.	26/9/15	Switzerland	9/12/17	9/12/18
Capt. W. D. JOHNSON.	26/9/15			11/9/17
Lieut. T. H. TAYLOR.	26/9/15	Holland	10/4/18	18/11/18
Lieut. B. H. PICKERING.	26/9/15	(*Died* 1/12/15 at Cologne).		
Lieut. F. D. MONTGOMERIE.	26/9/15	Holland	10/4/18	12/10/18
Lieut. S. VAUGHAN.	26/9/15	Holland	10/4/18	18/11/18
2/Lt. R. B. CARROW.	26/9/15	Holland	10/4/18	18/11/18

10th Battalion.

Name.	Missing.	Interned.		Repatriated.
Lieut. F. D. WILKINSON.	21/9/18			3/12/18

KING'S OWN ROYAL LANCASTER REGIMENT.
1st and 2nd Battalions.

Name.	Missing.	Interned.		Repatriated.
Lieut. C. G. S. IRVINE.	10/9/14	Holland	5/1/18	16/11/18
Lieut. A. S. D. B. DOUGLAS.	–/–/14	Switzerland	30/5/16	26/12/17
Lieut. J. A. BEVAN.	21/10/14	Holland	6/2/18	18/11/18
Lieut. J. H. C. COULSTON.	21/10/14	Switzerland	12/8/16	30/11/17
Capt. C. W. GROVER.	10/5/15	Holland	23/3/18	19/12/18
Lieut. F. H. ELLIS.	10/5/15			13/9/17
Lieut. A. D. SEDDON.	10/5/15	Holland	10/4/18	18/11/18
2/Lt. A. O. D. TAYLOR.	10/5/15	Holland	23/3/18	18/11/18
2/Lt. N. N. HART.	17/11/17			27/11/18
*2/Lt. P. J. ALLAN.	28/3/18	(*Died* 22/5/18 at Hamburg).		
2/Lt. P. S. ROBERTSHAW.	18/4/18			13/12/18
2/Lt. J. S. NEVARD.	18/4/18			18/12/18
2/Lt. A. W. WALL.	18/4/18			18/12/18
Capt. H. J. T. De CARTERET.	22/10/14	Holland	2/3/18	22/11/18

4th Battalion.

Name.	Missing.	Interned.		Repatriated.
Capt. W. G. PEARSON.	16/6/15			–/9/17
Capt. H. A. BROCKLEBANK.	31/7/17			14/12/18
2/Lt. G. FIELD.	20/11/17			23/2/18
Lieut. A. S. LATHAM.	9/4/18			10/12/18
2/Lt. H. THREADGOLD.	9/4/18			8/12/18
2/Lt. E. D. OSGOOD.	9/4/18			11/12/18
2/Lt. R. A. TAYLOR.	9/4/18			11/12/18
2/Lt. W. HOLMES.	9/4/18			18/12/18
2/Lt. W. McANDREW.	9/4/18			18/12/18

† Attached from Royal West Kent Regiment.
* Attached T.M.B.

KING'S OWN ROYAL LANCASTER REGIMENT—continued.

5th Battalion.

Name.	Missing.	Interned.	Repatriated.
*2/Lt. K. St. C. H. TOOVEY.	30/11/17	(Died –/10/18 at Frankfort).	
2/Lt. E. STAINTON.	30/11/17		3/12/18
2/Lt. W. HARRISON.	30/11/17		25/12/18
2/Lt. J. E. FISHER.	30/11/17		19/5/18
Capt. O. G. HUNT.	9/4/18		29/11/18
2/Lt. A. J. WHITE.	9/4/18		8/12/18
2/Lt. W. YOUNG.	9/4/18		8/12/18
2/Lt. F. BUCKLEY.	9/4/18		8/12/18
2/Lt. G. STEEL.	9/4/18		10/12/18
2/Lt. B. PERCIVAL.	9/4/18		11/12/18
2/Lt. G. CONHEENY.	9/4/18	(Killed 5/12/18 at Stralsund).	
2/Lt. H. J. WARBRICK.	11–12/4/18		28/11/18
2/Lt. J. ALEXANDER.	22/4/18		–/11/18
2/Lt. W. McE. YACOMENI.	22/4/18		29/11/18
2/Lt. H. F. WOODCOCK.	10/7/18		13/12/18
2/Lt. J. MANN.	30/8/18		8/12/18
2/Lt. M. SWINBURNE.	30/8/18	(doubtful).	
†2/Lt. F. A. DANSON.	28/9/18		29/11/18

7th Battalion.

Capt. H. G. DAVIES.	31/7/17	Switzerland	13/5/18

8th Battalion.

2/Lt. H. C. BROWN.	18/8/16	Holland	12/10/18	18/11/17
Capt. W. C. SKERRETT.	28/3/18			10/12/18
Capt. A. HOLLAND.	28/3/18			28/11/18
2/Lt. W. CROMPTON.	28/3/18			28/11/18
2/Lt. R. M. RAE.	28/3/18			28/11/18
2/Lt. S. G. GODDARD.	12/4/18			4/12/18

11th Battalion.

2/Lt. J. C. BESWICK.	21/4/17	(Died 22/4/17 at Cambrai).	

NORTHUMBERLAND FUSILIERS.

1st Battalion.

Capt. H. O. SUTHERLAND.	16/9/14	Switzerland	12/8/16	11/9/17
Lieut. D. CONDON.	1/11/14	(Died –/8/17).		
Capt. G. O. SLOPER.	16/6/15	Holland	16/5/18	18/11/18
Capt. W. R. ALLEN.	28/3/18			25/12/18
2/Lt. E. I. LAWRENCE.	28/3/18			–/12/18
2/Lt. J. RICHARDS.	28/3/18	(Died at Ferin 30/3/18).		
2/Lt. H. P. MULLEN.	28/3/18			–/12/18
2/Lt. J. C. THOMPSON.	28/3/18			18/12/18
Lieut. D. STORY.	22/8/18			13/12/18

2nd Battalion.

2/Lt. W. TAYLOR.	9/5/15	Holland	10/4/18	5/12/18
Lt.-Col. S. H. ENDERBY.	11/5/15	Holland	23/3/18	17/11/18
Capt. R. T. K. AULD.	11/5/15	Holland	23/3/18	18/11/18
Capt. B. E. S. MAHON.	11/5/15	Holland	10/4/18	
2/Lt. F. B. A. CARDEW.	11/5/15	Holland	23/8/18	23/11/18
2/Lt. V. C. HARDY.	11/5/15	Holland	10/4/18	21/1/19

* Attached T.M.B.   † Attached from Loyal North Lancs.

NORTHUMBERLAND FUSILIERS—continued.

3rd Battalion.

Name.	Missing.	Interned.	Repatriated.
*2/Lt. J. SOWERBY.	27/5/18		14/12/18

4th Battalion.

Name.	Missing.	Interned.	Repatriated.
Capt. W. B. HICKS.	26/3/18		1/12/18
2/Lt. A. N. LAWSON.	10/4/18		18/12/18
Capt. C. G. GASSON.	27/5/18		30/12/18
Capt. R. ALLEN.	27/5/18		25/12/18
Capt. A. WILLIS.	27/5/18		1/12/18
Lieut. F. J. IVES.	27/5/18		9/1/19
Lieut. J. J. HOLME.	27/5/18		-/12/18
2/Lt. H. E. FINDLEY.	27/5/18		-/12/18
2/Lt. J. W. MARSDEN.	27/5/18		17/12/18
2/Lt. W. L. McLEAN.	27/5/18		17/12/18
2/Lt. A. H. ROYLE.	27/5/18		30/12/18
2/Lt. F. PEDDIE.	27/5/18		1/1/19
2/Lt. J. A. McINTYRE.	27/5/18		17/12/18
2/Lt. W. J. MAXFIELD.	27/5/18		21/1/19
Lieut. F. H. BEDFORD.	28/5/18		-/12/18
2/Lt. H. R. REES.	28/5/18		-/12/18
Lieut. H. H. HARRISON.	14/6/18		30/12/18

5th Battalion.

Name.	Missing.	Interned.	Repatriated.
2/Lt. T. A. CROFTS.	22/3/18		25/12/18
2/Lt. W. H. J. MARKHAM.	22/3/18	(*Died* at Belleglise 27/3/18).	
Capt. F. W. GRINLING.	9/4/18		25/12/18
Lieut. J. W. LOUGH.	10/4/18		-/12/18
Capt. G. BRANFOOT.	11/4/18		25/12/18
Lt. R. G. SMITH.	11/4/18		29/11/18
Lieut. P. GRAHAM.	11/4/18		25/12/18
Capt. H. G. DODDS.	27/5/18		-/1/19
2/Lt. R. H. QUINE.	27/5/18		-/12/18
†2/Lt. R. T. DENNIS.	27/5/18	(*Died* 19/12/18 at Wimereux).	
2/Lt. G. E. D. BURBIDGE.	27/5/18		-/12/18
2/Lt. A. E. BROWN.	27/5/18		18/12/18
2/Lt. S. WEATERTON.	27/5/18		-/12/18

6th Battalion.

Name.	Missing.	Interned.	Repatriated.
Lieut. C. A. BALDEN.	22/3/18		28/11/18
Lieut. G. A. OSWALD.	22/3/18		12/10/18
Lieut. S. MORPETH.	10/4/18		29/11/18
Lieut. A. THOMPSON.	12/4/18		28/11/18
Lt.-Col. E. TEMPERLEY.	27/5/18		25/12/18
Capt. H. GRAHAM.	27/5/18		26/12/18
Capt. R. E. M. HEANLEY.	27/5/18		25/12/18
Capt. J. G. GARRARD.	27/5/18		21/1/19
Lieut. J. WATSON.	27/5/18		-/12/18
Lieut. J. W. CRAKE.	27/5/18		25/12/18
Lieut. W. M. McLARE.	27/5/18		6/1/19
Lieut. C. O. MARSHALL.	27/5/18		14/12/18
Lieut. H. V. RUSSELL.	27/5/18		18/12/18
2/Lt. W. R. DODD.	27/5/18		-/12/18
‡2/Lt. A. E. GLANVILLE.	27/5/18		8/12/18
2/Lt. J. GRAY.	27/5/18		2/1/19
2/Lt. J. S. STOKOE.	27/5/18		-/12/18

* Attached T.M.B.   † Attached from R. Irish Rifles.
‡ Attached from R. Dublin Fus.

NORTHUMBERLAND FUSILIERS—continued.

6th Battalion—continued.

Name.	Missing.	Interned.	Repatriated.
2/Lt. A. S. TAYLOR.	27/5/18		30/12/18
*2/Lt. T. R. LEES.	27/5/18		18/12/18
*2/Lt. H. R. B. BELLERBY.	27/5/18		25/12/18
†2/Lt. A. P. ANDERSON.	27/5/18		–/12/18

8th Battalion.

2/Lt. C. TOLKIEN.	27/5/18		18/12/18

9th Battalion.

2/Lt. H. E. WOODS.	23/4/17	(Died).	
2/Lt. L. W. FEATHERSTONE.	9/4/18		18/12/18

12th and 13th Battalions.

Name.	Missing.	Interned.	Repatriated.
2/Lt. C. R. M. GREENFIELD.	25/1/18		17/12/18
2/Lt. B. E. ASTBURY.	26/1/18		17/12/18
Major G. WHITE.	21/3/18		17/12/18
Capt. J. McKINNON.	21/3/18		–/1/19
Capt. J. O. BYRNE.	21/3/18		10/12/18
Lieut. A. P. HARROWER.	21/3/18	(Died at Roisel 26/3/18).	
Lieut. F. L. SMART.	21/3/18		14/12/18
2/Lt. A. WILLIAMSON.	21/3/18		18/12/18
2/Lt. R. H. COMLEY.	21/3/18		2/12/18
2/Lt. H. L. JOHNSON.	21/3/18		–/12/18
2/Lt. G. COPELAND.	21/3/18		5/12/18
2/Lt. H. F. DODD.	21/3/18		17/12/18
2/Lt. G. H. R. DOMAN.	21/3/18	(Died at Ostrove 11/6/18).	
2/Lt. J. RICHARDSON.	21/3/18		12/10/18
‡Capt. J. R. SHORT.	22/3/18		8/12/18
Capt. C. R. LINGWOOD.	16/4/18		13/12/18
Lieut. J. R. RITZEMA.	16/4/18		11/12/18
2/Lt. H. V. GATESHILL.	16/4/18		18/12/18
2/Lt. W. BRIGHAM.	16/4/18		11/12/18
2/Lt. G. W. LACEY.	16/4/18		25/12/18
2/Lt. H. W. DICKINSON.	16/4/18	(Died 9/8/18).	
Lieut. J. N. HALL.	27/5/18		25/12/18
Lieut. E. R. BRAIN.	27/5/18		25/12/18
Lieut. I. W. MAKEPEACE.	27/5/18		17/12/18
2/Lt. P. J. PASCOE.	27/5/18		–/12/18
2/Lt. B. H. CLARKE.	27/5/18		–/1/19
2/Lt. D. GEGGIE.	27/5/18		25/12/18
2/Lt. J. B. JACKSON.	27/5/18		–/1/19
2/Lt. W. C. DICKINSON.	27/5/18		26/12/18
2/Lt. R. E. FISHER.	27/5/18		10/12/18

18th Battalion.

Capt. F. J. REIDY.	16/6/17		2/1/19
2/Lt. A. INGLE.	16/6/17		6/12/18
2/Lt. S. J. KERR.	16/6/17		6/12/18

* Attached from R. Irish Rifles.
† Attached from Durham Light Infantry.
‡ Attached from Yorkshire Regiment.

NORTHUMBERLAND FUSILIERS—continued.
14th Battalion.

Name.	Missing.	Interned.	Repatriated.
2/Lt. J. E. HENDERSON.	22/3/18	(*Died*).	
2/Lt. T. D. LAWSON.	22/3/18		18/12/18
2/Lt. J. P. SOWERBY.	23/3/18		1/12/18
2/Lt. M. S. BRYCE.	27/5/18		-/12/18
2/Lt. F. T. DAVIS.	27/5/18		-/12/18
2/Lt. S. B. MILNE.	27/5/18		-/12/18
2/Lt. J. PARSONS.	27/5/18		30/12/18
Capt. S. A. HOLMAN.	28/5/18		20/12/18
Capt. C. E. MAYNARD.	28/5/18		-/1/19
2/Lt. L. LANGLEY.	28/5/18		-/12/18
2/Lt. A. GIBSON.	28/5/18		-/12/18

17th Battalion.

Name.	Missing.	Interned.	Repatriated.
2/Lt. E. TURNBULL.	10/4/18		18/12/18

20th Battalion.

Name.	Missing.	Interned.	Repatriated.
2/Lt. T. P. CONOLLY.	3/7/16	Holland 16/5/18	2/12/18
2/Lt. H. SEARS.	22/10/17		3/12/18

22nd Battalion.

Name.	Missing.	Interned.	Repatriated.
2/Lt. D. A. ROGERS.	22/10/17		3/12/18
Lieut. J. H. FAULDER.	21/3/18		1/12/18
Lieut. A. E. CARTER.	21/3/18		29/11/18
2/Lt. F. G. OLIVER.	21/3/18		1/12/18
2/Lt. N. C. HENRY.	21/3/18		8/12/18
2/Lt. J. H. GRANT.	21/3/18		18/12/18
2/Lt. N. DAVIDSON.	21/3/18		18/12/18
2/Lt. B. PEACOCK.	21/3/18		11/12/18
2/Lt. J. ROBINSON.	21/3/18		11/12/18
Lieut. J. H. NICHOLSON.	11/4/18		25/12/18
Capt. A. W. D. MARK.	13/4/18		13/12/18
2/Lt. R. L. NISBET.	13/4/18		29/11/18
2/Lt. G. M. GIBSON.	3/9/18		13/12/18

23rd Battalion.

Name.	Missing.	Interned.	Repatriated.
2/Lt. A. A. MORRIS.	29/4/17		14/12/18
Lt.-Col. G. CHARLTON.	21/3/18		28/11/18
Capt. W. M. DODDS.	21/3/18	(*Died* at Posen).	14/10/18
Capt. S. H. MATTHEWS.	21/3/18		2/12/18
Capt. J. T. V. WIGGANS.	21/3/18		2/12/18
Capt. G. A. BROWN.	21/3/18		28/11/18
Lieut. S. J. WILLMOTT.	21/3/18		29/11/18
Lieut. W. WATSON.	21/3/18		1/12/18
Lieut. A. R. LIDDELL.	21/3/18		11/12/18
2/Lt. H. J. WILSON.	21/3/18		18/12/18
2/Lt. W. R. T. COLE.	21/3/18		1/12/18
2/Lt. J. C. RODGER.	21/3/18		11/12/18
2/Lt. W. L. BOWMAN.	21/3/18		18/12/18
2/Lt. W. BOYD.	21/3/18		11/1/19
2/Lt. A. LAMBERT.	21/3/18		18/12/18
2/Lt. H. H. DAVIES.	21/3/18		27/11/18
2/Lt. G. R. JEFFERSON.	21/3/18		-/12/18
Capt. A. MORLIDGE.	11/4/18		3/12/18
2/Lt. J. P. HUGHES.	12/4/18		-/12/18
2/Lt. A. N. THOMPSON.	12/4/18		3/12/18
2/Lt. L. F. LEATHARD.	12/4/18		3/12/18
2/Lt. S. F. EGAN.	13/4/18		1/12/18

NORTHUMBERLAND FUSILIERS—continued.
24th Battalion.

Name.	Missing.	Interned.	Repatriated.
2/Lt. R. G. LENNARD.	20/4/17	(Died).	

25th Battalion.

Lt.-Col. N. LEITH-HAY-CLARK.	21/3/18	Switzerland 21/10/18	9/12/18
Capt. F. McKELLEN.	21/3/18		10/12/18
Capt. J. G. KIRKUP.	21/3/18		10/12/18
2/Lt. T. H. TAYLOR.	21/3/18		1/12/18
2/Lt. F. A. HARRISON.	21/3/18		18/12/18
2/Lt. G. C. SNOWDON.	21/3/18		8/12/18
Lieut. G. HARDY.	11/4/18		1/12/18

26th Battalion.

Lieut. P. A. GAMBLE.	21/3/18		–/1/19

ROYAL WARWICKSHIRE REGIMENT.
1st and 2nd Battalions.

Lieut. C. F. MAUNSELL.	26/8/14	Switzerland 9/12/17	6/12/18
Major R. MEIKLEJOHN.	4/9/14	Switzerland 30/5/16	24/3/18
Lieut. C. H. J. CHICHESTER-CONSTABLE.	4/9/14		1/1/19
Capt. J. B. B. MACKY.	25/9/14	Switzerland 9/12/17	23/12/18
Capt. P. E. BESANT.	30/9/14	Switzerland 9/12/17	14/6/18
Major D. A. L. DAY.	1/10/14	Holland 22/1/18	18/11/18
Capt. J. H. W. KNIGHT-BRUCE.	1/10/14		11/9/17
Capt. E. G. SYDENHAM.	20/10/14	Switzerland 27/12/17	14/6/18
Capt. N. B. F. COLLINS.	23/10/14	Holland 6/2/18	22/11/18
Lieut. J. METCALFE.	23/10/14	Holland 6/2/18	27/11/18
Lieut. G. H. R. B. SOMERVILLE.	3/10/14		9/4/18
Capt. J. M. LUCAS.	31/10/14	Holland 24/2/18	18/11/18
Capt. E. M. ONSLOW.	31/10/14	Holland 7/10/18	15/10/18
Capt. H. W. OZANNE.	31/10/14	Holland 24/2/18	21/11/18
Capt. A. J. PECK.	31/10/14	Holland 24/2/18	21/5/18
Major P. J. FOSTER.	31/11/14	Switzerland 9/12/17	9/12/18
Capt. I. A. BROWN.	31/11/14		26/12/18
Capt. J. B. HADDON.	18/12/14	Holland 24/2/18	18/11/18
2/Lt. P. F. W. HERBAGE.	26/9/15		18/11/18
2/Lt. G. S. M. NATHAN.	3/5/17		11/1/19
2/Lt. J. PARKER.	3/5/17		4/1/19
2/Lt. A. H. WILLES.	3/5/17		31/12/18
2/Lt. P. H. HORSLEY.	9/8/18		17/12/18
2/Lt. J. E. C. GUEST.	9/9/18	(Died).	

5th Battalion.

*Capt. F. W. BLANCHARD.	3/12/17	(Died 26/1/18).	
Capt. H. P. CHURCHOUSE.	3/12/17		17/12/18
2/Lt. A. W. BARNES.	3/12/17		19/1/19
2/Lt. R. T. HARRIS.	3/12/17		17/12/18
2/Lt. A. E. WINTER.	3/12/17		18/12/18
2/Lt. A. A. C. BROWN.	15/6/18		20/11/18
Capt. E. P. Q. CARTER.	15/6/18		12/11/18
Capt. J. B. FLORENCE.	15/6/18		12/11/18

2/5th Battalion.

†Capt. G. W. S. HOPKINS.	23/3/18		3/12/18

* Attached from D.C.L.I.   † Attached T.M.B.

ROYAL WARWICKSHIRE REGIMENT—continued.

2/6th Battalion.

Name.	Missing.	Interned.	Repatriated.
Capt. F. AYRE.	21/3/18		1/12/18
Capt. A. PHELPS.	22/3/18		-/12/18
2/Lt. J. W. CROFT.	22/3/18		29/11/18
2/Lt. F. HARDY.	22/3/18		25/12/18
Capt. F. J. BREEDON.	14/4/18		2/12/18
Capt. B. K. PARSONS.	14/4/18		2/12/18
2/Lt. H. G. CHELLINGWORTH.	4/4/18		3/12/18
2/Lt. T. T. HAWORTH.	14/4/18		13/12/18
*2/Lt. R. H ATTWELL.	29/6/18		29/11/18
2/Lt. A. E. CLARKE.	2/7/16	(Died at Cologne 9/7/16).	

2/7th Battalion.

Name.	Missing.	Interned.	Repatriated.
2/Lt. R. H. ADAMS.	22/3/18		25/12/18
2/Lt. W. CROOK.	22/3/18		29/11/18
Capt. G. L. GRAHAM.	23/3/18	(Died at Seboncourt 11/4/18).	
2/Lt. H. V. DAVIES.	23/3/18		1/12/18
2/Lt. A. R. JONES.	23/3/18	(Died).	
2/Lt. W. J. MOON.	23/3/18		30/12/18
Lieut. H. N. SMITH.	24/3/18		13/12/18

8th Battalion.

Name.	Missing.	Interned.	Repatriated.
Capt. G. C. FIELD.	26/6/16	Switzerland 8/12/17	14/6/18
Lieut. F. A. BRETTELL.	1/7/16		24/3/18
2/Lt. H. S. TOOGOOD.	27/8/16		18/12/18

2/8th Battalion.

Name.	Missing.	Interned.	Repatriated.
†Lieut. F. G. LEIGH.	22/3/18		19/12/18

10th Battalion.

Name.	Missing.	Interned.	Repatriated.
Capt. A. B. O'DONNELL.	17/8/16		23/10/18
Capt. J. R. GRIBBLE.	23/3/18	(Died at Mainz 25/11/18).	
Lieut. J. G. H. MANDER.	23/3/18		25/12/18
2/Lt. H. L. KEENE.	23/3/18		26/12/18
2/Lt. C. G. BAGLEY.	23/3/18		1/12/18
Capt. S. St. G. S. KINGDON.	10/4/18		1/1/19
Capt. C. MARTINEAU.	10/4/18	(Died at Kortryk 5/5/18).	
Lieut. R. ASTON.	10/4/18		13/12/18

11th Battalion.

Name.	Missing.	Interned.	Repatriated.
Capt. J. W. GRIFFIN.	22/3/18		-/12/18

14th Battalion.

Name.	Missing.	Interned.	Repatriated.
2/Lt. J. P. IVENS.	25/6/17		2/1/19
Lieut. F. C. ILETT.			1/12/18

15th Battalion.

Name.	Missing.	Interned.	Repatriated.
2/Lt. E. C. HOBSON.	9/5/17		20/5/17
2/Lt. A. H. THORPE.	25/10/17		5/12/18
Capt. A. C. COLDICOTT.	28/6/18	(Died at Dortmund 16/8/18).	

16th Battalion.

Name.	Missing.	Interned.	Repatriated.
2/Lt. G. ELTHAM.	27/5/17	Switzerland 29/12/17	23/12/18
Lieut. G. H. HADLEY.	14/4/17		29/11/18
2/Lt. J. E. GOPSILL.	9/10/17		14/12/18

* Attached from Suffolk Regiment.
† Attached T.M.B.

ROYAL FUSILIERS.
1st and 2nd Battalions.

Name.	Missing.	Interned.		Repatriated.
Lieut. F. A. SAMPSON.	26/8/14	Holland	5/1/18	23/9/18
Capt. Mowbray COLE.	14/9/14	(*Died*).		
Lieut. R. W. JACKSON.	20/10/14	Holland	24/2/18	22/1/19
Lieut. L. C. RUSSELL.	1/7/16		(Escaped)	30/11/17
2/Lt. A. HEDGES.	1/7/16	Switzerland	–/12/16	11/9/17
2/Lt. W. W. LINE.	30/11/17			27/11/18
2/Lt. W. DIMMOCK.	30/11/17			17/12/18
2/Lt. W. R. SPIKESMAN.	21–25/3/18			28/11/18
Capt. G. A. JONES.	22/3/18			–/11/18
2/Lt. S. W. WALLIS.	22/3/18			11/12/18
2/Lt. W. T. GOULD.	11/4/18			31/12/18

3rd Battalion.

Name.	Missing.	Interned.		Repatriated.
Lieut. J. A. BREWSTER.	25/5/15	Switzerland	12/8/16	11/9/17
2/Lt. T. ROBERTSON.	25/5/15	Holland	10/4/18	30/12/18

5th Battalion.

Name.	Missing.	Interned.		Repatriated.
Capt. R. S. SCHOLEFIELD.	25/9/15	Switzerland	19/12/16	13/9/17

7th Battalion.

Name.	Missing.	Interned.	Repatriated.
2/Lt. W. R. TRICKER.	30/12/17		27/11/18
2/Lt. G. W. MARPLE.	30/12/17		27/11/18
2/Lt. H. R. POOLEY.	30/12/17		27/11/18
2/Lt. H. M. P. PHELPS.	30/12/17		17/12/18
2]Lt. G. R. J. DUCKWORTH.	25/3/18		19/12/18
2/Lt. S. W. DUNTHORNE.	25/3/18		25/12/18
2/Lt. R. W. POLLARD.	25/3/18		29/11/18
2/Lt. A. E. V. BUDGE.	4/4/18		25/12/18
*Lieut. S. H. YOUNG.	26/8/18		13/12/18
Lieut. A. W. WHITLOCK.	27/8/18		18/12/18

8th Battalion.

Name.	Missing.	Interned.	Repatriated.
Col. N. B. ELLIOTT-COOPER.	30/11/17	(*Died* 11/2/18).	
Capt. F. W. GADE.	30/11/17		31/12/18
Lieut. W. CARMICHAEL.	30/11/17		3/12/18
2/Lt. G. F. PARFECT.	30/11/17		25/12/18
2/Lt. D. A. B. FRY.	30/11/17		25/12/18
2/Lt. G. F. STEARNE.	30/11/17		3/12/18
2/Lt. C. PATERSON.	7/10/16		18/12/18

9th Battalion.

Name.	Missing.	Interned.		Repatriated.
Lieut. T. B. JONES.	3/5/17			31/12/18
2/Lt. H. H. BROOKER.	21/11/17	Holland	30/4/18	23/11/18
2/Lt. A. V. EDWARDS.	30/11/17			3/12/18
2/Lt. A. H. ELLIOTT.	30/11/17			17/12/18
2/Lt. S. POTTER.	30/11/17			17/12/18

10th Battalion.

Name.	Missing.	Interned.	Repatriated.
2/Lt. S. J. THOMPSON.	14/9/18		9/12/18

11th Battalion.

Name.	Missing.	Interned.	Repatriated.
2/Lt. W. H. PRIOR.	3/5/17		1/1/19
Lieut. H. R. CRESSY.	10/8/17		14/12/18
2/Lt. G. W. H. ROGERS.	10/8/17		14/12/18
2/Lt. G. A. RENDLE.	10/8/17		19/12/18
Major G. DEKIN.	23/3/18		18/12/18
Capt. G. S. PEARCY.	23/3/18		10/12/18

* Attached 17th L.T.M.B.
† Attached from Royal Sussex Regiment.

ROYAL FUSILIERS—continued.
11th Battalion—continued.

Name.	Missing.	Interned.		Repatriated.
2/Lt. W. R. ROE.	3/5/17	(*Died* at Henn Lenglet 11/5/17).		
Capt. H. W. BROOKLING.	23/3/18			1/12/18
2/Lt. G. WILCOX.	23/3/18			-/12/18
2/Lt. G. M. GIBBS.	23/3/18			18/12/18
2/Lt. E. JAMES.	23/3/18			-/12/18
2/Lt. J. P. CRUIKSHANK.	23/3/18			18/12/18
2/Lt. A. H. MATTHEWS.	23/3/18			18/12/18

12th Battalion.

2/Lt. C. H. L. SKEET.	25/9/15	Holland	19/4/18	18/11/18
2/Lt. J. EASTON.	26/9/15	Holland	19/4/18	18/11/18

13th Battalion.

2/Lt. L. E. SHORMAN.	30/9/17			13/12/18
*2/Lt. T. W. SENIOR.	23/10/18			8/12/18

21st Battalion.

Capt. R. H. WHITTINGTON.	1/2/16	Holland	19/4/18	18/11/18

22nd Battalion.

2/Lt. J. H. E. ELLISON.	17/2/17			30/12/18
†2/Lt. J. W. IRELAND.	25/3/18			18/12/18

23rd Battalion.

2/Lt. C. H. DEACON.	17/2/17			17/12/18
2/Lt. F. K. HADDEN.	16/4/17			4/12/18
2/Lt. E. E. PENGILLEY.	3/5/17			14/12/18
2/Lt. C. D. ROWE.	23/3/18			11/12/18
Major N. A. LEWIS.	25/3/18			25/12/18
Capt. H. A. NICHOLSON.	25/3/18			18/12/18
Lieut. R. J. EVANS.	25/3/18			13/12/18
Lieut. J. LEIGHTON.	25/3/18			1/12/18
Lieut. N. THORNHILL.	25/3/18			30/12/18
2/Lt. H. WILLIAMS.	25/3/18			2/12/18
2/Lt. J. F. MANCE.	25/3/18			18/12/18
2/Lt. H. D. BIRD.	25/3/18			23/9/18
2/Lt. G. S. B. ANDREW.	25/3/18			18/12/18
2/Lt. W. H. RITCHIE.	25/3/18			18/12/18
2/Lt. P. PIPER.	25/3/18			31/12/18
2/Lt. C. PEARCE.	7/9/18			8/12/18

24th Battalion.

2/Lt. G. C. CLIFFORD.	29/4/17			6/12/18
Lieut. A. WING.	24/3/18			3/1/19
2/Lt. H. W. H. MOORE.				18/12/18
2/Lt. S. C. LAMBERT.	25/3/18			18/12/18
2/Lt. R. W. WINKWORTH.	25/3/18			18/12/18

LIVERPOOL REGIMENT.
1st Battalion.

Capt. F. L. KING.	8/8/16	Holland	12/10/18	21/1/19
Lieut. T. P. BREMNER.	8/8/16	Holland	12/10/18	22/11/18
Lieut. W. B. MOORHEAD.	8/8/16	Holland	12/10/18	22/11/18
2/Lt. C. R. D. BUSTARD.	8/8/16	Holland	12/10/18	9/12/18
2/Lt. H. W. SHAPTON.	30/11/17			3/12/18

* Attached from Northumberland Fusiliers.
† Attached T.M.B.

LIVERPOOL REGIMENT—continued.
1st Battalion—continued.

Name.	Missing.	Interned.	Repatriated.
2/Lt. A. H. ALEXANDER.	30/11/17		23/12/18
2/Lt. T. BOX.	30/11/17		17/12/18
2/Lt. J. DICKINSON.	30/11/17		25/12/18
2/Lt. J. H. S. GIBSON.	30/11/17		17/12/18
*Lieut. S. J. HENDRY.	24/3/18		–/12/18
2/Lt. G. H. EDWARDS.	24/3/18		25/12/18
Lieut. F. L. CHEETHAM.	27/9/18		28/11/18

4th Battalion.

2/Lt. S. THOMPSON.	15/4/18		–/12/18
Capt. D. H. PACK.	16/4/18		18/12/18
†2/Lt. A. O. WARD.	16/4/18		25/12/18
2/Lt. J. SPENCER.	16/4/18		25/12/18
2/Lt. S. E. BIRKUMSHAW.	16/4/18		30/12/18
2/Lt. J. F. MARRION.	16/4/18		1/12/18
2/Lt. L. COLLINGS.	16/4/18		18/12/18
2/Lt. C. NEWMAN.	16/4/18		25/12/18
2/Lt. F. WHEELER.	16/4/18		25/12/18
Lieut. W. J. KENDALL.	26/4/18		18/12/18

5th Battalion.

2/Lt. H. F. STEWART.	22/11/16		6/1/19
Lieut. T. W. SAUNDERS.	8/4/18		11/12/18
Capt. E. S. FORSTER.	9/4/18		11/12/18
Capt. G. B. EDWARDS.	9/4/18		8/12/18
2/Lt. R. W. FOULKES.	9/4/18		11/12/18
2/Lt. F. W. HARKIN.	9/4/18		11/12/18
2/Lt. K. R. A. ALLBON-BENNETT.	9/4/18		11/12/18
2/Lt. R. H. RICHARDS.	9/4/18		11/12/18
2/Lt. W. B. LEITHEAD.	9/4/18		11/12/18
2/Lt. J. A. NICHOLSON.	9/4/18		11/12/18
2/Lt. E. CLARK.	9/4/18		28/11/18
2/Lt. M. B. JONES.	9/4/18		25/12/18
2/Lt. F. M. KNIVETON.	9/4/18		11/12/18
2/Lt. F. WHITEHEAD.	9/4/18		11/12/18
2/Lt. P. GRUNDY.	9/4/18		29/11/18
2/Lt. F. W. FIRMINGER.	3/5/18		29/11/18

6th Battalion.

Capt. G. D. TYSON.	30/11/17		13/12/18
Lieut. V. R. BOWERS.	30/11/17		4/12/18
Lieut. R. R. STEWART.	30/11/17		6/1/19
2/Lt. E. S. ROGERS.	30/11/17		25/12/18
2/Lt. C. V. WATTS.	30/11/17		29/11/18
2/Lt. W. R. SMITH.	30/11/17		25/12/18
2/Lt. H. J. SHEPPARD.	30/11/17		3/12/18
2/Lt. W. K. DAVY.	30/11/17		2/12/18
2/Lt. C. F. COLE.	30/6/18		18/12/18

7th Battalion.

2/Lt. G. TAYLOR.	23/3/18		6/12/18
Lieut. S. B. POOLE.	9/4/18		25/12/18
2/Lt. W. P. SMART.	16/6/18		–/12/18
2/Lt. E. JONES.	29/9/18		13/12/18

* Attached from Border Regiment.   † Attached from Devonshire Regiment.

LIVERPOOL REGIMENT—continued.
8th Battalion.

Name.	Missing.	Interned.		Repatriated.
Capt. E. M. MURPHY.	8/8/16	Holland	12/10/18	21/1/19
Lieut. W. D. N. LILLEY.	8/8/16	(*Died* 11/8/16 at St. Quentin).		
Lieut. W. DUNCAN.	8/8/16		Escaped	16/2/18
2/Lt. H. WHITESIDE.	8/8/16			22/11/18
2/Lt. J. A. SISSON.	8/8/16	Holland	12/10/18	25/11/18
2/Lt. R. BURROW.	8/8/16	Holland	12/10/18	22/11/18
2/Lt. C. B. J. COLLISON.	8/8/16	Holland	12/10/18	21/1/19
2/Lt. W. N. SPARGO.	8/8/16			11/9/17
2/Lt. B. MALLINSON.	22/2/17			6/1/19
Lieut. E. F. G. ORCHARD.	31/7/17	(*Died*).		
2/Lt. C. W. VICK.	20/11/17			13/12/18
2/Lt. P. A. R. GEORGE.	20/11/17			13/12/18
2/Lt. R. A. DAVIES.	22/11/17			3/12/18
2/Lt. F. A. FREE.	22/12/17			29/11/18
*Capt. W. B. DOWSON.	21/3/18			10/12/18
2/Lt. O. P. CASEY.	31/3/18			2/1/19

10th Battalion.

Name.	Missing.	Interned.	Repatriated.
Capt. J. R. WILLIAMS.	10/8/16	(*Died* 13/8/16 at St. Quentin).	
2/Lt. G. R. HUGHES.	11/10/17		13/12/18
Capt. A. T. SALVIDGE.	30/11/17		28/11/18
Lieut. S. F. VELHO.	30/11/17		25/12/18
2/Lt. G. L. DICKSON.	30/11/17		3/12/18
2/Lt. J. D. GULICH.	30/11/17		27/11/18
*2/Lt. H. M. LOCKE.	30/11/17		17/12/18
†2/Lt. W. GARROW.	30/11/17		3/12/18
2/Lt. F. H. LOWE.	30/11/17		15/11/18
2/Lt. A. MANTLE.	30/11/17		17/12/18
2/Lt. I. A. STEWART.	30/11/17		3/12/18

11th Battalion.

Name.	Missing.	Repatriated.
Lieut. J. E. ACHESON.	23/3/18	18/12/18

12th Battalion.

Name.	Missing.	Repatriated.
2/Lt. J. BELL.	30/11/17	14/12/18
2/Lt. C. D. TAYLOR.	30/11/17	27/11/18
2/Lt. F. L. MULLIS.	30/11/17	3/12/18
2/Lt. C. M. SWATMAN.	—/3/18	18/12/18
2/Lt. G. M. GATHERAL.	21/3/18	25/12/18
Capt. J. E. B. PLUMMER.	21/3—3/4/18	16/12/18
Lieut. F. W. BUDD.	21/3—3/4/18	29/11/18
Lieut. J. S. MIDDLETON.	21/3—3/4/18	2/1/19
2/Lt. J. O'N. KENNEDY.	21/3—3/4/18	12/10/18

13th Battalion.

Name.	Missing.	Repatriated.
‡2/Lt. McC. DALY.	3/5/17	6/12/18
2/Lt. A. RICHARDS.	28/8/17	14/12/18
2/Lt. A. CHALLIS.	23/3/18	—/12/18
Lieut. B. W. GRAY.	28/3/18	18/12/18
§2/Lt. C. J. ALLISON.	28/3/18	2/12/18
2/Lt. H. HALEY.	28/3/18	2/1/19
2/Lt. A. R. TETLOW.	28/3/18	25/12/18
2/Lt. W. S. LITTLE.	28/3/18	2/1/19
2/Lt. S. MITCHELL.	28/3/18	11/12/18
Capt. S. T. J. PERRY.	31/8/18	10/12/18

* Attached T.M.B. † Attached from Cameron Highlanders.
‡ Attached from K.O.R.L. § Attached from Household Battalion.

LIVERPOOL REGIMENT—continued.

17th Battalion.

Name.	Missing.	Interned.	Repatriated.
Lieut. E. S. ASHCROFT.	1/5/18	(*Died* 12/5/18 at Lauwe).	
2/Lt. A. H. ELLIS.	2/5/18		6/12/18

18th Battalion.

Capt. E. B. BEAZLEY.	18/10/16	Switzerland 9/12/17	14/6/18
Capt. F. M. SHEARD.	21/3/18	(*Died* 2/4/18 at Bohain).	
*2/Lt. S. HOPE.	21/3/18		11/12/18
2/Lt. A. E. BARLOW.	23/3/18		18/12/18
2/Lt. A. G. COX.	23/3/18		18/12/18

19th Battalion.

Lt.-Col. J. N. PECK.	22/3/18		18/12/18
Capt. H. T. WILLMER.	22/3/18		10/12/18
Lieut. J. C. MUIR.	22/3/18		–/12/18
2/Lt. L. D. OWEN.	22/3/18		18/12/18
2/Lt. J. ROSS.	22/3/18		29/11/18
2/Lt. A. BRADBURY.	22/3/18		11/12/18
2/Lt. J. P. KING.	22/3/18		28/11/18
2/Lt. G. P. KING.	22/3/18		28/11/18

20th Battalion.

Lieut. G. W. LAMB.	30/7/16	Holland 15/6/18	18/11/18
2/Lt. H. K. BUSH.	30/7/16	Holland 15/6/18	22/11/18
2/Lt. A. E. WILSON.	30/7/16	(Escaped)	12/5/18
2/Lt. H. DERBYSHIRE.	24/3/18		25/12/18

25th Battalion.

2/Lt. S. B. CARSON.	9/10/18		8/12/18
2/Lt. T. E. GEORGE.	10/10/18		–/11/18

NORFOLK REGIMENT.

1st and 2nd Battalions.

Capt. R. REDDIE.	24/8/14	Escaped	4/8/17
Lieut. J. OAKES.	24/8/14	Holland 29/12/17	17/11/18
Lieut. G. PAGET.	11/9/14	Holland 29/12/17	17/11/18
Lieut. A. REEVE.	11/9/14	Holland 29/12/17	17/11/18
Lieut. G. P. BURLTON.	4/6/16	(*Died* 5/6/16).	
Lieut. O. S. D. WILLS.	26/3/18		1/12/18

7th Battalion.

2/Lt. W. G. FERGUSON.	2/8/17		29/11/18
2/Lt. D. C. WHITE.	14/10/17		3/12/18
Capt. K. R. POTTER.	30/11/17		14/12/18
Lieut. W. G. COLLINS.	30/11/17	(*Died* 21/1/18 at Hamburg).	
2/Lt. G. D. SUMMERS.	30/11/17		17/12/18
2/Lt. H. E. A. PAYNE.	30/11/17		2/1/19
‡Lt.-Col. E. T. REES.	27/3/18		–/1/19
2/Lt. W. H. BARTER.	27/3/18		25/12/18
§2/Lt. A. C. L. HILL.	27/3/18		18/12/18
§2/Lt. H. P. HOPTON.	27/3/18		18/12/18
§2/Lt. H. J. PHELPS.	27/3/18		–/12/18
2/Lt. E. G. U. CLARK.	27/3/18		–/1/19
2/Lt. F. A. HAYLOCK.	27/3/18		18/12/18

* Attached T.M.B.
† Attached from Northants Regiment.
‡ Attached from South Wales Borderers.   § Attached from Royal Warwicks.

NORFOLK REGIMENT—continued.
9th Battalion.

Name.	Missing.	Interned.	Repatriated.
2/Lt. F. T. BURTON.	21/3/18		29/11/18
2/Lt. J. R. C. LANE.	21/3/18		2/12/18
2/Lt. R. L. PERCIVAL.	21/3/18		29/11/18
Capt. J. W. HOWLETT.	13/4/18		18/12/18
2/Lt. C. J. W. TRENDELL.	16/4/18		18/12/18

LINCOLNSHIRE REGIMENT.
1st and 2nd Battalions.

Name	Missing	Interned	Repatriated
Capt. F. C. ROSE.	23/8/14	Switzerland 9/12/17	9/12/18
Major C. TOOGOOD.	10/9/14	Holland 5/1/18	23/9/18
Lieut. F. R. BRISLEE.	4/3/16	Holland 30/4/18	-/11/18
2/Lt. W. C. C. COX.	4/3/17		30/12/18
*Capt. L. Coleman SMITH.	16/8/17		25/12/18
2/Lt. S. J. BUSTON.	16/1/18		25/12/18
†2/Lt. F. G. COLE.	21/3/18		17/12/18
†2/Lt. C. E. WILLCOX.	22/3/18		17/12/18
†2/Lt. R. H. STAFFORD.	22/3/18		17/12/18
2/Lt. R. O. EDWARDS.	22/3/18		18/12/18
2/Lt. W. A. CROFT.	16/4/18		11/12/18
Lt.-Col. R. BASTARD.	27/5/18		-/1/19
Capt. H. MARSHALL.	27/5/18		25/12/18
Capt. J. T. PRESTON.	27/5/18		25/12/18
Lieut. G. R. HOLLIDAY.	27/5/18		30/12/18
Lieut. G. MATSON.	27/5/18		-/1/19
Lieut. H. G. CALDER.	27/5/18		11/1/19
2/Lt. J. HIGGINS.	27/5/18		11/1/19
2/Lt. L. J. TURNER.	27/5/18		-/12/18
2/Lt. S. G. SOLE.	27/5/18		2/1/19
2/Lt. C. RACE.	27/5/18		-/12/18
2/Lt. E. L. JONES.	27/5/18		18/12/18
2/Lt. B. W. PYE.	27/5/18		-/1/19
2/Lt. R. W. OSGERBY.	27/5/18		-/12/18
2/Lt. F. DONELL.	27/5/18		-/1/19
2/Lt. V. NOCTON.	27/5/18		-/1/19
2/Lt. A. R. BRADDY.	27/5/18		2/1/19
2/Lt. M. D. GRIEVE.	27/5/18		-/12/19
2/Lt. R. W. HARTLEY.	29/5/18		13/12/18
Lieut. H. W. FIRTH.	17/8/18		10/12/18

3rd Battalion.

Capt. R. F. PESKETT.		Switzerland 24/12/16	11/9/17

4th Battalion.

2/Lt. J. W. E. JOHNSON.	6/12/17		13/12/18
2/Lt. C. BLAMIRES.	-/3/18		18/12/18

5th Battalion.

2/Lt. R. W. ALSTON.	11/4/17		1/1/19
2/Lt. F. L. ROSE.	3/10/17		27/11/18
Capt. E. R. J. HETT.	21/3/18		18/12/18
2/Lt. W. G. ALLEN.	21/3/18		-/12/18
2/Lt. F. SHARPE.	21/3/18		11/12/18
2/Lt. F. R. GIBBONS.	21/3/18		18/12/18
2/Lt. A. J. ELSTON.	21/3/18		18/12/18
Lieut. P. E. COTTIS.	27/3/18		11/12/18
Capt. B. H. CHALLENOR.	31/3/18		18/12/18
Lieut. W. G. FENTON.	15/4/18		29/11/18
2/Lt. J. C. MYERS.	15/4/18		28/1/19

* Attached from South Staffs. † Attached from Royal Warwicks.

LINCOLNSHIRE REGIMENT—continued.

7th Battalion.

Name.	Missing.	Interned.	Repatriated.
Capt. E. de G. CARR.	23/3/18		6/12/18
Capt. H. C. F. WOTHERSPOON.	24/3/18		29/11/18
*Lieut. L. A. E. E. HOMMERT.	24/3/18		11/12/18

8th Battalion.

Name.	Missing.	Interned.		Repatriated.
Capt. L. D. McN. DAVIS.	25/9/15	Holland	10/4/18	18/11/18
Lieut. M. A. HALL.	25/9/15	Switzerland	9/12/17	7/12/18
Lieut. J. W. REYNOLDS.	25/9/15	Switzerland	30/5/16	14/9/17
Lieut. G. W. PARKER.	25/9/15	(*Died* 29/5/16).		
2/Lt. E. C. Van SOMERAN.	25/9/15	Holland	10/4/18	18/11/18
2/Lt. J. H. ALCOCK.	25/9/15	Holland	10/4/18	18/11/18
Lieut. L. D. EDWARDS.	16/11/16	Holland	9/4/18	16/8/18
2/Lt. B. W. GREGORY.	28/4/17			6/12/18
2/Lt. N. M. TIMPSON.	1/8/17			-/12/18

9th Battalion.

Name.	Missing.	Interned.	Repatriated.
2/Lt. N. G. WOODROW.	10/4/18		10/12/18

10th Battalion.

Name.	Missing.	Interned.	Repatriated.
Lieut. E. de L. W. ROEBUCK.	28/4/17		17/12/18
2/Lt. J. S. HILL.	28/4/17		31/12/18
2/Lt. H. J. LODGE.	28/4/17		6/12/18
2/Lt. A. R. MacKAY.	10/4/18		1/12/18
Lieut. W. S. ABBOTT.	10/4/18		18/12/18

DEVONSHIRE REGIMENT.

1st and 2nd Battalions.

Name.	Missing.	Interned.	Repatriated.
2/Lt. A. R. ABELL.	23/4/17	(*Died* 10/6/17).	
2/Lt. J. L. GREGORY.	25/11/17		6/11/18
2/Lt. C. E. CARPENTER.	22/3/18		1/12/18
2/Lt. R. TADMAN.	24/3/18		18/12/18
2/Lt. W. J. HANNAM.	26/3/18		11/12/18
2/Lt. W. E. DYSON.	24/4/18		29/11/18
Capt. U. B. BURKE.	27/5/18		23/10/18
*Capt. G. O. OPENSHAW.	27/5/18	(*Died* 9/8/18).	
*Capt. James MILNER.	27/5/18		6/12/18
*Capt. F. H. MILLMAN.	27/5/18		30/12/18
*Capt. S. H. COX.	27/5/18		-/12/18
*Capt. E. A. MILLAR.	27/5/18		30/12/18
Capt. W. L. CLEGG.	27/5/18		9/12/18
Capt. J. A. FERGUSSON.	27/5/18		30/12/18
Lieut. A. E. RUTLEDGE.	27/5/18		-/12/18
Lieut. T. OERTON.	27/5/18		31/12/18
‡Lieut. F. E. HARRIS.	27/5/18		13/12/18
*2/Lt. W. L. BARRETT.	27/5/18		14/12/18
2/Lt. R. F. B. HILL.	27/5/18		31/12/18
2/Lt. W. T. CROSS.	27/5/18		31/12/18
2/Lt. W. CANDLER.	27/5/18		-/12/18
2/Lt. F. MALKIN.	27/3/18		17/12/18
2/Lt. W. C. MAUNDER.	27/5/18		-/1/19
2/Lt. C. WREFORD.	27/5/18		-/12/18
2/Lt. R. LAMBERT.	27/5/18		31/12/18
2/Lt. A. M. HARVEY.	27/10/18		-/2/19

* Attached from A.S.C.
* Attached Portuguese Mission.
‡ Attached from South Staffs.

DEVONSHIRE REGIMENT—continued.
7th Battalion.

Name.	Missing.	Interned.	Repatriated.
*Lieut. J. N. HURRELL.	21/3/18		2/12/18

8th Battalion.

2/Lt. G. A. DREW.	26/10/17		3/12/18
2/Lt. W. J. REED.	26/10/17	(Died at Kortryk 28/10/17).	

9th Battalion.

2/Lt. H. E. B. DICKSON.		Switzerland 27/12/17	24/3/18
2/Lt. B. W. BLIGHT.	26/10/17		2/7/18
2/Lt. W. G. EVANS.	26/10/17		-/1/19
2/Lt. W. T. SANDERS.	26/10/17		16/12/18

SUFFOLK REGIMENT.
1st and 2nd Battalions.

Capt. E. PEARSON.	9/9/14	Holland 22/1/18	18/11/18
Lieut. V. G. M. PHILLIPS.	9/9/14	Holland 29/12/17	22/11/18
Major S. BARNARDISTON.	10/9/14	Holland 5/1/18	15/12/18
Major E. C. DOUGHTY.	10/9/14		13/9/17
Major A. PEEBLES.	10/9/14		13/9/17
Major F. T. WILSON.	10/9/14	Holland 5/1/18	30/11/18
Capt. W. M. CAMPBELL.	10/9/14		-/4/17
Capt. L. HEPWORTH.	10/9/14	(Died 10/3/17)	
Capt. A. CUTBILL.	10/9/14	Holland 22/1/18	21/12/18
Capt. E. ORFORD.	10/9/14		13/9/17
Lieut. E. H. W. BACKHOUSE.	10/9/14	Holland 22/1/18	21/1/19
Lieut. F. C. BERRILL.	10/9/14	Holland 5/1/18	18/11/18
Lieut. N. A. BITTLESTON.	10/9/14	Holland 22/1/18	18/11/18
Lieut. T. GEORGE	10/9/14	Holland 5/1/18	15/2/19
Lieut. R. G. HARVEY.	10/9/14	Holland 22/1/18	23/9/18
Lieut. J. B. MORGAN.	10/9/14		-/8/16
Lieut. C. B. NICHOLLS.	10/9/14	Holland 22/1/18	14/1/19
2/Lieut. H. P. JAMES	10/9/14	Holland 29/12/17	10/12/18
2/Lieut. A. F. KEMBLE.		Holland 10/4/18	23/10/18
Lieut. P. CARTHEW.	15/9/14	Holland 22/1/18	18/11/18
Lieut. H. BIGGS.	16/12/14	Holland 1/3/18	ret. for duty
Colonel W. B. WALLACE.	10/5/15	Holland 23/3/18	18/11/18
Capt. F. MOYSEY.	10/5/15	Holland 1/3/18	27/11/18
Lieut. C. AINSLEY.	10/5/15	Holland 23/3/18	22/11/18
Lieut. F. V. C. PEREIRA.		Holland 22/1/18	18/11/18
2/Lt. K. H. E. CAYLEY.	10/5/15	Holland 23/3/18	18/11/18
2/Lt. D. COX.	10/5/15	(Died 31/5/15)	
2/Lt. A. G. B. PATTEN.	21/7/16		22/11/18
2/Lt. H. W. WRIGHT.	13–15/11/16		18/12/18
2/Lt. K. M. DINGLEY.	13–15/11/16		18/12/18
Capt. W. L. SIMPSON.	22/3/18		10/12/18
2/L. H. J. BAYLIS	23/3/18		29/11/18
Capt. L. J. BAKER.	28/3/18		2/12/18
†Lieut. D. U. STONEHOUSE.	28/3/18		25/12/18
2/Lt. A. H. WARD.	28/3/18		29/11/18
2/Lt. H. W. WHITE.	28/3/18		11/12/18
2/Lt. E. H. HAMMONDS.	29/8/18		28/11/18

* Attached T.M.B.   † Attached from Norfolk Regiment.

SUFFOLK REGIMENT—Continued.

7th Battalion.

Name.	Missing.	Interned.	Repatriated.
Major P. S. WALKER.	30/11/17		11/1/19
Capt. L. A. G. BOWEN.	30/11/17		3/12/18
Capt. J. W. HAUGHTON.	30/11/17		3/12/18
2/Lt. H. W. CROOK.	30/11/17		2/12/18
2/Lt. J. C. DABBS.	30/11/17		3/12/18
*2/Lt. H. F. T. HAMILTON.	30/11/17		3/12/18
2/Lt. T. HAWKINS.	30/11/17		17/12/18
2/Lt. C. G. POULTER.	30/11/17	(Died 6/3/18)	
2/Lt. W. E. TEAGER.	30/11/17		27/11/18
2/Lt. H. THOMSON.	30/11/17		27/11/18

9th Battalion.

Name.	Missing.	Interned.	Repatriated.
2/Lt. H. L. FRAMPTON.	22/3/18		17/12/18

11th Battalion.

Name.	Missing.	Interned.	Repatriated.
2/Lt. W. A. MUDD.	28/4/17		1/1/19
2/Lt. J. M. HARMER.	28/4/17		1/1/19
2/Lt. F. W. BENNETT.	22/3/18		18/12/18
Capt. L. H. RODWELL.	6/4/18		18/12/18
2/Lt. R. S. SHEPHERD.	10/4/18		2/12/18
2/Lt. G. S. KEIGHTLEY.	13/4/18		1/12/18
2/Lt. J. A. SIMMONS.	13/4/18		18/12/18
2/Lt. G. C. LLOYD.	15/4/18		18/12/18

12th Battalion.

Name.	Missing.	Interned.	Repatriated.
2/Lt. K. PEARCE.	24/11/17		3/6/18
Capt. R. ENGLAND.	22/3/18		18/12/18
Lieut. G. HOPKINS.	22/3/18		18/12/18
Lieut. H. C. MATHEW.	22/3/18		28/11/18
2/Lt. J. A. BLANCH.	22/3/18		18/12/18
2/Lt. S. E. CLARKE.	22/3/18		1/12/18
2/Lt. G. HALLSMITH.	22/3/18		8/12/18
2/Lt C. H. HITCHCOCK.	22/3/18		10/12/18
2/Lt. G. T. TAYLOR.	22/3/18		18/12/18
2/Lt. E. L. TURNER.	22/3/18		18/12/18
2/Lt. A. J. WELLS.	22/3/18		18/12/18

SOMERSET LIGHT INFANTRY.

1st and 2nd Battalions.

Name.	Missing.	Interned.		Repatriated.
Lieut. J. G. SWAYNE.	26/8/14	Holland	22/1/18	returned on duty.
Capt. A. HARGREAVES.	6/9/14			11/9/17
Capt. J. BRODERIP.	25/9/14	Holland	22/1/18	24/12/18
Lieut. J. C. W. MACBRYAN.	25/9/14	Holland	22/1/18	18/11/18
Lieut. G. B. PHILBY.	25/9/14	Holland	22/1/18	21/12/18
Lieut. J. TAYLOR.	25/9/14	Holland	22/1/18	18/11/18
2/Lt. K. G. G. DENNYS.	19/12/14			11/9/17
2/Lt. H. W. V. TILLEY.	1/7/16	Holland	16/5/18	23/9/18
Lieut. Godwin NEWTON.				18/12/18

* Attached from Norfolk Regiment.
† Attached Trench Mortar Battery.

SOMERSET LIGHT INFANTRY—continued.
6th Battalion.

Name.	Missing.	Interned.	Repatriated.
Capt. H. S. BURRINGTON.	21/3/18		10/12/18
Capt. H. E. MAKINS.	21/3/18		31/12/18
*Capt. J. YELLOWLEES.	21/3/18		10/12/18
†Lieut. H. F. BOYCE.	21/3/18		8/12/18
Lieut. A. E. COTTRELL.	21/3/18		29/11/19
Lieut. R. G. C. DRAKE.	21/3/18		18/12/18
Lieut. I. A. ESTRIDGE.	21/3/18		10/12/18
Lieut. F. A. LEIVERS.	21/3/18		10/12/18
Lieut. W. A. N. THATCHER.	21/3/18		10/12/18
2/Lt. F. G. BURGESS.	21/3/18		11/12/18
2/Lt. A. C. V. HOSTLER.	21/3/18		11/12/18
2/Lt. W. D. SCOTT.	21/3/18		11/12/18
2/Lt. A. STAFFORD.	21/3/18		11/12/18
2/Lt. R. J. TUCKER.	21/3/18		11/12/18
2/Lt. T. F. TWIST.	21/3/18		11/12/18
2/Lt. W. J. WILCE.	21/3/18		18/12/18

7th Battalion.

Name.	Missing.	Interned.	Repatriated.
2/Lt. R H. FRYE.	15/6/17		6/12/18
Capt. A. A. ANDREWS.	30/11/17		15/12/18
2/Lt. W. B. PAUL.	30/11/17		9/5/18
Capt. H. A. FOLEY.	21/3–3/4/18		1/12/18
Lieut. R. ANDERSON.	21/3–3/4/18		28/12/18
2/Lt. H. A. COPE.	21/3–3/4/18		25/12/18
2/Lt. H. J. DUNCAN.	21/3–3/4/18		–/12/18
2/Lt. T. MITCHELL.	21/3–3/4/18		25/12/18
†2/Lt. F. PALMER.	21/3–3/4/18		18/12/18
2/Lt. H. M. SQUIBB.	21/3–3/4/18		2/12/18
Capt. G. D. J. McMURTRIE.	23/3/18		1/12/18
2/Lt. T. W. R. ELLIS.	8/4/18		25/12/18
2/Lt. D. C. J. CONSTABLE.	29/6/18		16/12/18

8th Battalion.

Name.	Missing.	Interned.	Repatriated.
Major W. H. NICHOLS.	26/9/15	(Died 15/10/15)	
†2/Lt. W. E. HAYES.	5/4/18		2/12/18
2/Lt. P. J. JONES.	5/4/18		–/1/19
2/Lt. S. T. DYTE.	5/4/18		25/12/18

12 Battalion.

Name.	Missing.	Interned.	Repatriated.
Capt. F. EDBROOKE.	1–11/9/18		29/11/18

WEST YORKSHIRE REGIMENT.
1st and 2nd Battalions.

Name.	Missing.	Interned.		Repatriated.
Capt. P. LOWE.	20/9/14	Switzerland	19/1/17	13/9/17
Capt. K. S. S. HENDERSON.	20/9/14	Holland	6/2/18	18/11/18
Capt. H. HARINGTON.	20/9/14	Holland	6/2/18	22/11/18
Capt. E. F. GRANT-DALTON.	20/9/14	Holland	6/2/18	1/11/18
Lieut. B. RATCLIFFE.	20/9/14		(Escaped)	–/4/17
Lieut. W. H. LANGRAN.	20/9/14	Holland	1/1/19	4/1/19
Lieut. P. FRYER.	20/9/14	Holland	6/2/18	14/1/19
Lieut. L. A. DAVIES.	20/9/14	Holland	6/2/18	24/1/19
Lieut. J. PARISH.	31/1/16	Holland	30/2/18	22/11/18
Lieut. W. E. H. SPICER.	17/4/17			1/1/19
2/Lt. J. EXLEY.	16/8/17			6/12/18

* Attached from Durham Light Infantry. † Attached from Devonshire Regiment.

WEST YORKSHIRE REGIMENT—Continued.
1st Battalion.

Name.	Missing.	Interned.	Rapatriated.
Lt.-Col. A. M. BOYALL.	21/3/18		28/11/18
Major H. A. W. COLE-HAMILTON	21/3/18		18/12/18
Capt. W. C. NEWSTEAD.	21/3/18		17/12/18
Capt. J. F. WALLACE.	21/3/18		17/12/18
Lieut. J. R. BEE.	21/3/18		29/11/18
Lieut. P. E. ADAMS.	21/3/18		29/11/18
Lieut. G. SERGEANT.	21/3/18		13/12/18
2/Lt. H. SALMONS.	21/3/18	(Died 1/4/18).	
2/Lt. A. E. H. PARROTT.	21/3/18		10/12/18
2/Lt. P. D. STEWART.	21/3/18		2/12/18
2/Lt. G. W. SMITH.	21/3/18		3/12/18
2/Lt. F. HODGES.	21/3/18		29/11/18
2/Lt. A. W. FRENCH.	21/3/18		-/12/18
2/Lt. J. LITTLEWOOD.	22/3/18		17/12/18
Capt. E. AMBLER.	24/3/18		29/11/18
2/Lt. E. BROOKS.	16/4/18		3/12/18
Lieut. A. J. DOYLE.	9/8/18		23/10/18

2nd Battalion.

Name.	Missing.	Interned.	Rapatriated.
2/Lt. W. H. DE VOIL.	27/3/18		18/12/18
Lieut. T. L. FIELDER.	24/4/18		29/11/18
2/Lt. H. PRESTON.	24/4/18		30/12/18
2/Lt. E. St. B. STUART-KELSO.	24/4/18		29/11/18
2/Lt. W. SMITH.	24/4/18		3/12/18
2/Lt. E. JOWETT.	24/4/18		29/11/18
2/Lt. S. S. L. JACKSON.	24/4/18		29/11/18
2/Lt. K. K. MAKIN.	24/4/18		25/12/18
Major F. H. TOUNSEND.	27/5/18		25/12/18
Lieut. N. O. TUCKER.	27/5/18		13/12/18
Lieut. G. W. HALL.	27/5/18		25/12/18
2/Lt. H. WIGGINS.	27/5/18		13/12/18
2/Lt. V. R. SCOTT.	27/5/18		31/12/18
2/Lt. H. J. RIGBY.	27/5/18		6/12/18
2/Lt. J. W. MARSDEN.	27/5/18		13/12/18
2/Lt. W. B. GERRITY.	27/5/18		17/12/18
*2/Lt. J. W. GARDNER.	27/5/18		25/12/18
2/Lt. D. G. GARBUTT.	27/5/18		-/12/18

5th Battalion.

Name.	Missing.	Interned.	Rapatriated.
2/Lt. H. WILCOX.	3/5/17		29/11/18
Lieut. P. CHEESMAN.	25/4/18		17/12/18
Lieut. A. D. CLUBB.	25/4/18		29/11/18
Lieut. J. SAYES.	25/4/18		-/12/18
2/Lt. S. R. MARDON.	25/4/18		29/11/18
2/Lt. J. HATTON.	25/4/18		11/12/18
2/Lt. C. R. FIRTH.	25/4/18		9/11/18
2/Lt. R. BLACKER.	25/4/18		3/12/18
2/Lt. J. W. DUNNINGTON.	25/4/18		2/12/18
Lieut. J. V. BATTERSBY-HARFORD.	29/4/18		1/12/18

6th Battalion.

Name.	Missing.	Interned.	Rapatriated.
2/Lt. S. Senior SMITH.	2/3/17	Holland 7/5/18	22/11/18
2/Lt. F. COOKSON.	14/4/18		18/12/18
Capt. F. W. WHITTAKER.	25/4/18		2/12/18
Capt. J. S. GORDON.	25/4/18		2/12/18

* Attached T.M.B.

WEST YORKSHIRE REGIMENT—continued.
6th Battalion—continued.

Name.	Missing.	Interned.	Repatriated.
Capt. G. SANDERS.	25/4/18		26/12/18
Lieut. E. BELDON.	25/4/18		-/12/18
Lieut. H. W. ROBINSON.	25/4/18		29/11/18
Lieut. T. L. SHIELD.	25/4/18		-/12/18
*2/Lt. H. E. JOWETT.	25/4/18		25/12/18
2/Lt. F. SUGDEN.	25/4/18		2/12/18
2/Lt. C. N. PEPPER.	25/4/18		2/12/18
2/Lt. G. MATTHEWS.	25/4/18	(*Died* 2/7/18 at Cologne).	
2/Lt. W. E. WARNER.	25/4/18		11/12/18
2/Lt. W. C. WHITING.	25/4/18		2/12/18
2/Lt. F. E. FAIRBANK.	25/4/18		1/12/18
2/Lt. T. BAIRSTOW.	25/4/18		12/10/18
2/Lt. B. ARCHER.	25/4/18		2/12/18
Capt. W. N. MOSSOP.	28/4/18	(*Died* 8/5/18 at Ghent).	

7th Battalion.

Name.	Missing.	Interned.	Repatriated.
2/Lt. C. C. FRANK.	1/7/16	Holland 16/5/18	23/9/18
2/Lt. A. L. H. CLELAND.	12/5/17		14/12/18
Capt. C. L. FOULDS.	-/3/18		17/12/18
2/Lt. L. W. METCALFE.	21/3/18		2/12/18
2/Lt. W. J. JEHU.	14/4/18		2/12/18
Capt. E. ROBERTS.	16/4/18		2/12/18
Lieut. R. W. HORSFALL.	16/4/18		3/12/18
2/Lt. G. J. NYE.	16/4/18		14/12/18
2/Lt. E. O. PANTING.	16/4/18		29/11/18
2/Lt. J. WILSON.	16/4/18		4/12/18
2/Lt. A. CHANDLER.	25/4/18		5/12/18
†2/Lt. T. CHAPMAN.	25/4/18		31/12/18
Lt.-Col. H. D. BOUSFIELD.	28/4/18		29/11/18

8th Battalion.

Name.	Missing.	Interned.	Repatriated.
Lieut. G. K. WILL.	3/9/16	(*Died* 11/9/16 at Velu)	
Lieut. V. TANSLEY.	3/5/17		3/12/18
2/Lt. W. D. MUIRHEAD.	3/5/17	Holland 7/5/18	19/7/18
Lieut. E. PEPPER.	24/5/18		3/1/19
2/Lt. J. D. PORTEOUS.			-/12/18
†2/Lt. W. R. WORRALL.	27/5/18		13/12/18
2/Lt. F. O. LAMB.	28/7/18		8/12/18
‡2/Lt. F. AXE.	27/9/18		29/11/18
2°Lt. W. I. WHITTELL.	27/9/18		-/11/18
2/Lt. R. L. A. TINGLE.	27/9/18		28/11/18
2/Lt. C. E. CROFT.	27/9/18		28/12/18

9th Battalion.

Name.	Missing.	Interned.	Repatriated.
Lieut. G. W. HOLLOWAY.	11/8/16	Holland 12/10/18	19/11/18
2/Lt. J. W. TOWNSEND.	15/12/17		23/12/18
2/Lt. R. B. WALKER.	5/11/18		-/11/18
2/Lt. F. G. MARSDEN.	5/11/18		5/1/19

10th Battalion.

Name.	Missing.	Interned.	Repatriated.
2/Lt. C. E. B. BERNARD.	1/7/16	Holland 16/5/18	25/11/18
2/Lt. M. COUCHMAN.	14/9/16		18/12/18
Lt.-Col. P. R. O. A. SIMNER.	25/3/18		24/12/18
Lieut. F. A. SHURROCK.	25/3/18		17/12/18
Lieut. F. D. DAMS.	21/4/18		18/12/18
Lieut. E. G. ADDINGTON.	24/8/18		13/12/18

*Attached 146/T.M.B.   ‡Attached from East Yorkshire Regiment.
†Attached T.M.B.

WEST YORKSHIRE REGIMENT—continued.

12th Battalion.

Name.	Missing.	Interned.		Repatriated.
Capt. H. G. S. BRANCH.	25/9/15	Holland	10/4/18	18/11/18
2/Lt. E. L. SHAWCROSS.	26/9/15	Holland	10/4/18	18/11/18
*Capt. R. H. T. SMITH.	30/11/17			27/11/18
*Lieut. E. K. G. PIROUET.	12/12/17			27/11/18
Lieut. A. J. DAVIS.	12/12/17			14/12/18
2/Lt. T. H. ENGLISH.	12/12/17			3/12/18
2/Lt. C. A. MONKS.	12/12/17			14/12/18
2/Lt. R. LEACH.	12/12/17			3/12/18

13th Battalion.

Name.	Missing.	Interned.		Repatriated.
2/Lt. T. S. PATTISON.	13/11/16			18/12/18

14th Battalion.

Name.	Missing.	Interned.		Repatriated.
2/Lt. J. H. BIRKINSHAW.	11/7/16	Holland	15/6/18	22/11/18
2/Lt. L. S. WALTON.	28/7/16	Holland	15/6/18	2/1/19

15th Battalion.

Name.	Missing.	Interned.		Repatriated.
Lieut. A. H. RILEY.	3/5/17	Holland	24/2/18	23/2/18
2/Lt. R. S. TATE.	3/5/17			14/12/18
†Lt.-Col. C. C. H. TWISS.	27/3/18			25/12/18
2/Lt. B. WILLEY.	27/3/18			13/12/18
2/Lt. E. KEIGHLEY.	27/3/18			23/12/18
2/Lt. J. G. PEDLEY.	27/3/18			25/12/18
‡2/Lt. A. W. ROBERTS.	27/3/18	(Died 18/12/18)		
2/Lt. E. G. STEVENS.	27/3/18			11/12/18
2/Lt. R. H. SMITH.	27/3/18			11/12/18
2/Lt. J. H. CLEGG.	12/14/18			13/12/18
2/Lt. W. STRONG.	27/4/18			31/12/18
2/Lt. G. WEATHERILL.	18/9/18			29/11/18

16th Battalion.

Name.	Missing.	Interned.		Repatriated.
Capt. O. ILLINGWORTH	3/5/17			2/12/18
Lieut. E. CROWTHER.	3/5/17			31/12/18
2/Lt. E. G. BANTOCK.	3/5/17			4/1/19
2/Lt. G. L. TUCKER.	3/5/17			31/12/18
2/Lt. N. PARKER.	3/5/17			4/1/19
2/Lt. L. ASHWORTH.	3/5/17			7/1/18

17th Battalion.

Name.	Missing.	Interned.		Repatriated.
2/Lt. O. DAY.	30/8/17	(*Died* at Candry 3/9/17).		
Lieut. J. C. ACHESON.	31/8/17	Holland	30/4/18	18/8/18
2/Lt. N. ODDY.	31/8/17			−/1/19
2/Lt. R. D. FITZPATRICK.	31/8/17			14/12/18

18th Battalion.

Name.	Missing.	Interned.		Repatriated.
Lieut. A. HOWARTH.	27/7/16	Holland	15/6/18	22/11/18
2/Lt. R. W. CLARKSON.	3/5/17			19/4/18
2/Lt. N. H. PRIDAY.	3/5/17			6/12/18
2/Lt. O. H. STAFF.	3/5/17	Switzerland	27/12/17	6/12/18

20th Battalion.

Name.	Missing.	Interned.		Repatriated.
Lieut. L. C. WATSON.	28/7/16	Holland	15/6/18	27/11/18

* Attached from A.S.C.
† Attached from East Yorkshire Regiment.   ‡ Attached from Durham L.I.

EAST YORKSHIRE REGIMENT.

1st Battalion.

Name.	Missing.	Interned.	Repatriated.
Capt. C. L. MacMAHON.	22/3/18		25/12/18
2/Lt. N. E. GASSON.	22/3/18		13/1/19
2/Lt. G. R. WARE.	17/4/18		11/12/18
Capt. W. F. SLEATH.	24/4/18		2/12/18
Capt. F. L. BALL.	24/4/18		-/12/18
2/Lt. W. E. WHITLEY.	24/4/18		31/12/18
2/Lt. A. TATLOW.	24/4/18		6/12/18
2/Lt. H. T. STEPHENS.	24/4/18		2/12/18
2/Lt. S. COVERDALE.	24/4/18		2/12/18
2/Lt. Lt. S. A. FARMER.	24/4/18		2/12/18
2/Lt. E. H. HARDY.	24/4/18		29/11/18
2/Lt. P. WALLIS.	24/4/18		-/12/18
2/Lt. G. W. WISBEY.	24/4/18		2/12/18
2/Lt. F. A. TOOGOOD.	24/4/18		-/12/18
2/Lt. T. G. MAYHEW.	24/4/18		1/12/18
Capt. E. B. ROBINSON.	26/4/18		2/12/18
*Lieut. O. GREENWOOD.	27/5/18		-/1/19
2/Lt. A. D. ROBINSON.	27/5/18		6/1/19
2/Lt. B. WAHL.	27/5/18		28/12/18
2/Lt. P. L. WRIGHT.	27/5/18		6/1/19
2/Lt. A. J. BOARDMAN.	27/5/18		-/12/18
*2/Lt. N. SPEEDY.	27/5/18		25/12/18
*Lieut. K. E. BLACK.	10/9/18		29/11/18
*Lieut. H. H. SCOBY.	10/9/18		13/12/18
2/Lt. J. WALKER.	10/9/18		29/11/18
2/Lt. F. O. RIDEOUT.	10/9/18		29/11/19

4th Battalion.

Name.	Missing.	Interned.	Repatriated.
2/Lt. B. V. HILDYARD.	23/4/17		31/12/18
2/Lt. F. STEVENSON.	23/4/17		30/12/18
2/Lt. W. C. WALGATE.	23/4/17		30/12/18
2/Lt. R. DUGGLEBY.	27/6/17	Switzerland 27/12/17	24/3/18
Capt. T. J. MORRILL.	28/6/17		2/1/19
2/Lt. F. LINSLEY.	28/6/17		6/12/18
Lieut. G. T. HOLLIS.	22/3/18		25/12/18
2/Lt. H. NEEDHAM.	22/3/18		2/1/19
2/Lt. C. R. INGHAM.	22/3/18		17/12/18
2/Lt. R. E. HATFIELD.	22/3/18		28/11/18
2/Lt. G. F. STEPHENSON.	23/3/18		12/10/18
2/Lt. S. B. WILSON.	25/3/18		18/12/18
2/Lt. C. W. PRETTY.	26/3/18		8/12/18
Capt. C. M. SLACK.	8/4/18		28/11/18
2/Lt. R. THOMPSON.	8–17/4/18		28/11/18
2/Lt. A. T. WOODCOCK.	8–17/4/18	(*Died 4/6/18 at Cologne*).	
Major H. B. JACKSON.	10/4/18		-/12/18
†Major H. R. HASLETT.	27/5/18		18/12/18
Capt. E. JOHNSON.	27/5/18		-/12/18
Capt. E. LAVERACK.	27/5/18		6/12/18
‡Lieut. E. WILLISON.	27/5/18		28/1/19
Lieut. W. E. HEWAT.	27/5/18		31/12/18
Lieut. C. S. JOHNSON.	27/5/18		31/12/18
†Lieut. J. F. STEVENSON.	27/5/18		-/12/18
†Lieut. P. S. MURRAY.	27/5/18		31/12/18
†2/Lt. T. K. DIGBY.	27/5/18		21/1/19

*Attached from Yorkshire Regiment. †Attached from Royal Irish Rifles.
‡Attached from Durham L.I.

EAST YORKSHIRE REGIMENT—continued.

4th Battalion—continued.

Name.	Missing.	Interned.	Repatriated.
†2/Lt. A. McB. SMITH.	27/5/18		–/12/18
†2/Lt. A. G. V. MARSH.	27/5/18		18/12/18
†2/Lt. B. C. BINER.	27/5/18	(*Died* 21/7/18).	
2/Lt. H. R. HOLLIS.	27/5/18		31/12/18
2/Lt. D. G. DANN.	27/5/18		31/12/18
2/Lt. J. W. CAMPBELL.	27/5/18		13/12/18
2/Lt. E. C. BROWN.	27/5/18		–/12/18
2/Lt. S. F. BASTOW.	27/5/18		–/12/18
2/Lt. W. J. WALKER.	27/5/18		–/12/18
2/Lt. W. C. WADDINGTON.	27/5/18	(*Died* 3/7/18 at Cassel).	
2/Lt. A. V. THRUSTLE.	27/5/18		–/12/18

5th Battalion.

Name.	Missing.	Interned.	Repatriated.
Capt. C. F. DICKINSON.	9/4/18		18/12/18

6th Battalion.

Name.	Missing.	Interned.	Repatriated.
*Capt. F. W. LAWE.	10/4/18		1/12/18

7th Battalion.

Name.	Missing.	Interned.	Repatriated.
2/Lt. W. CLARKSON.	23/2/16		14/12/18
Capt. J. HIRST.	24/3/18		–/12/18
Lieut. N. GIBSON.	24/3/18		18/12/18
2/Lt. H. F. ALLEN.	25/3/18		25/12/18
2/Lt. E. G. PICKERING.	25/3/18		25/12/18

8th Battalion.

Name.	Missing.	Interned.	Repatriated.
2/Lt. J. M. LAMB.	15/3/17		4/1/19
2/Lt. G. F. BUCKLAND.	26/9/17	Switzerland 3/8/18	6/12/18

10th Battalion.

Name.	Missing.	Interned.	Repatriated.
Capt. S. E. JONES.	27/2/17	Switzerland 27/12/18	24/3/18
Lieut. D. R. MORRISH.	3/5/17		19/12/18
2/Lt. L. M. BUTT.	3/5/17		31/12/18
2/Lt. G. AKESTER.	3/5/17		17/12/18
Lieut. J. H. LAWES.	3/11/17		3/12/18
2/Lt. A. F. W. MARSHALL.	15/8/18	(*Died* 26/9/18 at Karlsruhe).	

11th Battalion.

Name.	Missing.	Interned.	Repatriated.
2/Lt. R. WOOLCOTT.	3/5/17	Switzerland 27/12/17	9/12/18
2/Lt. E. WRIGHT.	27/3/18		25/12/18
2Lt. R. F. PITZ.	27/3/18		29/11/18
Capt. H. A. C. FITZPATRICK.	10/4/18		18/12/18
Major C. W. WAITE.	12/4/18	(*Died* 31/1/19).	–/12/18
Major L. A. CATTLEY.	12/4/18		29/12/18
Lieut. F. G. NICHOLS.	12/4/18		31/12/18
Lieut. G. SUTHRIEN.	12/4/18		31/12/18
Lieut. C. GOUGH.	8/9/18		
‡2/Lt. G. W. KOPLIK.	28/9/18		13/12/18

12th Battalion.

Name.	Missing.	Interned.	Repatriated.
2/Lt. C. FENWICK.	3/5/17		4/1/19
2/Lt. E. P. COOPER.	3/5/17	Switzerland 24/4/18	9/12/18

* Attached Portuguese Mission. † Attached from Royal Irish Rifles.
‡ Attached T.M.B.

EAST YORKSHIRE REGIMENT—continued.
13th Battalion.

Name.	Missing.	Interned.	Repatriated.
Capt. R. M. WOOLLEY.	13/11/16		6/1/19
2/Lt. C. CLOVER.	13/11/16		6/1/19
2/Lt. E. G. BRINDLEY.	13/11/16		18/12/18
2/Lt. W. J. LUCAS.	10/4/18		25/12/18

15th Battalion.

2/Lt. F. CAIRNS.	18/9/18		8/12/18

BEDFORDSHIRE REGIMENT.
1st and 2nd Battalions.

Name	Missing	Interned	Repatriated
Lieut. W. WAGSTAFF.	9/9/14	Holland 22/1/18	18/11/18
Capt. A. B. LEMON.	14/11/14	Holland 24/2/18	18/11/18
Lieut. C. POPE.	14/11/14	Holland 24/1/18	18/11/18
2/Lt. I. T. M. COLLINS.	28/7/17		3/6/18
2/Lt. F. E. THOMPSON.	21/3/18		11/12/18
Capt. F. W. PARKER.	23/3/18		1/12/18
2/Lt. W. R. SHAW.	23/3/18		14/12/18
Lieut. C. HAYWOOD.	25/3/18		15/12/18
Capt. G. A. ANSTEE.	28/3/18		1/12/18
*Lieut. H. W. H. DRUITT.	26/4/18		28/11/18
*2/Lt. A. H. CHANDLER.	26/4/18		3/12/18
Lieut. A. H. BAKER.	9/5/18		6/12/18
Lieut. A. F. WOODFORD.	6/8/18		-/12/18
Lieut. D. D. WARREN.	6/8/18		-/12/18
2/Lt. R. W. SMITH.	21/9/18		8/12/18

4th Battalion.

2/Lt. V. B. SHOTT.	11/2/17		15/12/18
Lieut. F. A. GIRLING.	23/3/16		23/10/18
2/Lt. MAX KRUGER.	23/3/18		29/11/18
2/Lt. E. M. L. GREEN.	24/3/18		25/12/18
2/Lt. R. G. COWELL.	25/3/18		-/12/18

5th Battalion.

Lieut. E. W. HASTINGS.	27/8/18		13/12/18

6th Battalion.

Lieut. J. H. A. LOVE.	28/4/17		30/12/18

7th Battalion.

2/Lt. E. J. F. SCOTT.	28/4/17		6/12/18
2/Lt. R. A. STILES.	22/3/18		29/11/18

LEICESTERSHIRE REGIMENT.
1st Battalion.

Capt. J. H. JOHN.	21/3/18		29/11/18
Capt. F. E. SHELTON.	21/3/18		29/11/18
Lieut. S. C. LAWRENCE.	21/3/18		4/12/18
Lieut. A. C. ANSELL.	21/3/18		17/12/18
Lieut. J. O. VESSEY.	21/3/18		17/12/18
2/Lt. T. C. A. CLARKE.	21/3/18		18/12/18
2/Lt. C. H. WATSON.	21/3/18		18/12/18
2/Lt. M. MILLS.	21/3/18		29/11/18
2/Lt. A. N. BAGSHAW.	21/3/18		25/12/18
2/Lt. L. W. E. RUSSELL.	-/3/18	(Died 1/11/18 at Mainz).	

*Attached from 2nd Wiltshire Regiment.

LEICESTERSHIRE REGIMENT—continued.

4th Battalion.

Name.	Missing.	Interned.	Repatriated.
Capt. F. S. PARR.	11–13/10/15	Holland –/4/18	18/11/18
Lieut. L. B. LAMBIE.	22/4/17		14/12/18
Capt. P. K. BLUNT.	24/3/18		2/12/18
Capt. G. B. WILLIAMS.	25/3/18		1/12/18
Lieut. C. D. BROWN.	25/3/18		25/12/18
2/Lt. E. ROBERTS.	25/3/18		1/12/18
2/Lt. A. G. RALEIGH.	25/3/18		29/11/18

5th Battalion.

Name.	Missing.	Interned.	Repatriated.
Lieut. L. H. PEARSON.	6/8/18		19/1/19

6th Battalion.

Name.	Missing.	Interned.	Repatriated.
2/Lt. M. J. S. DYSON.	21/3/18		18/12/18
*2/Lt. B. L. ASQUITH.	21/3/18		17/12/18
Lieut. W. E. MAJOR.	22/3/18		11/12/18
2/Lt. J. H. SMEDLEY.	22/3/18		28/11/18
2/Lt. N. S. HOGGARTH.	22/3/18	(*Died* 30/5/18 at Cassel).	
2/Lt. E. G. LANE-ROBERTS.	22/3/18		18/12/18
Capt. G. B. F. RUDD.	27/4/18		18/12/18
2/Lt. P. J. STRONG.	27/4/18		18/12/18
†2/Lt. A. F. CLARK.	27/5/18		–/12/18
†2/Lt. C. W. MARTEN.	27/5/18		14/12/18
Lieut. W. T. STEVENS.	28/5/18		3/1/19
2/Lt. W. A. BAGULEY.	28/5/18		6/1/19
‡Lt.-Col. M. C. MARTYN.	25/8/18		13/12/18

7th Battalion.

Name.	Missing.	Interned.	Repatriated.
2/Lt. W. STUBBS.	22/3/18		11/12/18
2/Lt. B. J. S. DODRIDGE.	22/3/18		28/11/18
2/Lt. C. G. SCARFE.	22/3/18		17/12/18
2/Lt. W. WOOD.	22/3/18		17/12/18
2/Lt. W. WATKINSON.	22/3/18		11/12/18
2/Lt. W. HOWITT.	22/3/18		–/12/18
2/Lt. A. D. GODFREY.	24/3/18		25/12/18
Capt. H. H. HEMPHILL.	27/5/18		–/12/18
Capt. W. A. EVANS.	27/5/18		–/12/18
Lieut. J. S. SHARPE.	27/5/18		31/12/18
2/Lt. J. ROYLE.	27/5/18		6/1/19
2/Lt. St. G. REDHEAD.	27/5/18		3/1/19
*2/Lt. A. W. ACOCKS.	27/5/18		25/12/18
*2/Lt. F. N. MORGAN.	27/5/18		2/1/19
2/Lt. F. B. STEVENSON.	27/5/18		31/12/18
2/Lt. H. J. CRESSWELL.	27/5/18		2/1/19
2/Lt. J. H. BONSHOR.	27/5/18		2/1/19

8th Battalion.

Name.	Missing.	Interned.	Repatriated.
2/Lt. F. W. H. CLARKE.	3/5/17		2/1/19
2/Lt. W. HARRIS.	3/5/17		31/12/18
2/Lt. E. B. PITTS.	3/5/17	(*Died* 17/5/17 at Bouchain).	
2/Lt. E. H. BONE.	20/3/18		18/12/18
2/Lt. S. HOBSON.	21/3/18		18/12/18
Lt.-Col. A. T. LE M. UTTERSON.	22/3/18		18/12/18

*Attached from Manchesters.   †Attached from Gloucesters.
‡Attached from Sherwood Foresters.

LEICESTERSHIRE REGIMENT.—continued.

8th Battalion.

Name.	Missing.	Interned.	Repatriated.
**Capt. R. M. R. DAVISON.	22/3/18		11/12/18
2/Lt. H. M. JACKSON.	22//318		11/12/18
2/Lt. H. JASPER.	26/5/18		5/12/18
Capt. W. S. MURPHY.	27/5/18		2/1/19
Lieut. A. HALKYARD.	27/5/18		25/12/18
Lieut. E. H. WRIGGLESWORTH.	27/5/18		6/1/19
*Lieut. W. SEAMAN.	27/5/18		26/12/18
2/Lt. C. S. DEARMAN.	27/5/18		6/1/19
2/Lt. A. H. T. CROWSON.	27/5/18		2/1/19
2/Lt. H. CARDALL.	27/5/18		2/1/19
2/Lt. E. W. ROGERSON.	27/5/18		11/12/18
2/Lt. A. E. RAYNER.	27/5/18		6/1/19
2/Lt. H. H. METTERS.	27/5/18		31/12/18
2/Lt. F. LARDER.	27/5/18		31/12/18
2/Lt. W. HANDFORD.	27/5/18		-/12/18
2/Lt. J. H. GREEN.	27/5/18		-/12/18
2/Lt. F. HARPER.	27/5/18		2/1/19

9th Battalion.

Name.	Missing.	Interned.	Repatriated.
Capt. H. E. MILBURN.	3/5/17		16/1/19
2/Lt. E. E. RAWLINGS.	3/5/17		17/12/18

11th Battalion.

Name.	Missing.	Interned.	Repatriated.
Lieut. A. L. HICKS.	21/3/18	(Died 4/4/18 at Auberchicourt).	

ROYAL IRISH REGIMENT.
1st and 2nd Battalions.

Name.	Missing.	Interned.		Repatriated.
Lieut. C. G. MAGRATH.	24/8/14	Holland	6/2/18	-/-/18
Lieut. A. E. B. ANDERSON.	24/8/14	Holland	6/2/18	18/11/18
Capt. J. B. GEORGE.	10/9/14			11/9/17
Capt. J. FITZGERALD.	10/9/14	Holland	6/2/18	19/7/18
Capt. G. ELLIOTT.	10/9/14	Holland	22/1/18	18/11/18
Lieut. R. E. G. PHILLIPS.	10/9/14			13/9/17
Lieut. A. FRAZER.	10/9/14	Holland	6/2/18	22/11/18
Lieut. C. F. T. O'B. FFRENCH.	10/9/14	Holland	29/12/17	18/11/18
Lieut. H. G. O. DOWNING.	10/10/14			13/9/17
Capt. J. A. SMITHWICK.	19/10/14			24/8/15
		(Died 10/11/15 in England).		
Capt. G. O. E. FURNELL.	19/10/14	Switzerland	9/12/17	14/6/18
Lieut. K. FOULKES.	19/10/14	Switzerland	27/12/17	2/6/18
2/Lt. W. E. BREDIN.	19/10/14	Holland	6/2/18	18/11/18
2/Lt. T. NICHOLSON.	19/10/14	Holland	6/2/18	16/8/18
2/Lt. J. MCLOUGHLIN.	19/10/14	Holland	6/2/18	18/11/18
Capt. M. C. C. HARRISON.	20/11/14			13/9/17
Capt. E. D. HANLEY.	21/5/15			14/9/17
Lieut. A. R. ROYALL.	3/9/16			13/9/17
2/Lt. J. P. CORCORAN.	30/10/16	Holland	15/4/18	2/7/18
*Lieut. E. G. LEE.	9/4/17			14/12/18
Capt. A. S. PIM.	21/3/18			14/12/18
Lieut. H. JORDAN.	21/3/18			-/12/18
Lieut. V. W. F. HICKS.	21/3/18			28/11/18
Lieut. J. A. MOUAT-BIGGS.	21/3/18	(Died 22/3/18 at Clary).		
Lieut. W. J. ROCHE.	21/3/18			5/12/18
Lieut. J. J. DONOVAN.	21/3/18			14/12/18

** Attached from North Staffs.
*Attached from A.S.C.

ROYAL IRISH REGIMENT—continued.
1st and 2nd Battalions.

Name.	Missing.	Interned.	Repatriated.
Lieut. V. FARQUHARSON-HICKS.	21/3/18		28/11/18
*2/Lt. C. H. SMITH.	21/3/18		18/12/18
**2/Lt. W. N. ABBOTT.	21/3/18		18/12/18
2/Lt. J. M. TERRY.	21/3/18		14/12/18
2/Lt. J. G. MAHAFFY.	21/3/18		28/11/18
2/Lt. J. T. FARRELL.	21/3/18		28/11/18
2/Lt. L. O'KEEFE.	21/3/18		3/12/18
2/Lt. J. BAILEY.	21//318		
*2/Lt. M. MULCAHY.	22/3/18		25/12/18
2/Lt. W. R. SIMMONS.	25/8/18		5/1/19

6th Battalion.

2/Lt. R. J. KELLY.	21/8/16		7/1/18

7th Battalion.

Major J. D. MORROGH.	21/3/18		15/12/18
Major FELIX CALL.	21/3/18		17/12/18
Capt. A. C. PATMAN.	21/3/18		2/12/18
Capt. P. N. SMITH.	21/3/18		14/12/18
*Capt J. M. WARDELL.	21/3/18		6/12/18
*Lieut. W. S. BARRETT.	21/3/18		3/12/18
*Lieut. J. S. MATTHEWS.	21/3/18		14/12/18
Lieut. P. J. GIBSON.	21/3/18		–/12/18
*2/Lt. A. B. HADDEN.	21/3/18		14/12/18
*2/Lt. J. A. WATTS.	21/3/18		20/12/18
*2/Lt. R. CONWAY.	21/3/18		25/12/18
2/Lt. H. J. JONES.	21/3/18	(Died 29/3/18 at Bertry).	
2/Lt. H. E. ROBINSON.	21/3/18		17/12/18
2/Lt. C. J. BAILEY.	21/3/18		8/12/18
2/Lt. R. W. M. HENDERSON.	17/9/18		28/11/18

8th Battalion.

Capt. T. BEDELL-SIVWRIGHT.	5/9/18		28/11/18
Lieut. S. RIVERS.	5/9/18		29/11/18
†Lieut. A. PATERSON.	5/9/18		29/11/18

YORKSHIRE REGIMENT.
1st and 2nd Battalions.

Name.	Missing.	Interned.		Repatriated.
Capt. R. LEDGARD.	10/9/14	Holland	5/1/18	12/11/18
Capt. W. WORSLEY.	30/10/14	Holland	24/2/18	22/1/19
Lieut. R. H. MIDDLEDITCH.	30/10/14	Switzerland	12/8/16	9/12/18
Lieut. A. C. BENTLEY.	26/9/15			6/1/19
Lieut. W. GRAY.	26/9/15	Holland	19/4/18	18/11/18
2/Lt. J. C. McINTYRE.	26/9/15	(Died).		

2nd Battalion.

2/Lt. J. J. COWNLEY.	21/3/18		29/11/18
2/Lt. G. F. LOCKWOOD.	21/3/18		29/11/18
2/Lt. W. VASEY.	21/3/18		18/12/18
2/Lt. J. W. WALKER.	21/3/18		13/12/18
2/Lt. N. MORANT.	22/3/18	(Died 27/3/18 at St. Quentin).	
2/Lt. C. A. BARKER.	23/3/18		11/12/18
‡Lieut. E. R. HARBOUR.	25/4/18		3/12/18
Capt. C. DAVISON.	8/5/18		1/12/18
2/Lt. J. E. HIBBERT.	8/5/18		13/12/18
Lieut. F. TENNEY.	6/11/18		11/12/18

*Attached from South Irish Horse. †Attached from Northumberland Fusiliers.
‡Attached T.M.B. ** Attached from 3rd Connaught Rangers.

YORKSHIRE REGIMENT—Continued.

4th Battalion.

Name.	Missing.	Interned.	Repatriated.
Capt. A. R. POWEYS.	23/3/18		29/11/18
2/Lt. W. THORNTON.	25/3/18		25/12/18
Major L. NEWCOMBE.	27/5/18		30/12/18
Capt. A. L. GORING.	27/5/18		30/12/18
Capt. R. M. HOWES.	27/5/18		30/12/18
Lieut. H. R. B. BAILEY.	27/5/18		-/12/18
Lieut. R. GATES.	27/5/18		14/12/18
Lieut. C. K. KELK.	27/5/18		-/12/18
Lieut. G. C. W. MacKAY.	27/5/18		13/12/18
Lieut. V. W. W. S. PURCELL.	27/5/18		-/12/18
Lieut. T. A. ROBSON.	27/5/18		13/12/18
Lieut. J. C. STORY.	27/5/18		13/12/18
2/Lt. A. W. APPLEBY.	27/5/18		-/12/18
2/Lt. A. E. BEDFORD.	27/5/18		25/12/18
2/Lt. H. A. CLIDERO.	27/5/18		13/12/18
2/Lt. J. H. DERRETT.	27/5/18		25/12/18
*2/Lt. J. A. A. FLYNN.	27/5/18		14/12/18
2/Lt. G. A. GREEN.	27/5/18		18/12/18
2/Lt. W. R. HOLMES.	27/5/18		-/12/18
2/Lt. C. W. STIRK.	27/5/18		-/12/18
2/Lt. H. E. WEBB.	27/5/18		13/12/18

5th Battalion.

Name.	Missing.	Interned.	Repatriated.
2/Lt. G. F. ROGERS.	24/4/17		2/1/19
Lieut. A. HEPTON.	22/3/18	(*Died* 13/4/18 at St. Quentin).	
†Lieut. H. P. GREGORY.	25/3/18		1/12/19
2/Lt. W. N. PEARSON.	25/3/18		29/12/18
2/Lt. A. H. STRONG.	26/3/18		13/12/18
Lieut. W. H. ALLIS.	8–17/4/18		25/12/18
Lieut. J. G. CROSS.	9/4/18		1/12/18
2/Lt. T. A. WILLIAMS.	12/4/18		11/12/18
Capt. H. G. AMIS.	27/5/18		26/12/18
Capt. G. A. MAXWELL.	27/5/18		30/12/18
Capt. G. MOSELEY.	27/5/18		30/12/18
Capt. G. THOMPSON.	27/5/18		1/1/19
Capt. E. H. WEIGHILL.	27/5/18		14/12/18
Capt. A. S. WOOD.	27/5/18		30/12/18
Lieut. G. W. COOPER.	27/5/18		30/12/18
Lieut. H. W. KNIGHT.	27/5/18		1/1/19
Lieut. E. A. LISTER.	27/5/18		-/12/18
Lieut. W. PATTERSON.	27/5/18		-/12/18
Lieut. C. B. R. REES.	27/5/18		-/12/18
Lieut. G. H. SMITH.	27/5/18		30/12/18
Lieut. J. H. E. WINSTON.	27/5/18		-/12/18
2/Lt. J. M. ATKINSON.	27/5/18		-/12/18
2/Lt. F. BARROWCLIFF.	27/5/18		-/12/18
*2/Lt. T. J. CAVANAGH.	27/5/18		25/12/18
*2/Lt. R. J. CHARTERS.	27/5/18		25/12/18
2/Lt. C. L. KING.	27/5/18		-/12/18
2/Lt. P. LAWSON.	27/5/18		-/12/18
2/Lt. H. T. ROBSON.	27/5/18		-/12/18
2/Lt. L. RYMER.	27/5/18		30/12/18

*Attached from Royal Irish Rifles.
†Attached T.M.B.

YORKSHIRE REGIMENT—Continued.

6th Battalion.

Name.	Missing.	Interned.	Repatriated.
2/Lt. W. A. BOOT.	27/9/16		4/1/19

10th Battalion.

2/Lt. F. E. STOKELD.	7/5/18		25/12/18

11th Battalion.

2/Lt. O. R. AGERSKOW.	12/4/18		18/12/18

12th Battalion.

2/Lt. H. D'A. CHAMPNEY.	9/4/18	(*Died* 29/4/18).	
Lieut. J. BINNS.	11/4/18		25/12/18

13th Battalion.

2/Lt. R. LANGLEY.	27/9/16		18/12/18
Capt. J. H. G. BAYLES.	23/11/17		24/12/18
2/Lt. W. HARDWICK.	23/11/17		14/12/18
2/Lt. P. R. THOMPSON.	23/11/17		19/5/18
Capt. R. G. De QUETTEVILLE.	10/4/18		28/11/18
Lieut. L. G. COLLINS.	10/4/18		–/12/18

LANCASHIRE FUSILIERS.

1st and 2nd Battalions.

Capt. J. A. DAVENPORT.	26/8/14	Holland	22/1/18	27/11/18
Lieut. F. F. CORBETT-WINDER.	25/9/14	Holland	22/1/18	18/11/18
2/Lt. H. S. CARTER.	20/2/16	Holland	19/4/18	21/5/18
Lieut. A. V. DAVIES.	1/7/16	Holland	7/10/18	22/11/18
2/Lt. W. O. BOLTON.	12/10/16			18/12/18
2/Lt. G. St. J. WRIGHT.	3/5/17			4/1/19
2/Lt. J. H. STOTT.	3/5/17			4/1/19
2/Lt. O. JAMES.	3/5/17			29/11/18
*2/Lt. J. ALLEN.	3/5/17			29/11/18
2/Lt. E. J. TOWNLEY.	31/5/17	Switzerland	27/12/17	24/3/18
2/Lt. A. M. THOMPSON.	11/7/17	(*Died* 31/7/17 at Douai).		
Lieut. C. CARMODY.	30/11/17			17/12/18
Capt. J. H. SPENCER.	12/4/18	(*Died* 15/7/18 at Limburg).		
2/Lt. L. TAYLOR.	12/4/18			–/12/18
2/Lt. F. W. GOODWIN.	13/4/18			29/12/18
†2/Lt. C. V. LONGLAND.	8/8/18			17/12/18

3rd Battalion.

Lieut. J. R. WILKINSON.	3/9/14	(*Died* 20/5/16 at Gradenfrei).	

5th Battalion.

2/Lt. H. M. AINSCOW.	28/6/16	Holland	16/5/18	4/10/18
Lieut. R. YOUNG.	31/7/17			14/12/18
2/Lt. V. A. TELFER.	31/7/17			6/12/18
2/Lt. S. KIRKPATRICK.	20/11/17	(*Died* –/10/18 at Saarbrucken).		
2/Lt. C. J. LEWIS.	21/3/18			3/12/18
Capt. G. GRAY.	26/3/18			8/12/18
‡Lieut. G. NICHOLSON.	26/3/18			5/12/18
2/Lt. A. WALLACE.	26/3/18			29/11/18
2/Lt. P. PLATT.	26/3/18			1/12/18

*Attached from 1/5 South Lancs. †Attached from Lincolns.
‡Attached from York and Lancaster Regiment.

LANCASHIRE FUSILIERS—Continued.

6th Battalion.

Name.	Missing.	Interned.	Repatriated.
2/Lt. F. C. NOXON.	6/9/17		17/12/18
Major W. WIKE.	21/3/18		18/12/18
Capt. J. L. LEE.	21/3/18		18/12/18
Capt. F. A. H. BEALEY.	21/3/18	(*Died* at Bad Colberg).	
Lieut. E. ORMEROD.	21/3/18		10/12/18
2/Lt. I. SKENE.	21/3/18	(*Died* 13/4/18 at Valenciennes).	
2/Lt. H. T. SMITH.	21/3/18		5/12/18
2/Lt. C. R. CURTIS.	21/3/18		5/12/18
2/Lt. V. DELANEY.	21/3/18		1/12/18
2/Lt. D. R. MacKAY.	21/3/18		18/12/18
2/Lt. H. HEWITT.	21/3/18		29/11/18
Lieut. C. GRAY.			–/12/18
Capt. L. M. ROBINSON.	22/3/18		10/12/18
2/Lt. C. H. VINES.	27/3/18		1/12/18
Capt. J. F. U. GRIFFIN.	6/9/17		11/1/19

7th Battalion.

Name.	Missing.	Interned.	Repatriated.
*Capt. S. E. REID.	21/3/18		5/12/18
Capt. K. L. KIRK.	21/3/18		6/12/18
Lieut. K. MUDIE.	21/3/18		2/12/18
Lieut. C. H. KELSALL.	21/3/18		3/12/18
2/Lt. D. W. HOWARD.	21/3/18		18/12/18
2/Lt. B. FURRELL.	21/3/18		17/12/18
2/Lt. H. PALMER.	21/3/18		3/1/19
2/Lt. S. MARSHALL.	21/3/18		
2/Lt. H. W. CULLEN.	21/3/18		2/12/18
2/Lt. D. MARSHALL.	21/3/18		10/12/18
2/Lt. F. A. BROWN.	21/3/18		2/12/18
2/Lt. J. G. ANDERSON.	21/3/18		29/11/18
2/Lt. H. W. WALTON.	21/3/18		2/12/18
2/Lt. E. PHILLIPSON.	21/3/18		29/11/18
2/Lt. H. ROSS.	21/3/18	(*Died* 8/4/18 at Le Cateau).	
Lieut. H. N. APPLEFORD.	26/3/18		12/10/18
†Lt.-Col. E. A. S. GELL.	27/3/18		25/12/18
2/Lt. A. G. CRUMP.	27/3/18		13/12/18

8th Battalion.

Name.	Missing.	Interned.	Repatriated.
2/Lt. J. C. COLLINGE.	4/10/17	(*Died* 25/10/17 at Hamburg).	
2]Lt. G. E. POWELL.	9/10/17		3/12/18
2/Lt. J. C. J. TOOMER.	2/2/18		25/12/18
‡Lt.-Col. H. G. ROBERTS.	21/3/18		6/12/18
†Lt.-Col. A. E. STOKES-ROBERTS.	21/3/18		11/1/19
Major T. J. BIDDOLPH.	21/3/18		–/11/18
Capt. J. EDGAR.	21/3/18		2/12/18
Capt. R. S. MORLEY.	21/3/18		9/12/18
Capt. R. L. BUSBY.	21/3/18		29/11/18
Lieut. G. H. YAPP.	21/3/18		2/12/18
Lieut. J. A. HOLDSWORTH.	21/3/18	(*Died* 17/6/18 at Zwickau).	
Lieut. E. S. ELLWOOD.	21/3/18		10/12/18
Lieut. H. HASTINGS.	21/3/18		3/12/18
2/Lt. G. LOFTHOUSE.	21/3/18		14/12/18
2/Lt. H. TYE.	21/3/18		3/12/18

*Attached from K.S.L.I. †Attached from Royal Fusiliers.
‡Attached from South Lancs. §Attached from Worcesters.

LANCASHIRE FUSILIERS—Continued.

8th Battalion—continued.

Name.	Missing.	Interned.	Repatriated.
2/Lt. J. HOWARTH.	21/3/18		29/11/18
2/Lt. E. J. DUNN.	21/3/18		2/12/18
2/Lt. H. M. NEWTON.	21/3/18		17/12/18
2/Lt. C. E. PALK.	21/3/18		2/12/18
*2/Lt. A. A. SIMPSON.	21/3/18		2/12/18
2/Lt. C. C. MOORE.	21/3/18		1/11/18
2/Lt. R. W. MABBETT.	21/3/18		2/12/18
2/Lt. J. BARLOW.	21/3/18		29/11/18
2/Lt. T. O. BOWEN.	21/3/18		2/12/18
2/Lt. G. MASSEY.	26/3/18		25/12/18
2/Lt. R. TOWERS.	27/3/18		18/12/18
Capt. H. THRUSH.	5/4/18		29/11/18
Lieut. J. H. RICK.	5/4/18		–/12/18
2/Lt. J. G. LYMER.	5/4/18		29/11/18

9th Battalion.

Name.	Missing.	Interned.	Repatriated.
Capt. E. H. DAVIES.	28–30/9/16	Holland 12/8/18	18/12/18
2/Lt. H. W. POTTER.	28–30/9/16		18/12/18

10th Battalion.

Name.	Missing.	Interned.	Repatriated.
2/Lt. G. BELL.	1/2/17		28/11/18
Capt. A. J. BARROW.	23/3/18	(*Died* 24/6/18 at Cassel).	
2/Lt. G. J. CUNNINGHAM.	26/3/18		25/12/18
Lieut. C. MANSBRIDGE.	4/6/18		8/12/18
2/Lt. H. L. HEELIS.	4/6/18		21/1/19
Capt. I. SANKEY.	25/8/18		28/11/18

11th Battalion.

Name.	Missing.	Interned.	Repatriated.
2/Lt. J. ADAMSON.	23/12/17		27/11/18
2/Lt. J. PORTEUS.	23/3/18		11/12/18
2/Lt. E. E. SHARP.	23/3/18		31/12/18
Lt.-Col. E. C. de R. MARTIN.	10/4/18		11/1/19
*Lt.-Col. G. P. POLLITT.	27/5/18		24/12/18
Capt. C. M. NEWMAN.	27/5/18		24/12/18
Lieut. F. EYRE.	27/5/18		14/12/18
2/Lt. E. A. NORTH.	27/5/18		–/12/18
†2/Lt. W. DALE.	27/5/18		14/12/18
†2/Lt. D. R. AUTY.	27/5/18		13/1/19
†2/Lt. G. A. BROADBENT.	27/5/18		18/12/18
†2/Lt. J. W. BOTTOMLEY.	27/5/18		25/12/18
†2/Lt. J. H. SMITH.	27/5/18		–/12/18
†2/Lt. F. H. GRAHAM.	28/5/18		31/12/18
†2/Lt. J. A. PIGHILLS.	28/5/18	(*Died* 29/5/18 at Rheims).	

15th Battalion.

Name.	Missing.	Interned.	Repatriated.
‡2/Lt. L. DE LOZEY.	2/11/18		9/12/18
2/Lt. E. H. EDWARDS.	2/11/18		–/12/18
2/Lt. J. A. CLARK.	2/11/18		11/12/18
2/Lt. F. R. CROCKFORD.	3/11/18		4/12/18

16th Battalion.

Name.	Missing.	Interned.	Repatriated.
2/Lt. N. H. ANDERTON.	11/3/16	Holland 30/4/18	18/11/18
Capt. F. F. WAUGH.	3/7/18		–/12/18
2/Lt. N. J. GILLMORE.	13/9/18		16/12/18

*Attached T.M.B.
†Attached from R.E.
‡Attached from North Staffs.

LANCASHIRE FUSILIERS—Continued.
17th Battalion.

Name.	Missing.	Interned.	Repatriated.
Capt. J. M. COWAN.	25/8/16		18/12/18
2/Lt. E. C. WEBSTER.	12/4/18		1/12/18

18th Battalion.

2/Lt. P. TORRANCE.	22/10/17		5/11/18
2/Lt. L. G. WILSON.	25/3/18		4/12/18
Lieut. H. B. ALMOND.	1/6/18		19/12/18

19th Battalion.

Major J. AMBROSE-SMITH.	25/4/18		8/12/18
Capt. H. W. HUXLEY.	25/4/18		8/12/18
Lieut. H. B. CARTWRIGHT.	25/4/18		—/12/18
Lieut. F. R. MUTCH.	25/4/18		31/12/18
Lieut. L. N. MIDDLETON.	25/4/18		11/12/18
Lieut. R. MARRIOTT.	25/4/18		6/12/18
2/Lt. H. W. SMITH.	25/4/18		6/12/18
2/Lt. S. BELCHER.	25/4/18		4/12/18
2/Lt. J. BALL.	25/4/18		29/11/18
2/Lt. E. J. WILSON.	25/4/18		18/12/18
2/Lt. M. WALKER.	25/4/18		29/11/18
2/Lt. J. CROSBIE.	25/4/18		—/12/18

20th Battalion.

2/Lt. H. BAKER.	2/10/16		30/12/18

23rd Battalion.

2/Lt. M. J. HENDERSON.	8/8/18		17/12/18
2/Lt. P. FARRELL.	8/8/18		18/12/18
2/Lt. G. S. CHARLTON.	27/9/18		8/12/18

ROYAL SCOTS FUSILIERS.
1st Battalion.

Name.	Missing.	Interned.		Repatriated.
Capt. T. A. ROSE.	10/9/14	(*Died*).		
Capt. R. W. S. STIVEN.	10/9/14	(*Died* —/9/15 at Mainz).		
Lieut. Cecil GRAVES.	10/9/14	Holland	5/1/18	15/12/18
Major A. H. McGREGOR.	30/10/14	Switzerland	9/12/17	24/3/18
Capt. A. LE GALLAIS.	30/10/14	Switzerland	9/12/17	9/12/18
Capt. J. FLEETWOOD.	8/11/14	Holland	24/2/18	28/11/18
Capt. R. M. BURGOYNE.	30/11/14	Switzerland	27/12/17	14/6/18
Lieut. E. P. O. BOYLE.	30/11/14	Holland	24/2/18	14/12/18
Lieut. J. L. BOWEN.	30/11/14	Switzerland	9/12/17	14/6/18
Capt. F. JUDGE.	15/12/14	Holland	24/2/18	23/9/18
2/Lt. A. G. LOCHHEAD.	13/11/16			18/12/18
2/Lt. P. DOBIE.	22/3/17			7/1/18
2/Lt. A. P. ORR.	29/3/18			5/1/19
2/Lt. W. McMINN.	10/4/18			1/12/18
Capt. R. G. FERGUSON.	18/5/18	(*Died* 11/6/18 at Habourdin).		
2/Lt. R. A. GERSTENBERG.	18/9/18			8/12/18

ROYAL SCOTS FUSILIERS—continued.

2nd Battalion.

Name.	Missing.	Interned.		Repatriated.
Lieut. H. STEWART.	30/10/14	Switzerland	9/12/17	14/6/18
Lt.-Col. A. G. BAIRD-SMITH.	14/12/14	Holland	24/2/18	17/11/18
2/Lt. P. McHUGH.	1/8/16	Holland	17/6/18	22/11/18
2/Lt. J. McA. C. GRACIE.	1/8/16	Switzerland	27/12/17	24/3/18
2/Lt. G. H. SLAUGHTER.	1/8/16	Switzerland	9/12/17	24/3/18
2/Lt. G. DICEY.	23/4/17			4/12/18
2/Lt. A. R. DOUGALL.	25/3/18			25/12/18
2/Lt. W. TEMPLETON.	26/3/18			18/12/18
Lieut. F. W. FRANCIS.	9/4/18			18/12/18

6th Battalion.

Name.	Missing.	Interned.		Repatriated.
Capt. G. ROBERTSON.	25/9/15	Holland	10/4/18	18/11/18
Capt. A. B. PURVES.	25/9/15	(*Died* 8/11/15 at Cologne).		
2/Lt. A. R. CARR.	12/8/16	Holland	12/10/18	21/1/19

6/7th Battalion.

Name.	Missing.	Interned.	Repatriated.
2/Lt. T. SMILLIE.	21/3/18		2/12/18
2/Lt. E. McQUAID.	21/3/18		19/12/18
2/Lt. G. P. CROCKETT.	30/3/18		2/12/18
2/Lt. N. B. FIFE.	21/4/18		—/12/18

7th Battalion.

Name.	Missing.	Interned.	Repatriated.
2/Lt. A. WEIR.	21/3/18		2/12/18

CHESHIRE REGIMENT.

1st and 2nd Battalions.

Name.	Missing.	Interned.		Repatriated.
Lt.-Col. D. C. BOGER.	24/8/14	Holland	29/12/17	23/9/17
Capt. W. G. R. ELLIOT.	31/8/14	Holland	29/12/17	30/11/18
Capt. A. J. L. DYER.	31/8/14	Holland	29/12/17	31/12/18
Capt. C. J. JOLLIFFE.	31/8/14			13/9/17
Capt. E. A. JACKSON.	31/8/14	Switzerland	9/12/17	24/3/18
Major B. CHETWYND-STAPYLTON.	4/9/14	Holland	29/12/17	23/10/18
Capt. B. E. MASSY.	4/9/14	Holland	5/1/18	18/11/18
Capt. C. A. K. MATTERSON.	4/9/14	Holland	5/1/18	13/11/18
Capt. C. H. RANDALL.	4/9/14	Holland	29/12/17	4/10/18
Capt. V. TAHOURDIN.	10/9/14	Switzerland	9/12/17	14/6/18
Capt. W. L. E. DUGMORE.	11/9/14	Holland	29/12/17	18/8/18
Lieut. W. L. STEWART.	11/9/14	Holland	6/2/18	18/11/18
Lieut. R. H. BOLTON.	11/9/14	Holland	29/12/17	23/11/18
Lieut. T. FAIRWEATHER.	11/9/14	Holland	29/12/17	17/11/18
Capt. S. BUTTERWORTH.	12/10/14	Holland	6/2/18	18/11/18
Major F. YOUNG.	13/10/14			13/9/17
Capt. H. N. HARRINGTON.	13/10/14	Switzerland	9/12/17	14/6/18
Lieut. W. THOMAS.	13/10/14	Holland	29/12/17	22/11/18
Capt. L. A. FORSTER.	22/10/14	(*Died*).		
Capt. J. L. SHORE.	22/10/14	Switzerland	9/12/17	4/3/19
Capt. G. W. LEICESTER.	22/10/14	Holland	24/2/18	18/11/18
Lieut. G. S. JACOBS.	4/11/14	Holland	29/12/17	12/12/18
Lieut. E. R. HARBORD.	13/11/14	Switzerland	9/12/17	24/3/18
Lieut. B. V. HAYES-NEWINGTON.	11/5/15	Holland	23/3/18	8/2/19
Lieut. H. FORMAN.	11/5/15			18/11/18
Lieut. W. A. WARD.	11/5/15			1/11/18
*2/Lt. A. Q. ROBINSON.	28/6/18			3/12/18

*Attached from Worcesters.

CHESHIRE REGIMENT—Continued.

4th Battalion.

Name.	Missing.	Interned.	Repatriated.
Lieut. H. R. WALL.	10/4/18		2/12/18

5th Battalion.

Lieut. T. MOULTON.	17/5/18		31/12/18

6th Battalion.

2/Lt. S. KING.	31/7/17		19/7/18
2/Lt. G. B. JORDAN.	27/5/18		18/12/18

7th Battalion.

2/Lt. J. C. JONES.	25/10/18		24/11/18
2/Lt. A. BRADLEY.	25/10/18		24/11/18
2/Lt. W. W. DAVIES.	25/10/18		1/12/18

9th Battalion.

Capt. J. A. BAIRD.			18/12/18
2/Lt. G. H. VERITY.	25/3/18		26/12/18
Lieut. G. W. DAY.	31/5/18		7/9/18

10th Battalion.

*Lt.-Col. W. E. WILLIAMS.	11/4/18		29/11/18
Capt. G. C. MEREDITH.	11/4/18		29/11/18
Lieut. E. J. SAUNDERS.	12/4/18		29/11/18
†2/Lt. H. G. EVANS.	12/4/18		1/12/18
2/Lt. E. M. GIBSON.	26/4/18		8/12/18
2/Lt. K. B. RALSTON.	26/4/18		12/10/18
2/Lt. S. A. ELLIS.	27/5/18		1/12/18
2/Lt. H. J. HOLLAMBY.	27/5/18		13/12/18
‡2/Lt. P. COOKSON.	27/5/18		13/12/18
‡2/Lt. W. P. HUNTER.	27–30/5/18		6/1/19

11th Battalion.

2/Lt. H. H. OWEN.	22/3/18		11/12/18
2/Lt. A. H. D. DUTTON.	22/3/18		29/11/18
2/Lt. E. F. BYRON.	22/3/18		29/11/18
Lieut. E. C. DIXON.	23/3/18		29/11/18
Lieut. A. H. KISSACK.	23/3/18		1/12/18
§Lieut. W. A. WILLIAMS.	23/3/18		18/12/18
2/Lt. W. R. JONES.	23/3/18		11/12/18
2/Lt. J. W. FOSTER.	23/3/18		18/12/18
2/Lt. R. S. COOLE.	23/3/18		5/1/19
2/Lt. W. M. BARRY.	23/3/18		18/12/18
Lieut. F. W. HARVEY.	10/4/18		29/11/18
Lieut. J. A. SNAPE.	10/4/18		13/12/18
Lieut. C. A. BEARD.	10/4/18		31/12/18
2/Lt. A. TAYLOR.	10/4/18		25/12/18
2/Lt. F. HAMMOND.	10/4/18		18/12/18
Capt. C. de Witte WOODYER.	27/5/18		
Lieut. H. R. CARSON.	27/5/18		–/12/18
2/Lt. W. RYDEN.	27/5/18		26/12/18
2/Lt. A. MAYOR.	27/5/18		13/12/18
2/Lt. J. S. BURGOYNE.	27/5/18		25/12/18
2/Lt. A. W. BYTHEWAY.	27/5/18		18/12/18
2/Lt. C. F. M. BARRETT.	27/5/18		22/12/18
Capt. H. M. WILKINSON.	28/5/18		14/12/18

*Attached from Middlesex. †Attached from R. W. Kents. ‡Attached from Manchesters.
§Attached from Liverpools.

CHESHIRE REGIMENT—Continued.
15th Battalion.

Name.	Missing.	Interned.	Repatriated.
Major H. F. A. Le MESURIER.	24/3/18		1/1/19
Capt. E. W. BIGLAND.	24/3/18		25/12/18
Capt. V. G. BARNETT.	24/3/18		13/12/18
Lieut. D. W. MILLS.	24/3/18		11/12/18
2/Lt. E. H. BANN.	24/3/18		11/12/18
2/Lt. A. CHUCK.	24/3/18		25/12/18
2/Lt. T. YOUNG.	24/3/18		25/12/18
*2/Lt. A. J. C. WALTERS.	10/4/18		29/11/18

ROYAL WELSH FUSILIERS.
1st Battalion.

Name.	Missing.	Interned.		Repatriated.
Capt. E. SKAIFE.	20/10/14	Holland	24/2/18	18/8/18
Capt. SMYTHE OSBORNE.	20/10/14	Holland	6/2/18	29/12/18
Lieut. Hon. R. BINGHAM.	20/10/14	Holland	24/2/18	14/1/19
Lieut. H. COURAGE.	20/10/14	Holland	6/2/18	18/11/18
Lieut. C. G. H. PEPPE.	20/10/14	Holland	24/2/18	22/1/19
Lieut. R. E. HINDSON.	23/10/14	Holland	6/2/18	18/11/18
2/Lt. E. WODEHOUSE.	30/10/14	Holland	6/2/18	18/11/18
Lieut. B. C. H. POOLE.	8/11/14	Holland	24/2/18	18/11/18
Lieut. D. M. BARCHARD.	-/-/14	Holland	6/2/18	22/11/18

2nd Battalion.

Name.	Missing.	Interned.		Repatriated.
Lieut. A. M. G. EVANS.	30/10/14	Holland	24/2/18	22/1/19
2/Lt. J. D. M. RICHARDS.	27/5/17	Switzerland	27/12/17	24/3/18
2/Lt. J. A. SOAMES.	5/5/17			7/1/18
2/Lt. C. P. CRABTREE.	1/9/18			28/11/18
2/Lt. D. JONES.	1/9/18			8/12/18
Lieut. E. C. TUNNICLIFFE.	1/9/18			11/12/18
2/Lt. T. ROWLAND.	27/3/17			8/1/17

4th Battalion.

Name.	Missing.	Repatriated.
Capt. P. R. FOULKES-ROBERTS.	23/3/18	28/11/18
Lieut. O. P. T. N. BLAKE.	24/3/18	1/12/18

9th Battalion.

Name.	Missing.	Repatriated.
2/Lt. R. E. SMITH.	23/3/18	11/12/18
Lieut. W. O. H. ELLIS.	24/3/18	17/12/18
Capt. J. M. WARDLAW.	10/4/18	8/12/18
2/Lt. W. B. BEDDOW.	10/4/18	18/12/18
2/Lt. A. C. CLOUGH.	10/4/18	17/12/18
2/Lt. G. H. WEBB.	10/4/18	29/11/18
†Capt. S. DARVELL.	30/5/18	14/12/18
Capt. J. R. WILLIAMS.	30/5/18	14/12/18
Lieut. R. S. R. PITTARD.	30/5/18	-/12/18
Lieut. A. WYNNE.	30/5/18	-/12/18
2/Lt. L. JONES.	30/5/18	11/1/19
2/Lt. E. C. THOMAS.	30/5/18	11/1/19
2/Lt. S. WATKINS.	30/5/18	28/12/18

*Attached from South Lancashire.
†Attached from Denbighshire Yeomanry.

ROYAL WELSH FUSILIERS—Continued.

13th Battalion.

Name.	Missing.	Interned.	Repatriated.
2/Lt. D. O. JONES.	10/3/18		25/12/18

14th Battalion.

2/Lt. C. PARKER.	19/9/18 (*Died*).		25/10/18
2/Lt. B. LAW.	7/10/18		29/11/18

15th Battalion.

Lieut. L. C. NEWMAN.	21/12/18 (*Died*).		

16th Battalion.

Lieut. P. A. ROBERTS.	2/12/16		7/1/19
2/Lt. J. RICHARDS.	18/9/18		
2/Lt. G. E. YOUNG.	18/9/18		2/12/18

18th Battalion.

Capt. E. W. BISHOP.	15/11/16		18/12/18
2/Lt. S. T. JONES.			18/11/18

25th Battalion.

Lieut. H. L. MORGAN.	21/9/18		8/12/18

SOUTH WALES BORDERERS.

1st and 2nd Battalions.

*Lieut. G. W. PHILLIMORE.	5/4/16			12/11/18
Lieut. C. DAVIDSON.	20/5/16	Holland	30/4/18	22/1/19
Capt. J. C. B. TRAGETT.	3/12/17			18/8/18
2/Lt. H. EDWARDS.	3/12/17			17/12/18
2/Lt. D. R. WINDSOR.	3/12/17			17/12/18
2/Lt. T. J. JORDAN.	13/12/17			25/12/18

2nd Battalion.

Major D. H. S. SOMERVILLE.	11/4/18		28/11/18
Capt. E. A. LLOYD.	11/4/18		25/12/18
Capt. J. B. STERNDALE-BENNETT.	11/4/18		25/12/18
Lieut. W. F. PAGE.	11/4/18		25/12/18
2/Lt. F. H. BEES.	11/4/18		–/1/19
2/Lt. S. F. HEARDER.	11/4/18		18/12/18
2/Lt. J. S. LEWIS.	11/4/18		18/12/18
†2/Lt. W. PARRY.	11/4/18		18/12/18
2/Lt. J. PEMBERTON.	11/4/18		18/12/18
2/Lt. G. F. SMITH.	11/4/18		18/12/18
†2/Lt. F. T. WILLIAMS.	11/4/18		25/12/18

6th Battalion.

‡Lieut. H. DAVIES.	27/5/18		17/12/18
†2/Lt. G. CARLYLE.	28/5/18		14/12/18
2/Lt. H. R. MURRAY.	28/5/18		18/12/18

11th Battalion.

§2/Lt. H. E. GRIFFITHS.	11/4/18		18/12/18

*Attached from Highland L.I. †Attached from Welsh Regiment.
*Attached from Royal Welsh Fusiliers. §Attached from Entrenching Battery.

SOUTH WALES BORDERERS—Continued.
12th Battalion.

Name.	Missing.	Interned.	Repatriated.
2/Lt. E. O. DAVIES.	24/11/17		17/12/18

K.O. SCOTTISH BORDERERS.
1st and 2nd Battalions.

Name	Missing	Interned		Repatriated
Capt. H. COBDEN.	26/8/14	Holland	22/1/1	18/11/18
Lieut. R. P. M. BELL.	26/8/14	Holland	5/1/18	2/1/19
Capt. R. JOYNSON.	27/8/14	Holland	22/1/18	18/11/18
Lt.-Col. C. M. STEPHENSON.	10/9/14	Switzerland	28/12/16	24/3/18
Lieut. W. N. SHEWEN.	10/9/14	Holland	5/1/18	20/12/18
Major A. E. HAIG.	10/9/14	Holland	22/1/18	23/10/18
Capt. E. W. MacDONALD.		Holland	11/8/18	7/9/18
Lieut. T. F. TEELING.		Holland	22/1/18	23/10/18
2/Lt. A. C. RANKINE.	13/12/16			14/12/18
2/Lt. N. MacLEOD.	28/1/17			14/12/18
2/Lt. U. A. BOND.	11/4/18			18/12/18
Capt. R. M. SHORTER.	11/4/18			17/12/18
2/Lt. W. C. TAYLOR.	11/4/18			25/12/18
2/Lt. A. W. ROBB.	11/4/18			11/12/18
2/Lt. E. C. J. CROFTS.	11/4/18	(*Died* 28/4/18 at Langensalza).		
2/Lt. W. R. COX.	18/9/18			28/11/18

4th Battalion.

Name	Missing			Repatriated
Lieut. L. T. O'HANLON.	18/9/18			29/11/18
2/Lt. D. L. SCOTT.	3/10/18			28/11/18

6th Battalion.

Name	Missing	Interned		Repatriated
2/Lt. J. S. FRANKLIN.	26/9/15			11/9/17
2/Lt. A. D. McKERRELL.	1/4/17			30/12/18
2/Lt. G. K. GREENAWAY.	3/5/11			5/1/19
*Capt. H. W. SAMSON.	3/5/17			2/12/18
2/Lt. J. H. NELSON.	3/5/17	Switzerland	27/12/17	14/6/18
2/Lt. J. MABEN.	22/3/18			29/11/18
2/Lt. J. R. MASSON.	26/3/18			25/12/18
2/Lt. J. D. STARK.	15/4/18	(*Died* 3/9/18 at Cologne).		
2/Lt. George PENMAN.	25/4/18			14/12/18
2/Lt. P. ORMISTON.	25/4/18			29/11/18
2/Lt. W. E. LIVINGSTONE.	25/4/18			29/11/18
2/Lt. A. D. ARCHIBALD.	25/4/18			29/11/18
Capt. H. J. WILKIE.	25/4/18			29/12/18
2/Lt. A. G. FARQUHARSON.	25/4/18			–/11/18
2/Lt. P. J. SPARKES.	16/10/18			13/12/18

*Attached from Royal Scots.

7th Battalion.

Name	Missing			Repatriated
Capt. T. BLACKBURN.	26/9/15			13/9/17
2/Lt. W. M. HONEYMAN.	23/7/18			–/12/18

8th Battalion.

Name	Missing	Interned		Repatriated
2/Lt. H. G. MITCHELL.	26/9/15	Switzerland	9/12/17	9/12/18
Lieut. P. M. ROSS.	26/9/15			18/11/18

CAMERONIANS.
(Scottish Rifles.)
1st and 2nd Battalions.

Name.	Missing.	Interned.	Repatriated.
Capt. A. R. MacALLAN.		Switzerland 12/8/16	13/9/17
*Capt. A. ARMSTRONG.	22/8/17		—/12/18
2/Lt. H. D. GRANT.	24/3/18		8/12/18
†Capt. P. J. BOOTH.	25/3/18		2/12/18
Capt. A. W. F. STEWART.	25/3/18		1/12/18
Capt. M. MALLACE.	25/3/18		1/12/18
Lieut. W. B. THOMAS.	25/3/18		—/12/18
2/Lt. J. E. MacKAY.	25/3/18		—/12/18
Lt.-Col. F. G. W. DRAFFEN.	9/5/18		1/12/18
Lieut. A. G. ROBB.	9/5/18	(*Died* 20/5/18 at Hanover).	

5/6th Battalions.

2/Lt. A. ANDERSON.	24/10/18		8/12/18

6th Battalion.

2/Lt. D. C. CALDWELL.	19/8/18		13/12/18

9th Battalion.

2/Lt. J. R. KAY.	28/12/16		17/12/18
Capt. A. L. BROWN.	3/5/17		17/12/18
Lieut. T. A. NEILSON.	23/3/18		29/11/18
2/Lt. R. O. LOCKHEAD.	2/7/18		17/12/18

10th Battalion.

Leiut. A. FLEMING.	1/8/17		6/12/18
Lieut. H. J. ROBISON.	19/8/18		11/12/18
Lieut. G. M. DREW.	19/8/18		29/11/18
2/Lt. L. McK. EWEN.	21/12/17		3/12/18

ROYAL INNISKILLING FUSILIERS.
1st Battalion.

Name	Missing	Interned	Repatriated
Lieut. S. W. AITCHISON.	19/5/17		—/12/18
‡2/Lt. J. CLANCY.	19/5/17	Switzerland 27/12/17	7/12/18
Capt. J. McMECHAN.	21/3/18		25/12/18
Lieut. S. McCONNELL.	21/3/18		28/11/18
2/Lt. F. S. MARCHANT.	21/3/18		18/12/18
2/Lt. C. GREGG.	21/3/18		—/12/18
Lt.-Col. J. N. CRAWFORD.	22/3/18		3/1/19
Capt. E. E. J. MOORE.	22/3/18		1/12/18
Capt. T. H. COCKBURN-MERCER.	22/3/18		11/1/19
Lieut. B. L. GRIGGS.	22/3/18		18/12/18
Lieut. W. G. BAKER.	22/3/18		25/12/18
2/Lt. S. S. HUNTER.	22/3/18		25/12/18
2/Lt. J. P. ROBINSON.	22/3/18		17/12/18
2/Lt. W. PRICE.	22/3/18		29/11/18
2/Lt. R. B. McCONNELL.	22/3/18		25/12/18
Capt. G. W. WILLOCK.	23/3/18		18/12/18

*Attached T.M.B.
‡Attached from Munster Fusiliers.
†Attached from Royal Scots Fusiliers.

ROYAL INNISKILLING FUSILIERS—Continued.

2nd Battalion.

Name.	Missing.	Interned.	Repatriated.
Capt. E. R. LLOYD.	-/-/14	(*Died* at Cambrai).	
Lieut. I. R. F. MILLER.	11/9/14	(*Died* 8/3/15).	
Lieut. C. F. BEVERLAND.	23/11/16	(*Died* 4/12/16 at Pronville).	
2/Lt. D. H. O'HARA.	27/2/17		18/12/18
Capt. J. A. S. HOPKINS.	21/3/18		1/12/18
Capt. R. M. VAUGHAN.	21/3/18		10/12/18
Capt. R. M. BOYLE.	21/3/18		8/12/18
Capt. C. C. MILLER.	21/3/18		29/11/18
Lieut. W. V. MORONY.	21/3/18		18/12/18
Lieut. F. W. DAVIDSON.	21/3/18		1/12/18
2/Lt. F. CINNAMOND.	21/3/18	(*Died* 13/11/18 at Graudenz).	
2/Lt. S. B. McCONNELL.	21/3/18		-/12/18
2/Lt. G. WATSON.	21/3/18		28/11/18
2/Lt. J. F. O'BRIEN.	21/3/18		2/12/18
2/Lt. P. HENNESSY.	21/3/18		18/12/18
2/Lt. G. M. BURKE.	21/3/18		20/12/18
*Lt.-Col. Lord A. K. FARNHAM.	21/3/18		17/12/18
Lieut. J. H. WHERRY.	21-29/3/18		17/12/18
†Lieut. C. J. ARMSTRONG.	21-29/3/18		10/12/18
‡Lieut. T. H. BIRD.	21-29/3/18		-/12/18
‡2/Lt. D. R. CLARK.	21-29/3/18		18/12/18
‡2/Lt. J. D. McCULLOUGH.	21-29/3/18		18/12/18
2/Lt. F. C. WILLIAMS.	21-29/3/18		29/11/18
2/Lt. R. B. W. IRWIN.	21-29/3/18		14/12/18
2/Lt. J. M. J. MARTIN.	24/3/18		17/12/18
Major E. F. EAGAR.	29/3/18		29/11/18

7th Battalion.

Name.	Missing.	Interned.	Repatriated.
2/Lt. H. W. RUDDOCK.	16/8/17	Switzerland 24/4/18	9/12/18
2/Lt. J. FISHER.	16/8/17		6/1/19
2/Lt. J. T. FLANAGAN.	16/8/17		18/12/18
Capt. H. P. McKENNA.	21/3/18		28/11/18
Capt. D. H. MORTON.	16/8/17		3/12/18

7/8th Battalion.

Name.	Missing.	Interned.	Repatriated.
Major V. H. PARR.	21/3/18		2/1/19
§Capt. L. W. L. LEADER.	21/3/18		-/12/18
Capt. L. W. P. YATES.	21/3/18		16/1/19
Lieut. E. W. McKEGNEY.	21/3/18		11/12/18
Lieut. W. J. A. H. AUCHINLECK.	21/3/18		13/12/18
2/Lt. T J. STACK.	21/3/18		3/12/18
2/Lt. J. G. O'NEILL.	21/3/18		23/9/18
†2/Lt. J. W. BURKE.	1/9/18		16/12/18

8th Battalion.

Name.	Missing.	Interned.	Repatriated.
2/Lt. J. L. CHARLESWORTH.	16/8/17		9/12/18

9th Battalion.

Name.	Missing.	Interned.	Repatriated.
Capt. A. B. DOUGLAS.	6/12/17		6/1/19
Lieut. J. F. PARKHOUSE.	21/3/18		29/11/18
2/Lt. J. F. R. DARBYSHIRE.	21-29/3/18		29/11/18
2/Lt. H. H. MURDOCH.	21-29/3/18		1/12/18
2/Lt. J. A. GIBSON.	23/3/18	(*Died* 24/9/18 at Trier).	
Lieut. G. M. K. MARTIN.	2/10/18		-/12/18

*Attached from Irish Horse.   †Attached from Royal Irish Fusiliers.
‡Attached from Royal Munster Fusiliers.   §Attached from Connaught Rangers.

ROYAL INNISKILLING FUSILIERS—Continued.
10th Battalion.

Name.	Missing.	Interned.	Repatriated.
2/Lt. J. H. SHANNON.	1/7/16		13/9/17

GLOUCESTERSHIRE REGIMENT.
1st and 2nd Battalions.

Capt. A. F. CHAPMAN.	29/10/14	Switzerland	24/3/18
Capt. D. A. GREENSLADE.	29/11/14	Holland 24/2/18	18/11/18
Lieut. C. F. L. TEMPLER.	22/12/14	Escaped	–/9/17
Capt. J. A. CAUNTER.		Escaped	–/6/17
Major R. CONNOR.		Exchanged	–/8/17
Lieut. P. P. KING.	23/3/18		–/12/18
2/Lt. I. SYKES.	23/3/18		6/1/19
Capt. R. F. RUBINSTEIN.	15/6/18		–/11/18

4th Battalion.

Lieut. C. M. COOTE.	24/7/16	Holland –/6/16	22/11/18
Capt. W. R. HUTCHINGS.	3/12/17		27/11/18
Lieut. W. G. SHIPWAY.	3/12/17		3/12/18
2/Lt. F. R. RAWLINGS.	3/12/17		3/12/18

5th Battalion.

2/Lt. F. W. HARVEY.	19/8/16	Holland 12/10/18	21/1/19
*2/Lt. F. G. L. WOOSTER.	29/8/17		20/12/18
Lieut. R. HOWELL.	22/3/18	(Died 30/5/18 at Heilbronn).	
2/Lt. T. E. MONDAY.	22/3/18		18/12/18
Lieut. A. F. BARNES.	23/3/18		15/12/18
2/Lt. R. A. FOTHERGILL.	23/3/18		25/12/18
2/Lt. W. PETTIGREW.	15/6/18		–/11/18
2/Lt. R. R. E. ELCOCK.	15/6/18		–/11/18
2/Lt. J. THOMAS.	15/6/18		21/11/18
†2/Lt. J. J. OVENSTONE.	15/6/18		–/11/18

6th Battalion.

2/Lt. E. B. CLARKE.	22/8/16	Holland 12/10/18	22/11/18
‡Capt. H. B. GOULDING.	3/12/17		22/3/18
2/Lt. G. M. SHEPPARD.	3/12/17		1/1/19
2/Lt. K. G. GURNEY.	3/12/17	(Died 17/12/17 at Selvigny).	

8th Battalion.

2/Lt. E. A. SQUIRE.	25/2/17		14/12/18
2/Lt. F. J. R. GARLAND.	25/2/17		14/12/18
Capt. M. A. JAMES.	23/3/18		25/12/18
Lieut. S. H. WATSON.	23/3/18		25/12/18
2/Lt. A. W. SHUBROOK.	23/3/18		17/12/18
2/Lt. G. ELLIS.	23/3/18		18/12/18
Capt. F. H. BOWLES.	10/4/18		2/12/18
2/Lt. H. COOPER.	10/4/18		18/12/18
2/Lt. R. W. NORRIS.	10/4/18		25/12/18
2/Lt. D. W. VICK.	10/4/18		29/11/18
2/Lt. C. MARFELL.	10/4/18		13/12/18
2/Lt. J. B. W. HUGHES.	22/9/18		23/1/19

*Attached from Norfolk Yeomanry.
†Attached from Dorsets.
‡Attached from R.A.M.C.

GLOUCESTERSHIRE REGIMENT—Continued.

12th Battalion.

Name.	Missing.	Interned.	Rapatriated.
Lieut. R. J. FITZGERALD.	8/5/17	Escaped	–/10/17
2/Lt. W. J. G. ABBOTT.	25/6/18		29/11/18

13th Battalion.

Name.	Missing.	Interned.	Rapatriated.
Lieut. F. C. BRIGHT.	23/3/18		18/12/18
Capt. G. M. HELE.	26/4/18		29/11/18
Capt. F. E. A. BERGER-WHEELER.	26/4/18		29/11/18
Lieut. A. C. BAKER.	26/4/18		31/12/18
Lieut. F. B. WHITTALL.	26/4/18		29/11/18
2/Lt. D. D. HERRING.	26/4/18		29/11/18
2/Lt. J. S. PAWSEY.	26/4/18		2/12/18
2/Lt. L. C. FARR.	26/4/18		29/11/18
2/Lt. F. S. SMITH.	26/4/18		29/11/18

WORCESTERSHIRE REGIMENT.

1st Battalion.

Name.	Missing.	Interned.	Rapatriated.
Capt. R. C. MARSHALL.	27/5/18		17/12/18
*Capt. A. B. PRATT.	27/5/18		8/12/18
†Lieut. T. G. MARTIN.	27/5/18		31/12/18
Lieut. F. PERCY.	27/5/18		–/12/18
Lieut. F. RODMAN.	27/5/18		–/12/18
Lieut. R. B. BERRY.	27/5/18		21/12/18
2/Lt. W. KELLY.	27/5/18		13/12/18
2/Lt. A. P. EDGAR.	27/5/18		13/12/18

2nd Battalion.

Name.	Missing.	Interned.	Rapatriated.
Capt. T. F. V. MATTHEWS.	13/4/18		18/12/18
Lieut. C. W. V. PEAKE.	13/4/18		1/12/18
2/Lt. A. HURLEY.	13/4/18		29/11/18
‡Major E. J. DONALDSON.	15/4/18		–/1/18
2/Lt. H. O. TREDWELL.	15/4/18		18/12/18
2/Lt. F. J. D. GUNSTON.	15/4/18	(*Died* 14/7/18).	

3rd Battalion.

Name.	Missing.	Interned.	Rapatriated.
Capt. C. V. BERESFORD.	10/9/14	Switzerland –/8/16	13/9/17
2/Lt. A. E. FRYER.	25/12/17		27/11/18
2/Lt. E. H. JONES.	25/12/17		27/11/18
2/Lt. C. LATHAM.	28/3/18		11/12/18
Lieut. H. U. RICHARDS.	–/4/18		–/11/18
Capt. E. A. HUMPHRIES.	27/5/18		11/1/19
2/Lt. R. O. GOOLDEN.	27/5/18		25/12/18
2/Lt. V. B. WASLEY.	27/5/18		31/12/18
2/Lt. E. V. MATTHEWS.	27/5/18		11/1/19
Lieut. W. E. J. WILL.	28/5/18		–/12/18
2/Lt. W. H. TODHUNTER.	28/5/18		–/12/18
2/Lt. A. J. SINCLAIR.	28/5/18		19/1/19
Lieut. A. S. ABRAHALL.	5/9/18		23/1/19

4th Battalion.

Name.	Missing.	Interned.	Rapatriated.
2/Lt. T. C. HAMBLING.	5/5/16	Holland 30/4/18	24/12/18
2/Lt. G. E. OVERBURY.	20/10/16		18/12/18
2/Lt. W. H. PITT.	23/4/17	Holland 30/10/18	23/11/18

*Attached from Leinsters. †Attached from Manchesters.
‡Attached from Lovats Scouts.

WORCESTERSHIRE REGIMENT—Continued.

5th Battalion.

Name.	Missing.	Interned.		Repatriated.
Capt. E. G. WILLIAMS.	31/10/14	Switzerland	9/12/17	24/3/18

7th Battalion.

Name.	Missing.	Interned.	Repatriated.
2/Lt. J. WHALE.	26/8/17		14/12/18
*Lieut. W. E. VACHER.	22/3/18		14/12/18
2/Lt. F. C. PERRETT.	27/5/18		13/12/18

8th Battalion.

Name.	Missing.	Interned.	Repatriated.
2/Lt. E. W. WELLS.	21/3/19		25/12/18
Major H. W. DAVIES.	22/3/18		4/12/18
Capt. A. T. BUTLER.	22/3/18		14/12/18
Capt. S. A. GODSALL.	22/3/18		14/12/18
2/Lt. J. A. GREAVES.	22/3/18		27/11/18
2/Lt. C. C. HAFFIELD.	22/3/18		–/12/18
2/Lt. W. G. JONES.	22/3/18		14/12/18
2/Lt. T. A. LANDRETH.	22/3/18		–/12/18
2/Lt. W. RUNDLE.	22/3/18		25/12/18
2/Lt. C. H. THOMAS.	22/3/18		31/12/18
2/Lt. J. G. PLAYER.	22/3/18		4/12/18
2/Lt. E. A. BROWN.	22/3/18		14/12/18
2/Lt. P. C. RUSHTON.	22/3/18		14/12/18
2/Lt. W. RADFORD.	22/3/18		6/12/18
2/Lt. C. W. LAWRENCE.	27/3/18		28/11/18
2/Lt. V. C. H. SPENCELAYH.	27/3/18		11/12/18
2/Lt. R. J. BURTON.	14/4/18	(*Died* 15/4/18 at Kortryk).	
Capt. C. R. PAWSEY.	2/8/18		–/11/18
2/Lt. A. G. GRANGER.	3/8/18		–/11/18
Lieut. R. S. MILLER.	23/10/18		16/12/18

10th Battalion.

Name.	Missing.	Interned.	Repatriated.
2/Lt. F. I. SMITH.	21/3/18		23/9/18
2/Lt. O. J. SHORT.	24/3/18	(*Died* 3/4/18 at Peruwelz).	
Capt. G. M. IRELAND-BLACKBURNE.	10/4/18		–/11/18
Capt. A. M. DICKINSON.	10/4/18		25/12/18
2/Lt. P. E. THOMPSON.	10/4/18		1/12/18
†Capt. H. STREET.	30/5/18	(*Died* 1/6/18 at Brouille).	

EAST LANCASHIRE REGIMENT.
1st and 2nd Battalions.

Name.	Missing.	Interned.		Repatriated.
Capt. C. F. HARGREAVES.	14/9/14	Holland	6/2/18	21/1/19
Major E. R. COLLINS.	17/9/14			9/12/18
Lieut. Kenneth HOOPER.	19/9/14	Holland	22/1/18	18/11/18
2/Lt. C. S. DODWELL.	10/4/15	Holland	10/4/18	18/11/18
Capt. G. MacK. SMITH.	14/5/15	Switzerland	27/12/17	9/12/18
2/Lt. W. H. T. HILPERN.	14/5/15	Holland	10/4/18	18/11/18
Capt. M. G. BROWNE.	1/7/16	Holland	16/5/18	16/12/18
Capt. C. WADDINGTON.	18/10/16			18/12/18
Capt. A. N. SCOTT.	18/10/16			18/12/18
Lieut. Mark QUAYLE.	18/10/16			23/10/18
2/Lt. J. M. WILKS.	18/10/16			18/12/18

*Attached 183/L.T.M.B.
†Attached from South Lancs Regiment.

EAST LANCASHIRE REGIMENT—Continued.

1st and 2nd Battalions.—continued.

Name.	Missing.	Interned.	Repatriated.
2/Lt. J. C. THOMPSON.	10/4/17		4/1/19
2/Lt. S. T. MARTIN.	21/3/18		11/12/18
Lieut. E. F. G. CHAPMAN.	24/3/18		8/12/18
2/Lt. H. E. ROBERTS.	24/3/18		19/1/19
2/Lt. B. H. RIDGARD.	10/4/18		11/12/18
Lieut. W. E. MILWARD.	11/4/18		3/12/18
2/Lt. J. ROWBOTTOM.	11/4/18		18/12/18
*2/Lt. E. L. FORD.	12/4/18		18/12/18
2/Lt. E. H. BURR.	24/4/18		3/12/18
Lt.-Col. G. E. M. HILL.	27/5/18		–/12/18
*Lieut. H V. SAMPSON.	27/5/18		23/12/18
Lieut. R PHILLIPS.	27/5/18		31/12/18
†2/Lt. W. YELLAND.	27/5/18		13/12/18
†2/Lt. G. FLETCHER.	27/5/18		–/12/18
†2/Lt. D. A. ROPER.	27/5/18		–/12/18
2/Lt. T. SHERIDAN.	27/5/18		31/12/18
2/Lt. G. H. HOWARTH.	27/5/18		31/12/18
*2/Lt. J. P. HAYLEY.	27/5/18		–/12/18
*2/Lt. F. J. COTTON.	28/5/18		30/12/18
2/Lt. W. A. LAUDERDALE.	28/5/18		31/12/18
*2/Lt. A. ROBINSON.	28/5/18		31/12/18

4th Battalion.

Name.	Missing.	Interned.	Repatriated.
Capt. A. D. S. A. FLETCHER.	21/3/18		2/12/18
Capt. H. A. MELLOWES.	21/3/18		2/12/18
‡Capt. R. CALEY.	21/3/18		28/11/18
‡Lieut. D. B. ROBERTSON.	21/3/18		28/11/18
Lieut. H. A. RILEY.	21/3/18		4/12/18
Lieut. E. M. SPICER.	21/3/18		14/12/18
†Lieut. P. A. PHILLIPS.	21/3/18		29/11/18
2/Lt. V. L. W. BROWN.	21/3/18		–/12/18
2/Lt. R. J. BARR.	21/3/18		18/12/18
2/Lt. A. E. QUAINTRELL.	21/3/18		29/11/18
2/Lt. H. W. VICCARS.	21/3/18		2/12/18
2/Lt. W. E. EADIE.	21/3/18		3/12/18
2/Lt. J. W. H. CRAIG.	21/3/18		29/11/18
2/Lt. J. C. MacDONALD.	29/3/18		17/12/18

†Attached from 23rd Londons.   †Attached T.M.B.

5th Battalion.

Name.	Missing.	Interned.	Repatriated.
2/Lt. N. J. HOWITT.	28/1/18		17/12/18
2/Lt. F. W. BROWN.	21/3/18		–/12/18
2/Lt. H. H. MASSEY.	21/3/18		13/12/18
2/Lt. L. PINDER.	21/3/18		2/12/18
2/Lt. A. K. HORN.	21/3/18		17/12/18
2/Lt. V. H. JOHNSTON.	21/3/18		–/12/18
2/Lt. E. B. OSBORNE.	21/3/18	(Died 1/4/18 at Le Cateau).	
2/Lt. G. V. MARSH.	22/3/18		11/12/18

8th Battalion.

Name.	Missing.	Interned.	Repatriated.
2/Lt. W. POWELL.	14/8/17		17/12/18
‡2/Lt. J. H. CALVERT.	22/3/18		18/12/18

*Attached from Lancashire Fusiliers.   †Attached from Manchesters.
‡Attached from South Lancs.   §Attached 15th Entrenching Battalion.

EAST LANCASHIRE REGIMENT—Continued.
11th Battalion.

Name.	Missing.	Interned.	Repatriated.
2/Lt. F. J. WILD.	8/3/17		6/12/18
Capt. C. H. MALLINSON.	4/12/17	(*Died* –/6/18 at Ingolstadt).	
2/Lt. E. TYER.	27/3/18		31/12/18
2/Lt. H. D. WALMSLEY.	5/9/18		8/12/18
2/Lt. J. MARSHALL.	5/9/18		8/12/18
2/Lt. T. C. ATKINSON.	5/9/18		29/11/18

EAST SURREY REGIMENT.
1st and 2nd Battalions.

Name	Missing	Interned	Repatriated
Capt. F. A. BOWRING.	–/–/14	Holland 6/2/18	18/11/18
Capt. R. CAMPBELL.	10/9/14	Holland 29/12/17	16/11/18
Lieut. W. G. MORRITT.	10/9/14	(*Killed* while escaping 27/6/17).	
Capt. R. J. HILLIER.	8/5/17		17/12/18
2/Lt. S. WINDEBANK.	8/5/17		6/12/18
2/Lt. E. A. WEEKS.	8/5/17		6/12/18
2/Lt. W. C. ROSER.	8/5/17		6/12/18
2/Lt. E. G. NEAME.	8/5/17		6/12/18
2/Lt. G. S. HEARN.	8/5/17	(*Died* 12/5/17).	

3rd Battalion.

2/Lt. W. G. PRICE.	9/4/18		10/12/18

7th Battalion.

2/Lt. J. A. ROSS.	12/8/16	Holland 12/10/18	6/12/18
2/Lt. J. L. McNAUGHTON.	3/5/17		31/12/18
2/Lt. F. W. GEE.	3/5/17		31/12/18
2/Lt. P. WARBURTON.	3/5/17		31/12/18
Lt.-Col. R. H. BALDWIN.	30/11/17		30/12/18
Capt. C. B. LITTLE.	30/11/17		3/12/18
Capt. K. ANNS.	30/11/17		14/12/18
2/Lt. H. M. BINSTEAD.	30/11/17		3/12/18
*2/Lt. E. E. W. BOWEN.	30/11/17		17/12/18
2/Lt. H. BUCK.	9/4/18		8/12/18

8th Battalion.

Capt. J. R. ACKERLEY.	3/5/17	Switzerland 27/12/17	23/12/18
Capt. C. J. LONERGAN.	3/5/17		18/8/18
2/Lt. G. S. FACER.	3/5/17		–/11/18
2/Lt. L. H. PEARSE.	3/5/17	Switzerland 27/12/17	23/12/18
2/Lt. J. F. McMILLAN.	3/5/17		6/12/18
2/Lt. H. T. SMITH.	23/3/18		–/12/18
Lieut. A. R. TOD.	4/4/18	(*Died* 18/4/18 at Caix).	

9th Battalion.

Capt. B. FENWICK.	26/9/15	Holland 10/4/18	7/12/18
Capt. C. E. BARNETT.	26/9/15	(*Died* 1/10/15 at Douai).	
Capt. W. B. BIRT.	26/9/15	(*Died* 18/4/16 at Cologne).	
Lieut. J. W. S. SEATON.	21/3/18		11/12/18
2/Lt. A. E. CLARE.	21/3/18		11/12/18
2/Lt. B. BISHOP.	22/3/18		18/12/18
2/Lt. R. B. CRABB.	22/3/18		18/12/18
2/Lt. A. F. ORCHARD.	23/3/18		25/12/18
Lieut. M. S. BLOWER.	25/3/18		–/12/18

*Attached T.M.B.

EAST SURREY REGIMENT—continued.
9th Battalion—continued.

Name.	Missing.	Interned.	Repatriated.
2/Lt. W. S. AUSTIN.	25/3/18		25/12/18
Major C. A. CLARK.	26/3/18		25/12/18
Capt. G. W. WARRE-DYMOND.	26/3/18		–/11/18
2/Lt. W. H. BABER.	16/10/18		11/12/18
*2/Lt. A. C. NILSON.	16/10/18		11/12/18

12th Battalion

2/Lt. L. H. JENNINGS.	5/8/17		25/12/18
2/Lt. F. A. SAMUELS.	5/8/17		31/12/18
Lieut. L. DAWSON.	25/3/18		29/11/18
2/Lt. R. C. JOHNS.	25/3/18		13/10/18

13th Battalion.

Lieut. F. W. LANHAM.	26/11/17		2/12/18
Lieut. R. H. HARKER.	26/11/17		3/12/18
†Major W. G. WEST.	9/4/18		31/12/18
Capt. F. S. AINGER.	9/4/18		11/12/18
Capt. C. E. LINGE.	9/4/18		9/12/18
Lieut. H. W. ALLASON.	9/4/18		10/12/18
Lieut. L. W. PINNICK.	9/4/18		29/11/18
Lieut. W. A. MORRIS.	9/4/18		10/12/18
2/Lt. R. R. WEBB.	9/4/18		18/12/18
2/Lt. W. B. PARKER.	9/4/18		–/11/18
2/Lt. J. A. V. CANT.	9/4/18		3/12/18
2/Lt. H. E. BLATCH.	9/4/18		31/12/18

DUKE OF CORNWALL'S LIGHT INFANTRY.
1st and 2nd Battalions

Major Paul PETAVEL.	10/9/14			7/1/18
Lieut. W. M. RICHARDSON.	10/9/14	Holland	5/1/18	4/10/18
Capt. F. H. SPAN.	21/10/14	Holland	24/2/18	18/11/18
Lieut. C. H. RUSSEL.	21/10/14	Holland	6/2/18	29/1/19
Lieut. H. S. LEVERTON.	21/10/14	Holland	6/2/18	18/11/18
Capt. E. E. BARROW.	30/11/14	Holland	24/2/18	18/11/18
2/Lt. F. R. NORTH.	24/7/16	Holland	15/6/18	26/11/18
2/Lt. H. M. SMAIL.	23/4/17			13/1/19
Lieut. J. L. A. CRAVEN.	15/4/18			18/12/18
2/Lt. G. B. ROBSON.	20/8/18			13/12/18
2/Lt. B. D. JOHNSTONE.	21/8/18			13/12/18

5th Battalion

2/Lt. H. A. BLACKLOCK.	12/4/18		13/12/18
2/Lt. P. L. MALTON.	20/8/18	(*Died* –/–/18 at Lille).	

6th Battalion.

Lieut. R. M. PADDISON.	4/4/17		14/12/18
*Lieut. A. DOWNING.	21/3/18		18/12/18

*Attached T.M.B.
†Attached from Sherwood Foresters.

DUKE OF CORNWALL'S LIGHT INFANTRY—continued.

7th Battalion.

Lieut. R. F. WHITELEY.	30/11/17		27/11/18
Lieut. H. RICKARD.	30/11/17	Switzerland —/4/18	6/12/18
2/Lt. WM. KING.	21/3/18	(*Died* 26/6/18).	
*Lt.-Col. H. G. R. BURGES-SHORT.	24/3/18		25/12/18
†Lieut. S. RUNDLE.	18/4/18	(*Died* 30/4/18 at Rouvin).	

WEST RIDING REGIMENT.

1st and 2nd Battalions.

Lieut. O. PRICE.	7/9/14	Holland	29/12/17	7/1/19
Lt.-Col. J. A. GIBBS.	10/9/14	Holland	29/12/17	16/8/18
Capt. E. JENKINS.	10/9/14	Holland	29/12/17	3/1/19
Lieut. M. C. B. K. YOUNG.	10/9/14	Holland	29/12/17	17/2/19
Major E. N. TOWNSEND.	19/9/14	Switzerland	9/12/17	9/12/18
2/Lt. H. G. HENDERSON.	8/11/14			11/9/17
Lieut. R. O'D. CAREY.	10/11/14	Holland	24/2/18	1/1/19
Lieut. J. BENNETT.	16/11/14	Holland	24/2/18	18/11/18
Lieut. E. B. DAVIS.	5/5/15	Holland	23/3/18	18/11/18
Lieut. G. W. OLIPHANT.		Holland	29/12/17	22/1/19
2/Lt. G. H. BEYFUS.	6/5/15			14/12/18
Capt. K. E. CUNNINGHAM.	3/5/17	(*Died*).		
2/Lt. J. F. RHODES.	3/5/17			6/12/18
2/Lt. A. H. LARCOMBE.	3/5/17			16/1/19
2/Lt. W. REES.	3/5/17			31/12/18
2/Lt. S. A. BELSHAW.	3/5/17			4/1/19
2/Lt. J. D. V. MACKINTOSH.	3/5/17			7/1/18
2/Lt. G. D. JOHNSTON.	10/10/17			6/12/18
‡Lieut. S. WALLER.	15/4/18			1/12/18

4th Battalion.

†2/Lt. J. MAUDE.	20/7/18	14/1/19

5th Battalion.

2/Lt. N. E. BENTLEY.	6/2/17		2/1/19
Capt. G. E. GLOVER.	3/5/17		6/1/19
2/Lt. T. W. M. HUTTON.	3/5/17		6/12/18
2/Lt. G. T. DARWENT.	3/5/17		4/1/19
2/Lt. T. C. JACOBS.	3/5/17		17/12/18
§2/Lt. E. G. MACKENZIE.	20/1/18		17/12/18
2/Lt. A. CAWTHRA.	28/3/18		6/12/18
Lieut. E. R. STORRY.	22/7/18		11/1/19
Capt. W. GRANTHAM.	11/10/18	(*Died* 30/11/18 at Gottingen).	

6th Battalion

Capt. W. K. LAW.	3/5/17	7/1/18
2/Lt. G. F. SWABY.	25/4/18	18/12/18

7th Battalion.

Capt. J. L. WATSON.	11/10/18	11/1/18

*Attached from Som. L.I. †Attached from A.S.C.
‡Attached from D.C.L.I. §Attached from West Yorks.

WEST RIDING REGIMENT—Continued.

9th Battalion.

Name.	Missing.	Interned.	Repatriated.
2/Lt. H. S. FORD.	13/8/17		2/1/19

13th Battalion.

2/Lt. H. E. L. PRIDAY.	14/10/18		16/12/18

BORDER REGIMENT.

1st and 2nd Batts.

Capt. H. SLEIGH.		Holland 24/2/18	18/11/18
2/Lt. H. T. THOMPSON.	14/8/17		14/12/18
2/Lt. J. W. ROBSON.	19/11/17		3/12/18
2/Lt. W. COE.	11/4/18		13/12/18
2/Lt. J. W. LITTLE.	29/10/18		—/11/18
2/Lt. A. EMSLIE.	29/10/18		—/12/18

5th Battalion.

Lieut. E. L. FLEMING.			18/12/18
2/Lt. T. H. ARNOTT.			29/11/18
2/Lt. W. D. BROWN.			3/12/18
*2/Lt. A. G. CROLL.	—/3/18		2/1/19
2/Lt. F. ROBERTSON.	—3/18	(*Died* 3/12/18 at Mainz).	
Capt. J. N. FRANKS.	21/3/18		29/11/18
Lieut. A. T. POTTER.	21/3/18		29/11/18
Lieut. J. S. TURNBULL.	21/3/18		28/11/18
2/Lt. C. H. CORBETT.	21/3/18		3/12/18
Capt. O. J. FEETHAM.	22/3/18		3/12/18
Lieut. N. GRAHAM.	24/3/18		18/12/18

7th Battalion.

2/Lt. H. L. MORGAN.	2/11/16		18/12/18
2/Lt. R. G. BIRD.	21/3/18		5/1/19
Lieut. H. S. TUCKETT.	20/10/18		16/12/18

8th Battalion.

†Capt. A. MISCAMPBELL.	27/5/18		26/12/18
Lieut. H. LANSLEY.	27/5/18		2/1/19
2/Lt. J. BROWN.	27/5/18		—/12/18
2/Lt. D. PHILIP.	27/5/18		—/12/18
2/Lt. C. SPENCE.	27/5/18		—/12/18
2/Lt. G. SUTCLIFFE.	27/5/18		—/12/18
2/Lt. W. T. THORNTON.	27/5/18		—/1/19

11th Battalion.

Capt. W. A. WELSH.	18/11/16		—/1/19
2/Lt. H. N. SPENCE.	18/11/16		17/12/18
2/Lt. J. G. NIXON.	18/11/16		
2/Lt. D. W. BRADY.	18/11/16		17/12/18
2/Lt. JOHN CHERRY.	10/7/17		17/12/18
Lieut. G. W. N. ROWSELL.	10/7/17		16/8/18
2/Lt. J. B. A. HOPE.	10/7/17		17/12/18
2/Lt. W. Y. FERNIE.	10/7/17		2/1/19
‡2/Lt. F. J. RIDGWAY.	10/7/17		14/12/18

*Attached from Durham L. I.
†Attached from A.S.C.
‡Attached T.M.B.

ROYAL SUSSEX REGIMENT.
1st and 2nd Battalions.

Name.	Missing.	Interned.	Repatriated.
2/Lt. J. J. RUSSELL.		Switzerland 12/8/16	–/10/17
2/Lt. A. J. HUTCHINS.	21/3/18	(*Died* 22/3/18 at Pithem)	
Lieut. A. H. SMART.	27/3/18		29/11/18

7th Battalion.

2/Lt. C. F. ROLFE.	4/8/16	Switzerland 27/12/17	9/12/18
2/Lt. A. D. BULLOCK.	25/7/17		17/12/18

9th Battalion.

Capt. H. BURY.	26/9/15		11/9/17
Capt. F. T. GODMAN.	26/9/15	(*Died* 12/10/17 at Holzminden)	
2/Lt. T. R. KIRKPATRICK.	26/9/15	Holland 10/4/18	20/11/18
Capt. H. SAXON.	21/3/18		11/12/18
Lieut. W. E. PALING.	21/3/18		10/12/18
2/Lt. C. CLERIHEW.	22/3/18		–/12/18
Capt. N. E. YOUNG.	25/3/18		14/12/18

11th Battalion.

2/Lt. C. H. CONWAY.	31/7/17		3/1/19
2/Lt. J. W. GIBBS.	21/3/18		3/12/18
2/Lt. H. ETHERTON.	22/3/18		31/12/18
Capt. C. LAPWORTH.	24/3/18		25/12/18
2/Lt. A. R. NORRIS.	24/3/18		21/1/19
2/Lt. E. C. PIPER.	26/3/18		3/12/18
*2/Lt. A. W. NEALE.	30/3/18		31/12/18
Lieut. H. V. BADCOCK.	26/4/18		31/12/18
2/Lt. C. A. VORLEY.	3/9/16	(*Died* at Cauldry 13/9/16).	

12th Battalion.

2/Lt. J. R. ARDILL.	30/6/16	Holland 16/5/18	22/11/18
2/Lt. F. W. MOYLE.	30/6/16		–/11/18
2/Lt. S. H. SWALLOW.	30/6/16	Holland 16/5/18	23/10/18

13th Battalion.

Capt. C. G. WALTER.	22/3/18		–/12/18
Lieut. R. L. J. CLEAN.	22/3/18		–/12/18
2/Lt. E. LEVETT.	22/3/18		17/12/18
2/Lt. L. G. WHISTLER.	22/3/18		28/11/18
2/Lt. S. W. COWAN.	22/3/18		14/12/18
2/Lt. R. A. LUSTY.	26/3/18		18/12/18
Lieut. H. C. HARVEY.	26/4/18		29/11/18
2/Lt. L. H. STOTT.	26/4/18		3/12/18
2/Lt. F. J. SOUTHERN.	26/4/18		29/11/18

16th Battalion.

Lieut. H. T. TRIGGS.	21/9/18		–/12/18

HAMPSHIRE REGIMENT.
1st and 2nd Battalions.

Name	Missing	Interned	Repatriated
Major N. W. BARLOW.	2/9/14	Switzerland 9/12/17	8/12/18
Capt. N. BAXTER.	10/9/14	Holland 5/1/18	22/11/18
Lt. Col. S. JACKSON.	13/9/14	Switzerland 19/1/17	14/9/17
Lieut. S. HALLS.	14/9/14	Holland 5/1/18	–/–/18
Lieut. J. LE HUNTE.	16/9/14	Switzerland 9/12/17	9/12/18

*Attached T.M.B.

HAMPSHIRE REGIMENT—continued.

1st and 2nd Battalions—continued.

Name.	Missing.	Interned.	Repatriated.
Lieut. G. T. ROSE.	25/9/14	Holland 22/1/18	18/11/18
Capt. N. C. ROBERTSON.	23/4/17	(*Died* 20/6/17)	
Lieut. P. A. CORNISH.	23/4/17		4/12/18
2/Lt. J. B. SIMONDS.	23/4/17		31/12/18
2/Lt. H. W. RENSHAW.	28/3/18		18/12/18
2/Lt. J. R. POUNCEY.	15/6/18		8/12/18

11th Battalion.

Name.	Missing.	Interned.	Repatriated.
*2/Lt. H. S. ROOTS.	21/3/18		17/12/18
2/Lt. R. F. COURTIER.	22/3/18		2/1/19
Major T. P. THYNE.	29/3/18		–/12/18
Major C. J. HAZARD.	29/3/18		–/1/19
2/Lt. J. SMITH.	29/3/18		18/12/18

14th Battalion.

Name.	Missing.	Interned.	Repatriated.
Lieut. R. SIMPSON.	3/9/16		18/12/18
2/Lt. J. S. HAYDON.	3/9/16		3/1/19
2/Lt. D. McL. TEW.	3/9/16		18/12/18

15th Battalion.

Name.	Missing.	Interned.	Repatriated.
2/Lt. R. E. MARTIN.	5/8/17		4/12/18

SOUTH STAFFORDSHIRE REGIMENT.

1st and 2nd Battalions.

Name.	Missing.	Interned.	Repatriated.
Capt. O. DE TRAFFORD.	20/10/14	Holland 24/2/18	18/11/18
Lieut. C. Boys ADAMS.	20/10/14	Holland 6/2/18	22/11/18
Lieut. R. R. RILEY.	20/10/14	Holland 24/2/18	18/11/18
Lieut. H. WILLOUGHBY.	31/10/14	Holland 6/2/18	18/11/18
Lieut. W. FOSTER.		(*Died* 14/11/14 at Frankfort).	
2/Lt. T. W. DOKE.	11/1/17		14/12/18
2/Lt. E. R. OXLADE.	17/2/17		29/11/18
Lieut. W. A. DICKINS.	28/3/17		14/12/18
Capt. W. A. SIMMONDS.	28/4/17		3/1/19
2/Lt. C. W. BLOOMFIELD.	28/4/17		6/12/18
2/Lt. V. HIELD.	26/10/17	Holland 30/4/18	7/9/18
2/Lt. A. E. CAUNT.	24/3/18		–/12/18
2/Lt. A. T. JACKSON.	24/3/18		18/12/18
2/Lt. S. J. BUCKLEY.	24/3/18	(*Died*)	
2/Lt. F. W. M. LAMBERT.	24/3/18		25/12/18
2/Lt. E. D. ROBERTS.	24/3/18		11/12/18
2/Lt. M. J. QUILL.	24/3/18		11/12/18
Capt. E. O. KAY.	25/3/18		25/12/18
2/Lt. J. W. MILLAR.	25/3/18		25/12/18
Capt. E. H. PAYNE.	24/3/18		10/12/18

4th Battalion.

Name.	Missing.	Interned.	Repatriated.
2/Lt. S. G. WHITAKER.	23/4/17	Switzerland 27/12/17	23/12/18
2/Lt. S. K. MOREY.	9/4/18		30/12/18
2/Lt. A. P. WALKER.	9/4/18		19/12/18
†Lt.-Col. L. H. K. FINCH.	11/4/18		6/12/18
Capt. A. H. NUTT.	26/4/18		14/12/18
Capt. H. R. WEBB.	26/4/18	(*Died* 7/3/18 at Deinye).	
‡2/Lt. L. PARAMORE.	27/5/18		6/1/19
2/Lt. A. St. LEDGER.	27/5/18		5/1/19

*Attached from Royal Dublin Fusiliers.
†Attached from Cheshire Regiment.
‡Attached T.M.B.

SOUTH STAFFORDSHIRE REGIMENT—continued.

5th Battalion.

Name.	Missing.	Interned.	Repatriated.
2/Lt. H. W. GREGORY.	21/3/18		18/12/18
2/Lt. R. BAXTER.	21/3/18		18/12/18
2/Lt. J. W. WRIGHT.	12/10/18		5/1/19

6th Battalion.

Name.	Missing.	Interned.	Repatriated.
2/Lt. A. DOWNES.	26/4/17		3/12/18
Capt. C. E. L. WHITEHOUSE.	21/3/18		13/12/18
Capt. W. A. JORDAN.	21/3/18		9/12/18
Capt. W. S. LYNES.	21/3/18		1/12/18
Capt. W. A. ADAM.	21/3/18		29/11/18
Lieut. L. J. SHELTON.	21/3/18		4/12/18
Lieut. R. G. BOYCOTT.	21/3/18		–/11/18
Lieut. W. T. BUTLER.	21/3/18		30/12/18
2/Lt. T. A. GOUGH.	21/3/18		11/12/18
2/Lt. J. A. GEYTON.	21/3/18		20/12/18
2/Lt. H. P. BUNN.	21/3/18		–/12/18
2/Lt. J. H. HICKMAN.	21/3/18		2/1/19
2/Lt. C. HAWORTH.	21/3/18		29/11/18
2/Lt. H. E. SHIPTON.	21/3/18		11/12/18
2/Lt. F. W. SPIBEY.	21/3/18		11/12/18
2/Lt. G. A. YATES.	21/3/18		19/12/18
2/Lt. J. BONSHOR.	21/3/18	(*Died* 26/7/18 at Stendal).	

DORSETSHIRE REGIMENT.

1st and 2nd Battalions.

Name.	Missing.	Interned.		Repatriated.
Lieut. G. A. BURNAND.	24/8/14	Holland	5/1/18	17/11/18
Lieut. W. LEISHMAN.	10/9/14	Holland	29/12/17	16/11/18
Capt. C. F. M. MARGETTS	14/9/14	Holland	5/1/18	18/11/18
2/Lt. C. WELLS.	14/9/14	Holland	24/2/18	4/10/18
Capt. A. CLUTTERBUCK.	13/10/14	Holland	6/2/18	–/11/18
Capt. A. S. FRASER.	13/10/14	Switzerland	12/8/17	11/9/17
Capt. J. KELSALL.	13/10/14	Holland	6/2/18	18/11/18
Lieut. L. GRANT-DALTON.	13/10/14	Holland	6/2/18	14/1/19
Capt. H. BEVERIDGE.	22/10/14	Holland	24/2/18	–/11/18
Lieut. C. H. WOODHOUSE.	22/10/14	Holland	10/4/18	18/11/18
*2/Lt. W. E. EDWARDS.	2/10/18			28/11/18
2/Lt. H. B. RATHBORNE.	2/10/18			28/12/18

5th Battalion.

Name.	Missing.	Repatriated.
2/Lt. K. S. B. BATEMAN.	11/1/17	–/12/18
2/Lt. R. L. STATHAM.	9/4/18	–/11/18

6th Battalion.

Name.	Missing.	Repatriated.
Lieut. E. L. B. LART.	25/3/18	25/8/18

SOUTH LANCASHIRE REGIMENT.

1st and 2nd Battalions.

Name.	Missing.	Interned.		Repatriated.
Major G. EWART.	10/9/14	Holland	29/12/17	1/2/19
Lieut. F. BERRY.	30/9/14	Holland	29/12/17	returned for duty.
Lieut. H. G. W. IRWIN.	10/9/14			13/9/17
Lieut. J. ICKE.	10/9/14	Holland	22/1/18	1/11/18

*Attached from Gloucesters.

SOUTH LANCASHIRE REGIMENT—continued.

1st and 2nd Battalions—continued.

Name.	Missing.	Interned.		Repatriated.
*Lieut. H. T. D. MEREDITH.	-/-/14	Switzerland	-/8/16	24/3/18
Capt. F. M. COLVILLE.	21/10/14	Holland	6/2/18	23/10/18
Lieut. A. F. THORP.	21/10/14	Holland	6/2/18	18/11/18
2/Lt. W. G. CLARK.	21/10/14	Holland	24/2/18	18/11/18
Capt. K. H. O. R. SADGROVE.	22/3/18			10/12/18
Lieut. A. C. GOSDEN.	22/3/18			22/12/18
2/Lt. L. G. MARTHEWS.	22/3/18	(Died 22/4/18 at Achen).		
†Capt. A. C. DEVLIN.	27/5/18			2/1/19
2/Lt. G. PARKIN.	27/5/18			11/12/18
2/Lt. W. NAPIER.	28/5/18			13/12/18
2/Lt. R. W. SIMPSON.	2/6/18			13/12/19

4th Battalion.

Name.	Missing.	Interned.		Repatriated.
Lieut. E. E. TOWLER.	28/8/18			11/12/18

5th Battalion.

Name.	Missing.	Interned.		Repatriated.
2/Lt. H. GAMBLE.	24/10/15	Holland	9/4/18	23/9/18
2/Lt. S. R. SMITH.	22/4/18			23/12/18
Lt.-Col. C. P. JAMES.	30/11/17			27/11/18
Capt. F. B. F. HARGREAVES.	30/11/17			27/11/18
Capt. H. G. WHITAKER.	30/11/17			17/12/18
Capt. J. SHUFFLEBOTHAM.	30/11/17			3/12/18
Capt. E. R. McLEOD.	30/11/17			17/12/18
Lieut. P. PLOWMAN.	30/11/17			25/12/18
Lieut. V. T. THIERENS.	30/11/17			14/12/18
‡2/Lt. E. KITCHEN.	30/11/17			17/12/18
‡2/Lt. L. B. TAYLOR.	30/11/17			17/12/18
2/Lt. D. DE PENNINGTON.	30/11/17			17/12/18
§2/Lt. F. H. FRANCIS.	30/11/17			14/12/18
2/Lt. W. DICKINSON.	30/11/17			3/12/18
2/Lt. A. E. EMBERSON.	30/11/17			17/12/18
2/Lt. H. C. INGHAM.	30/11/17			17/12/18
2/Lt. F. V. CLIFFE.	30/11/17			25/12/18
2/Lt. J. .G. HALL.	30/12/17			24/12/18
2/Lt. E. G. GIBSON.	27/5/18			25/12/18
2/Lt. A. S. LATTA.	22/10/18			8/12/18
2/Lt. J. C. O. COCKING.	10/4/17	(Died).		24/9/17

11th Battalion.

Name.	Missing.	Interned.		Repatriated.
2/Lt. R. CARR.	23/10/18			30/12/18

WELSH REGIMENT.

1st and 2nd Battalions.

Name.	Missing.	Interned.		Repatriated.
Major L. I. O. ROBINS.	14/9/14			13/9/17
Capt. T. MARSHALL.	21/10/14	Holland	24/2/18	12/10/18
2/Lt. A. LEACH.	21/10/14	Holland	24/2/18	18/11/18
Lieut. E. M. DOUGLAS.	20/2/15	Holland	1/3/18	8/1/19
Major A. G. PROTHERO.	26/9/15	Holland	10/4/18	23/9/18
Lieut. E. W. PIDDUCK.	26/9/15	Holland	10/4/18	18/11/18
2/Lt. A. N. HAZELL.	2/10/15	Switzerland	19/12/16	11/9/17
Capt. C. E. H. JAMES.	21/5/16	Holland	30/4/18	29/1/19
2/Lt. E. C. MCGROARTY.	26/7/16	Switzerland	9/12/17	22/12/18
2/Lt. L. C. GARBETT.	12/5/18			18/12/18

*Attached from Liverpool Regiment. †Attached T.M.B.
‡Attached from Somerset L.I. §Attached from Buffs.

WELSH REGIMENT—Continued.

3rd Battalion.

Name.	Missing.	Interned.	Repatriated.
2/Lt. T. C. S. HUSS.			28/11/18

9th Battalion.

Name.	Missing.	Interned.	Repatriated.
Lieut. E. EMBLEM.	23/3/18		29/11/18
2/Lt. H. W. THOMPSON.	25/3/18		13/12/18
Major E. W. BROAKES.	30/5/18		-/12/18
Capt. T. SUGRUE.	30/5/18		1/1/19
Capt. D. H. THOMAS.	30/5/18		1/1/19
Lieut. F. M. ST. H. EVANS.	30/5/18		14/12/18
2/Lt. J. BODYCOMBE.	30/5/18		16/1/19
2/Lt. J. EVANS.	30/5/18		17/12/18
2/Lt. T. E. NOBLE.	30/5/18		31/12/18
2/Lt. G. WILLIAMS.	30/5/18		30/12/18

14th Battalion.

Name.	Missing.	Interned.	Repatriated.
Capt. J. S. STRANGE.	10/5/18		18/12/18

15th Battalion.

Name.	Missing.	Interned.	Repatriated.
2/Lt. D. I. REES.	10/5/18		23/10/18

17th Battalion.

Name.	Missing.	Interned.	Repatriated.
Lieut. W. J. MOULD.	24/11/17		25/12/18
2/Lt. F. S. J. McK. LEWIS.	25/11/17		27/11/18

18th Battalion.

Name.	Missing.	Interned.	Repatriated.
Capt. T. G. WHITE.	9/4/18		18/12/18
Lieut. E. V. EVANS.	9/4/18		10/12/18
Lieut. J. S. G. HACKNEY.	9/4/18		23/9/18
Lieut. R. O. OWEN.	9/4/18		13/12/18
Lieut. J. I. RICHARDS.	9/4/18		-/12/18
Lieut. O. SALISBURY.	9/4/18		23/9/18
Lieut. G. I. TURNBULL.	9/4/18	(*Died* at Lille).	
2/Lt. D. M. DAVIES.	9/4/18		2/12/18
2/Lt. W. P. GARNER.	9/4/18		
*2/Lt. G. OWENS.	9/4/18		29/11/18
2/Lt. C. S. THOMAS.	9/4/18		25/12/18
2/Lt. J. C. TUCKER.	9/4/18		25/12/18
2/Lt. W. M. WILLIAMS.	9/4/18		1/12/18
2/Lt. J. C. HILL.	9/4/18		2/12/18

24th Battalion.

Name.	Missing.	Interned.	Repatriated.
Lieut. H. C. WATKINS.	21/9/18	(*Died* at Le Cateau 23/10/18).	

BLACK WATCH.

1st and 2nd Battalions.

Name.	Missing.	Interned.		Repatriated.
Capt. A. D. CAMPBELL KROOK.	29/11/14	Holland	24/2/18	4/10/18
2/Lt. L. MACLEOD.	2/11/15	Holland	-/4/18	18/11/18
Capt. R. K. ARBUTHNOT, M.C.	18/4/18			29/11/18
Lieut. G. T. KIRKCALDY.	18/4/18			6/12/18
Lieut. J. C. STEPHEN.	18/4/18			18/12/18
Lieut. D. C. STEWART-SMITH.	18/4/18			13/12/18
2/Lt. R. M. HUME.	18/4/18			-/1/19
2/Lt. P. W. MACKAY.	18/4/18			13/12/18
2/Lt. R. W. RAMSAY.	18/4/18			1/12/18
†2/Lt. M. JAMESON.	18/4/18			18/12/18

*Attached from Royal Welsh Fusiliers. †Attached from A.S.C.

BLACK WATCH—continued.

4th Battalion.

Name.	Missing.	Interned.	Repatriated.
Capt. C. M. COUPER.	26/9/15	(*Died* 28/9/15 at Sainghain).	
Capt. O. MOODIE.	26/9/15	Switzerland 9/12/17	
2/Lt. G. A. ANDERSON.	12/4/18		1/12/18

4/5th Battalion.

Lieut. J. D. STEWART.	22/3/18		1/1/19
2/Lt. D. McNICOL.	22/3/18		25/12/18
Lieut. W. L. GILLIES.	23/3/18		17/12/18
Lieut. J. F. McL. WILKIE.	26/3/18		–/12/18
2/Lt. G. R. FARRAR.	26/4/18		6/12/18
2/Lt. W. K. M GREGOR.	28/7/18		13/12/18
2/Lt. T. C. BELL.	21/8/18		13/12/18

5th Battalion.

Capt. J. M. R. KEILLER.	23/3/18		18/12/18
Lieut. G. W. YOUNG.		(*Died* 8/4/18).	

6th Battalion.

Capt. J. LINDSAY, M.C.	21/3/18		19/12/18
Capt. D. CABLE.	21/3/18		29/12/18
Lieut. J. PATRICK.	21/3/18		18/12/18
2/Lt. A. REID.	21/3/18		18/12/18
2/Lt. N. A. LAUGHLAND.	21/3/18		18/12/18
2/Lt. H. S. GUTHRIE.	21/3/18	(*Died* 31/3/18 at Bouchain).	
2/Lt. C. C. MACINTYRE.	22/3/18		11/12/18
2/Lt. W. ROBSON.	11/4/18		2/12/18

7th Battalion.

Capt. D. S. GREIG.	21/3/18		19/12/18
Capt. A. M. MOODIE.	21/3/18		10/12/18
Lieut. T. W. BERRY.	21/3/18		29/11/18
Lieut. J. R. GORDON.	21/3/18		–/12/18
Lieut. J. MACLENNAN.	21/3/18		3/1/19
2/Lt. A. KERR.	21/3/18		18/12/18
2/Lt. J. HISLOP.	21/3/18		11/12/18
Lieut. A. L. MILLER.	22/3/18		25/12/18
2/Lt. I. K. MACKINTOSH.	22/3/18		10/12/18
2/Lt. A. M. SIMPSON.	22/3/18		18/12/18
2/Lt. J. McCRACKEN.	27/3/18		11/12/18

8th Battalion.

Lieut. T. D. SHAW-MACLAREN.	22/3/18		–/11/18
2/Lt. J. B. POLLOCK.	22/3/18		29/11/18
2/Lt. H. F. C. GOVAN.	23/3/18		11/12/18
2/Lt. G. R. B. HENDERSON.	24/3/18		25/12/18

9th Battalion.

2/Lt. E. P. M. WALCOTT.	28/3/18		–/12/18
2/Lt. W. A. FORREST.	28/3/18		29/11/18
2/Lt. R. B. ANDERSON.	10/4/18		2/12/18

*Attached from American Red Cross.

OXFORDSHIRE AND BUCKINGHAMSHIRE LIGHT INFANTRY.

1st and 2nd Battalions.

Name.	Missing.	Interned.	Repatriated.
Lieut. G. T. BUTTON.	25/9/14	Switzerland 27/12/17	9/12/18
Capt. P. GODSAL.	8/10/14	(Escaped)	–/4/17
Capt. D. T. BARNES.	25/3/18		–/12/18

Bucks Battalion.

Capt. G. G. JACKSON.	21/7/16		1/11/18
*2/Lt. H. F. HORNE.	30/3/18		1/12/18

4th Battalion.

2/Lt. T. W. F. GUILDFORD.	28/2/17		1/1/19
2/Lt. C. B. HUNT.	28/2/17		18/12/18
Capt. G. V. ROWBOTHAM.	21/3/18		2/12/18
Capt. K. E. BROWN.	21/3/18	(Died 12/4/18 at Hautmont).	
Capt. C. E. P. FORESHEW.	21/3/18		14/12/18
†Lieut. R. OSTLER.	21/3/18		2/12/18
2/Lt. C. H. WALLINGTON.	21/3/18		14/12/18
2/Lt. G. SHELLEY.	21/3/18		–/12/18
2/Lt. J. C. CUNNINGHAM.	21/3/18		14/12/18
2/Lt. C. C. HALL.	21/3/18		–/12/18
2/Lt. V. C. GRAY.	21/3/18		–/12/18
2/Lt. R. G. H. GOUGH.	21/3/18		14/12/18
2/Lt. P. J. SIMMS.	21/3/18		14/12/18
2/Lt. C. H. LEACH.	21/3/18		14/12/18
2/Lt. E. LITTLE.	21/3/18		14/12/18
2/Lt. F. A. NAYLOR.	21/3/18		14/12/18
Major H. J. BENNETT.	30/3/18		–/12/18
2/Lt. H. G. LEDGER.	6/4/18		1/12/18
2/Lt. G. A. ROWLERSON.	13/9/18		13/12/18
2/Lt. P. E. CRADDOCK.	29/9/18		29/11/18

5th Battalion.

2/Lt. R. J. RICHARDS.	3/5/17	(Died 12/5/17 at Ferin).	
‡Lieut. W. A. RAMSAY.	21/3/18		11/12/18
2/Lt. F. J. COLLINGE.	21/3/18		8/12/18
Lieut. E. C. COOK.	21–23/3/18		1/12/18
2/Lt. R. G. CRESWELL.	21–23/3/18		10/12/18
Capt D. J. BANKS.	23/3/18		10/12/18
Capt. H. MONEY.	23/3/18		–/12/18
2/Lt. H. M. GRAY.	29/3/18		25/12/18
Major A. M. LABOUCHERE.	4/4/18	(Died 30/4/18 at Valenciennes).	
Lieut. L. V. D. OWEN.	4/4/18		3/12/18

6th Battalion.

§2/Lt. A K. STANDAGE.	10/4/18		1/12/18

ESSEX REGIMENT.

1st and 2nd Battalions.

Name.	Missing.	Interned.	Repatriated.
Lieut. G. DALE.	–/–/14	Holland 24/2/18	Returned for Duty.
2/Lt. J. P. PEARCE.	21/10/14	Holland 6/2/18	1/11/18
2/Lt. A. L. PIPER.	14/4/17	Holland –/4/18	19/7/18
2/Lt. G. D. TURK.	14/4/17	(Died 23/6/17).	

*Attached Entrenching Batt.   †Attached from A.S.C.
‡Attached T.M.B.   §Attached Portuguese Corps.

ESSEX REGIMENT—continued.

1st and 2nd Battalions—continued.

Name.	Missing.	Interned.	Repatriated.
Capt. O. W. HORNE.	3/5/17		6/12/18
Lieut. C. J. T. F. HOPEGOOD.	20/11/17		29/11/18
2/Lt. F. HAVILL.	21/3/18		18/12/18
Capt. B. C. N. WILLMOTT.	28/3/18		10/12/18
Lieut. H. L. HUGHES.	28/3/18		18/12/18
2/Lt. L. H. PULFER.	28/3/18		11/12/18
2/Lt. E. A. PATTERSON.	28/3/18		13/12/18
2/Lt. M. S. CLAYDON.	28/3/18		11/12/18
2/Lt. G. B. ARNOLD.	28/3/18		11/12/18
2/Lt. F C. YOUNG.	28/3/18		25/12/18
*2/Lt. W. HOPWOOD.	28/3/18		8/12/18
2/Lt. S. STORER.	19/4/18		1/12/18
†2/Lt. W. R. FITCH.	27/5/18		26/12/18

9th Battalion.

2/Lt. V. C. H. YOUNG.	17/3/17		14/12/18
2/Lt. S. A. CLARK.	11/7/17		13/5/18
†Capt. C. COLLINS.	30/11/17		27/11/18
Capt. E. R. CAPPER.	30/11/17	(*Died* 8/12/17 at Coblenz).	
Lieut. H. S. COPE.	27/3/18		26/12/18
Lieut. H. E. D. ELLIOTT.	27/3/18		25/12/18
‡2/Lt. T. W. BETTS.	18/9/18		14/12/18
2/Lt. S. G. LOWSON.	18/9/18		29/11/18

10th Battalion.

§2/Lt. G. M. TURNER.	30/11/17		14/12/18
2/Lt. J. G. CULVER.	21/3/18		19/1/19
Lieut. J. P. AMPS.	23/3/18		27/11/18
‖Lieut. A. H. GALLIE.	23/3/18		1/12/18
Lieut. P. C. CLEALL.	8/8/18	(*Died* 26/8/18 at Longavesnes).	
2/Lt. A. WOODS.	8/8/18		8/12/18

11th Battalion.

Major J. L. DAVIES.	26/9/15	(*Died*).	
Lieut. B. L. MIDDLETON.	26/9/15	Holland —/4/18	24/1/19
Lieut. P. E. DALE.	26/9/15		12/5/18
Capt. J. S. MARKS.	21/3/18		—/12/18
Capt. W. F. MARTINSON.	21/3/18		19/1/19
Capt. G. SIMPSON.	22/3/18		29/11/18
2/Lt. R. V. BULLEN.	22/3/18		3/12/18
2/Lt. H. J. WIDGERY.	12/10/18		13/12/18

13th Battalion.

2/Lt. C. C. N. MARSHALL.	14/11/16		7/1/18
2/Lt. H. P. TURNER.	28/4/17		6/12/18
2/Lt. A. C. LEECH.	28/4/17		7/1/19
2/Lt. W. FREEMAN.	28/4/17		17/12/17
Capt. H. T. JESSOP.	29/11/17		18/12/18
Lieut. J. D. ROBINSON.	29/11/17		25/12/18
2/Lt. E. L. CORPS.	29/11/17		31/12/18
†2/Lt. R. J. TREBILCO.	30/11/17		6/1/19
2/Lt. C. W. PHILLIPS.	2/12/17		25/12/18
2/Lt. V. E. BLOOMFIELD.	21/3/18		27/11/18

*Attached from Liverpools. †Attached T.M.B.
‡ Attached from Hunts Cyclists. §Attached from Glasgow Yeomanry.
‖Attached 35 /T.M.B.

SHERWOOD FORESTERS.
1st and 2nd Battalions.

Name.	Missing.	Interned.		Repatriated.
Capt. W. DRURY-LOWE.	20/10/14	Holland	6/2/18	18/11/18
Capt. W. H. WILKIN.	20/10/14	Holland	6/2/18	18/11/18
Lieut. T. E. DAVEY.	20/10/14	Holland	6/2/18	18/11/18
Lieut. G. EDWARDS	20/10/14	Holland	6/2/18	17/11/18
Lieut. T. HUDSON.	20/10/14	Switzerland	9/12/17	9/12/18
Lieut. R. G. S. MAY.	20/10/14	Holland	6/2/18	19/1/19
Lieut. C. SCHNEIDER	20/10/14	Holland	6/2/18	18/11/18
Lieut. A. TROOPS	20/10/14	Holland	6/2/18	Returned for Duty

1st Battalion.

Name.	Missing.	Repatriated.
Lieut. R. W. ROUNDS.	25/3/18	25/12/18
2/Lt. J. T. SIDDONS.	25/3/18	-/1/19
2/Lt. W. GREENSMITH.	26/3/18	-/12/18
*Capt. E. B. GREENSMITH.	27/5/18	25/12/18
Capt. C. HARRISON.	27/5/18	-/12/18
Capt. J. F. MENZIES.	27/5/18	30/12/18
*Lieut. J. E. M. WALKER.	27/5/18	30/12/18
2/Lt. W. E. BROWN.	27/5/18	-/12/18
2/Lt. T. E. INMAN.	27/5/18	-/12/18
2/Lt. A. NEILD.	27/5/18	13/12/18
2/Lt. FitzD. SEVERN.	27/5/18	30/12/18
2/Lt. D. M. START.	29/5/18	13/12/18
2/Lt. G. W. WEBB.	29/5/18	13/12/18

2nd Battalion.

Name.	Missing.	Interned.	Repatriated.
Capt. N. H. BEEDHAM.	21/3/18		13/12/18
Capt. L. H. FINCH.	21/3/18		14/1/19
Capt. T. THORNTON.	21/3/18		18/12/18
2/Lt. E. BOOTHROYD	21/3/18	(*Died* 20/4/18 at Aachen).	
2/Lt. G. S. W. PROFIT	21/3/18		17/12/18
2/Lt. H. STIRLAND.	21/3/18		-/12/18
2/Lt. H. G. TAYLOR.	21/3/18		29/11/18

5th Battalion.

Name.	Missing.	Interned.		Repatriated.
Lieut. M. S. FRYAR.	1/7/16			22/11/18
Capt. F. H. M. LEWES.	2/7/16	(*Died*).		
2/Lt. T. F. C. DOWNMAN.	2/7/16			15/12/18
2/Lt. H. H. LILLY.	2/7/16	Holland	15/5/18	
2/Lt. W. T. GREENFIELD.	30/6/17			6/12/18

2/5th Battalion.

Name.	Missing.	Interned.	Repatriated.
Lt.-Col. H. R. GADD.	21/3/18		8/12/18
Capt. F. E. ANDREWS.	21/3/18		
Capt. R. J. CASE.	21/3/18		1/12/18
Capt. H. WATERHOUSE.	21/3/18		25/12/18
Lieut. R. E. A. GRONER.	21/3/18		20/12/18
Lieut. T. L. HILL.	21/3/18		2/1/19
Lieut. F. H. SUTHERLAND.	21/3/18		30/12/18
2/Lt. H. E. BARKER.	21/3/18		18/12/18
2/Lt. A. H. CHAMBERS.	21/3/18		13/12/18
2/Lt. L. De MAUNY.	21/3/18		11/12/18
2/Lt. S. E. GRAYSTON.	21/3/18		29/11/18
2/Lt. W. HAGUE.	21/3/18	(*Died* 31/3/18 at Mons).	
*2/Lt. A. C. HARRIS.	21/3/18		15/2/19

*Attached T.M.B.

SHERWOOD FORESTERS—continued.
2/5th Battalion—continued.

Name.	Missing.	Interned.	Repatriated.
2/Lt. J. W. JAGO.	21/3/18		21/12/18
2/Lt. P. A. MURPHY.	21/3/18		29/11/18
2/Lt. H. C. PICKTHALL.	21/3/18		29/11/18
2/Lt. A. E. SILVERWOOD.	21/3/18		13/12/18
2/Lt. A. J. SMITH.	21/3/18		29/11/18
2/Lt. R. STONE.	21/3/18		14/12/18
2/Lt. C. M. WRIGHT.	21/3/18		18/12/18
2/Lt. G. A. MIDDLEMISS.	23/3/18		1/12/18

6th Battalion.

Name.	Missing.	Interned.	Repatriated.
2/Lt. T. O. COLLES.	7/4/17		9/12/18
2/Lt. S. M. JOHNSON.	21/3/18		–/14/18
2/Lt. H. NUTTALL.	22/3/18		29/11/18

2/6th Battalion.

Name.	Missing.	Interned.	Repatriated.
*Col. H. S. HODGKIN.	21/3/18		1/12/18
Major A. C. CLARKE.	21/3/18		29/12/18
†Capt. H. P. GREAVES.	21/3/12		18/12/18
Capt. S. A. ROGERS.	21/3/18	(Died).	
Lieut. A. G. F. ELLWOOD.	21/3/18		29/11/18
‡Lieut. F. P. FOSTER.	21/3/18		5/12/18
2/Lt. L. W. ALLEN.	21/3/18		17/12/18
2/Lt. H. C. BARHAM.	21/3/18		1/12/18
2/Lt. R. B. BRACE.	21/3/18		13/12/18
2/Lt. W. A. COTTON.	21/3/18		11/12/18
2/Lt. C. G. HASLAM.	21/3/18		18/12/18
2/Lt. H. HICKMAN.	21/3/18		11/12/18
§2/Lt. P. E. JACKSON.	21/3/18		29/12/18
2/Lt. G. V. MIDDLETON.	21/3/18		31/12/18
2/Lt. S. C. RAYMENT.	21/3/18		29/12/18
2/Lt. C. STARK.	21/3/18		1/12/18
2/Lt. W. H. V. WOODROW.	21/3/18		11/12/18

7th Battalion.

Name.	Missing.	Interned.	Repatriated.
Lieut. J. M. McBAIN.	1/7/16	(Died 9/7/16).	
Capt. C. GASCOYNE.	2/4/17	(Died 8/5/17).	
‖Lt.-Col. W. S. N. TOLLER.	21/3/18		8/12/18
Capt. A. S. BRIGHT.	21/3/18		23/9/18
Capt. F. PRAGNELL.	21/3/18		29/11/18
Capt. W. PRITCHETT.	21/3/18		17/12/18
Lieut. F. H. CLARK.	21/3/18		29/11/18
Lieut. R. B. EMMETT.	21/3/18		18/12/18
Lieut. J. E. HARTSHORN.	21/3/18		26/12/18
Lieut. C. F. PARRY.	21/3/18		31/12/18
‖Lieut. E. WRIGHTON.	21/3/18		10/12/18
2/Lt. T. ALLEN.	21/3/18		25/12/18
2/Lt. G. A. BREACH.	21/3/18		29/11/18
2/Lt. F. G. ELLIS.	21/3/18		3/12/18
2/Lt. G. L. THORPE.	21/3/18		25/12/18
2/Lt. A. P. WARD.	21/3/18		29/11/18
2/Lt. J. F. BISHOP.	1/4/16		18/11/18

*Attached from Dragoon Guards.
†Attached T.M.B.
‖ Attached from Leicester Regiment.
‡Attached from Derby Yeomanry.
§Attached from S. Notts. Hussars.

SHERWOOD FORESTERS—continued.

8th Battalion.

Name.	Missing.	Interned.		Repatriated.
2/Lt. R. T. SKINNER.	23/4/17			1/1/19

9th Battalion.

2/Lt. F. J. ARCHER.	19/12/17			3/12/18

10th Battalion.

Capt. E. T. R. CARLYON.	16/2/16	Switzerland	19/12/16	6/12/18
Lieut. P. KNOX-SHAW.	16/2/16	Holland	19/4/18	18/11/18
Lieut. E. A. TOLLEMACHE.	16/2/16	Holland	10/4/18	18/11/18
2/Lt. R. MILWARD.	16/2/16	Holland	19/4/18	23/10/18
Lt.-Col. L. GILBERT.	23/4/17			18/12/18
Lieut. R. A. PAGE.	23/3/18			18/12/18
Lieut. T. C. NUGENT.	21/4/18			3/1/19

12th Battalion.

2/Lt. E. N. TAYLOR.	21/3/18			11/12/18
Capt. W. J. ASHER.	28/3/18			-/12/18

15th Battalion.

Capt. R. W. AINSWORTH.	31/5/16	Holland	19/4/18	29/12/18
2/Lt. E. WARBURTON.	25/10/16	Switzerland	9/12/17	24/3/18
2/Lt. J. S. BECKETT.	24/3/18	Switzerland	25/9/18	7/12/18
2/Lt. F. HEMSTOCK.	24/3/18			17/12/18
2/Lt. J. KEELING.	24/3/18			1/12/18
2/Lt. C. J. McDONNELL.	24/3/18			1/12/18
2/Lt. M. H. STEPHENSON.	24/3/18			-/12/18
2/Lt. H. J. WICKENDEN.	25/3/18			25/12/18
Lieut. T. WILLIAMSON.	20/10/18			13/12/18
2/Lt. J. F. POWELL.	20/10/18			12/12/18

16th Battalion.

2/Lt. F. NURSE.	30/3/18			18/12/18
2/Lt. H. B. BUSWELL.	21/3/18			2/12/18

LOYAL NORTH LANCASHIRE REGIMENT.

1st and 2nd Battalions.

Name.	Missing.	Interned.		Repatriated.
2/Lt. C .E. WALLIS.	14/9/14			13/9/17
Capt. A. COLLEY.	2/11/14			13/9/17
Lieut. D. GARDEN.	2/11/14	Holland	24/2/18	18/11/18
Lieut. J. GRIFFITH.	2/11/14	Holland	24/2/18	11/1/19
Capt. G. T. BODY.	22/12/14	(Died).		
Lieut. S. H. BATTY-SMITH.	22/12/14	Holland	23/8/18	22/11/18
2/Lt. L. G. GILLILAND.	22/12/14	Escaped.		-/4/17
Lieut. F. R. C. BARRETT.	10/7/17			6/12/18
2/Lt. S. E. MATTHEWS.	10/7/17	Holland	15/4/18	19/7/18
Lieut. E. GLADDING.	18/4/18			-/11/18
2/Lt. C. G. CLARIDGE.	18/4/18			25/12/18
2/Lt. H. E. SMITH.	18/4/18			6/1/19
*2/Lt. E. H. NORMAN.	18/4/18			18/12/18
*Capt. A. HARRISON.	27/5/18			5/1/19
2/Lt. H. J. McCOVEY.	2/10/18			-/11/18

*Attached T.M.B.

LOYAL NORTH LANCASHIRE REGIMENT—continued.

4th Battalion.

Name.	Missing.	Interned.		Repatriated.
2/Lt. J. F. HOLDEN.	8/8/16	Holland	12/10/18	22/11/18
2/Lt. O. H. DUCKSBURY.	8/8/16	Holland	12/10/18	22/11/18
2/Lt. C. RIGBY.	31/7/17			2/1/19
2/Lt. D. H. McSWEENY.	31/7/17			17/12/18
2/Lt. H. S. HOLDEN,	31/7/17			3/12/18
2/Lt. G. H. VARAH.	10/4/18			2/12/18
*2/Lt. E. IVES.	2/10/18			13/12/18
2/Lt. W. G. E. TAYLOR.	13/10/18			13/12/18
2/Lt. G. A. BLOUNT.	22/10/18			–/12/18
2/Lt. JAMES CHAMBERS.	22/10/18			8/12/18

5th Battalion.

Name	Missing	Interned		Repatriated
Capt. R. K. G. MARSEILLE	6/7/17	Switzerland	27/12/17	24/3/18
Capt. T. A. BARTER.	30/11/17			17/12/18
2/Lt. C. A. BRYAN.	30/11/17			27/11/18
2/Lt. C. B. WRAY.	30/11/17			2/12/18
2/Lt. W. WADWORTH.	30/11/17			14/12/18
†2/Lt. C. A. ROBERTSON.	30/11/17			17/12/18
2/Lt. W. MARSDEN.	30/11/17			14/12/18
2/Lt. H. N. HOBSON.	30/11/17			14/12/18
2/Lt. E. N. O. WEIGHILL.	30/11/17			19/5/18
‡2/Lt. W. H. INCE.	22/3/18			14/12/18
‡2/Lt. N. ENTWISLE.	11/4/18			1/12/18
2/Lt. H. WHITEHEAD.	18/4/18			18/12/18
2/Lt. A. W. KITCH.	13/9/18			8/12/18
Lieut. J. FORSHAW.	1/10/18			–/1/19

8th Battalion.

Name	Missing		Repatriated
*Lieut. G. W. TOLLETT.	12/4/18		2/12/18

9th Battalion.

Name	Missing		Repatriated
2/Lt. R. WILSON.	21/3/18		2/12/18
2/Lt. F. N. SCOTT.	22/3/18		11/12/18
2/Lt. G. HOLT.	23/3/18		11/12/18
2/Lt. H. S. A. BRIEN.	23/3/18		4/12/18
Capt. R. J. P. HEWETSON.	27/5/18	(Died –/7/18 at Beaurieux).	
Capt. P. R. SHIELDS.	27/5/18		6/12/18

10th Battalion.

Name	Missing		Repatriated
Capt. P. BEE.	22/3/18		2/12/18
Lieut. B. W. PEACHEY.	22/3/18		14/12/18
2/Lt. A. W. BELLIS.	22/3/18		2/12/18
2/Lt. J. F. MILLS.	22/3/18		18/12/18
2/Lt. F. B. HEWITT.	22/3/18		6/12/18
2/Lt. J. A. JACKSON.	22/3/18		25/12/18
2/Lt. C. H. LAW.	22/3/18		14/12/18
2/Lt. E. WRIGLEY.	22/3/18		25/12/18
†Lieut. F. HAYES.			14/12/18

*Attached from Yorkshire Regiment.   †Attached from Manchester Regiment.
‡Attached Entrenching Battalion.

NORTHAMPTONSHIRE REGIMENT.

1st and 2nd Battalions.

Name.	Missing.	Interned.		Repatriated.
2/Lt. H. F. W. BARNETT.	20/7/16	Holland	15/6/18	21/9/19
2/Lt. T. E. BOURDILLON.	22/7/16	Holland	15/6/18	19/11/18
2/Lt. B. J. F. WYLDE.	26/4/17			30/12/18
Lt.-Col. Hon. D. P. TOLLEMACHE.	10/7/17			4/12/18
Capt. C. CHISHOLM.	10/7/17			6/12/18
Capt. E. R. C. AYLETT.	10/7/17			6/12/18
Lieut. G. R. C. D. LINDLEY.	10/7/17			6/12/18
Lieut. J. H. A. WOOD.	10/7/17			6/12/18
Lieut. T. C. BLANDFORD.	10/7/17			17/12/18
2/Lt. E. C. AIRTH.	10/7/17			6/12/18
2/Lt. N. H. V. COGILL.	10/7/17			17/12/18
2/Lt. A. R. McANALLY.	10/7/17			6/12/18
2/Lt. E. H. JONES.	10/7/17			17/12/18
2/Lt. R. P. NEEDHAM.	10/7/17			17/12/18
2/Lt. J. L. JENNINGS.	10/7/17			17/12/18
2/Lt. J. BOSTON.	10/7/17			17/12/18
2/Lt. R. L. COWLEY.	10/7/17			17/12/18
2/Lt. R. C. SAXTON.	10/7/17			14/12/18
2/Lt. C. E. BORROW.	10/7/17			2/1/19
Lieut. R. MACPHERSON.	24/3/18			18/12/18
Lieut. J. E. JARVIS.	26/3/18			1/12/18
Lieut. W. GILLITT.	26/3/18			1/12/18
*Lieut. L. L. L. LEMAN.	26/3/18			17/12/18
†2/Lt. B. E. DAVEY.	26/3/18			18/12/18
2/Lt. J. CALDWELL.	20/4/18			1/12/18
‡Capt. J. HANDLEY.	27/5/18			14/1/19
Capt. A. M. WILLIAMS.	27/5/18			16/1/19
Lieut. G. M. EDMONDS.	27/5/18			14/12/18
Lieut. W. H. DENTON.	27/5/18			26/12/18
Lieut. J. S. DENTON.	27/5/18			26/12/18
*Lieut. C. H. TOLLEMACHE.	27/5/18			13/12/18
Lieut. W. H. SHAW.	27/5/18			30/12/18
2/Lt. H. JONES.	27/5/18			31/12/18
2/Lt. L. A. JOSLAND.	27/5/18			-/12/18
2/Lt. J. T. HIGSON.	27/5/18	(Died 8/8/18).		
2/Lt. J. L. HUTTON.	27/5/18			31/12/18
§2/Lt. H. GRIFFIN.	27/5/18			-/12/18
§2/Lt. E. G. PARTRIDGE.	27/5/18			31/12/18
2/Lt. W. H. KENNEDY.	27/5/18			26/12/18
2/Lt. S. E. FARBON.	27/5/18			31/12/18
2/Lt. M. V. EYDEN.	27/5/18			-/12/18

5th Battalion.

2/Lt. H. J. WATT.	30/11/17		27/11/18

6th Battalion.

2/Lt. A. B. SWAIN.	17/2/17	Switzerland 27/12/17	24/3/18
Capt. H. C. GRACE.	10/8/17	(Died 2/9/17 at Courtrai).	
Lieut. D. I. GOTCH.	23/3/18		18/12/18
2/Lt. A. C. HERRING.	23/3/18		18/12/18
2/Lt. I. McNALLY.	23/3/18		18/12/18

*Attached from A.S.C.
†Attached from Middlesex Regiment. ‡Attached from Essex Regiment.
§Attached from South Staffs Regiment.

NORTHAMPTONSHIRE REGIMENT—continued.

6th Battalion.

Name.	Missing.	Interned.	Repatriated.
*2/Lt. G. W. GREEN.	23/3/18		18/12/18
*2/Lt. E. P. PARRISH.	23/3/18		11/12/18
*2/Lt. C. W. CASWELL.	5/4/18		11/12/18
2/Lt. M. WEBBER.	31/8/18		28/11/18
†Lieut. H. G. TEBB.	21/9/18		11/12/18

7th Battalion.

2/Lt. L. J. P. LAYCOCK.	13/7/17	(*Died*).	
2/Lt. F. COMPTON.	25/3/18		18/12/18

ROYAL BERKSHIRE REGIMENT.

1st and 2nd Battalions.

Name.	Missing.	Interned.	Repatriated.
Major A. S. TURNER.	10/9/14	Holland 5/1/18	16/11/18
Capt. D. A. MacGREGOR.	9/5/15	(*Died* 15/8/15 at Hanover).	
2/Lt. A. E. HENLEY.	3/5/17	Holland 30/4/18	19/7/18
2/Lt. G. R. THRELFELL.	16/8/17		14/12/18
2/Lt. S. M. LOUDAN.	16/8/17		6/12/18
2/Lt. A. E. BERRY.	16/8/17		7/1/18
2/Lt. E. L. THOMPSON.	16/8/17		14/12/18
2/Lt. A. C. URRY.	24/3/18		25/12/18
2/Lt. H. T. L. WOOSTER.	24/3/18		28/12/18
Capt. H. A. CURTIS.	25/3/18		12/10/18
2/Lt. A. E. FARMER.	25/3/18		1/12/18
‡Lt.-Col. J. A. A. GRIFFIN.	27/5/18		25/12/18
§Capt. C. W. FOWLER.	27/5/18		1/11/19
Capt. A. D. CLARE.	27/5/18		25/12/18
Capt. R. WHITTAKER.	27/5/18		3/1/19
Lieut. R. B. GILLIAT.	27/5/18	(*Died* 28/5/18 at Sevigny).	
‖Lieut. Oscar WILD.	27/5/18		25/12/18
‖Lieut. R. de C. McDONNELL.	27/5/18		31/12/18
‖Lieut. E. S. HAIGHTON.	27/5/18		25/12/18
2/Lt. W. VAUGHAN.	27/5/18		-/12/18
**2/Lt. G. S. HALLEY.	27/5/18		-/12/18
** 2/Lt. R. B. HADDOW.	27/5/18		31/12/18
**2/Lt. H. E. FLIGHT.	27/5/18		21/12/18
††2/Lt. C. D. WILLIAMS.	27/5/18		-/12/18
‡‡2/Lt. J. M. BENNETT.	27/5/18		-/12/18
2/Lt. W. A. UPTON.	27/5/18		25/12/18
2/Lt. C. A. N. BOSTON.	21/9/18		28/11/18
2/Lt. S. H. OSWELL.	21/9/18		6/12/18
Lieut. A. J. EASTMAN.	14/10/18		11/12/18

2/4th Battalion.

2/Lt. J. LAWRENCE.	21/3/18		11/1/19
2/Lt. J. TULLETT.	21/3/18		-/12/18
§§2/Lt. G. W. DE ST. LEGIER.	21/3/18		14/12/18
‖Capt. G. HINCHLIFFE.	28/3/18		28/12/18
Lieut. H. W. FRY.	11/5/18		-/12/18

*Attached from Middlesex Regiment.   †Attached from Herts Regiment.
‡Attached from Lincolns.   §Attached from R.A.M.C.
‖Attached from Manchesters.
**Attached from Hants.   ††Attached from Worcs.   ‡‡Attached from Sussex.
§§Attached from Devons.

ROYAL BERKSHIRE REGIMENT—continued.

5th Battalion.

Name.	Missing.	Interned.		Repatriated.
2/Lt. R. HAYWOOD.	3/7/16	Holland	16/5/18	22/11/18
2/Lt. C. P. HOLLOWAY.	3/7/16	Holland	16/5/18	22/11/18
2*Lt. F. C. R. HILL.	30/11/17			2/1/19
2/Lt. H. SCHOFIELD.	30/11/17			2/1/19
2/Lt. E. JONES.	30/11/17			25/12/18
*2/Lt. W. BARKER.	5/4/18			18/12/18
2/Lt. B. MILES.	5/4/18			11/12/18
2/Lt. P. L. HOWARD.	24/6/18			-/12/18

7th Battalion.

2/Lt. W. L. HAILE.	22/3/18			17/12/18

8th Battalion.

Capt. C. GENTRY-BIRCH.	21/3/18			28/11/18
Capt. D. J. FOOTMAN.	21/3/18			28/11/18
Capt. H. R. FENNER.	21/3/18			18/12/18
Lieut. E. J. MECEY.	21/3/18			18/12/18
Lieut. C. F. R. BLAND.	21/3/18			28/11/18
Lieut. G. R. GOODSHIP.	21/3/18			28/11//8
Lieut. N. LANGSTON.	21/3/18			28/11/18
*2/Lt. T. H. ROBERTS.	21/3/18			28/11/18
2/Lt. E. F. JOHNSON.	21/3/18			28/11/18
2/Lt. G. CAPES.	21/3/18			16/12/18
2/Lt. W. V. HEALE.	21/3/18			1/12/18
2/Lt. W. C. A. HANNEY.	21/3/18			18/12/18
2/Lt. J. R. McMULLEN.	21/3/18			28/11/18
*2/Lt. A. G. WILLIAMS.	26/3/18			17/12/18

9th Battalion.

2/Lt. J. A. V. WOOD.	14/11/16			-/12/18

ROYAL WEST KENT REGIMENT.

1st and 2nd Battalions.

Capt. G. D. LISTER.	23/8/14	Switzerland	9/12/17	14/6/18
Lieut. A. A. CHITTY.	-/-/14	Switzerland	12/9/16	11/9/17
2/Lt. H. E. FRY.	26/10/17			13/5/18
Capt. A. M. CAMPBELL.	-/-/16			-/-/18

6th Battalion.

Capt. G. A. L. HATTON.	3/7/16	Holland	16/5/18	18/11/18
Lieut. H. B. ANTILL.	3/5/17			6/12/18
2/Lt. L. PYRKE.	3/5/17	Switzerland	27/12/17	9/12/18
2/Lt. E. N. ALLEN.	3/5/17			6/12/18
2/Lt. L. W. BROWNING.	3/5/17			6/12/18
2/Lt. H. HIBBETT.	3/5/17			6/12/18
2/Lt. E. J. W. ELY.	3/5/17			17/12/18
Capt. W. B. HODSON-SMITH.	30/11/17	Holland	30/4/18	18/8/18
Lieut. S. G. WRIGHT.	30/11/17			5/12/18
Lieut. S. E. ROBERTS.	30/11/17			3/12/18
2/Lt. V. S. LEATHER.	30/11/17			5/12/18
2/Lt. M. W. J. SWALLOW.	30/11/17			2/12/18
2/Lt. W. S. NEWSHOLME.	30/11/17			11/12/18
2/Lt. J. W. LOWE.	30/11/17			27/11/18
2/Lt. J. E. ABEL.	30/11/17	(*Died* 22/12/17 at Sevigny).		

*Attached from Worcs.

ROYAL WEST KENT REGIMENT—continued.

7th Battalion.

Name.	Missing.	Interned.	Repatriated.
Lieut. C. S. STEVENSON.	19/11/16		26/12/18
2/Lt. K. G. FRYER.	19/11/16		17/12/18
*Lt.-Col. J. D. CROSTHWAITE.	21/3/18		3/1/19
Capt. E. WATTS.	21/3/18		29/11/18
Capt. A. GODLY.	21/3/18		2/12/18
Lieut. P. B. WHITROW.	21/3/18		5/12/18
Lieut. A. A. EASON.	21/3/18		3/12/18
2/Lt. W. F. DRAIN.	21/3/18		8/12/18
2/Lt. S. H. WEBB.	21/3/18	(*Died* 26/3/18 at Ribemont).	
2/Lt. E. V. SAWYER.	21/3/18		18/12/18
2/Lt. B. VAUGHAN.	21/3/18		13/12/18
2/Lt. G. M. HEAPHY.	21/3/18		25/12/18
2/Lt. H. LYNCH-WATSON	21/3/18		11/12/18
†2/Lt. J. A. HORTON.	21/3/18		–/12/18
2/Lt. G. T. M. LEWIS.	21/3/18		27/11/18
2/Lt. H. P. RIMINGTON.	21/3/18		29/11/18
2/Lt. W. U. C. TAYLOR.	21/3/18		5/12/18
‡2/Lt. J. H. BENTLEY.	4/4/18		18/12/18

8th Battalion.

Name.	Missing.	Interned.	Repatriated.
Col. E. VANSITTART.	26/9/15		13/9/17
Major J. C. CHILLINGWORTH.	26/9/15	Switzerland 27/12/17	17/12/18
Capt. C. de C. MIDDLETON.	26/9/15	Switzerland 27/12/17	12/6/18
Capt. C. A. HUTCHINSON.	26/9/15		13/9/17
Lieut. R. M. OLD.	26/9/15	Holland 10/4/18	22/11/18
2/Lt. N. S. ELL.	26/9/15	(Exchanged)	7/12/15
2/Lt. J. S. CRIGHTON.	3/2/18		25/1/19
Capt. C. R. H. ALLWORTH.	21/3/18		10/12/18
2/Lt. H. W. BEATTIE.	21/3/18		28/11/18
2/Lt. J. BOWSKILL.	21/3/18		–/11/18
2/Lt. C. D. WHITBOURN.	21/3/18		29/11/18
2/Lt. E. LEVEY.	21/3/18		29/11/18
2/Lt. D. C. M. OLIVER.	21/3/18		25/12/18

9th Battalion.

Name.	Missing.	Interned.	Repatriated.
2/Lt. A. L. HART.	30/11/17		25/12/18

10th Battalion.

Name.	Missing.	Interned.	Repatriated.
Capt. F. W. ROBERTS.	21/9/17	(*Died*).	
2/Lt. F. C. RENNELLS.	22/3/18		11/12/18
Lt.-Col. A. C. CORFE.	23/3/18		18/12/18
Major A. J. JIMENEZ.	23/3/18		18/12/18
Capt. C. F. HALL.	23/3/18		29/11/18
Capt. F. W. WAYDELIN.	23/3/18		18/12/18
§Lieut. L. E. HALE.	23/3/18		29/11/18
Lieut. L. A. PANCHAUD.	23/3/18		10/12/18
2/Lt. F. C. VASS.	23/3/18		1/12/18
2/Lt. J. R. PHILLIPS.	23/3/18		25/12/18
2/Lt. B. E. LONG.	23/3/18		25/12/18
2/Lt. R. H. CHANDLER.	23/3/18		1/12/18

*Attached from 1st Londons. †Attached T.M.B. ‡Attached from Gloucester Regiment.
§Attached from Scottish Rifles.

KING'S OWN YORKSHIRE LIGHT INFANTRY.

1st and 2nd Battalions.

Name.	Missing.	Interned.		Repatriated.
Lt.-Col. R. C. BOND.	10/9/14	Holland	5/1/18	27/11/18
Capt. W. E. GATACRE.	10/9/14	Holland	5/1/18	18/11/18
Capt. A. R. KEPPEL.	10/9/14	Holland	5/1/18	returned for duty.
Capt. A. C. G. LUTHER.	10/9/14	Holland	6/2/18	18/11/18
Capt. L. SIMPSON.	10/9/14	Holland	5/1/18	18/11/18
Lieut. T. BUTT.	10/9/14			11/9/17
Lieut. H. D. HIBBERT.	10/9/14	Holland	22/1/18	18/11/18
Lieut. C. H. RAWDON.	10/9/14	Holland	5/1/18	18/11/18
Lieut. T. REYNOLDS.	10/9/14	Holland	5/1/18	18/11/18
Lieut. W. H. UNETT.	10/9/14	Holland	5/1/18	18/11/18
Lieut. G. C. WYNNE.	10/9/14			18/2/18
Capt. C. H. ACKROYD.	10/10/14	Holland	5/1/18	21/1/19
*Capt. T. H. CLEMSON.	27/10/14	Holland	24/2/18	18/11/18
2/Lt. J. B. NOEL.	30/10/14	Holland	5/1/18	18/11/18
Lieut. W. BATEMAN.	10/5/15	Holland	23/3/18	18/11/18
2/Lt. J. A. ARMITAGE.	18/11/16	Switzerland	27/12/17	14/6/18
2/Lt. R. F. CORLETT.	18/11/16			4/1/19
2/Lt. A. RYLETT.	18/11/16	Holland	20/4/18	18/8/18
2/Lt. A. L. WESTWOOD.	18/11/16			28/11/18

4th Battalion.

Name	Missing	Interned		Repatriated
Capt. C. H. PLACKETT.	5/7/16	Holland	16/5/18	18/11/18
Capt. W. M. WILLIAMSON.	6/7/16	Holland	15/6/18	21/1/19
Lieut. J. C. PLEWS.	23/7/16	Holland	15/6/18	returned for duty.
†2/Lt. H. W. SAMPSON.	14/4/18			2/12/18

2/4th Battalion.

Name	Missing			Repatriated
Capt. A. E. PILLEY.	27/3/18			25/12/18
2/Lt. D. O. C. MAGGS.	27/3/18			18/12/18
2/Lt. H. W. SPINK.	27/3/18			2/12/18
Capt. G. L. HUDSON.	28/3/18			–/12/18
‡2/Lt. J. W. POWNALL.	28/3/18			25/12/18

5th Battalion.

Name	Missing			Repatriated
Lieut. R. GRIGG.	27/3/18			2/12/18
Capt. B. A. BEACH.	28/3/18			29/11/18
Capt. E. ROBERTS.	28/3/18			29/11/18
§Capt. A. D. THOMSON.	28/3/18			3/12/18
†2/Lt. R. APPLETON.	28/3/18			29/11/18
2/Lt. W. IBBOTT.	28/3/18			2/12/18
2/Lt. B. P. JENKINSON.	28/3/18			6/12/18
2/Lt. H. G. NORTHEY.	28/3/18			2/12/18
†2/Lt. T. WELDON.	28/3/18			2/12/18
2/Lt. A. H. FEHR.	14/4/18			2/12/18

6th Battalion.

Name	Missing			Repatriated
**2/Lt. G. B. JUBB.	21/3/18			14/12/18

*Attached from Dorset Regiment.
†Attached from K.O.R. Lanc. Regiment.
§Attached from A.S.C.
‡Attached from W. Yorks Regiment.
**Attached T.M.B.

KING'S OWN YORKSHIRE LIGHT INFANTRY—continued.
7th Battalion.

Name.	Missing.	Interned.	Repatriated.
Capt. R. CLIBBORN.	23/9/16		18/12/18
2/Lt. C. ELLIS.	18/10/17		6/12/18
2/Lt. J. D. AITKEN.	24/4/18		25/12/18

9th Battalion.

Lieut. J. F. LITTLEDALE.	23/3/18		11/12/18
Lieut. D. EVANS.	23/3/18		–/12/18
2/Lt. H. HUTSON.	23/3/18	(*Died* at Villers Fancon)	26/3/18
2/Lt. J. MAGIN.	23/3/18		2/1/19
Capt. G. F. ELLENBERGER.	27/5/18		25/12/18
Lieut. F. P. NILEN.	27/5/18		–/12/18
2/Lt. R. H. L. DAVIS.	27/5/18		–/1/19
2/Lt. J. W. DORE.	27/5/18		–/1/19
2/Lt. F. A. MARSDEN.	27/5/18		–/1/19
2/Lt. C. E. SCOTT.	27/5/18		25/12/18
2/Lt. C. E. TAYLOR.	27/5/18		30/12/18

10th Battalion.

*2/Lt. R. J. CARLESS.	22/8/18		5/1/19

12th Battalion.

Lieut. L. FORSDIKE.	13/4/18		18/12/18
Lieut. J. R. WILSON.	13/4/18		18/12/18
2/Lt. J. B. CLARKE.	13/4/18		13/12/18

KING'S SHROPSHIRE LIGHT INFANTRY.
1st Battalion.

Lt.-Col. H. M. SMITH.	21/3/18		17/12/18
†Major H. P. OSBORNE.	21/3/18		1/1/19
Capt. E. BIRD.	21/3/18		25/12/18
Capt. J. DEEDES.	21/3/18		19/12/18
Lieut. B. E. CRAIGIE.	21/3/18		18/12/18
‡Lieut. G. P. LLOYD.	21/3/18		2/12/18
Lieut. N. V. WEBBER.	21/3/18		–/12/18
†Lieut. A. C. WELBOURNE.	21/3/18		29/11/18
2/Lt. H. W. D. EVANS.	21/3/18		–/12/18
2/Lt. A. W. LEPPER.	21/3/18		13/12/18
2/Lt. W. H. MORRIS.	21/3/18		9/1/19
2/Lt. L. A. T. SPEER.	21/3/18		2/12/18
2/Lt. C. VAN HUMBEECK.	21/3/18		2/12/18
†2/Lt. S. G. WHITE.	21/3/18		17/12/18
2/Lt. M. H. WRIGHT.	21/3/18		25/12/18

2nd Battalion.

Capt. H. G. BRYANT.	27/4/15	(*Died* –/5/15).	
2/Lt. R. du B. EVANS.	27/4/15	Switzerland 19/12/16	6/12/18
2/Lt. F. W. VOELKER.	27/4/15	Holland 23/3/18	18/11/18
2/Lt. T. S. LANYON.	7/12/17		18/12/18

*Attached from K. Shrop. L.I.
†Attached from Middlesex Regiment. ‡Attached from Herefordshire Regiment.

KING'S SHROPSHIRE LIGHT INFANTRY—continued

4th Battalion.

Name.	Missing.	Interned.	Repatriated.
Capt. C. E. R. LITT.			27/11/18
Lieut. F. J. K. SMITH.	25/3/18		8/12/18
2/Lt. R. H. FRANCIS.	25/3/18		-/1/19
2/Lt. J. SANDERSON.	25/3/18		21/1/19

6th Battalion.

Name	Missing	Interned	Repatriated
2/Lt. J. P. SHAW.	3/9/16		18/12/18
2/Lt. D. T. FOULDS.	21/3/18		18/12/18
*2/Lt. L. S. MUNN.	21/3/18		18/12/18
Capt. M. J. HELLIER.	22/3/18		18/12/18
†Capt. F. A. H. STANIER.	22/3/18		14/12/18
*Lieut. C. C. KELLY.	22/3/18		-/12/18
2/Lt. W. BULLOCK.	22/3/18		18/12/18
‡2/Lt. De W. HOWARD.	22/3/18		18/12/18
‡2/Lt. C. H. KING.	22/3/18		1/12/18
2/Lt. A. M. A. LYLE.	22/3/18		19/12/18
2/Lt. G. R. MATHER.	22/3/18		18/12/18
Capt. T. MILLYARD.	24/3/18		23/10/18
Capt. R. H. BANKS.	28/3/18		18/12/18

7th Battalion.

Name	Missing	Interned	Repatriated
2/Lt. G. V. JONES.	28/3/18	(*Died* at Duisburg 24/4/18).	

10th Battalion.

Name	Missing	Interned	Repatriated
2/Lt. A. F. McEWEN.	22/8/18		8/12/18

MIDDLESEX REGIMENT.

1st to 4th Battalions.

Name	Missing	Interned		Repatriated
Capt. H. A. CARTWRIGHT.	3/9/14			16/8/18
Capt. L. J. GRAHAM-TOLER.	3/9/14			1/1/19
Capt. L. F. SLOANE-STANLEY.	10/9/14	Holland	29/12/17	22/12/18
Capt. L. H. O. JOSEPHS.	10/9/14	Holland	29/12/17	22/11/18
Capt. H. E. L. GLASS.	10/9/14	Switzerland	9/12/17	21/1/19
Lieut. E. R. RUSHTON.	10/9/14	Holland	29/12/17	18/11/18
Lieut. G. C. DRUCE.	10/9/14	Holland	29/12/17	18/11/18
Capt. H. F. SPENCE.	11/9/14	Switzerland	27/12/17	24/3/18
2/Lt. B. G. HORROCKS.	21/10/14			17/12/18
Major W. H. C. DAVY.	-/-/14			Exchange 17/2/15
2/Lt. F. E. BEACHAMP.	31/7/17			10/12/18
2/Lt. W. S. BERTIOLI.	25/9/17			6/12/18
2/Lt. J. C. OLIVER.	24/3/18			18/12/18
§2/Lt. F. S. PENFOLD.	24/3/18			18/12/18
Lieut. E. FRAYNE.	25/3/18	(*Died*).		
2/Lt. J. L. WENN.	27/3/18			18/12/18
2/Lt. J. R. S. CHAPMAN.	27/3/18			18/12/18
Lieut. H. E. WHITE.	28/3/18			1/12/18
2/Lt. H. CAWDRON.	28/3/18			8/12/18
2/Lt. P. H. E. FAIRCLOUGH.	1/4/18			18/12/18
§Capt. H. C. KILLINGBACK.	9/4/18			10/12/18
**Lieut. W. J. FRANCIS.	24/4/18			1/12/18
**Lieut. J. H. F. HARVEY.	24/4/18			29/11/18
**2/Lt. A. H. PALIN.	24/4/18			15/12/18
**2/Lt. J. G. MORTON.	24/4/18			29/11/18
†2/Lt. S. SLAVITZ.	24/4/18			29/11/18
†2/Lt. H. HOWARTH.	24/4/18			16/12/18

*Attached from Herefordshire Regiment.   †Attached from Shropshire Yeomanry.
‡Attached from Berkshire Regiment.
§Attached T.M.B.   **Attached from Gloucester Regiment.

MIDDLESEX REGIMENT—continued.

1st to 4th Battalions—continued.

Name.	Missing.	Interned.	Repatriated.
2/Lt. F. POND.	24/4/18		—/11/18
2/Lt. F. W. STAFFORD.	24/4/18		29/11/18
2/Lt. F. D. AITKEN.	24/4/18		29/11/18
Major C. A. S. PAGE.	27/5/18		12/10/18
Capt. H. L. McILWAINE.	27/5/18		—/12/18
Capt. T. C. MANDERS.	27/5/18		6/12/18
Capt. W. G. S. JONES.	27/5/18		31/12/18
Capt. S. F. DEL COURT.	27/5/18		19/1/19
2/Lt. A/Capt. L. WANSTALL.	27/5/18		13/12/18
Lieut. R. GREIG.	27/5/18		13/12/18
Lieut. R. D. HORNBY.	27/5/18		—/12/18
Lieut. G. D. HARVEY-SAMUEL.	27/5/18		2/1/19
Lieut. J. E. MAYNARD.	27/5/18		17/12/18
2/Lt. W. J. MARTIN.	27/5/18		13/1/19
2/Lt. H. T. BYE.	27/5/18		—/12/18
2/Lt. C. S. LEWIS.	27/5/18		30/12/18
2/Lt. J. H. MARKS.	27/5/18		17/12/18
2/Lt. C. T. M. HALL.	27/5/18		—/12/18
2/Lt. J. HAYER.	27/5/18		13/12/18
2/Lt. G. OEHL.	27/5/18		11/1/19
2/Lt. A. N. OVERELL.	27/5/18		30/12/18
2/Lt. S. F. CORNWELL.	27/5/18		25/12/18
2/Lt. T. F. COLLINGWOOD.	27/5/18		8/12/18
2/Lt. W. O. PEARSON.	27/5/18		30/12/18
2/Lt. C. E. CADE.	24/10/18		8/12/18

6th Battalion.

Name.	Missing.	Interned.	Repatriated.
Lieut. A. B. W. ALLISTONE.	10/9/14	Switzerland 13/2/17	9/12/18

7th Battalion.

Name.	Missing.	Interned.	Repatriated.
Capt. J. W. CATER.	3/5/17	(*Died* 9/7/17 at Cassel).	
2/Lt. F. A. PEARSON.	26/8/18		28/11/18

8th Battalion.

Name.	Missing.	Interned.	Repatriated.
Lieut. E. B. BUDDEN.		Holland 5/1/18	18/11/18
Lieut. H. BROUGH.	31/5/15	(Exchanged)	26/8/15
Capt, G. W. TREMLETT.	19/5/17	Switzerland 27/12/17	7/12/18
Capt. H. C. VAUX.	30/11/17		14/12/18
Lieut. W. S. SIMPSON.	30/11/17	Switzerland 2/10/18	25/12/18
Lieut. G. D. DOWTY.	30/11/17		14/12/18
Lieut. J. E. BAYLISS.	30/11/17		28/11/18
Lieut. V. L. H. MEYERS.	30/11/17		6/12/18
2/Lt. C. J. N. JEFFREYS.	30/11/17		4/12/18
2/Lt. C. R. BIRD.	30/11/17		14/12/18
2/Lt. R. W. SMART.	30/11/17		14/12/18
2/Lt. C. H. JACKSON.	30/11/17		3/12/18
2/Lt. F. C. W. LAGDEN.	15/5/18		31/12/18

12th Battalion.

Name.	Missing.	Interned.	Repatriated.
Capt. F. G. SKINNER.	3/5/17		20/1/18
Capt. H. PERKS.	3/5/17	Holland 15/4/18	20/7/18
Lieut. F. S. HEARD.	3/5/17		3/1/19
*Capt. H. F. PEARSON.	24/3/18		29/11/18

*Attached Entrenching Battalion.

MIDDLESEX REGIMENT—continued.

13th Battalion.

Lieut. C. E. HARMAN.	27/9/15	Holland	10/4/18	22/11/18
2/Lt. A. R. HAYFORD.	22/3/18			25/12/18

16th Battalion.

Capt. E. W. HALL.	1/7/16		11/9/17
Capt. F. S. COCKRAM.	1/7/16	Switzerland 27/12/17	9/12/18
2/Lt. R. F. MICHELMORE.	1/7/16	(*Died* 7/7/16 at Velu).	
Lieut. L. J. LUFFINGHAM.	31/5/17		17/12/18
2/Lt. D. S. B. STARNES.	31/5/17		17/12/18
2/Lt. T. W. LANE.	30/11/17		1/1/19

17th Battalion.

Lieut. E. W. MARCHANT.	13–15/11/16		14/12/18
2/Lt. A. M. MURRAY.	13–15/11/16		18/12/18
2/Lt. C. KOOP.	13–15/11/16	Switzerland 9/12/17	23/12/18
2/Lt. C. FLINT.			14/12/18
2/Lt. E. S. KING.	21/1/17		17/12/18
Capt. E. PARFITT.	28/4/17	(*Died* 28/5/17 at Kempton).	
Lieut. J. H. K. SEBRIGHT.	28/4/17		3/1/19
2/Lt. P. G. CARRUTHERS.	28/4/17		2/1/19
Lieut. H. W. SANDERS.	5/6/17		7/12/18

19th Battalion.

Major O. S. PRATT.	24/3/18	8/12/18

20th Battalion.

Lieut. W. WELLS.	22/3/18	11/12/18
2/Lt. E. T. HOOPER.	22/3/18	25/12/18
Capt. E. D. SAMUEL.	9/4/18	9/12/18
Lieut. H. P. CRITTALL.	9/4/18	18/12/18
2/Lt. A. R. HULLS.	9/4/18	11/12/18
2/Lt. J. A. ROLLS.	9/4/18	11/12/18
2/Lt. T. W. R. FAIRALL.	9/4/18	28/11/18
2/Lt. R. D. STEINBERG.	9/4/18	29/11/18
2/Lt. L. W. FREEMAN.	9/4/18	8/12/18
2/Lt. G. F. WHITBREAD.	9/4/18	13/12/18
2/Lt. F. IZOD.	9/4/18	29/11/18
2/Lt. H. G. BAYLIS.	9/4/18	9/12/18
2/Lt. T. S. MOORE.	9/4/18	5/12/18
Major F. R. HILL.	10/4/18	17/12/18
Capt. L. PRICE.	10/4/18	23/12/18
Lieut. D. O. LIGHT.	10/4/18	10/12/18

21st Battalion.

*2/Lt. A. S. T. SMURTHWAITE.	28/8/17		14/12/18
Capt. H. J. SKILL.	24/3/18	(*Died* 7/4/18).	
Capt. J. H. DALGARNO.	9/4/18		11/12/18
Capt. A. P. HEARD.	9/4/18		–/1/19
2/Lt. G. HENDERSON.	9/4/18		18/12/18
2/Lt. P. M. BESTER.	9/4/18		11/12/18
2/Lt. E. J. CONYNHAM.	9/4/18		18/12/18
2/Lt. R. L. SEARS.	9/4/18		2/1/19
2/Lt. C. H. SULLENS.	9/4/18		–/12/18
Capt. R. C. SHEEN.	11/4/18		10/12/18

* Attached T.M.B.

MIDDLESEX REGIMENT—continued.
23rd Battalion.

Name.	Missing.	Interned.	Repatriated.
Capt. B. T. FOSS.	23/3/18		29/11/18

KING'S ROYAL RIFLE CORPS.
1st to 4th Battalions.

Name.	Missing.	Interned.		Repatriated.
Capt. W. P. LYNES.				8/10/16
		(Died at Q.A.M. Hosp.		14/10/16)
Lieut. J. F. E. GOAD.	31/10/14	Holland	24/2/18	21/1/19
Lieut. T. WADNER.	1/11/14	Holland	24/2/18	14/1/18
Lieut. A. M. WAKEFIELD-SAUNDERS.	2/11/14	Holland	24/2/18	16/11/18
Lieut. C. F. SCHOON.	2/11/14	Holland	24/2/18	5/1/18
Lieut. S. LUCAS.	2/11/14	Holland	24/2/18	15/10/18
Lieut. G. V. H. GOUGH.	2/11/14	Holland	24/2/18	18/11/18
2/Lt. R. RICHARDS.	2/11/14	Holland	24/2/18	18/11/18
2/Lt. C. H. REYNARD.	2/11/14			18/9/17
2/Lt. K. H. Wodehouse WARD.	14/3/15	Switzerland	12/8/16	13/9/17
2/Lt. J. S. POOLE.	9/5/15			—/11/16
2/Lt. M. B. HOPE.	9/5/15	Holland	10/4/18	18/11/18
2/Lt. H. CHEVIS.	10/7/17			2/1/19
Capt. W. L. CLINTON.	10/7/17	(Died at Belgrade		22/11/18).
Lieut. W. H. E. GOTT.	10/7/17			3/12/18
Lieut. H. J. F. MILLS.	10/7/17			4/12/18
Lieut. A. PINNOCK.	10/7/17			1/1/19
2/Lt. A. SIMPSON.	10/7/17			7/12/18
2/Lt. H. J. LINDSAY.	10/7/17			14/12/18
2/Lt. D. H. TAYLOR.	10/7/17			7/12/18
2/Lt. R. MADELEY.	10/7/17			17/12/18
*Lieut. C. E. S. S. ECCLES.	21/3/18			25/12/18
Lt.-Col. H. M. GOSLING.	23/3/18			4/12/18
2/Lt. H. M. BARNET.	24/3/18	(Died at Langensalza		21/4/18).
2/Lt. O. L. MARLOW.	19/9/18			2/12/18

7th Battalion.

Name.	Missing.	Repatriated.
Capt. W. BORTHWICK.	21/3/18	12/12/18
Lieut. W. L. SANDERS.	21/3/18	18/12/18
2/Lt. C. ALLEN.	21/3/18	11/12/18
2/Lt. H. M. DAY.	21/3/18	11/12/18
2/Lt. H. A. JACKSON.	21/3/18	18/12/18
2/Lt. H. J. RATHBONE.	21/3/18	8/12/18
Lt.-Col. J. G. BIRCH.	22/3/18	2/12/18

8th Battalion.

Name.	Missing.	Repatriated.
Capt. J. W. LESLEY.	3/5/17	31/12/18
2/Lt. H. M. COOK.	3/5/17	30/12/18
2/Lt. H. H. LIDDLE.	3/5/17	7/1/18
Major N. E. BARBER.	21/3/18	—/12/18
Major R. L. BOWEN.	21/3/18	6/12/18
Capt. P. M. POPE.		2/12/18
Capt. C. L. DOMVILLE.	21/3/18	6/12/18
†Capt. W. J. REYNOLDS.	21/3/18	6/12/18
Capt. F. G. SCOTT.	21/3/18	14/12/18

*Attached T.M.B. †Attached from London Regiment.

KING'S ROYAL RIFLE CORPS.—continued.

8th Battalion—continued.

Name.	Missing.	Interned.	Repatriated.
*Lieut. F. B. ADAMS.	21/3/18		25/12/18
†Lieut. A. J. BELL.	21/3/18		3/1/19
‡Lieut. J. E. GIBSON.	21/3/18		11/12/18
2/Lt. J. D. K. BEIGHTON.	21/3/18		6/12/18
§2/Lt. L. C. BUTLER.	21/3/18		14/12/18
2/Lt. E. BUTTIFANT.	21/3/18		6/12/18
**2/Lt. F. G. W. CONNON.	21/3/18		6/12/18
2/Lt. D. S. FORSYTH.	21/3/18		-/12/18
2/Lt. W. S. P. GOW.	21/3/18		6/12/18
2/Lt. P. JOHNSON.	21/3/18		-/12/18
‡‡P2/Lt. C. RAYNER.	21/3/18		11/12/18
**2/Lt. R. ROBERTSON.	21/3/18		10/12/18
2/Lt. S. R. C. SHARP.	21/3/18		6/12/18
2/Lt. W. STUART.	21/3/18		6/12/18
2/Lt. G. TUXFORD.	21/3/18		6/12/18
2/Lt. P. J. JEFFREYS.	4/4/18		18/12/18

9th Battalion.

Name.	Missing.	Interned.	Repatriated.
Lt.-Col. C. H. HOWARD-BURY.			-/12/18
Capt. E. R. VICKERS.	21/3/18		10/12/18
Capt. R. P. GRAHAM.	21/3/18		4/12/18
Capt. H. M. GRIFFITH.	21/3/18		10/12/18
Capt. R. T. RIDLEY.	21/3/18		10/12/18
Lieut. A. J. D'ALTON.	21/3/18		10/12/18
2/Lt. C. G. BAKER.	21/3/18		11/12/18
2/Lt. E. H. V. BURGESS.	21/3/18		11/12/18
2/Lt. J. S. CHOWN.	21/3/18		11/12/18
2/Lt. L. S. DAGG.			11/12/18
2/Lt. L. G. MACKIE.	21/3/18		11/12/18
2/Lt. R. R. MITCHELL.	21/3/18		11/12/18
2/Lt. P. D. ROGERS.	21/3/18		11/12/18
**2/Lt. A. F. PARSONS.	21/31/8		11/12/18
2/Lt. W. E. ROOKE.	21/3/18		11/12/18
2/Lt. P. J. WHITE.	21/3/18		18/12/18

10th Battalion.

Name.	Missing.	Interned.		Repatriated.
2/Lt. R. D. EVANS.	14/8/16	Holland	12/10/18	22/12/18
Capt. H. C. H. ILLINGWORTH.	28/2/17	Switzerland	9/12/17	18/12/18
Capt. R. L. JONES.	10/8/17			11/1/19
‖2/Lt. J. M. LOVATT.	12/8/17			25/12/18
Capt. F. G. FISON.	30/11/17			9/12/18
Lieut. E. G. PRIOR.	30/11/17			14/12/18
2/Lt. J. HUNTER.	30/11/17			28/11/18
2/Lt. A. MACKENZIE.	30/11/17			27/11/18
2/Lt. J. T. KING.	30/11/17			3/12/18
2/Lt. N. A. MACLEAN.	30/11/17			17/12/18
2/Lt. W. E. PRISTO.	30/11/17			25/12/18
2/Lt. P. B. DIPLOCK.	30/11/17			2/12/18
2/Lt. J. J. LEE.	30/11/17			15/1/19
2/Lt. C. M. PENNEY.	30/11/17			4/12/18

*Attached from Liverpool Regiment.
†Attached from A.S.C.
‡Attached from Scottish Rifles.
§Attached from Manchester Regiment.
**Attached from London Regiment.
††Attached T.M.B.
‖Attached from Dorset Regiment.
‖Attached from N. Staffs.

KING'S ROYAL RIFLE CORPS.—continued.

11th Battalion.

Name.	Missing.	Interned.	Repatriated.
Capt. C. N. BARLOW.	30/11/17		13/5/18
Lieut. C. P. E. De PARAVICINI.	30/11/17		25/12/18
2/Lt. G. P. LOWE.	30/11/17		3/12/18
2/Lt. W. P. MORRIS.	30/11/17	(*Died* at Rouen 20/12/18).	
2/Lt. J. S. PORTEOUS.	30/11/17		25/12/18
2/Lt. R. READER.	30/11/17		17/12/18
2/Lt. G. H. WILLIS.	30/11/17		17/12/18
2/Lt. A. G. E. TAYLOR.	30/11/17		3/12/18
Capt. J. A. WATT.	30/11/17		9/12/18
*Lieut. L. E. JAMES.	23/3/18		18/12/18
2/Lt. E. C. GRIFFITHS.	24/3/18		18/12/18
†P2/Lt. A. J. SUTTERS.	24/3/18		3/12/18
Capt. C. G. WEBB.	25/3/18		3/12/18
2/Lt. B. JOHNSTON.	29/3/18	(*Died*).	

12th Battalion.

Name.	Missing.	Interned.	Repatriated.
2/Lt. H. PRATT.	19/2/16	Holland 7/10/18	22/11/18
Lieut. W. L. WARD-DAVIS.	21/3/18		4/12/18
2/Lt. J. C. CALDWELL.	21/3/18		–/12/18
2/Lt. P. SMITTEN.	21/3/18		31/12/18
Lt.-Col. L. G. MOORE.	23/3/18		–/12/18
2/Lt. W. H. TAYLOR.	25/3/18		29/11/18
2/Lt. J. W. EVERETT.	29/3/18	(*Died* at Beaufort 12/4/18).	
Capt. A. N. CRANSWICK.	31/3/18		10/12/18

13th Battalion.

Name.	Missing.	Interned.	Repatriated.
2/Lt. A. J. WIGGETT.	8/3/16	(Died 15/3/16).	

16th Battalion.

Name.	Missing.	Interned.	Repatriated.
Capt. A. B. BERNARD.	23/4/17	(*Died* at Munster 4/5/17).	
Capt. L. E. FRANCIS.	12/4/18		25/12/18
2/Lt. R. H. M. LEA.	13/4/18		–/12/18
2/Lt. W. SULLIVAN.	13/4/18		2/12/18
Capt. C. H. CORK.	14/4/18		4/12/18
Lieut. E. F. SARGENT.	15/4/18		25/12/18
2/Lt. L. J. GOLDSACK.	15/4/18		23/9/18
2/Lt. J. E. RICHES.	15/4/18		6/1/19
Lieut. C. E. HOWARD.	16/4/18		2/12/18
2/Lt. H. W. H. CONSIDINE.	16/4/18		25/12/18
2/Lt. R. W. EDWARDS.	16/4/18		4/12/18
2/Lt. J. HANNAY.	16/4/18		–/12/18
2/Lt. W. H. McLEAN.	16/4/18		4/12/18
2/Lt. G. S. HOGAN.	24/9/18		16/12/18
2/Lt. A. H. VILLIERS.	12/10/18		18/12/18

17th Battalion.

Name.	Missing.	Interned.	Repatriated.
‡Capt. A. W. HARVEY.	22/3/18	(*Died* at Walincourt 27/3/18).	
2/Lt. W. McINTYRE.	22/3/18		25/12/18
2/Lt. J. P. BUNCE.	29/3/18		6/1/19
2/Lt. T. J. G. EASTMAN.	30/3/18		–/12/18

18th Battalion.

Name.	Missing.	Interned.	Repatriated.
Lieut. F. W. PARISH.	14/6/16	Holland 30/4/18	22/11/18
Capt. J. B. GRAY.	24/3/18		2/12/18
2/Lt. G. CALDER.	24/3/18		3/12/18
2/Lt. J. A. HARRIS.	24/3/18		18/12/18
2/Lt. H. J. PICKUP.	24/3/18		10/12/18
2/Lt. G. RICHARDSON.	24/3/18		11/12/18

*Attached from London Regiment. †Attached from T.M.B.
‡Attached from Scottish Rifles.

KING'S ROYAL RIFLE CORPS—continued.

18th Battalion—continued.

Name.	Missing.	Interned.	Repatriated.
2/Lt. E. P. W. SHEPHEARD.	24/3/18		–/12/18
2/Lt. C. T. UREN.	24/3/18		2/12/18
2/Lt. W. A. F. BINNS.	11/8/18		13/12/18
Lieut. S. PYE.	22/10/18		8/12/18
2/Lt. E. J. HACKING.	22/10/18		–/12/18

20th Battalion.

Name.	Missing.	Interned.	Repatriated.
Lieut. C. W. YOUNG.	2/10/18		28/11/18

21st Battalion.

Name.	Missing.	Interned.	Repatriated.
Lieut. J. A. BEARN.	21/3/18		2/12/18

WILTSHIRE REGIMENT.

1st and 2nd Battalions.

Name.	Missing.	Interned.		Repatriated.
Lieut. W. LODER-SYMONDS.	10/9/14			14/3/18
		(*Killed* 30/5/18 at Thetford).		
Major J. R. WYNDHAM.	24/10/14	Holland	24/2/18	31/8/18
Capt. A. W. TIMMIS.	24/10/14	Holland	24/2/18	20/11/18
Capt. R. SMITH.	24/10/14	Holland	24/2/18	18/11/18
Capt. C. H. E. MOORE.	24/10/14	Holland	24/2/18	18/11/18
Lieut. R. P. ROGERS.	24/10/14	Switzerland	9/12/17	6/12/18
Lieut. H. B. ROSE.	27/10/14	Holland	24/2/18	18/11/18
Lieut. J. H. WAND-TETLEY.	27/10/14	Holland	24/2/18	19/11/18
Lieut. F. B. RILEY.	27/10/14	Holland	24/2/18	15/9/18
Lieut. K. J. P. OLIPHANT.	27/10/14	Holland	24/2/18	17/11/18
Lieut. H. W. C. LLOYD.	27/10/14	(Escaped)		–/1/17
2/Lt. W. MARTIN.	27/10/14	Holland	24/2/18	Returned for duty.
Lieut. M. R. WATSON.	29/10/14	Holland	24/2/18	20/12/18
Capt. E. L. HENSLOW.	8/11/14	Holland	24/2/18	29/1/19
Capt. R. CULVER.	1/11/14	Holland	24/2/18	18/11/18
Lt.-Col. J. N. FORBES.	24/11/14	Holland	6/2/18	–/–/18
Major C. LAW.	24/11/14	Holland	24/2/18	8/2/19
Capt. G. LE HUQUET.	24/11/14	Holland	24/2/18	18/11/18
Capt. H. F. CODDINGTON.	24/11/14	Holland	24/2/18	1/11/18
Lieut. A. K. BLECKLY.	24/11/14	Switzerland	–/12/17	7/12/18
Lieut. E. L. BETTS.	24/11/14	Holland	24/2/18	18/11/18
Lieut. C. H. R. BARNES.	24/11/14	Holland	6/2/18	18/11/18
Lieut. D. A. ANSTED.	24/11/14	Holland	24/2/18	21/11/18
Lieut. A. S. HOOPER.	24/11/14	Holland	20/12/17	18/11/18
2/Lt. G. P. OLDFIELD.	24/11/14	Holland	24/2/18	21/1/19
2/Lt. F. RYLANDS.	14/1/15	Holland	24/2/18	Returned for duty.
Capt. A. E. STICKINGS.	16/6/15			11/9/17
2/Lt. H. G. DEHN.	9/7/16	Switzerland	9/12/17	14/6/18
2/Lt. C. H. BLAKE.	15/12/16			17/12/18

1st Battalion.

Name.	Missing.	Interned.	Repatriated.
2/Lt. S. C. SMITH.	24/3/18		11/12/18
2/Lt. A. V. S. GRANT.	24/3/18		23/9/18
Capt. F. SMITH.	10/4/18		25/12/18
2/Lt. S. J. PARKER.	11/4/18		29/11/18
Lt.-Col. S. S. OGILVIE.	12/4/18		4/12/18
Capt. C. H. G. THOMAS.	12/4/18		9/1/19
Lt.-Col. E. K. B. FURZE.	27/5/18		21/12/18
Capt. J. F. ARNOTT.	27/5/18		18/12/18
Lieut. H. C. REID.	27/5/18		18/12/18
2/Lt. J. B. STANLEY.	27/5/18		–/12/18
2/Lt. S. T. DOWSON.	15/8/18		13/12/18
2/Lt. D. H. DAVIES.	30/8/18	(*Died* at Gottingen 18/11/18

WILTSHIRE REGIMENT—continued.

2nd Battalion.

Name.	Missing.	Interned.	Repatriated.
Lt.-Col. A. V. P. MARTIN.	21/3/18		6/12/18
Capt. L. C. MAKEHAM.	21/3/18		6/12/18
Lieut. R. M. P. BEAVEN.	21/3/18		-/12/18
Lieut. S. S. MILLER.	21/3/18		6/12/18
2/Lt. J. F. F. McQUEEN.	21/3/18		6/12/18
2/Lt. C. D. BAKER.	21/3/18		-/12/18
2/Lt. R. H. EDWARDS.	21/31/8		6/12/18
2/Lt. E. W. APPS.	21/3/18		6/12/18
2/Lt. P. E. KING-SMITH.	21/3/18		14/12/18
2/Lt. B. M. IVISON.	21/3/18		14/12/18
2/Lt. H. J. HULBERT.	21/3/18		25/12/18
2/Lt. A. R. MOORE.	21/3/18		6/12/18
Lieut. F. J. LONDON.	24/3/18		10/12/18
Lieut. C. L. USHER.	28/3/18	(*Died* 23/4/18).	
2/Lt. F. J. E. SPENCER.	26/4/18		9/11/18
Lt. T. W. GLYNN.	21/3/18		6/12/18

6th Battalion.

Lieut. E. E. PEGGE.	22/3/18		10/12/18
*Lieut. M. G. SUMNER.	23/3/18		28/11/18
Lieut. S. H. WILLIAMS.	24/3/18		25/12/18
Lieut. J. STOGDEN.	24/3/18		10/12/18
Lieut. L. R. MILLERSHIP.	24/3/18		11/12/18
2/Lt. A. G. AUSTIN.	24/3/18		18/12/18
Capt. N. L. FLOWER.	25/3/18		13/1/19
*2/Lt. D. B. CAMPBELL.	25/3/18		-/1/19
Capt. G. C. H. KENT.	10/4/18		25/12/18
*Lieut. B. M. KNOWLES.	10/4/18		-/12/18
†2/Lt. P. G. HART.	10/4/18		25/12/18
Capt. W. M. AUSTIN.	11/4/18		-/12/18

MANCHESTER REGIMENT.

1st and 2nd Battalions.

Capt. C. MORLEY.	30/8/14			13/9/17
Lieut. R. F. G. BURROWS.	30/8/14	Holland	5/1/18	18/11/18
2/Lt. R. T. MILLER.	3/9/14	Switzerland	12/8/16	23/3/18
Capt. G. P. WYMER.	10/9/14	Holland	22/1/18	18/8/18
2/Lt. W. BUTLER.				2/1/19
Capt. B. L. ERSKINE.	18/11/16			5/1/19
Lieut. M. R. DAVIDSON.	18/11/16			1/1/19
2/Lt. G. B. GRIFFIN.	18/11/16			1/1/19
2/Lt. E. E. J. HENDERSON.	18/11/16			17/12/18
2/Lt. N. F. HARLEY.	18/11/16			17/12/18
2/Lt. F. HARBRON.	18/11/16			29/11/18
2/Lt. B. W. SPROWELL.	2/10/18			13/12/18

4th Battalion.

2/Lt. G. A. HALSTEAD.	25/3/18		26/12/18

*Attached from Wiltshire Yeomanry.
†Attached T.M.B.

MANCHESTER REGIMENT—continued.

5th Battalion.

Name.	Missing.	Interned.	Repatriated.
Capt. R. P. PORTER.	21/3/18		29/11/18
Capt. G. TWEEDALE.	21/3/18		10/12/18
Lieut. W. A. E. URIE.	21/3/18		8/12/18
*Lieut. W. H. E. N. GRIFFITH.	21/3/18		29/11/18
Lieut. S. R. ELLIS.	21/3/18		2/12/18
Lieut. H. D. ATKIN.	21/3/18		2/12/18
Lieut. R. A. THORNTON.	21/3/18		14/12/18
2/Lt. A. B. C. DYER.	21/3/18		29/11/18
2/Lt. J. H. WELLARD.	21/3/18		2/12/18
2/Lt. J. R. GRIFFITH.	21/3/18		25/12/18
2/Lt. S. KEYS.	21/3/18		–/12/18
2/Lt. J. CHANDLER.	21/3/18		14/12/18
2/Lt. H. ELLISON.	21/3/18		–/12/18
2/Lt. F. C. G. BENSON.	21/3/18		29/11/18
2/Lt. J. F. SCHOFIELD.	21/3/18		2/12/18
2/Lt. L. PULPHER.	21/3/18		14/12/18
Major E. L. FISHER.	22/3/18		18/12/18
Lieut. T. NICHOLSON.	22/3/18		28/11/18
2/Lt. W. A. CHURCH.	22/3/18		14/12/18
Capt. K. G. MAXWELL.	23/3/18		–/12/18
2/Lt. W. J. McBEATH.	24/3/18		25/12/18

6th Battalion.

Name.	Missing.	Interned.	Repatriated.
Lieut. J. H. B. SEWELL.	21/3/18		29/11/18
Lieut. H. MAKINSON.	21/3/18		–/11/19
2/Lt. H. BAGGS.	21/3/18		29/11/18
2/Lt. H. W. H. ORAM.	21/3/18		18/12/18
2/Lt. E. WILKINSON.	21/3/18		25/12/18
2/Lt. F. BRADLEY.	22/3/18		29/11/18
Capt. S. L. BRIDGFORD.	23/3/18	(Died 6/4/18 at Ghent).	
2/Lt. R. P. HOLLAND.	24/3/18		29/11/18
2/Lt. B. K. WHITTAKER.	25/3/18		28/11/18
2/Lt. F. L. C. SIMONS.	25/3/18		2/12/18

7th Battalion.

Name.	Missing.	Interned.	Repatriated.
*Major N. A. B. BAILLIE-HAMILTON.	21/3/18		18/12/18
Capt. J. A. SCHOLFIELD.	21/3/18		–/12/18
Lieut. A. G. ALDRED.	21/3/18		11/12/18
Lieut. E. H. SHAW.	21/3/18		29/11/18
Lieut. R. W. FOX.	21/3/18		25/12/18
2/Lt. J. N. HODGKINSON.	21/3/18		18/12/18
2/Lt. F. P. FREEMAN.	21/3/18		29/11/18
2/Lt. J. M. HAYES.	21/3/18		5/12/18
2/Lt. F. ANDREW.	25/3/18	(Died 31/3/18 at Bohain).	

8th Battalion.

Name.	Missing.	Interned.	Repatriated.
Capt. K. V. BAILEY.	21/3/18		14/12/18
Lieut. W. GIBBONS.	21/3/18		–/11/18
2/Lt. F. ROBSON.	21/3/18		12/10/18
2/Lt. A. N. TONGUE.	21/3/18		6/12/18
2/Lt. G. PARSONS.	21/3/18		29/11/18
2/Lt. C. HASLAM.	25/3/18		–/12/18
Lieut. A. S. WOMERSLEY.	12/4/18		1/12/18

*Attached T.M.B.   *Attached from Black Watch.

MANCHESTER REGIMENT—continued.

9th Battalion.

Name.	Missing.	Interned.	Repatriated.
Capt. H. E. BUTTERWORTH.	21/3/18		25/12/18
*Capt. F. WOOD.	21/3/18		29/11/18
2/Lt. G. HUNT.	21/3/18		18/12/18
2/Lt. W. WITTY.	4/4/18		2/12/18

10th Battalion.

Name.	Missing.	Interned.	Repatriated.
*Major E. G. SOTHAM.	21/3/18		6/12/18
2/Lt. F. J. DURRANT.	21/3/18		8/12/18

12th Battalion.

Name.	Missing.	Interned.	Repatriated.
Capt. J. T. BROMLEY.	8/9/17		6/12/18
Lieut. R. B. HAMER.	21/3/18		18/12/18
2/Lt. M. LIGGETT.	24/3/18		18/12/18
2/Lt. F. F. TAYLOR.	24/3/18		17/12/18
2/Lt. A. H. JACOBS.	24/3/18		18/12/18
2/Lt. G. S. BAILEY.	8/9/18		28/11/18
2/Lt. E. WINDER.	12/10/18		8/12/18
†2/Lt. J. BRADLEY.	12/10/18		16/12/18

14th Battalion.

Name.	Missing.	Interned.	Repatriated.
2/Lt. J. S. PARTINGTON.	1/7/16	Holland 15/6/18	22/11/18
2/Lt. F. S. SHAW.	26/4/18		2/12/18

16th Battalion.

Name.	Missing.	Interned.	Repatriated.
Major R. N. R. GIBBON.	21/3/18		13/12/18
Capt. J. GUEST.	21/3/18		2/1/19
Capt. O. T. PRICHARD.	21/3/18		14/12/18
Capt. P. H. HEYWOOD.	21/3/18		14/12/18
Lieut. E. T. HOLLINS.	21/31/8		18/12/18
Lieut. M. D. PLEASANCE.	21/3/18		14/12/18
Lieut. J. CLARKE.	21/3/18	(*Died* at Cologne).	
2/Lt. F. HAYES.	21/3/18		–/12/18
2/Lt. J. A. BIRCHENOUGH.	21/3/18		11/12/18
2/Lt. W. DEAN.	21/3/18		14/12/18
2/Lt. J. A. BENTLEY.	21/3/18		27/11/18
2/Lt. W. McQUINN.	21/3/18	(*Died* 6/8/18 at Wittenberg).	
2/Lt. F. W. KEELING.	22/3/18		14/12/18
2/Lt. A. WOODACRE.	26/4/18		2/12/18
2/Lt. H. T. RINGHAM.	26/4/18		3/12/18
2/Lt. E. JONES.	26/4/18		6/12/18
2/Lt. E. BRADWELL.	26/4/18		2/12/18

17th Battalion.

Name.	Missing.	Interned.	Repatriated.
2/Lt. C. W. ROBERTSON.	10–11/7/16	(*Died* 22/8/16 at Le Cateau).	
Lieut. L. B. HUMPHREYS.	11/7/16		22/1/19
Lieut. W. F. SWIFT.	23/4/17		4/1/19
2/Lt. A. T. S. HOLT.	23/4/17		4/12/18
Capt. W. G. WOODWARD.	22/3/18		2/12/18
Capt. J. L. CLAYTON.	22/3/18		1/12/18
Lieut. G. DUNSCOMBE.	22/3/18	(*Died* at Graudenz).	
2/Lt. F. V. HARRISON.	22/3/18		18/12/18
2/Lt. C. S. MILES.	22/3/18		12/12/18

*Attached from Lancashire Fusiliers.
†Attached from South Lancs.

MANCHESTER REGIMENT—continued.
17th Battalion—continued.

Name.	Missing.	Interned.	Repatriated.
2/Lt. T. LONGWORTH.	22/3/18		18/12/18
2/Lt. S. A. JACKSON.	22/3/18		18/12/18
2/Lt. W. H. SMITH.	26/4/18		2/12/18
2/Lt. L. RATHBONE.	26/4/18		3/12/18
2/Lt. S. W. CANNON.	26/4/18		–/12/18
2/Lt. J. HILLIAN.	26/4/18		2/12/18
2/Lt. C. T. M. MARSHALL.	26/4/18		2/12/18

18th Battalion.

Name	Missing	Interned		Repatriated
2/Lt. D. BLENKIRON.	29/1/16	Holland	19/4/18	23/10/18
Capt. F. WOLFENDEN.	1/8/16			29/11/18
Capt. W. F. ROUTLEY.	1/8/16	Switzerland	9/12/17	24/3/18
Capt. J. O. McELROY.	14/12/17			3/12/18
2/Lt. H. WHINCUP.	14/12/17			27/11/18
*Capt. H. A. HENDRIE.	21/3/18			10/12/18
*Lieut. W. EVANS.	21/3/18			25/12/18

19th Battalion.

Name	Missing	Interned		Repatriated
Capt. W. M. CLARKE.	24/7/16	Switzerland	19/12/16	14/6/18
Lieut. J. A. CALDWELL.	24/7/16	Holland	15/6/18	1/2/19
Lieut. G. LERESCHE.	24/7/16			22/11/18
2/Lt. N. H. CRASTON.	24/7/16	Holland	15/6/18	22/11/18

20th Battalion.

Name	Missing	Interned	Repatriated
Lieut. R. K. MATHESON.	3/9/16	(*Died* 8/9/16).	
Lieut. F. H. BISHOP.	18/4/18		14/12/18

21st Battalion.

Name	Missing	Repatriated
2/Lt. S. R. SMITH.	15/5/17	23/12/18
2/Lt. W. B. PURVIS.	26/10/17	2/12/18

22nd Battalion.

Name	Missing	Repatriated
Lieut. H. GRIMWOOD.	14/3/17	–/11/18
2/Lt. H. WILLIAMS.	6/10/17	13/12/18

NORTH STAFFORDSHIRE REGIMENT.
1st and 2nd Battalions.

Name	Missing	Interned		Repatriated
Lieut. L. J. JONES.	28/10/14	Holland	24/2/18	28/1/19
Lieut. J. ADAMS.		Holland	24/2/18	22/11/18
Lieut. J. R. WHYTE.		Switzerland	27/12/17	14/6/18
Capt. C. B. STARTIN.	21/3/18			10/12/18
Capt. D. M. SMYTH.	21/3/18			10/12/18
*2/Lt. R. MANSELL.	21/3/18			11/1/19
2/Lt. H. V. TATTERSALL.	21/3/18	(*Died* 22/4/18 at Halle).		
2/Lt. L. REDFERN.	21/3/18			11/12/18
2/Lt. F. J. SHUTT.	21/3/18			11/12/18

4th Battalion.

Name	Missing	Repatriated
†2/Lt. F. M. W. SIEMS.	3/11/17	3/12/18

*Attached T.M.B.   †Attached from 7th Londons.

NORTH STAFFORDSHIRE REGIMENT—continued.

5th Battalion.

Name.	Missing.	Interned.	Repatriated.
2/Lt. G. E. E. WILLIAMS.	14/3/17		7/1/18
2/Lt. P. B. ROSS.	1/7/17		6/12/18
2/Lt. R. F. JOHNSON.	1-5/7/17		6/12/18
Colonel H. JOHNSON.	21/3/18		8/12/18
Capt. T. E. TILDESLEY.	21/3/18		29/11/18
Capt. L. C. GRICE.	21/3/18		52/12/18
Capt. V. B. SHELLEY.	21/3/18		29/11/18
Capt. M. SETTLE.	21/3/18	(*Died* 23/12/18).	
2/Lt. G. L. KING.	21/3/18		3/12/18
2/Lt. A. M. JONES.	21/3/18		-/11/18
2/Lt. W. A. BERESFORD.	21/3/18		29/11/18
2/Lt. H. ST. J. B. WATSON.	21/3/18		11/12/18
2/Lt. F. R. TUNNICLIFFE.	21/3/18		29/11/18
2/Lt. L. M. McKNIGHT.	17/4/18		25/12/18

6th Battalion.

Name.	Missing.	Interned.		Repatriated.
2/Lt. G. D. COLLIS.	2/7/16	Holland	16/5/18	21/1/19
2/Lt. C. W. WHITEHURST.	2/7/16	Holland	16/5/18	22/11/18
Major O. J. F. KEATING.	21/3/18			29/11/18
*Capt. N. ST. C. PALMER.	21/3/18			13/12/18
Capt. C. W. SMITH.	21/3/18			10/12/18
Capt. G. ADAMS.	21/3/18			2/1/19
Lieut. G. P. RATHBONE.	21/3/18			5/12/18
†2/Lt. J. PAXTON.	21/3/18			13/12/18
†2/Lt. W. N. PRICE.	21/3/18			-/12/18
†2/Lt. J. S. COLBOURNE.	21/3/18			11/12/18
†2/Lt. S. P. HUDSON.	21/3/18			18/12/18
2/Lt. S. G. HOWE.	21/3/18			11/12/18
2/Lt. R. HEATON.	21/1/18			2/12/18
2/Lt. O. L. PAGET.	21/3/18			29/11/18
2/Lt. E. M. COPE.	21/3/18			25/12/18
‡2/Lt. J. C. V. JENNINGS.	21/3/18			6/12/18
2/Lt. P. H. BATCHELOR.	21/3/18	(*Died*).		
§2/Lt. A. C. IRVINE.	21/3/18			25/12/18
Capt. A. G. PAXTON.	15/4/18			25/12/18
Lieut. W. P. SHORT.	15/4/18			25/12/18
2/Lt. E. BENTLEY.	15/4/18			-/12/18
2/Lt. J. STANSBY.	-/-/16	Holland	16/5/18	22/12/18

8th Battalion.

Name.	Missing.	Interned.		Repatriated.
2/Lt. T. MAUGHFLING.	17-20/11/16	Switzerland	27/12/17	24/3/18
Lt. Col. C. L. ANDERSSON.	18/11/16	Switzerland	27/12/17	-/2/19
Capt. G. C. JAMES.	18/11/16			17/12/18
2/Lt. G. S. CARVER.	24/3/18			3/12/18

YORK AND LANCASTER REGIMENT.
1st Battalion.

Name.	Missing.	Interned.		Repatriated.
Lieut. G. C. R. MARTIN.	20/10/14	Holland	6/2/18	
		(*Died* 12/9/18).		
Lieut. S. H. TAYLOR.	20/10/14	Holland	6/2/18	18/11/18

*Attached from Hertfordshire Regiment.   †Attached from Warwickshire Regiment.
‡Attached from K.O.R.L.   §Attached from Border Regiment.

YORK AND LANCASTER REGIMENT—continued.

2nd Battalion.

Name.	Missing.	Interned.		Repatriated.
Capt. W. E. SHEPHERD.	21/3/18			—/12/18
2/Lt. H. CAMERON.	21/3/18			13/12/18
2/Lt. F. J. W. LYONS.	21/3/18			18/12/18
2/Lt. E. MERRALL.	21/3/18			17/12/18
2/Lt. W. R. MUFF.	21/3/18			2/12/18
2/Lt. A. L. NORMAN.	21/3/18			3/12/18
*2/Lt. A. RACE.	21/3/18			3/12/18
†2/Lt. H. SINGLETON.	21/3/18			23/10/18
2/Lt. M. J. WHITEHEAD.	21/3/18			2/12/18

4th Battalion.

Name.	Missing.	Interned.		Repatriated.
Lieut. C. UTLEY.	12/4/18			1/12/18
Lieut. E. A. HOLMES.	14/4/18			2/12/18
Lieut. R. H. WALKER.	14/4/18			2/12/18
Lieut. J. D. M. MORTON.	13/10/18			24/11/18
2/Lt. S. E. WARBURTON.	13/10/18			27/11/18

5th Battalion.

Name.	Missing.	Interned.		Repatriated.
Lieut. J. HAIGH.	2/7/16	Holland	16/5/18	22/11/18
2/Lt. H. M. GREENHOW.	7/7/16	Holland	16/5/18	18/11/18
Capt. A. S. FURNISS.	22/2/17	Holland	7/5/18	23/10/18
Lieut. A. H. HICKS.	22/2/17			31/12/18
*2/Lt. L. M. C. COLLINS.	9/1/18			27/11/18
2/Lt. E. COOKE.	26/3/18			14/12/18
2/Lt. J. W. KIRKBY.	11/4/18			3/12/18
Capt. J. W. BEAUMONT.	13/10/18			3/12/18

6th Battalion.

Name.	Missing.	Interned.		Repatriated.
Lieut. A. S. C. BARNARD.	9/10/17			6/12/18

9th Battalion.

Name.	Missing.	Interned.		Repatriated.
2/Lt. F. KEMPTON.	15/6/18			20/11/18

10th Battalion.

Name.	Missing.	Interned.		Repatriated.
Lieut. G. J. WHITAKER.	26/9/15	Holland	19/4/18	18/11/18
2/Lt. H. D. HUGHES.	21/3/18			18/12/18

13th Battalion.

Name.	Missing.	Interned.		Repatriated.
Lieut. F. H. WESTBY.	26/3/18			10/12/18
2/Lt. C. S. SMITH.	12/4/18			—/12/18

DURHAM LIGHT INFANTRY.

2nd Battalion.

Name.	Missing.	Interned.	Repatriated.
Major G. SOPWITH.	21/3/18		14/12/18
Capt. E. FAWCETT.	21/3/18		29/11/18
Capt. M. P. GRIFFITH-JONES.	21/3/18		3/12/18
Capt. H. A. PICKERING.	21/3/18		29/11/18
Lieut. MILES HUTCHINSON.	21/3/18		25/12/18
Lieut. R. M. HOGG.	21/3/18	(*Died* 1/4/18 at Cologne).	
Lieut. E. W. TUFFS.	21/3/18		18/12/18

* Attached from West Riding Regiment. † Attached from East Lancashire Regiment.

DURHAM LIGHT INFANTRY—continued.

2nd Battalion—continued.

Name.	Missing.	Interned.	Repatriated.
Lieut. L. A. HARTSHORN.	21/3/18	(*Died* 26/3/18 at Zancourt).	
Lieut. W. HENDERSON.	21/3/18		
2/Lt. K. E. ALEXANDER.	21/3/18		-/1/19
2/Lt. N. BROWN.	21/3/18		29/11/18
2/Lt. J. J. LUNN.	21/3/18		
2/Lt. H. H. CARMICHAEL.	21/3/18		29/11/18
2/Lt. J. E. ECCLES.	22/3/18		17/12/18
2/Lt. M. R. PINKNEY.	28/3/18		6/12/18
*Lieut. L. SILBURN.	24/9/18		8/12/18

5th Battalion.

Name.	Missing.	Interned.	Repatriated.
2/Lt. A. E. W. PEREIRA	23/4/17		25/12/18
2/Lt. H. J. W. SCOTT	23/3/18		12/10/18
Capt. L. W. TAYLOR.	27/3/18		25/12/18
Lieut. J. N. SLACK.	27/3/18		10/12/18
Lieut. G. F. ROWE.	11/4/18		25/12/18
2/Lt. C. L. HADDON.	11/4/18		18/12/18
Capt. F. W. B. JOHNSON.	27/5/18		-/12/18
Capt. A. B. HILL.	27/5/18		-/12/18
Lieut. R. W. B. ROBINSON.	27/5/18		30/12/18
Lieut. O. J. WILLIAMS.	27/5/18		13/12/18
Lieut. A. L. B. CHILDE.	27/5/18		31/12/18
†Lieut. J. LEIGH.	27/5/18		2/1/19
†2/Lt. K. McN. PHILLIPS.	27/5/18		2/1/19
†2/Lt. W. S. WRAY.	27/5/18		-/12/18
2/Lt. R. J. HADDON.	27/5/18		30/12/18
2/Lt. E. J. LOWES.	27/5/18	(*Died* 2/6/18 at Liesse).	
‡2/Lt. P. GODDING.	27/5/18		6/12/18
§P2/Lt. W. S. KIRKUP.	27/5/18		30/12/18
Lieut. W. A. CAMPBELL.	21/7/18		30/12/18

6th Battalion.

Name.	Missing.	Interned.	Repatriated.
2/Lt. A. DOBSON.	31/3/18		18/12/18
2/Lt. R. RAILTON.	9/4/18		11/12/18
Capt. P. H. Bowes LYON.	27/5/18		18/12/18
‡Lieut. L. W. WILSON.	27/5/18		-/12/18
‡2/Lt. T. F. GRAVES.	27/5/18		-/12/18
Lieut. G. P. RUDGE.	27/5/18		30/12/18
Lieut. G. D. ROBERTS.	27/5/18		13/12/18
Lieut. R. GREEN.	27/5/18		25/12/18
2/Lt. A. B. GILES.	27/5/18		13/12/18
2/Lt. J. L. GOTT.	27/5/18		25/12/18
2/Lt. G. A. GRAY.	27/5/18		-/12/18
§2/Lt. H. C. HOWELL.	27/5/18		31/12/18
§2/Lt. B. HOWARTH.	27/5/18		17/12/18
2/Lt. W. E. G. PRIEST.	27/5/18		-/12/18
2/Lt. N. B. THOMPSON.	27/5/18		17/12/18
2/Lt. C. BROWN.	27/5/18		-/12/18
2/Lt. A. S. BOSTOCK.	27/5/18		17/12/18
**Lieut. C. H. SYMES.	28/5/18		31/12/18

* Attached from A.S.C.
† Attached from Northumberland Fusiliers.
‡ Attached from Royal Irish Rifles.
§ Attached from Border Regiment.
** Attached from Gloucesters.

DURHAM LIGHT INFANTRY—continued.

7th Battalion.

Name.	Missing.	Interned.	Repatriated.
Lieut. A. V. GRAYSTON.			29/11/18
2/Lt. G. NIXON.	29/3/18		18/12/18
Lieut. F. W. R. NESBITT.	11/4/18	(*Died* 19/4/18 at Lille).	
Capt. L. BENNETT.	27/5/18		17/12/18
Capt. W. F. LAING.	27/5/18		-/12/18
Capt. H. H. JOSEPH.	27/5/18		6/12/18
*pCapt. R. W. W. PARKER.	27/5/18		14/12/18
Lieut. R. V. ILES.	27/5/18		31/12/18
Lieut. G. W. BOSUSTOW.	25/7/18		-/12/18
Lieut. P. WALKER.	27/5/18		-/12/18
Lieut. F. GRAHAM.	27/5/18		-/12/18
Lieut. J. P. B. GREY.	27/5/18		25/12/18
Lieut. L. J. FOSTER.	27/5/18		-/12/18
2/Lt. P. GIBSON.	27/5/18		-/12/18
2/Lt. F. C. MAJOR.	27/5/18		-/12/18
2/Lt. E. B. F. ARTHY.	27/5/18		13/12/18

8th Battalion.

Name.	Missing.	Interned.		Repatriated.
Major J. R. RITSON.	27/4/15	Holland	23/3/18	1/11/18
Capt. W. H. COULSON.	27/4/15	Holland	17/8/18	23/10/18
Lieut. G. E. BLACKETT.	27/4/15	Holland	23/3/18	1/11/18
Lieut. E. A. LEYBOURNE.	27/4/15			3/12/17
Lieut. C. SAYER.	27/4/15	(*Died* 7/6/15).		
Lieut. J. L. WOOD.	27/4/15	Holland	19/3/18	18/11/18
2/Lt. J. O. WILSON.	27/4/15	Holland	19/3/18	4/10/18
2/Lt. D. H. RICHARDSON.	27/4/15	(*Died* 31/5/15).		
2/Lt. A. W. NESBITT.	27/4/15	Holland	23/3/18	18/11/18
2/Lt. J. N. ROGERS.	27/4/15	Holland	19/3/18	22/11/18
Capt. R. BURDON.	21/3/18			2/12/18
Capt. H. J. MOWLAM.	28/3/18			12/10/18
2/Lt. W. J. RICHARDSON.	28/3/18			-/1/19
Lieut. A. RANSON.	10/4/18			29/11/18
2/Lt. H. I'ANSON.	10/4/18			8/12/18
Lieut. A. G. N. GREEN.	11/4/18			2/12/18
Capt. H. WILKINSON.	27/5/18			-/12/18
Capt. J. HUTCHINSON.	27/5/18			14/12/18
Capt. J. H. BURRELL.	27/5/18			-/12/18
Capt. J. W. E. TURNBULL.	27/5/18			-/12/18
Capt. R. H. WHARRIER.	27/5/18			14/12/18
Lieut. A. L. WILSON.	27/5/18			-/12/18
Lieut. F. ARKLESS.	27/5/18			-/12/18
Lieut. E. A. ARMBRISTER	27/5/18			25/12/18
Lieut. W. R. HILL.	27/5/18	(*Died* 6/11/18 at Stralsund).		
Lieut. M. HOPPER.	27/5/18			25/12/18
Lieut. E. A. PIKE.	27/5/18			-/12/18
†Lieut. A. N. MONTGOMERY.	27/5/18			31/12/18
†2/Lt. D. SLOANE.	27/5/18			31/12/18
†2/Lt. T. E. McQUISTON.	27/5/18			31/12/18
2/Lt. F. C. S. HARRISON	27/5/18			30/12/18
2/Lt. C. A. MACE.	27/5/18			15/12/18

* Attached from Army Cyclist Corps. † Attached from Royal Irish Rifles.

DURHAM LIGHT INFANTRY—continued.

9th Battalion.

Name.	Missing.	Interned.	Repatriated.
2/Lt. E. W. MANNERS.	5/11/16		21/12/18
2/Lt. L. A. HOWE.	5/11/16		18/12/18
2/Lt. T. E. COULSON.	5/11/16		18/12/18

11th Battalion.

Name.	Missing.	Interned.	Repatriated.
2/Lt. H. RUTHERFORD.	22/3/18		1/12/18
2/Lt. W. T. ALEXANDER.	22/3/18		18/12/18
*2/Lt. C. A. MORRIS.	22/3/18		18/12/18
2/Lt. W. G. CRAIG.	22/3/18	(*Died* at Graudenz).	
2/Lt. F. NAYLOR.	23/3/18		17/12/18
Lieut. R. BUSHELL.	29/3/18		1/12/18
2/Lt. D. E. ELLWOOD.	29/3/18		14/12/18
2/Lt. T. W. APPLEGARTH.	29/3/18	(*Died*).	

13th Battalion.

Name.	Missing.	Interned.	Repatriated.
2/Lt. E. A. CROSLAND.	6/4/16	Holland 30/4/18	18/11/18
2/Lt. F. AUDAS.	5/10/18		29/11/18

14th Battalion.

Name.	Missing.	Interned.	Repatriated.
2/Lt. C. E. BROGDEN.			25/12/18
*2/Lt. R. M. MALCOLM.	3/12/17		3/12/18
2/Lt. H. FORBES.	3/12/17		27/11/18

15th Battalion.

Name.	Missing.	Interned.	Repatriated.
2/Lt. A. SHEARER.	22/12/17		7/11/18
Capt. T. A. L. WELCH.	24/3/18		-/12/18
2/Lt. V. G. DAVIES.	27/5/18		30/12/18
2/Lt. F. BURGESS.	27/5/18		13/12/18
†2/Lt. E. JOICEY.	27/5/18		5/1/19
†2/Lt. A. E. FOSTER.	28/5/18		-/12/18
Capt. J. B. CUNNINGHAM.	24/8/18		29/11/18

20th Battalion.

Name.	Missing.	Interned.	Repatriated.
2/Lt. G. OLIVER.			3/12/18

22nd Battalion.

Name.	Missing.	Interned.	Repatriated.
Lieut. H. E. RAINE.			18/12/18
2/Lt. J. AITCHISON.	22/3/18		18/12/18
Lieut. J. H. PATTISON.	24/3/18		-/12/18
2/Lt. C. B. PICKARD.	25/3/18		-/1/19
2/Lt. W. H. O'DELL.	25/3/18		18/12/18
2/Lt. J. W. JAMIESON.	25/3/18		18/12/18
2/Lt. R. WHITE.	27/3/18		18/12/18
Capt. J. ATKINSON.	27/5/18		19/1/19
2/Lt. W. H. DAVIES.	27/5/18		25/12/18
2/Lt. C. H. LISTER.	27/5/18		-/12/18

29th Battalion.

Name.	Missing.	Interned.	Repatriated.
2/Lt. H. M. RIDLEY.	19/4/18	(*Died* 23/5/18 at Iseghem).	

* Attached from Border Regiment.
† Attached from Northumberland Fusiliers.

HIGHLAND LIGHT INFANTRY.

1st and 2nd Battalions.

Name.	Missing.		Interned.	Repatriated.
Lieut. D. D. BARRY.	21/12/14	Holland	1/3/18	18/11/18
2/Lt. T. A. GRAY.	27/1/15	Holland	1/3/18	14/12/18
Lieut. W. ROLLO.	26/9/15	Holland	6/2/18	28/11/18
2/Lt. J. F. HOLMS.	25/2/17			29/11/18
Capt M. A. KINCAID-SMITH.	24/3/18			13/12/18
Capt. W. NEILSON.	24/3/18			25/12/18
Lieut. W. J. DONELLY.	24/3/18			–/12/18
*Capt. J. GILLIES.				29/11/18

5th Battalion.

Name.	Missing.	Repatriated.
2/Lt. P. F. LEITH.	–/3/18	18/12/18
Capt. R. M. MILLER.	24/8/18	13/12/18
Lieut. J. W. PARR.	24/8/18	13/12/18
2/Lt. J. McKIE.	24/8/18	13/12/18

9th Battalion.

Name.	Missing.	Repatriated.
2/Lt. W. M. ANDREW.	20/5/17	8/12/18
2/Lt. A. G. M. WATT.	12/4/18	11/12/18
Lieut. T. H. DICKIE.	29/9/18	28/11/18
2/Lt. R. MENZIES.	29/9/18	28/11/18
Lieut. J. R. PATERSON.	26/10/18	8/12/18

10th Battalion.

Name.	Missing.	Repatriated.
2/Lt. M. G. HOOD.	21/3/18	29/11/18
2/Lt. M. G. CAMPBELL.	22/3/18	18/12/18
Lieut. A. McKAY.	31/8/18	29/11/18

10/11th Battalions.

Name.	Missing.	Repatriated.
2/Lt. C. D. THOMSON.	1/8/17	14/12/18
2/Lt. A. W. GILL.	1/8/17	14/12/18
2/Lt. K. D. McNEILL.	1/8/17	17/12/18
2/Lt. J. C. WHYTE.	1/8/17	13/12/18
Capt. H. T. KINLOCH.	22/3/18	1/12/18
Lieut. J. B. BLACK.	22/3/18	3/12/18
2/Lt. W. D. WHITE.	22/3/18	6/12/18
2/Lt. L. A. SHUTTE.	22/3/18	21/12/18
†2/Lt. R. F. FRANCIS.	22/3/18	21/12/18
2/Lt. I. D. MacNEILL.	25/3/18	14/1/18
Capt. T. CHRISTIE.	9/4/18	3/12/18
Lieut. R. A. CUTHBERTSON.	9/4/18	29/11/19
Lieut. A. A. BOWMAN.	9/4/18	29/11/18
Lieut. D. STALKER.	9/4/18	8/12/18
2/Lt. P. HUGHES.	9/4/18	3/12/18
‡2/Lt. J. ELLIS.	9/4/18	29/11/18

12th Battalion.

Name.	Missing.	Repatriated.
Lieut. J. HUNTER.	25/3/18	10/12/18

* Attached T.M.B.
† Attached from Suffolks.　　‡ Attached from Lovat's Scouts.

HIGHLAND LIGHT INFANTRY—continued.
14th Battalion.

Name.	Missing.	Interned.	Repatriated.
2/Lt. J. BEVERIDGE.	24/11/17		3/12/18
Capt. G. C. SMITH.	26/11/17		22/12/18
Lieut. R. HADDOCK.	26/11/17		3/6/18
2/Lt. W. B. McGEORGE.	26/11/17		2/1/19
2/Lt. A. R. SCLANDERS.	26/11/17		3/12/18
2/Lt. A. WATT.	26/11/17		3/12/18
2/Lt. H. W. M. THOMAS.	26/11/17		3/12/18
2/Lt. G. E. B. McINDOE.	26/11/17		31/10/18
2/Lt. F. G. McLEOD.	26/11/17		3/12/18
2/Lt. S. SOUDEN.	26/11/17		3/12/18
Capt. J. G. B. WALKER.	25/3/18		10/12/18
2/Lt. KENNETH REID.	3/4/18		4/12/18
Capt. R. D. BLACKLEDGE.	9/4/18		8/12/18
Capt. H. N. S. MUMMERY.	9/4/18	(*Died* 6/8/18 at Pforzheim).	
Capt. H. Y. G. HENDERSON.	9/4/18		10/12/18
Lieut. G. W. WOTHERSPOON.	9/4/18		29/11/18
Lieut. G. L. DICKSON.	9/4/18		18/12/18
Lieut. A. C. CURLE.	9/4/18		8/12/18
2/Lt. J. S. ROBERTSON.	9/4/18		3/12/18
2/Lt. J. C. PICKEN.	9/4/18		3/12/18
2/Lt. C. C. JENNINGS.	9/4/18		10/12/18
2/Lt. J. D. EDWARD.	9/4/18	(*Died* 26/4/18).	

15th Battalion.

Name.	Missing.	Interned.		Repatriated.
Capt. W. T. MITCHELL.	3/7/16	Holland	16/5/18	22/11/18
2/Lt. H. A. ADAMSON.	4/3/17			

16th Battalion.

Name.	Missing.	Repatriated.
Lieut. A. SKENE.	18/11/16	4/12/18
2/Lt. J. STEWART.	18/11/16	17/12/18
2/Lt. F. SCOTT.	18/11/16	17/12/18
2/Lt. M. M. LYON.		29/11/18

SEAFORTH HIGHLANDERS.
2nd Battalion.

Name.	Missing.	Repatriated.
2/Lt. J. TOOTHILL.	23/10/18	27/11/18

4th Battalion.

Name.	Missing.	Repatriated.
Capt. T. H. PEVERELL.	21/11/17	19/5/18
2/Lt. G. M. COOPER.	22/3/18	18/12/18
Capt. F. W. BROWN.	23/3/18	1/12/18
Capt. P. C. KNIGHT.	23/3/18	10/12/18
Lieut. A. MACRAE.	23/3/18	25/12/18
2/Lt. J. DAVIDSON.	23/3/18	9/1/19
2/Lt. W. WEIR.	11/4/18	11/12/18
*Major M. JOBSON.	12/4/18	(*Died* at Tourcoing 3/5/18).
Lieut. J. A. HERMON.	28/10/18	30/12/18
2/Lt. C. T. BOYD.	28/10/18	27/11/18

* Attached from King's Own Scottish Borderers.

SEAFORTH HIGHLANDERS—continued.

5th Battalion.

Name.	Missing.	Interned.	Repatriated.
Capt. J. R. BLACK.	21/3/18		28/11/18
Capt. R. F. SINCLAIR.	21/3/18		–/1/19
Lieut. L. A. MEREDITH.	21/3/18		13/12/18
2/Lt. A. MOWAT.	23/3/18		11/12/18
2/Lt. W. NOBLE.	10/4/18		18/12/18
2/Lt. I. G. MACDONALD.	11/4/18		–/12/18
Lieut. J. B. SIMPSON.	12/4/18		2/12/18

2/5th Battalions.

Name.	Missing.	Interned.	Repatriated.
Lieut. G. CUMMING.	12/4/18		29/11/18

6th Battalion.

Name.	Missing.	Interned.	Repatriated.
2/Lt. J. W. BLAIR.	12/12/16		17/12/18
Capt. W. LEGGE.	23–25/4/17		31/12/18
Capt. W. R. PETRIE.	23–25/4/17		14/12/18
Lieut. D. M. FORSYTH.	23–25/4/17		31/12/18
2/Lt. P. MOTTRAM.	15/5/17		6/12/18
Major W. H. DOIG.	25/3/18		18/12/18
Capt. L. FRASER.	25/3/18		–/12/18
Capt. W. STEWART.	25/3/18	(*Died* at Beaulencourt)	
2/Lt. A. A. GUNN.	25/3/18		29/12/18
Lieut. S. C. M. DOUGLAS.	11/4/18		–/12/18
Lieut. H. OLIVER.	11/4/18		11/12/18
2/Lt. R. F. CUMMING.	11/4/18		25/12/18
2/Lt. R. A. L. FRASER-MACKENZIE.	11/4/18		13/12/18
2/Lt. A. F. HEDLEY.	11/4/18		2/12/18
Lieut. W. M. ASHER.	12/4/18		12/12/18
2/Lt. J. MACDONALD.	12/4/18		18/12/18
2/Lt. C. W. STEWART.	12/4/18		18/12/18

7th Battalion.

Name.	Missing.	Interned.	Repatriated.
Lieut. R. A. BEGG.	21/3/18		10/12/18
Lieut. J. W. M. MACKAY.	23/3/18		18/12/18
2/Lt. M. MOWAT.	24/3/18		18/12/18

8th Battalion.

Name.	Missing.	Interned.	Repatriated.
2/Lt. A. McKENZIE.	8/7/17		27/11/18
Lieut. R. F. W. PATRICK.	28/7/18		13/12/18

9th Battalion.

Name.	Missing.	Interned.	Repatriated.
Lieut. J. H. ANDERSON.	24/3/18		–/12/18

GORDON HIGHLANDERS.

1st and 2nd Battalions.

Name.	Missing.	Interned.		Repatriated.
Colonel F. H. NEISH.	10/9/14	Switzerland	12/8/16	11/9/17
Colonel W. E. GORDON.	10/9/14		Exchanged	25/1/16
Major C. J. SIMPSON.	10/9/14	Switzerland	19/1/17	13/9/17
Capt. W. NEISH.	10/9/14	Holland	6/2/18	22/11/18
Capt. Hon. A. A. FRASER.	10/9/14	Holland	22/1/18	22/11/18
Capt. H. L. PELHAM BURN.	10/9/14	Holland	22/1/18	–/12/18

GORDON HIGHLANDERS—continued.
1st and 2nd Battalions.—continued.

Name.	Missing.	Interned.		Repatriated.
Capt. I. PICTON-WARLOW.	10/9/14	Holland	22/1/18	22/11/18
Capt. F. BELL.	10/9/14	Switzerland	–/12/17	23/12/18
Lieut. A. D. L. STEWART.	10/9/14	Holland	22/1/18	23/10/18
Lieut. D. W. HUNTER-BLAIR.	10/9/14	Holland	6/2/18	23/11/18
Lieut. J. F. H. HOULDSWORTH.	10/9/14	Holland	6/2/18	23/10/18
Lieut. I. B. M. HAMILTON.	10/9/14	Holland	6/2/18	16/11/18
2/Lt. R. D. GILLESPIE.	10/9/14	Holland	1/3/18	9/1/19
2/Lt. A. W. M. ROBERTSON.		Holland	6/2/18	22/11/18
Lieut. C. M. USHER.	16/9/14	Holland	22/1/18	18/11/18
Capt. M. H. O. FORBES.	24/10/14	Holland	24/2/18	18/11/18
Capt. G. H. G. FOWKE.	24/10/14	Holland	24/2/18	18/11/18
Lieut. H. S. KEVILLE-DAVIES.	24/10/14	Holland	24/2/18	23/9/18
Lieut. A. E. S. MILLER-STERLING.	24/10/14	Holland	24/2/18	18/11/18
Lieut. J. F. J. WATSON.	24/10/14	Holland	24/2/18	18/11/18
2/Lt. G. W. NELSON.	18/7/16	Switzerland	13/12/16	13/9/17
Capt. I. CUMMING.	21/3/18			18/12/18
2/Lt. A. THOMPSON.	28/3/18			30/12/18
2/Lt. G. N. McLEAN.	31/10/14			14/1/19

4th Battalion.

Name.	Missing.	Interned.	Repatriated.
2/Lt. W. ADDISON.	26/9/15	Holland	18/11/18
2/Lt. J. CAMPBELL.	21/3/18		19/12/18
2/Lt. W. A. N. ROSS.	22/3/18		1/12/18
2/Lt. J. T. STEPHEN.	22/3/18		11/12/18
2/Lt. W. PRING.	22/3/18		11/12/18
2/Lt. A. MILNE.	22/3/18		28/11/18
Lieut. G. L. ALLARDYCE.	20/10/18		1/12/18
Lieut. R. T. L. MITCHELL.	27/10/18	(*Died* 30/11/18 at Louvain).	
2/Lt. A. CLARK.	27/10/18		3/12/18

5th Battalion.

Name.	Missing.	Interned.	Repatriated.
*Lt. Col. M. F. McTAGGART.	20–21/3/18		–/12/18
Major C. T. A. ROBERTSON.	21/3/18	(*Died* 23/3/18).	
Capt. A. KELLY.	21/3/18		29/11/18
2/Lt. W. ENDSON.	21/3/18		29/11/18
2/Lt. A. CRUDEN.	21/3/18		13/12/18
2/Lt. J. J. CHALMERS.	21/3/18		20/11/18
2/Lt. W. GORDON.	21/3/18		18/12/18
†2/Lt. A. G. McPHAIL.	21/3/18		–/12/18
2/Lt. A. R. MURRAY.	21/3/18		2/12/18
2/Lt. J. MORT.	21/3/18		19/12/18
2/Lt. C. W. HODGINS.	21/3/18		18/12/18
2/Lt. G. HENDERSON.	21/3/18		13/12/18

6th Battalion.

Name.	Missing.	Interned.		Repatriated.
Lieut. J. B. TURNBULL.	26/9/15	Holland	–/4/18	22/11/18
Lieut. A. G. McLEAN.				2/12/18
2/Lt. T. B. TURNER.	21/3/18			2/12/18
2/Lt. B. CARRE.	21/3/18			5/1/19
Major C. E. CORNWALL.	25/3/18			21/12/18
2/Lt. G. RUTHERFORD.	25/3/18			11/12/18
Capt. J. R. CHRISTIE.	10/4/18			17/12/18
Lieut. P. W. LYON.	10/4/18			3/12/18
2/Lt. A. D. MILLER.	10/4/18			5/12/18

* Attached from 5th Lancers. † Attached from Black Watch.

GORDON HIGHLANDERS—continued.

7th Battalion.

Name.	Missing.	Interned.	Repatriated.
*Lieut. W. H. BURGESS.	21/3/18		13/12/18
*Lieut. W. N. BUYERS.	21/3/18		12/12/18
*2/Lt. N. K. ROBSON.	21/3/18		–/12/18
Capt. B. M. HENDERSON.	22/3/18		
Lieut. G. H. E. HAZLEWOOD.	22/3/18		10/12/18
2/Lt. J. C. E. MURRAY.	22/3/18		11/12/18
2/Lt. G. J. ROBERTSON.	22/3/18		11/12/18
2/Lt. H. G. FRYER.	22/3/18		2/12/18
2/Lt. R. I. MAPLETON.	22/3/18		11/12/18
Lieut. J. J. FERGUSON.	25/3/18		18/12/18
†2/Lt. B. A. MORRIS.	25/3/18		18/12/18
2/Lt. D. W. MILNE.	25/3/18		18/12/18
2/Lt. A. S. CLARK.	25/3/18		18/12/18
2/Lt. W. J. M. BROWN.	25/5/18		–/1/19

8th Battalion.

Name.	Missing.	Interned.	Repatriated.
Lieut. W. C. L. SMITH.	9/11/15	(*Died* 10/11/15).	

10th Battalion.

Name.	Missing.	Interned.	Repatriated.
†Lieut. R. S. KNOX.	28/3/18		10/12/18
2/Lt. A. CANTLAY.	24/5/18		–/12/18

CAMERON HIGHLANDERS.

1st and 2nd Battalions.

Name.	Missing.	Interned.	Repatriated.
Major G. SOREL-CAMERON.	Holland	24/2/18	23/10/18
Capt. Lord J. T. STEWART-MURRAY.		Holland 1/3/18	21/1/19
Lieut. J. R. CUMMING.		Holland 24/2/18	3/1/19
Major D. A. NICHOLSON.		(*Died* 25/9/15 at Crefeld).	
Capt. L. NAPIER.	22/7/16	(*Died*).	

4th Battalion.

Name.	Missing.	Interned.	Repatriated.
*Lieut. W. FALCONER.	28/3/18		18/12/18

5th Battalion.

Name.	Missing.	Interned.	Repatriated.
Lieut. D. H. SOUTAR.	22/3/18		10/12/18
Capt. W. H. RIACH.	23/3/18	(*Died* 5/5/18).	
Lieut. W. ELLIOT.	25/4/18		13/12/18
Lieut. H. H. T. DAVIES.	25/4/18		14/12/18
Lieut. J. McINNES.	29/4/18		4/12/18

6th Battalion.

Name.	Missing.	Interned.	Repatriated.
Capt. H. S. WALKER.	27/2/16	Holland	16/5/18
2/Lt. G. HAMILTON.	31/7/17		13/5/18
2/Lt. F. S. SANDEMAN.	1/8/17		1/12/18
2/Lt. A. G. McGRUER.	1/8/17		17/12/18
2/Lt. J. R. MacKAY.	1/8/17		1/12/18
2/Lt. J. G. GIBSON.	1/8/17	(*Died* 12/9/17 at Langensalza).	
‡2/Lt. T. P. PHILLIPS.	26/3/18		8/12/18
Lieut. A. D. MILLIGAN.	28/3/18		–/12/18
2/Lt. J. W. DOGHERTY.	28/3/18		2/12/18
‡2/Lt. G. R. JOHNSTONE.	28/3/18		13/12/18

* Attached T.M.B.
† Attached from Royal Scots.
‡ Attached from 14th Londons (London Scottish).

CAMERON HIGHLANDERS—continued.
7th Battalion.

Name.	Missing.	Interned.		Repatriated.
Capt. E. K. CAMERON.	26/9/15	Holland	7/10/18	8/12/18
2/Lt. D. TAYLOR.	18/7/16	Holland	—/6/18	22/11/18
2/Lt. A. C. McCUISH.	23/12/16			17/12/18
2/Lt. Lacplan McLEOD.	23/3/18			1/12/18
*2/Lt. H. R. RENNIE.	28/3/18	(*Died* 10/7/18 at Posen).		
*2/Lt. P. DRUMMOND.	28/3/18			—/1/19
2/Lt. J. S. McNAB.	28/3/18			1/12/18
2/Lt. J. A. DONALD.	28/3/18			25/12/18
2/Lt. T. S. DENHOLM.	28/3/18	(*Died* 5/4/18 at Douai).		
2/Lt. W. F. GRIEVE.	28/3/18			1/12/18

11th Battalion.

2/Lt. I. CAMPBELL.	17/9/18			8/12/18

ROYAL IRISH RIFLES.
1st and 2nd Battalions.

Name	Missing	Interned		Repatriated
Lieut. Qmr. W. CLARKE.	10/9/14	Holland	5/1/18	28/10/18
Capt. A. T. JONSSON.	27/10/14	Holland	6/2/18	18/11/18
Lieut. F. L. FINLAY.	27/10/14	Holland	24/2/18	19/12/18
Major H. R. CHARLEY.	21/3/15			11/9/17
2/Lt. A. DAVISON.	23/10/17			3/12/18
Lieut. S. H. WALKER.	21/3/18			6/12/18
Capt. J. C. BRYANS.	24/3/18			29/11/18
Lieut. J. K. BOYLE.	24/3/18	(*Died* —/—/18 at Cologne).		
2/Lt. E. C. STROHM.	24/3/18			11/12/18
2/Lt. A. W. WALKER.	2/10/18			8/12/18
2/Lt. A. A. L. MacMANUS.	2/10/18			13/12/18
2/Lt. J. T. GARDINER.	21/10/18			

6th Battalion.

2/Lt. L. J. ROSS.	27/5/18			31/12/18

8th Battalion.

Lieut. S. HUNTER.	29/11/15	Holland	19/4/18	18/11/18
2/Lt. S. W. MAXWELL.	1/7/16	(*Died*).		

9th Battalion.

Capt. J. H. BERRY.	1/7/16			11/9/17
Lieut. L. N. RICHARDSON.	1/7/16	Switzerland	9/12/17	9/12/18
2/Lt. K. W. GOULD.	1/7/16	Switzerland	27/12/17	14/6/18
Lieut. R. H. MORTON.	2/7/16	Holland	16/5/18	22/11/18
2/Lt. A. W. HENRY.	27/3/18			25/12/18

10th Battalion.

2/Lt. F. A. J. DAVIDSON.	9/10/16			7/1/18
Lieut.-Qmr. C. H. T. DAWSON.	24/3/18	(*Died*).		

11th Battalion.

Major Adam JENKINS.	1/7/16			11/9/17
Capt. C. C. CRAIG.	1/7/16	Holland	15/6/18	4/10/18
Lieut. E. VANCE.	1/7/16	(*Died* 15/7/16).		
2/Lt. J. W. SALTER.	1/7/16	Holland	16/5/18	22/11/18

* Attached from 14th London (London Scottish).

ROYAL IRISH RIFLES—continued.
11/13th Battalions.

Name.	Missing.	Interned.	Repatriated.
2/Lt. W. T. W. ELLIOT.	28/3/18		19/12/18
2/Lt. J. S. ADAIR.	28/3/18		25/12/18

12th Battalion.

Name	Missing	Interned	Repatriated
2/Lt. W. A. HAYDEN.	16/8/17		17/12/18
Major A. H. HALL.	21/3/18		28/11/18
Capt. L. J. JOHNSTON.	21/3/18		8/12/18
Capt. H. ST. J. MORRISON.	21/3/18		18/12/18
Capt. T. S. ADAMSON.	21/3/18		–/11/18
Lieut. T. A. BLACKWOOD.	21/3/18		29/11/18
Lieut. T. H. WILSON.	21/3/18		10/12/18
2/Lt. A. SMITH.	21/3/18		11/12/18
2/Lt. H. D. SWAYNE.	21/3/18		28/11/18
2/Lt. J. BURNSIDE.	21/3/18		25/12/18
2/Lt. R. J. RAGGETT.	21/3/18		25/12/18
2/Lt. A. T. BELL.	21/3/18		28/11/18
2/Lt. J. ROBINSON.	21/3/18		11/12/18
2/Lt. H. F. WALDEN.	21/3/18		11/12/18
2/Lt. A. H. OSBOROUGH.	21/3/18		11/12/18
*2/Lt. W. F. IRVINE.	21/3/18		11/12/18
2/Lt. J. A. C. KENNEDY.	21/3/18		6/12/18
†2/Lt. E. W. JOHNSTON.	21/3/18		25/12/18
2/Lt. T. SHEARER.	21/3/13		11/12/18
2/Lt. J. G. MALONE.	21/3/18		8/12/18
2/Lt. J. MORTON.	21/3/18		29/11/18
2/Lt. H. L. WEIR.	21/3/18	(*Died* / /18 at Cologne).	
2/Lt. R. MONTEITH.	22/3/18		28/11/18
2/Lt. H. L. KEMPSON.	23/3/18		17/12/18
2/Lt. W. FERGUSON.	23/3/18		29/11/18
2/Lt. H. YOUNG.	15/4/18		5/12/18

13th Battalion.

Name	Missing	Interned	Repatriated
2/Lt. R. C. KINNIBURGH.	1/7/16	Holland 16/5/18	1/2/19
2/Lt. D. J. McGILTON.	21/3/18		6/12/18
Capt. R. M. PRYDE.	24/3/18		6/12/18

14th Battalion.

Name	Missing	Interned	Repatriated
2/Lt. R. V. GRACEY.	1/7/16		13/9/17
Lieut. A. J. E. GIBSON.	23/3/18		13/12/18
Lieut. D. B. TAYLOR.	24/3/18		18/12/18

15th Battalion.

Name	Missing	Interned	Repatriated
2/Lt. J. BARRY BROWN.	5/7/16	Switzerland 19/12/16	23/12/18
2/Lt. H. G. BUCHANAN.	22/11/17		3/12/18
Colonel C. G. COLE-HAMILTON.	21/3/18		14/12/18
Capt. J. H. STEWART.	21/3/18		6/12/18
Capt. J. E. S. CONDON.	21/3/18		6/12/18
Lieut. W. WILSON.	21/3/18		6/12/18
Lieut. S. A. LYNCH.	21/3/18		6/12/18
Lieut. W. CLARKE.	21/3/18		25/12/18
2/Lt. S. C. HUGHES.	21/3/18		6/12/18
2/Lt. P. HILDER.	21/3/18		4/12/18
2/Lt. L. K. REID.	21/3/18		6/12/18

* Attached from Royal Irish Fusiliers.   † Attached T.M.B.

ROYAL IRISH RIFLES—continued.
15th Battalion—continued.

Name.	Missing.	Interned.	Repatriated.
2/Lt. H. G. CARDOZO.	21/3/18		6/12/18
2/Lt. J. ARMSTRONG.	21/3/18		14/12/18
2/Lt. A. SCOTT.	21/3/18		6/12/18
2/Lt. C. P. SEATH.	21/3/18		11/12/18
2/Lt. R. SPROTT.	21/3/18		6/12/18
2/Lt. J. K. WYLIE.	21/3/18		14/12/18
2/Lt. C. HIND.	23-25/3/18		-/12/18
2/Lt. A. E. TODD.	31/3/18		6/12/18

16th Battalion.

Name.	Missing.	Interned.	Repatriated.
2/Lt. J. W. FURBISHER.	21/3/18		28/11/18
2/Lt. J. H. K. FREELAND.	21/3/18		28/11/18
2/Lt. E. CROKER.	21/3/18		28/11/18
2/Lt. G. A. DAY.	21/3/18		10/12/18
2/Lt. W. Q. REA.	21/3/18		17/12/18
2/Lt. W. H. K. GIBSON.	21/3/18		28/11/18
2/Lt. N. F. IRWIN.	21/3/18		14/12/18
2/Lt. C. HALLINAN.	21/3/18		14/12/18

17th Battalion.

Name.	Missing.	Interned.	Repatriated.
2/Lt. W. C. HATHERALL.	27/5/18		31/12/18

ROYAL IRISH FUSILIERS.
1st Battalion.

Name.	Missing.	Interned.	Repatriated.
Major R. A. GRAY.	17/9/14	Holland 6/2/18	18/11/18
Lieut. H. A. H. WARNOCK.	13/8/15	(*Died* 16/8/15 at Bapaume).	
Lieut. A. V. OLPHERT.		Holland 24/2/18	21/1/19
Lieut. J. POLLACK.	11/4/17		8/1/18
2/Lt. E. E. HARRIS.	11/4/17	(*Died* 21/4/17 at Julich).	
2/Lt. C. M. HARRIS.	3/5/17		6/12/18
Capt. W. W. NEVILLE.	21/3/18		25/12/18
Capt. G. A. DEANE.	21/3/18	(*Died* 11/4/18).	
Lieut. W. D. BRADLEY.	21/3/18		1/12/18
2/Lt. G. H. LEMON.	21/3/18		25/12/18
2/Lt. T. F. HALL.	21/3/18		28/11/18
Colonel M. FURNELL.	26/3/18		2/12/18
Major S. U. L. CLEMENTS.	27/3/18		29/11/18
Capt. B. ST. J. GALVIN.	27/3/18		25/12/18
Lieut. B. J. EYRE.	27/3/18		25/12/18
Lieut. T. HOUSTON.	27/3/18		18/12/18
Lieut. H. GRAY.	27/3/18		-/12/18
2/Lt. T. S. HASWELL.	27/3/18		25/12/18
2/Lt. C. N. McKENNY.	27/3/18		25/12/18
2/Lt. R. M. MOORE.	27/3/18		-/12/18
2/Lt. R. E. GLOVER.	28/3/18		25/12/18
2/Lt. T. R. COGHLAN.	23/10/18		

2nd Battalion.

Name.	Missing.	Interned.	Repatriated.
2/Lt. L. J. HARRISON.	21/3/18	(*Died* -/4/18 at Germersheim).	

4th Battalion.

Name.	Missing.	Interned.	Repatriated.
2/Lt. J. F. CALDWELL.			18/12/18
2/Lt. O. B. McMANUS.	24/3/18		18/12/18

ROYAL IRISH FUSILIERS—continued.

Name.	Missing.	Interned.	Repatriated.
6th Battalion.			
2/Lt. R. L. V. WINTER.	21/3/18		25/12/18
Lieut. A. JOULE.	27/3/18		11/12/18
7th Battalion.			
Lieut. H. H. E. Q. COLES.	27/3/18		25/12/18
8th Battalion.			
2/Lt. J. H. DICKSON.	16/8/17		14/12/18
9th Battalion.			
2/Lt. D. H. WRIGHT.	16/8/17		14/12/18
2/Lt. C. J. T. PERKINS.	21/3/18		11/12/18
2/Lt. J. H. CONNOR.	22/3/18		25/12/18
Capt. T. SLATTER.	24/3/18		1/12/18
Capt. M. HENEHAN.	24/3/18		18/12/18
2/Lt. E. H. GILMER.	26/3/18		25/12/18
Lieut. G. I. O'F. JOHNSTON.	27/3/18		10/12/18
Lieut. J. J. McE. POLLOCK.	27/3/18		4/12/18
2/Lt. T. BREMNER.	27/3/18		18/12/18
2/Lt. N. CLARKE.	27/3/18		18/12/18
2/Lt. F. L. H. DONALDSON.	27/3/18		25/12/18
2/Lt. R. L. SMITH.	27/3/18		-/12/18
2/Lt. J. SCOTT.	27/3/18		25/12/18
2/Lt. G. HARDY.	12/4/18	(*Died* 31/4/18 at Kortryk).	
Capt. J. BENSON.	11/8/18		13/12/18
2/Lt. R. A. RICHEY.	30/9/18		13/12/18
12th Battalion.			
2/Lt. G. FOY.	23/3/18		17/12/18

CONNAUGHT RANGERS.

Name.	Missing.	Interned.	Repatriated.
1st and 2nd Battalions.			
Lieut. C. A. TURNER.	-/8/14		13/9/17
Lt.-Col. A. W. ABERCROMBIE.	10/9/14	(*Died* 25/11/15 at Magdeburg).	
Capt. W. G. S. BARKER.	10/9/14		Exchanged 29/6/15 (*Died*). 2/6/16
Capt. W. W. ROCHE.	10/9/14	Holland 6/2/18	10/1/19
Lieut. J. L. HARDY.	10/9/14		14/3/18
Lieut. W. H. REES.	20/10/14	Holland 6/2/18	28/11/18
2/Lt. H. S. KIRKWOOD.	21/3/18		31/12/18
5th Battalion.			
Lieut. H. J. SHANLEY.	10/10/18		8/12/18
2/Lt. H. MATTISON.	10/10/18		1/1/19
6th Battalion.			
2/Lt. P. L. N. GORDON-RALPH.	19/2/17		7/12/18
Capt. B. J. START.	21/3/18		17/12/18
Capt. R. ROUSSEL.	21/3/18		29/11/18
Lieut. J. A. V. KENT, M.C.	21/3/18		13/12/18
Lieut. A. RIBBONS.	21/3/18		14/12/18
2/Lt. H. E. HALL.	21/3/18		13/12/18
2/Lt. H. E. TAGGERT.	21/3/18		14/12/18

ARGYLL AND SUTHERLAND HIGHLANDERS.
1st and 2nd Battalions.

Name.	Missing.	Interned.		Repatriated.
Capt. A. J. H. MacLEAN.	6/9/14	Holland	24/1/18	1/11/18
Lieut. G. F. CONNAL ROWAN.	11/9/14	Holland	1/5/18	22/1/19
Capt. A. STIRLING.	11/9/14	Holland	1/5/18	1/2/19
Capt. M. G. SANDEMAN.	21/10/14	Holland	24/2/18	18/11/18
Lieut. C. L. CAMPBELL.	21/10/14	Holland	6/2/18	7/9/18
Capt. J. D. TYSON.	11/12/17			6/12/18
2/Lt. W. H. DUNCAN.	24/9/18			10/12/18
2/Lt. O. L. DUNLEY.	12/12/17			3/12/18

6th Battalion.

Name.	Missing.	Repatriated.
Capt. T. GREENLEES.	18/10/18	27/11/18

7th Battalion.

Name.	Missing.	Repatriated.
Capt. E. R. ORR.	22/11/17	25/12/18
Lieut. James McLAREN.	21/3/18	18/12/18
Capt. J. CUNNINGHAM.	23/3/18	3/12/18
2/Lt. T. GEMMELL.	23/3/18	(*Died* 7/5/18 at Valenciennes).
2/Lt. F. CAMERON.	23/3/18	25/12/18
Lieut. Wm. SCOTT.	25/3/18	11/12/18
Lieut. W. S. JOHNSTON.	21/3/18	(*Died* 23/3/18 at Inchy).
Major W. McCRACKEN.	27/5/18	13/12/18

8th Battalion.

Name.	Missing.	Repatriated.
2/Lt. A. D. HUMBLE.	15/5/17	2/1/19
2/Lt. T. P. JOHNSTON.	15/5/17	2/1/19
Lieut. W. Mc.N. SNADDEN.	15/5/17	14/12/18
2/Lt. G. C. HALDANE.	6/9/17	30/12/18
*2/Lt. D. McCHLEARY.	21/3/18	14/12/18
2/Lt. A. S. MURRAY.	22/3/18	–/1/19
Capt. James ROSS.	22/3/18	8/12/18
Lieut. G. C. CAMPBELL.	1/4/18	18/12/18

9th Battalion.

Name.	Missing.	Repatriated.
Lieut. O. A. OWEN.	21/7/15	22/11/18

10th Battalion.

Name.	Missing.	Repatriated.
2/Lt. James BLAIR.	30/9/18	8/12/18

11th Battalion.

Name.	Missing.	Repatriated.
Lieut. A. H. D. RICHMOND.	22/8/17	14/12/18

14th Battalion.

Name.	Missing.	Repatriated.
Capt. H. Boswell SANDEMAN.	21/3/18	10/12/18
Capt. A. McMILLAN.	25/3/18	10/12/18

LEINSTER REGIMENT.
1st and 2nd Battalions.

Name.	Missing.	Interned.		Repatriated.
Lieut. A. W. BARTON.	21/10/14	Holland	6/2/18	18/11/18
Lieut. G. S. HAMILTON.	21/10/14	Holland	6/2/18	18/11/18
Lieu. R. D. O'CONNOR.	21/10/14	Holland	19/3/18	18/11/18
Capt. B. DEANE.	15/2/15	Holland	19/3/18	29/11/18
Lieut. H. C. BERNE.	2/12/16			17/12/18
2/Lt. G. C. PARKS.	22/3/18			2/12/18
2/Lt. E. C. SMYTH.	22/3/18			3/1/19
2/Lt. W. M. SURTEES.	22/3/18			17/12/18
Lieut. R. G. HOLMES.	25/3/18			18/12/18
2/Lt. E. DANIEL.	28/3/18			25/12/18

* Attached T.M.B.

LEINSTER REGIMENT—continued.

11th Battalion.

Name.	Missing.	Interned.	Repatriated.
2/Lt. C. H. SPENCER.	21/3/18		18/12/18

ROYAL MUNSTER FUSILIERS.

1st Battalion.

Name.	Missing.	Interned.	Repatriated.
Capt. C. D. DRAKE.		Holland 22/1/18	18/11/18
Capt. C. R. RAWLINSON.	29/8/14	Holland 22/1/18	20/7/18
Capt. H. S. JERVIS.	29/8/14	Holland 6/2/18	31/8/18
Capt. C. R. HALL.	29/8/14	Switzerland 27/12/17	24/3/18
Lieut. J. F. O'MALLEY.	29/8/14	Holland 6/2/18	22/11/18
Lieut. H. A. NEWSON.	16/9/14	Holland 6/2/18	18/11/18
Lieut. R. A. D. MOSELEY.	16/9/14	Holland 6/2/18	18/11/18
Capt. D. WISE.	29/9/14	Holland 6/2/18	18/11/18
Lieut. E. W. GOWER.	29/9/14	Holland 6/2/18	
Lieut. H. G. WHELAN.	21/3/18	(*Died* 11/4/18 at Rastatt).	
2/Lt. T. F. O'DONNELL.	22/3/18		8/12/18
2/Lt. O. J. O'HARE.	22/3/18		2/12/18
2/Lt. L. W. R. MURPHY.	22/3/18		28/11/18
2/Lt. C. BOURCHIER.	22/3/18		2/12/18
2/Lt. T. G. CAHILL.	22/3/18		-/12/18

2nd Battalion.

Name.	Missing.	Interned.	Repatriated.
2/Lt. T. T. PRICE.	9/5/15	Holland 10/4/18	1/2/19
Capt. A. H. BATTEN-POOLL.	10/11/17	Switzerland 27/12/17	24/3/18
Capt. J. C. R. DELMEGE.	10/11/17		3/12/18
Lieut. H. B. FISHER.	10/11/17	(*Died* 23/11/17).	
2/Lt. H. J. McELNEA.	21/3/18		1/12/18
2/Lt. P. A. DENAHY.	21/3/18		6/12/18
*2/Lt. L. A. CARTER.	21/3/18		18/12/18
Lieut. C. E. O'CALLAGHAN.	27/3/18		18/12/18
*2/Lt. A. H. STRACHAN.	27/3/18		18/12/18
*2/Lt. J. F. NASH.	27/3/18		1/12/18
†2/Lt. P. M. J. ARDAGH.	27/3/18		1/12/18
2/Lt. J. DOORLEY.	27/3/18		18/12/18
‡Major M. M. HARTIGAN.	31/3/18		-/12/18

3rd Battalion.

Name.	Missing.	Interned.	Repatriated.
Capt. R. W. THOMAS.	16/9/14		13/9/17

ROYAL DUBLIN FUSILIERS.

1st Battalion.

Name.	Missing.	Interned.	Repatriated.
Major H. M. SHEWIN.	4/9/14		25/11/18
Lieut. J. E. VERNON.	4/9/14	Exchanged	26/8/15
Lieut. F. DOBBS.	4/9/14		17/11/18
Lieut. F. E. S. MACKY.	4/9/14	Holland 6/2/18	8/2/19
Lieut. C. H. L'E. WEST.	4/9/14	Holland 6/2/18	22/1/19
Major G. S. HIGINSON.	13/9/14	Switzerland 9/12/17	24/3/18
Capt. R. L. H. CONLAN.	13/9/14	Switzerland 9/12/17	24/3/18
2/Lt. A. L. KENT.	28/2/17		4/12/18
2/Lt. A. J. McCANN.	5/10/17	Switzerland 21/10/18	8/12/18
Capt. G. E. COWLEY.	21/3/18	(*Died* 18/6/18 at Le Cateau).	
Capt. H. M. LETCHWORTH.	21/3/18		29/11/18
Lieut. G. H. CHANDLER.	21/3/18		-/1/19

* Attached from Royal Dublin Fusiliers. † Attached from Jersey Militia.
‡ Attached from South African Force.

ROYAL DUBLIN FUSILIERS—continued.

1st Battalion—continued.

Name.	Missing.	Interned.	Repatriated.
Lieut. R. PEACEY.	21/3/18		—/12/18
2/Lt. W. N. GOURLAY.	21/3/18		29/11/18
2/Lt. P. McCARTHY.	21/3/18		21/12/18
2/Lt. R. G. HUNTER.	21/3/18	(Died 25/4/18 at Stettin).	
2/Lt. G. A. CLARKE.	21/3/18	(Died 22/3/18 at Cambrai).	
2/Lt. W. R. W. BRISCOE.	27/3/18		25/12/18
2/Lt. G. P. G. CRAWFORD.	27/3/18		
2/Lt. F. M. LAIRD.	27/3/18		25/12/18
2/Lt. C. K. KIRWAN.	3/6/18		—/1/19
2/Lt. JAMES OWENS.	4/9/18		29/11/18

2nd Battalion.

Name	Missing	Interned		Repatriated
2/Lt. W. Y. SHANKS.	25/5/15	Holland	10/4/18	26/12/18
Lieut. W. BRADDELL.	6/7/15	Holland	6/2/18	23/9/18
*2/Lt. V. M. MacKEAG.	14/7/15	Holland	10/4/18	18/11/18
Lieut. J. P. SCOTT.	27/5/17			7/1/18
2/Lt. A. HOLMES.	27/5/17			14/12/18
2/Lt. M. W. O'CONNELL.	21/3/18			17/12/18
2/Lt. W. J. GREENE.	21/3/18			8/12/18
2/Lt. G. PETIT	21/3/18			
2/Lt. F. E. KENNEDY.	21/3/18			3/12/18
2/Lt. M. AHERN.	21/3/18			25/12/18
2/Lt. F. G. W. WILKIN.	21/3/18			2/12/18
2/Lt. D. F. WARREN.	21/3/18			2/12/18
2/Lt. H. FIELDING.	21/3/18			2/12/18
Capt. S. DUFF-TAYLOR.	27/3/18			25/12/18
Capt. A. S. TRIGONNA.	11/4/18			10/12/18

9th Battalion.

Name	Missing	Repatriated
2/Lt. N. V. FORREST.	27/4/17	1/1/19

10th Battalion.

Name	Missing	Interned		Repatriated
Lieut. W. J. MOUNT.	14/10/16	Holland	7/9/18	18/12/18
2/Lt. C. ADAMS.	1/2/17			14/12/18
Capt. R. BOYD.	27/3/18			8/12/18

11th Battalion.

Name	Missing	Repatriated
2/Lt. A. F. McCANN.	21/3/18	2/12/18

RIFLE BRIGADE.

1st and 2nd Battalions.

Name	Missing	Interned		Repatriated
Capt. G. E. W. LANE.	26/8/14	Switzerland	27/12/17	9/12/18
Lieut. E. W. S. FOLJAMBE.	13/9/14			13/9/17
Capt. W. W. YOUNG.	24/8/16	Holland	12/10/18	21/1/19
2/Lt. B. W. DENNIS.	20/1/17			2/1/19
2/Lt. H. BARKER.	16/8/17			17/12/18
2/Lt. T. C. LEWIS.	24/3/18			13/12/18
Capt. R. C. S. STEVENSON.	24/4/18			3/12/18
2/Lt. R. K. GARNER.	24/4/18			29/11/18
2/Lt. D'A. F. THUILLIER.	24/4/18			3/12/18

* Attached from Leinsters.

RIFLE BRIGADE—continued.
1st and 2nd Battalions—continued.

Name.	Missing.	Interned.	Repatriated.
*2/Lt. W. LOFTUS.	24/4/18		3/12/18
†2/Lt. E. A. H. ODDY.	24/4/18		3/12/18
2/Lt. W. MacKECHNIE.	24/4/18		29/11/18
2/Lt. A. H. BURMAN.	24/4/18		3/12/18
2/Lt. H. YOUNG.	24/4/18		29/11/18
Major A. A. TOD.	27/5/18		25/12/18
Capt. E. W. CREMER.	27/5/18		25/12/18
Capt. G. H. G. ANDERSON.	27/5/18		23/12/18
Lieut. A. N. WARREN.	27/5/18		30/12/18
Lieut. G. PURVES.	27/5/18		31/12/18
†2/Lt. J. FARRELL.	27/5/18		-/12/18
2/Lt. H. N. ABERCROMBIE.	27/5/18		25/12/18
2/Lt. R. BEATTIE.	27/5/18		25/12/18
2/Lt. O. BRUCE.	27/5/18	(*Died* 21/6/18).	
2/Lt. E. P. HORGAN.	27/5/18		31/12/18
‡2/Lt. W. H. HARRIS.	27/5/18		-/12/18
2/Lt. R. T. CALDWELL.	27/5/18		-/12/18
Capt. A. W. M. RISSIK.	2/9/18		8/12/18

3rd Battalion.

Name.	Missing.	Interned.	Repatriated.
2/Lt. J. MUNDAY.	20/1/18		14/12/18
2/Lt. G. G. F. GREIG.	21/3/18		18/12/18
2/Lt. A. E. WARD.	21/3/18		25/12/18

7th Battalion.

Name.	Missing.	Interned.	Repatriated.
Lt.-Col. A. J. H. SLOGGETT.	21/3/18		19/1/19
Capt. F. A. HAWKINS.	21/3/18		28/11/18
Capt. J. A. SAUNDERS.	21/3/18		29/11/18
Lieut. M. D. CHILD.	21/3/18		29/11/18
Lieut. J. A. SOWERBUTTS.	21/3/18		29/11/18
2/Lt. H. P. GRAHAM.	21/3/18		28/11/18
2/Lt. W. BAKEL.	21/3/18		18/12/18
§2/Lt. W. A. ROBBINS.	21/3/18		29/11/18
2/Lt. W. P. McCAFFREY.	21/3/18		18/12/18
2/Lt. F. ATTERTON.	21/3/18		28/11/18
2/Lt. S. ARNOLD.	21/3/18		18/12/18
2/Lt. M. J. MONAGHAN.	21/3/18		-/11/18
2/Lt. W. G. MILLS.	21/3/18		28/11/18
2/Lt. D. B. McPHERSON.	21/3/18		29/11/18
2/Lt. C. HOLBROOK.	21/3/18		18/12/18
2/Lt. A. McALLISTER.	21/3/18		18/12/18
2/Lt. G. H. KING.	21/3/18		18/12/18
2/Lt. H. W. LETHBRIDGE.	21/3/18		29/11/18
2/Lt. W. D. ORCHARD.	21/3/18		28/11/18
2/Lt. W. WOODHEAD.	23/3/18		18/12/18

8th Battalion.

Name.	Missing.	Interned.		Repatriated.
2/Lt. D. H. MILLER.	24/3/16	Holland	30/4/18	18/11/18
2/Lt. J. F. SMITH.	23/3/18			-/12/18
**2/Lt. E. P. BLUNDELL.	23/3/18			29/11/18
2/Lt. A. W. McCRORIE.	24/3/18			29/11/18
††2/Lt. A. GRAY.	4/4/18			25/12/18
2/Lt. F. W. RICHARDS.	4/4/18			-/12/18

* Attached from King's Own Yorkshire Light Infantry.
† Attached King's Royal Rifles.
‡ Attached T.M.B.
§ Attached from Liverpools.
‖ Attached Signals, R.E.
** Attached from Liverpool Regiment.
†† Attached from Yorkshire Regiment.

RIFLE BRIGADE—continued.

9th Battalion.

Name.	Missing.	Interned.	Repatriated.
Capt. Ralph WILSON.	20/3/18		—/12/18
2/Lt. W McGEOCH.	21/3/18		2/12/18
*Major J. H. BOARDMAN.	23/3/18	(*Died* 25/4/18 at Heilbronn).	
2/Lt. W. L. McKECHNIE.	23/3/18		—/12/18
2/Lt. H. CHANDLER.	23/3/18		18/12/18
2/Lt. Robert WILSON.	23/3/18		17/12/18

10th Battalion.

Name.	Missing.	Interned.	Repatriated.
2/Lt. R. T. URRY.	20/2/17		17/12/18
2/Lt. A. W. B. FINCH.	20/2/17		29/11/18
Lt.-Col. L. H. W. TROUGHTON.	30/11/17		30/12/18
2/Lt. M. A. YOUNG.	30/11/17		21/1/19
2/Lt. W. H. RODGER.	30/11/17		27/11/18
2/Lt. S. EIDMANS.	30/11/17		23/3/18

11th Battalion.

Name.	Missing.	Interned.	Repatriated.
Lieut. G. DAVIDSON.	24/3/18		18/12/18
†2/Lt. H. A. HOGG.	24/3/18		6/12/18

12th Battalion.

Name.	Missing.	Interned.	Repatriated.
2/Lt. B. R. C. READ.	14/2/16	Holland 9/4/18	18/11/18
2/Lt. F. W. BLOORE.	22/3/18		18/12/18
2/Lt. D. H. DE PASS.	22/3/18		2/12/18
2/Lt. G. L. RUMBLE.	22/3/18		11/12/18
2/Lt. W. I. HENDERSON.	30/3/18		29/11/18

16th Battalion.

Name.	Missing.	Interned.	Repatriated.
Capt. E. F. H. SMITH.	22/3/18		6/1/19
Capt. G. C. COOPER.	22/3/18		18/12/18
2/Lt. H. BARNABY.	22/3/18		2/12/18
2/Lt. H. A. SYKES.	22/3/18		2/12/18
2/Lt. J. H. SUMMERSKILL.	26/3/18		25/12/18
2/Lt. C. A. BENNETT.	27/3/18		1/12/18

ARMY CYCLISTS CORPS.

Name.	Missing.	Interned.	Repatriated.
Major D. P. DAVIES.	9/4/18		25/12/18
Capt. A. S. LUCAS.	9/4/18		25/12/18
Capt. D. E. WIGGANS.	9/4/18		29/11/18
Lieut. F. E. STARKEY.	9/4/18		18/12/18
‡Lieut. C. H. SCOTT.	9/4/18		25/12/18
§Lieut. G. F. LOWSON.	9/4/18		18/12/18
Lieut. E. R. BEWLEY.	9/4/18		18/12/18

MACHINE GUN CORPS.

Name.	Missing.	Interned.	Repatriated.
2/Lt. T. C. NICHOLAS.		Holland —/6/18	21/1/19
2/Lt. A. L. HYSLOP.	2/4/17		1/1/19
Lieut. C. S. HADDEN.	23/4/17		31/12/18
2/Lt. A. S. DRABBLE.	29/4/17		1/1/19
2/Lt. A. YOUNG.	16/5/17		6/12/18

* Attached from Oxford and Bucks Light Infantry. † Attached from Border Regiment.
‡ Attached from Liverpools.   § Attached from East Yorks.

MACHINE GUN CORPS—continued.

Name.	Missing.	Interned.	Repatriated.
2/Lt. H. BAKER.	10/7/17		17/12/18
Lieut. E. PEARCE.	31/7/17	Switzerland 27/10/17	9/12/18
2/Lt. A. McLEOD.	1/8/17		6/1/19
Capt. R. L. HARTLEY.	1/8/17		14/12/18
2/Lt. L. R. FORSTER.	5/8/17		14/12/18
2/Lt. J. S. ANDERSON.	25/9/17		3/12/18
2/Lt. W. B. PARKER.	26/9/17		6/12/18
2/Lt. T. BOWKER.	22/10/17		28/11/18
Lieut. M. M. HOLDEN.	30/11/17		14/12/18
Lieut. J. E. McERVEL.	30/11/17		3/12/18
Lieut. H. WILSON.	30/11/17		6/1/19
Lieut. H. J. DAVEY.	30/11/17		1/1/19
2/Lt. W. BAILEY.	30/11/17		25/12/18
2/Lt. S. S. IRWIN.	30/11/17		6/12/18
2/Lt. J. H. KINAHAN.	30/11/17		17/12/18
2/Lt. J. B. HILL.	30/11/17		17/12/18
2/Lt. G. GAY.	30/11/17		27/11/18
2/Lt. F. W. SHEBBEARE.	1/12/17		23/2/18
2/Lt. J. H. WALMSLEY.	1/12/17		27/11/18
Lieut. P. P. PERRY.	2/12/17		14/12/18
2/Lt. E. D. KIPPEN.	3/12/17		14/12/18
2/Lt. A. S. PAYNE.	3/12/17		6/1/19
2/Lt. G. CHAMBERS.	6/12/17		14/12/18
Capt. G. R. GOLDINGHAM.	30/12/17		27/11/18
2/Lt. A. W. DACOMBE.	31/1/18		1/1/19
Lieut. J. A. ROBOTHAM.	21/3/18		11/12/18
2/Lt. H. I. KAY.	21/3/18		2/12/18
Capt. A. WOODS.	23/3/18		6/12/18
2/Lt. T. GUYATT.	24/3/18		25/12/18
2/Lt. F. G. H. SMALL.	24/3/18	(*Died* 9/6/18 at Cassel).	
2/Lt. N. ROBERTS.	24/3/18		28/11/18
2/Lt. R. METCALF.	26/3/18		13/12/18
Lieut. L. S. WINN.	28/3/18		1/12/18
2/Lt. H. J. C. ALBRECHT.	9/4/18		28/11/18
2/Lt. R. MORRISON.	10/4/18	(*Died* 14/4/18 at Vignies).	
2/Lt. H. A. WHARTON.	27/5/18		13/12/18
Lieut. A. M. DUNAND.	24/8/18		13/12/18
Lt. Col. Sir W. R. CODRINGTON.	31/10/18		–/12/18
Lieut. C. W. F. WOOLNOUGH.			
2/Lt. G. WARBURTON.			17/12/18
2/Lt. N. D. DALTON.			11/12/18

1st Battalion.

Capt. L. MARSH.	31/10/18		

2nd Battalion.

Lieut. A. WAUGH.	28/3/18		4/12/18
Lieut. T. SIME.	28/3/18		17/12/18

5th Battalion.

2/Lt. A. MacFARLANE.	21/3/18		18/12/18

MACHINE GUN CORPS—continued.

6th Battalion.

Name.	Missing.	Interned.	Repatriated.
Lieut. J. J. ANDERSON.	21/3/18		3/1/19
2/Lt. T. F. NEWBERY.	21/3/18		15/12/18
2/Lt. A. A. DODD.	21/3/18		–/12/18
2/Lt. S. G. BALL.	21/3/18		11/12/18
2/Lt. F. W. HOCKADAY.	21/3/18		17/12/18
Lieut. W. T. REDGRAVE.	22/3/18		18/12/18
Lieut. H. McCORMICK.	26/4/17	(*Died* 8/5/17).	

8th Battalion.

Name.	Missing.	Interned.	Repatriated.
2/Lt. J. M. EMERSON.	23/3/18	(*Died* 2/4/18 at Rosiers).	
2/Lt. W. H. SKINNER.	25/3/18	(*Died* 27/3/18).	
Lieut. W. HARDY.	24/4/18		–/12/18
Lieut. D. E. S. BROWNE.	24/4/18		3/12/18
2/Lt. J. M. HOOD.	24/4/18		3/12/18
2/Lt. C. H. REEVES.	24/4/18		3/12/18
Capt. W. TONKS.	27/5/18		–/12/18
Lieut. G. E. CROWDER.	27/5/18		8/12/18
Lieut. F. W. ARTHURTON.	27/5/18		25/12/18
Lieut. F. R. LOCKHART.	27/5/18		–/12/18
Lieut. A. C. CRONE.	27/5/18		25/12/18
Lieut. H. E. WALKER.	27/5/18		–/12/18
2/Lt. A. A. TARVER.	27/5/18		–/12/18
2/Lt. S. TELFER.	27/5/18		–/12/18
2/Lt. R. W. BROWN.	27/5/18		–/12/18
2/Lt. S. ROBEY.	27/5/18		–/12/18
2/Lt. W. B MILLS	27/5/18		–/12/18
2/Lt. E. J. JOBERNS.	27/5/18		–/12/18
2/Lt. S. H. KEEN.	27/5/18		–/12/18
2/Lt. L. L CLARKE.	27/5/18		25/12/18
2/Lt. L. F. DOWDEN.	27/5/18		31/12/18

9th Battalion.

Name.	Missing.	Interned.	Repatriated.
Lieut. F. J. BRIDGES.	21/3/18		4/12/18
2/Lt. P. A. KENNEDY.	21/3/18		18/12/18
Lieut. G. A. HISKENS.	16/4/18		1/12/18
Lieut. R. B. ROBB.	16/4/18		3/12/18
Lieut. W. L. W. LEACH.	25/4/18		3/12/18

10th Battalion.

Name.	Missing.	Interned.	Repatriated.
Lieut. E. F. HARDMAN.	28/3/18		1/12/18

12th Battalion.

Name.	Missing.	Interned.	Repatriated.
Lieut. J. S. PHILLIPS.	30/10/18		8/11/18

14th Battalion.

Name.	Missing.	Interned.	Repatriated.
Lieut. R. E. DAVENHILL.	21/3/18		14/12/18
Lieut. W. F. PORTEOUS.			14/12/18
Lieut. J. ROLPH.	21/3/18		26/12/18
Lieut. T. C. SKINNER.	21/3/18		14/12/18
Lieut. G. N. MASKELL.	21/3/18		10/12/18
2/Lt. G. ROBBINS.	21/3/18		2/12/18
2/Lt. E. G. BELL.	21/3/18		
2/Lt. S. C. WOOD.	21/3/18		11/12/18
2/Lt. H. D. GREEN.	21/3/18		14/12/18
2/Lt. H. LATHAM.	22/11/16		2/1/19

MACHINE GUN CORPS—continued.

15th Battalion.

Name.	Missing.	Interned.	Rapatriated.
2/Lt. J. C. ASHBURNER.	28/3/18		17/12/18
2/Lt. W. J. TAYLOR.	28/3/18		2/12/18

16th Battalion.

Lieut. F. A. KIRKLAND.	21/3/18		–/12/18
Lieut. E. S. F. TURNER.	21/3/18		2/12/18
2/Lt. J. DONALDSON.	29/3/18		8/12/18

18th Battalion.

Lieut. A. B. JONES.	21/3/18		2/12/18
2/Lt. F. C. CHEESEMAN.	21/3/18		2/12/18
2/Lt. R. F. GALBRAITH.	21/3/18		18/12/18

19th Battalion.

Lieut. G. W. HARGRAVES.	22/3/18		18/12/18
2/Lt. S. BOWKER.	24/3/18		25/12/18
2/Lt. W. G. BARUGH.	24/3/18		18/12/18
2/Lt. H. E. BAGGS.	24/3/18	(*Died* 30/6/18 at Cassel).	
Capt. L. E. JONES.	25/3/18		2/11/18
Lieut. B. B. GASCOYNE.	25/3/18		11/12/18
Lieut. J. ANDERSON.	10/4/18		29/11/18
2/Lt. M. C. GREGORY.	10/4/18		18/12/18
2/Lt. J. S. SPEAR.	10/4/18		29/11/18
Capt. F. P. DAVIS.	11/4/18		18/12/18
2/Lt. E. D. JONES.	11/4/18		25/11/18
2/Lt. A. M. HODGSON.	12/4/18		18/12/18

20th Battalion.

2/Lt. W. HILL.	20/3/18		18/12/18
2/Lt. R. DELL.	22/3/18	(*Died* 8/5/18 Avesnes).	
Lieut. J. T. CUFFLEY.	24/3/18	(*Died* 31/3/18 at Dury).	

21st Battalion.

2/Lt. F. O. LANE.	21/3/18		22/12/18
Lieut. F. A. R. WADSWORTH.	22/3/18		29/11/18
2/Lt. W. G. ATTER.	22/3/18		23/1/19
2/Lt. S. EDMUNDSON.	22/3/18		17/12/18
2/Lt. G. W. JACK.	22/3/18		18/12/18
2/Lt. G. LESLIE.	23/3/18		–/12/18
Capt. S. J. CHITTENDEN.	24/3/18		1/12/18
Lieut. J. E. ENRIGHT.	24/3/18		–/2/19
Lieut. J. P. AINSCOUGH.	24/3/18		–/12/18
2/Lt. A. W. H. BLACK.	24/3/18		2/12/18
Lieut. W. E. BARCLAY.	24/3/18		12/12/18
2/Lt. L. J. DILLIWAY.	24/3/18		18/12/18
2/Lt. C. E. SANDERS.	24/3/18		11/12/18
Lieut. J. CAMPBELL.	28/4/18		18/12/18
2/Lt. E. MYERS.	27/5/18		17/12/18
2/Lt. H. W. KNOTT.	27/5/18		17/12/18
2/Lt. S. E. SINCLAIR.	27/5/18		–/12/18

22nd Battalion.

Capt. T. C. B. UDALL.	27/5/18		17/12/18

MACHINE GUN CORPS—continued.

24th Battalion.

Name.	Missing.	Interned.	Repatriated.
Capt. R. DARBY.	21/3/18		4/12/18
Lieut. C. D. ARMSTRONG.	21/3/18		18/12/18
2/Lt. S. M. WILLIAMS.	21/3/18		12/12/18
2/Lt. J. G. HOLT.	21/3/18		23/9/18
Capt. R. G. DUMARESQ.	11/4/18		3/12/18

25th Battalion.

2/Lt. F. BENTLEY.	21/3/18		1/12/18
Major L. E. FABER.	23/3/18		28/11/18
Lieut. F. O. RHODES.	23/3/18		11/12/18
Lieut. W. D. LAWSON.	23/3/18		10/12/18
Lieut. F. P. SPOONER.	25/3/18		1/12/18
Lieut. F. W. JACOB.	10/4/18		29/11/18
Lieut. E. J. C. MADDISON.	10/4/18		29/11/18
Lieut. F. H. C. REDINGTON.	14/4/18		2/12/18
Lieut. S. MORRISON.	17/4/18		2/12/18
2/Lt. H. M. PERRYMAN.	18/4/18		3/12/18
2/Lt. H. F. HAYES.	25/4/18		2/12/18
Lieut. A. S. CALVERT.	27/5/18		25/12/18
Lieut. G. H. COATON.	27/5/18		–/12/18
Lieut. D. J. COLEMAN.	27/5/18		10/1/19
Lieut. R. H. COCKSEDGE.	27/4/18		14/12/18
Lieut. W. K. RENNIE.	27/5/18		–/12/18

29th Battalion.

2/Lt. A. H. SUTCLIFFE.	12/4/18		25/12/18
2/Lt. P. JAMIESON.	11/4/18		–/1/19

30th Battalion.

Lieut. T. W. ASHLEY.	21/3/18		–/1/19
2/Lt. R. B. MORISON.	21/3/18		1/12/18
2/Lt. H. FIELD.	21/3/18		16/1/19
2/Lt. H. T. MORGAN.	21/3/18		7/12/18
2/Lt. W. T. HOWARTH.	21/3/18		11/1/19
2/Lt. A. McCOLL.	23/3/18		18/12/18

31st Battalion.

Capt. D. M. CULE.	12/4/18		18/12/18
2/Lt. J. W. E. PALMER.	12/4/18	(*Died* at Lille).	
2/Lt. A. F. ADAMS.	12/4/18		1/12/18

33rd Battalion.

2/Lt. A. S. HUNT.	2/10/18		28/11/18

34th Battalion.

2/Lt. J. R. LLOYD-ATKINS.	21/3/18		1/12/18
2/Lt. F. C. BENSON.	21/3/18		25/12/18
2/Lt. G. R. W. LAWSON.	21/3/18		25/12/18
2/Lt. W. STENSON.	21/3/18		1/12/18
2/Lt. J. H. PATON.	21/3/18		11/12/18
2/Lt. W. H. HANCOCK.	10/4/18		25/12/18
2/Lt. E. N. MATHIESON.	13/4/18		1/12/18
2/Lt. J. S. PEGG.	13/4/18		18/12/18
Lieut. A. JACKSON.	29/7/18		14/12/18

MACHINE GUN CORPS—continued.

36th Battalion.

Name.	Missing.	Interned.	Repatriated.
Lieut. V. E. OSBORNE.	21/3/18	(*Killed* while trying to escape).	
Lieut. T. B. REYNOLDS.	21/3/18		14/12/18
Lieut. A. J. LAMPORT.	21/3/18		-/12/18
Lieut. J. BARKER.	21/3/18		14/12/18
Lieut. H. W. ROOT.	21/3/18	(*Died* 22/3/18 Labancourt).	
Lieut. J. T. SAUNDERS.	21/3/18		29/11/18
2/Lt. J. W. J. SLOAN.	21/3/18		10/12/18
2/Lt. T. G. WEALL.	21/3/18		17/12/18

38th Battalion.

Name.	Missing.	Interned.	Repatriated.
2/Lt. E. P. MARTIN.	24/3/18		2/12/18

39th Battalion.

Name.	Missing.	Interned.	Repatriated.
2/Lt. R. J. PRITCHARD.	23/3/18		2/12/18
2/Lt. W. A. NEWMAN.	30/3/18		7/9/18

40th Battalion.

Name.	Missing.	Interned.	Repatriated.
2/Lt. J. GORDON.	22/3/18		18/12/18
2/Lt. B. HOWARD.	24/3/18		11/12/18
Lieut. J. G. ELMITT.	9/4/18		10/12/18
2/Lt. W. G. FINCH.	9/4/18		11/12/18
2/Lt. W. C. WICKHAM.	9/4/18		8/12/18
2/Lt. E. L. WILLIAMS.	9/4/18		8/12/18
2/Lt. C. P. DUNN.	9/4/18		11/12/18

41st Battalion.

Name.	Missing.	Interned.	Repatriated.
2/Lt. L. S. P. H. RAYNER.	21/3/18		8/12/18
Capt. A. McK. REID.	24/3/18		14/12/18

47th Battalion.

Name.	Missing.	Interned.	Repatriated.
2/Lt. S. F. PETERS.	21/3/18		11/12/18
Lieut. E. H. TAYLOR.	24/3/18		4/12/18
Lieut. V. R. L. HUTCHINGS.	24/3/18		8/12/18
Lieut. N. H. L. BARNI.	24/3/18	(*Died* 29/3/18 at Lesdain).	
2/Lt. A. C. BLACK.			22/11/18

48th Battalion.

Name.	Missing.	Interned.	Repatriated.
2/Lt. P. OSWIN.	21/3/18		14/12/18
2/Lt. F. S. S. DAWKINS.	25/4/18		-/12/18

49th Battalion.

Name.	Missing.	Interned.	Repatriated.
2/Lt. F. P. HARRISON.	21/3/18		28/11/18
2/Lt. H. CLARKE.	14/4/18		18/12/18
2/Lt. J. C. LAMONT.	16/4/18		2/12/18
Major W. MILNE.	25/4/18	(*Died* at Munster 25/7/18).	
Capt. M. FitzG. KINDER.	25/4/18		1/12/18
Lieut. J. B. BROWN.	25/4/18		13/12/18
Lieut. A. K. STEEL.	26/4/18		18/12/18
2/Lt. A. H. CLARK.	26/4/18	(*Died*).	

MACHINE GUN CORPS—continued.

50th Battalion.

Name.	Missing.	Interned.	Repatriated.
Lieut. P. H. HIGHT.	22/3/18		18/12/18
2/Lt. T. WAINWRIGHT.	22/3/18		28/11/18
Capt. W. R. THOMSON.	11/4/18		–/12/18
Lieut. E. HAZELEY.	11/4/18		13/12/18
2/Lt. B. M. BALBI.	11/4/18		18/12/18
Major J. S. DAWBARN.	27/5/18		–/12/18
Major R. C. MOON.	27/5/18		–/12/18
Major M. B. DOUGLAS.	27/5/18		–/12/18
Capt. G. R. McPHAIL.	27/5/18		25/12/18
Capt. A. O. COOPER.	27/5/18		31/12/18
Capt. T. H. NEEDHAM.	27/5/18		–/12/18
Lieut. I. A. LAUDER.	27/5/18		30/12/18
Lieut. F. F. MUNRO.	27/5/18		26/12/18
Lieut. A. SPENCER.	27/5/18		11/1/19
Lieut. J. R. GRAHAM.	27/5/18		25/12/18
Lieut. B. BURDETT.	27/5/18		2/1/19
Lieut. G. C. J. BURTON.	27/5/18		30/12/18
Lieut. G. C. ODOM.	27/5/18		–/12/18
Lieut. T. W. WALDING.	27/5/18		14/12/18
2/Lt. R. ROPNER.	27/5/18		–/12/18
2/Lt. R. S. ROBERTSON.	27/5/18		–/12/18
2/Lt. W. J. S. RANKEN.	27/5/18		–/12/18
2/Lt. H. J. P. TEAGUE.	27/5/18		25/12/18
2/Lt. F. BETHELL.	27/5/18		–/12/18
2/Lt. J. S. McVEY.	27/5/18		8/12/18
2/Lt. W. T. HUNTER.	27/5/18		–/12/18

51st Battalion.

Name.	Missing.	Interned.	Repatriated.
Lieut. J. EDGAR.	21/3/18		
2/Lt. W. SIMPSON.	21/3/18		25/12/18
2/Lt. G. E. MOSS.	21/3/18		11/12/18
2/Lt. T. G. MANNERS.	21/3/18		11/12/18
2/Lt. J. R. McC. MITCHELL.	–/3/18		11/12/18
2/Lt. R. A. BARKER.	21/3/18		29/11/18
Lieut. J. N. HENDRY.	22/3/18		28/11/18
Lieut. D. MENZIES.	22/3/18		29/11/18
2/Lt. H. BIRCHWOOD.	22/3/18		19/12/18
Lieut. S. E. CHARLTON.	23/3/18		1/12/18
Lieut. L. V. CULY.	24/3/18		18/12/18
2/Lt. C. M. APPERLEY.	24/3/18	(Died 28/3/18).	
Lieut. R. S. MORPETH.	11/4/18		29/11/18
2/Lt. E. H. SINCLAIR.			18/12/18
2/Lt. E. F. HARTLEY.	12/4/18		2/12/18
2/Lt. F. J. FRENCH.	12/4/18		18/12/18

55th Battalion.

Name.	Missing.	Interned.	Repatriated.
2/Lt. W. ADDISON.	9/4/18		25/12/18

56th Battalion.

Name.	Missing.	Interned.	Repatriated.
2/Lt. W. J. BATTING.	28/3/18		18/12/18

57th Battalion.

Name.	Missing.	Interned.	Repatriated.
Lieut. E. C. JONES.	4/10/18		25/12/18

MACHINE GUN CORPS—continued.

58th Battalion.

Name.	Missing.	Interned.	Repatriated.
2/Lt. T. OWEN.	22/3/18		2/12/18
2/Lt. J. ROBERTSON.	22/3/18		2/12/18
2/Lt. J. D. HAMPTON.	24/8/18		13/12/18

59th Battalion.

2/Lt. E. D. LANE.	30/11/17	(*Died* 8/12/17 at Candry).	
Capt. E. NEEDHAM.	21/3/18		25/12/18
Lieut. D. YATES.	21/3/18		11/12/18
Lieut. F. C. WILSON.	21/3/18		29/12/18
2/Lt. E. J. FRIEND.	21/3/18		18/12/18
2/Lt. R. A. EDKINS.	21/3/18		14/12/18
2/Lt. G. H. BANDEY.	21/3/18	(*Died* at Graudenz).	
2/Lt. J. G. TOWNSEND.	21/3/18		29/11/18
2/Lt. T. A. MAY.	21/3/18		1/12/18

61st Battalion.

Lieut. F. W. CASWELL.	21/3/18		–/12/18
Lieut. E. C. DOUGLASS.	21/3/18		2/12/18
Lieut. A. E. KER.	21/3/18		16/12/18
Lieut. W. O. JONES.	21/3/18		2/12/18
Lieut. H. KAY.	21/3/18		28/11/18
Lieut. S. C. GOODE.	21/3/18		6/12/18
2/Lt. S. P. GREER.	21/3/18		13/12/18
2/Lt. E. R. FORWARD.	21/3/18		8/12/16
2/Lt. L. N. FENN.	21/3/18		29/11/18
2/Lt. G. H. FARROW.	21/3/18		6/12/18
2/Lt. P. ORGILL.	21/3/18	(*Died* 31/3/18 at Bohain).	
2/Lt. G. EARL.	21/3/18		6/12/18
2/Lt. W. E. WICKS.	21/3/18		6/12/18
2/Lt. H. G. JONES.	12/4/18		18/12/18

63rd Battalion.

2/Lieut. R. E. W. SANDISON.	22/3/18		17/12/18

66th Battalion.

Lieut. E. S. HAY.	21/3/18		5/12/18
Lieut. T. S. BICKERSTAFFE.	21/3/18		2/12/18
2/Lt. W. B. HOLWILL.	21/3/18	(*Died* 16/5/18).	
2/Lt. S. S. MARSH.	21/3/18		3/12/18
2/Lt. H. B. JONES.	22/3/18		25/12/18
Lieut. H. B. BEAUMONT.	27/3/18		18/12/18

103rd Battalion.

Lieut. H. H. LESLIE.	21/3/18		13/12/18

109th Battalion.

2/Lt. G. R. ROLSTON.	21/3/18		–/12/18

117th Battalion.

Lieut. R. WILSON.	21/3/18		25/12/18

197th Battalion.

Capt. R. W. H. MOLINE.	22/3/18		28/11/18

MACHINE GUN CORPS—continued.

200th Battalion.

Name.	Missing.	Interned.	Repatriated.
2/Lt. A. R. ANDREW.	21/3/18		18/12/18

TANK CORPS.

"A" Battalion.

Lieut. J. K. LIPSCOMB.	20/11/17		18/12/18

"B" Battalion.

Capt. F. VANS-AGNEW.	23/11/17		31/1/19
Lieut. A. A. DALBY.	23/11/17		2/1/19

"C" Battalion.

2/Lt. D. F. BRUNDRITT.	20/11/17		25/12/18
2/Lt. H. W. ASHWORTH.	20/11/17		27/11/18

"D" Battalion.

2/Lt. D. R. LEWIS.	22/8/17		2/1/19
Major E. N. MARRIS.	20/11/17		–/1/19
2/Lt. J. de B. SHAW.	20/11/17		3/12/18

"E" Battalion.

Capt. A. H. TATNELL.	23/11/17		3/12/18

"F" Battalion.

Capt. A. E. ARNOLD.	22/8/17		6/12/18
Lieut. C. W. CARLES.	21/11/17		2/12/18
Lieut. A. E. SMITH.	27/11/17		27/11/18
2/Lt. H. D. CURRY.	27/11/17		14/12/18
2/Lt. K. ASHCROFT.	27/11/17		2/12/18
2/Lt. C. I. H. TOLLEY.	27/11/17		23/12/18
2/Lt. J. P. WETENHALL	27/11/17		3/12/18
Capt. V. DUPREE.	1/12/17		3/12/18

"H" Battalion.

2/Lt. E. L. BOSTOCK.	25/10/17		17/12/18

"I" Battalion.

2/Lt. G. E. WILLIAMS	23/11/17		13/12/18

1st Battalion.

2/Lt. A. J. HUME.	3/5/18	(*Died* 21/5/18 at Le Quesnoy).	
Capt. S. HOULTON.	8/8/18		13/12/18
2/Lt. T. RHODES.	8/8/18		–/1/19
2/Lt. E. R. FRISBY.	8/8/18		31/12/18
2/Lt. A. AYERS.	8/8/18		13/12/18

2nd Battalion.

2/Lt. F. G. SINKINSON.	22/3/18	(*Died* 26/3/18 at Ghent).	
2/Lt. J. TURNER.	22/3/18	(*Died* 13/4/18 at Cassel).	
*Capt. F. A. HAMLET	18/9/18		10/12/18

* Attached from Royal Dublin Fusiliers.

TANK CORPS—continued.

3rd Battalion.

Name.	Missing.	Interned.	Repatriated.
2/Lt. F. L. A. FIELD.	9/8/18		13/12/18
2/Lt. P. RIDLEY.	9/8/18		28/11/18
Lieut. L. B. HORE.	21/8/18		28/11/18

4th Battalion.

Lieut. R. F. NALDER.	22/3/18		17/12/18
2/Lt. J. C. ELLIS.	22/3/18	(*Died* 21/4/18 at Villers Faucon).	
2/Lt. R. G. VERGETTE.	12/4/18		18/12/18
2/Lt. W. J. BEALE.	9/8/18		13/12/18
2/Lt. F. CARTMELL.	10/8/18		13/12/18

5th Battalion.

2/Lt. E. C. REES.	22/3/18		14/12/18
2/Lt. J. LANDERS.	22/3/18		29/11/18
2/Lt. C. B. BROWN.	16/4/18		25/12/18
2/Lt. G. BRIDGE.	16/4/18		–/1/19
2/Lt. C. W. MIDGLEY.	16/4/18		25/12/18
2/Lt. A. E. BAKER.	16/4/18		25/12/18
2/Lt. V. E. JONES.	17/4/18		30/12/18

6th Battalion.

Lieut. C. B. ARNOLD.	9/8/18		6/12/18
2/Lt. N. O. BENNETT.	9/8/18		14/12/18
Lieut. C. B. PLANT.	6/11/18		18/12/18
2/Lt. H. F. JONES.	6/11/18		20/12/18

7th Battalion.

2/Lt. G. G. KING.	15/4/18		18/12/18
*2/Lt. R. B. YENDELL.	29/9/18		28/11/18

8th Battalion.

2/Lt. J. G. W. FERGUSON.	21/3/18		25/12/18
2/Lt. M. WILSON.	24/3/18		17/12/18

9th Battalion.

2/Lt. R. H. HARROP.	23/8/18		28/11/18

10th Battalion.

2/Lt. J. P. CHAMPNEY.	9/8/18		13/12/18
2/Lt. G. T. L. BAYLIFF.	21/8/18		13/12/18
2/Lt. J. R. HAMILTON.	21/8/18		28/11/18
2/Lt. C. WEBB.	21/8/18		13/12/18

11th Battalion.

Lieut. F. A. BURTON.	25/8/18		29/11/18
2/Lt. B. BOLGER.	29/9/18		11/12/18

12th Battalion.

Lieut. R. ACKROYD.	31/8/18		8/12/18
Lieut. S. GANLEY.	2/9/18		8/12/18
2/Lt. G. C. SOUTAR.	2/9/18		13/12/18

Attached from Monmouthshire Regiment.

TANK CORPS—continued.
13th Battalion.

Name.	Missing.	Interned.	Repatriated.
Capt. H. P. WHITE.	25/4/18		12/10/18
*2/Lt. G. SMITH.	25/4/18		3/12/18
2/Lt. T. DOWER.	8/8/18		–/12/18
2/Lt. H. BENSON.	24/9/18		13/12/18

14th Battalion.

Lieut. T. F. MURPHY.	9/8/18		13/12/18
2/Lt. A. F. C. LUMLEY.	9/8/18		13/12/18
2/Lt. H. S. GINGER.	9/8/18		13/12/18

16th Battalion.

2/Lt. H. E. DUPRE.	20/9/18		27/11/18

17th Battalion.

2/Lt. J. H. DAVIES.	27/9/18		29/11/18
2/Lt. F. H. PHIPPARD.	29/9/18		29/11/18

LABOUR CORPS.

2/Lt. D. E. A. HORNE	30/11/17		14/12/18

MONMOUTHSHIRE REGIMENT.
1st and Second Battalions.

Name.	Missing.	Interned.		Repatriated.
Lieut. R. E. LONES.	26/4/15	Holland	23/3/18	23/10/18
Lieut. J. COTTRELL.	26/4/15	Holland	23/3/18	23/11/18
Lieut. E. T. STEALEY.	8/5/15	Holland	23/3/18	25/11/18
Capt. F. G. DAWSON.	11/5/15	Holland	10/4/18	23/10/18
Capt. M. C. LLEWELLIN.	11/5/15	Holland	23/3/18	22/11/18
Lieut. D. G. C. MURPHY.	11/5/15	Holland	23/3/18	18/11/18
Lieut. L. LLEWELLIN.	11/5/15			26/8/15
2/Lt. N. C. NEWLAND.	11/5/15	(*Died* 31/5/15/.		
2/Lt. T. G. LOWE.	11/5/15	Holland	23/3/18	18/11/18
Lieut. J. F. C. RAIKES.	13/10/15			11/9/17
Capt. G. E. FOSTER.	12/4/18			18/12/18
Lieut. F. C. STRONG.	12/4/18			–/12/18
2/Lt. R. S. DAVIES.	12/4/18			13/12/18

CAMBRIDGE REGIMENT.
1st and 2nd Battalions.

Lieut. G. E. RAWLINSON.	20/7/16	(*Died* at Seclin).	
Lieut. W. SHAW.	16/9/16	(*Died* 27/9/16 at Cambrai).	
2/Lt. W. C. BROWN.	24/3/18		18/12/18
2/Lt. C. L. SHAW.	26/3/18		1/12/18
2/Lt. R. W. T. ROLFE.	26/4/18		13/12/18
2/Lt. J. N. McNISH.	8/10/18		8/12/18
†2/Lt. J. V. MEYER.	12/10/18		24/11/18

LONDON REGIMENT.
1st Battalion.

2/Lt. G. B. HOOPER.	16/8/17		17/12/18
*Lieut. F. S. WARREN.	21/3/18		2/12/18

* Attached from York and Lancaster Regiment.   ‡ Attached T.M.B.
† Attached from Suffolks.

LONDON REGIMENT—continued.

43
2nd Battalion.

Name.	Missing.	Interned.	Repatriated.
2/Lt. C. A. FIELD.	14/1/17		30/12/18
2/Lt. A. N. B. CLARK.	3/5/17		1/1/19
2/Lt. R. Y. ROSS.	16/8/17		16/12/18
2/Lt. A. PHILLIPS.	16/8/17		14/12/18
2/Lt. L. H. NEWTON.	26/10/17		21/12/18
Lt.-Col. A. R. RICHARDSON.	21/3/18		29/11/18
Capt. B. J. BARTON.	21/3/18		6/12/18
Capt. J. HOWIE.	21/3/18		1/12/18
Lieut. L. W. BINDON.	21/3/18		18/12/18
2/Lt. P. M. WITH.	21/3/18		18/12/18
2/Lt. L. MOUTRIE.	21/3/18		1/12/18
2/Lt. W. G. PHILPOTT.	21/3/18		-/12/18
2/Lt. G. T. ROBERTS.	21/3/18		2/12/18
2/Lt. L. W. DIXON.	21/3/18		28/11/18
2/Lt. S. W. B. CLAPHAM.	21/3/18		25/12/18
2/Lt. R. J. H. BROWN.	21/3/18		-/11/18
2/Lt. H. F. BOON.	21/3/18		18/12/18
2/Lt. T. H. GLADSTONE.	21/3/18		12/12/18
2/Lt. D. de F. GILLINGS.	21/3/18		20/12/18
2/Lt. P. D. GIBSON.	21/3/18		28/11/18
2/Lt. M. L. HARPER.	21/3/18		18/12/18
*2/Lt. J. E. MUNDY.	24/4/18	(Died).	
*2/Lt. W. E. MAY.	24/4/18		18/12/18
*2/Lt. F. G. HAYES.	24/4/18		18/12/18
2/Lt. G. G. SHADBOLT.	24/4/18		11/12/18
Lieut. N. GARDINER.	25/4/18		18/12/18
2/Lt. A. H. STREETS.	25/4/18		31/12/18
2/Lt. P. R. TAYLOR.	25/4/18		18/12/18
2/Lt. H. G. MITCHINER.	25/4/18		18/12/18
2/Lt. A. H. EDGE.	10/9/18		11/12/18
2/Lt. A. R. FOX.	10/9/18		28/11/18
2/Lt. J. H. J. DEWEY.	10/9/18		8/12/18
2/Lt. H. A. GRAHAM.	10/9/18		5/1/19
2/Lt. T. W. N. WATSON.	13/10/18		29/12/18
2/Lt. J. M. STOTESBURY.	6/11/18		10/12/18

3rd Battalion.

Name.	Missing.	Interned.		Repatriated.
Capt. E. N. WILCOX.	4/5/17	Switzerland	27/12/17	3/2/19
2/Lt. E. W. CUNNINGHAM.	4/5/17			1/1/19
Capt. H. Seppings LIDIARD	26/10/17			17/12/18
†2/Lt. W. N. HARRIS.	21/3/18			25/12/18
Capt. P. W. HERAPATH.	21/3–4/4/18			18/12/18
Lieut. S. JOHNSON.	21/3–4/4/18			2/12/18
2/Lt. A. J. CORRIE.	21/3–4/4/18			18/12/18
2/Lt. F. BUCKLE.	23/3/18			25/12/18
2/Lt. C. E. CARR.	26/3/18			2/12/18
2/Lt. F. de C. CALLENDER.	24/4/18			17/12/18
2/Lt. S. N. CLEMOW.	24/4/18			18/12/18
2/Lt. G. D. HAIGH.	8/8/18			13/12/18

4th Battalion.

Name.	Missing.	Interned.		Repatriated.
Lieut. A. G. BLUNN.	1/7/16			14/12/18
2/Lt. R. McDOWELL	15/6/17			23/12/18
2/Lt. E. MONKMAN.	15/6/17			6/1/19
2/Lt. E. A. STEVENSON.	16/6/17	Holland	7/5/18	18/8/18
Lieut. H. W. DURLACHER.	21/3/18			2/12/18

* Attached from Middlesex Regiment. † Attached T.M.B.

LONDON REGIMENT—continued.
4th Battalion—continued.

Name.	Missing.	Interned.	Repatriated.
2/Lt. L. F. WARDLE.	21/3/18		2/12/18
2/Lt. S. H. E. CRANE.	21/3–4/4/18		2/12/18
2/Lt. G. E. LESTER.	21/3–4/4/18		2/12/18
Lieut. C. W. FRY.	24/3/18		1/12/18
2/Lt. H. O. MORRIS.	28/3/18		28/11/18
*2/Lt. C. W. DENNING.	28/3/18		29/11/18
2/Lt. D. F. CRAWFORD.	30/3–4/4/18		25/12/18

5th Battalion.

Name.	Missing.	Interned.	Repatriated.
2/Lt. A. R. L. GOODSON.	3/6/16	Holland 30/4/18	18/11/18
Capt. A. T. B. DE COLAGAN.	1/7/16	Holland 16/5/18	12/1/19
Capt. W. J. GRACE	28/3/18		3/12/18
2/Lt. R. C. THOMPSON.	28/3/18		4/12/18
†2/Lt. C. S. TRESILIAN.	28/3/18		13/12/18
2/Lt. F. C. SILLS.	28/3/18		11/12/18
2/Lt. W. R. B. KETTLE.	28/3/18		27/12/18
2/Lt. R. F. L. HEWLETT.	28/3/18		11/12/18
2/Lt. H. G. HIGHAM.	28/3/18		11/12/18
2/Lt. P. ADAMS.	28/3/18		18/12/18
2/Lt. T. C. K. POWELL.	28/3/18		10/12/18
2/Lt. J. A. T. DERHAM.	5/5/18		18/12/18
2/Lt. C. M. KING.	5/11/18		17/12/18
2/Lt. S. GOULD.	28/3/17		18/12/18

6th Battalion.

Name.	Missing.	Interned.	Repatriated.
Capt. H. G. NOBBS.	9/9/16		9/12/16
2/Lt. E. O. COZENS.	21/5/17		23/9/18
Capt. A. T. CANNON.	29/11/17		25/12/18
2/Lt. H. K. FORSTER.	29/11/17	(*Died* at Bouchain).	
2/Lt. C. H. FARRINGTON.	29/11/17		–/12/18
2/Lt. C. H. RAVEN.	28/3/18		11/12/18

7th Battalion.

Name.	Missing.	Interned.	Repatriated.
Capt. F. M. DAVIS.	21/5/16	Holland 30/4/18	4/10/18
2/Lt. W. V. BROOKS.	21–22/5/16	Holland 16/5/18	15/11/18
2/Lt. M. JURISS.	21–22/5/16	Holland 27/6/18	23/10/18
2/Lt. G. B. SLATER.	7/10/16		18/12/18
2/Lt. A. C. ROBINSON.	23/3/18		1/1/19
2/Lt. C. J. A. COULSHAW.	18/4/18		14/12/18
Lieut. F. E. MOYLAN.	26/8/18		13/12/18
2/Lt. H. COCKROFT.	26/8/18		13/12/18
2/Lt. C. D. MENZIES.	16/8/17		14/12/18

8th Battalion.

Name.	Missing.	Interned.	Repatriated.
2/Lt. C. L'E. WALLACE.	21/5/16	Holland 30/4/18	21/1/19
Capt. G. M. B. PORTMAN.	21–22/5/16	Holland 30/4/18	21/12/18
Capt. G. N. CLARK.	21–22/5/16	Holland 30/4/18	19/12/18
2/Lt. J. GURNEY.	21–22/5/16	Holland 30/4/18	22/11/18
2/Lt. N. L. AMES.	21–22/5/16	Holland 30/4/18	13/12/18
2/Lt. E. A. HOWELL.	21–22/5/16	Holland 30/4/18	23/11/18
2/Lt. V. WHEELER.	22/3/18		8/12/18
2/Lt. D. F. WILKINSON.	22/3/18		1/12/18
2/Lt. W. G. HEWETT.	22/3/18		2/12/18
2/Lt. A. H. MILLER.	23/3/18		29/11/18
2/Lt. A. ODDLAFSON.	23/3/18		1/12/18
2/Lt. H. R. STONE.	23/3/18	(*Died* 17/4/18 at Valenciennes).	
2/Lt. S. R. POWL.	14/10/18		13/12/18
2/Lt. E. M. ROBINSON.	14/10/18		13/12/18

* Attached T.M.B. † Attached from Middlesex Regiment.

LONDON REGIMENT—continued.

9th Battalion.

Name.	Missing.	Interned.	Repatriated.
2/Lt. C. P. FLEETWOOD.	1/7/16	(*Died* 12/7/16 at Le Cateau).	
2/Lt. R. BENNETT.	1/7/16	Holland 16/5/18	–/1/19

10th Battalion.

2/Lt. J. C. HEROLD.			8/12/18

12th Battalion.

Lieut. G. F. RICKETT.	8/5/15	Holland 23/3/18	18/11/18
2/Lt. W. G. PARKER.	1/7/16	Holland 7/10/18	19/11/18
2/Lt. T. W. S. GARNHAM.	24/8/18		14/12/18
Capt. K. H. J. ANDERSON.	12/9/18		28/11/18
Lieut. K. H. S. CLARKE.	12/9/18		29/11/18
Lieut. A. A. BAKER.	12/9/18		29/11/18

13th Battalion.

2/Lt. R. C. MALBY.		Holland 10/4/18	18/11/18
2/Lt. P. R. PIKE.	1/7/16	Holland 16/5/18	22/11/18

14th Battalion.

Capt. IAN HENDERSON.	1/11/14	Switzerland 30/5/16	9/12/18
Lieut. T. H. K. ALLSOP.	1/11/14	Switzerland 9/12/18	6/12/18
Capt. F. C. WALKER.	24/11/17		17/12/18
Capt. H. L. LAMB.	24/11/17		19/1/19
2/Lt. A. L. WISDON.	28/3/18		18/12/18

15th Battalion.

Major H. F. M. WARNE.	6/12/17		6/1/19
Capt. L. L. BURTT.	6/12/17		2/1/19
Lieut. W. A. S. HOUSLOP.	6/12/17		3/12/18
2/Lt. J. P. POTTS.	6/12/17	Holland 6/2/18	23/10/18
2/Lt. A. E. KING.	6/12/17		17/12/18
Capt. R. MIDDLETON.	22/3/18	(Doubtful)	
2/Lt. F. A. BRIGHT.	22/3/18		11/12/18
2/Lt. J. A. SCHOFIELD.	25/4/18		18/12/18
2/Lt. F. GRAY.	2/9/18		8/12/18

16th Battalion.

Lieut. P. SPENCER SMITH.		Holland 16/5/18	19/12/18
Capt. G. E. COCKERILL.	1/7/16	(*Died* 3/7/16 at Vrancourt).	
Lieut. D. F. UPTON.	1/7/16	Switzerland 9/12/17	24/3/18

17th Battalion.

Lieut. G. B. LOVELL.	–/3/18		11/12/18
2/Lt. C. S. RICHARDS.	28/3/18		11/12/18
2/Lt. G. A. MARCHANT.	10/9/18		–/12/18
2/Lt. S. A. STROUD.	10/9/18		6/12/18

18th Battalion.

2/Lt. P. R. PARKES.	21–26/3/18	(*Died* 4/4/18 at Le Cateau).	
*Lieut. G. B. NEWTON.	22/3/18		11/12/18
†2/Lt. A. ELTRINGHAM.	22/3/18		25/12/18
Lieut. R. W. MONYPENY.	23/3/18		29/11/18
2/Lt. A. M. PILCHER.	23/3/18	(*Died* 6/6/18 at Valenciennes).	
2/Lt. C. E. HENNING.	23/3/18		29/11/18
2/Lt. J. W. CARRINGTON.	24/3/18		11/12/18
Capt. R. MACDONALD.	3/10/18		29/11/18

*Attached T.M.B. † Attached from 3rd London Yeomanry.

LONDON REGIMENT—continued.
19th Battalion.

Name.	Missing.	Interned.	Repatriated.
Capt. H. FOX.	24/3/18		10/12/18
Capt. J. B. MORRISON.	24/3/18		10/12/18
*Capt. C. H. SMITH.	24/3/18		29/11/18
*Lieut. A. D. BATES.	24/3/18		6/12/18
Lieut. J. A. McFIE.	24/3/18		29/11/18
2/Lt. I. C. SMITH.	24/3/18		11/12/18
2/Lt. A. C. BALL.	24/3/18		11/12/18
2/Lt. L. L. KIRBY.	24/3/18		11/12/18
2/Lt. H. F. McELROY.	24/3/18		11/12/18
†2/Lt. W. E. S. JOTCHAM.	28/3/18		11/12/18

20th Battalion.

Name.	Missing.	Interned.	Repatriated.
Lt.-Col. F. R. GRIMWOOD.	24/3/18		14/1/19
Capt. R. E. PERRETT.	24/3/18		20/1/19
Capt. W. R. WOOD.	24/3/18		25/12/18
Capt. W. T. C. CAVE.	24/3/18		25/12/18
Lieut. W. R. CRESSWELL.	24/3/18		25/12/18
Lieut. C. J. ADAMS.	24/3/18		25/12/18
2/Lt. S. J. CONSTABLE.	24/3/18		25/12/18
2/Lt. R. MATTHEWS.	24/3/18		28/11/18
2/Lt. O. L. FULLER.	25/3/18	(*Died* 18/10/18 at Cologne).	

22nd Battalion.

Name.	Missing.	Interned.	Repatriated.
Lieut. E. J. PORTER.	16/9/16	(*Died* 22/9/16 at Cambrai).	
Major L. A. BOOSEY.	25/3/18		25/12/18

23rd Battalion.

Name.	Missing.	Interned.	Repatriated.
Capt. G. BRETT.	21/3/18		6/12/18
Lieut. R. K. LANGLEY.	21/3/18		11/12/18
2/Lt. P. B. BRAMBROUGH.	21/3/18		2/1/19
2/Lt. W. G. PARISH.	23/3/18		11/12/18
2/Lt. F. J. C. SPURGE.	23/3/18		11/12/18
2/Lt. A. H. AMEY.	24/3/18		11/12/18
2/Lt. W. J. KEMP.	5/4/18		25/12/18
2/Lt. G. CRISP.	5/4/18		8/12/18
Capt. A. J. HARMAN.	22/8/18		10/12/18
Capt. G. C. PHILLIPS.	22/8/18		8/12/18
2/Lt. R. P. GOLDSMITH.	22/8/18		13/12/18
2/Lt. J. H. HORNBY.	22/8/18		29/11/18
2/Lt. H. T. CLEMENTS.	22/8/18		13/12/18

24th Battalion.

Name.	Missing.	Interned.	Repatriated.
Capt. L. C. GAMAGE.	23/3/18		10/12/18
Capt. G. N. C. DALZIEL.	23/3/18		25/12/18
Capt. R. F. SIEVERS.	22/8/18		29/11/18
2/Lt. C. C. B. MARSHALL.	5/11/18		6/1/19

28th Battalion.

Name.	Missing.	Interned.	Repatriated.
2/Lt. E. HARVEY.	2/7/16	Holland 16/5/18	22/11/18
*2/Lt. C. A. R. PARK.	30/12/17		27/11/18
Capt. G. C. KITCHING.	24/3/18		25/12/18
Lieut. R. E. PETLEY.	24/3/18		25/12/18
2/Lt F. H. SILCOCK.	24/3/18		–/1/19

* Attached from 3rd London Yeomanry. † Attached T.M.B.

LONDON REGIMENT—continued.
34th Battalion.

Name.	Missing.	Interned.	Repatriated.
2/Lt. W. H. BOND.	2/9/18		13/12/18

HERTFORDSHIRE REGIMENT.
1st Battalion.

Lieut. W. F. FRANCIS.	31/7/17		14/12/18
Lieut. R. L. HARDY.	31/7/17		6/1/19
2/Lt. W. THOMPSON.	31/7/17		14/12/18
2/Lt. F. S. WALTHEW.	31/7/17		6/1/19
Lieut. G. F. C. GUDGEON.	22/3/18		14/12/18
2/Lt. R. F. B. BORRODALE.	22/3/18		14/12/18
2/Lt. E. FREEDMAN.	22/3/18		14/12/18
Lt.-Col. E. C. M. PHILLIPS.	23/3/18		25/12/18
2/Lt. F. E. ALLEN.	23/3/18		17/12/18

HEREFORDSHIRE REGIMENT.
1st Battalion.

2/Lt. A. C. EDWARDS.	4/9/18		13/12/18

ARMY SERVICE CORPS.

Lt.-Col. C. D. CHRISTOPHER.		Switzerland 30/5/18	13/9/17
Lieut. D. POTTS.		Holland 6/2/18	23/10/18
Lieut. L. G. HUMPHREYS.		Holland 6/2/18	15/12/18
Capt. J. A. D. BELL.		Holland 6/2/18	23/10/18
2/Lt. C. V. EVITT.	15/5/18		18/12/18
2/Lt. W. L. MALLABAR.	27/5/18		18/12/18

ROYAL ARMY MEDICAL CORPS.
(See also page 131A*).*

Major W. FRY.	(*Died* 17/3/15 at Wittenberg)	31/8/14	
Capt. A. SUTCLIFF.	(*Died* 26/4/15 at Wittenberg)	31/8/14	
Capt. H. E. PRIESTLY.		12/9/14	282//16
Capt. A. C. VIDAL.		13/9/14	28/2/16
Lieut. J. LAUDER.		8/10/14	29/1/16
Capt. B. JOHNSON.	*Att.* 16th Lancers.	10/10/14	15/12/15
Capt. C. EDMUNDS.		-/-/14	13/1/16
Lieut. J. M. GILLESPIE.	*Att.* 2/*Northumberland Fus.*	26/5/15	1/7/15
Capt. D. A. LAIRD.	*Att.* 2/*Yorkshire Regt.*	25/9/15	29/1/16
Lieut. J. R. SPENSLEY.	*Att.* 8/*East Kent Regt.* (*Died* 10/11/15 at Mainz)	26/9/15	
Capt. V. D. O. LOGAN.	*Att.* 7/*Suffolk Regt.*	3/7/16	23/2/18
Capt. E. D. F. HAYES.	*Att.* 1/*Northants Regt.*	10/7/17	23/2/18
Capt. H. K. WARD.	*Att.* 2/*K.R.R.C.*	10/7/17	23/2/18
Lieut. J. RICKARDS.		1/8/17	
Lt.-Col. G. S. WILLIAMSON.		29/8/17	23/2/18
Lieut. K. ATKIN.	*Att.* 2/6th *South Staffs.*	22/9/17	23/2/18
Capt. R. T. BRUCE.		22/11/17	23/2/18
Lt.-Col. C. D. RANKIN.		30/11/17	23/2/18
Capt. H. D. CLEMENTI-SMITH.		30/11/17	23/2/18
Capt. F. W. FAWSETT.	*Att.* 5/*Loyal North Lancs.*	30/11/17	23/2/18
Capt. C. F. DILLON-KELLY.	*Att.* 7/*East Surrey Regt.*	30/11/17	23/2/18

ROYAL ARMY MEDICAL CORPS.—continued.

Name.	Missing.	Exchanged.
Capt. W. BEAMAN.	31/8/14	29/6/15
Lieut. A. BROWN.	12/9/14	29/6/15
Major J. BRUNSKILL.	12/9/14	29/6/15
Lieut. P. BUTLER.	21/8/14	29/6/15
Lieut. W. CRYMBLE.	-/-/14	1/7/15
Capt. R. J. CAHILL.	11/9/14	29/6/15
Major P. H. COLLINGWOOD.	-/-/14	1/7/15
Capt. D. M. CORBETT.	17/10/14	29/6/15
Capt. W. CROKER.	-/-/14	1/7/15
Capt. A. E. G. FRAZER.	27/10/14	29/6/15
Capt. F. G. GARLAND.	22/9/14	29/6/15
Major J. FURNESS.	12/9/14	29/6/15
Capt. J. GRAHAM.	-/-/14	26/8/15
Lieut. Y. R. HAYMAN.	23/10/14	29/6/15
Lieut. T. E. HEPPER.	26/10/14	29/6/15
Lieut. H. HILLS.	-/-/14	1/7/15
Lieut. J. L. JACKSON.	-/-/14	1/7/15
Major H. LONG.	10/9/14	29/6/15
Capt. J. P. LYNCH.	-/-/14	1/7/15
Surg. M. B. LEARY.	11/9/14	1/7/15
Major H. Kelly.	13/8/14	29/6/15
Capt. A. A. MEADON.	3/11/14	29/6/15
Capt. E. MIDDLETON.	13/9/14	29/6/15
Capt. W. MITCHELL	6/9/14	29/6/15
Lieut. A. PRESTON.	-/-/14	1/7/15
Capt. A. M. POLLARD.	30/10/14	29/6/15
Capt. H. PERRY.	10/9/14	29/6/15
Capt. A. D. O'CARROLL.	-/-/14	29/6/15
Lieut. G. STEVENSON.	26/8/14	29/6/15
Lieut. J. A. STENHOUSE.	27/4/15	29/6/15
Capt. W. T. THOMPSON.	26/8/14	29/6/15
Major A. M. THOMPSON.	12/9/14	29/6/15
Lieut. — WINTER.	1/11/14	29/6/15
Lieut. E. DAVIES.	-/-/14	1/7/15
Capt. P. DAVY.	16/9/14	1/7/15
Lieut. R. DOLBEY.	-/-/14	1/7/15
Capt. W. EGAN.	-/-/14	1/7/15
Lieut. L. ROUTH.	12/9/14	29/6/15
Capt. A. M. ROSE.	3/11/14	29/6/15

ROYAL ARMY MEDICAL CORPS—continued.

Name.	Missing.	Interned.	Repatriated.
Capt. F. M. WALKER.	Att. R.H.A.	30/11/17	22/3/18
Capt. G. A. D. McARTHUR.	Att. 11/K.R.R.C.	30/11/17	22/3/18
Capt. E. L. F. NASH.		30/11/17	23/2/18
Capt. C. R. WILLS.	Att. 10/Rifle Brigade.	30/11/17	23/2/18
Capt. F. B. RYAN.	Att. R.E.	30/11/17	23/2/18
Capt. A. G. BRYCE.	Att. 7/Suffolk Regt.	30/11/17	22/3/18
Lieut. T. F. RYAN.		30/11/17	23/2/18
Capt. H. H. FAIRFAX.	Att 2/5th Warwick Regt.	3/12/17	22/3/18
Capt. H. J. DAVIDSON.	Att. 7/Royal Fusiliers	30/12/17	22/3/18
*Lieut. F. K. MILLER.	Att. 9/Royal Welsh Fus.	20/3/18	11/1/19
Major A. C. HEPBURN.	Att. 97/Field Ambulance.	21/3/18	1/11/18
Major J. KENNEDY.		21/3/18	1/11/18
Major J. S. McCONNACHIE.		21/3/18	1/11/18
Capt. F. T. H. DAVIES.	Att. 7/Sherwood Foresters.	21/3/18	13/12/18
Capt. D. McNAIR.	Att. 6/Sherwood Foresters.	21/3/18	1/11/18
Capt. Colin MEARNE.	Att. 5/Sherwood Foresters.	21/3/18	1/11/18
Capt. W. WARBURTON.	Att. 2/Royal Dublin Fus.	21/3/18	1/11/18
Capt. J. C. MUIR.	Att. 2/Durham L.I.	21/3/18	1/11/18
Capt. S. SMITH.	Att. 1/West Yorkshire Regt.	21/3/18	26/12/18
Capt. H. A. SANDIFORD.	Att. 8/Lancashire Fus.	21/3/18	6/12/18
Capt. D. C. HANSON.	Att. 9/K.R.R.C.	21/3/18	30/12/18
Capt. G. B. BUCKLEY.	Att. 8/K.R.R.C.	21/3/18	-/1/19
Capt. J. ANDERSON.	Att. 6/Black Watch	21/3/18	-/1/19
Capt. C. E. P. HUSBAND.	Att. 22/Northumberland Fus.	21/3/18	1/11/18
Capt. E. H. GRIFFIN.	Att. 13/15 Northumberland Fus.	21/3/18	1/11/18
Capt. P. B. CORBETT.	Att. 25/Northumberland Fus.	21/3/18	-/1/19
Capt. H. S. MOORE.	Att. 7/Royal West Kents.	21/3/18	10/1/19
Capt. G. R. LIPP.	Att. 5/North Staffs Regt.	21/3/18	18/1/19
Capt. W. M. CHRISTIE.	Att. 6/South Staffs Regt.	21/3/18	8/12/18
Capt. D. M. SPRING.	Att. 5/East Lancs. Regt.	21/3/18	5/1/19
Capt. R. HODGSON JONES.	Att. 1/R. Inniskilling Fus.	21/3/18	1/11/18
Capt. L. S. H. GLANVILLE.	Att. 13/Royal Irish Rifles	21/3/18	1/11/18
*Capt. F. J. CAHILL.	Att. 2/4 Ox. & Bucks. L.I.	21/3/18	
Capt. D. A. WILSON.	Att. 2/1 North Midland Field Ambulance	21/3/18	1/11/18
Capt. F. P. SMITH.	Att. 2/1 East Lancs. Field Ambulance	21/3/18	1/11/18
*Capt. R. M. DEMING.	Att. 1/2 Highland Field Ambulance, with 5/Seaforths	21/3/18	
Capt. M. T. ASCOUGH.	Att. 2/1 Field Ambulance	21/3/18	1/11/18
Capt. A. T. C. MacDONALD.	Att. 2/1 Field Ambulance	21/3/18	30/12/18
Capt. G. TORRANCE.	Att. 2/1 Field Ambulance	21/3/18	1/11/18
Capt. J. G. ELDER.	Att. 2/1 Field Ambulance	21/3/18	1/11/18
Capt. D. F. DOBSON.	Att. 2/2 Field Ambulance	21/3/18	30/12/18
Capt. E. A. WALKER.	Att. 98/Field Ambulance	21/3/18	-/12/18
Capt. J. A. GILFILLAN.	Att. 98/Field Ambulance	21/3/18	17/12/18
Capt. E. UNDERHILL.	Att. 109/Field Ambulance	21/3/18	13/12/18
Capt. D. R. E. ROBERTS.		21/3/18	5/1/19
Capt. C. E. REDMAN.		21/3/18	28/11/18
Capt. W. A. ARNOTT.		21/3/18	1/11/18
Capt. C. H. C. BRYNE.		21/3/18	28/11/18
Capt. James TATE.		21/3/18	1/11/18
Capt. F. R. TICKLE.	(Died 5/11/18 in London)	21/3/18	1/11/18
Capt. T. E. A. CARR.		21/3/18	27/12/18
Capt. R. R. DUNCAN.		21/3/18	6/12/18

* U.S.A.

ROYAL ARMY MEDICAL CORPS—continued.

Name.	Regiment.	Missing.	Repatriated.
Capt. W. O'BRIAN.		21/3/18	1/11/18
Capt. C. C. G. GIBSON.		21/3/18	10/12/18
Capt. T. W. LEIGHTON.		21/3/18	29/12/18
Lieut. H. M. GILBERTSON.	Att. 6/Somerset L.I.	21/3/18	
*Lieut. J. E. QUIGLEY.	Att. 6/Black Watch.	21/3/18	
*Lieut. A. STRAUSS.	Att. /Connaught Rangers	21/3/18	
Lieut. O. L. F. MILBURN.	Att. 1/R. Dublin Fusiliers	21/3/18	1/11/18
Lieut. J. F. POWER.	Att. 2/R. Inniskilling Fus.	21/3/18	1/11/18
Lieut. W. H. ROWDEN.		21/3/18	1/11/18
Lieut. H. CRASSWELLER.	Att. 11/Royal Sussex Regt.	21/3/18	1/11/18
Capt. W. H. McCARTER.	Att. 5/Leinster Regt.	22/3/18	30/12/18
Capt. H. B. JONES.	Att. 2/Bedfordshire Regt.	22/3/18	13/12/18
Capt. J. P. THIERENS.	Att 6/Leicester Regt.	22/3/18	6/12/18
Capt. A. G. BISSET.	Att. 1/R. Munster Fus.	22/3/18	1/11/18
Capt. D. F. TORRENS.	Att. 6/North Staffs. Regt.	22/3/18	10/12/18
*Lieut. S. MILLER.	Att. 8/Worcestershire Regt.	22/3/18	
Lieut. E. S. PHILLIPS.		22/3/18	1/11/18
Capt. A. J. CHILLINGWORTH.	Att. 10/Royal West Kents	23/3/18	11/12/18
Capt. S. J. DARKE.	Att. Royal West Surrey Regt.	23/3/18	1/11/18
Capt. I. C. MacLEAN.	Att. 2/Rifle Brigade (Died 4/4/18 at Bohain).	24/3/18	
Capt. G. L. JONES.	Att. Scottish Rifles	24/3/18	1/11/18
*Lieut. H. A. GOODRICH.	At. 6/Wiltshire Regt.	24/3/18	30/12/18
Capt. F. DALLIMORE.	Att. 22/London Regt.	25/3/18	24/1/19
*Lieut. J. A. GORDON.	Att. 63/Royal Naval Division	25/3/18	
Capt. W. J. HIRST.		26/3/18	30/12/18
Capt. P. H. GREEN.	Att. 21/South Midland Field Ambulance	26/3/18	1/11/18
Capt. J. B. BALL.	Att. 15/West Yorkshire Regt.	27/3/18	17/12/18
Capt. R. M. SOAMES.	Att. 7/Norfolk Regt.	27/3/18	1/11/18
Lieut. J. A. LOUGHBRIDGE.		27/3/18	13/12/18
Capt. R. A. LEEMBRUGGEN.	Att. 2/Suffolk Regt.	28/3/18	1/1/19
Capt. E. E. MATHER.	Att. 8/Durham L.I.		5/12/18
Capt. J. G. MOLONY.	Att. 4/London Regt.	28/3/18	5/1/19
Lieut. E. N. P. MARTLAND.	Att. 5/London Regt.	28/3/18	8/12/18
*Lieut. R. B. RHETT.	Att. 16/London Regt.	28/3/18	
*Lieut. B. J. GALLAGHER.	Att. Gloucestershire Regt.	29/3/18	
Capt. S. A. FORBES.		4/4/18	25/12/18
Capt. C. A. MEADEN.	Att. Middlesex Regt.	9/4/18	1/11/18
Capt. C. K. O'MALLEY.	Att. 21/Middlesex Regt.	9/4/18	18/1/19
Capt. A. H. LITTLE.	Att. 11/Loyal North Lancs.	9/4/18	–/12/18
Capt. J. SULLIVAN.	Att. 5/Manchester Regt.	9/4/18	1/11/18
*Lieut. F. B. PEDRICK.	Att. 13/East Surrey Regt.	9/4/18	
Capt. F. C. NICHOLS.	Att. 4/South Staffs. Regt.	10/4/18	1/11/18
*Lieut. P. W. HUNTER.	Att. 10/Worcesters	10/4/18	
Capt. W. J. ISBISTER.	Att. 8/Border Regt.	11/4/18	1/11/18
Capt. F. J. NATTRASS.	Att. 2/South Wales Bordrs.	11/4/18	30/12/18
*Lieut. L. M. EDENS.	Att. 1/Wiltshire Regt.	11/4/18	
Capt. J. R. H. ROSS.	Att. 8/Royal Scots		1/11/18
Capt. S. S. MEIGHAM.	Att. 2/Highland Field Ambulance	12/4/18	10/1/19
*Lieut. M. S. REDMOND.	Att. 10/Cheshire Regt.	12/4/18	

* U.S.A.

ROYAL ARMY MEDICAL CORPS—continued.

Name.	Regiment.	Missing.	Repatriated.
Capt. S. V. P. PILL.	Att. 1/Wiltshire Regt.	13/4/18	1/11/18
Capt. A. G. CLARK.	Att. 2/South Lancs. Regt.	13/4/18	18/12/18
Capt. A. B. CLUCKIE.	Att. 19/Lancashire Fus.	25/4/18	30/12/18
Lieut. D. ROBERTSON.	Att. 12/Royal Scots	25/4/18	1/11/18
Col. A. MILNE-THOMSON.		–/5/18	1/11/18
Lt.-Col. H. B. KELLY.	Att. 77/Field Ambulance	27/5/18	1/11/18
Major A. M. WOOD.		27/5/18	27/12/18
Major F. G. LESCHER.	Att. 77/Field Ambulance	27/5/18	14/12/18
Major N. A. A. HUGHES.	Att. 25/Field Ambulance	27/5/18	–/12/18
Major R. M. HANDFIELD-JONES.		27/5/18	1/11/18
Capt. R. M. COALBANK.	Att. 11/Lancashire Fus.	27/5/18	24/1/19
*Capt. H. F. KANE.	Att. 2/Devonshire Regt.	27/5/18	
Capt. R. W. PEARSON.	Att. 22/Durham L.I.	27/5/18	1/11/18
Capt. D. Munro SMITH.	Att. 2/Northants Regt.	27/5/18	8/12/18
Capt. W. A. REES.	Att. 250/Bde. R.F.A.	27/5/18	1/11/18
Capt. T. BLACKWOOD.	Att. 33/Bde. R.F.A.	27/5/18	1/11/18
Capt. M. S. ESLER.	Att. 2/Middlesex Regt.	27/5/18	1/11/18
Capt. C. R. CROWTHER.	Att. 25/Field Ambulance	27/5/18	1/11/18
Capt. A. B. SIMPSON.	Att. 25/Field Ambulance	27/5/18	1/11/18
Capt. W. T. P. MEADE-KING.	Att. 25/Field Ambulance	27/5/18	1/11/18
Capt. M. DONALDSON.	Att. 37/Casualty Clearing Station	27/5/18	13/12/18
Capt. J. D. GENESE.	Att. 37/Casualty Clearing	27/5/18	13/12/18
Capt. F. C. H. BENNETT.		27/5/18	13/12/18
Capt. F. H. McCAUGHEY.		27/5/18	30/12/18
Capt. J. M. MacKENZIE.		27/5/18	1/11/18
Capt. W. G. HARNETT.		27/5/18	1/11/18
Capt. D. GILLESPIE.		27/5/18	1/11/18
Capt. C. W. FOWLER.	Att. 2/Royal Berks Regt.	27/5/18	1/11/18
Capt. W. F. DUNLOP.	Att. 12/13 Northumberland Fus.	27/5/18	1/11/18
Lieut. A. M. McCORMICK.	Att. 12/13 Northumberland Fus.	27/5/18	1/11/18
*Lieut. G. D. TIBBETTS.	Att. 4/East Yorks Regt.	27/5/18	
Lieut. J. W. JONES.	Att. Rifle Brigade	27/5/18	1/11/18
Lieut. J. FINDLAY.	Att. Worcestershire Regt.	27/5/18	–/1/19
Lieut A. S. FINDLAY.	Att. 77/Field Ambulance	27/5/18	–/12/18
Lieut. F. W. D. CARTER.	Att. 24/Field Ambulance	27/5/18	1/11/18
Lieut. A. BOYLE.	Att. 24/Field Ambulance	27/5/18	1/11/18
Lieut. F. W. M. LAMB.	Att. 26/Field Ambulance	27/5/18	18/1/19
Lieut. F. B. O'DOWD.		27/5/18	1/11/18
Lieut. G. V. W. ANDERSON.		27/5/18	–/12/18
Lt.-Col. A. C. H. GRAY.	Att. 37/Casualty Clearing Station	28/5/18	1/11/18
Major E. J. TILBURY.	Att. 37/Casualty Clearing Station	28/5/18	8/12/18
Capt. F. G. P. HEATHCOTE.	Att. 2/East Lancs. Regt.	28/5/18	1/11/18
Lieut. A. M. CLARE.	Att. 6/Durham L.I.	27/6/18	13/12/18
Capt. C. WITTS.		19/7/18	1/11/18
Capt. E. H. JONES.	Att. 37/Casualty Clearing Station	25/7/18	13/12/18
Capt. C. Crawford JONES.			6/1/19

*U.S.A.

M.O.R.C., U.S.A.
(With British Army.)

Name.	Regiment.	Missing.	Repatriated.
Capt. B. BURPEE.			
Lieut. C. W. MAXSON.	Att. 26/Field Ambulance		
Capt. A. S. ROBINSON.			
Lieut. C. P. NASH.			
Lieut. Julian N. DOW.			

ARMY CHAPLAINS' DEPARTMENT.

Name	Regiment	Missing	Repatriated
Rev. A. GRANT.	Att. Highland Field Ambulance	22/11/17	23/2/18
Rev. C. B. PIKE.	Att. 5/Loyal North Lancs.	30/11/17	22/3/18
Rev. P. SINCLAIR.	Att. Highland Field Ambulance	21/3/18	1/11/18
Rev. P. CASEY.		21/3/18	14/12/18
Rev. R. BIRD.		21/3/18	-/12/18
Rev. J. K. MITCHELSON.	Att. 25/Northumberland Fus.	21/3/18	10/12/18
Rev. A. B. L. KARNEY.	Att. 22/Northumberland Fus.	21/3/18	1/11/18
Rev. A. F. PENTNEY.		21/3/18	28/11/18
Rev. W. AMCOATS.		21/3/18	1/11/18
Rev. H. A. SMITH-MASTERS.	Att. 178/L.T.M.B.	21/3/18	25/12/18
Rev. W. P. YOUNG.	Att. 1/5 Seaforths	21/3/18	1/11/18
Rev. J. C. DAVIES.	Att. 1/North Staffs.	21/3/18	1/11/18
Rev. G. C. R. COOKE.	Att. 7/Royal West Kents	21/3/18	6/12/18
Rev. W. FITZMAURICE.	Att. 2/Royal Irish Regt.	21/3/18	1/11/18
Rev. W. F. MORRIS.	Att. 15/Royal Irish Rifles	21/3/18	1/11/18
Rev. W. A. SCANLEN.	Att. Royal Field Arty.	21/3/18	9/1/19
Rev. E. DALY.	Att. 18/Field Ambulance	21/3/18	28/11/18
Rev. J. G. LANE-DAVIES.	Att. 2/Durham L.I.	21/3/18	13/12/18
Rev. T. F. DUGGAN.		22/3/18	1/11/18
Rev. N. L. LYCETT.		22/3/18	27/11/18
Rev. W. R. A. BROWN.		24/3/18	1/11/18
Rev. H. DAVIES.	Att. 20/Middlesex Regt.	9/4/18	-/1/19
Rev. L. N. FORSE.	Att. King's Liverpools	9/4/18	1/11/18
Rev. J. L. A. EDWARDS.	Att. 4/East Yorks	27/5/18	1/11/18
Rev. E. HERBERT.	Att. 23/Durham L.I.	27/5/18	1/11/18
Rev. C. G. BROWN.	Att. 22/Durham L.I.	27/5/18	1/11/18
Rev. J. NOLAN.		27/5/18	1/11/18
Rev. C. STEER, M.C.	Att. Royal Field Arty.	27-31/5/18	1/11/18
Rev. G. A. WESTON.			4/10/18
Rev. H. J. CHAPMAN.			6/12/18
Rev. C. S. ROSE.			6/12/18
Rev. J. G. SMITH.			7/12/18
Rev. E. H. BEATTIE.			9/12/18
Rev. T. E. GRIFFITHS.			9/12/18
Rev. J. TODD.			23/12/18
Rev. J. HILL-WILLIAMS.			31/1/19
Rev. O. RORKE.	4/Field Ambulance	-/-/14	1/7/15

ROYAL GUERNSEY LIGHT INFANTRY.
1st Battalion.

Name.	Missing.	Interned.	Repatriated.
Lieut J C. O. BEUTTLER.	30/11/17		14/12/18
Lieut. G. K. F. BORRETT.	30/11/17		14/12/18
*Lieut. A. V. ANDREWS.	30/11/17		3/12/18
Lieut. F. A. HOVIL.	12/4/18		18/12/18
Lieut. I. F. MacALPINE.	12/4/18		14/1/19
2/Lt. P. STRANGER.	12/4/18		18/12/18

*Attached from Buffs.

AUSTRALIANS.

Infantry.

Name.	Missing.	Interned.		Repatriated.
Lieut. N. G. BLANCHARD.	6/5/16	Holland	16/5/18	
2/Lt. M. B. DOBIE.	28/5/16	(*Died*).		
Capt. A. G. FOX.		Switzerland	9/12/17	9/12/18
Lieut. A. W. M. BOWMAN.	19/7/16	Holland	7/10/18	21/1/19
Capt. C. ARBLASTER.	19/7/16	(*Died* 24/7/16 at Douai).		
Capt. F. R. RANSON.	19/7/16	Holland	30/8/18	
Capt. R. A. KEAY.	20/7/16	Holland	–/6/18	
Major J. J. HUGHES.	20/7/16			21/1/19
Capt. C. MILLS.	20/7/16	Switzerland	9/12/17	12/1/19
Lieut. J. H. MATTHEWS.	20/7/16	Switzerland	27/12/17	7/12/18
Lieut. V. D. BERNARD.	20/7/16	Switzerland	27/12/17	7/12/18
Lieut. H. R. LOVEJOY.	20/7/16	Holland	–/6/18	21/1/19
2/Lt. G. D'A. FOLKARD.	20/7/16	Holland	–/6/18	
2/Lt. G. CUMMINS.	20/7/16	Holland	–/6/18	25/11/18
Capt. A. S. ROBERTSON.				18/12/18
2/Lt. T. BRINE.	24/7/16	Holland	–/6/18	4/10/18
Capt. A. K. KENNEDY.	28/7/16	(*Died* 26/8/16 at Gottingen).		
2/Lt. A. McGOWN.	12/8/16	Holland	12/10/18	19/11/18
Capt. F. J. S. HOAD.	18/8/16	Switzerland	9/12/17	7/12/18
2/Lt. R. H. DABB.	18/8/16	(*Died* 22-28/9/16 at Munster).		
2/Lt. L. C. O'KELLY.	18/8/16			6/1/19
Lieut. H. C. ANTHONY.	19/8/16	Holland	12/10/18	
Lieut. E. H. CHINNER.		(*Died*).		
Lieut. C. B. MEYER.		Switzerland	–/12/16	14/9/17
Lieut. W. A. HALVORSEN.				31/12/18
Capt. W. H. GURTRELL.	14/11/16	(*Died* at Morchies).		
Lieut. A. E. DENT.	14/11/16	Switzerland	27/12/17	14/6/18
2/Lt. L. GRIEVE.	21/11/16			14/12/18
2/Lt. W. MURDOCH.	2/2/17			31/12/18
Capt. W. A. CULL.	26/2/17	Switzerland	29/12/17	24/3/18
2/Lt. V. W. CHARKER.	27/3/17			31/12/18
Capt. D. L. TODD.	3/4/17			14/12/18
Lieut. M. GORE.	3/4/17			14/12/18
Lieut. J. E. EDWARDS.	3/4/17			17/12/18
Major V. J. WAINE.	11/4/17			25/12/18
Capt. H. S. HUMMERSTON.	11/4/17			31/12/18
Capt. A. LANAGAN.	11/4/17			31/12/18
Capt. G. G. GARDINER.	11/4/17			14/12/18
Capt. D. DUNSWORTH.	11/4/17	Holland	–/4/18	18/8/18
Capt. D. P. WELLS.	11/4/17	Switzerland	27/12/17	14/6/18
Capt. J. E. MOTT.	11/4/17			11/10/17
Lieut. O. C. D. GOWER.	11/4/17			2/1/19
Lieut. R. H. O. CUMMING.	11/4/17			31/12/18
Lieut. P. McCALLUM.	11/4/17			30/12/18
Lieut. W. STONES.	11/4/17	Switzerland	29/12/17	10/2/19
Lieut. R. MORRIS.	11/4/17			25/12/18
Lieut. R. E. SANDERS.	11/4/17			–/12/18
Lieut. J. H. HONEYSETT.	11/4/17			17/12/18
Lieut. A. J. McQUIGGAN.	11/4/17			7/1/18
Lieut. O. S. GLUYAS.	11/4/17			3/12/18
Lieut. J. M. COONEY.	11/4/17			31/12/18
Lieut. M. F. BURKE.				4/12/18
2/Lt. G. D. McLEAN.	11/4/17			26/12/18

AUSTRALIANS—Infantry—continued.

Name.	Missing.	Interned.	Repatriated.
2/Lt. K. L. JOHNSON.	11/4/17		1/1/19
2/Lt. J. P. M. COURTNEY.	11/4/17		10/1/19
2/Lt. J. R. GALLAGHER.	11/4/17		4/12/18
2/Lt. G. C. SMITH.	11/4/17		31/12/18
2/Lt. E. J. L. EDMONDS.	11/4/17		29/11/18
2/Lt. W. J. LYON.	11/4/17		
2/Lt. E. BINNINGTON.	11/4/17		2/1/19
2/Lt. A. M. MARSHALL.	11/4/17		14/12/18
2/Lt. M. J. D'ARCY.	11/4/17		31/12/18
2/Lt. J. INGRAM.	11/4/17		6/12/18
2/Lt. F. N. CULVERWELL.	11/4/17		1/1/19
2/Lt. J. H. WATSON.	11/4/17		31/12/18
2/Lt. M. J. WALTON.	11/4/17		1/1/19
2/Lt. L. P. RIDGWELL.	11/4/17		14/12/18
2/Lt. F. BROOMFIELD.	11/4/17		14/12/18
2/Lt. A. V. WATKINSON.	11/4/17		4/12/18
Lieut. R. BEATTIE.	15/4/17		31/12/18
Lieut. C. W. HOOPER.	15/4/17		31/12/18
Lieut. P. W. LYON.	15/4/17		26/12/18
2/Lt. J. E. A. STUART.	15/4/17		10/2/19
Lieut. A. W. B. PETTIT.	16/4/17		1/1/19
2/Lt. S. B. SMITH.		(Died).	
2/Lt. K. AHNALL.		(Died).	
Lieut. H. S. RAMSAY.	3/5/17		16/8/18
2/Lt. H. C. FITZGERALD	3/5/17		25/12/18
2/Lt. W. L. THOMASON.	16/5/17	Switzerland 27/12/17	14/6/18
2/Lt. N. J. HILL.	26/9/17		6/12/18
Lieut. H. F. B. CASTLE.	26/9/17		3/12/18
Lieut. L. A. WHITINGTON.			17/12/18
Lieut. L. E. THOMPSON.			
Capt. D. LESLIE.			
2/Lt. J. D. A. COLLIER.	13/10/17		15/12/18
2/Lt. A. C. H. GIBBS.	13/10/17		19/7/18
Lieut. L. C. BOASE.	4/4/18		25/12/18
2/Lt. H. T. LEWIS.	4/4/18		11/12/18
Capt. A. H. FRASER.	5/4/18		2/12/18
Lieut. W. GOODSALL.	5/4/18		1/12/18
Lieut. H. W. MARSON.	5/4/18		31/12/18
Lieut. J. E. SMITH.	5/4/18		1/12/18
Lieut. E. ROBINSON.	5/4/18		1/12/18
2/Lt. J. H. ALLEN.	5/4/18		1/12/18
Lieut. W. J. KILPATRICK.	7/4/18		1/12/18
Capt. P. H. AULD.	25/4/18		1/12/18
Capt. H. H. McMINN.	8/5/18		1/12/18
Lieut. L. S. McMAHON.	8/5/18		1/12/18
Lieut. A. J. FELL.	8/5/18		1/12/18
Lieut. G. C. W. REID.	14/5/18		
Lieut. L. N. JENNINGS.	14/5/18		1/12/18
Lieut. A. T. DOIG.	23/5/18	(Died 27/6/18 at Le Quesnoy).	
Lieut. H. C. MORRISON.	10/8/18		4/12/18
Lieut. F. FEARNSIDE.	12/8/18		12/12/18
2/Lt. W. S. MISSINGHAM.	11/4/17		30/12/18
2/Lt. H. L. KILLINGSWORTH.	28/5/17	(Died).	
Lieut. J. H. B. ARMSTRONG.	18/8/18		29/11/18
Lieut. R. MALLINSON.	18/8/18		29/11/18

AUSTRALIANS—Infantry—continued.

Name.	Missing.	Interned.	Repatriated.
Lieut. H. A. RIGBY.	18/8/18		29/11/18
Lieut. E. J. COX.	30/8/18		8/12/18
2/Lt. J. W. PEACOCK.	5/10/18		13/1/19
Lieut. N. CUMMING.	-/-/16		2/7/18

Engineers.

Name.	Missing.	Interned.	Repatriated.
2/Lt. W. M. MORTENSEN.			2/1/19

Machine Gun Corps.

Name.	Missing.	Interned.	Repatriated.
Lieut. G. C. DODD.	11/4/17		1/1/19
Lieut. G. KIRKLAND.	11/4/17	(Died 13/4/17 at Hem-Lenglet).	
2/Lt. V. G. VENESS.	11/4/17		1/1/19
2/Lt. W. J. COX.	11/4/17		31/12/18
2/Lt. H. JOHNSON.	15/4/17		30/11/17
2/Lt. H. A. FERGUSON.	20/9/17		14/12/18
Lieut. C. C. DIGHT.			1/12/18
Lieut. J. S. COOLAHAN.	-/4/18	(Died 3/5/18).	
Lieut. F. C. A. MYERS.	5/4/18		-/12/18
2/Lt. W. A. CARNE.	31/8/18		11/12/18
Major T. R. MARSDEN.	17/9/18		28/11/18

Flying Corps.

Name.	Missing.	Interned.	Repatriated.
2/Lt. A. WEARNE.	26/7/17		14/12/18
2/Lt. I. C. F. AGNEW.	2/10/17		29/11/18
2/Lt. V. J. PARKINSON.	-/3/18		
2/Lt. W. H. NICHOLLS.	16/3/18		14/12/18
Lieut. O. T. FLIGHT.	28/3/18		13/12/18
Lieut. C. M. FEEZ.			13/12/18
Lieut. H. K. LOVE.	10/4/18		1/12/18
Lieut. A. R. RACKETT.	1/6/18		30/12/18
2/Lt. A. RINTOUL.	1/6/18		13/12/18
Lieut. R. C. NELSON.	14/7/18		26/12/18
2/Lt. A. F. G. McCULLOCH.	28/7/18		13/12/18
Lieut. L. TAPLIN.	5/9/18		28/12/18
Lieut. George COX.	21/9/18		23/12/18
Lieut. M. J. KILSBY.	30/10/18		24/12/18
Lieut. E. J. GOODSON.	5/11/18		27/11/18
Lieut. C. W. RHODES.	5/11/18		26/11/18

CANADIANS.
Infantry.

Name.	Missing.	Interned.		Repatriated.
Lieut. V. A. McLEAN	24/4/15	Holland	19/3/18	18/11/18
Capt. E. C. CULLING.	26/4/15			
Capt. W. H. V. HOOPER.	26/4/15	Switzerland	19/12/17	24/3/18
Lieut. J. E. McLURG.	26/4/15			22/12/17
Lieut. C. R. SCOTT.	26/4/15			11/9/17
Major A. E. KIRKPATRICK	27/4/15			3/12/18
Major D. R. McCUAIG.	27/4/15	Holland	23/3/18	12/10/18
Capt. L. S. MORRISON.	27/4/15	Switzerland	9/12/17	
Capt. P. J. LOCKE.	27/4/15	Holland	19/3/18	18/11/18
Capt. J. E. L. STREIGHT.	27/4/15	Switzerland	9/12/17	24/3/18
Lieut. C. G. PITBLADO.	27/4/15	Holland	23/3/18	18/11/18
Lieut. B. L. JOHNSTON.	27/4/15	Holland	19/3/18	

CANADIANS—Infantry—continued.

Name.	Missing.	Interned.		Repatriated.
Lieut. G. E. D. GREENE.	27/4/15	Holland	10/4/18	18/11/18
Lieut. D. G. ALLAN.	27/4/15	Holland	19/3/18	18/11/18
Capt. T. V. S. SCUDAMORE.	28/4/15	Switzerland	19/12/16	24/3/18
Capt. C. FRYER.	28/4/15	Switzerland	9/12/17	2/6/18
Capt. G. M. ALEXANDER.	28/4/15	Holland	19/3/18	18/11/18
Capt. R. S. CORY.	28/4/15	Holland	19/3/18	18/11/18
Capt. J. E. OSBORNE.	28/4/15	Holland	19/3/18	18/11/18
Capt. G. ANDREWS.	28/4/15	Holland	19/3/18	18/11/18
Capt. G. W. NORTHWOOD	28/4/15	Holland	19/3/18	
Capt. R. HARVEY.	28/4/15	(*Died* 8/5/15).		
Lieut. E. C. BATH.	28/4/15	Holland	19/3/18	1/11/18
Lieut. R. P. STEEVES.	28/4/15	Holland	19/3/18	
Lieut. V. A. G. MacDOWELL.	28/4/15	Holland	19/3/18	
Lieut. E. D. BELLEW.	28/4/15	Switzerland	27/12/17	9/12/18
Lieut. G. A. COLDWELL.	28/4/15	Holland	1/3/18	
Lieut. H. A. BARWICK.	28/4/15	Holland	19/3/18	18/11/18
Lieut. J. K. BELL.	28/4/15	Switzerland	27/12/17	9/12/18
Lieut. H. E. L. OWEN.	28/4/15	Holland	19/3/18	
Lieut. F. G. SMITH.	28/4/15	Holland	19/3/18	29/1/19
Lieut. R. R. McKESSOCK.	28/4/15	Holland	4/3/18	12/10/18
Lieut. F. H. C. MacDONALD.	28/4/15	Holland	19/3/18	20/12/18
Lieut. F. V. JONES.	28/4/15	Holland	19/3/18	
Lieut. C. V. FESSENDEN.	28/4/15	Holland	23/3/18	18/11/18
Lieut. J. C. THORN.	28/4/15	Holland	23/3/18	31/8/18
Lieut. W. de C. O'GRADY.	28/4/15			11/9/17
Lieut. G. N. GORDON.	14/8/15	Holland	10/4/18	18/11/18
Lieut. D. W. ELLIOTT.	8/4/16	Switzerland	7/5/18	7/12/18
Lieut. H. St. J. BIGGS.	20/4/16	Holland	30/4/18	16/11/18
Major-General V. WILLIAMS.	3/6/16	Switzerland	27/12/17	24/3/18
Major S. L. JONES.	3/6/16	(*Died* 8/6/16).		
Major P. BYNG HALL.		Holland	19/3/18	18/11/18
Lieut. A. W. SIME.	3/6/16	Holland	30/4/18	31/8/18
Lieut. W. G. COLQUHOUN.		Holland	1/3/18	
Lieut. H. W. MacDONNELL.	5/6/16	Switzerland	13/12/16	29/6/18
Lieut. C. J. LAWRENCE.	6/6/16	Holland	30/4/18	23/9/18
Lieut. K. JARVIS.	7/6/16	Holland	30/4/18	18/11/18
Lieut. R. W. NEIL.	7/6/16	Holland	30/4/18	
Lieut. G. G. D. MURPHY.	7/6/16	Holland	30/4/18	18/11/18
Lieut. F. C. R. ANSTEY.	9/7/16	Holland	16/5/18	
Lieut. J. G. MURRAY.	8/9/16			–/11/18
Lieut. F. C. HOWARD.	9/9/16	(*Died* 9/9/16).		
Lieut. W. CLARK.	25/9/16	Holland	5/1/18	23/10/18
Lieut. E. W. MINGO.				18/12/18
Lieut. E. H. SIMPSON.	8/10/16			18/12/18
Lieut. J. W. H. ELLIS.	8/10/16			18/12/18
Lieut. H. E. BALFOUR.	8–10/10/16			31/1/19
Lieut. G. C. HAMILTON.	9/10/16			18/12/18
Lieut. J. D. GUNN.	9/10/16	Switzerland	27/12/17	14/6/18
Lieut. R. S. W. FORDHAM.	9/10/16	Switzerland	27/12/17	24/3/18
Capt. R. SNOWDEN.		Switzerland	–/2/17	
Capt. Russell TAYLOR.		Switzerland	–/2/17	
Lieut. W. L. BACK.	23/12/16			7/1/19
Lieut. A. C. LUMSDEN.	1/3/17			31/12/18
Lieut. C. G. ROBERTSON.	9–12/4/17			7/1/19
Lieut. H. S. LEWIS.	9–12/4/17	(*Died*).		
Lieut. J. LADLER.	25/4/17	(*Died* 2/5/17).		

CANADIANS—Infantry—continued.

Name.	Missing.	Interned.		Repatriated.
Lieut. F. G. LAWSON.	8/5/17			6/12/18
Lieut. W. D. HARDING.	9/4/17			30/12/18
Lieut. H. E. BRIDGE.	8/5/17	Holland	15/4/18	31/8/18
Capt. R. A. BRODIE.	15/8/17			6/12/18
Lieut. J. B. ROSE.	19/8/17			3/12/18
Lieut. K. R. M. MORRISON.	23/8/17			14/12/18
Lieut. C. L. HEATHER, M.C.	11/11/17			1/1/19
Lieut. A. W. BANNARD.	11/12/17			27/11/18
Lieut. B. E. MOBERLY, M.C.	25/3/18			-/11/18
Lieut. D. CLELLAND.	12/4/18			29/11/18
Lieut. G. A. CLOUTIER.	24/5/18			26/12/18
Lieut. A. B. PIKE.	21/6/18			26/12/18
Lieut. R. CARLETON.	14/8/18			13/12/18
Lieut. J. STEWART.	6/9/18			30/12/18
Lieut. A. E. P. PALMER.	29/9/18			30/12/18
Capt. W. W. JOHNSON.	1/10/18			30/12/18
Lieut. H. CAMPBELL.	1/10/18			28/11/18
Lieut. J. C. LITTLE.	10/10/18			-/12/18
Lieut. J. A. ROSS.	10/10/18			-/12/18
Lieut. J. H. MOLSON.	10/10/18			-/12/18
Lieut. D. G. L. CUNNINGTON.				26/12/18
Lieut. B. STEVENS.	8/11/18			25/11/18
Lieut. G. S. LENNOX.	27/7/17	(*Died* at Henin-Lietard).		

Army Medical Corps.

Capt. W. M. HART.	27/4/15	Exchanged		29/6/15
Capt. W. R. W. HAIGHT.				23/2/18

Engineers.

Lieut. R. G. BARNES	3/6/16			13/9/17
Lieut. A. GAUL.	3/6/16	Holland	30/4/18	
Lieut. J. D. WILSON.	3/7/16	Holland	30/4/18	
Lieut. W. E. MASSEY-COOKE.	3/6/16	Holland	30/4/18	14/1/19
Capt. G. B. FIELD.	30/9/18			29/11/18

Machine Gun Corps.

Lieut. R. BABB.	24/3/18			18/12/18
Lieut. J. A. S. GARDINER.	8/8/18			13/12/18
Lieut. W. W. BENNY.	1/10/18			

Chaplains' Department.

Capt. Rev. A. G. WILKEN.	3/6/16			23/2/18

Mounted Rifles.

Lt.-Col. J. F. H. USSHER.	3/6/16	Switzerland	9/12/17	9/12/18
Capt. H. N. FRASER.	3/6/16	Holland	30/4/18	18/11/18
Capt. A. F. CROSSMAN.	3/6/16	Holland	8/10/18	
Capt. M. A. SCOVIL.	3/6/16	Holland	30/4/18	
Capt. F. S. PARK.	3/6/16			23/2/18
Capt. A. H. LIGHTBOURNE.	3/6/16	Holland	30/4/18	19/12/18
Capt. J. E. LATTIMER.	3/6/16	Switzerland	9/12/17	24/3/18
Lieut. J. R. MARTIN.	3/6/16	Switzerland	9/12/18	24/3/18
Lieut. H. G. ROGERS.				17/12/18
Lieut. J. H. DOUGLAS.	3/6/16			11/9/17
Lieut. N. L. WELLS.	3/6/16	Holland	30/4/18	

CANADIANS—Mounted Rifles—continued.

Name.	Missing.	Interned.		Repatriated.
Lieut. F. S. HUBBS.	3/6/16	Switzerland	13/12/16	14/6/18
Lieut. S. E. GOODERHAM.	3/6/16	Holland	30/4/18	18/11/18
Lieut. H. E. SMITH.	3/6/16	Holland	30/4/18	
Lieut. F. H. WOOD.	3/6/16	Holland	30/4/18	
Lieut. C. B. GADD.	3/6/17	Holland	30/4/18	1/11/18
Lieut. E. SMITH.	3/6/16			11/9/17
Major F. PALMER.	5/6/16	Holland	30/4/18	12/10/18
Capt. G. A. B. BUCHANAN.	5/6/16			18/11/18
Cpat. H. R. RICHARDSON.	5/6/16	Holland	30/4/18	25/11/18
Lieut. J. WALKER.	5/6/16	Holland	30/4/18	1/11/18
Lieut. F. H. WILSON.	5/6/16			31/12/18
Lieut. E. S. SKEAD.	5/6/16	Switzerland	27/12/17	23/12/18
Lieut. E. H. HALL.	11/5/17			6/1/18

NEWFOUNDLAND REGIMENT.

2/Lt. A. M. CLOUSTON.	14/4/17			14/12/18
2/Lt. A. B. BAIRD.	14/4/17	Switzerland	27/12/17	6/12/18
2/Lt. W. A. GRACE.	14/4/17			14/12/18
2/Lt. L. MOORE.	12/4/18			8/12/18

NEW ZEALAND FORCE.
Rifle Brigade.

Capt. G. A. AVEY.	26/6/17		14/12/18
Lieut. W. A. GRAY.	8/8/17		12/10/18
Lieut. R. J. RICHARDS.	26/10/18		8/12/18

Auckland Battalion.

Lieut. D. MILLAR.	1/10/18	29/11/18

Engineers.

Lieut. W. M. DURANT.	14/9/16	(*Died* 14/9/16 near Arras)

Canterbury Battalion.

2/Lt. A. L. OWEN.	29/9/18	28/11/18

Wellington Battalion.

2/Lt. J. T. THOMAS.	26/4/18	18/12/18

SOUTH AFRICAN FORCE.

Brig.-General F. S. DAWSON.	24/3/18	30/12/18

1st Infantry.

Lieut. C. J. BATE.	20/7/16			17/11/18
Lieut. W. D. HENRY.	20/7/16	Holland	15/6/18	14/1/19
2/Lt. E. C. K. O'KEEFE.	19/10/16			18/12/18
2/Lt. E. A. BUDGEON.	19/10/16			18/12/18
Major T. ORMISTON.	23/3/18			–/1/19
Capt. E. A. DAVIES.	23/3/18			29/11/18
Capt. A. W. LIEFELDT.	23/3/18			28/11/18
Lieut. A. FRIELINGHAUS.	23/3/18			1/12/18
Lieut. P. W. FURMIDGE.	23/3/18			29/11/18
Lieut. F. P. MacKENZIE.	23/3/18			2/12/18
Lieut. M. A. GRAHAM.	23/3/18			1/12/18

SOUTH AFRICAN FORCE—1st Infantry—continued.

Name.	Missing.	Interned.		Repatriated.
Lieut. W. C. ROBERTSON.	23/3/18			25/12/18
Lieut. W. SCALLEN.	23/3/18			2/12/18
2/Lt. T. VUCOVITCH.	23/3/18			1/12/18
2/Lt. C. STRADLING.	23/3/18			28/11/18
2/Lt. W. F. FAULDS.	23/3/18			28/11/18
2/Lt. H. F. ROFFE.	23/3/18			28/11/18
2/Lt. J. D. GIBBS.	23/3/18			1/12/18
2/Lt. G. CURTIS.	23/3/18			1/12/18
2/Lt. E. CARTER.	23/3/18			1/12/18

2nd Infantry.

Name.	Missing.	Interned.		Repatriated.
Capt. S. E. ROGERS.	22/3/18			18/8/18
Lt.-Col. E. CHRISTIAN.	23/3/18			25/12/18
Major I. McDOUGALL.	23/3/18			17/12/18
Capt. J. ADDISON.	23/3/18			3/12/18
Capt. C. J. STEIN.	23/3/18			10/12/18
Lieut. T. GARSTANG.	23/3/18			2/12/18
Lieut. D. F. BELL.	23/3/18			30/11/18
2/Lt. G. E. MARSHALL.	23/3/18			29/11/18
2/Lt. G. V. MERRIMAN.	23/3/18			2/12/18
2/Lt. J. C. CRAGG.	23/3/18			5/12/18
2/Lt. W. HADLOW.	23/3/18			14/12/18
2/Lt. J. A. GOODING.	23/3/18			18/12/18

3rd Infantry.

Name.	Missing.	Interned.		Repatriated.
Capt. R. F. C. MEDLICOTT.		Holland	15/6/18	–/11/18
Capt. D. A. PIRIE.		Holland	15/6/18	
Lieut. H. HIRTZEL.		Holland	15/6/18	–/10/18
2/Lt. F. K. St. M. RITCHIE.		Holland	30/4/18	23/9/18
2/Lt. S. G. GUARD.	20/7/16	Holland	15/6/18	–/2/19
Lieut. G. H. de B. THOMAS.		Holland	15/6/18	

4th Infantry.

Name.	Missing.	Interned.		Repatriated.
Lieut. H. M. NEWSON.		Holland	15/6/18	19/11/18
2/Lt. K. S. EARP.	22/3/18			3/12/18
2/Lt. D. R. MacINTOSH.	22/3/18			29/11/18
2/Lt. E. H. de M. McINTOSH.	22/3/18			25/12/18
2/Lt. J. KIRKPATRICK.	22/3/18			3/12/18
Capt. H. BUNCE.	23/3/18			1/12/18
*2/Lt. R. K. ANDERSON.	23/3/18			1/12/18
2/Lt. A. D. MITCHELL.	23/3/18			29/11/18
Capt. B. H. L. DOUGHERTY.	24/3/18			–/12/18
Lieut. G. LEIGHTON.	24/3/18			–/12/18
2/Lt. R. B. CORNOCK.	24/3/18			–/12/18
2/Lt. W. A. COOK.	24/3/18			–/11/18
2/Lt. H. E. SULSTON.	24/3/18			2/12/18
2/Lt. R. C. COOK.	24/3/18			–/11/18
2/Lt. W. L. BELL.	24/3/18			1/12/18
2/Lt. S. S. SLATEM.	24/3/18			3/12/18
2/Lt. V. MOGRIDGE.	24/3/18			29/11/18
2/Lt. C. R. ROBINSON.	24/3/18			–/12/18
2/Lt. H. M. RETHMAN.	24/3/18			3/12/18
2/Lt. R. J. READ.	24/3/18			5/12/18
2/Lt. F. PEACOCK.	24/3/18			5/12/18
2/Lt. C. G. MASON.	24/3/18			28/11/18
Lieut. W. H. THOMPSON.	11/4/18			–/12/18

* Attached T.B.M.

SOUTH AFRICAN FORCE—continued.

Chaplains' Department.

Name.	Missing.	Interned.	Repatriated.
Capt. E. St. C. HILL.	–/3/18		–/12/18

Medical Corps.

Capt. P. J. MONAGHAN.	27/3/18		–/11/18

INDIAN ARMY.

129th Baluchis.

Capt. R. D. DAVIES.	20/12/14	Holland	1/3/18

9th Bhopal Infantry.

Capt. R. W. GASKELL.	24/11/14	Holland	24/2/18
Lieut. J. C. D. MULLALY.	24/11/14	Holland	24/2/18	14/1/19

97th Deccan Infantry.

Capt. W. T. FLETCHER.	24/11/14	Holland	24/2/18	1/11/18

Gurkha Rifles.

Capt. MacL. WYLIE.		Holland	1/3/18	15/12/18
Capt. R. D. ALEXANDER.		Switzerland	30/5/16	13/9/17

Punjabis.

Capt. C. B. HARCOURT.	25/9/15	Holland	10/4/18	23/9/18
Capt. H. J. DANIELL.		(*Died*)		
Lieut. J. P. GULLAND.		Holland	10/4/18	18/11/18

24th Sikh Pioneers.

Capt. G. E. H. WILSON.		Holland	24/2/18	28/2/19

Indian Medical Service.

*Lieut. A. S. GAREWAL.	30/11/17	Holland	19/3/18	22/3/18

Nigerian Regiment.

Capt. G. SECCOMBE.	Taken on S.S. "Appam"			6/12/18
Capt. W. T. McG. BATE.	Taken on S.S. "Appam"			17/11/18

ROYAL NAVAL DIVISION.

Capt. F. C. GROVER.		Holland	6/2/18	18/11/18
Commodore W. HENDERSON.				
Lieut. R. PRICE.		Holland	6/2/18	
Major R. CROSSMAN.				24/3/18

188th T.M.B.

Sub-Lt. E. H. C. McNAUGHTON.	24/3/18			6/1/19

190th T.M.B.

Lieut. R. E. HOLROYDE.	25/3/18			25/12/18

63rd Div. M.G. Battalion.

Lieut. D. A. DAVIDSON.	5/4/18			

* Attached 2nd Lancers.

ROYAL NAVAL DIVISION—continued.

R.M.L.I.

Name.	Missing.	Interned.	Repatriated.
2/Lt. W. E. LLEWELYN.	28/4/17		31/12/18
2/Lt. A. FARMER.	28/4/17		17/12/18
2/Lt. R. R. BLACKBURN.	28/4/17		6/12/18
2/Lt. E. G. VAGG.	28/4/17		28/11/18
Lieut. W. C. GWYNNE.	23/3/18		
Capt. R. J. WILLIAMS.	24/3/18		17/12/18
Lieut. P. WATTS.	24/3/18		17/12/18
2/Lt. F. DEATON.	24/3/18		17/12/18
Surgeon H. C. BROADHURST.	24–28/3/18		18/12/18
Sub-Lt. C. V. ENGLISH.	24–28/3/18		25/12/18
Sub-Lt. R. G. GRAY.	24–28/3/18		25/12/18
2/Lt. M. E. TAYLOR.	24–28/3/18		17/12/18
2/Lt. H. J. IRWIN.	24–28/3/18		29/12/18
2/Lt. S. S. CAILES.	24–28/3/18		17/12/18
2/Lt. W. G. STUART.	28/3/18		5/12/18
Capt. J. M. PALMER.	22–23/4/18		
Lieut. J. HAMMOND.	–/–/15	Switzerland 9/12/17	24/3/18

"Anson" Battalion.

Name.	Missing.	Interned.	Repatriated.
Sub-Lt. F. BLAKE.	26/10/17		3/12/18
Sub-Lt. W. JOHNSTON.	26/3/18	(*Died* at Graudenz)	
*Capt. C. A. SCOTTT.	25/8/18		13/12/18
Sub-Lt. D. A. INGLIS.	25/8/18		28/11/18
Sub-Lt. S. V. WILD.	30/9/18		28/11/18

"Collingwood" Battalion.

Name.	Missing.	Interned.	Repatriated.
Lieut. M. A. M. DILLON.			1/12/18

"Drake" Battalion.

Name.	Missing.	Interned.	Repatriated.
Sub-Lt. H. K. LUNN.	5/2/17		29/11/18
Sub-Lt. G. M. LOVE.	30/12/17		27/11/18
Sub-Lt. W. M. HUME.	30/12/17		
Sub-Lt. T. H. BENNETT.	30/12/17		27/11/18
Capt. E. E. CONSTABLE.	24/3/18		31/12/18
Surgeon W. A. McKERROW.	24/28/3/18		6/12/18
Lieut. W. C. JOHNSON.	24–28/3/18		14/1/19
Lieut. J. BARCLAY.	25/3/18		29/11/18
Sub-Lt. H. J. COLLINGS.	25/3/18		13/12/18
Lt.-Com. J. W. TURRELL.	28/3/18		14/1/19
Sub-Lt. R. DONALDSON.	3/9/18		8/12/18

"Hawke" Battalion.

Name.	Missing.	Interned.	Repatriated.
Lieut. J. L. BROMFIELD.			1/12/18
Sub-Lt. A. M. PERRY.	21/3/18		18/12/18
Sub-Lt. L. STEPHENSON.	25/8/18		13/12/18
Sub-Lt. A. A. LEIGHTON.	25/8/18		

"Hood" Battalion.

Name.	Missing.	Interned.	Repatriated.
Sub-Lt. A. FULLERTON.	22/1/17		14/12/18
Sub-Lt. A. W. M. HILLAM.	4/2/17		6/1/19
Sub-Lt. H. BEARDSMORE.	31/12/17		27/11/18
Sub-Lt. S. W. GIBBONS.	31/12/17		27/11/18
Lieut. T. M. FOX.	24/3/18		29/11/18
Lieut. H. GRANT-DALTON.	24/3/18	(*Died* 28/4/18 at Ohrdruf).	

* Attached from South Staffs Regiment.

ROYAL NAVAL DIVISION—continued.

"Hood" Battalion—continued.

Name.	Missing.	Interned.	Repatriated.
Sub-Lt. H. HAWKER.	24/3/18		25/12/18
Sub-Lt. H. W. BISHOP.	24/3/18		3/12/18
Sub-Lt. J. H. COWAN.	24/3/18		25/12/18
Sub-Lt. A. WALPOLE.	24/3/18		4/12/18
Sub-Lt. W. S. PARRY.	24/3/18		2/12/18
Sub-Lt. H. RAWSON.	24/3/18		2/12/18
Sub-Lt. R. STRONG.	24/3/18		2/12/18
Sub-Lt. J. W. STOTT.	24/3/18		14/12/18
Sub-Lt. J. RAMWELL.	24/3/18		18/12/18
2/Lt. T. H. DICKSON.	24/3/18		18/12/18

"Howe" Battalion.

Name.	Missing.	Interned.	Repatriated.
Sub-Lt. W. R. McCHLERY.	30/12/17		27/11/18
Sub-Lt. E. R. CRUMMER.	30/12/17		27/11/18
Sub-Lt. W. S. DAIN.	30/12/17		27/11/18
Sub-Lt. J. M. CALDWELL.	24/3/18		29/11/18

ROYAL NAVAL RESERVE.

Name.	Missing.	Interned.	Repatriated.
Sub-Lt. W. H. D. GARDNER.			14/12/18
Lieut. J. W. JOHNSON.			14/12/18
Sub-Lt. B. W. DURRANT.			9/12/18
Lieut. G. N. S. JOHNSTON.			
Capt. W. OLPHERT.		Holland	24/2/18
Lieut. A. B. LAMBLE.		Holland	19/4/18
Lieut. H. HARRIS.	24/6/17		17/12/18
Lieut. W. S. LANE.			
Lieut. J. COODE-BATE.			
Lieut. W. M. M. HUTCHINGS.	26/7/17		14/12/18

R.N.V.R.

Sub-Lt. G. MARCUS.

ROYAL AIR FORCE.

Name.	Missing.	Interned.		Repatriated.
Capt. D. S. CROSBIE	-/-/14			18/11/18
Lieut. H. T. MAYNE.				
Lieut. V. S. E. LINDOP.	9/9/14	Holland	6/2/18	22/11/18
Capt. R. GREY.	5/10/14	Holland	6/2/18	4/10/18
Capt. R. A. BOGER.	5/10/14	Holland	6/2/18	30/1/19
Lieut. K. RAWSON-SHAW.	27/10/14	Holland	24/2/18	21/1/19
Lieut. H. G. L. MAYNE.	27/10/14	Holland	24/2/18	22/11/18
Lt. Joubert de la FERTE.				-/2/18
2/Lt. M. R. CHIDSON.	28/2/15	Holland	1/3/18	17/12/18
2/Lt. D. C. W. SANDERS.	28/2/15	Switzerland	30/5/16	-/8/17
Lieut. E. H. EASTWOOD.	10/3/15	Escaped		2/8/15
Lieut. O. MANSEL MOULLIN.	12/3/15			15/11/18
Lieut. G. N. HUMPHREYS.	20/3/15	Holland	1/3/18	14/1/19
Lieut. D. M. VETCH.	21/3/15	Escaped		12/10/15
2/Lt. T. E. H. DAVIES.	22/3/15	Holland	23/8/18	21/1/19
Lieut. C. A. GLADSTONE.	30/4/15	Holland	23/3/18	18/11/18
Lieut. S. A. SANFORD.	9/5/15	Holland	10/4/18	-/11/18
Lieut. E. E. HODGSON.	5/6/15	(19/11/18—R.A.F., rep. escaped).		
Capt. A. D. GAYE.	5/6/15	Holland (interned)		31/10/18
2/Lt. F. B. ADAMS.	3/7/15	Holland (interned)		11/11/18
2/Lt. G. E. R. MEAKIN.	3/7/15	Holland (interned)		5/10/18
Capt. J. C. LEECH.	4/7/15	Holland	23/1/18	-/11/18
Lieut. E. WALKER.	4/7/15			7/12/18
Sub-Lieut. J. O. GROVES.	5/7/15	Switzerland	22/5/18	
2/Lt. W. M. CRABBE.	14/7/15	Holland	10/4/18	17/11/18
2/t. H. M. GOODE.	14/7/15			11/9/17
Capt. R. E. B. HUNT.	21/7/15	Holland (interned)		21/11/18
Lieut. F. H. JACKSON.	21/7/15	Holland (interned)		
Lieut. H. F. HANKIN.	26/7/15	Holland	10/4/18	21/1/19
Lieut. A. G. WEIR.	26/7/15	Holland	10/4/18	22/11/18
Lieut. P. A. BRODER.	29/7/15	Holland	10/4/18	22/11/18
2/Lt. R. C. MacPHERSON.	29/7/15	Holland	10/4/18	29/1/19
2/Lt. W. REID.	1/8/15	Switzerland	30/5/16	11/3/18
Lieut. W. DALZELL.	6/8/15	Holland	10/4/18	23/10/18
2/Lt. C. DOLLINGSMITH.	6/8/15	Holland	10/4/18	18/11/18
2/Lt. D. D. DRURY.	16/8/15	Switzerland	27/12/17	24/3/18
2/Lt. W. A. MacLEAN.	16/8/15			10/11/18
Capt. F. J. C. WILSON.	1/9/15	Switzerland	12/8/16	11/7/17
Lieut. E. R. C. SCHOLEFIELD.	1/9/15	Holland	10/4/18	18/11/18
Capt. T. W. M. MORGAN.	13/9/15	Escaped		-/4/17
Capt. J. N. S. STOTT.	19/9/15	Holland	10/4/18	25/11/18
Lieut. W. SUGDEN-WILSON.	21/9/15	Holland	10/4/18	25/11/18
2/Lt. M. W. GREENHOW.	25/9/15	Holland	10/4/18	18/11/18
2/Lt. J. N. C. WASHINGTON.	25/9/15	(Died at Bapaume 2/10/15)		
Capt. F. B. BINNEY.	26/9/15			14/6/18
Lieut. N. C. SPRATT.	28/9/15	Holland	10/4/18	17/11/18
2/Lt. H. B. STUBBS.	28/9/15	Holland	10/4/15	18/11/18
Lieut. D. LEESON.	10/10/15	Holland	19/4/18	18/11/18
Lieut. R. POTTER.	10/10/15	Holland	10/4/18	22/11/18
2/Lt. B. WILKIN.	11/10/15	Holland	19/4/18	18/11/18
2/Lt. A. J. BURNIE.	11/10/15	Holland	19/4/18	18/11/18
2/Lt. A. C. COLLIER.	22/10/15	Holland	19/4/18	26/11/18
Capt. G. C. DARLEY.	26/10/15	Switzerland	30/5/16	14/6/17
2/Lt. R. J. SLADE.	26/10/15	Holland	19/4/18	18/11/18
Lieut. F. H. EBERLI.	9/5/15	Holland	10/4/18	18/11/18

ROYAL AIR FORCE—continued.

Name.	Missing.	Interned.	Repatriated.
2/Lt. J. B. ROBINSON.	2/11/15		—/5/18
Lieut. A. W. BROWN.	9/11/15	Switzerland 19/1/17	11/9/17
2/Lt. H. W. MEDLICOTT.	10/11/15	(—/6/18 shot in trying to escape)	
2/Lt. J. E. P. HOWEY.	11/11/15	Switzerland 13/2/17	19/7/17
2/Lt. V. M. GRANTHAM.	11/11/15	Holland 19/4/18	22/11/18
Lieut. W. A. HARVEY.	11/11/15	(*Died* in Switzerland 7/11/17)	
Lieut. T. C. SHILLINGTON.	19/11/15	Switzerland 12/8/16	11/9/17
2/Lt. H. S. WARD.	30/11/15	Escaped	—/4/16
Lieut. S. E. BUCKLEY.	30/11/15	Escaped	—/6/17
Lieut. D. W. GRINNELL-MILNE.	1/12/15	Escaped	—/4/18
Capt. C. C. STRONG.	1/12/15	Holland 19/4/18	18/11/18
2/Lt. G. S. M. INSALL.	14/12/15	Escaped	—/9/17
Lieut. G. T. PORTER.	27/12/15	Holland 19/4/18	18/11/18
Lieut. E. J. STROVER.	28/12/15	Holland 19/4/18	18/11/18
2/Lt. A. L. RUSSELL.	—/1/16	Holland 19/4/18	22/11/18
Lieut. G. C. FORMILLI.	5/1/16	Holland 18/4/18	18/11/18
2/Lt. W. E. SOMERVELL.	5/1/16	Holland 19/4/18	18/11/18
2/Lt. F. ADAMS.	10/1/16	Holland 19/4/18	2/7/18
2/Lt. J. G. McEWAN.	10/1/16	Holland 19/4/18	22/11/18
2/Lt. H. T. KEMP.	12/1/16	Holland 19/4/18	18/11/18
Lieut. K. W. GRAY.	12/1/16	Holland 19/4/18	—/11/18
Lieut. C. B. WILSON.	19/1/16	Holland 19/4/18	10/7/18
2/Lt. L. J. PEARSON.	5/2/16	Holland 7/10/18	22/11/18
Lieut. E. ALEXANDER.	5/2/16	Holland 19/4/18	
2/Lt. L. A. NEWBOLD.	29/2/16	Holland 30/4/18	Ret. for duty
2/Lt. H. F. CHAMPION.	29/2/16		—/3/16
2/Lt. C. W. PALMER.	2/3/16	(*Died* 29/3/16)	
2/Lt. L. R. HEYWOOD.	9/3/16	Holland 7/10/18	19/11/18
2/Lt. D. B. GAYFORD.	9/3/16	Switzerland 24/4/18	8/12/18
2/Lt. M. A. H. ORDE.	13/3/16	Switzerland 27/12/17	14/6/18
2/Lt. O. LERWILL.	25/3/16	Holland 30/4/18	22/11/18
2/Lt. A. E. HALFORD.	29/3/16	Holland 7/10/18	22/11/18
2/Lt. F. G. PINDER.	29/3/16	Switzerland 9/12/17	24/3/18
2/Lt. T. C. WILSON.	30/3/16		14/8/18
2/Lt. W. JOYCE.	31/3/16	Holland 30/4/18	29/1/19
2/Lt. G. S. CASTLE.	31/3/16	Holland 30/4/18	18/11/18
2/Lt. F. N. GRIMWADE.	1/4/16	Switzerland 6/6/17	11/9/17
2/Lt. H. G. FROST.	1/4/16	Switzerland	13/9/17
2/Lt. C. W. P. SELBY.	16/4/16	Switzerland 24/12/16	11/9/17
2/Lt. N. A. G. SCOTT-BROWN.	23/4/16		
2/Lt. MORTIMER-PHELAN.	23/4/16	Holland 30/4/18	18/11/18
Capt. D. GRINNELL-MILNE.	16/5/16	Holland 30/4/18	20/11/18
2/Lt. H. L. C. AKED.	21/5/16	Holland 30/4/18	18/11/18
Lieut. A. CAIRNDUFF.	31/5/16	Holland 30/4/18	18/11/18
2/Lt. G. E. MAXWELL.	31/5/16	Holland 30/4/18	18/11/18
Lieut. S. C. T. LITTLEWOOD.	1/6/16	Holland 30/4/18	1/1/19
Capt. D. L. GRANT.	1/6/16	Holland 30/4/18	17/11/18
2/Lt. A. R. L. GOODSON.	3/6/16	Holland 30/4/18	18/11/18
Lieut. H. B. RUSSELL.	26/6/16	Switzerland 9/12/17	24/3/18
Lieut. J. R. DENNISTOUN.	26/6/16	(*Died* 9/8/16).	
Lieut. W. TUDOR-HART.	1/7/16		22/11/18
Capt. T. W. P. L. CHALONER.	1/7/16	Holland 16/5/18	21/1/19
2/Lt. L. A. WINGFIELD.	1/7/16	Escaped	21/10/17
2/Lt. C. T. Van NOSTRAND.	1/7/16	Holland 16/5/18	11/12/18
2/Lt. J. H. FIRSTBROOK.	1/7/16	Switzerland 13/12/16	11/9/17
2/Lt. J. W. TOONE.	2/7/16	Holland 16/5/18	11/12/18

ROYAL AIR FORCE—continued.

Name.	Missing.	Interned.		Repatriated.
2/Lt. S. H. ELLIS.	3/7/16			7/1/18
Lieut. W. CASTLE.	3/7/16	Holland	16/5/18	26/11/18
2/Lt. W. B. ELLIS.	3/7/16	Holland	16/5/16	16/11/18
2/Lt. R. W. NICHOL.	9/7/16	Holland	16/5/18	-/11/18
2/Lt. D. H. MACINTYRE.	9/7/16	Holland	16/5/18	Ret. for duty
2/Lt. H. FLOYD.	9/7/16	(Died at Fabreuil 11/7/16)		
Capt. W. W. JEFFERD.	10/7/16	Holland	16/5/18	22/11/18
Lieut. W. J. M. TOMSON.	10/7/16	Holland	16/5/18	11/12/18
2/Lt. C. KERR.	11/7/16	Holland	16/5/18	19/12/18
2/Lt. H. O. LONG.	16/7/16	Holland	15/6/18	22/11/18
Lieut. H. C. FINNERTY.	19/7/16	Holland	15/6/18	22/11/18
Capt. A. J. EVANS.		Escaped		-/6/17
Lieut. NORMAN ROBINSON.				
Lieut. D. S. C. MacASKIE.	20/7/16	Switzerland	24/12/16	14/9/17
2/Lt. C. J. SANDYS-THOMAS.	20/7/16	Holland	15/6/18	15/11/18
Lieut. R. M. WILSON-BROWNE.	21/7/16	(Died)		
2/Lt. J. G. ROBERTSON.	25/7/16	Holland	15/6/18	-/11/18
2/Lt. L. N. GRAHAM.	30/7/16	Holland	15/6/18	21/1/19
Lieut. E. R. FARMER.	30/7/16	Holland	15/6/18	15/1/19
Capt. C. W. SNOOK.	2/8/16	Holland	15/4/18	7/9/18
2/Lt. J. A. N. ORMSBY.	2/8/16	(Died 5/8/16).		
Lieut. J. C. TURNER.	3/8/16	(Died at Namur 3/8/16)		
2/Lt. C. W. BLAIN.	7/8/16	Escaped		-/8/18
2/Lt. C. D. GRIFFITHS.	7/8/16	Holland	12/10/18	22/11/18
Capt. E. W. LEGGATT.	9/8/16	Escaped		-/8/18
2/Lt. C. GEEN.	13/8/16	Holland	12/10/18	22/11/18
Lieut. H. H. WHITEHEAD.	20/8/16	(Died at Remy 21/8/16)		
2/Lt. R. T. GRIFFIN.	20/8/16	Holland	12/10/18	22/11/18
2/Lt. K. K. TURNER.	25/8/16			21/1/19
2/Lt. C. SMITH.	25/8/16			18/12/18
Lieut. R. D. WALKER.	25/8/16			18/12/18
2/Lt. A. W. REYNELL.	27/8/16			18/12/18
Lieut. H. M. CORBOLD.	-/8/16	(Died at Roisel 26/8/16)		
2/Lt. S. P. BRIGGS.	27/8/16			18/12/18
2/Lt. B. M. WAINWRIGHT.	28/8/16			1/1/19
Lieut. H. F. MASE.	28/8/16			18/12/18
Lieut. G. V. ODLING.	28/8/16	Holland	12/10/18	22/11/18
2/Lt. D. S. CAIRNS.	29/8/16			18/12/18
2/Lt. K. E. TULLOCH.	29/8/16	Switzerland	10/7/18	6/12/18
Capt. O. L. WHITTLE.	31/8/16			18/12/18
2/Lt. H. M. STRANGE.	31/8/16			18/12/18
2/Lt. A. J. O. O'BYRNE.	31/8/16	Switzerland	27/12/17	24/3/18
2/Lt. F. G. MACINTOSH.	31/8/16	Switzerland	9/12/17	24/3/18
2/Lt. J. D. A. MACFIE.	31/8/16	Switzerland	13/12/16	14/9/17
Lieut. D. STEWART.	2/9/16	Escaped		-/4/17
2/Lieut. F. W. GRIFFITHS.	2/9/16	(2/1/19—R.A.F. rep. escaped)		
2/Lt. E. BURTON.	2/9/16			18/12/18
Capt. R. E. WILSON.	2/9/16			18/12/18
Capt. H. G. SALMOND.	2/9/16			18/12/18
2/Lt. A. F. ORGAN.				18/12/18
2/Lt. F. D. H. SAMS.	3/9/16			18/12/18
2/Lt. J. C. TAYLOR.	6/9/16	Switzerland	27/12/17	9/12/18
2/Lt. J. N. TULLIS.	6/9/16	Escaped		-/8/18
Lieut. L. R. BRIGGS.	11/9/16	Switzerland	9/12/17	9/12/18
2/Lt. J. V. BOWRING.	14/9/16			16/12/18
2/Lt. C. J. KENNEDY.	15/9/16			18/12/18
Capt. J. D. F. McEWAN.	16/7/16	Holland	15/6/18	4/1/19
2/Lt. C. A. RIDLEY.	3/8/16	Escaped		16/8/18

ROYAL AIR FORCE—continued.

Name.	Missing.	Interned.	Repatriated.
2/Lt. F. H. BOWYER.	15/9/16		7/1/18
2/Lt. C. ELPHINSTON.	15/9/16		18/12/18
2/Lt. D. CUSHING.	16/9/16		18/12/18
Lieut. G. KLINGENSTEIN.	16/9/16		7/1/18
Lieut. J. W. SANDERS.	16/9/16		18/12/18
2/Lt. A. L. PINKERTON.	16/9/16		18/12/18
2/Lt. L. F. B. MORRIS.	17/9/16	(*Died* at Cambrai)	
Lieut. R. R. N. MONEY.	17/9/16		18/12/18
Lieut. L. B. HELDER.	17/9/16		18/12/18
Capt. D. B. GRAY.	17/9/16	Escaped	-/8/18
2/Lt. R. WOOD.	17/9/16	Holland 9/4/18	2/7/18
Lieut. W. H. S. CHANCE.	17/9/16		18/12/18
2/Lt. A. F. A. PATTERSON.	17/9/16	(*Died* at Cambrai 25/9/16)	
2/Lt. T. P. L. MOLLOY.	17/9/16		18/12/18
2/Lt. R. N. CARTER.	21/9/16		18/12/18
2/Lt. W. J. GRAY.	21/9/16		21/1/19
2/Lt. F. A. A. HEWSON.	22/9/16		18/12/18
2/Lt. R. D. HERMAN.	22/9/16	(*Died* at Epehy)	
2/Lt. J. L. TIBBETTS.	23/9/16		30/12/18
2/Lt. E. N. WINGFIELD.	24/9/16	Holland 12/10/18	29/1/19
2/Lt. S. DENDRINO.	27/9/16	(*Died* 27/9/16)	
Leiut. J. H. LOWSON.	27/9/16		18/12/18
2/Lt. M. S. FARADAY.	27/9/16		18/12/18
2/Lt. A. T. EASON.	28/9/16		18/12/18
2/Lt. W. R. C. CARMICHAEL.	2/10/16	Switzerland 17/12/17	24/3/18
2/Lt. C. KENNARD.	9/10/16	Escaped	-/8/18
Lieut. G. WADDEN.	10/10/16		18/12/18
Lieut. J. B. LAWTON.	10/10/16		18/12/18
Lieut. A. H. M. COPELAND.	10/10/16		14/12/18
2/Lt. N. MIDDLEBROOK.	11/10/16		18/12/18
2/Lt. A. R. CRISP.	16/10/16		18/12/18
2/Lt. C. MOORE KELLY.	16/10/16		20/1/18
2/Lt. C. L. ROBERTS.	17/10/16		-/12/18
2/Lt. J. K. PARKER.	17/10/16		-/1/19
Lieut. W. H. N. WHITEHEAD.	19/10/16		27/1/19
2/Lt. R. L. DINGLEY.	19/10/16		17/12/18
2/Lt. W. BLACK.	20/10/16	Switzerland 27/12/17	14/6/18
Lieut. A. B. RAYMOND-BARKER.	21/10/16		18/12/18
2/Lt. A. L. M. SHEPHERD.	22/10/16	(*Died* at Vitry 3/11/16)	
2/Lt. W. T. WILLCOX.	22/10/16		18/12/18
2/Lt. R. WATTS.	22/10/16		27/1/19
2/Lt. P. F. HEPPEL.	27/10/16	Holland 9/4/18	18/8/18
2/Lt. H. B. O. MITCHELL.	27/10/16	Holland 9/4/18	16/8/18
Lieut. T. M. JOHNS.	31/10/16		18/12/18
Lieut. G. H. NICHOLSON.	31/10/16		18/12/18
2/Lt. W. E. KNOWLDEN.	3/11/16		18/12/18
Lieut. A. ANDERSON.	3/11/16		-/12/18
2/Lt. L. C. L. COOK.	3/11/16	Holland 9/4/18	4/10/18
2/Lt. H. A. HALLAM.	9/11/16		18/12/18
2/Lt. B. W. A. ORDISH.	9/11/16	Holland 9/4/18	7/9/18
Lieut. G. F. KNIGHT.	9/11/16	Escaped	13/9/17
Capt. T. MAPPLEBECK.	9/11/16		29/1/19
2/Lt. T. CURLEWIS.	9/11/16		7/1/18
Capt. A. C. BOLTON.	9/11/16		7/1/18
Lieut. T. H. CLARKE.	20/11/16		17/12/18
2/Lt. J. C. LEES.	20/11/16		1/1/19
2/Lt. K. F. HUNT.	22/9/16		18/12/18
2/Lt. H. F. EVANS.	9/11/16		2/6/18

ROYAL AIR FORCE—continued.

Name.	Missing.	Interned.		Rapatriated.
Lieut. R. CORBETT.	22/11/16	Switzerland	27/12/17	24/3/18
2/Lt. B. W. BLAYNEY.	24/11/16			30/12/18
2/Lt. W. B. CLARK.	26/11/16			-/12/18
2/Lt. G. S. DEANE.	26/11/16			17/12/18
Lieut. B. P. G. HUNT.	11/12/16	Holland	9/4/18	18/11/18
Lieut. C. H. WINDRUM.	20/12/16			-/12/18
Lieut. J. A. HOLLIS.	20/12/16			17/12/18
2/Lt. D. W. DAVIS.	21/12/16	Holland	7/5/18	27/11/18
2/Lt. F. N. INSOLL.	26/12/16			-/12/18
2/Lt. F. A. MANN.	7/1/17			18/12/18
2/Lt. J. E. McLENNAN.	24/1/17			2/1/19
Capt. O. GREIG.	24/1/17			22/12/18
2/Lt. S. ALDER.	25/1/17			-/12/18
Lieut. R. W. WHITE.	25/1/17			28/11/18
2/Lt. F. H. BRONSKILL.	28/1/17			2/1/19
Lieut. C. B. BIRD.	28/1/17			-/12/18
2/Lt. W. A. REEVES.	1/2/17	Retained in Germany for duty		
Lieut. T. G. HOLLEY.	2/2/17			14/12/18
2/Lt. R. T. WHITNEY.	2/2/17			-/1/19
Capt. A. P. V. DALY.	-/2/17	Holland	7/5/18	31/8/18
2/Lt. H. BLYTHE.	2/2/17	(*Died* at Croissiles 10/2/17)		
Flight Sub-Lt. G. BOWLES.		(Interned in Holland)		
Flight Sub-Lt. BRANTFORD.		(Interned in Holland)		
2/Lt. M. E. WOODS.	6/2/17			30/12/18
2/Lt. J. V. FAIRBAIRN.	14/2/17	Holland	15/4/18	18/8/18
Lieut. C. H. MARCH.	15/2/17			2/1/19
Capt. A. LEES.	4/3/17			14/12/18
2/Lt. M.J.J.G. MARE-MONTEMBAULT.	5/3/17			-/1/19
2/Lt. A. G. RYALL.	6/3/17			14/12/18
Lieut. F. E. HILLS.	6/3/17			17/12/18
2/Lt. V. O. LONSDALE	6/3/17			28/11/18
Capt. W. S. R. BLOOMFIELD.	6/3/17			2/1/19
Lieut. H. G. SOUTHON.	6/3/17	Switzerland	29/12/17	-/5/18
2/Lt. T. SHEPARD.	9/3/17			1/1/19
2/Lt. W. B. HILLS.	9/3/17			17/12/18
2/Lt. G. F. HASELER	9/3/17			17/12/18
Lieut. A. D. WHITEHEAD.	11/3/17			20/1/18
2/Lt. A. HOLDEN.	11/3/17			1/1/19
2/Lt. C. A. R. SHUM.	11/3/17			15/12/18
2/Lt. R. W. CROSS.	17/3/17			22/12/18
Lieut. W. ANDERSON.	17/3/17			-/1/19
Lieut. C. F. LODGE.	17/3/17			31/12/18
Lieut. D. B. WOOLLEY.	17/3/17			-/1/19
2/Lt. P. E. H. VanBAERLE.	18/3/17			17/12/18
Lieut. S. HARRYMAN.	18/3/17	(*Died* at Hambaline)		
2/Lt. C. R. DOUGALL.	18/3/17			2/1/19
Lieut. F. H. WILSON.	19/3/17			31/12/18
2/Lt. T. W. JAY.	19/3/17			18/12/18
2/Lt. S. S. B. PURVES.	19/3/17	Escaped		-/8/18
Lieut. J. R. MIDDLETON.	24/3/17	(*Died* at Mulheim 21/6/17)		
Lieut. H. S. WHITESIDE.	24/3/17			11/1/19
Capt. W. H. COSTELLO.	24/3/17			2/1/19
Lieut. C. G. GILBERT.	25/3/17			2/12/18
Lieut. R. P. BAKER.	25/3/17			22/12/18
Lieut. C. S. VANE TEMPEST.	25/3/17	(*Died* at Ligny 27/3/17)		
Lieut. F. ALLINSON.	25/3/17	(*Died* at Ligny 27/3/17)		
2/Lt. C. D. BENNETT.	14/2/17			6/12/18
2/Lt. F. C. COOPS.	11/3/17			18/12/18

ROYAL AIR FORCE—continued.

Name.	Missing.	Interned.	Repatriated.
Sub-Lieut. H. W. OWEN.	28/3/17		14/1/19
2/Lt. N. L. KNIGHT.	28/3/17		14/12/18
2/Lt. L. A. T. STRANGE.	31/3/17		31/12/18
2/Lt. A. P. WARREN.	2/4/17		17/12/18
2/Lt. N. C. DENISON.	2/4/17		3/1/19
Capt. H. TOMLINSON.	2/4/17	(*Died* at Oignies)	
Lt.-Col. C. E. H. RATHBONE.	–//417	Escaped	–/8/18
Lieut. G. P. HARDING.	–/4/17	Escaped	–/10/17
Lieut. L. DODSON.	3/4/17		22/12/18
2/Lt. S. A. SHARPE.	3/4/17		3/1/19
2/Lt. D. P. MacDONALD.	3/4/17		–/12/18
2/Lt. E. L. HEYWORTH.	3/4/17		18/8/18
2/Lt. C. P. THORNTON.	5/4/17		25/12/18
2/Lt. E. D. WARBURTON.	5/4/17		14/12/18
Capt. W. L. ROBINSON.	5/4/17	(*Died* 31/12/18)	14/12/18
Lieut. A. T. ADAMS.	5/4/17		14/12/18
Lieut. D. J. STEWART.	5/4/17		31/12/18
2/Lt. W. T. B. TASKER.	5/4/17		17/12/18
Lieut. H. A. COOPER.	5/4/17		20/1/18
Lieut. H. D. K. GEORGE.	5/4/17	(*Died*)	
2/Lt. A. BOLDISON.	5/4/17		2/1/19
Lieut. N. A. BIRKS.	5/4/17		14/12/18
2/Lt. V. C. MORRIS.	6/4/17		2/1/19
2/Lt. H. D. HAMILTON.	6/4/17		1/1/19
2/Lt. A. R. M. RICKARDS.	6/4/17		14/12/18
Lieut. E. J. D. TOWNESEND.	6/4/17		20/1/18
2/Lt. M. LEWIS.	6/4/17		17/12/18
Lieut. R. T. B. SCHREIBER.	6/4/17		–/12/18
Lieut. T. F. BURRILL.	6/4/17		14/12/18
Lieut. J. K. BOUSFIELD.	6/4/17	Holland 4/8/18	Escaped
2/Lt. A. C. PEPPER.	6/4/17		17/12/18
Capt. M. B. KNOWLES.	7/4/17		17/12/18
Lieut. R. J. BEVINGTON.	7/4/17		17/11/18
2/Lt. D. C. BIRCH.	8/4/17		18/12/18
2/Lt. L. BUTLER.	8/4/17		31/12/18
2/Lt. R. A. LOGAN.	8/4/17		2/1/19
Lieut. F. R. HENRY.	8/4/17		14/12/18
2/Lt. E. A. V. BELL.	8/4/17		11/12/18
2/Lt. J. S. HEAGERTY.	8/4/17		17/12/18
Lieut. A. H. K. McCALLUM.	8/4/17		16/12/18
2/Lt. H. E. HERVEY.	8/4/17		17/12/18
2/Lt. F. B. GOODISON.	8/4/17	(*Died* at Mainz 26/5/17)	
2/Lt. S. ROCHE.	11/4/17		17/12/18
2/Lt. F. MATTHEWS.	11/4/17		2/1/19
2/Lt. G. N. BROCKHURST.	11/4/17		31/12/18
2/Lt. C. B. BOUGHTON.	11/4/17		31/12/18
Capt. D. W. TIDMARSH.	11/4/17		–/12/18
2/Lt. C. B. HOLLAND.	11/4/17		30/12/18
2/Lt. R. E. ADENEY.	11/4/17	(*Died* at Douai)	
2/Lt. E. T. DUNFORD.	11/4/17	(*Died* at Douai)	
Lieut. A. TODD.	12/4/17	(*Died*)	
Lieut. O. D. MAXTED.	12/4/17		2/1/19
2/Lt. H. D. DAVIES.	13/4/17		17/12/18
2/Lt. R. S. L. WORSLEY.	13/4/17		1/1/19
Lieut. W. H. GREEN.	13/4/17	Switzerland 21/10/18	8/12/18
2/Lt. C. W. D. HOLMES.	14/4/17		14/12/18
2/Lt. A. N. LECKLER.	5/4/17	Holland 9/4/18	7/9/18

ROYAL AIR FORCE—continued.

Name.	Missing.	Interned.	Repatriated.
Lieut. H. R. DAVIES.	14/4/17		18/12/18
Lieut. W. O. RUSSELL.	14/4/17		2/1/19
Lieut. J. R. SAMUEL.	14/4/17		2/1/19
2/Lt. E. R. LAW.	14/4/17		31/12/18
Capt. A. BINNIE.	14/4/17		7/1/18
Lieut. W. HARLE.	14/4/17	Switzerland 27/12/17	14/6/18
2/Lt. A. WATSON.	14/4/17		19/5/18
2/Lt. A. E. CRISP.	20/4/17		-/12/18
2/Lt. G. A. NEWENHAM.	20/4/17		-/12/18
2/Lt. F. C. CRAIG.	22/4/17		14/12/18
2/Lt. K. R. FURNISS.	22/4/17	(*Died* at Cambrai 31/4/17)	
Lieut. A. W. WOOD.	22/4/17		7/12/18
2/Lt. J. G. H. FREW.	-/4/17		23/2/18
2/Lt. R. S. CAPON.	24/4/17		31/12/18
Lieut. G. E. HICKS.	24/4/17		17/12/18
Lieut. E. J. DILLNUTT.	25/4/17		14/12/18
2/Lt. J. D. M. STEWART.	25/4/17		17/12/18
2/Lt. G. O. McENTEE.	26/4/17		-/12/18
Lieut. G. M. HOPKINS.	26/4/17		17/12/18
2/Lt. J. H. PRICE.	26/4/17		30/12/18
Capt. H. R. HAWKINS.	26/4/17		14/12/18
Lieut. A. V. BURBURY.	26/4/17		14/12/18
2/Lt. F. STEDMAN.	27/4/17		1/1/19
2/Lt. J. A. CAIRNS.	27/4/17		3/1/19
2/Lt. F. J. KIRKHAM.	28/4/17		31/12/18
2/Lt. A. A. BAERLEIN.	28/4/17		25/12/18
2/Lt. J. V. WISCHER.	28/4/17		6/1/19
Lieut. D. K. PARIS.	28/4/17		1/1/19
2/Lt. C. REECE.	28/4/17		16/1/19
2/Lt. V. L. A. BURNS.	29/4/17		25/12/18
2/Lt. E. PERCIVAL.	29/4/17		14/12/18
2/Lt. F. A. W. HANDLEY.	29/4/17		31/12/18
Lieut. H. B. MILLING.	29/4/17		31/12/18
2/Lt. D. L. HOUGHTON.	29/4/17		28/11/18
Lieut. W. N. HAMILTON.	29/4/17		1/1/19
2/Lt. J. E. DAVIES.	29/4/17		-/12/18
2/Lt. R. H. UPSON.	30/4/17		31/12/18
Lieut. J. R. LINGARD.	30/4/17		31/12/18
2/Lt. S. T. WILLS.	30/4/17		17/12/18
2/Lt. A. E. FEREMAN.	30/4/17		2/1/19
Lieut. P. T. BOWERS.	30/4/17		14/12/18
2/Lt. E. D. JENNINGS.	30/4/17		30/12/18
2/Lt. D. McTAVISH.	30/4/17		1/1/19
2/Lt. H. KIRBY.			-/1/19
Lieut. C. R. O'BRIEN.	1/5/17		-/12/18
2/Lt. E. L. EDWARDS.	1/5/17		18/12/18
Lieut. G. S. FRENCH.	1/5/17		14/12/18
2/Lt. A. FRASER.	3/5/17		22/12/18
2/Lt. V. H. ADAMS.	4/5/17	(*Died* 5/5/17)	
2/Lt. L. G. BACON.	5/5/17		7/1/18
2/Lt. G. D. HUNTER.	6/5/17		20/1/18
2/Lt. C. W. McKISSOCK.	6/5/17		17/12/18
2/Lt. A. W. MARTIN.	7/5/17		30/12/18
2/Lt. M. M. KAIZER.	7/5/17		25/12/18
Lieut. J. B. B. DE M. HARVEY.	9/5/17		17/12/18
2/Lt. F. D. WOOLLIAMS.	9/5/17		17/12/18

ROYAL AIR FORCE—continued.

Name.	Missing.	Interned.	Repatriated.
2/Lt. C. W. LANE.	9/5/17		2/1/19
2/Lt. C. A. FURLONGER.	9/5/17		3/1/19
2/Lt. G. C. T. HADRILL.	9/5/17		1/1/19
Lieut. T. H. WICKETT.	10/5/17		3/6/18
2/Lt. W. O. B. WINKLER.	11/5/17		30/12/18
2/Lt. J. DANIEL.	11/5/17		2/1/19
2/Lt. E. S. MOORE.	11/5/17		1/1/19
Lieut. A. B. RAYMOND.	13/5/17		-/1/19
2/Lt. A. M. SUTHERLAND.	13/5/17		1/1/19
Sub-Lieut. E. J. GROUT.	15/5/17		12/12/18
2/Lt. J. D. V. HOLMES.	18/5/17		2/1/19
2/Lt. T. H. LINES.	18/5/17		14/12/18
2/Lt. S. T. ALLABARTON.	19/5/17		3/1/19
Lieut. C. E. FRENCH.	20/5/17		14/12/18
Lieut. A. C. LEE.	20/5/17		1/1/19
Lieut. J. H. BLACKALL.	21/5/17		17/12/18
2/Lt. B. C. MOODY.	21/5/17		17/12/18
Lieut. R. A. P. JOHNS.	23/5/17		-/1/19
Capt. L. A. SMITH.	24/5/17	Switzerland 27/12/17	14/6/18
Lieut. C. C. F. OSBORN.	24/5/17		17/12/18
Lieut. J. H. H. GOODALL.	24/5/17		1/1/19
2/Lt. L. HOLMAN.	24/5/17		17/12/18
2/Lt. W. GILCHRIST.	25/5/17		17/11/18
2/Lt. T. S. MILLAR.	25/5/17		-/12/18
2/Lt. J. JOHNSTONE.	25/5/17		2/1/19
2/Lt. R. R. MacINTOSH.	26/5/17		-/12/18
2/Lt. Y. TOOGOOD.	26/5/17	Switzerland 27/12/17	24/3/18
Lieut. C. F. SMITH.	26/5/17		14/12/18
2/Lt. G. M. ROBERTSON.	26/5/17	Switzerland 27/12/17	7/12/18
Lieut. S. S. HUME.	27/5/17		28/8/18
2/Lt. E. A. L. LLOYD.	27/5/17		2/1/19
Lieut. T. N. SOUTNORN.	27/5/17		17/12/18
Lieut. V. SMITH.	28/5/17		-/12/18
2/Lt. E. H. STEVENS.	28/5/17	(*Died* at Tournai 16/6/17)	
Capt. A. De SELINCOURT.	28/5/17		17/12/18
Lieut. H. COTTON.	28/5/17		14/12/18
Lieut. R. M. ROBERTS.	28/5/17		17/12/18
Lieut. F. W. KANTEL.	30/5/17		14/12/18
2/Lt. B. S. LISTER.	1/6/17		14/12/18
Lieut. E. A. STEWARDSON.	1/6/17		30/12/18
2/Lt. F. BARRIE.	2/6/17		31/12/18
2/Lt. H. E. WATERS.	2/6/17		14/12/18
Lieut. D. R. CAMERON.	3/6/17		14/12/18
Lieut. A. S. BOURINOT.	3/6/17		14/12/18
2/Lt. D. T. STEEVES.	4/6/17		17/12/18
2/Lt. C. D. GRIERSON.	5/6/17		17/12/18
Lieut. B. SMITH.	5/6/17		17/12/18
2/Lt. B. G. CHALMERS.	5/6/17		26/12/18
Capt. F. P. DON.	5/6/17		-/1/18
2/Lt. H. HARRIS.	5/6/17		17/12/18
Lieut. T. M. DICKINSON.	6/6/17		19/1/19
2/Lt. F. DURKIN.	7/6/17		18/12/18
Lieut. A. P. MITCHELL.	7/6/17		2/1/19
2/Lt. Count L. T. B. Di BALME.	7/6/17		14/12/18
2/Lt. N. B. HAIR.	7/6/17		17/12/18
2/Lt. F. W. ILLINGWORTH.	7/6/17		-/12/18

ROYAL AIR FORCE—continued.

Name.	Missing.	Interned.	Repatriated.
Lieut. J. W. SHAW.	7/6/17		17/12/18
2/Lt. R. M. MARSH.	7/6/17		17/12/18
2/Lt. G. C. STEAD.	7/6/17		-/1/19
2/Lt. R. S. L. BOOTE.	8/6/17		18/12/18
2/Lt. F. D. SLEE.	8/6/17		5/12/18
Lieut. F. SHARPE.	9/6/17		2/1/19
2/Lt. W. J. MUSSARED.	9/6/17		15/12/18
Lieut. H. ROGERSON.	14/6/17		31/12/18
Lieut. W. T. COLES.	17/6/17		31/12/18
Lieut. H. D. SPEARPOINT.	17/6/17		17/12/18
Capt. T. DAVIDSON.	19/6/17		14/12/18
2/Lt. G. C. ATKINS.	19/6/17		5/12/18
2/Lt. G. T. HARKER.	23/6/17		28/12/18
2/Lt. T. M. STURGESS.	24/6/17		17/12/18
2/Lt. F. E. VIPOND.	26/6/17		17/12/18
Lieut. D. C. G. MURRAY.	27/6/17	Switzerland 27/12/17	9/12/18
Lieut. G. P. SIMON.	27/6/17		2/1/19
Lieut. V. A. NORVILL.	29/6/17		8/1/18
Lieut. J. C. MacGOWN.	7/7/17		17/12/18
2/Lt. A. J. SAVORY.	11/7/17		2/1/19
2/Lt. R. TRATTLES.	11/7/17		31/12/18
2/Lt. W. A. STRICKLAND.	12/7/17		31/12/18
2/Lt. H. M. LEWIS.	12/7/17		17/12/18
Lieut. D. S. WELD.	12/7/17		14/12/18
2/Lt. J. C. GRIFFITH.	12/7/17		25/12/18
2/Lt. W. C. SMITH.	13/7/17		7/1/18
Lieut. C. G. MATHEW.	13/7/17		17/12/18
Lieut. F. W. WINTERBOTHAM.	13/7/17		6/1/19
Capt. F. N. HUDSON.	13/7/17		19/12/18
Lieut. E. D. SLITER.	13/7/17		19/5/18
2/Lt. D. H. PALMER.	14/7/17		17/12/18
2/Lt. N. H. MARSHALL.	14/7/17		14/1/19
2/Lt. G. DAVIS.	14/7/17		18/12/18
2/Lt. V. C. COOMBS.	15/7/17		14/12/18
2/Lt. H. M. TAYLER.	15/7/17		20/1/18
2/Lt. G. A. H. PARKES.	15/7/17		23/12/18
2/Lt. C. T. FELTON.	17/7/17		20/1/18
Lieut. O. J. PARTINGTON.	17/7/17		2/1/19
Lieut. W. E. GROSSERT.	17/7/17		23/12/18
2/Lt. J. C. TRULOCK.	22/7/17		25/8/18
Lieut. C. C. KNIGHT.	22/7/17	Holland 30/4/18	18/11/18
Lieut. M. MOORE.	22/7/17		1/1/19
Capt. G. H. COCK.	23/7/17		-/12/18
Lieut. W. D. CULLEN.			14/12/18
2/Lt. A. B. HILL.	24/7/17		14/12/18
Lieut. W. B. MACKAY.	27/7/17		14/12/18
2/Lt. J. CHAPMAN.	27/7/17		-/1/19
2/Lt. T. W. WHITE.	27/7/17		25/12/18
2/Lt. A. S. SHEPHERD.	27/7/17	(*Died* at Fandvoorde)	
2/Lt. J. B. HINE.	28/7/17		2/1/19
2/Lt. R. C. HUME.	28/7/17		2/1/19
Capt. H. O. D. WILKINS.	28/7/17		14/12/18
Lieut. A. C. MALLOCH.	28/7/17		14/12/18
Lieut. H. O. MACDONALD.	29/7/17		16/1/19
Lieut. C. H. BELDAM.	31/7/17		28/12/18
2/Lt. W. B. KELLOG.	31/7/17		13/12/18

ROYAL AIR FORCE—continued.

Name.	Missing.	Interned.	Repatriated.
Lt. M. T. WRIGHT.	16/8/17		8/12/18
Lt. C. B. WATERS.	16/8/17		19/12/18
2/Lt. W. H. WATT.	31/7/17		-/1/19
Lieut. H. J. ELLAM.	5/8/17		29/11/18
Lieut. C. A. S. BEAN.	9/8/17		-/1/19
Lieut. W. H. HOWES.	9/8/17		17/12/18
2/Lt. W. R. K. SKINNER.	9/8/17		17/12/18
2/Lt. J. F. HENDERSON.	10/8/17		2/1/19
Lieut. E. P. FULTON.	10/8/17		14/12/18
2/Lt. A. N. BARLOW.	10/8/17		2/1/19
2/Lt. C. G. MALLOUS.	10/8/17		25/12/18
Lieut. C. D. HUTCHINSON.	10/8/17	(*Died* at Menlebeke 12/8/17)	
2/Lt. R. N. W. JEFF.	11/8/17		-/12/18
2/Lt. H. G. TINNEY.	11/8/17		6/1/19
2/Lt. G. COLLEDGE.	11/8/17		18/12/18
2/Lt. C. G. GUY.	11/8/17	(*Died* Wynendaele 12/8/17)	
2/Lt. L. READ.	12/8/17		17/12/18
2/Lt. J. G. YOUNG.	14/8/17		2/1/19
Capt. A. R. HUDSON.	16/8/17		29/11/18
2/Lt. A. T. SHIPWRIGHT.	16/8/17		25/12/18
Lieut. C. D. THOMPSON.	16/8/17		25/12/18
Lieut. A. E. S. BARTON.	16/8/17		27/12/18
2/Lt. G. M. SMITH.	16/8/17		5/1/19
2/Lt. P. A. O'BRIEN.	17/8/17	Escaped	-/11/17
2/Lt. R. S. PHELAN.	17/8/17		17/12/18
Lieut. D. S. WILKINSON.	17/8/17	(*Died* Kortryk 26/8/17)	
Lieut. R. T. LEIGHTON.	17/8/17		-/1/19
2/Lt. G. A. ROSE.	18/8/17		2/1/19
2/Lt. W. B. STYLES.	18/8/17		17/12/18
Capt. H. N. RUSHWORTH.	18/8/17		12/10/18
Lieut. H. R. HART-DAVIES.	19/8/17		28/11/18
2/Lt. S. F. THOMPSON.	19/8/17		6/1/19
2/Lt. C. R. RICHARDS.	19/8/17		2/1/19
2/Lt. H. E. A. WARING.	19/8/17		-/1/19
2/Lt. C. P. ADAMSON.	20/8/17		18/12/18
2/Lt. Sidney THOMPSON.	21/8/17		17/12/18
2/Lt. C. W. DAVIES.	21/8/17		17/12/18
Lieut. W. B. HUTCHESON.	21/8/17		14/12/18
Lieut. J. A. MANNERS SMITH.	21/8/17		-/12/18
2/Lt. E. H. GARLAND.	22/8/17		-/11/18
2/Lt. L. WIGLEY.	23/8/17		19/12/18
2/Lt. H. G. TAMBLING.	23/8/17		14/12/1-8
Lieut. J. B. C. MADGE.	1/9/17		17/12/18
2/Lt. W. A. L. SPENCER.	2/9/17		30/11/18
Lieut. S. W. WILLIAMS.	3/9/17		17/12/18
Lieut. A. F. BIRD.	3/9/17		14/12/18
Lieut. K. W. MACDONALD.	3/9/17	(*Died* at Menin)	
2/Lt. A. C. PICKETT.	3/9/17		2/1/19
2/Lt. F. SCARBOROUGH.	3/9/17		17/12/18
Capt. C. C. SHARP.	4/9/17		2/1/19
Lieut. S. A. HARPER	4/9/17		2/1/19
2/Lt. T. M. WEBSTER.	5/9/17		14/12/18
Lieut. J. W. F. NEILL.	5/9/17	Holland 9/4/18	31/8/18
2/Lt. J. C. HUGGARD.	5/9/17		14/12/18
2/Lt. E. G. C. QUILTER.	6/9/17		18/12/18
2/Lt. W. E. DE B. DIAMOND.	9/9/17		18/12/18
Lieut. N. C. SAWARD.	9/9/17		6/1/19
2/Lt. G. P. ROBERTSON.	10/9/17		25/12/18
2/Lt. D. P. COLLIS.	10/8/17		4/1/19
2/Lt. J. W. GILLESPIE.	19/8/17		2/1/19
2/Lt. J. J. MacFARLANE	17/8/17	(*Died* 26/8/17)	

ROYAL AIR FORCE—continued.

Name.	Missing.	Interned.		Repatriated.
2/Lt. A. F. ORR-EWING	20/9/17			3/1/19
2/Lt. H. T. HAMMOND.	14/9/17			31/12/18
2/Lt. E. B. DENISON.	11/9/17			3/1/19
Sub-Lt. E. D. ABBOTT.	13/9/17			17/12/18
2/Lt. S. H. TAYLOR.	14/9/17			6/1/19
Lieut. E. G. C. SEN.	14/9/17			17/12/18
2/Lt. J. B. H. WYMAN.	15/9/17	Holland	7/5/18	-/1/19
2/Lt. H. IBBOTSON.	15/9/17			29/11/18
2/Lt. E. E. F. LOYD.	15/9/17			17/12/18
Lieut. T. G. DEASON.	15/9/17			17/12/18
2/Lt. A. H. SKINNER.	16/9/17			17/12/18
2/Lt. L. F. WHEELER.	16/9/17			17/12/18
Lieut. G. B. McMICHAEL.	16/9/17			-/1/19
2/Lt. L. M. SHADWELL.	16/9/17			17/12/18
2/Lt. C. A. SUTCLIFFE.	19/9/17			17/12/18
Lieut. G. W. MUMFORD.	19/9/17			14/12/18
2/Lt. N. J. TAYLOR.	19/9/17			14/12/18
2/Lt. C. G. D. GRAY.	20/9/17			14/12/18
2/Lt. C. H. F. NOBBS.	20/9/17			2/1/19
2/Lt. T. HUMBLE.	20/9/17			2/1/19
Capt. A. C. HATFIELD.	20/9/17			13/12/18
2/Lt. R. R. MACGREGOR.	20/9/17			-/12/18
2/Lt. D. P. FitzG. UNIACKE.	21/9/17			-/12/18
2/Lt. E. A. COOKE.	21/9/17			19/12/18
2/Lt. G. R. BAYNTON.	23/9/17			25/12/18
2/Lt. H. ROTHERY.	23/9/17			-/12/18
2/Lt. W. ENGLISH.	24/9/17			14/12/18
2/Lt. M. E. HALL.	24/9/17			14/12/18
2/Lt. P. J. CASEY.	24/9/17			18/12/18
2/Lt. F. C. ANDREWS.	26/9/17			5/12/18
2/Lt. C. N. L. LOMAX.	26/9/17			-/12/18
2/Lt. A. L. SUTCLIFFE.	26/9/17			23/2/18
2/Lt. C. E. STUART.	26/9/17			6/1/19
2/Lt. T. B. FENWICK.	26/9/17			7/12/18
2/Lt. A. TAYLOR.	26/9/17			-/12/18
2/Lt. J. L. HAIGHT.	28/9/17			17/12/18,
2/Lt. J. W. FROST.	29/9/17			15/11/18
2/Lt. F. L. SMITH.	29/9/17			15/11/18
Lieut. G. F. WESTCOTT.	29/9/17			-/12/18
2/Lt. E. A. V. ELLERBECK.	29/9/17			14/12/18
Lieut. J. W. BOUMPHREY.	30/9/17			14/12/18
2/Lt. J. F. BUSHE.	1/10/17			2/1/19
2/Lt. L. A. COLBERT.	1/10/17			17/12/18
Lieut. F. H. BERRY.	2/10/17			14/12/18
2/Lt. C. G. CRANE.	2/10/17			17/12/18
2/Lt. F. M. NASH.	3/10/17			2/1/19
Lieut. C. H. JEFFS.	5/10/17			17/12/18
2/Lt. J. G. STEVENSON.	5/10/17			-/1/19
2/Lt. J. J. FITZGERALD.	5/10/17			17/12/18
Capt. D. D. WALROND-SKINNER.	5/10/17			10/1/19
Lieut. G. R. LONG.	6/10/17			14/12/19
2/Lt. R. H. RICHARDSON.	6/10/17			2/1/19
Lieut. E. Cola CARROLL.	6/10/17			14/12/18
Lieut. W. D. CHAMBERS.	8/10/17			-/1/19
2/Lt. M. A. PEACOCK.	9/10/17			-/1/19
Lieut. D. G. POWELL.	10/10/17			-/12/18
Lieut. R. F. HILL.	10/10/17			-/1/19
Lieut. R. I. V. HILL.	11/10/17			14/12/18
2/Lt. K. G. CRUIKSHANK.	11/9/17	(Died 29/9/17).		
2/Lt. S. W. DRONSFIELD.	12/9/17			2/1/19

ROYAL AIR FORCE—continued.

Name.	Missing.	Interned.	Repatriated.
2/Lt. S. L. WHITEHOUSE.	27/10/17		27/11/18
2/Lt. R. S. GILBERT.	11/10/17		24/1/19
2/Lt. A. E. TURVEY.	11/10/17		6/1/19
2/Lt. W. H. WINTER.	11/10/17		13/12/18
2/Lt. W. G. MORGAN.	12/10/17	(*Died* 23/10/17)	
2/Lt. W. NEWCOMB.	12/10/17		2/1/19
2/Lt. H. PUGHE-EVANS.	12/10/17		13/12/18
2/Lt. F. W. TALBOT.	12/10/17	Holland 9/4/18	-/11/18
2/Lt. G. W. ARMSTRONG.	12/10/17		17/12/18
2/Lt. R. W. B. MATTHEWSON.	12/10/17		2/1/19
2/Lt. J. M. ATKINSON.	12/10/17	Holland 30/4/18	18/8/18
2/Lt. P. C. NORTON.	13/10/17		13/12/18
2/Lt. W. W. VICK.	13/10/17		13/12/18
2/Lt. J. C. GARRETT.	14/10/17		17/12/18
2/Lt. B. F. BRAITHWAITE.	14/10/17		18/12/18
Lieut. C. SMYTHE.	14/10/17		25/12/18
2/Lt. A. A. WARD.	14/10/17		14/12/18
2/Lt. T. Vernon LORD.	14/10/17		2/1/19
2/Lt. H. S. WELLBY.	15/10/17		-/12/18
2/Lt. F. J. ORTWEILER.	16/10/17	Escaped	-/10/18
Fl. Sub.-Lt. M. T. WATSON.			19/12/18
2/Lt. E. SCHOLTZ.	17/10/17		16/12/18
2/Lt. E. L. FOSSE.	17/10/17		19/5/18
2/Lt. H. C. WOOKEY.	17/10/17		16/12/18
Lieut. S. M. PARK.	18/10/17		17/12/18
2/Lt. G. W. FORBES.	18/10/17		
Lieut. B. B. PERRY.	18/10/17		2/1/19
Capt. H. PATCH.	18/10/17	(*Died* at Bevereu 19/10/17)	
Lieut. C. H. BARTLETT.	18/10/17		17/12/18
2/Lt. W. E. WATTS.	20/10/17		-/1/19
2/Lt. F. B. FARQUHARSON.	20/10/17		2/1/19
2/Lt. G. R. EDWARDS.	21/10/17		14/1/19
2/Lt. O. M. HILLS.	21/10/17		2/1/19
2/Lt. D. McLAURIN.	21/10/17		2/1/19
2/Lt. F. L. YEOMANS.	21/10/17		17/12/18
Capt. D. OWEN.	21/10/17	Holland 30/4/18	16/8/18
2/Lt. A. E. HEMPEL.	21/10/17		17/12/18
2/Lt. B. HARKER.	21/10/17		3/6/18
2/Lt. P. GOODBEHERE.	22/10/17		17/12/18
Fl. Sub.-Lt. H. G. B. LINNELL.			14/12/18
Lieut. J. S. GODDARD.	24/10/17		17/12/18
2/Lt. K. L. GOLDING.	24/10/17		18/8/18
Lieut. R. L. GREENSLADE.	24/10/17		14/12/18
2/Lt. L. N. ARCHIBALD.	24/10/17		17/12/18
2/Lt. E. C. S. RINGER.	25/10/17		17/12/18
2/Lt. J. A. M. FLEMING.	25/10/17		5/12/18
2/Lt. E. A. L. F. SMITH.	26/10/17		17/12/18
Lieut. R. J. E. P. GOODE.	27/10/17		17/12/18
2/Lt. R. A. CARTLEDGE.	27/10/17		14/12/18
2/Lt. A. W. RUSH.	28/10/17		14/12/18
2/Lt. W. H. JONES.	29/10/17		17/12/18
2/Lt. F. S. CLARK.	29/10/17		18/12/18
2/Lt. N. H. KEMP.	31/10/17		17/12/18
2/Lt. R. M. SMITH.	31/10/17		17/12/18
2/Lt. H. G. ROBINSON.	3/11/17		-/12/18
Lieut. T. B. BRUCE.	6/11/17	Escaped.	-/1/18
2/Lt. E. H. CUTBILL.	6/11/17		14/12/18
2/Lt. R. G. FRITH.	5/11/17		2/12/18
2/Lt. J. D. LAING.	24/10/17	(*Died* 28/1/18).	

ROYAL AIR FORCE—continued.

Name.	Missing.	Interned.		Repatriated.
2/Lt. A. G. CRIBB.	6/11/17			17/12/18
2/Lt. E. P. WILMOT.	6/11/17			17/12/18
2/Lt. E. G. S. GORDON.	6/11/17			14/12/18
Lieut. R. C. TAYLOR.	6/11/17			17/12/18
2/Lt. F. G. BAKER.	6/11/17			17/12/18
Lieut. W. L. HARRISON.	6/11/17			27/11/18
2/Lt. W. C. PRUDEN.	8/11/17			1/12/18
2/Lt. W. R. KINGSLAND.	8/11/17			-/12/18
Lieut. F. R. C. COBBOLD.	8/11/17			12/12/18
2/Lt. F. J. B. HAMMERSLEY.	8/11/17			6/1/19
Lieut. W. G. MEGGITT.	8/11/17			2/6/18
2/Lt. A. THOMPSON.	9/11/17			17/12/18
Lieut. K. S. MORRISON.	12/11/17	Holland	14/4/18	18/8/18
2/Lt. T. P. MORGAN.	15/11/17			27/11/18
2/Lt. S. S. HENRY.	15/11/17			27/11/18
Lieut. J. M. LEACH.	15/11/17			13/12/18
2/Lt. T. J. KENT.	20/11/17			14/12/18
2/Lt. M. B. W. STEAD.	20/11/17			14/12/18
Lieut. T. MORSE.	20/11/17			
Lieut. J. MacRAE.	20/11/17			14/12/18
Lieut. L. N. WARD.	20/11/17			13/12/18
2/Lt. T. L. ATKINSON.	22/11/17			17/12/18
Capt. G. B. CROLE.	22/11/17			18/12/18
2/Lt. E. F. MARCHAND.	22/11/17			2/1/19
Lieut. C. F. KELLER.	23/11/17			17/12/18
2/Lt. R. MAIN.	23/11/17			29/12/18
2/Lt. A. MUIR.	24/11/17			17/12/18
Lieut. L. KERT.	27/11/17			14/12/18
2/Lt. C. H. BROWN.	28/11/17			22/11/18
Lieut. A. DODDS.	29/11/17			18/12/18
2/Lt. L. W. TIMMIS.	30/11/17			14/12/18
Lieut. R. E. DUSGATE.	30/11/17	*(Died)*		
Capt. D. B. KING.	30/11/17			14/1/19
Lieut. H. WHITWORTH.	30/11/17			17/12/18
2/Lt. G. G. W. PETERSON.	2/12/17			14/12/18
2/Lt. S. G. SPIRO.	2/12/17			17/12/18
Capt. J. E. JOHNSTON.	2/12/17			-/12/18
2/Lt. D. MILLER.	2/12/17			17/12/18
2/Lt. A. F. GOODCHAP.	3/12/17			14/12/18
2/Lt A. H. MIDDLETON.	3/12/17			14/12/18
2/Lt. C. E. OGDEN.	5/12/17			17/12/18
2/Lt. L. G. NIXON.	5/12/17			17/12/18
2/Lt. S. KENDALL.	5/12/17			17/12/18
2/Lt. H. A. YEO.	7/12/17			17/12/18
2/Lt. A. W. PALMER.	7/12/17			17/12/18
2/Lt. T. W. CALVERT.	7/12/17			28/12/18
2/Lt. J. A. M. ROBERTSON.	8/12/17			4/12/18
Lieut. H. V. CAUNT.	15/12/17			14/12/18
2/Lt. I. D. CAMERON.	18/12/17			18/12/18
2/Lt. R. H. COWAN.	18/12/17			14/12/18
Lieut. James BRENT.		Holland.		
Lieut. L. B. MAY.	19/12/17			29/11/18
2/Lt. G. F. TURNER.	24/12/17			17/12/18
2/Lt. A. F. CASTLE	24/12/17			18/12/18
2/Lt A. L. CLARK.	-/12/17			11/1/19
2/Lt. J. BRYDONE.	28/12/17			18/12/18

ROYAL AIR FORCE—continued.

Name.	Missing.	Interned.	Repatriated.
2/Lt. H. E. GALER.	29/12/17		17/12/18
2/Lt. A. L. KIDD.	1/1/18		17/12/18
2/Lt. R. J. G. STEWART.	3/1/18		22/12/18
2/Lt. A. F. WYNNE.	4/1/18		17/12/18
Capt. E. E. E. POPE.	4/1/18		17/12/18
2/Lt. O. THAMER.	6/1/18	Holland	22/11/18
Lieut. C. W. LEGGATT.	10/1/18		17/12/18
2/Lt. J. H. YOUNG.	12/1/18	(*Died* at Seboncourt)	
Lieut. J. D. BARNES.	12/1/18		20/11/18
Lieut. G. N. GOLDIE.	12/1/18		21/11/18
Lieut. J. BOYD.	12/1/18		18/12/18
2/Lt. T. B. URWIN.	12/1/18	(*Died* at Bohain)	
2/Lt. F. B. WILLMOTT.	13/1/18		14/12/18
2/Lt. H. V. BIDDINGTON.	13/1/18		14/12/18
2/Lt. H. E. DAVIES.	13/1/18		14/12/18
2/Lt. A. M. OHRT.	19/1/18		17/12/18
Lieut. C. W. REID.	21/1/18		17/12/18
2/Lt. F. W. DOGHERTY.	22/1/18		18/12/18
2/Lt. L. G. TAYLOR.	21/1/18		17/12/18
2/Lt. F. E. Le FEVRE.	24/1/18		17/12/18
2/Lt. H. S. CLEMONS.	25/1/18		1/12/18
2/Lt. L. J. WILLIAMS.	28/1/18		17/12/18
Lieut. K. M. RODGER.	29/1/18		13/12/18
2/Lt. A. H. PEILE.	31/1/18		14/12/18
Major J. F. POWELL.	2/2/18		–/12/18
2/Lt. F. D. C. GORE.	2/2/18		29/12/18
2/Lt. P. C. C. MARTIN.	3/2/18	Escaped.	–/8/18
Lieut. E. G. GREEN.	3/2/18		2/12/18
2/Lt. A. C. BALL.	5/2/18		14/12/18
2/Lt. E. O. CUDMORE.	5/2/18		18/12/18
2/Lt. A. G. D. ALDERSON.	6/2/18		17/12/18
2/Lt. A. FIELDING-CLARKE.	9/2/18		18/12/18
2/Lt. O. B. SWART.	9/2/18		17/12/18
2/Lt. G. A. C. MANLEY.	9/2/18		14/12/18
Capt. S. J. SIBLEY.	14/2/18		14/12/18
2/Lt. F. C. GILBERT.	16/2/18		14/12/18
2/Lt. R. MACDONALD.	16/2/18		29/11/18
2/Lt. O. G. S. CRAWFORD.	17/2/18		17/12/18
2/Lt. C. J. W. McKEOWN.	18/2/18		17/12/18
2/Lt. G. G. JACKSON.	18/2/18		14/12/18
2/Lt. H. A. HEWITT.	19/2/18		17/12/18
Lieut. W. ROSS.	19/2/18		17/12/18
2/Lt. G. C. LOGAN.	21/2/18		11/12/18
2/Lt. S. G. WILLIAMS.	21/2/18	Escaped.	1/5/18
2/Lt. A. COUSTON.	21/2/18		19/12/18
2/Lt. B. C. WINDLE.	21/2/18		17/12/18
2/Lt. W. B. RANDELL.	24/2/18		14/12/18
Capt. K. B. MONTGOMERY.	22/2/18		20/11/18
2/Lt. G. R. T. MARSH.	24/2/18		13/12/18
2/Lt. C. H. S. ACKERS.	26/2/18		14/12/18
2/Lt. H. F. DOUGALL.	26/2/18		–/12/18
Lieut. J. R. LAW.	26/2/18		14/12/18
2/Lt. J. M. ALLEN.	26/2/18		13/12/18
2/Lt. C. H. CROSBIE.	26/2/18		18/12/18
2/Lt. D. C. DOYLE.	26/2/18		14/12/18
Lieut. G. M. SHAW.	26/2/18		18/12/18
Capt. BIHELLER.	19/1/18		23/9/18
Lt. D. C. WRIGHT.	20/2/18	(*Died* at Vienna 22/2/18).	

ROYAL AIR FORCE—continued.

Name.	Missing.	Interned.	Repatriated.
2/Lt. R. A. MAYNE.	16/3/18		19/12/18
Flt.Sub.-Lt. K. D. CAMPBELL.			14/12/18
Lieut. W. F. POULTER.	5/3/18	(*Died* at Outreaux 6/3/18)	
Lieut. R. E. DUKE.	6/3/18		17/12/18
2/Lt. A. P. C. WIGAN.	6/3/18		14/12/18
Lieut. R. H. TOPLISS.	8/3/18		17/12/18
Lieut. H. R. CASGRAIN.	8/3/18		7/12/18
2/Lt. P. La T. FOSTER.	9/3/18		14/12/18
2/Lt. R. CALDECOTT.	10/3/18		17/12/18
Lieut. C. H. FLERE.	10/3/18		14/12/18
2/Lt. E. P. P. EDMONDS.	10/3/18	(*Died* at Denain 18/3/18)	
Lieut. G. P. F. THOMAS.	10/3/18		14/12/18
Lieut. H. B. P. BOYCE.	12/3/18		14/12/18
2/Lt. C. B. FENTON.	12/3/18		17/12/18
2/Lt. J. A. A. FERGUSON.	12/3/18		18/12/18
2/Lt. H. J. SPARKS.	12/3/18		13/12/18
2/Lt. L. C. F. CLUTTERBUCK.	12/3/18		17/12/18
Lieut. G. R. CRAMMOND.	13/3/18		14/12/18
Lieut. E. E. HEATH.	13/3/18		25/12/18
2/Lt. T. S. WILSON.	13/3/18		17/12/18
2/Lt. N. B. WELLS.	13/3/18		17/12/18
2/Lt. N. T. WATSON.	13/3/18		25/12/18
2/Lt. W. H. TAYLOR.	16/3/18		14/12/18
2/Lt. C. V. SHAKESBY.	16/3/18		17/12/18
2/Lt. A. L. T. TAYLOR.	16/3/18		14/12/18
Flt. Commdr. R. P. MINIFIE.	17/3/18		14/12/18
2/Lt. W. J. IVAMY.	18/3/18		14/12/18
Capt. F. L. LUXMOORE.	18/3/18		17/12/18
Lieut. E. B. LEE.	18/3/18		17/12/18
Capt. A. P. MacLEAN.	18/3/18	(*Died*)	
2/Lt. A. W. MATSON.	18/3/18		14/12/18
Lieut. G. T. STEEVES.	18/3/18		17/12/18
Lieut. J. H. WENSLEY.	18/3/18		14/12/18
2/Lt. A. T. ISBELL.	21/3/18		18/12/18
2/Lt. F. K. KNELLER.	21/3/18	(*Died*)	
2/Lt. R. B. SMITH.	21/3/18		17/12/18
2/Lt. T. E H. BIRLEY.	22/3/18		13/12/18
2/Lt. H. K. CASSELS.	22/3/18		17/12/18
Lieut. R. W. COUTTS.	22/3/18		17/12/18
2/Lt. C. H. CLARKE.	23/3/18		13/12/18
2/Lt. H. P. BLAKE.	23/3/18		17/12/18
2/Lt. A. F. G. CLARKE.	23/3/18		14/12/18
Lieut. R. H. EDELSTON.	23/3/18		23/12/18
Lieut. D. W. KENT-JONES.	23/3/18		26/12/18
Lieut. W. G. FLUKE.	24/3/18		17/12/18
Lieut. C. W. COOK.	24/3/18		25/12/18
2/Lt. R. M. WYNNE-EYTON.	24/3/18		15/11/18
2/Lt. J. O. BUTLER.	24/3/18	(*Died* at Mons 11/4/18)	
Lieut. J. D. CURRIE.	24/3/18		14/12/18
2/Lt. N. H. THACKRAH.	24/3/18		14/12/18
2/Lt. A. A. MILES.	24/3/18		14/12/18
2/Lt. C. F. WESTING.	24/3/18		1/12/18
Lieut. E. M. CHANT.	25/3/18	(*Died* at Cambrai 4/4/18)	
2/Lt. G. G. NEWBURY.	25/3/18		13/12/18
2/Lt. W. M. R. GRAY.	26/3/18		14/12/18
Lieut. A. HOLLIS.	26/3/18		1/12/18
2/Lt. A. T. W. LINDSAY.	26/3/18		1/12/18
Lieut. G. D. FALKENBERG.	12/3/18		18/12/18

ROYAL AIR FORCE—continued.

Name.	Missing.	Interned.	Repatriated.
2/Lt. G. R. NORMAN.	26/3/18		14/12/18
2/Lt. R. C. D. OLIVER.	26/3/18		17/12/18
Lieut. F. J. WESTFIELD.	26/3/18		17/12/18
2/Lt. F. C. B. WEDGWOOD.	27/3/18		–/1/19
2/Lt. D. VAUGHAN.	27/3/18		17/12/18
Lieut. J. C. THOMPSON.	27/3/18		17/12/18
2/Lt. E. W. PICKFORD.	27/3/18		1/12/18
Capt. J. H. HEDLEY.	27/3/18		17/12/18
Capt. R. K. KIRKMAN.	27/3/18		17/12/18
Capt. E. B. CAHUSAC.	27/3/18		14/12/18
Capt. T. S. SHARPE.	27/3/18		–/12/18
Lieut. H. S. REDPATH.	28/3/18		18/12/18
2/Lt. A. D. POPE.	28/3/18		1/12/18
2/Lt. R. J. OWEN.	28/3/18		1/12/18
Lieut. D. D. RICHARDSON.	28/3/18		2/12/18
2/Lt. F. D. SHREEVE.	29/3/18		18/12/18
Lieut. A. JERRARD.	30/3/18		–/11/18
2/Lt. H. W. BROWNE.	30/3/18		1/12/18
2/Lt. A. S. HANNA.	31/3/18		18/12/18
2/Lt. C. B. COLEMAN.	31/3/18		18/12/18
2/Lt. R. A. BURNARD.	31/3/18		18/12/18
Lieut. F. BEAUMONT.	1/4/18		17/12/18
2/Lt. B. MACPHERSON.	1/4/18		25/12/18
2/Lt. J. J. MEREDITH.	1/4/18		1/12/18
Capt. J. L. TROLLOPE.			12/10/18
2/Lt. A. K. LOMAX.	2/4/18		1/12/18
2/Lt. H. DEAN.	3/4/18		18/12/18
2/Lt. L. L. F. TOWNE.	3/4/18		–/12/18
2/Lt. S. R. WELLS.	5/4/18		17/12/18
Lieut. P. H. O'LIEFF.	5/4/18		17/12/18
Lieut. D. G. GOLD.	6/4/18		17/12/18
Lieut. H. G. DUGAN.	6/4/18		–/12/18
2/Lt. M. F. PEILER.	6/4/18		1/12/18
2/Lt. F. D. HUDSON.	6/4/18	(*Died* at Paderborn)	
2/Lt. T. R. V. HILL.	6/4/18		17/12/18
2/Lt. E. SMITHERS.	6/4/18		1/12/18
Lt. A. G. WINGATE GRAY.	6/4/18	Switzerland –/10/18	25/12/18
Lieut. R. G. H. ADAMS.	7/4/18		17/12/18
Flt. Lieut. K. R. COLE.	7/4/18		18/12/18
Lieut. D. C. HOPEWELL.	7/4/18		17/12/18
Lieut. G. A. MERCER.	9/4/18		1/12/18
2/Lt. F. J. HOPGOOD.	10/4/18		18/12/18
Lieut. G. G. McPHEE.	10/4/18		1/12/18
Capt. W. D. PATRICK.	10/4/18		14/12/18
Lieut. H. INMAN.	11/4/18		18/12/18
2/Lt. L. M. GERSON.	11/4/18		18/12/18
2/Lt. R. G. LAWSON.	11/4/18		–/1/19
Lieut. A. C. DEAN.	12/4/18		14/12/18
2/Lt. A. L. PEMBERTON.	12/4/18		13/12/18
Lieut. C. McCANN.	12/4/18		1/12/18
Lieut. A. W. MILLER.	12/4/18		18/12/18
Lieut. F. R. KNAPP.	16/4/18		–/12/18
2/Lt. D. G. LEWIS.	20/4/18		1/12/18
2/Lt. B. W. ROBINSON.	20/4/18		6/12/18
Lieut. S. C. H. BEGBIE.	21/4/18	(*Died* at Lille 22/4/18)	
2/Lt. C. J. FITZGIBBON.	21/4/18		17/12/18

ROYAL AIR FORCE—continued.

Name.	Missing.	Interned.	Repatriated.
Lieut. W. RUDMAN.	21/4/18		18/12/18
2/Lt. C. St. C. PARSONS.	22/4/18		-/12/18
Capt. C. J. THOMSEN.	23/4/18		27/11/18
Lieut. H. V. N. BANKES.	24/4/18		25/11/18
2/Lt. P. G. RATLIFF.	24/4/18		4/12/18
Lieut. H. B. D. HARRINGTON.	24/4/18		1/12/18
Capt. T. COLVILL-JONES.	25/4/18	(*Died* at Frankfurt 14/5/18)	
Lieut. C. J. GILLAN.	25/4/18		1/12/18
Lieut. W. DUCE.	25/4/18		1/12/18
Lieut. C. G. TYSOE.	29/4/18		25/12/18
2/Lt. C. V. CARR.	29/4/18		30/12/18
Capt. E. G. S. WALKER.			7/12/18
Lieut. M. T. McKELVEY.	11/4/18		13/12/18
Flt. Sub.-Lt. J. H. T. CARRE.		R.N.A.S.	14/12/18
Sub.-Lt. N. J. ATTWOOD.			
2/Lt. W. J. PRIER.			17/12/18
2/Lt. W. H. TAYLOR.			-/12/18
Lieut. G. HAMILTON.	2/5/18		19/12/18
2/Lt. A. C. G. BROWN.	3/5/18	(*Died* at Herleville 7/5/18)	
Capt. G. CHADWICK.	3/5/18		2/1/19
2/Lt. A. F. DAWES.	3/5/18		18/12/18
Lieut. P. R. HAMPTON.	3/5/18		13/12/18
Lieut. L. C. LANE.	3/5/18		-/12/18
2/Lt. R. L. G. SKINNER.	3/5/18	(*Died*)	
2/Lt. R. A. SLIPPER.	4/5/18		30/12/18
Lieut. S. A. HUSTWITT.	6/5/18		1/12/18
Lieut. N. A. SMITH.	6/5/18		18/12/18
2/Lt. J. C. WOOD.	8/5/18		13/12/18
Capt. C. C. CLARK.	8/5/18		14/12/18
Lieut. S. BIRCH.	9/5/18		1/1/19
Lieut. T. RATCLIFFE.	9/5/18		1/1/19
2/Lt. A. V. JONES.	10/5/18		13/12/18
Lieut. Geraint THOMAS.	10/4/18		14/12/18
Lieut. E. G. FORDER.	11/5/18		28/11/18
Lieut. A. P. BOLLINS.	12/5/18		30/12/18
Lieut. C. E. TYLOR.	12/5/18		30/12/18
Lieut. J. B. BIRKHEAD.	12/5/18		-/12/18
Lieut. J. HANDLEY.	12/5/18		25/12/18
2/Lt. L. R. SINCLAIR.	14/5/18		29/11/18
Capt. EDWARDS.		(*Died* at Mossel 14/5/18)	
2/Lt. D. S. ANDERSON.	15/5/18		18/12/18
Lieut. W. L. ANDREW.	15/5/18		-/12/18
2/Lt. W. LAMONT.	15/5/18		25/12/18
Lieut. C. C. ROBSON.	15/5/18		-/12/18
Lieut. H. B. B. WILSON.	15/5/18		
2/Lt. F. E. BOULTON.	16/5/18		-/12/18
Capt. P. R. WHITE.	16/5/18		25/12/18
Lieut. W. E. COWAN.	16/5/18		-/12/18
2/Lt. H. G. HOLMAN.	16/5/18		6/12/18
Lieut. W. A. LESLIE.	16/5/18		30/12/18
2/Lt. J. C. WILLIAMSON.	17/5/18		30/12/18
Lieut. N. F. PENRUDDOCKE.	17/5/18		31/12/18
2/Lieut. M. F. SUTTON.	17/5/18		-/12/18
2/Lt. A. S. CROSS.	17/5/18		30/12/18
Lieut. H. J. LEAVITT.	17/5/18		-/12/18
2/Lt. V. W. HILLYARD.	17/5/18		13/12/18

ROYAL AIR FORCE—continued.

Name.	Missing.	Interned.	Repatriated.
2/Lt. D. J. RUSSELL.	17/5/18		—/12/18
2/Lt. K. HUNT.	17/5/18		8/12/18
Lieut. W. F. SCOTT-KERR.	18/5/18		26/12/18
2/Lt. C. B. LAW.	18/5/18		—/12/18
Major A. D. CARTER.	18/5/18		13/12/18
2/Lt. F. J. BULL.	18/5/18		—/12/18
Lieut. F. ATKINSON.	19/5/18	(*Died*)	
2/Lt. H. A. CLARKE.	19/5/18		—/12/18
Capt. H. CLAYE.	19/5/18		30/12/18
2/Lt. H. MITCHELL.	19/5/18		30/12/18
2/Lt. A. J. PATENAUDE.	19/5/18		1/1/19
Lieut. H. C. HUNTER.	19/5/18		8/12/18
Lieut. L. SEYMOUR.	19/5/18		9/1/18
2/Lt. S. B. REECE.	21/5/18		1/1/19
Lieut. R. W. PEAT.	21/5/18		—/12/18
2/Lt. T. G. DREW-BROOK.	21/5/18		17/12/18
2/Lt. N. B. HARRIS.	21/5/18		13/12/18
2/Lt. H. E. TANSLEY.	21/5/18		30/12/18
Lieut. H. E. TOWNSEND.	21/5/18		14/12/18
2/Lt. G. A. RAINIER.	22/5/18		13/12/18
2/Lt. W. I. CRAWFORD.	23/5/18		4/1/19
Lieut. H. L. Le ROY.	23/5/18		—/12/18
2/Lt. F. H. BLAXILL.	27/5/18		—/12/18
Lieut. D. A. MacDONALD.	27/5/18		30/12/18
Lt.-Col. P. F. M. FELLOWES.	27/5/18		28/11/18
Capt. D. J. BELL.	27/5/18	(*Died*)	
2/Lt. V. R. BROWN.	28/5/18		14/1/19
2/Lt. R. S. MILANI.	28/5/18		17/12/18
Lieut. W. A. SCOTT.	30/5/18		30/12/18
Lieut. J. A. EATON.	30/5/18	*Holland*	
Flt. Lieut. E. F. BENSLEY.			13/12/18
Lieut. H. C. E. BOCKETT-PUGH.			29/11/18
2/Lt. J. L. H. ANDERSON.	31/5/18	(*Died* at Karlsruhe)	
Lieut. E. McN. HAND.	1/6/18		14/11/18
Lieut. I. A. PEERS.	1/6/18		31/12/18
Lieut. J. R. ZIEMAN.	2/6/18		30/12/18
2/Lt. A. R. COWAN.	3/6/18		14/12/18
Lieut. B. A. BIRD.	3/6/18		6/12/18
Capt. R. F. L. DICKEY.	4/6/18		—/8/18
Capt. R. F. PAUL.	4/6/18	Holland	
Lieut. A. G. HODGSON.	4/6/18	Holland	21/7/18
2/Lt. A. JOHNSON.			
2/Lt. R. J. GREGORY.	5/6/18		13/12/18
2/Lt. E. A. MAGEE.	5/6/18		—/12/18
2/Lt. J. E. W. SUGDEN.	5/6/18		13/12/18
Lieut. C. H. DUNSTER.	5/6/18		18/12/18
Lieut. F. CLARKE.			
Lieut. A. F. BARTLETT.	6/6/18		6/12/18
Lieut. L. A. HACKLETT.	7/6/18		13/12/18
Lieut. G. D. McLEOD.	8/6/18		21/11/18
2/Lt. E. M. BROWN.	9/6/18		12/12/18
Lieut. C. A. GORDON.	9/6/18		20/11/18
Lieut. C. MARSDEN.	9/6/18		13/12/18
2/Lt. W. BRECKENRIDGE.	9/6/18		—/1/19
Lieut. J. H. JOHNSON.	9/6/18		
Lieut. J. F. PATTINSON.		Holland	
2/Lt. H. TANNENBAUM.	2/6/18		1/1/19

ROYAL AIR FORCE—continued.

Name.	Missing.	Interned.	Repatriated.
Lieut. R. J. R. D. FYFE.		Holland.	15/11/18
Lieut. B. W. DE LEYSON.	10/6/18		
2/Lt. J. L. BROWN.	12/6/18		18/12/18
Capt. J. WEAVER.	12/6/18		17/12/18
Lieut. G. F. THOMSON.	12/6/18		13/12/18
Lieut. H. H. GILE.	13/6/18	U.S.A.	
Lieut. C. R. HALL.	13/6/18		13/12/18
2/Lt. R. G. LEWIS.	13/6/18		13/12/18
2/Lt. E. M. NICHOLAS.	13/6/18		13/12/18
2/Lt. W. H. A. RICKETT.	16/6/18		13/12/18
Capt. R. O. PURRY.	16/6/18		14/1/19
2/Lt. C. E. WHARTON.	16/6/18		13/12/18
Lieut. J. W. PRYOR.	16/6/18		13/12/18
Lieut. H. VICK.	16/6/18		30/12/18
Lieut. H. E. THOMSON.	16/6/18		13/12/18
2/Lt. G. H. GLASSPOOLE.	16/6/18		14/12/18
2/Lt. V. MERCER-SMITH.	16/6/18		13/12/18
2/Lt. P. KEMP.	16/6/18		13/12/18
2/Lt. J. R. JACKMAN.	17/6/18	(*Died*)	
Lieut. G. D. COWARD.	17/6/18		21/11/18
Lieut. J. F. REID.	17/6/18		15/11/18
2/Lt. W. J. T. ATKINS.	17/6/18		13/12/18
2/Lt. S. M. CONNOLLY.	18/6/18		23/12/18
Lieut. S. M. ROBINS.	19/6/18		20/11/18
Lieut. H. MASON.	20/6/18		13/12/18
Lieut. H. S. COLLETT.	21/6/18		12/12/18
Lieut. H. B. EVANS.	21/6/18		13/12/18
2/Lt. R. G. CARR.	21/6/18	Escaped	18/7/18
Lieut. K. W. J. HALL.	21/6/18		13/12/18
Lieut. W. K. WILSON.	21/6/18		30/12/18
2/Lt. A. J. COBBIN.	23/6/18	(*Died* at Le Quesnoy 14/7/18)	
Lieut. A. D. R. JONES.	23/6/18		13/12/18
Lieut. J. W. THOMSON.	23/6/18		13/12/18
Lieut. L. J. W. INGRAM.	23/6/18		13/12/18
Lieut. C. W. PECKHAM.	23/6/18		4/12/18
Flt. Lieut. MURTON.			17/12/18
2/Lt. W. C. TEMPEST.	24/6/18		31/12/18
2/Lt. W. TURNER.	24/6/18		13/12/18
2/Lt. E. ROBERTS.	25/6/18		13/12/18
Lieut. N. H. MUIRDEN.	25/6/18		
Lieut. F. DALTREY.	25/6/18		1/1/19
2/Lt. J. ARNOLD.	25/6/18		13/12/18
Lieut. S. C. M. PONTIN.	25/6/18		13/12/18
Lt. O. J. F. JONES-LLOYD.	25/6/18		13/12/18
Lieut. W. H. STUBBS.	25/6/18	(*Died*)	
2/Lt. A. J. ELVIN.	26/6/18		13/12/18
Lieut. J. E. DOE.	26/6/18		13/12/18
Lieut. C. BOOTHMAN.	26/6/18	(*Died*)	
Lieut. F. F. H. BRYAN.	26/6/18		14/12/18
Lieut. C. G. JENYNS.	26/6/18		13/12/18
Lieut. J. WEBSTER.	27/6/18		30/12/18
Lieut. G. M. GRAY.	27/5/18		17/12/18
Lieut. J. C. ROBINSON.	27/6/18		13/12/18
2/Lt. L. G. COCKING.	27/6/18		13/12/18
Capt. J. A. GRAY.	27/6/18	Holland	12/11/18
Lieut. S. C. WELINKER.	27/6/18	(*Died* 30/6/18)	

ROYAL AIR FORCE—continued.

Name.	Missing.	Interned.	Repatriated.
2/Lt. J. J. COMERFORD.	27/6/18	Holland	12/11/18
Capt. W. A. FORSYTH.	27/6/18	(*Died*)	
2/Lt. J. FULTON.	27/6/18		13/12/18
Lieut. A. L. GARRETT.	28/6/18		13/12/18
Lieut. H. AUSTIN.	28/6/18		13/12/18
Lieut. A. E. BINGHAM.	28/6/18		13/12/18
2/Lt. J. L. SMITH.	28/6/18		–/12/18
Lieut. P. C. MICHELL.	28/6/18		13/12/18
Lieut. C. EATON.	29/6/18		14/12/18
Lieut. G. BALLANCE.	29/6/18		–/12/18
Lieut. R. P. WHYTE.	29/6/18		13/12/18
2/Lt. D. BOE.	29/6/18		13/12/18
Lieut. E. G. TURNER.	29/6/18		13/12/18
Lieut. E. W. TATNALL.	29/6/18		13/12/18
Lieut. J. D. VANCE.	30/6/18		15/11/18
Lieut. J. E. SYDIE.	30/6/18		16/1/19
2/Lt. K. C. B. WOODMAN.	1/7/18		13/12/18
Lieut. W. G. NORDEN.	1/7/18		13/12/18
Lieut. G. C. BODY.	1/7/18		13/12/18
Lieut. G. L. CASTLE.	1/7/18		18/12/18
Lieut. A. H. HARRISON.	1/7/18		13/12/18
Lieut. J. D. MANCE.	1/7/18	Holland	
2/Lt. S. B. PORTER.	1/7/18	Holland	15/11/18
Capt. H. V. PUCKRIDGE.	1/7/18		13/12/18
Lieut. T. L. MacCONCHIE.	1/7/18		5/12/18
Lieut. A. J. FRICKER.	4/7/18		17/12/18
2/Lt. W. J. SAUNDERS.	6/7/18		13/12/18
Lieut. M. J. DUCRAY.	7/7/18		26/11/18
Lieut. A. MOORE.	7/7/18		13/12/18
2/Lt. H. W. BURRY.	8/7/18		14/12/18
Lieut. J. A. CHUBB.	8/7/18		14/12/18
2/Lt. H. K. SCRIVENER.	8/7/18		13/12/18
2/Lt. R. H. DUNN.	9/7/18		17/12/18
2/Lt. H. E. HINCHLIFFE.	9/7/18		11/1/19
Lieut. M. H. K. KANE.	10/7/18		14/12/18
Lieut. J. LOUPINSKI.	10/7/18		13/12/18
Lieut. C. B. RIDLEY.	10/7/18		13/12/18
Lieut. T. F. BLIGHT.	11/7/18		23/1/19
2/Lt. A. T. SIMONS.	11/7/18		26/12/18
2/Lt. H. R. WHITEHEAD.	11/7/18		18/1/19
2/Lt. R. ARNOTT.	11/7/18		23/9/18
2/Lt. D. MALLETT.	14/7/18		13/12/18
2/Lt. J. S. BURN	14/7/18		13/12/18
2/Lt. B. N. GARRETT.	14/7/18		16/12/18
Lieut. R. A. YATES.	14/7/18		13/12/18
2/Lt. N. H. MARSHALL.	14/7/18		14/1/19
Lieut. R. H. GRAY.	15/7/18		13/12/18
Lieut. E. B. CRICKMORE.	16/7/18		13/12/18
Lieut. J. A. PUGH.	16/7/18		13/12/18
2/Lt. R. E. WHITE.	17/7/18		5/12/18
Lieut. R. A. STRANG.	17/7/18		27/11/18
Lieut. G. ROSE.	18/7/18		13/12/18
Lieut. F. KEMP.	18/7/18		17/12/18
Lieut. W. M. F. BAYLISS.	18/7/18		13/12/18
Lieut. A. SMITH.	18/7/18		13/12/18
Lieut. R. A. VOSPER.	18/7/18		13/12/18

ROYAL AIR FORCE—continued.

Name.	Missing.	Interned.	Repatriated.
Lieut. H. BOSHER.	18/7/18		14/12/18
Lieut. L. W. D. T. TRATMAN.	18/7/18		23/12/18
Lieut. J. A. Van TILBURG.	19/7/18		14/12/18
2/Lt. H. L. CROSS.	19/7/18		13/12/18
Lieut. A. M. ROBERTS.	19/7/18	U.S.A.S.	
Lieut. E. SCADDING.	19/7/18		17/12/18
Lieut. A. R. JONES.	19/7/18		14/12/18
Lieut. F. G. THOMPSON.	20/7/18		28/12/18
2/Lt. K. R. ANGUS.	20/7/18		13/12/18
2/Lt. S. C. THORNLEY.	20/7/18		13/12/18
Lieut. A. J. CYR.	20/7/18		13/12/18
Lieut. T. CONLAN.	20/7/18		8/12/18
2/Lt. E. J. RILEY.	20/7/18		23/12/18
Lieut. A. SOMMERFELT.	21/7/18		13/12/18
Lieut. A. LEWIS.	21/7/18		14/12/18
2/Lt. J. GONDRE.	21/7/18		13/12/18
2/Lt. B. M. BATTEY.	21/7/18		12/12/18
Lieut. WILLIAMS.	21/7/18	Holland	
Lieut. JACKSON.	21/7/18	Holland	
2/Lt. E. DAWSON.	21/7/18	Holland	26/12/18
Lieut. W. E. COULSON.	22/7/18		13/12/18
2/Lt. W. H. E. LABATT.	22/7/18		13/12/18
Lieut. E. BULLEN.	22/7/18		13/12/18
Lieut. W. S. G. KIDDER.	22/7/18		5/12/18
Lieut. H. C. TUSSAUD.	22/7/18		29/11/18
Lieut. W. R. HENDERSON.	22/7/18		13/12/18
Lieut. C. F. BROWN.	25/7/18	(Died 3/8/18)	
2/Lt. A. G. S. BLAKE.	25/7/18		13/12/18
Lieut. F. S. COGHILL.	25/7/18		13/12/18
2/Lt. K. S. LAURIE.	25/7/18		13/12/18
Lieut. H. M. STRUBEN.	25/7/18		13/12/18
2/Lt. N. WILSON.	25/7/18	(*Died* at Munster 18/10/18)	
Lieut. W. A. CARVETH.	26/7/18		13/12/18
2/Lt. G. TRAVERS.	26/7/18		13/12/18
Lieut. W. S. STEPHENSON.	28/7/18		30/12/18
Lieut. R. V. IRWIN.	28/7/18	(*Died* at Cologne 2/10/18)	
Lieut. L. C. GILMOUR.	31/7/18		13/12/18
Lieut. W. H. SHELL.	31/7/18		13/12/18
Lieut. R. L. HOLLINGSWORTH.	31/7/18		5/12/18
Lieut. J. FARQUHAR.	31/7/18	(*Died* near Rooselaure 1/8/18)	
Lieut. D. C. TOWNLEY.	31/7/18		13/12/18
Lieut. J. E. GOW.	31/7/18	(*Died* 10/8/18)	
Lieut. W. J. HUTCHINSON.	31/7/18		23/12/18
Lieut. L. W. C. PEARCE.	31/7/18	Holland	12/11/18
2/Lt. F. H. BUGGE.	31/7/18	Holland	12/11/18
Lieut. G. H. STEPHENSON.	31/7/18		13/12/18
2/Lt. F. SMITH.	31/7/18		13/12/18
2/Lt. E. SINGLETON.	31/7/18		13/12/18
2/Lt. T. M. RITCHIE.	31/7/18		13/12/18
Lieut. M. T. S. PAPENFUS.	31/7/18		13/12/18
Lieut. W. J. GARRITY.	31/7/18		-/12/18
2/Lt. K. H. ASHTON.	31/7/18		13/12/18
Lieut. A. L. BENJAMIN.	31/7/18		29/11/18
Lieut. S. McB. BLACK.	31/7/18		-/12/18
Lieut. D. W. WILSON.	2/8/18	Holland	
Lieut. L. C. BOWER.	2/8/18	Holland	

ROYAL AIR FORCE.—continued.

Name.	Missing.	Interned.	Repatriated.
Capt. E. P. HARDMAN.	2/8/18		20/11/18
2/Lt. E. S. COOMBES.	3/8/18		13/12/18
Lieut. A. F. FORSYTH.	3/8/18		13/12/18
Lieut. ALBERTSON.	4/8/18	U.S.A.S.	
Lieut. J. D. ANDERSON.	7/8/18		17/12/18
2/Lt. C. E. A. LOVELL.	7/8/18		13/12/18
2/Lt. B. C. PEARSON.	8/8/18		13/12/18
Lieut. J. C. NUTTALL.	8/8/18		23/12/18
Lieut. L. H. RIDDELL.	8/8/18		3/1/19
Lieut. R. H. HEMMENS.	8/8/18		14/12/18
2/Lt. L. K. DAVIDSON.	8/8/18	Holland	12/11/18
2/Lt. W. L. BING.	8/8/18	Holland	12/11/18
Lieut. R. E. TAYLOR.	8/8/18		23/12/18
Capt. G. H. P. WHITFIELD.	8/8/18		13/12/18
2/Lt. G. WIGNALL.	8/8/18		13/12/18
Capt. F. G. POWELL.	8/8/18		25/12/18
Lieut. W. GOFFE.	8/8/18		5/1/19
2/Lt. D. E. CHASE.	8/8/18		29/12/18
Lieut. G. W. GORMAN.	8/8/18		5/12/18
2/Lt. G. L. CARTER.	8/8/18		23/12/18
Capt. M. E. GONNE.	8/8/18	(*Died* at Villers-Carbonnel)	
2/Lt. C. F. W. ILLINGWORTH.	8/8/18		30/12/18
Lieut. F. C. RUSSELL.	8/8/18		13/12/18
2/Lt. M. TISON.	8/8/18		23/12/18
Lieut. G. R. TOUCHSTONE.	8/8/18		8/12/18
Capt. R. MANZER.	8/8/18		13/12/18
Capt. H. RAMPLING.	8/8/18	Holland.	
Lieut. J. A. YATES.	8/8/18		23/12/18
2/Lt. G. R. SCHOOLING.	8/8/18		13/12/18
Lieut. H. P. MALLETT.	8/8/18		13/12/18
2/Lt. R. KELLY.	8/8/18		–/12/18
Lieut. F. E. BEAUCHAMP.	8/8/18		14/12/18
Lieut. F. I. ROGERS.	8/8/18		17/12/18
2/Lt. H. ELLIOTT	8/8/18		13/12/18
Lieut. L. L. BROWN.	8/8/18		13/12/18
2/Lt. A. E. DONCASTER.	8/8/18		13/12/18
Lieut. N. O. N. FOGGO.	8/8/18		5/1/19
2/Lt. W. COX.	8/8/18		13/12/18
Lieut. H. M. BROWN.	8/8/18		24/12/18
Lieut. L. H. FORREST.	8/8/18		12/12/18
Lieut. S. W. P. FOSTER-SUTTON.	8/8/18		25/11/18
Lieut. A. McCONNELL-WOOD.	8/8/18		17/12/18
Lieut. C. B. H. LEFROY.	8/8/18		4/2/19
Lieut. F. CARPENTER.	9/8/18		13/12/18
2/Lt. H. S. MUSGROVE.	9/8/18		
2/Lt. A. S. SINCLAIR.	9/8/18		23/12/18
Lieut. W. E. JACKSON.	9/8/18		13/12/18
2/Lt. P. T. A. REVELEY.	9/8/18		30/12/18
Lieut. L. H. BUTTON.	9/8/18		29/1/19
Lieut. B. HALL.	9/8/18		5/12/18
Lieut. L. A. CLACK.	9/8/18		13/12/18
Lieut. J. E. T. SUTCLIFFE.	9/8/18		1/1/19
Lieut. S. R. COWARD.	9/8/18		10/1/19
2/Lt. S. J. HILL.	9/8/18		13/12/18
2/Lt. H. HARTLEY.	10/8/18		11/12/18
Lieut. H. T. FLINTOPP.	10/8/18		12/12/18

ROYAL AIR FORCE—continued.

Name.	Missing.	Interned.	Repatriated.
Lieut. G. S. HARVEY.	10/8/18		5/12/18
Lieut. T. T. SHIPMAN.	10/8/18		1/1/19
Lieut. C. L. WOOD.	10/8/18	(*Died* at Tournai 17/8/18)	
2/Lt. E. H. CLAYTON.	11/8/18	(*Died*)	
Lieut. S. D. CONNOLLY.	11/8/18		–/12/18
Lieut. W. W. BRADFORD.	11/8/18		26/11/18
2/Lt. J. E. PARKE.	11/8/18		26/11/18
2/Lt. J. M. McPHERSON.	11/8/18		10/12/18
2/Lt. J. V. RISK.	11/8/18		13/12/18
2/Lt. G. F. METSON.	11/8/18		14/12/18
2/Lt. C. A. ATKINS.	12/8/18		13/12/18
2/Lt. J. IVENS.	12/8/18		18/1/19
Lieut. O. F. MEYER.	12/8/18		13/12/18
Lieut. G. H. PATMAN.	12/8/18		13/12/18
Lieut. S. C. J. ASKIN.	12/8/18		23/12/18
Lieut. A. R. STEDMAN.	12/8/18		
Capt. I. K. SUMMERS.	12/8/18		23/12/18
Lieut. H. H. WOOD.	12/8/18		17/12/18
Lieut. J. L. C. SUTHERLAND.	13/8/18	(*Died* at Metz 19/8/18)	
Lieut. E. J. C. McCRACKEN.	13/8/18		14/12/18
2/Lt. G. R. HOWARD.	14/8/18		16/12/18
2/Lt. J. HILLS.	14/8/18		23/12/18
2/Lt. H. A. O'SHEA.	14/8/18		
2/Lt. C. E. THORPE.	14/8/18		23/12/18
2/Lt. G. A. R. HILL.	14/8/18		18/12/18
Lieut. A. G. LAWE.	15/8/18		13/12/18
Lieut. T. J. ARTHUR.	15/8/18		14/12/18
Lieut. D. E. CULVER.	15/8/18		
2/Lt. J. MUNRO.	16/8/18	Holland	
Lieut. A. C. LLOYD.	16/8/18	Holland	15/11/18
2/Lt. M. G. WILSON.	16/8/18	Holland	15/11/18
2/Lt. T. B. DODWELL.	16/8/18	Holland	15/11/18
Lieut. C. H. DENNY	16/8/18		13/12/18
Lieut. E. H. KILBOURNE.	16/8/18		13/12/18
2/Lt. D. E. STEPHENS.	16/8/18	(*Died* at Karlsruhe)	
Lieut. A. T. PARTRIDGE.			25/12/18
Lieut. W. H. POLLARD.	16/8/18		18/1/19
2/Lt. B. P. JENKINS.	16/8/18	(*Died* at Aachen)	
2/Lt. F. J. KEBLE.	16/8/18		8/12/18
Lieut. H. BURTON.	16/8/18		
2/Lt. J. R. FOX.	16/8/18	(*Died*)	
Lieut. D. R. HARRIS.	16/8/18	Holland	
Lieut. W. G. CLAXTON.	17/8/18		1/12/18
Capt. R. S. S. INGRAM.	18/8/18		10/12/18
2/Lt. A. W. WYNCOLL.	18/8/18		11/12/18
Capt. C. J. VENTER.	18/8/18		13/12/18
2/Lt. J. M. DUNLOP.	19/8/18		11/12/18
2/Lt. F. F. SCHORN.	19/8/18		11/12/18
Lieut. N. E. WILLIAMS.	19/8/18		10/11/18
2/Lt. A. C. PORTER.	19/8/18		30/12/18
2/Lt. J. WOODING.	21/8/18		13/12/18
Lieut. R. H. ELLIS.	21/8/18	U.S.A.S.	
Lieut. R. A. C. BRIE.	22/8/18		13/12/18
Lieut. N. E. GWYER.	22/8/18		19/11/18
2/Lt. T. R. HILTON.	22/8/18		20/11/18
Capt. D. LATIMER.	22/8/18		31/12/18

ROYAL AIR FORCE—continued.

Name.	Missing.	Interned.	Repatriated.
Lieut. J. S. ANDREWS.	22/8/18		13/12/18
Lieut. M. E. BURNHAM.	22/8/18		13/12/18
Lieut. D. F. BURTON.	22/8/18		13/12/18
2/Lt. C. K. DAVID.	22/8/18		13/12/18
2/Lt. G. ROCHESTER.	22/8/18		13/12/18
Lieut. H. P. WELLS.	22/8/18	U.S.A.S.	
Lieut. J. VALENTINE.	22/8/18		17/12/18
Lieut. G. H. B. SMITH.	22/8/18		8/12/18
2/Lt. R. J. SEARLE.	22/8/18		15/12/18
2/Lt. J. H. RADFIELD.	22/8/18		
Capt. E. A. MACKAY.	22/8/18		8/12/18
Capt. J. B. H. HAY.	22/8/18		13/12/18
2/Lt. C. G. HITCHCOCK.	22/8/18		13/12/18
2/Lt. R. F. GLAZEBROOK.	23/8/18		13/12/18
Lieut. C. E. G. GILL.	23/8/18		18/11/18
Lieut. M. K. CURTIS.	24/8/18	U.S.A.S.	
Lieut. J. A. DEAR.	24/8/18	Holland	15/11/18
2/Lt. J. F. J. PETERS.	24/8/18	Holland	15/11/18
Lieut. H. J. W. ROBERTS.	24/8/18		23/12/18
Lieut. C. H. STEPHENS.	25/8/18		23/12/18
2/Lt. L. G. TAYLOR.	25/8/18		23/12/18
Lieut. F. M. SELLARS.	27/8/18		4/12/18
2/Lt. A. R. HEAVER.	27/8/18		23/12/18
Lieut. A. H. BELLIVEAU.	27/8/18		1/1/19
Capt. S. G. GILMOUR.	28/8/18		13/12/18
Lieut. P. H. GOODHUGH.	28/8/18		
Lieut. W. K. MacFARLANE.	29/8/18		11/12/18
Capt. L. G. LOUDOUN.	29/8/18		23/12/18
2/Lt. S. E. CROOKELL.	29/8/18		8/12/18
2/Lt. W. T. S. LEWIS.	29/8/18		9/12/18
2/Lt. W. R. JACKSON.	30/8/18		8/12/18
Lieut. K. A. W. LEIGHTON.	30/8/18		23/12/18
2/Lt. A. S. PAPWORTH.	30/8/18		23/12/18
Lieut. H. H. DOEHLER.	30/8/18	U.S.A.S.	
2/Lt. A. J. C. GORMLEY.	30/8/18		23/12/18
Lieut. J. MACDONALD.	30/8/18		–/11/18
Lieut. R. B. LUARD.	30/8/18		8/12/18
2/Lt. G. E. HERRING.	31/8/18		6/12/18
Capt. W. G. SHEDEL.	31/8/18		23/12/18
Capt. J. MACKERETH.	31/8/18		17/12/18
2/Lt. G. PURYEAR.		U.S.A.S.	
Capt. R. MARSHALL.			
2/Lt. C. H. A. BRIDGE.	31/8/18		
2/Lt. Z. MILLER.			
Lieut. W. S. MARS.	–/9/18	Holland	15/11/18
Lieut. G. L. BARRITT.	1/9/18		28/11/18
2/Lt. R. BOYS.	1/9/18		23/12/18
2/Lt. M. E. CHALLIS.	1/9/18		23/12/18
2/Lt. R. D. HUGHES.	1/9/18		23/12/18
2/Lt. J. G. DUGDALE.	1/9/18		13/12/18
Lieut. H. V. FELLOWES.	1/9/18		8/12/18
Lieut. D. A. MARTIN.	1/9/18		22/12/18
2/Lt. R. L. SCARFF.	1/9/18		30/12/18
2/Lt. H. V. PEELING.	1/9/18		8/12/18
2/Lt. L. B. RAYMOND.	1/9/18		2/12/18
2/Lt. F. B. ROBINSON.	1/9/18		8/12/18

ROYAL AIR FORCE—continued.

Name.	Missing.	Interned.	Repatriated.
Lieut. O. O'CONNOR.	2/9/18		8/12/18
2/Lt. I. M. McCULLOCH.	2/9/18		11/12/18
Lieut. J. J. AMBLER.	2/9/18		8/12/18
2/Lt. D. ROSE.	2/9/18		24/12/18
2/Lt. J. B. COCKIN.	2/9/18		18/1/19
Lieut. W. A. HALL.	2/9/18		11/12/18
2/Lt. C. H. LIVING.	2/9/18		8/12/18
2/Lt. O. MANDEL.	2/9/18		
2/Lt. J. S. STRINGER.	2/9/18		11/12/18
Lieut. R. A. B. POPE.	2/9/18		8/12/18
2/Lt. H. A. SCRIVENER.	2/9/18		2/1/19
2/Lt. D. B. SINCLAIR.	2/9/18		8/12/18
Lieut. W. M. STRATHEARNE.	2/9/18		8/12/18
2/Lt. J. C. BOYLE.	4/9/18		30/12/18
2/Lt. G. T. COLES.	4/9/18		8/12/18
Lieut. J. LEVESON-GOWER.	4/9/18		10/12/18
Lieut. R. McPHEE.	4/9/18		-/12/18
Lieut. S. W. ROCHFORD.	4/9/18		11/12/18
Lieut. W. M. HERRIOT.	4/9/18		11/12/18
Capt. J. H. FORMAN.	4/9/18		10/12/18
Lieut. W. K. SWAYZE.	4/9/18		4/1/19
Lieut. W. E. HALL.	4/9/18		24/12/18
2/Lt. C. H. P. KILLICK.	4/9/18		23/12/18
Lieut. E. R. SPROULE.	4/9/18		5/1/19
2/Lt. A. M. MILLER.	5/9/18		23/12/18
2/Lt. R. BEESLEY.	5/9/18		8/12/18
2/Lt. V. HARLEY.	5/9/18		23/12/18
Lieut. W. A. F. COWGILL.	5/9/18		13/12/18
2/Lt. C. E. FRANCIS.	5/9/18		8/12/18
Lieut. E. V. HOLLAND.	5/9/18		11/12/18
Capt. H. A. PATEY.	5/9/18		22/12/18
2/Lt. A. PRESTON.	5/9/18		-/1/19
2/Lt. A. R. THATCHER.	5/9/18		23/12/18
Capt. G. A. WELLS.	5/9/18		8/12/18
Lieut. L. YEREX.	5/9/18		-/12/18
2/Lt. T. W. BRODIE.	6/9/18	Holland	-/11/18
Lieut. J. G. MUNRO.	6/9/18	Holland	-/11/18
Lieut. M. A. DUNN.	7/9/18		5/12/18
Lieut. G. BROADBENT.	7/9/18		10/12/18
2/Lt. W. E. L. COURTNEY.	7/9/18		29/11/18
2/Lt. J. E. KEMP.	7/9/18		23/12/18
2/Lt. A. R. SABEY.	7/9/18	(*Died* 10/9/18)	
2/Lt. E. B. SMAILES.	7/9/18	(*Died* 13/9/18)	
Lieut. J. C. WALKER.	7/9/18		13/1/19
Capt. J. E. DOYLE.	8/9/18		19/12/18
Lieut. R. A. HENRY.	8/9/18		8/12/18
Lieut. J. P. LLOYD.	10/9/18		1/1/19
Lieut. H. A. COLE.	12/9/18		8/12/18
2/Lt. C. R. GAGE.	12/9/18		13/12/18
2/Lt. W. A. JOHNSTON.	14/9/18		28/11/18
Lieut. J. E. REID.	14/9/18		13/12/18
2/Lt. G. A. SHIPTON.	14/9/18		26/11/18
Lieut. W. F. OGILVY.	14/9/18		-/11/18
Lieut. E. F. WRIGHT.	15/9/18		13/12/18
Lieut. J. H. M. YEOMANS.	15/9/18		11/12/18
Capt. O. C. HOLLERAN.	15/9/18		5/12/18

ROYAL AIR FORCE—continued.

Name.	Missing.	Interned.	Repatriated.
2/Lt. J. A. MATTHEWS.	15/9/18		8/12/18
Lieut. E. J. STOCKMAN.	15/9/18		8/12/18
2/Lt. P. PAYNE.	15/9/18		8/12/18
2/Lt. E. A. MARCHANT.	15/9/18		-/12/18
Lieut. R. W. HEINE.	15/9/18		13/12/18
Lieut. F. F. JEWETT.	15/9/18	U.S.A.S.	
2/Lt. H. MERCER.	15/9/18		13/12/18
Lieut. C. B. NAYLOR.	15/9/18		8/12/18
2/Lt. G. C. RUSSELL.	15/9/18		13/12/18
2/Lt. F. E. FINCH.	15/9/18		13/12/18
Lieut. G. F. ANDERSON.	15/9/18		13/12/18
2/Lt. C. THOMAS.	15/9/18	Holland	15/11/18
Lieut. J. J. MacDONALD.	15/9/18	Holland	15/11/18
2/Lt. F. B. COX.	15/9/18	Holland	15/11/18
2/Lt. G. E. McMANUS.	15/9/18	Holland	15/11/18
2/Lt. J. B. RICHARDSON.	15/9/18		1/1/19
2/Lt. A. TAPPING.	15/9/18		23/12/18
2/Lt. C. GUILD.	15/9/18		23/12/18
2/Lt. H. DAVIES.	15/9/18		1/1/19
2/Lt. W. J. N. CHALKLIN.	15/9/18		23/12/18
2/Lt. A. G. HARRISON.	15/9/18		23/12/18
2/Lt. L. G. HALL.	15/9/18	U.S.A.S.	
2/Lt. W. D. EVANS.	15/9/18		23/12/18
2/Lt. E. L. BADDELY.	15/9/18		23/12/18
2/Lt. R. H. ROSE.	15/9/18		24/12/18
2/Lt. H. T. HEMPSALL.	15/9/18		-/12/18
Capt. W. R. E. HARRISON.	15/9/18	Holland	15/11/18
Sub-Lieut. A. B. D. CAMPBELL.	15/9/18		13/12/18
2/Lt. C. H. SENECAL.	16/9/18		13/12/18
2/Lt. E. J. NORRIS.	16/9/18		29/12/18
2/Lt. A. HINDER.	16/9/18	(Died)	
2/Lt. P. J. A. FLEMING.	16/9/18		8/12/18
2/Lt. W. E. JOHNS.	16/9/18		25/12/18
2/Lt. R. H. STONE.	16/9/18		8/12/18
Lieut. N. F. ADAMS.	16/9/18		9/12/18
2/Lt. F. F. ANSLOW.	16/9/18		1/1/19
Capt. AYRTON (F. A.)	16/9/18		18/12/18
2/Lt. R. S. LIPSETT.	16/9/18		23/12/18
Lieut. H. V. BRISBIN.	16/9/18		11/12/18
Lieut. R. C. PITMAN.	17/9/18		24/12/18
2/Lt. F. H. CHAINEY.	17/9/18		23/12/18
Lieut. F. R. JOHNSON.	17/9/18		24/12/18
2/Lt. H. H. SENIOR.	17/9/18		6/12/18
2/Lt. W. A. WILSON.	17/9/18		29/11/18
2/Lt. C. E. USHER-SOMERS.	17/9/18		12/12/18
Lieut. W. W. CHREIMAN	17/9/18		5/12/18
2/Lt. F. W. KING.	17/9/18		13/12/18
Lieut. B. NORCROSS.	17/9/18		28/12/18
2/Lt. R. H. COLE.	17/9/18	(Died 30/9/19)	
Lieut. E. G. GALLAGHER.	17/9/18	Luxemburg	28/11/18
Lieut. R. S. COBHAM.	17/9/18	Luxemburg	28/11/18
Lieut. E. E. TAYLOR.	17/9/18	Luxemburg	28/11/18
2/Lt. C. C. FISHER.	17/9/18	Holland	15/11/18
2/Lt. R. S. OAKLEY.	17/9/18	Holland	15/11/18
Lieut. J. B. LACY.	17/9/18		-/12/18
Lieut. G. H. LOCKE.	17/9/18	Holland	

ROYAL AIR FORCE—continued.

Name.	Missing.	Interned.	Repatriated.
Lieut. H. B. MONAGHAN.	17/9/18		13/12/18
2/Lt. A. FAIRHURST.	17/9/18		8/12/18
2/Lt. E. C. JEFFKINS.	17/9/18		26/11/18
Lieut. H. E. HYDE.	17/9/18		8/12/18
2/Lt. R. T. DOWN.	17/9/18		1/1/19
2/Lt. C. N. YELVERTON.	17/9/18		23/12/18
Lieut. G. W. MITCHEL.	17/9/18		–/12/18
Lieut. C. M. HOLBROOK.	18/9/18		8/12/18
Lieut. E. G. ROLPH.	20/9/18		13/12/18
2/Lt. T. NEWEY.	20/9/18		22/11/18
2/Lt. C. G. MILNE.	20/9/18		23/12/18
Lieut. E. P. LARRABEE.	20/9/18		5/12/18
2/Lt. J. N. KIER.	20/9/18		23/12/18
Lieut. G. F. C. CASWELL.	20/9/18		8/12/18
Capt. S. CARLIN.	21/9/18		13/12/18
Lieut. D. A. NEVILLE.	22/9/18		13/12/18
2/Lt. J. C. GUNN.	22/9/18		28/11/18
2/Lt. T. WARBURTON.	24/9/18		13/12/18
2/Lt. J. M. DANDY.	24/9/18		5/12/18
Lieut. H. S. MANTLE.	24/9/18		13/12/18
Lieut. N. N. COOPE.	24/9/18		29/11/18
Lieut. H. J. BENNETT.	24/9/18		
2/Lt. R. H. ARMSTRONG.	24/9/18		13/12/18
2/Lt. H. J. PRETTY.	24/9/18		14/12/18
Lieut. C. C. CONOVER.	24/9/18		10/12/18
2/Lt. J. OLERENSHAW.	24/9/18	Holland	15/11/18
2/Lt. R. L. KINGHAM.	24/9/18	Holland	15/11/18
2/Lt. H. J. C. ELWIG.	25/9/18		13/12/18
Lieut. C. R. GROSS.	25/9/18		28/11/18
Capt. A. LINDLEY.	25/9/18		29/11/18
2/Lt. J. W. BROWN.	25/9/18		13/12/18
Lieut. B. H. KEWLEY.	25/9/18		29/11/18
2/Lt. A. B. HENDERSON.	25/9/18		30/12/18
Lieut. N. W. HELWIG.	25/9/18		29/11/18
Lieut. C. B. E. LLOYD.	25/9/18		13/12/18
Capt. C. CRAWFORD.	25/9/18		29/11/18
Lieut. C. P. SPARKES.	25/9/18		16/12/18
2/Lt. C. B. SANDERSON.	25/9/18	*(Died* at Hautmont 17/10/18)	
2/Lt. R. C. PRETTY.	25/9/18		13/12/18
2/Lt. A. C. HEYES.	25/9/18		13/12/18
Lieut. G. B. DUNLOP.	25/9/18		13/12/18
2/Lt. G. R. BARTLETT.	25/9/18		13/12/18
Lieut. E. FULFORD.	26/9/18		28/11/18
2/Lt. W. H. COGHILL.	26/9/18		13/12/18
Lieut. H. CROSSLEY.	26/9/18		–/11/18
2/Lt. W. H. G. GILLET.	26/9/18		13/12/18
Lieut. T. H. SWANN.	26/9/18		26/11/18
Capt. P. E. WELCHMAN.	26/9/18		28/11/18
Lieut. W. R. THORNTON.	26/9/18		13/12/18
2/Lt. L. G. SMITH.	26/9/18	*(Died)*	
Lieut. J. A. PARKINSON.	26/9/18		13/12/18
2/Lt. O. R. HIBBERT.	26/9/18		19/12/18
Capt. J. F. CHISHOLM.	26/9/18	Holland	15/11/18
Lieut. F. H. STRINGER.			13/12/18
2/Lt. J. O. WOOD.	27/9/18		13/12/18
Lieut. N. D. WILLIS.	27/9/18		14/12/18

ROYAL AIR FORCE—continued.

Name.	Missing.	Interned.	Repatriated.
2/Lt. N. F. MOXON.	29/9/18		31/1/19
2/Lt. C. H. WILCOX.	27/9/18		25/12/18
Lieut. P. M. WALLACE.	27/9/18		13/12/18
Lieut. P. S. MANLEY.	27/9/18		–/12/18
2/Lt. C. A. HARRISON.	27/9/18		13/12/18
2/Lt. C. F. CAWLEY.	27/9/18		27/11/18
Lieut. R. C. BENNETT.	27/9/18		29/12/18
Capt. R. J. MORGAN.	28/9/18		5/12/18
Lieut. G. J. SMITH.	28/9/18		29/11/18
Lieut. T. M. STEELE.	28/9/18		16/12/18
Lieut. D. L. MELVIN.	28/9/18		13/12/18
Lieut. W. A. RANKIN.	28/9/18		13/12/18
Lieut. P. C. JENNER.	28/9/18		28/11/18
2/Lt. A. FLETCHER.	28/9/18		13/12/18
Lieut. R. C. MITTEN.	28/9/18		17/12/18
2/Lt. J. C. MALCOLMSON.	28/9/18		13/12/18
Lieut. J. M. McLENNAN.	28/9/18		13/12/18
Lieut. F. EDSTEAD.	28/9/18		5/12/18
Lieut. D. A. O'LEARY.	28/9/18		10/12/18
Lieut. B. R. ROLFE.	28/9/18		8/12/18
Capt. E. C. HOY.	28/9/18		28/11/18
Lieut. W. L. DOUGAN.	28/9/18		26/12/18
2/Lt. W. MITCHELL.	28/9/18	(*Died* at Lenze)	
2/Lt. H. B. HEWAT.	28/9/18		13/1/19
Lieut. P. B. COOKE.	28/9/18		29/11/18
2/Lt. G. GEDGE.	28/9/18		13/12/18
Lieut. H. P. BRUMMELL.	28/9/18		29/12/18
Capt. A. V. BOWATER.	28/9/18		8/12/18
2/Lt. E. DARBY.	28/9/18		13/12/18
Lieut. C. R. MOORE.	28/9/18		8/12/18
Lieut. A. F. SMITH.	28/9/18		13/12/18
2/Lt. H. C. TELFER.	28/9/18		13/12/18
2/Lt. D. A. THOMSON.	28/9/18		29/11/18
2/Lt. O. V. JUDKINS.	28/9/18		2/1/19
2/Lt. W. J. JOHNSON.	28/9/18		
2/Lt. D. M. JOHN.	28/9/18	Holland	15/11/18
Lieut. F. G. PYM.	–/9/18		30/12/18
2/Lt. A. C. J. PAYNE.	29/9/18		13/12/18
Lieut. M. R. MAHONY.	–/9/18		23/12/18
Lieut. R. M. MacDONALD.	29/9/18		29/11/18
Lieut. C. W. M. THOMPSON.	29/9/18		30/12/18
Lieut. L. R. JAMES.	29/9/18		28/11/18
Lieut. W. HENLEY-MOONEY.	29/9/18	U.S.A.S.	
Lieut. L. ELWORTHY.	29/9/18		13/12/18
2/Lt. A. M. ALLAN.	29/9/18		–/12/18
2/Lt. J. M. KELLY.			12/11/18
Lieut. T. BECK.	1/10/18	(*Died*)	
Capt. W. BUCKINGHAM.	1/10/18		13/12/18
2/Lt. F. R. EVELEIGH.	1/10/18		13/12/18
Lieut. A. M. MATHESON.	1/10/18		29/12/18
2/Lt. R. J. HAGENBUSH.	1/10/18	U.S.A.S.	
Lieut. F. L. STRANGWARD.	2/10/18		13/12/18
Lieut. R. HALL.	2/10/18		13/12/18
2/Lt. J. E. JENNINGS.	2/10/18		13/12/18
Lieut. J. K. SHOOK.	2/10/18		13/12/18
Lieut. I. W. AWDE.	5/10/18		25/12/18
2/Lt. H. M. D. SPEAGELL.	5/10/18		13/12/18
Lieut. E. C. LANSDALE.	30/9/16	(*Died* as Prisoner 1/12/16)	

ROYAL AIR FORCE—continued.

Name.	Missing.	Interned.	Repatriated.
Capt. A. G. INGLIS.	5/10/18		13/12/18
Lieut. W. G. L. BODLEY.	5/10/18		29/1/19
2/Lt. A. BRANDRICK.	5/10/18		21/12/18
Lieut. F. E. BOND.	5/10/18		13/12/18
2/Lt. C. V. A. BUCKNALL.	5/10/18		13/12/18
2/Lt. D. P. DAVIES.	5/10/18		13/12/18
Lieut. C. KNIGHT.	5/10/18		26/12/18
Lieut. C. HANCOCK.	5/10/18		14/12/18
2/Lt. H. L. PRIME.	5/10/18		
2/Lt. J. H. PERRING.	5/10/18		13/12/18
Lieut. R. CALROW.	6/10/18		–/11/18
2/Lt. W. T. S. CAIRNS.	6/10/18		13/12/18
2/Lt. W. PENDLETON.		Holland	15/11/18
2/Lt. B. LOCKEY.	7/10/18	Holland	15/11/18
2/Lt. H. E. POWER.		Holland	15/11/18
2/Lt. F. CORNWALL.	8/10/18		1/1/19
2/Lt. R. W. HOPPER.	8/10/18		13/12/18
Lieut. J. P. MURPHY.	8/10/18		–/12/18
Lieut. W. E. BARDGETT.	9/10/18		2/12/18
Lieut. C. F. PINEAU.	9/10/18		–/12/18
Lieut. J. E. SITCH.	9/10/18		27/11/18
Lieut. D. S. FOX.	9/10/18		14/11/18
Lieut. C. HOULGRAVE.	9/10/18		30/12/18
2/Lt. H. H. WHITLOCK.	14/10/18		30/12/18
Capt. E. W. CORNISH.	14/10/18		11/12/18
Lieut. R. J. FARQUHARSON.	14/10/18		8/12/18
2/Lt. P. C. S. McCREA.	14/10/18		13/12/18
2/Lt. P. L. PHILLIPS.	14/10/18		–/12/18
2/Lt. J. C. J. McDONALD.	14/10/18		15/12/18
2/Lt. L. TIMMINS.	18/10/18		13/12/18
2/Lt. R. COULTHARD.	18/10/18		13/12/18
2/Lt. G. E. HUGHES.	21/10/18		–/11/18
2/Lt. A. L. MAWER.	21/10/18		18/11/18
Lieut. M. H. WINKLER.	21/10/18		5/12/18
Capt. W. E. WINDOVER.	21/10/18		8/12/18
Lieut. R. W. L. THOMSON.	21/10/18		8/12/18
2/Lt. J. A. SIMSON.	21/10/18		8/12/18
Major L. G. S. REYNOLDS.	21/10/18		13/12/18
2/Lt. R. RIFFKIN.	21/10/18		8/12/18
Lieut. J. M. PEARSON.	21/10/18		25/11/18
Lieut. S. L. MUCKLOW.	21/10/18		8/12/18
2/Lt. P. KING.	21/10/18		26/11/18
2/Lt. A. W. R. EVANS.	21/10/18		8/12/18
2/Lt. M. W. DUNN.	21/10/18		–/12/18
Lieut. R. W. SILK.	23/10/18		11/1/19
2/Lt. F. H. REED.	23/10/18		
Lieut. J. T. SORLEY.	23/10/18		8/12/18
2/Lt. A. P. C. BRUCE.	23/10/18		8/12/18
2/Lt. H. H. ROFE.	23/10/18		8/12/18
2/Lt. B. S. CASE.	23/10/18	(*Died* 31/10/18)	
2/Lt. H. BRIDGER.	23/10/18		26/11/18
2/Lt. J. C. COLLINS.	23/10/18		8/12/18
Lieut. L. H. SMITH.	25/10/18		8/12/18
Lieut. H. E. HASTIE.	25/10/18		–/11/18
2/Lt. F. H. V. COOMBER.	26/10/18		7/12/18
2/Lt. H. THOMAS.	26/10/18		7/12/18

ROYAL AIR FORCE—continued.

Name.	Missing.	Interned.	Repatriated.
2/Lt. M. McLEAN.	26/10/18		8/12/18
2/Lt. K. O. BRACKEN.	27/10/18		30/11/18
Lieut. E. W. O. HALL.	27/10/18		27/11/18
Capt. C. L. KING.	27/10/18		30/11/18
2/Lt. N. SMITH.	27/10/18		-/11 '18
2/Lt. W. SANDERS.	27/10/18		13/12/18
Lieut. H. G. LEWIS.	27/10/18		-/12/18
2/Lt. A. R. PRATT.	27/10/18		11/12/18
2/Lt. C. A. CRICHTON.	27/10/18		19/11/18
Lieut. I. O. GAZE.	28/10/18		27/11/18
Lieut. N. T. TREMBATH.	28/10/18		22/1/19
2/Lt. L. G. STOCKWELL.	28/10/18		8/12/18
2/Lt. J. P. COLEMAN.	28/19/18		8/12/18
2/Lt. C. M. ALLAN.	28/10/18		10/12/18
Lieut. J. E. HALLENQUIST.	29/10/18		25/11/18
2/Lt. L. H. EYRES.	29/10/18		8/12/18
Lieut. H. F. MULHALL.	30/10/18		5/1/19
2/Lt. T. W. SLEIGHT.	30/10/18		19/11/18
2/Lt. W. AMORY.	30/10/18		18/12/18
Lieut. F. LYNN.	30/10/18		13/12/18
2/Lt. R. V. MURRAY.	30/10/18		13/12/18
2/Lt. C. N. BOYD.	30/10/18		27/11/18
Lieut. R. W. DUFF.	30/10/18		22/11/18
Lieut. A. BUCHANAN.	30/10/18		19/12/18
2/Lt. J. B. VICKERS.	30/10/18		26/11/18
2/Lt. S. J. GOODFELLOW.	30/10/18		8/12/18
2/Lt. J. B. ISAACS.	30/10/18		5/12/18
2/Lt. H. LANSDALE.	31/10/18		23/1/19
2/Lt. H. J. GEMMEL.	31/10/18		4/12/18
Lieut. R. G. DOBESON.	1/11/18		-/12/18
2/Lt. F. G. MILLS.	1/11/18		29/12/18
2/Lt. W. G. GADD.	1/11/18		8/12/18
2/Lt. J. M. PAYNE.	1/11/18		8/12/18
2/Lt. P. S. TENNANT.	2/11/18		31/12/18
2/Lt. G. L. P. DRUMMOND.	2/11/18		10/12/18
2/Lt. H. R. ABEY.	2/11/18		-/12/18
Lieut. F. S. BOWLES.	3/11/18		9/12/18
Lieut. P. G. GREENWOOD.	3/11/18		27/11/18
Lieut. W. SHACKLETON.	4/11/18		8/12/18
Lieut. J. E. RADLEY.	4/11/18		8/12/18
2/Lt. D. M. DEE.	4/11/18		27/11/18
2/Lt. J. PUGH.	4/11/18		29/11/18
2/Lt. J. F. McNAMARA.	4/11/18		27/11/18
Capt. A. A. HARCOURT-VERNON.	4/11/18		27/11/18
2/Lt. W. J. POTTS.	4/11/18		17/12/18
Lieut. C. W. NEWSTEAD.	4/11/18		28/11/18
Lieut. A. C. MacAULAY	4/11/18		25/11/18
2/Lt. H. G. LUTHER.	4/11/18		29/11/18
2/Lt. D. C. MacDONALD.	4/11/18		27/11/18
Lieut. J. G. CAREY.	4/11/18		27/11/18
Lieut. H. J. BERRY.	5/11/18		29/11/18
2/Lt. H. A. HAMLET.	5/11/18		27/11/18
2/Lt. E. W. THRESHER.	6/11/18		1/12/18
Lt. G. T. RICHARDSON.	6/11/18		29/1/19
2/Lt. W. H. TRESHAM.	6/11/18		1/12/18
Lieut. H. L. WREN.	6/11/18		28/12/18

ROYAL AIR FORCE—continued.

Name.	Missing.	Interned.	Repatriated.
Lieut. H. W. RUSSELL.	8/11/18		28/11/18
Lieut. E. O. AMM.	9/11/18		28/11/18
2/Lt. F. B. CANDY.	9/11/18	Holland	
2/Lt. O. E. COLEMAN.	9/11/18	Holland	
2/Lt. J. FREEMAN.	9/11/18	Holland	
2/Lt. C. H. THOMAS.	10/11/18	—	28/2/19
Lieut. A. M. ROSENBLEET.	10/11/18		25/11/18
2/Lt. H. T. C. GOMPERTZ.	10/11/18		–/11/18
2/Lt. S. COATES.	10/11/18		23/11/18
Lieut. A. B. AGNEW.	10/11/18		23/11/18
2/Lt. E. A. C. BRITTON.	10/11/18		25/11/18
Lieut. J. MARTIN.		Holland	–/12/18
Lieut. J. LISTER.		Holland	15/11/18
Lieut. C. J. LOCKE.		Holland	15/11/18
Lieut. F. N. HUDSON.		Holland	15/11/18
2/Lt. T. N. ENRIGHT.		Holland	14/11/18
Capt. F. E. FRYER.		Holland	15/11/18
Lieut. E. S. FARRAND.			14/12/18
Capt. W. E. FOSTER.			27/11/18
Lieut. J. B. HULME.			27/11/18
Capt. T. E. LANDER.			27/11/18
Capt. C. B. WILSON.			19/11/18
Lt. E. J. COOPER.			7/2/19
Lt. A. COPLEY.			9/2/19
Lt. G. WALLACE SIMPSON.			9/2/19
Capt. G. C. F. OWEN.			4/2/19

ROYAL NAVAL AIR SERVICE.

Name	Missing	Interned		Repatriated
Lieut. R. INGE.		Holland	30/4/18	26/11/18
Lieut. A. T. COWLEY.		Holland	30/4/18	18/11/18
Lieut. H. G. REID.		Holland	27/6/18	31/8/18
Midshipman J. M. D'ARCY LEVY.		Holland	9/4/18	18/11/18
Lieut. D. C. TOOKE.		Holland	12/10/18	21/2/19
Lieut. F. W. MARDOCK.				19/12/18
Lieut. J. F. BAILEY.		Holland	15/6/18	21/1/19
Lieut. C. BUTTERWORTH.		Holland	6/2/18	18/11/18
Lieut. C. NEWMAN.				18/12/18
Lieut. J. ROCKEY.				18/12/18
Flt. Sub.-Lieut. C. G. KNIGHT.		Holland	30/4/18	
Flt. Lieut. G. G. G. HODGE.				12/12/18
Lieut. G. LLEWELLYN-DAVIES.				6/1/19
Lieut. W. WALKER.				19/12/18
Lieut. G. L. ELLIOTT.				14/12/18
Flt. Sub.-Lieut. L. P. PAINE.				14/1/19
Lieut. S. R. HIBBARD.				13/12/18
Capt. G. FLEMING.		(Died 17/4/17)		
Lieut. H. C. VEREKER.				3/1/19
2/Lt. H. EDWARDS.				14/1/19
Lieut. J. C. CROFT.				6/1/19
Flt. Sub.-Lieut. H. M. BURTON.				
Lieut. N. M. HEWITT.				20/12/18
Sub.-Lieut. A. J. BEATTIE.	3/1/18			16/12/18
Lieut. A. C. STEVENS.	28/11/16			17/12/18

ROYAL NAVAL AIR SERVICE—continued.

Name.	Missing.	Interned.	Repatriated.
Lieut. C. RATTBORNE.			5/8/18
Lieut. K. SLATER.			6/1/19
Sub.-Lieut. A. MATHER.			31/12/18
Flt. Sub.-Lt. W. R. WING.			
Flt. Sub.-Lt. C. LAURENCE.			14/12/18
Sub.-Lt. L. J. BENNETT.	Holland	4/8/18	16/8/18
Flt. Lieut. G. E. NASH.			1/1/19
Sub.-Lt. R. L. KENT.			1/1/19
Flt. Sub.-Lt. A. B. HOLCROFT.			19/12/18
Flt. Sub.-Lt. V. G. AUSTEN.			25/12/18
Sub.-Lt. A. D. M. LEWIS.			25/12/18
Flt. Sub.-Lt. N. D. HALL.			2/1/19
Flt. Sub.-Lt. H. H. BOOTH.			14/12/18
Flt. Sub.-Lt. E. W. DESBARATS.			6/1/19
Capt. R. MACK.			20/1/18
Flt. Sub.-Lt. J. R. WILFORD.			14/12/18
Flt. Sub.-Lt. H. S. BROUGHALL.			25/12/18
Flt. Sub.-Lt. R. E. MacMILLAN.			14/12/18
Lieut. D. F. LEWIS.			
Flt. Sub.-Lt. W. INGLESON.			17/12/18
Flt. Sub.-Lt. A. W. PHILLIPS.			26/12/18
Flt. Sub.-Lt. E. FOSTER.			2/1/19
Flt. Lieut. W. PERHAM.	Holland	26/10/17	
Sub.-Lt. H. C. GOOCH.			15/11/18
Flt. Sub.-Lt. J. C. AKESTER.			18/12/18
Flt. Sub.-Lt. W. E. B. OAKLEY.			14/12/18
Flt. Sub.-Lt. G. ANDREWS.			17/12/18
Flt. Sub.-Lt. A. MacDONALD.			17/12/18
Flt. Sub.-Lt. J. S. SERCOMBE SMITH.			18/12/18
Flt. Lieut. L. G. SIEVEKING.			17/12/18
Lieut. S. E. HOBLYN.	Holland	30/4/18	26/11/18
Flt. Lieut. W. S. MAGRATH.	Holland	6/5/18	14/12/18
Lieut. A. A. D. GREY.			1/1/19
Lieut. J. HAY.	Holland	19/4/18	4/10/18
Flt. Sub.-Lt. J. G. CLARK.			18/12/18
Sub.-Lt. H. WHITE.			19/12/18
Sub.-Lt. H. P. SALTER.			31/12/18
Flt. Sub.-Lt. H. St. J. E. YOUENS.			14/12/18
Flt. Sub.-Lt. J. H. T. CARR.	25/1/18		18/12/18

EAST THEATRE OF WAR.

TURKISH PRISONERS.
DARDANELLES.

Name.	Regiment.	Missing.	Repatriated.
Lieut. Sir R. J. PAUL.	R.E. att. French Flying Corps		17/12/18
Capt. B. S. ATKINS.	11/Rajputs att. R.A.F.	16/9/15	7/12/18
Lieut. Douglas BRANSON.	R.N.A.S.	–/2/16	16/12/18
Lieut. R. T. A. MacDONALD.	16/Australian Inf.	30/4/15	9/1/19
Lieut. W. E. ELSTON.	16/Australian Inf.	30/4/15	–/11/18
Lieut. S. L. STORMOUTH.	15/Australian Inf.	7/6/15	16/12/18
2/Lt. L. H. LUSCOMBE.	14/Australian Inf.		16/12/18
Lieut. S. R. JORDAN.	9/Australian Inf.		8/12/18
Capt. W. H. TRELOAR.	Australian Flying Corps	16/9/15	–/11/18
Lieut. S. T. W. GOODWIN.	6/Australian Inf.	20/12/15	16/12/18
Lieut. John L. STONE.	4/Worcestershire Regt.	6/8/15	–/12/18
Capt. J. M. B. ENTWHISTLE.	4/Worcestershire Regt. (Died 2/12/18 at Alexandria)	6/8/15	
Capt. H. A. BRETT.	9/Lincolnshire Regt.	6/8/15	7/12/18
Capt. R. D. ELLIOT.	5/East Yorks Regt.	7-11/8/15	16/12/18
Lieut. R. A. RAWSTORNE.	6/East Yorks Regt.	7-11/8/15	13/12/18
Lieut. J. STILL.	6/East Yorks Regt.	7-11/8/15	7/12/18
Capt. H. DYSON.	8/West Riding Regt.	7-11/8/15	7/12/18
2/Lt. H. DAVENPORT.	9/West Yorks Regt.	11/8/15	16/12/18
Capt. A. C. M. COXON.	5/Norfolk Regt.	12/8/15	16/12/18
2/Lt. W. G. S. FAWKES.	5/Norfolk Regt.	12/8/15	16/12/18
Lieut. S. WHITE.	Egyptian Police		24/11/18
Capt. A. J. DAWES.	9/Somerset L.I. att. Gurkhas (Died 22/6/17 at Constantinople)	14/8/15	
Lieut. A. D. PASS.	1/Dorset Yeomanry	21/9/15	16/12/18

PALESTINE.

Name.	Regiment.	Missing.	Repatriated.
Lieut. A. W. M. BUDGETT.	Berkshire Yeomanry	28/11/17	16/12/18
Capt. S. R. E. SNOW.	Devon Yeomanry	1/12/17	7/12/18
Lieut. S. E. ARMITAGE.	Dorset Yeomanry att. from Dragoon Guards	12/11/17	7/12/18
Lieut. A. W. STRICKLAND.	Gloucestershire Yeomanry	23/4/16	16/12/18
2/Lt. C. C. HERBERT.	Gloucestershire Yeomanry	23/4/16	7/12/18
Lt.-Col. Hon. C. J. COVENTRY.	Worcestershire Yeomanry	23/4/16	7/12/18
Major F. S. WILLIAMS THOMAS.	Worcestershire Yeomanry	23/4/16	–/12/18
Capt. W. R. O'FARRELL.	R.A.M.C. att. Worcestershire Yeomanry	23/4/16	29/12/18
Capt. E. S. WARD.	Worcestershire Yeomanry	23/4/16	7/12/18
Lieut. W. BELL.	Worcestershire Yeomanry	23/4/16	7/12/18
Lieut. J. H. T. DAWSON.	Worcestershire Yeomanry	23/4/16	1/1/19
Lieut. A. V. HOLYOAKE.	Worcestershire Yeomanry	23/4/16	1/1/19
2/Lt. W. B. CHAMBERLAIN.	Worcestershire Yeomanry	23/4/16	1/1/19
2/Lt. A. HICKMAN.	Worcestershire Yeomanry	23/4/16	1/1/19
2/Lt. B. A. JERVIS.	Worcestershire Yeomanry	23/4/16	23/12/18
2/Lt. J. MARSH.	Worcestershire Yeomanry (Died at Yozgad 23/10/18)	23/4/16	
2/Lt. F. W. OSBORNE.	Worcestershire Yeomanry att. from Dragoon Guards	23/4/16	7/12/18
2/Lt. G. B. WRIGHT.	Worcestershire Yeomanry	23/4/16	7/12/18
2/Lt. J. A. TWINBERROW.	Worcestershire Yeomanry	23/4/16	11/12/18

PALESTINE—continued.

Name.	Regiment.	Missing.	Repatriated.
Lieut. C. W. HILL.	*Royal Air Force*	23/4/16	11/12/18
Capt. R. J. TIPTON.	*Royal Air Force*	18/6/16	24/10/17
2/Lt. A. LAZARUS-BARLOW.	*Royal Air Force*	15/2/17	9/12/18
Lieut. E. A. FLOYER.	*Royal Air Force*	5/3/17	7/12/18
2/Lt. C. B. PALMER.	*Royal Air Force*	5/3/17	8/12/18
Lieut. L. W. HEATHCOTE.	*Royal Air Force*		8/12/18
2/Lt. E. A. NEWTON.	*Royal Naval Air Service*	11/10/17	18/12/18
Lieut. P. PARKINSON.	*Royal Air Force*	10/1/18	
Lieut. C. G. BRONSON.	*Royal Naval Air Service*		16/12/18
Lieut. F. W. HANCOCK.	*Royal Air Force*		16/12/18
2/Lt. A. A. POOLE.	*Royal Air Force*		16/12/18
Lt. L. H. PAKENHAM-WALSH.	*Royal Air Force*	28/1/18	16/12/18
Capt. A. J. BOTT.	*Royal Air Force*	22/4/18	16/12/18
Major M. R. McG. TURNBULL.	*Royal Air Force*	25/4/18	–/1/19
2/Lt. R. T. CHALLONOR.	*Australian Flying Corps*	1/5/18	24/11/18
2/Lt. J. McELLIGOTT.	*Australian Flying Corps*	1/5/18	24/11/18
Lieut. F. W. HAIG.	*Australian Flying Corps*		16/12/18
Lieut. J. N. GARNETT.	*Royal Air Force*	15/7/18	
Lieut. J. S. WESSON.	*Royal Air Force*	29/9/18	4/1/19
Lieut. W. STEELE.	*Royal Air Force*	29/9/18	9/1/19
Capt. F. N. G. TAYLOR.	*Royal Engineers*	23/4/16	20/12/18
Lieut. O. H. LITTLE.	*Royal Engineers*	23/4/16	1/1/19
Lieut. D. S. McGHIE.	*Royal Engineers*	23/4/16	16/12/18
2/Lt. J. KILLIN.	*Royal Engineers*	23/4/16	16/12/18
Lt.-Col. S. F. NEWCOMBE.	*Royal Engineers*	1/11/17	4/11/18
2/Lt. F. C. CARR.	*Machine Gun Corps* (*Died* of wounds 24/4/17)	19/4/17	
Lieut. W. STUART.	*Machine Gun Corps*	27/10/17	16/12/18
2/Lt. C. D. McMILLAN.	*Machine Gun Corps*	1/11/17	16/12/18
2/Lt. H. J. BRADSHAW.	4/*Norfolk Regt.* (*Died* at Nazareth)	19/4/17	
Capt. W. C. GARDINER.	5/*Norfolk Regt.*	2/11/17	16/12/18
2/Lt. G. H. L. TALLENT.	5/*Norfolk Regt. att. from Northants.*	29/11/17	16/12/18
2/Lt. J. WINDSOR.	16/*Devonshire Regt.*	3/12/17	16/12/18
2/Lt. H. G. WITHERS.	16/*Devonshire Regt. att. Devon Yeomanry*	3/12/17	27/11/18
2/Lt. K. M. WATT.	5/*Bedfordshire Regt.* (*Died* of wounds)	1/10/17	
2/Lt. E. E. DENNIS.	5/*Bedfordshire Regt. att. from R. Berks.*	1/10/17	9/1/19
Capt. J. F. FERGUSON.	2/*Leicestershire Regt. att. from Durham L.I.*	17/4/18	–/1/19
2/Lt. F. M. PRYCE.	25/*R. Welsh Fusiliers att. from S. Wales Borderers*	30/11/17	16/12/18
2/Lt. G. B. JOHNSTON.	4/*Royal Sussex Regt.* (*Died* at Yozgad 23/10/18)	27/3/17	
2/Lt. A. T. C. ASKIN.	8/*Hampshire Regt.*	19/4/17	16/12/18
2/Lt. R. A. BLOFIELD.	*Hampshire Regt.* (*Died* of wounds 20/4/17)	19/4/17	
2/Lt. H. A. COX.	8/*Hampshire Regt.*	19/4/17	7/12/18
2/Lt. W. S. ROBERTS.	8/*Hampshire Regt.*	19/4/17	16/12/18
2/Lt. V. C. SCLATER.	2/4 *Dorsetshire Regt.*	9/4/18	–/12/18
Major D. H. PEARSON.	7/*Essex Regt.*	27/3/17	7/12/18
2/Lt. S. C. RIDGEWELL.	7/*Essex Regt.* (*Died*)	27/11/17	

PALESTINE—continued.

Name.	Regiment.	Missing.	Repatriated.
Capt. P. G. THOMPSON.	2/4 Royal West Kent Regt.	28/3/17	27/11/18
2/Lt. B. K. CATTELL.	2/10 Middlesex Regt.	1/11/17	13/12/18
2/Lt. W. DICK.	6/Highland Light Infantry att. from A. & S. Hldrs.	10/8/17	8/12/18
2/Lt. F. G. CHALLIS.	1/Herefordshire Regt.	26/3/17	16/12/18
2/Lt. R. E. M. Du CANE.	10th London Regt.	19/4/17	8/12/18
2/Lt. D. R. WARE.	2/14 London Regt.	8/3/18	7/12/18
Lt. W. S. L. M. PEARSON.	17/London Regt.	2/5/18	16/12/18
Lieut. H. M. JUSTICE.	2/21 London Regt.	28/3/18	16/12/18
Lieut. J. BROWN.	Royal Army Medical Corps		-/1/19
Capt. A. J. WILCOX.	Army Chaplains Department	23/4/16	9/1/19
2/Lt. F. ALLSUPP.	Auckland Mtd. Rifles N.Z.	3/8/16	-/11/18
2/Lt. F. S. SHERIDAN.	Indian Army Reserve of Officers	25/3/17	8/12/18
Lieut. P. M. G. BALDWIN.	Indian Lancers att. Mysore Cavalry	14/7/17	3/1/19
Lieut. W. F. PATTON.	3/Gurkha Rifles	19/4/18	16/12/18
Capt. D. St. P. BUNBURY.	Camel Corps		7/12/18
Lieut. W. MILLER.	Camel Corps att. from Rifle Bde.	1/11/17	24/11/18

PERSIAN GULF.

Name.	Regiment.	Missing.	Repatriated.
Major H. L. REILLY.	R.A.F. att. from 82/Punjabis	-/11/15	16/12/18
2/Lt. E. J. FULTON.	R.A.F. att. from 1/Lancers	23/11/15	-/11/18
Lieut. C. R. GOAD.	Royal Indian Marines	-/11/15	16/12/18
Capt. H. G. BRODIE.	103/Mahratta L.I. (Died 26/4/17 at Constantinople)	-/12/15	
Lieut J. G. STILWELL.	1/4th Hampshire Regt.	23/1/16	27/11/18

MESOPOTAMIA.

Name.	Regiment.	Missing.	Repatriated.
Commander G. B. DACRE.	R.A.F.	1/16	16/12/18
Lieut. A. J. BARLOW.	R.A.F.	15/2/17	9/1/19
Sub.-Lt. G. T. BYSSHE.	R.A.F.		16/12/18
Lieut. B. A. TREACHMAN.	R.A.F.		16/12/18
Lieut. T. E. LANDER.	R.A.F.		27/11/18
2/Lt. M. L. MAGUIRE.	R.A.F. (Died -/5/17)	28/4/17	
Capt. J. R. PHILPOTT.	R.A.F. (Died 15/1/18 at Afion)	25/9/17	
Lieut. M. G. BEGG.	R.A.F.	25/9/17	16/12/18
Lieut. E. M. BAILLON.	R.A.F.	25/9/17	16/12/18
2/Lt. J. W. BLAKE.	R.A.F.		24/11/18
Lieut. J. D. G. McRAE.	R.A.F.	5/10/17	16/12/18
2/Lt. P. PRICE.	R.A.F.	19/10/17	
2/Lt. J. B. WELMAN.	R.A.F.	31/10/17	7/12/18
Lieut. A. S. MILLS.	R.A.F.	17/1/18	16/12/18
2/Lt. W. TAYLOR.	R.A.F.	17/1/18	16/12/18
Lieut. E. ROBINSON.	R.A.F.	/18	
Lieut. J. C. JENKS.	R.A.F.	/18	
Capt. A. J. EVERARD.	R.A.F.		
Capt. W. L. HAIGHT.	R.A.F.	12/3/18	16/12/18
Capt. D. W. RUTHERFORD.	R.A.F.		-/11/18
Lieut. H. L. N. HANCOCK.	R.A.F.		16/12/18
Lieut. EDWARDS.	R.A.F. (Died 14/5/18 at Mosul)	2/5/18	
Lieut. A. WARD.	R.A.F.		7/12/18
Lieut. G. J. WILLIAMS.	R.A.F.		16/12/18

MESOPOTAMIA—continued.

Name.	Regiment.	Missing.	Repatriated.
Lt. A. A. CULLEN.	R.A.F.	31/8/18	–/1/19
Major A. J. EVANS.	R.A.F.		7/12/18
Lieut. E. P. OSMOND.	R.A.F.		–/11/18
2/Lt. H. G. PENWARDEN.	R.A.F.		–/11/18
Capt. S. L. PETTIT.	R.A.F.	29/7/18	16/12/18
Capt. T. W. WHITE.	Australian Flying Corps	12/11/15	–/12/18
Capt. F. C. YEATS-BROWN.	Australian Flying Corps	12/11/15	6/12/18
2/Lt. N. L. STEELE.	Australian Flying Corps		(Died)
2/Lt. C. H. VAUTIN.	Australian Flying Corps	8/7/17	16/12/18
Commander A. W. CLEMSON.	Australian Flying Corps	11/10/17	16/12/18
Capt. R. A. AUSTIN.	Australian Flying Corps	19/3/18	24/11/18
Lieut. M. C. LEE.	Australian Flying Corps	19/3/18	24/11/18
Lieut. V. J. PARKINSON.	Australian Flying Corps		–/10/18
Lieut. L. H. SMITH.	Australian Flying Corps		–/10/18
2/Lt. C. B. GASSON.	R.N.A.S.		
Lieut. A. MAITLAND-HERIOT.	R.N.A.S.		6/12/18
Lieut. W. C. JAMESON.	R.N.A.S.		
Lieut. P. WOODLAND.	R.N.A.S.		30/12/18
Lieut. A. J. NIGHTINGALE.	R.N.A.S.		30/12/18
Sub.-Lt. W. E. FOSTER.	R.N.A.S.		27/11/18
Sub.-Lt. H. BURNS.	R.N.A.S.		16/12/18
Lieut. J. W. ALCOCK.	R.N.A.S.		16/12/18
Commander T. HACKMAN.	R.N.A.S.	22/2/18	7/12/18
Lieut. T. H. PIPER.	R.N.A.S.	22/2/18	16/12/18
Capt. L. MURPHY.	R.A.M.C.		1/1/19
Capt. W. L. E. FRETZ.	R.A.M.C.	(Exchanged	–/–/16)
Capt. A. S. CANE.	R.A.M.C.	(Exchanged	–/–/16)
Capt. J. BUCHANAN.	R.A.M.C. att. 9/Warwicks	2/9/18	30/12/18
Father P. J. MULLAN.	Army Chaplains' Department		7/12/18
2/Lt. E. A. PINNINGTON.	13/Hussars	5/3/17	18/2/18
Lieut. T. WILLIAMS-TAYLOR.	13/Hussars	5/11/17	–/12/18
2/Lt. E. H. JONES.	R.F.A.		18/11/18
Lieut. P. S. LEWIS.	R.F.A. 10/Brigade	(Exchanged	–/–/16)
Lieut. H. S. D. McNEAL.	R.F.A. 10/Brigade	(Exchanged	–/–/16)
Major H. G. THOMSON.	R.F.A.	(Exchanged	–/–/16)
Lieut. C. K. WOOLLEY.	R.F.A.		16/12/18
2/Lt. T. W. ABBOTT.	Royal Engineers	(Exchanged	–/–/16)
Major G. A. BEAZELEY.	Royal Engineers	2/5/18	16/12/18
2/Lt. F. W. WOODFIELD.	2/Leicestershire Regt.	11/3/16	16/12/18
2/Lt. F. H. E. WATSON.	10/Norfolk (Exchanged –/–/16)	15–16/3/16	
2/Lt. H. BIRCH.	8/Royal Welsh Fus.	9/4/16	(Died)
2/Lt. T. H. R. DANIELS.	6/K.O. Royal Lancaster Regt.	9.4.16	
Lieut. W. B. H. PARKER.	8/Cheshire Regt. (Died 26/4/16)	–/4/16	
2/Lt. A. B. JONES.	8/Cheshire Regt.	30/4/17	16/12/18
Lieut. J. H. T. BRABAZON.	4/Connaught Rangers	17–18/4/16	9/12/18
2/Lt. J. A. SHANNON.	Highland Light Infantry	17–18/4/16	16/12/18
2/Lt. T. McK. COWIE.	2/Black Watch	17/2/17	1/3/17
2/Lt. A. H. QUINE.	2/Black Watch	21/4/17	16/12/18
Capt. T. M. JENKINS.	4/South Wales Borderers	30/4/17	1/1/19
Capt. E. G. STAPLES.	4/South Wales Borderers	30/4/17	16/12/18
2/Lt. Sir J. W. L. NAPIER.	4/South Wales Borderers	30/4/17	16/12/18
2/Lt. A. W. BROCKS.	16/Devonshire Regt. att. from 3/Cheshires) (Died 10/3/18 at Afion-kara-Hissar)	3/12/17	

MESOPOTAMIA—continued.

Name.	Regiment.	Missing.	Repatriated.
Lieut. C. W. ROGERS.	9/Royal Warwickshire Regt.	1/9/18	28/11/18
Lieut. H. L. COLLINS.	South African Field Arty.	16/2/18	16/12/18
Major S. BOSE.	Indian Medical Service	(Exchanged –/–/16)	
Asst. Surg. A. DE SOUZA.	Indian Medical Service		
Asst. Surg. A. J. HIXON.	Indian Medical Service		
Asst. Surg. R. P. LEWIS.	Indian Medical Service		
Asst. Surg. D. MacKAY.	Indian Medical Service		
Capt. P. O. WESTON.	Indian Medical Service		
Capt. J. S. S. MARTIN.	Indian Medical Service		7/12/18
Capt. M. L. PURJ.	Indian Medical Service		6/10/18
Lieut. A. PAEO.	Indian Medical Service		1/1/19
Asst. Surg. H. W. STEWART.	Indian Medical Service		17/12/18
Asst. Surg. H. A. T. WELLS.	Indian Medical Service		17/12/18
Asst. Surg. E. DUCKWORTH.	Indian Medical Service		17/12/18
Lieut. J. M. BALLIN.	Supply & Transport Corps I.A.		17/12/18
2/Lt. G. E. C. FLYNN.	103/Mahratta L.I., I.A.	1–2/12/15	7/12/18
Capt. P. WOOD.	89/Punjabis, I.A.	11/3/16	(Died)
Capt. R. CLIFFORD.	24/Punjabis, I.A.		
Lieut. H. G. TRANCHELL.	2/Rajputs, I.A.	(Exchanged –/–/16)	
2/Lt. H. SOUTHERN.	47/Sikhs, I.A.	17–18/4/16	
Capt. W. K. COOK.	Indian Army		16/12/18
Lieut. E. P. LARKIN.	20/Deccan Horse I.A.	10/7/18	16/12/18
Lieut. W. R. BOYCE.	I.A.R.O.		28/12/18

KUT GARRISON.

Name.	Regiment.	Missing.	Repatriated.
General C. V. F. TOWNSHEND.			9/11/18
Brig.-General N. W. EVANS.			11/11/18
Brig.-General HAMILTON-HAMILTON.			27/11/18
Major-General DELAMAIN.			27/11/18
Major-General C. G. MELLIS.			11/11/18
Major E. G. DUNN.	General Staff		7/12/18
Major B. G. PEEL.	General Staff		30/12/18
Capt. E. S. HALFORD.	Staff		7/12/18
Lt. F. T. DRAKE-BROCKMAN.	7/Lancers		24/11/18
Lieut. C. A. FORBES.	7/Lancers		7/12/18
Capt. C. H. KIRKWOOD.	23/Daly's Horse		16/12/18
Lieut. R. BRIERLEY.	23/Daly's Horse		7/12/18
Lieut. C. H. C. MONROE.	33/Indian Cavalry		16/12/18
Lt.-Col. J. DAVIE.	34/Poona Horse		7/12/18
Lt.-Col. McV. CRICHTON.	Indian Army Reserve		7/12/18
Major H. J. COTTON.	Indian Army Reserve	(Died)	
Major C. W. NEUMANN.	Indian Army Reserve		24/11/18
Capt. E. W. BURDETT.	Indian Army Reserve		16/12/18
Capt. L. V. HOYNE-FOX.	Indian Army Reserve		
Capt. H. G. MORRELL.	Indian Army att. Div. Signal Coy.		16/12/18
Capt. H. M. SPINK.	Indian Army Reserve		30/12/18
Lieut. J. L. BATEY.	Indian Army Reserve		1/1/19
Lieut. H. S. CHESHIRE.	Indian Army Reserve att. Sappers and Miners		16/12/18
Lieut. E. S. FAIRBROTHER.	Indian Army Reserve		8/12/18
Lieut. LABOTHER.	Indian Army Reserve.		
Lieut. LECKYARD.	Indian Army Reserve		
2/Lt. DUXBURY.	Indian Army Reserve		8/12/18
Lieut. H. A. CLIFTON.	Staff		19/12/18

KUT GARRISON—continued.

Name.	Regiment.	Missing.	Repatriated.
2/Lt. O. G. KIERNANDER	*Indian Army Reserve*		11/11/18
2/Lt. G. R. LEIGH-BENNETT.	*Indian Army Reserve*		7/12/18
2/Lt. C. LESMOND.	*Indian Army Reserve*		6/1/19
2/Lt. G. N. ROGERS.	*Indian Army Reserve*		24/11/18
2/Lt. M. L. C. SMITH.	*Indian Army Reserve*		
Lt.-Col. H. O. PARR.	*7/Rajputs*		–/11/18
Major F. C. TREGEAR.	*7/Rajputs*		7/12/18
Capt. A. R. THOMSON.	*7/Rajputs*		29/12/18
Lieut. M. CORBEY-SMITH.	*7/Rajputs*		24/11/18
Lieut. W. S. HALLILEY.	*7/Rajputs*		30/12/18
2/Lt. T. E. FURNEAUX.	*7/Rajputs.*		9/1/19
Capt. G. R. RAE.	*9/Rajputs*		28/11/18
Major J. C. McKENNA.	*16/Rajputs*		7/12/18
Capt. H. J. DANIELL.	*20/Punjabis*	(Died at Mossul 19/8/16)	
Major A. SUTHERLAND.	*22/Punjabis*		6/12/18
Capt. W. WALLACE.	*22/Punjabis*		7/12/18
Capt. C. T. WARNER.	*22/Punjabis*		16/12/18
Lieut. G. R. HUDDLESTON.	*22/Punjabis*		16/12/18
Lieut. H. MEARS.	*22/Punjabis*		16/12/18
Lieut. L. R. POTTER.	*22/Punjabis*		24/11/18
Lt.-Col. H. A. V. CUMMINS.	*24/Punjabis*		27/11/18
Capt. A. B. HAIG.	*24/Punjabis*		18/9/18
Capt. A. C. H. TREVOR.	*24/Punjabis*		16/12/18
Lieut. W. A. PHILLIPS.	*24/Punjabis*		1/1/19
2/Lt. H. BROWNE.	*24/Punjabis*		
Lieut. H. E. STAPLETON.	*25/Punjabis*		16/12/18
Capt. H. CARDEW.	*29/Rifles*		29/12/18
Capt. A. GATHERER.	*46/Punjabis*		30/12/18
Colonel A. J. N. HARVARD.	*48/Pioneers*		27/11/18
Major M. E. S. JOHNSON.	*48/Pioneers*		7/12/18
Capt. BIGNELL.	*48/Pioneers*		
Capt. R. D. CORBETT.	*48/Pioneers*	(Died at Krangri 25/12/17)	
Capt. C. A. RAYNOR.	*48/Pioneers*		7/12/18
2/Lt. S. W. BIDEN.	*48/Pioneers*		16/12/18
2/Lt. L. F. SOUTER.	*48/Pioneers*		13/12/18
Major W. F. G. GILCHRIST.	*52/Sikhs*		29/12/18
Lt.-Col. A. MOORE.	*66/Punjabis*		10/1/19
Capt. C. H. STOCKLEY.	*66/Punjabis*		9/1/19
2/Lt. H. W. BISHOP.	*66/Punjabis*		24/10/17
2/Lt. A. R. UBSDELL.	*66/Punjabis*		16/12/18
Major C. E. S. COX.	*67/Punjabis*		16/12/18
Capt. R. F. ATKINS.	*67/Punjabis*		16/12/18
Capt. R. A. P. GRANT.	*67/Punjabis*		16/10/18
Lt. F. N. C. ARMSTRONG.	*67/Punjabis*		7/12/18
Major E. MILFORD.	*76/Punjabis*		11/11/18
Major N. V. I. RYBOT.	*76/Punjabis*		7/12/18
Capt. S. Van B. LAING.	*76/Punjabis*		16/12/18
Capt. G. R. REYNE.	*76/Punjabis*		16/12/18
Capt. J. HOOD.	*83/Punjabis*	(Died at Bagdad 6/4/16)	
Colonel W. H. BROWN.	*103/Mahratta Light Infantry*		28/11/18
Major A. C. THORNE.	*103/Mahratta Light Infantry*		29/12/18
Capt. H. W. GOLDFRAP.	*103/Mahratta Light Infantry*		7/12/18
Lieut. B. W. REYNOLDS.	*103/Mahratta Light Infantry* (Died at Castamouni 20/7/16)		
Capt. C. M. S. MANNERS.	*104/Wellesley Rifles*		16/12/18
Lieut. B. AYER.	*104/Wellesley Rifles*		

KUT GARRISON—continued.

Name.	Regiment.	Missing.	Repatriated.
2/Lt. L. BELL-SYER.	*104/Wellesley Rifles*		16/12/18
2/Lt. A. C. LOCH.	*104/Wellesley Rifles* (Died at Castamouni 1/8/16)		
2/Lt. F. N. PUNCHARD.	*104/Wellesley Rifles*		9/1/19
Major C. H. HILL.	*110/Mahratta Light Infantry*		7/12/18
Capt. A. D. GUNN.	*110/Mahratta Light Infantry*		10/1/19
Lieut. R. O. CHAMIER.	*110/Mahratta Light Infantry*		9/1/19
Lt. C. V. HERON-JONES.	*110/Mahratta Light Infantry*		1/1/19
2/Lt. A. MacFADYEN.	*110/Mahratta Light Infantry*		7/12/18
2/Lt. J. H. O'DONOGHUE.	*110/Mahratta Light Infantry* (Died at Nisiebin 27/6/16)		
Capt. S. A. HUNGERFORD.	*117/Mahratta Light Infantry*		–/1/19
Lieut. A. TAYLOR.	*117/Mahratta Light Infantry*		24/11/18
2/Lt. H. D. STEARNS.	*117/Mahratta Light Infantry*		9/1/19
Brev.-Col. W. W. CHITTY.	*119/Mooltan Regt.*		27/11/18
Capt. F. I. BRICKMANN.	*119/Mooltan Regt.*		16/12/18
Lieut. E. Le PATOUREL.	*119/Mooltan Regt.*		6/1/19
2/Lt. E. H. KEELING.	*119/Mooltan Regt.*		6/10/17
Major P. F. POCOCK.	*120/Rajput Infantry*		16/12/18
Capt. W. L. MISKIN.	*120/Rajput Infantry*		16/12/18
Lieut. W. GALLOWAY.	*120/Rajput Infantry*		16/12/18
Lieut. R. LECKY.	*120/Rajput Infantry*		1/1/19
Lieut. H. H. RICH.	*120/Rajput Infantry*		20/1/19
Major J. BARRARD.	*128/Pioneers* (Died at Bagdad 7/5/16)		
Lieut. L. MATHIAS.	*128/Pioneers*		29/12/18
Lt.-Col. A. N. TAYLOR.	*7/Gurkha Rifles*		7/12/18
Capt. G. R. CHANNER.	*7/Gurkha Rifles*		28/11/18
Capt. N. M. WILSON.	*7/Gurkha Rifles*		28/11/18
Lt.-Col. W. B. POWELL.	*2/7 Gurkha Rifles*		24/11/18
Major W. JOHNSTON.	*2/7 Gurkha Rifles*		7/12/18
Lieut. R. BAMPTON.	*2/7 Gurkha Rifles*		16/12/18
Lieut. R. SWEET.	*2/7 Gurkha Rifles* (Died at Yozgad)		
2/Lt. A. M. CLARK.	*2/7Gurkha Rifles*		17/12/18
Brig.-General H. D. GRIER.	*Indian Mounted Artillery Brigade*		26/11/18
Lieut. R. D. MERRIMAN.	*Royal Indian Marines*		29/12/18
Colonel P. HEHIR.	*Indian Medical Service.*		25/9/16
Major McM. PEARSON.	*Indian Medical Service.*		27/11/18
Major E. A. WALKER.	*Indian Medical Service.*		7/12/18
Capt. L. A. P. ANDERSON.	*Indian Medical Service.*		7/12/18
Capt. F. AQUINO.	*Indian Medical Service.*		17/12/18
Capt. D. ARTHUR.	*Indian Medical Service.* (Died at Entelli 31/7/17).		
Capt. L. H. FOX.	*Indian Medical Service.* (Died at Yozgad).		
Capt. S. HAUGHTON.	*Indian Medical Service.*		7/12/18
Capt. H. KING.	*Indian Medical Service.*		25/9/16
Capt. C. NEWCOMB.	*Indian Medical Service.*		7/12/18
Capt. J. S. STARTIN.	*Indian Medical Service.*		17/12/18
Lieut. P. E. DONOGHUE.	*Indian Medical Service.*		1/1/19
Lieut. R. V. MARTIN.	*Indian Medical Service.*		9/1/19
Lieut. W. O. SPACKMAN.	*Indian Medical Service.*		16/12/18
Brig.-Gen. G. B. SMITH.	*6/Division Royal Artillery.*		2/12/18
Lt.-Col. H. S. MAULE.	*Royal Field Artillery.*		7/12/18
Lt.-Col. H. B. SMITH.	*Royal Field Artillery.*		–/12/18
Major A. J. ANDERSON.	*Royal Field Artillery.*		7/12/18

KUT GARRISON—continued.

Name.	Regiment.	Missing.	Repatriated.
Major E. CORBOULD-WARREN.	*Royal Field Artillery.*		6/11/18
Major W. C. R. FARMAR.	*Royal Field Artillery.*		11/12/18
Major A. F. B. HARVEY.	*Royal Field Artillery*		16/12/18
Major O. S. LLOYD.	*Royal Field Artillery.*		16/12/18
Capt. E. L. J. BAYLEY.	*Royal Field Artillery*		7/12/18
Capt. T. R. M. CARLISLE.	*Royal Field Artillery*		29/12/18
Capt. L. H. G. DORLING.	*Royal Field Artillery*		–/12/18
Capt. K. F. FREELAND.	*Royal Field Artillery*		29/12/18
Capt. V. R. GUISE.	*Royal Field Artillery*		16/12/18
Capt. E. T. MARTIN.	*Royal Field Artillery.*		16/11/16
Capt. V. R. REEKS.	*Royal Field Artillery*		
Lieut. F. DAVERN.	*Royal Field Artillery*		8/12/18
Lieut. W. DEVEREUX.	*Royal Field Artillery*		16/12/18
Lieut. P. EDMONDS.	*Royal Field Artillery*		11/11/18
Lieut. H. C. GALLUP.	*Royal Field Artillery*		8/12/18
Lieut. M. A. B. JOHNSTON.	*Royal Field Artillery.*		16/10/18
Lieut. H. E. JONES.	*Royal Field Artillery.*		
Lieut. E. O. MOUSLEY.	*Royal Field Artillery*		–/12/18
Lieut. R. SPENCE.	*Royal Field Artillery*		1/1/19
Lieut. W. TOZER.	*Royal Field Artillery.*	(*Died*).	
Lieut. F. W. B. WILSON.	*Royal Field Artillery.*		16/12/18
2/Lt. W. E. TRAFFORD.	*Royal Field Artillery.*		16/12/18
Major R. C. ALEXANDER.	*Royal Garrison Artillery*		7/12/18
Capt. R. C. LOWNDES.	*Royal Garrison Artillery*		1/1/19
Lieut. R. L. FLUX.	*Royal Garrison Artillery*		7/12/18
Lieut. R. G. PARSONS.	*Royal Garrison Artillery*		24/11/18
Lieut. E. J. WILLIAMS.	*Royal Garrison Artillery*		16/12/18
Lieut. F. P. G. WILLIAMS.	*Royal Garrison Artillery*		7/12/18
Lt.-Col. F. A. WILSON.	*Royal Engineers*		27/11/18
Major J. S. BARKER.	*Royal Engineers*		7/12/18
Major F. BOOTH.	*Royal Engineers (Signal Service) att. from K.O.R. Lancs.*		6/12/18
Major H. E. WINSLOE.	*Royal Engineers.*		16/11/16
Capt. C. E. COLBECK.	*Royal Engineers.*		7/12/18
Capt. E. W. C. SANDES.	*Royal Engineers.*		–/12/18
Capt. R. E. STACE.	*Royal Engineers.*		7/12/18
Capt. H. W. TOMLINSON.	*Royal Engineers.*		7/12/18
Capt. K. D. YEARSLEY.	*Royal Engineers.*		16/10/18
Lieut. W. BOYES.	*Royal Engineers.*		10/12/18
Lieut. K. B. S. CRAWFORD.	*Royal Engineers.*		16/12/18
Lieut. C. L. E. GREENWOOD.	*Royal Engineers.*		7/12/18
Lieut. A. B. MATTHEWS.	*Royal Engineers.*		6/1/19
Lieut. J. A. POCOCK.	*Royal Engineers.*		8/12/18
2/Lt. J. McCONVILLE.	*Sappers and Miners att. from King's Liverpool Regt.*		17/12/18
Lieut. F. MAYO.	*Sappers and Miners*		7/12/18
Col. A. S. R. ANNESLEY.	*Supply and Transport Corps.*		27/11/18
Major T. L. BALL.	*Supply and Transport Corps.*		16/12/18
Major H. W. DAVIES.	*Supply and Transport Corps.*		17/12/18
Major E. E. FORBES.	*Supply and Transport Corps.*		20/1/19
Mjaor T. LEESON-BALL.	*Supply and Transport Corps.*		
Major R. W. H. MIDDLEMASS.	*Supply and Transport Corps.*		16/12/18
Major H. W. PRICE.	*Supply and Transport Corps.*		24/11/18
Major P. C. SAUNDERS.	*Supply and Transport Corps.*		16/12/18
Major A. F. STEWART.	*Supply and Transport Corps.*		16/12/18
Major H. H. SYER.	*Supply and Transport Corps.*		16/12/18

KUT GARRISON—continued.

Name.	Regiment.	Missing.	Repatriated.
Capt. G. H. BURROUGHS.	*Supply and Transport Corps.*		7/12/18
Capt. C. B. HEREPATH.	*Supply and Transport Corps.*		24/11/18
Capt. J. W. PHILIPS.	*Supply and Transport Corps.*		29/12/18
Capt. G. WHITE.	*Supply and Transport Corps.*		7/12/18
Lieut. R. BAIRD.	*Supply and Transport Corps.*		16/12/18
Lieut. S. FOWLES.	*Supply and Transport Corps.*		17/12/18
Lieut. J. H. C. GAYER.	*Supply and Transport Corps.*		24/11/18
Lieut. A. LANG.	*Supply and Transport Corps.*		17/12/18
Lieut. F. C. SLY.	*Supply and Transport Corps.*		8/12/18
2/Lt. C. H. McDERMOTT.	*Supply and Transport Corps.*		8/12/18
Lieut. J. C. HORWOOD.	*Mechanical Transport Corps.*		16/12/18
2/Lt. J. A. DOOLEY.	*Mechanical Transport Corps.*		9/1/19
Capt. C. B. MUNDEY.	*Royal Flying Corps.*		–/11/18
Capt. T. A. WELLS.	*Royal Flying Corps.*		7/12/18
Capt. S. C. WINFIELD-SMITH.	*Royal Flying Corps.*		7/12/18
Lieut. H. STEPHENSON.	*Army Veterinary Corps.*		16/12/18
Lieut. W. B. K. ANDEESN.	*Postal Department.*		17/12/18
Lieut. W. APPLEBY.	*Postal Department*		
Capt. H. SPOONER.	*Army Chaplains Department*		1/1/19
Capt. A. Y. WRIGHT.	*Army Chaplains Department*		16/12/18
Colonel H. O. B. BROWNE-MASON.	*Royal Army Medical Corps*		16/11/16
Lt.-Col. E. F. BAINES.	*Royal Army Medical Corps.*		7/12/18
Lt.-Col. J. HENNESSY.	*Royal Army Medical Corps.*		16/11/16
Major E. V. AYLEN.	*Royal Army Medical Corps.*		16/11/16
Major C. H. BARBER.	*Royal Army Medical Corps.*		25/9/16
Major E. BENNETT.	*Royal Army Medical Corps.*		11/11/18
Major T. JENKINSON.	*Royal Army Medical Corps'* (Died at Mosul 8/7/16).		
Capt. L. ANDERSON.	*Royal Army Medical Corps.*		
Capt. E. G. S. CANE.	*Royal Army Medical Corps.*		16/12/18
Capt. R. C. CLIFFORD.	*Royal Army Medical Corps.*		14/12/18
Capt. C. E. JONES.	*Royal Army Medical Corps.*		9/1/19
Capt. A. T. S. McCREARY.	*Royal Army Medical Corps.*		16/11/16
Capt. J. D. MARTIN.	*Royal Army Medical Corps.*		
Capt. T. E. OSMOND.	*Royal Army Medical Corps.*		7/12/18
Capt. P. E. O'DONOGHUE.	*Royal Army Medical Corps.*		10/12/18
Lieut. J. W. NEWBOLD.	*Royal Army Medical Corps.*		
Lieut. J. S. TWINBERROW.	*Worcestershire Yeomanry.*		1/1/19
Major W. THOMAS.	*Worcestershire Yeomanry.*		
Lieut. E. B. BURNS.	*2/East Kent Regt.*		7/12/18
Lt.-Col. F. C. LODGE.	*2/Norfolk Regt.*		7/12/18
Major W. E. CRAMER-ROBERTS.	*2/Norfolk Regt.*		7/12/18
Capt. G. de GREY.	*2/Norfolk Regt.*		
Capt. A. B. FLOYD.	*2/Norfolk Regt.*		30/12/18
Capt. A. J. SHAKESHAFT.	*2/Norfolks.*		1/1/19
Lieut. T. CAMPBELL.	*2/Norfolk Regt.*		30/12/18
Lieut. H. L. PEACOCK.	*2/Norfolk Regt.*		1/12/18
Lieut. J. F. W. READ.	*2/Norfolk Regt.*		1/1/19
Lieut. J. P. RICHARDSON.	*2/Norfolk Regt.*		16/11/16
Lieut. S. B. GREGORY.	*4/Devonshire Regt.* (Died at Mosul 3/6/16).		
Lieut. W. SNELL.	*4/Devonshire Regt.*		8/12/18
Capt. F. R. ELLIS.	*4/Duke of Cornwall's L.I.*		16/10/18
2/Lt. P. W. KEARNEY.	*4/Duke of Cornwall's L.I.*		9/1/19
Major S. JULIUS.	*1/Royal Sussex Regt.*		13/1/19

KUT GARRISON—continued.

Name.	Regiment.	Missing.	Repatriated.
Major F. L. FOOTNER.	4/Hampshire Regt.		9/1/19
Capt. N. REEKS.	4/Hampshire Regt.		16/12/18
Lieut. G. ELTON.	4/Hampshire Regt.		16/12/18
Lieut. A. G. FORBES.	4/Hampshire Regt.		27/11/18
Lieut. J. H. HARRIS.	4/Hampshire Regt.		16/10/18
Lieut. R. S. LACY.	4/Hampshire Regt.		6/12/18
Lieut. F. J. PATMORE.	4/Hampshire Regt.		6/12/18
2/Lt. C. CHITTY.	4/Hampshire Regt.		16/12/18
Major G. M. HERBERT.	2/Dorsetshire Regt.		7/12/18
Major J. McKENNA.	2/Dorsetshire Regt.		
Capt. G. W. R. BISHOP.	2/Dorsetshire Regt., att. from Somerset L.I.		10/12/18
Capt. A. BROWN.	2/Dorsetshire Regt.		29/12/18
Capt. C. T. HIGHETT.	2/Dorsetshire Regt.		1/1/19
Capt. W. H. MILES.	2/Dorsetshire Regt.		7/12/18
Lieut. S. MILLER.	2/Dorsetshire Regt.		30/12/18
Lieut. D. A. SIMMONS.	2/Dorsetshire Regt.		30/12/18
Lieut. H. G. WALDRAM.	2/Dorsetshire Regt., att. from Devonshire Regt.		30/12/18
2/Lt. W. BARTON.	2/Dorsetshire Regt.		5/1/19
2/Lt. C. P. CRAWLEY.	2/Dorsetshire Regt.		8/1/19
Lt.-Col. E. LETHBRIDGE.	1/Oxford & Bucks L.I.		7/12/18
Major C. F. HENLEY.	1/Oxford & Bucks L.I.		7/12/18
Capt. T. IVEY.	1/Oxford & Bucks L.I.		7/12/18
Capt. W. MORLAND.	1/Oxford & Bucks L.I.		21/11/18
Lieut. G. L. HEAWOOD.	1/Oxford & Bucks L.I., att. from Wilshire Regt.		20/11/16
Lieut. A. E. MASON.	1/Oxford & Bucks L.I.		8/12/18
Lieut. J. S. P. MELLOR.	1/Oxford & Bucks L.I., att. from Somerset L.I.		16/12/18
Lieut. G. NAYLOR.	1/Oxford & Bucks L.I.		16/12/18
Major J. W. NELSON.	2/Royal West Kent Regt.		16/12/18
Capt. V. S. CLARKE.	2/Royal West Kent Regt.		–/9/18
Capt. M. J. DINWIDDY.	2/Royal West Kent Regt.		16/12/18
Capt. O. Y. HIBBERT.	2/Royal West Kent Regt.		7/12/18
2/Lt. J. MILLS.	2/Royal West Kent Regt.		16/12/18
Lieut. T. E. GRANGER.	7/Manchester Regt.		16/12/18
Lieut. J. M. McCOMBIE.	Gordon Highlanders		16/12/18
Lieut. W. REED.	Royal Navy		16/12/18
Lieut. L. TUDWAY.	Royal Navy		7/12/18
Lieut. S. NICHOLSON.	H.M.S. "Zaida"		16/12/18
Lieut. H. DUNLOP.	H.M.S. "Zaida"		16/12/18

AEGEAN GROUP.

Name.	Regiment.	Missing.	Repatriated.
Lieut. C. G. CLARK.	R.A.F.	29/7/18	16/12/18
Major J. P. B. FERRAND.	R.A.F.	–/9/18	9/1/19
Lieut. S. P. O. HAUGHTON.	R.A.F.	21/9/18	9/1/19
Lieut. Kenneth WITHERS.	R.A.F.	17/10/18	–/12/18
Lieut. W. BAMBER.	R.A.F.	17/10/18	–/12/18

BALKANS.

Name.	Regiment.	Missing.	Repatriated.
Sub.-Lt. B. A. MILLARD.	R.A.F. (late R.N.A.S.)		3/1/19
2/Lt. A. N. D. POCOCK.	R.A.F.	5/1/17	19/10/18
2/Lt. S. SMITH.	R.A.F.	21/7/17	–/11/18
2/Lt. A. C. STOPHER	R.A.F.	12/2/17	28/11/18

BALKANS—continued.

Name.	Regiment.	Missing.	Repatriated.
Lieut. J. C. F. OWEN.	R.A.F.	18/2/17	16/10/18
2/Lt. A. LESLIE-MOORE.	R.A.F.	18/6/17	19/1/18
Capt. J. E. A. O'DWYER.	R.A.F.	8/7/17	28/11/17
Lieut. S. WISE.	R.A.F.	1/10/17	8/12/18
2/Lt. J. R. F. GUBBINS. (Died 20/11/17)	R.A.F.	29/10/17	
Lieut. A. ROWAN.	R.A.F.	3/1/18	29/11/18
2/Lt. H. A. TRACEY.	R.A.F.	3/1/18	29/11/18
2/Lt. H. F. GAYNOR.	R.A.F.	15/3/18	28/11/18
2/Lt. G. HANNAN.	R.A.F.	14/4/18	28/11/18
Sub.-Lt. G. BLANDY.	R.N.A.S.		–/10/18
Lieut. E. J. COOPER.	R.N.A.S.		22/10/18
Sub.-Lt. R. W. FRAZIER.	R.N.A.S.	–/12/16	28/11/18
2/Lt. C. W. GREIG.	R.N.A.S. (Died 12/9/18)		
Sub.-Lt. S. G. BEARE.	R.N.A.S.		28/11/18
2/Lt. E. P. HYDE.	R.N.A.S.		21/9/18
Viscount TORRINGTON.	R.N.A.S.		25/10/18
Lieut. B. J. BRADY.	R.N.A.S.		21/9/18
Sub.-Lt. L. MARSH.	R.N.A.S.		–/10/18
Capt. G. B. BAKER.	R.N.A.S.		
Lieut. Hugh AIRD.	R.N.A.S.	30/9/17	16/12/18
2/Lt. M. MALONEY.	6/Royal Dublin Fus.	6–11/12/15	–/10/18
2/Lt. R. G. HOWE.	6/Royal Dublin Fus.	6–11/12/15	–/10/18
Capt. S. SPIRA.	9/K.O. Royal Lancaster Regt.	12/12/15	–/10/18
Capt. L. W. HARRIES.	9/K.O. Royal Lancaster Regt.	12/12/15	–/10/18
2/Lt. G. H. COLE.	2/K.O. Royal Lancaster Regt.	27/10/17	28/11/18
Lieut. G. T. BENNETT.	10/Hampshire Regt.	31/5/16	–/11/18
2/Lt. S. C. BARBER.	11/Northumberland Fus.	10/9/16	–/10/18
2/Lt. H. G. TAYLOR.	2/Northumberland Fus.	10/9/16	21/9/18
Capt. H. U. SCRUTTON.	2/Northumberland Fus.	10/9/17	(Died)
Capt. R. E. WALKER.	1/York & Lancaster Regt.	12/10/16	–/10/18
2/Lt. G. C. TUNBRIDGE. (Died 27/4/18)	1/York & Lancaster Regt.	18/4/18	
Lieut. J. L. W. CRAIG.	11/Royal Welsh Fus.	21/2/17	20/1/18
Lieut. R. A. W. P. RICHARDES.	11/Royal Welsh Fus.	22/9/18	6/1/19
2/Lt. R. B. LLOYD.	11/Worcestershire Regt.	25/4/17	11/1/19
2/Lt. C. DE. LEMOS.	11/Worcestershire Regt.	–/18	21/9/18
Lieut. A. A. TOWNSEND.	7/Royal Munster Fus.	6–11/12/15	–/10/18
Lieut. D. J. COWAN.	5/Connaught Rangers	6–11/12/15	–/10/18
Lieut. W. E. GILLILAND.	10/Norfolk Regt.	6–11/12/15	–/11/18
2/Lt. G. ALEXANDER.	3/Royal Irish Rifles	24/10/16	29/11/18
2/Lt. E. L. FOOKS.	R.F.A.	31/10/16	(Died)
2/Lt. L. G. H. DEAN.	3/Middlesex Regt.	8/4/17	–/10/18
2/Lt. T. W. GREENSTREET.	2/Royal Irish Fus. att. from 3/Northants	20/4/17	21/9/18
Lieut. J. A. TAYLOR.	7/Wiltshire Regt.	24–25/4/17	21/9/18
2/Lt. J. D. WALLIS.	12/Argyll & Sutherland Highlanders att. from Scottish Horse	8–9/5/17	–/10/18
2/Lt. W. S. EBDEN.	8/K. Shropshire L.I. att. from 11/Gloucesters	16/5/17	28/11/18
Lieut. A. B. RIDDLE.	2/5th Durham L.I.	7/6/17	28/11/18
Capt. H. S. STEWART.	1/Lothian & Border Horse	19/9/17	24/12/18
2/Lt. P. STEWART.	9/South Lancs. Regt.	15/10/18	29/11/18
Lieut. J. N. HERAPATH.	10/Devonshire Regt.	26/1/18	–/11/18
2/Lt. A. J. JONES.	2/Cheshire Regt. att. from Royal Berks.	14/4/18	29/12/18

BALKANS—continued.

Name.	Regiment.	Missing.	Repatriated.
Lieut. J. A. READ.	4/Rifle Brigade	15/4/18	29/11/18
Capt. J. E. STONES.	8/Royal Scots. Fus. att. from 11/Middlesex	19/9/18	25/12/18
Lieut. F. H. MITCHELL.	R.N.V.R.	2/12/16	(Died)
Lieut. R. G. BLAKESLEY.	R.N.V.R.		22/10/18

WEST AFRICA.

Name.	Regiment.	Missing.	Repatriated.
Capt. A. L. DE C. STRETTON.	South Lancs. att. W.A.F.F.	6/9/14	8/1/16
Capt. M. J. PARKER.	South Staffs. att. W.A.F.F.	6/9/14	8/1/16
Lieut. O. G. BODY.	R.A. att. W.A.F.F.	6/9/14	8/1/16
Lieut. R. R. TAYLOR.	K.O.S.B. att. W.A.F.F.	6/9/14	8/1/16

EAST AFRICA.

Name.	Regiment.	Missing.	Repatriated.
Lieut. G. S. FRAME.	R.A.F.	-/-/17	10/10/17
2/Lt. C. F. STRANGHAM.	R.A.F.	-/-/17	18/11/17
Lieut. G. G. R. WILLIAMS.	2/Loyal North Lancs. Regt.	-/-/15	18/11/17
Capt. H. STOKES.	R.A.M.C.	-/-/17	-/-/17
Lieut. J. R. McGREGOR.	R.A.M.C.	3/7/18	27/8/18
Capt. G. PERKINS.	R.A.M.C.	22/7/18	9/9/18
Lieut. C. MURRAY.	R.A.M.C.	24/8/18	-/10/18
Lieut. G. HOARE.	A.S.C.	-/12/16	(Released)
Capt. H. G. SEALY.	130/Baluchis I.A.	-/16	18/11/17
Major J. H. G. BULLER.	57/Wilde's Rifles, I.A.	10/8/16	
Lieut. D. POWELL.	30/Punjabis, I.A.	3/8/17	1/10/17
Lieut. G. W. PALIN.	129/Baluchis, I.A.	5/8/17	18/11/17
Lieut. T. WILSON.	South African Engineers	-/12/16	(Released)
Capt. H. WALLIS.	8/South African Inf.	19/7/17	18/11/17
Lieut. H. E. W. BARRETT.	1/South African Horse	10/3/16	18/11/17
Lieut. A. H. G. BARR.	9/South African Horse	1/1/17	18/11/17
Lieut. S. G. INGLESBY.	9/South African Horse	1/1/17	18/11/17
Lieut. S. G. CHAMPION.	2/King's African Rifles	-/2/17	(Died)
Lieut. C. V. GRAY.	2/King's African Rifles	25/4/17	18/11/18
Lieut. F. H. BLACKIE.	1/King's African Rifles.	16/5/17	
Lieut. P. NOTTIDGE.	3/King's African Rifles	19/7/17	18/11/17
Capt. V. H. SMITH.	1/King's African Rifles	11/4/18	21/5/18
Lt.-Col. H. C. DICKINSON.	3/King's African Rifles	22/7/18	-/11/18
Capt. J. E. G. RANSOME.	3/King's African Rifles	22/7/18	-/11/18
Lieut. S. H. JARDINE.	3/King's African Rifles	22/7/18	-/11/18
Lieut. H. M. SHAW.	3/King's African Rifles	22/7/18	-/11/18
Lieut. W. JOHNSON.	4/King's African Rifles	22/7/18	3/11/18
Capt. F. H. BUSTARD.	3/King's African Rifles	23/7/18	-/9/18
Lieut. C. H. McELROY.	3/King's African Rifles	23/7/18	-/11/18
Lieut. J. M. BRINK.	3/King's African Rifles	23/7/18	18/10/18
Lieut. H. N. TITTERTON.	3/King's African Rifles	23/7/18	-/11/18
Major P. GARRARD.	4/King's African Rifles (Died 18/9/18)	24/8/18	
Lieut. K. E. ISAACS.	Gold Coast Regt.	12/10/16	18/11/17
Lieut. E. STRINGER.	Nyasaland Field Force	-/12/16	(Released)
Major R. D. GARDNER.	3/Nigerian Regt.	29/1/17	18/11/17
Lieut. M. D. E. JEFFREYS.	3/Nigerian Regt.	29/1/17	18/11/17
Lieut. E. B. B. SHAW.	4/Nigerian Carrier Corps	16/10/17	18/11/17
Agent G. PERKS.	Intelligence Dept.	-/16	15/11/17
Agent R. S. HALL.	Intelligence Dept.	-/16	18/11/17

INDEX.

Name	Page
Abbott, E. D., Sub-Lt.	156
—— T. W., 2/Lt.	181
—— W. J. G., 2/Lt.	62
—— W. N., 2/Lt.	48
—— W. S., Lieut.	36
Abel, J. E., 2/Lt.	83
Abell, A. R., 2/Lt.	36
Abercrombie, H. N., 2/Lt.	115
—— A. W., Lt.-Col.	111
Abey, H. R., 2/Lt.	175
—— H. W., 2/Lt.	14
Abrahall, A. S., Lieut.	62
Abraham, Michael, Lieut.	10
Acheson, J. E., Lieut.	33
—— G. J., Lieut.	42
Ackerley, J. R., Capt.	65
Ackroyd, C. H., Capt.	85
—— Reginald, Lieut.	125
Ackers, C. H. S., 2/Lt.	159
Acocks, A. W., 2/Lt.	46
Adair, J. Sinclair, 2/Lt.	109
Adam, W. A., Capt.	71
Adams, A., F., 2/Lt.	120
—— A. T., Lieut.	151
—— C., 2/Lt.	114
—— C. Boys, Capt.	70
—— C. J., Lieut.	130
—— F., 2/Lt.	147
—— F. B., Lieut.	91
—— F. B., 2/Lt.	146
—— Godfrey, Capt.	98
—— J., 2/Lt.	97
—— N. F., Lieut.	171
—— P., 2/Lt.	128
—— P. E., Lieut.	40
—— R. G. H., Lieut.	161
—— R. H., 2/Lt.	29
—— V. H., 2/Lt.	152
Adamson, C. P., 2/Lt.	155
—— H. A., 2/Lt.	104
—— J., 2/Lt.	52
—— T. S., Capt.	109
Addington, E. G., Lieut.	41
Addison, Julian, Capt.	142
—— W., 2/Lt.	106
—— Wm., 2/Lt.	122
Adeney, R. E., 2/Lt.	151
Agerskow, O. Randall, 2/Lt.	50
Agnew, A. B., Lieut.	176
—— I. C. F., 2/Lt.	138
Ahnall, K., 2/Lt.	137
Ahern, M., 2/Lt.	114
Ainger, Frank S., Capt.	66
Ainscough, J. P., Lieut.	119
Ainscow, H. M., 2/Lt.	50
Ainsley, C., Capt.	37
Ainsworth, R. W., Capt.	79
Aird, Hugh, Fl. Lt.	188
Airth, E. C., 2/Lt.	81
Aitchison, J., 2/Lt.	102
—— S. W., Lieut.	59
Aitken, Frank Douglas, 2/Lt.	88
—— J. D., 2/Lt.	86
—— J. S., 2/Lt.	20
Aked, H. L. C., 2/Lt.	147
Akester, Gordon, 2/Lt.	44
—— J. C., Fl.Sub-Lt.	177
Albert, C. H., 2/Lt.	63
Albertson, Lieut.	167
Albrecht, Henry J. C. 2/Lt.	117
Alcock, J. H., 2/Lt.	36
—— J. W., Fl. Lt.	181
Alder, S., 2/Lt.	150
Alderson, A. G. w., 2/Lt	159
Aldred, A. G., Lieut.	95
Alexander, A. H., 2/Lt.	32
—— E., Lieut.	147
—— G., 2/Lt.	188
—— G. M., Capt.	139
—— J., 2/Lt.	24
—— K. E., 2/Lt.	100
—— P. S., Capt.	9
—— R. C., Major	185
—— R. D., Capt.	143
—— W. T., 2/Lt	102
Allabarton, S. T., 2/Lt.	153
Alison, J. S., 2/Lt.	18
Allan, A. M., 2/Lt.	173
—— C. Maitland, 2/Lt.	175
—— D. G., Lieut.	139
—— P. J., 2/Lt.	23
Allardyce, G. L., Lieut.	106
Allason, H. W., Lieut.	66
Allbon-Bennett, K. R. A., 2/Lt.	32
Allen, C., 2/Lt.	90
—— E. N., 2/Lt.	83
—— F. E., 2/Lt.	131
—— H. F., 2/Lt.	44
—— John, 2/Lt.	50
—— J. H., 2/Lt.	137
—— J. M., 2/Lt.	159
—— L. T. M., 2/Lt.	22
—— L. W., 2/Lt.	78
—— R., Capt.	25
—— T., 2/Lt.	78
—— W. G., 2/Lt.	35
—— Wm. R., Capt.	24
Alleyne, W. H. Capt.	21
Allinson, F., Lieut.	150
Allis, W. Henry	49
Allison, C. J., 2/Lt	33
Allistone, A. B. W. Lieut.	88
Allsop, H., 2/Lt.	15
—— T. H. K., Lieut.	129
Allsupp, F., 2/Lt.	180
Allworth, C. R. H., Capt.	84
Almond, H. B., Lieut.	53
Alston, R. W., 2/Lt.	35
Ambler, E., Capt.	40
—— J. J., Lieut.	170
Ambrose-Smith, J., Major	53
Amcoats, W., Capt, the Rev.	135
Ames, N. L., 2/Lt.	128
Amey, A. H., 2/Lt.	130
Amis, H. G., Capt.	49
Amm, E. O., Lieut.	176
Amory, W., 2/Lt.	175
Amps, J. P., Lieut.	76
Andeesn, W. B. K., Lieut.	186
Anderson, A., Lieut.	149
—— Alex., 2/Lt.	59
—— A. E. B., Capt.	47
—— A. J., Major	184
—— A. P., 2/Lt.	26
—— D. S., 2/Lt.	162
—— G. A., 2/Lt.	74
—— G. F., Lieut.	171
—— G. H. G., Capt.	115
Anderson, G. V. W., Lieut.	134
—— H. S., Lieut.	11
—— J., Lieut.	119
—— James, Capt.	132
—— J. D., Lieut.	167
—— J. G., 2/Lt.	51
—— J. H., Lieut.	105
—— J. J., Lieut.	118
—— J. L. H., 2/Lt.	163
—— J. S., 2/Lt.	117
—— K. H. J., Capt.	129
—— L., Capt.	186
—— L. A. P., Capt.	184
Anderson, Robert	39
—— R. B., 2/Lt.	74
—— R. K., 2/Lt.	142
—— W., Lieut.	150
Andersson, C. L., Lt.-Col	98
Anderton, N. H., 2/Lt.	52
Andrew, A. R., 2/Lt.	124
—— Frank, 2/Lt.	95
—— G. S. B., 2/Lt.	31
—— R., 2/Lt.	20
—— W. Leslie, Lieut.	162
—— W. M., 2/Lt.	103
Andrews, A. A., Capt.	39
—— A. V., Lieut.	135
—— F. C., 2/Lt.	156
—— F. E., 2/Lt., A/Capt.	77
—— Geoffrey, Fl. Sub.-Lt.	177
—— G. M., Capt.	139
—— J. S., Lieut.	169
Angus, K. R., 2/Lt.	166
Annandale, J. R., 2/Lt.	10
Annesley, A. S. R., Col.	185
Anns. K., Capt., Adj., M.C.	65
Ansell, A. C., Lieut.	45
Anslow, F. F., 2/Lt.	171
Ansted, D. A., Lieut.	93
Anstee, G. A., Capt.	45
Anstey, F. C. R., Lieut.	139
Anthony, H. C., Lieut.	136
Antill, H. B., Lieut.	83
Apperley, Charles M., 2/Lt.	122
Appleby, A. W., 2/Lt.	49
—— W., Lieut.	186
Appleford, H. N., Lieut.	51
Applegarth, Thomas W., 2/Lt.	102
Appleton, Richard, 2/Lt.	85
Apps, E. W., 2/Lt.	94
Aquino, F., Med. Officer	184
Arblaster, C., Capt.	136
Arbuthnott, R. K., Capt., M.C.	73
Archer, Ben., 2/Lt.	41
—— F. J., 2/Lt.	79
Archibald, A. D., 2/Lt.	58
—— L. N., 2/Lt.	157
Ardagh, P. M. J., 2/Lt.	113
Ardill, J. R., 2/Lt.	69
Arkless, Frank, Lieut.	101
Armbrister, E. A., Lieut.	101
Armitage, E. L., Lieut.	10
—— J. A., 2/Lt.	85
—— S. E., Lieut.	178
Armstrong, A., Capt.	59
—— C. D., Lieut.	120
Armstrong, C. J., Lieut.	60
—— F. N. C., Lieut.	183
—— G. W., 2/Lt.	157
—— J., 2/Lt.	110
—— J. H. B., Lieut.	137
—— R. H., 2/Lt.	172
Arnold, A. E., Capt., M.C.	124
—— C. B., Lieut.	125
—— G. B., 2/Lt.	76
—— J., 2/Lt.	164
—— S., 2/Lt.	115
Arnott, J. F., Capt., M.C.	93
—— R., 2/Lt.	165
—— T. H., 2/Lt.	68
—— W. A., Capt.	132
Arthur, D., Capt.	184
—— T. J., Lieut.	168
Arthurton, F. W., Lieut.	118
Arthy, E. B. F., 2/Lt.	101
Ashburner, J. C., 2/Lt.	119
Ascough, M. T., Capt.	132
Ashby, J., 2/Lt.	18
Ashcroft, E. S., Lieut.	34
—— K., 2/Lt.	124
Asher, W. J., Capt.	79
—— W. M., Lieut.	105
Ashforth, H. W., 2/Lt.	124
Ashley, T. W.	130
Ashton, H. C. S., Capt.	0
—— K. H., 2/Lt.	166
Ashworth, L., 2/Lt.	42
Askin, A. T. C., 2/Lt.	179
—— S. C. J., Lieut.	168
Asquith, B. I., 2/Lt.	46
Astbury, B. E., 2/Lt.	26
Aston, R., Lieut.	29
Atkin, H. D., Lieut.	95
—— K., Lieut.	131
Atkins, C. A., 2/Lt.	168
—— B. S., Capt.	178
—— G. C., 2/Lt.	154
—— R. F., Capt.	183
—— W. J. T., 2/Lt.	164
Atkinson, Alan, 2/Lt.	17
—— F., Lieut.	163
—— J., Capt. (? 2/Lt.)	102
—— J. M., 2/Lt.	49
—— J. M., 2/Lt.	157
—— T. C., 2/Lt.	65
—— T. L., 2/Lt.	158
Attenborough, E. G., Lieut.	14
Atter, W. G., 2/Lt.	119
Atterton, F., 2/Lt.	115
Attwell, R. H., 2/Lt.	29
Attwood, N. J., Sub.-Lt.	162
Auchinleck, W. J. A. H., Lieut.	60
Audas, Francis, Lieut.	102
Auld, R. T. K., Capt.	24
—— P. H., Capt.	137
Austen, V. G., Fl.Sub-Lt.	177
Austin, A. G., 2/Lt.	94
—— R. A., Capt.	181
—— H., Lieut.	165
—— W. M., Capt.	94
—— W. S., 2/Lt.	66
Auty, D. R., 2/Lt.	52
Avey, G. A., Capt.	141
Awde, I. W., Lieut.	173
Axe, F., 2/Lt.	41

Ayer, B., Lieut.	183
Ayers, Austin, 2/Lt.	124
Aylen, E. V., Major	186
Aylett, E. R. C., Capt., M.C.	81
Ayre, F., Capt.	29
Ayrton, F. A., Capt.	171
Babb, R., Lieut.	140
Baber, W. H., 2/Lt.	66
Back, W. L., Lieut.	139
Backhouse, E. H. W., Lieut.	37
Bacon, L. G., 2/Lt.	152
Badcock, H. V., Lieut.	69
Baddely, E. L., 2/Lt.	171
Baerlein, A. A., 2/Lt.	152
Baggs, H., 2/Lt.	95
———— H. E., 2/Lt.	119
Bagley, C. G., 2/Lt.	29
Bagshaw, A. N., 2/Lt.	45
Baguley, W. A., 2/Lt.	46
Bailey, C. J., 2/Lt.	48
———— F. J., Lieut.	176
———— G. S., 2/Lt.	96
———— H. R. B., Lieut.	49
———— J., 2/Lt.	48
———— K. V., Capt.	95
———— P. J., Major, D.S.O.	9
———— V. T., Brig.-Gen.	7
———— W., 2/Lt.	117
Baillie-Hamilton, Major A/Col.	95
Baillon, E. M., Lieut.	180
Baines, E. F., Lt.-Col.	186
Baird, A. B., 2/Lt.	141
———— J. A., Capt.	55
———— R., Lt.	186
Baird-Smith, A. G., Lieut.-Col.	54
Bairstow, T., 2/Lt.	41
Bakel, W., 2/Lt.	115
Baker, A. A., Lieut.	129
———— A. C., Lieut.	62
———— A. E., 2/Lt.	125
———— A. H., Lieut.	45
———— C. D., 2/Lt.	94
———— C. G., 2/Lt.	91
———— F. G., 2/Lt.	158
———— G. B., Capt.	188
———— H., 2/Lt.	53
———— H., 2/Lt.	117
———— L. J., Capt.	37
———— R. P., Lieut.	150
———— W. G., Lieut.	59
Balbi, B. M., 2/Lt.	122
Balden, C. A., Lieut.	25
Baldwin, P. M. G., Lieut.	180
———— R. H., Lt.-Col.	65
Balfour, O., Lieut.	16
———— H. E., Lieut.	139
Ball, A. C., 2/Lt.	130
———— A. C., 2/Lt.	159
———— F. L., Capt.	43
———— F. S., Capt.	21
———— John, 2/Lt.	53
———— J. B., Capt.	133
———— S. G., 2/Lt.	118
———— S. W., 2/Lt.	11
———— T. L., Major	185
Ballance, G., Lieut.	165
Ballin, J., Lieut.	182
Bamber, Walter, Lieut.	187
Bambrough, P. B., 2/Lt.	130
Bampton, R., Lt.	184
Bandey, G. H., 2/Lt.	123
Banks, D. J., Capt.	75
———— R. H., Capt., M.C.	87
Bankes, H. V. N., Lieut.	162
Bann, E. H., 2/Lt.	56
Bannard, A. W., Lieut.	140
Bantock, E. G., 2/Lt.	42
Barber, C. H., Major	186
———— N. E., Major	90
———— S. C., 2/Lt.	188
Barchard, D. M., Lieut.	56
Barclay, James, Lieut.	144
———— W. E., Lieut.	119
Bardgett, W. E., Lieut.	174
Bardsley, R. J., Lieut.	14
Barham, H. C., 2/Lt.	78
Barker, C. A., 2/Lt.	48
———— H., 2/Lt.	114
———— H. E., 2/Lt.	77
———— J., Lieut.	121
———— J. S., Major	185
———— R. A., 2/Lt.	122
———— W., 2/Lt.	83
———— W. G. S., Lieut.	111
Barlow, A. E., 2/Lt.	34
———— A. J., Lieut.	180
———— A. N., 2/Lt.	155
———— C. N., Capt.	92
———— John, 2/Lt.	52
———— N. W., Major	69
Barnaby, H., 2/Lt.	116
Barnard, A. S. C., Lieut.	99
Barnardiston, S., Major	37
Barnes, A. F., Lieut.	61
———— A. W., 2/Lt.	28
———— C. H. R., Lieut.	93
———— D. T., Capt.	75
———— J. D., Lieut.	159
———— R. G., Lieut.	140
Barnet, H. F. W., 2/Lt.	81
Barnett, H. M., 2/Lt.	90
———— C. E., Capt.	65
———— V. G., Capt.	56
Barni, N. H. L., Lieut.	121
Barr, A. H. G., Lieut.	189
———— R. J., 2/Lt.	64
Barrard, James, Major	184
Barrell, K. C., Lt.	16
Barrett, C. F. M., 2/Lt.	55
———— F. R. C., Lieut.	79
———— H. E. W. C., Lt.	189
———— W. S., Lieut.	48
———— W. L., 2/Lt.	36
Barrie, Frank, 2/Lt.	153
Barritt, G. L., Lieut.	169
Barrow, A. J., Capt.	52
———— E. E., Capt.	66
Barrowcliff, F., 2/Lt.	49
Barry, D. D., Lieut.	103
———— W. M., Capt.	55
Barter, T. A., Capt.	80
———— W. H., Capt.	34
Bartlett, A. F., Lieut.	163
———— C. H., 2/Lt.	157
———— G. R., Lieut.	172
Barton, A. E. S., Lieut.	155
———— A. W., Lieut.	112
———— B. J., Capt.	127
———— Basil K., Capt.	21
———— E. de L., Capt.	21
———— W., 2/Lt.	187
Barugh, W. G., 2/Lt.	119
Barwick, H. A., Lieut.	139
Bastard, R., Lt.-Col.	35
Bastow, S. F., 2/Lt.	44
Batchelor, P. H., 2/Lt.	96
Bate, C. I., Lieut.	141
———— W. T. McGuire, Capt.	143
Bateman, K. S. B., 2/Lt.	71
———— W., Lieut.	85
Bates, A. D., Lieut.	130
Batey, J. L., Lieut.	182
Bath, E. O., Lieut.	139
Batten, E. V., 2/Lt.	21
Batten-Pooll, A. H., Capt., V.C., M.C.	113
Battersby-Harford, J. V., Lieut.	40
Battey, B. M., 2/Lt.	166
Batting, W. J., 2/Lt.	122
Battle, T. H. N., Lieut.	15
Batty, E. A. F., 2/Lt.	7
Batty-Smith, S. H., Lieut.	79
Baxter, N. E., Capt.	69
———— R., 2/Lt.	71
Bayles, J. H. G., Capt.	50
Bayley, E. L. J., Capt.	185
Bayliff, G. T. L., 2/Lt.	125
Baylis, H. G., 2/Lt.	89
———— H. J., 2/Lt.	37
Bayliss, J. E., Lieut.	88
———— W. Murray F., Lieut.	165
Bayly, A. R., Major	10
Baynton, G. R., Lieut.	156
Beach, B. A., Capt.	85
Beale, W. J., 2/Lt.	125
Bealey, F. A. H., Capt.	51
Beaman, W., Capt.	131
Bean, C. A. S., Lieut.	155
Beard, C. A., Lieut.	55
Beardsmore, H., Sub-Lt.	144
Beare, S. G., Fl.-Sub-Lt.	188
Bearn, J. A., —	93
Beattie, A. J., Sub.-Lt.	176
———— E. H., Rev.	135
———— H. W., 2/Lt.	84
———— R., 2/Lt.	115
———— R., Lt.	137
Beauchamp, F. E., 2/Lt.	87
———— F. E., Lieut.	167
Beaumont, F., Lieut.	161
———— H. B., Lieut.	123
———— J. W., Capt.	99
———— W. S., 2/Lt.	16
Beavan, W. F., Lieut.	22
Beazley, E. B., Capt.	34
Beazeley, G. A., Major	181
Beck, T., Lieut.	173
Beckett, J. S., 2/Lt.	79
Beddow, W. E., 2/Lt.	56
Bedell-Sivwright, T., Capt.	48
Bedford, A. E., 2/Lt.	49
———— F. H., Lieut.	25
Bee, J. R., Lieut.	40
———— Percy, Capt.	80
Beedham, N. H., Capt.	77
Bees, F. H., 2/Lt.	57
Beesley, R., 2/Lt.	170
Begbie, S. C. H., Lieut.	161
Begg, M. G., Lieut.	180
———— R. A., Lieut.	105
Beighton, J. D. K., 2/Lt.	91
Belcher, S., 2/Lt.	53
Beldam, C. H., Lieut.	154
Beldon, Eric, Lieut.	41
Bell, A. J., Lieut.	91
———— A. T., 2/Lt.	109
———— D. F., Lieut.	142
———— D. J., Capt.	163
———— E. A. V., 2/Lt.	151
———— E. G., 2/Lt.	118
———— F., Capt.	106
———— G., 2/Lt.	52
———— J., 2/Lt.	33
———— J. A. D., Major	131
———— J. K., Lieut.	139
———— R. P. M., Capt.	58
———— T. C., 2/Lt.	74
———— W., Lieut.	178
———— W. L., 2/Lt.	142
Bell-Syer, L., 2/Lt.	184
Bellerby, H. R. B., 2/Lt.	26
Bellew, E. D., Lieut.	139
Bellingham, E. H. C. P., Brig.-Gen.	7
Bellis, A. W., 2/Lt.	80
Belliveau, A. H., Lieut.	169
Bellville, G. E., Capt.	9
Belshaw, S. A., 2/Lt.	67
Benedictus, J. H., 2/Lt.	15
Benjamin, A. L., Lieut.	166
Bennett, C. A., 2/Lt.	116
———— C. D., 2/Lt.	150
———— E., Major	186
———— F. C. H., Capt.	134
———— F. W., 2/Lt.	38
———— G. T., Lieut.	188
———— H. J., Major	75
———— H. J., Lieut.	172
———— J., Lieut.	67
———— J. B., 2/Lt.	12
———— J. M., 2/Lt.	82
———— L., Capt.	101
———— L. J., Sub-Lt.	177
———— N. O., 2/Lt.	125
———— R., 2/Lt.	129
———— R. C., Lieut.	173
———— T. H., Sub-Lt.	144
Benny, W. W., Lieut.	140
Bensley, E. F., Fl.-Lt.	163
Benson, F. C., 2/Lt.	120
———— John, Capt.	111
———— F. C. G., 2/Lt.	95
———— H., 2/Lt.	126
Bentley, A. C., Lieut.	48
———— Ernest, 2/Lt.	98
———— F., 2/Lt.	120
———— J. A., 2/Lt.	96
———— J. H., 2/Lt.	84
———— N. E., 2/Lt.	67
Beresford, C. V., Capt.	62
———— M. de la P., 2/Lt.	13
———— W. A., 2/Lt.	98
Berger-Wheeler, F. E. Allister, Capt.	62
Bernard, A. B., Capt.	92
———— C. E. B., 2/Lt.	41
———— V. D., Lieut.	136
Berne, H. C., Lieut.	112
Berney-Ficklin, H. P. M., Capt.	7
Berrill, F. C., Lieut.	37
Berry, A. E., 2/Lt.	82
———— F., Lieut.	71
———— F. H., Lieut.	156
———— H. J., Lieut.	175
———— J. H., Capt.	108
———— R. B., Lieut.	62
———— T. W., Lieut.	74
Bertioli, W. S., 2/Lt.	87

Name	Page	Name	Page	Name	Page	Name	Page
Besant, P. E., Capt.	28	Black, J. R., Capt.	105	Bolton, R. H., Lieut.	54	Box, T., 2/Lt.	32
Besley, E. M., Capt.	16	——— K. E., Lieut.	43	——— W. E., 2/Lt.	12	Boyall, A. M., Lt.-Col.	40
Bester, P. M., 2/Lt.	89	——— S. McBrayne, Lieut.	166	——— W. O., 2/Lt.	50	Boyce, H. B. P., Lieut.	160
Beswick, J. C., 2/Lt.	24	——— W., 2/Lt.	149	Bond, F. E., Lieut.	174	——— W. R., Lieut.	182
Bethell, F., 2/Lt.	122	Blackall, J. H., 2/Lt.	153	——— R. C., Lt.-Col.	85	——— H. F., Lieut.	39
Betts, E. L., Lieut.	93	Blackburn, R. R., 2]Lt.	144	——— U. A., 2/Lt.	58	Boycott, R. G., Lieut.	71
——— T. W., 2/Lt.	76	——— T., Capt.	58	——— W. H., 2/Lt.	131	Boyd, C. N., 2/Lt.	175
Beuttler, J. C. O., Lieut.	135	Blacker, R., 2/Lt.	40	Bone, Ernest H., 2/Lt.	46	——— C. T., 2/Lt.	104
Bevan, F. H.,	7	Blackett, G. E., Capt.	101	Bonshor, John, 2/Lt.	71	——— J., Lieut.	159
——— J. A., Lieut.	23	Blackledge, R. D., Capt., M.C.	104	——— J. H., 2/Lt.	46	——— R., Capt.	114
Beveridge, H., Capt.	71	Blackie, F. H., Lieut.	189	Boon, H. F., 2/Lt.	127	——— W., 2/Lt.	27
——— J., 2/Lt.	104	Blacklock, H. A., 2/Lt.	66	Boosey, L. A., Major	130	Boyes, W., Lieut.	185
Beverland, C. F., Lieut.	60	Blackwell, K. R., 2/Lt.	13	Boot, W. A., 2/Lt.	50	Boyle, A., Lieut.	134
Beverley, R., Capt., M.C.	7	Blackwood, T., Capt.	134	Boote, R. S. L., 2/Lt.	154	——— E. P. O., Lieut.	53
Bevington, R. J., Lieut.	151	——— T. A., Lieut.	109	Booth, F., Major	185	——— J. C., 2/Lt.	170
Bewley, E. R., Lieut.	116	Blain, C. W., 2/Lt.	148	——— H. H., Fl. Sub.-Lt.	177	——— J. K., Lieut., M.C.	108
Beyfus, G. H., 2/Lt.	67	Blair, James, 2/Lt.	112	——— P. J., Capt.	59	——— R. M., Capt.	60
Bibby, J. D., Capt.	9	——— J. W., 2/Lt.	105	——— W. R., Lieut.	13	Boys, Randolph, 2/Lt.	169
Bickerstaffe, T. S., Lieut.	123	Blake, A. G. S., 2/Lt.	166	Boothman, C., Lieut.	164	Brabazon, J. H. T., Lieut.	181
Biddington, H. V., 2/Lt.	159	——— C. H., 2/Lt.	93	Boothroyd, E., 2/Lt.	77	Brace, R. B., 2/Lt.	78
Biddolph, N., Capt.	20	——— F., Sub.-Lt.	144	Boraston, C. A., Lieut.	17	Bracken, K. O., 2/Lt.	175
——— T. J., Major	51	——— H. P., 2/Lt.	160	Borrett, G. K. F., Lieut.	135	Bradbury, A., 2/Lt.	34
Biden, S. W., 2/Lt.	183	——— J. W., 2/Lt.	180	Borrodale, R. F. B., 2/Lt.	131	Braddell, W., Capt.	114
Biggs, Henry, Lieut.	37	——— N. G., 2/Lt.	22	Borrow, C. E., 2/Lt.	81	Braddy, A. R., 2/Lt.	35
——— H. St. J., Lt.	139	——— O. P. T. N., Lieut.	56	Borthwick, W., Capt., Hon.	90	Bradford, W. W., Lieut.	168
Bigland, E. W., Capt.	56	Blakesley, R. G., Lieut.	189	Boscawen, G.; Maj. The Hon.	13	Bradley, Arthur, 2/Lt.	55
Bignell, Capt.	183	Blamires, Charles, 2/Lt.	35	Bose, S., Major	182	——— C. E., Brig.-Gen.	7
Biheller, W., Capt.	159	Blanch, J. A., 2/Lt.	38	Bosher, H., Lieut.	166	——— F., 2/Lt.	95
Bindon, L. W., Lieut.	127	Blanchard, F. W., Capt.	28	Bostock, A., Lieut.	14	——— James, 2/Lt.	96
Biner, B. C., 2/Lt.	44	——— N. G., Lieut.	136	——— A. S., 2/Lt.	100	——— W. D., Lieut.	110
Bing, W. L., 2/Lt.	167	Bland, C. F. R., Lieut.	83	——— E. L., 2/Lt.	124	Bradshaw. H. J., 2/Lt.	179
Bingham, A. E., Lieut.	165	Blandford, T. C., Lieut.	81	Boston, C. A. N., 2/Lt.	82	Bradwell, E., 2/Lt.	96
——— Hon. R., Lieut.	56	Blandy, G., Sub.-Lt.	188	——— J., 2/Lt.	81	Brady, D. W., 2/Lt.	68
Binney, F. B., Capt.	146	Blatch, H. E., 2/Lt.	66	Bosustow, G. W., Lieut.	101	——— B. J., Fl.-Lt.	188
Binnie, Alan, Capt.	152	Blaxill, F. H., 2/Lt.	163	Boswell, K. C., 2/Lt.	15	Brailsford, J., 2/Lt.	13
Binnington, E., 2/Lt.	137	Blayney, B. W., 2/Lt.	150	Bott, A. J., Capt.	179	Brain, E. R., Lieut.	26
Binns, John	50	Bleckly, A. K., Lieut.	93	Bottomley, J. W., 2/Lt.	52	Braithwaite, B. F., 2/Lt.	157
——— W. A. F., 2/Lt.	95	Blenkiron, D., 2/Lt.	97	Botton, O. V., 2/Lt.	21	Brakell, J. F., 2/Lt.	9
Birch, D. C., 2/Lt.	151	Blight, B. W., 2/Lt.	37	Boughton, C. B., 2/Lt.	151	Branch, H. G. S., Capt.	42
——— H., 2/Lt.	181	——— T. F., Lieut.	165	Boulton, F. E., 2/Lt.	162	Brander, G. L., Lieut.	19
——— J. G., Lt.-Col.	90	Blofield, R. A., 2/Lt.	179	Boumphrey, J. W., Lieut.	156	Brandon, G., Lieut.	16
——— S., Lieut.	162	Bloomfield, C. W., 2/Lt.	70	Bourchier, C., 2/Lt.	113	Brandrick, Arthur, 2/Lt.	174
Birchenough, J. A., 2/Lt.	96	——— V. E., 2/Lt.	76	Bourdillon, T. E., 2/Lt.	81	Branfoot, G., Capt.	25
Birchwood, H., 2/Lt.	122	——— W. S. R., Capt.	150	Bourinot, A. S., Lieut.	153	Branson, D., Lieut.	178
Bird, A. F., Lieut.	155	Bloore, W., 2/Lt.	116	Bousfield, Hugh D., Lt.-Col.	41	Brantford, Fl. Sub.-Lt.	150
——— B. A., Lieut.	163	Blount, G. A., 2/Lt.	80	——— J. K., Lieut.	151	Brattle, C. C., 2/Lt.	22
——— C. B., Lieut.	150	Blower, M. S., Lieut.	65	Bowater, A. V., Capt.	173	Breach, G. A., 2/Lt.	78
——— C. R., 2/Lt.	88	Blundell, E. P., 2/Lt.	115	Bowen, E. E. W., 2/Lt.	65	Breckenridge, W., 2/Lt.	163
——— E., Capt.	86	——— H. A., 2/Lt.	12	——— J. L., Lieut.	53	Bredin, W. E., 2/Lt.	47
——— H. D., 2/Lt.	31	Blunn, A. G., Lieut.	127	——— L. A. G., Capt., M.C.	38	Breedon, F. J., Capt., M.C.	29
——— R., Rev.	135	Blunt, P. K., Capt.	46	——— R. L., Major	90	Breen, T.	7
——— R. G., 2/Lt.	68	Blythe, H., 2/Lt.	150	——— T. O., 2/Lt.	52	Bremner, T., 2/Lt.	111
——— T. H., Lieut.	60	Blythe Lamble, A. E., Lieut.	145	Bower, L. C., Lieut.	166	——— T. P., Lieut.	31
——— W. H. F., Lieut.	11	Boardman, A. J., 2/Lt.	43	Bowers, P. T., Lieut.	152	Brent, James, Lieut.	158
Birkhead, J. B., Lieut.	162	——— J. H., Major	116	——— V. R., Lieut.	32	Breton. B. W. F., 2/Lt.	15
Birkinshaw, J. H., 2/Lt.	42	Boase, L. C., Lt.	137	Bowker, S., 2/Lt.	119	Brett, G., Capt.	130
Birkumshaw, S. E., 2/Lt.	32	Bockett-Pugh, H. C. E., Lieut.	163	——— T., 2/Lt.	117	——— H. A., Capt.	178
Birks, N. A., Lieut.	151	Bodley, W. G. L., 2/Lt.	174	Bowles, F. H., Capt.	61	Brettell, F. A., Lieut.	29
Birley, R. A., Major	10	Body, G. C., Lieut.	165	——— F. S., Lieut.	175	Brewer, B. D. M., Lieut.	11
——— T. E. H., 2/Lt.	160	——— G. T., Capt.	79	——— G. P., Fl. Sub.-Lt.	150	Brewster, J. A., Lieut.	30
Birt, W. B., Capt.	65	——— O. G., Lieut.	189	Bowman, A. A., Lieut.	103	Brickmann, F. I., Capt.	184
Bishop, B., 2/Lt.	65	Bodycombe, J., 2/Lt.	73	——— A. W. M., Lieut.	136	Bridge, C. H. A., 2/Lt.	169
——— E. W., Capt.	57	Boe, D., 2/Lt.	165	——— W. L., 2/Lt.	27	——— Gordon, 2/Lt.	125
——— F. H., Lieut.	97	Boger, D. C., Lt.-Col.	54	Bowring, F. A., Capt.	65	——— H. E., Lieut.	140
——— G. W. R., Capt.	187	——— R. A., Capt.	146	——— J. V., 2/Lt.	148	Bridger, H., 2/Lt.	174
——— H. C. W., 2/Lt.	183	Bodycombe, J., 2/Lt.	73	Bowskill, J., 2/Lt.	84	Bridges, F. J., Lieut, M.C.	118
——— H. W., Sub.-Lt.	145	Boldison, A., 2/Lt.	151	Bowyer, F. H., 2/Lt.	149	Bridgford, S. L., Capt.	95
——— J. F., 2/Lt.	78	Bolger, B., 2/Lt.	125			Brie, R. A. C., Lieut.	168
Bisset, A. G., Capt.	133	Bollam, A. D., Capt.	11			Brien, H. S. A., 2/Lt.	80
Bittleston, N. A., Lieut.	37	Bollins, A. P., Lieut.	162			Brierley, R., Lt.	182
Binsted, H. M., 2/Lt.	65	Bolton, A. C., Capt.	149			Brigham, W., 2/Lt.	26
Black, A. C., 2/Lt.	121	——— R. G. I., Lt.-Col.	18			Briggs, L. P., Lieut.	148
——— A. W. H., 2/Lt.	119						
——— J. B., Lieut.	103						

	PAGE		PAGE		PAGE		PAGE
Briggs, S. P., 2/Lt.	148	Brown, I. L., Lieut.	167	Burdett, Basil, Lieut.	122	Bye, H. T., 2/Lt.	88
Bright, A. S., Capt.	78	——— K. E., Capt.	75	——— E. W., Capt.	182	Byng Hall, P., Major, D.S.O.	139
——— F. A., 2/Lt.	129	——— N., 2/Lt.	100	Burdon, Rowland, Capt.	101		
——— F. C., Lieut.	62	——— R. P. M., 2/Lt.	15	Burges-Short, H. G. R., Lt.-Col.	67	Byrne, C. H. C., Capt.	132
Brindley, E. G., 2/Lt.	45	——— R. S., 2/Lt.	22			——— J. O., Capt., M.C.	26
Brine, T., 2/Lt.	136	——— R. J. H., 2/Lt.	127	Burgess, E. H. V., 2/Lt.	91		
Brink, J. M., Lieut.	189	——— R. W., 2/Lt.	118	——— F., 2/Lt.	102	Byron, E. F., 2/Lt.	55
Brisbin, H. V., Lieut.	171	——— S. J., Capt.	20	——— F. G., 2/Lt.	39	Bysshe, G. T., Sub.-Lt.	180
Briscoe, W. R. W., 2/Lt.	114	——— V. L. W., 2/Lt.	64	——— P. G., 2/Lt.	21	Bytheway, A. W., 2/Lt.	55
Brislee, F. R., 2/Lt.	35	——— V. R., 2/Lt.	163	——— W. H., Lieut.	107		
Britton, E. A. C., 2/Lt.	176	——— W. C., 2/Lt.	126	Burgoyne, J. S., 2/Lt.	55	Cable, D., Capt., Adj.	74
Broackes, E. W., Major	73	——— W. D., 2/Lt.	68	——— R. M., Capt.	53	Cade, C. E., 2/Lt.	88
Broadbent, G., Lieut.	170	——— W. E., 2/Lt.	77	Burke, G. M., 2/Lt.	60	Cahill, F. J., Capt.	132
——— G. A., 2/Lt.	52	——— W. H., Col.	183	——— J. W., 2/Lt.	60	——— T. G., 2/Lt.	113
Broadhurst, H. C., Surg.	144	——— W. J. M., 2/Lt.	107	——— M. F., Lieut.	136	——— R. J., Capt.	131
Broadwood, J., Capt.	7	——— W. R. A., Capt., Rev.	135	——— U. B., Capt.	36	Cahusac, E. B., Capt., M.C.	161
Brockhurst, G. N., 2/Lt.	151			Burlton, G. P., Lieut.	34		
Brocklebank, H. A., Capt.	23	Browne, D. E. S., Lt.	118	Burman, A. H., 2/Lt.	115	Cailes, S. S., 2/Lt.	144
Brocks, A. W., 2/Lt.	181	——— H., 2/Lt.	183	Burn, H. L. P., Capt.	105	Cairnduff, A., Lieut.	147
Brockwell, S. G., Lieut.	9	——— M. G., Capt.	63	——— J. S., 2/Lt.	165	Cairnes, D. S., 2/Lt.	148
Broder, P. A., Lieut.	146	——— H. W., 2/Lt.	161	Burnand, G. A., Lieut.	71	Cairns, Fred., 2/Lt.	45
Broderip, J. Y. M., Capt.	38	Browne-Mason, H. O. B., Col.	186	Burnard, R. A., 2/Lt.	161	——— J. A., 2/Lt.	152
Brodhurst-Hill, R., Capt.	21			Burnham, M. E., Lieut.	169	——— W. T. S., 2/Lt.	174
Brodie, H. G., Capt.	180	Browning, L. W., 2/Lt.	83	Burnie, A. J., 2/Lt.	146	Caldecott, R., 2/Lt.	160
——— R. A., Capt.	140	Bruce, A. P. C., 2/Lt.	174	Burnley, C. P., 2/Lt.	21	Calder, G., 2/Lt.	92
——— T. W., 2/Lt.	170	——— C. D., Brig.-Gen.	7	Burns, E. B., Lt.	186	——— H. G., Lieut.	35
Brogden, C. E., 2/Lt.	102	——— O., 2/Lt.	115	——— H., Fl. Sub-Lt.	181	Caldwell, D. C., 2/Lt.	59
Bromfield, J. L., Lieut.	144	——— R. T., Capt.	131	——— V. I. A., 2/Lt.	152	——— J., 2/Lt.	81
Bromley, J. T., Capt.	96	——— T. B., Lieut.	157	Burnside, J., 2/Lt.	109	——— J. A., Lieut.	97
Bronskill, F. H., 2/Lt.	150	——— W. F., Major	16	Burpee, B., Capt.	135	——— J. F., 2/Lt.	110
Bronson, C. G., Lieut.	179	Brumell, H. P., Lieut.	173	Burr, E. H., 2/Lt.	64	——— J. M., Sub.-Lt.	145
Brooker, H. H., 2/Lt.	30	Brundritt, D. F., 2/Lt.	124	Burr, P., Lieut.	17	——— J. C., 2/Lt.	92
Brookes, A. A., 2/Lt.	21	Brunskill, J., Major	131	Burrell, J. H., Capt. and Adjt.	101	——— R. T., 2/Lt.	115
Brookfield, C. W., 2/Lt.	12	Bryan, C. A., 2/Lt.	80			Caley, R., 2/Lt.	64
Brookling, H. W., Capt.	31	——— E. F., 2/Lt.	13	Burrill, T. F., Lieut.	151	Call, Felix, Major	48
Brooks, Edgar, 2/Lt.	40	——— F. F. H., Lieut.	164	Burrington, H. S., Capt.	39	Callender, F. de C., 2/Lt.	127
——— W. J., Capt.	13	Bryans, J. C., Capt.	108	Burroughs, G. H., Capt.	186	Calrow, Richard, Lieut.	174
——— W. V., 2/Lt.	128	Bryant, H. G., Capt.	86	Burrow, R., 2/Lt.	33	Calvert, A. S., Lieut.	120
Broomfield, F., 2/Lt.	137	——— J. W., Lieut.	23	Burrows, M. B., Lieut.	8	——— J. H., 2/Lt.	64
Brough, Harry, Lieut.	88	Bryce, A. G., Capt.	132	——— R. F. G., Lieut.	94	——— T. W., 2/Lt.	158
Broughall, H. S., F. Sub.-Lt.	177	——— M. S., 2/Lt.	27	Burry, H. W., 2/Lt.	165	Cameron, D. R., Lieut.	153
		Brydone, James, 2/Lt.	158	Burt, G. C., Lieut.	17	——— E. K., Capt.	108
Brown, A., Lieut.	131	Buchanan, A., Lieut.	175	Burton, D. F., Lieut.	169	——— F., 2/Lt.	112
——— A., Capt.	187	——— G. A. B., Capt.	141	——— E., 2/Lt.	148	——— G. W., Lieut.	23
——— A. A. C., 2/Lt.	28	——— H. P., 2/Lt.	109	——— F. A., Lieut.	125	——— H., 2/Lt.	99
——— A. C. G., 2/Lt.	162	——— John, Capt.	181	——— F. T., 2/Lt.	35	——— I. D., 2/Lt.	158
——— A. E., 2/Lt.	25	Buck, Harry, 2/Lt.	65	——— G. C. J., Lieut.	122	Campbell, A. B. D., Sub-Lt.	171
——— A. G., 2/Lt.	23	Buckingham, W., Capt., M.C.	173	——— H. M., Fl. Sub.-Lt.	176		
——— A. L., Capt.	59					——— A. J., Lieut.	8
——— A. W., Lieut.	147	Buckland, G. F., 2/Lt.	44	——— R. J., 2/Lt.	63	——— A. M., Capt.	83
——— C., 2/Lt.	100	Buckle, F., 2/Lt.	127	Burtt, L. L., Capt.	129	——— C. L., Lieut.	112
——— C. B., 2/Lt.	125	Buckley, F., 2/Lt.	24	Bury, H., Capt.	69	——— D. B., 2/Lt.	94
——— C. D., Lieut.	46	——— G. B., Capt.	132	Busby, R. I., Capt.	51	——— G. C., Lieut.	112
——— C. F., Lieut.	166	——— S. E., Lieut.	147	Bush, H. K., 2/Lt.	34	——— H., Lieut.	140
——— C. G., 2/Lt.	21	——— S. J., 2/Lt.	70	Bushe, J. F., 2/Lt.	156	——— Ivan, 2/Lt.	108
——— C. G., Capt., Rev.	135	Bucknall, C. V. A., /Lt.	174	Bushell, R., Lieut.	102	——— J., 2/Lt.	106
——— C. H., 2/Lt.	158	Budd, F. W., Lieut.	33	Bustard, C. R. D., 2/Lt.	31	——— James, Lt.	119
——— E. A., 2/Lt.	63	Budden, E. B., Lieut.	88	——— F. H., Capt.	189	——— J. W., 2/Lt.	44
——— E. C., 2/Lt.	44	Budge, A. E. V., 2/Lt.	30	Buston, S. J., 2/Lt.	35	——— K. D., Fl. Sub-Lt.	160
——— E. M., 2/Lt.	163	Budgeon, E. A., 2/Lt.	141	Buswell, H. B., 2/Lt.	79		
——— F. A., 2/Lt.	51	Budgett, A. W. M., Lieut.	178	Butler, A. T., Capt.	63	——— M. G., 2/Lt.	103
——— F. W., Capt.	104	Bugge, F. H., 2/Lt.	166	——— J. O., 2/Lt.	160	——— Robert, Capt.	65
——— F. W., 2/Lt.	64	Bull, F. J., 2/Lt.	163	——— L., 2/Lt.	151	——— T., Lieut.	186
——— G. A., Capt.	27	Bullen, Edward, Lieut.	166	——— L. C., 2/Lt.	91	——— W. A., Lieut.	100
——— H. C., 2/Lt.	24	——— R. V., 2/Lt.	76	——— P., Lieut.	131	——— W. M., Capt.	37
——— H. M., Lieut.	167	Buller, J. H. G., Major	189	——— W., 2/Lt.	94	Candler, W., 2/Lt.	36
——— I. A., Capt.	28	Bulling, H., 2/Lt.	14	——— W. T., Lieut.	71	Candy, F. B., 2/Lt.	176
——— J., 2/Lt.	68	Bullock, A. D., 2/Lt.	69	Butt, L. M., 2/Lt.	44	Cane, A. S., Capt.	181
——— J., Lieut.	180	——— W., 2/Lt.	87	——— Thomas, Lieut.	85	——— E. G. S., Capt.	186
——— J. A., 2/Lt.	15	Bunbury, D. St. P., Capt.	180	Butterworth, C., Lieut.	176	Cannon, A. T., Capt.	128
——— J. A., 2/Lt.	12	Bunce, H., Capt.	142	——— H. E., Capt.	96	——— S. W., 2/Lt.	97
——— J. B., 2/Lt.	109	——— J. P., 2/Lt.	92	——— S., Capt.	54	Cant, J. A. V., 2/Lt.	66
——— J. B., Lieut.	121	Bunn, H. P., 2/Lt.	71	Buttifant, E., 2/Lt.	91	Cantlay, A., 2/Lt.	107
——— J. L., 2/Lt.	164	Burbidge, G. E. D., 2/Lt.	25	Button, G. T., Lieut.	75	Capes, G., 2/Lt.	83
——— J. W., 2/Lt.	172	Burbury, A. V., Lieut.	152	——— L. H., Lieut.	167	Capon, R. S., 2/Lt.	152
				Buyers, W. N., Lieut.	107	Capper, E. R., Capt., M.C.	76

Name	Page	Name	Page	Name	Page	Name	Page
Cardall, H., 2/Lt.	47	Caunt, A. E., 2/Lt.	70	Childe, A. L. B., Lieut.	100	Clarke, J., Lieut.	96
Cardew, H., Capt.	183	—— H. V., Lieut.	158	Chillingworth, A. J., Capt.	133	—— J. B., 2/Lt.	86
—— F. B. A., 2/Lt.	24	Caunter, J. A., Capt.	61	—— Major	84	—— K. H. S., Lieut.	129
Cardozo, H. G., 2/Lt.	110	Causton, L. P., Capt.	22	Chinner, E. H., Lieut.	136	—— L. L., 2/Lt.	118
Carey, J. G., Lieut.	175	Cavanagh, T. J., 2/Lt.	49	Chisholm, D. C., Lieut.	81	—— N., 2/Lt.	111
—— R. O'D., Lieut.	67	Cave, W. T. C., Capt.	130	—— J. F., Capt.	172	—— S. E., 2/Lt.	38
Carles, C. W., Lieut.	124	Cawdron, Harold, 2/Lt.	87	Chittenden, S. J., Capt.	119	—— T. C. A., 2/Lt.	45
Carless, R. J., 2/Lt.	86	Cawley, C. F., 2/Lt.	173	Chitty, A. A. E., Lt.	83	—— T. H., Lieut.	149
Carleton, R., Lieut.	140	Cawthra, A., 2/Lt.	67	—— C., 2/Lt.	187	—— V. S., Capt.	187
Carlisle, T. R. M., Capt.	185	Cayley, A., Lieut.	15	—— W. W., Brevet-Col.	184	—— Wm., Lieut.	109
Carlin, S., Capt.	172	—— K. H. E., 2/Lt.	37	Chown, J. S., 2/Lt.	91	—— W. E., 2/Lt.	14
Carlyon, E. T. R., Capt.	79	Cayzer, C. W., Lt., Sir	9	Chreiman, W. W., Lieut.	171	—— W. M., Capt.	97
Carlyle, Geo., 2/Lt.	57	Chadwick, C. R., 2/Lt.	15	Christian, Ewan, Lt.-Col. D.S.O.	142	Clarkson, R. W., 2/Lt.	42
Carmichael, H. H., 2/Lt.	100	—— Geo., Capt.	162	Christie, J. R., Capt.	106	—— W., 2/Lt.	44
—— W., Lieut.	30	Chainey, F. H., 2/Lt.	171	—— T., Capt.	103	Claxton, W. G., Lieut.	168
—— W. R. C., 2/Lt.	149	Chalklin, W. J. N., 2/Lt.	171	—— W. M., Capt.	132	Claydon, M. S., 2/Lt.	76
Carmody, C., Capt., M.C.	50	Challenor, B. H., Capt.	35	Christie-Miller, E., Capt.	18	Claye, H., Capt.	163
Carne, W. A., 2/Lt.	138	Challinor, R. T., 2/Lt.	179	Christopher, C. D., Lt.-Col.	131	Clayton, F. H., 2/Lt.	168
Carpenter, C. E., 2/Lt.	36	Challis, A., 2/Lt.	33	Chubb, J. A., Lieut.	165	—— J. L., Capt.	96
—— F., Lt.	167	—— F. G., 2/Lt.	180	—— J. E. V., 2/Lt.	20	Cleall, P. C., Lieut.	76
Carr, A. M., 2/Lt.	18	—— M. E., 2/Lt.	169	Chuck, Arthur, 2/Lt.	56	Clean, R. L. J., Lieut.	69
—— A. R., 2/Lt.	54	Chalmers, B. G., 2/Lt.	153	Church, W. A., 2/Lt.	95	Clegg, J. H., 2/Lt.	42
—— C. E., 2/Lt.	127	—— J. J., 2/Lt.	106	Churchill, W. F. N., 2/Lt.	12	—— W. L., Capt.	36
—— E. de G., Capt.	36	Chaloner, T. W. P. L., Capt., Hon.	147	Churchouse, H. P., Capt.	28	Cleland, A. L. H., 2/Lt.	41
—— F. C., 2/Lt.	179	Chamberlain, W. B., 2/Lt.	178	Cinnamond, F., 2/Lt.	60	Clelland, David, 2/Lt.	140
—— G. W., 2/Lt.	12	Chambers, A. H., 2/Lt.	77	Clack, L. A., Lieut.	167	Clementi-Smith, H. D., Capt.	131
—— C. V., 2/Lt.	162	—— G., 2/Lt.	117	Clancy, J., 2/Lt.	59	Clements, H. T., 2/Lt.	130
—— R., 2/Lt.	72	—— James, 2/Lt.	80	Clapham, S. W. B., 2/Lt.	127	—— S. U. L., Major	110
—— R. G., 2/Lt.	164	—— W. D., Lieut.	156	Clare, A. D.	82	Clemons, H. S., 2/Lt.	159
—— T. E. A., Capt.	132	Chamier, R. O., Lieut.	184	—— A. E., 2/Lt.	65	Clemow, S. N., 2/Lt.	127
Carre, B., 2/Lt.	106	Champion, H. T., 2/Lt.	147	—— A. M., Lieut.	134	Clemson, E. G., 2/Lt.	14
—— J. H. T., Fl. Sub.-Lt.	162	—— S. G., Lieut.	189	Claret, A. E., Lieut.	22	—— A. W., Fl. Com.	181
Carrington, J. W., 2/Lt.	129	Champney, H. D'A., 2/Lt.	50	Claridge, C. G., 2/Lt.	79	—— T. H., Capt.	85
Carroll, E. Cola, Lieut.	156	—— J. P., 2/Lt.	125	Clark, Alex., 2/Lt.	106	Clenshaw, W. F., Lieut.	21
Carrow, R. B., 2/Lt.	23	Chance, W. H. S., Lieut.	149	—— A. F., 2/Lt.	46	Clerihew, Clive, 2/Lt.	69
Carruthers, P. G., 2/Lt.	89	Chandler, A., 2/Lt.	41	—— A. G., Capt.	134	Clibborn, R., Capt.	86
Carson, H. R., Lieut.	55	—— A. H., 2/Lt.	45	—— A. H., 2/Lt.	121	Clidero, H. A., 2/Lt.	49
—— S. B., 2/Lt.	34	—— G. H., Lieut.	113	—— A. L., 2/Lt.	158	Cliffe, F. V., 2/Lt.	72
Carter, A. D., Major	163	—— H., 2/Lt.	116	—— A. M., 2/Lt.	184	Clifford, G. C., 2/Lt.	31
—— A. E., Lieut.	27	—— J., 2/Lt.	95	—— A. N. B., 2/Lt.	127	—— R., Capt.	182
—— C. W., 2/Lt.	14	—— R. H., 2/Lt.	84	—— A. S., 2/Lt.	107	—— R. C., Capt.	186
—— E., 2/Lt.	142	Channer, R., Capt.	184	—— C. A., Major, M.C.	66	Clifton, H. A., Lieut.	182
—— E. P. Q., Capt.	98	Chant, W. F., Capt.	22	—— C. C., Capt.	162	—— H. N., 2/Lt.	18
—— F. W. B., Lt. and Qtmr.	134	—— E. M., Lieut.	160	—— C. G., Lieut.	187	Clinton, W. L., Capt.	90
—— G. L., 2/Lt.	167	Chantrill, A. I., Capt.	14	—— D. R., 2/Lt.	60	Clough, A. C., 2/Lt.	56
—— H. S., 2/Lt.	50	Chapman, A. F., Capt.	61	—— E., 2/Lt.	32	Clouston, A. M., 2/Lt.	141
—— L. A., 2/Lt.	113	—— E. F. G., Lieut.	64	—— E. G. U., 2/Lt.	34	Cloutier, G. A., Lieut.	140
—— R. N., 2/Lt.	149	—— G., Major	13	—— F. H. B., 2/Lt.	14	Clubb, A. D., Lieut.	40
Carthew, P. R., Lieut.	37	—— H. J., Capt.	135	—— F. H., Lieut.	78	Cluckie, A. B., Capt.	134
Cartledge, R. A., 2/Lt.	157	—— J., 2/Lt.	154	—— F. S., 2/Lt.	157	Clutterbuck, A., Capt.	71
Cartmell, F., 2/Lt.	125	—— J. R. S., 2/Lt.	87	—— G. N., Capt.	128	—— L. C. F., 2/Lt.	160
Cartwright, H. A., Capt.	87	—— T., 2/Lt.	41	—— J. A., 2/Lt.	52	Coalbank, R. M., Capt.	134
—— H. B., Lieut.	53	Charker, V. W., 2/Lt.	136	—— J. G., Fl. Sub.-Lt.	177	Coates, S., 2/Lt.	176
Carver, G. S., 2/Lt.	98	Charlesworth, J. L., 2/Lt.	60	—— S. A., 2/Lt.	76	Coaton, G. H., Lieut.	120
Carveth, W. A., Lt.	166	Charley, H. R., Major	108	—— W. Lieut.	139	Cobbin, A. J., 2/Lt.	164
Case, B. S., 2/Lt.	174	Charlton, G., Lt.-Col.	27	—— W., Lieut. and Qtmr.	108	Cobbold, F. R. C., Lieut.	158
—— R. J., Capt.	77	—— G. S., 2/Lt.	53	—— W. B., 2/Lt.	150	Cobden, H., Capt.	58
Casey, O. P., 2/Lt.	33	—— S. E., Lieut.	122	—— W., 2/Lt.	72	Cobham, R. S., Lieut.	171
—— Pat, Rev.	135	Charters, R. J., 2/Lt.	49	Clarke, A. C., Major	78	Cochrane, D. C., 2/Lt.	19
—— P. J., 2/Lt.	156	Chase, D. E., 2/Lt.	167	—— A. E., 2/Lt.	29	—— W. A., 2/Lt.	15
Casgrain, H. R., Lt.	160	Cheeseman, F. C., 2/Lt.	119	—— A. F. G., 2/Lt.	160	Cock, G. H., Capt., M.C.	154
Cassels, H. K., 2/Lt.	160	Cheesman, P., Lieut.	40	—— B. H., 2/Lt.	26	Cockburn, J. S., Lieut., M.C.	9
Castelli, G. D., 2/Lt.	11	Cheetham, F. L., Lieut.	32	—— C. H., 2/Lt.	160	Cockburn-Mercer, T. H., Capt.	59
Castle, A. F., 2/Lt.	158	Chellingworth, H. G., 2/Lt.	29	—— E. B., 2/Lt.	61	Cockerill, G. E., Capt.	129
—— G. Lloyd, Lieut.	165	Cherry, John, 2/Lt.	68	—— F., Lieut.	163	Cockin, John B., 2/Lt.	170
—— G. S., 2/Lt.	147	Cheshire, H. S., Lt.	182	—— F. W. H., 2/Lt.	46	Cocking, J. C. O., Capt.	72
—— H. F. B., Lieut.	137	Chetwynd-Stapleton, B., Major	54	—— G. A., 2/Lt.	114	—— L. G., 2/Lt.	164
—— W., Lieut.	148	Chevis, H., 2/Lt.	90	—— Harold, 2/Lt.	121	Cockram, F. S., Capt.	89
Caswell, C. W., 2/Lt.	82	Cheyne, C. L., 2/Lt.	19	—— H. A., 2/Lt.	163	Cockroft, H., 2/Lt.	128
—— F. W., Lieut.	123	Chichester-Constable, C. H. J., Lieut.	28			Cocksedge, R. H., Lieut.	120
—— G. F. C., Lieut.	172	Chidson, M. R., 2/Lt.	145			Coddington, H. F., Capt.	93
Cater, J. W., Capt.	88	Child, M. D., Lieut.	115			Codrington, W. R., Lt.-Col. Sir	117
Cattell, B. K., 2/Lt.	180						
Cattley, L. A., Major	44						

Coe, W., 2/Lt. 68	Connor, J. H., 2/Lt. ... 111	Costello, W. H., Capt. 150	Crane, S. H. E., 2/Lt. ... 128
Coghill, F. S., Lieut. ... 166	——— R., Major ... 61	Cottis, P. E., Lieut. ... 35	Cranswick, A. N., Capt. 92
——— W. H., 2/Lt.... 172	Conover, C. C., Lieut. ... 172	Cotton, F. J., 2/Lt. ... 64	Crassweller, H., Capt. ... 133
Coghlan, T. R., 2/Lt. ... 110	Considine, H. W. H., 2/Lt. 92	——— H., Lieut. ... 153	Craston, N. H., 2/Lt. ... 97
Cogill, N. H. V., 2/Lt. ... 81	Constable, D. C. J., 2/Lt. 39	——— H. J., Major... 182	Craven, J. L. A., Lieut. 66
Cohen, W. R., Lieut. ... 21	——— E. E., Capt.... 144	——— W. A., 2/Lt.... 78	Crawford, Ch., Capt. ... 172
Coke, J., Capt. The Hon. 18	——— S. J., 2/Lt. ... 130	Cottrell, A. E., Lieut. ... 39	——— D. F., 2/Lt. ... 128
Colbeck, C. E., Capt. ... 185	Conway, C. H., 2/Lt. ... 69	——— J., Lieut. ... 126	——— G. P. G., 2/Lt. 114
Colbert, L. A., 2/Lt. ... 156	——— R., 2/Lt. ... 48	Couchman, M., 2/Lt. ... 41	——— J. N., Lt.-Col.,
Colbourne, J. S., 2/Lt. ... 98	Conyngham, E. J., 2/Lt. 89	Coulshaw, C. J. A., 2/Lt. 128	D.S.O. ... 59
Coldicott, A. C., Capt.,	Coode-Bate, J., Lieut.... 145	Coulson, A., Lieut. ... 10	——— K. B. S., Lieut. 185
M.C. 29	Cook, C. W., Lieut. ... 160	——— T. E., 2/Lt. ... 102	——— O. G. S., 2/Lt. 159
Coldwell, G. A., Lieut.... 139	——— E. C., Lieut.... 75	——— W. H., Capt. 101	——— W. I., 2/Lt. ... 163
Cole, C. F., 2/Lt. ... 32	——— H. M., 2/Lt.... 90	——— W. E., Lieut. 166	Crawley, C. P., 2/Lt. ... 187
——— F. G., 2/Lt. ... 35	——— L. C. L., 2/Lt. 149	Coulston, J. H. C., Lieut. 23	Cremer, E. W., Capt. ... 115
——— H. A., Lieut. 170	——— R. C., 2/Lt. ... 142	Coulthard, Robert, 2/Lt. 174	Cresswell, H. J., 2/Lt.... 46
——— G. H., 2/Lt. 188	——— W. A., 2/Lt. ... 142	Couper, C. M., Capt. ... 74	——— W. R., Lieut. 130
——— K. R., Fl.Lieut.161	Cooke, E., 2/Lt. ... 99	——— J. M., Lieut.... 11	Cressy, H. R., Lieut. ... 30
——— M., Capt. ... 30	——— E. A., 2/Lt. ... 156	Courage, H., Lieut. ... 56	Creswell, R. G., 2/Lt. ... 75
——— O. J. B., 2/Lt. 15	——— G. C. R., Rev.,	Courteir, R F., 2/Lt. ... 70	Cribb, A. G., 2/Lt. ... 158
——— R. H., 2/Lt.... 171	M.C. ... 135	Courtney, J. P. M., 2/Lt. 137	Crichton, C. A., 2/Lt. ... 175
——— W. R. T., 2/Lt. 27	——— P. B., Lieut. 173	——— W. E. L., 2/Lt. 170	Crichton, McV., Lt.-Col. 182
Cole-Hamilton, G. C.,	——— W. K., Capt. 182	Couston, A., 2/Lt. ... 159	Crickmore, E. B., Lieut. 165
Col., C.M.G., D.S.O.... 109	Cookson, F., 2/Lt. ... 40	Coutts, R. W., Lieut. ... 160	Crighton, J. S., 2/Lt. ... 84
——— H. A. W., Major 40	——— P., 2/Lt. ... 55	Coventry, the Hon. C. J.,	Crisp, A. E., 2/Lt. ... 152
Coleman, C. B., 2/Lt. ... 161	Coolahan, J. S., Lieut. ... 138	Lt.-Col. 178	——— A. R., 2/Lt. ... 149
——— D. J., Lieut. ... 120	Coole, R. S., 2/Lt. ... 55	Coverdale, S., 2/Lt. ... 43	——— G., 2/Lt. ... 130
——— J. P., 2/Lt. ... 175	Coombes, E. S., 2/Lt. ... 167	Cowan, A. R., 2/Lt. ... 163	Crittall, H. P., Lieut. ... 89
——— O. E., 2/Lt. ... 176	Coomber, F. H. V., 2/Lt. 174	——— D. J., Lieut.... 188	Croal, B. V., 2/Lt. ... 14
Coles, G. T., 2/Lt. ... 170	Coombs, V. C., 2/Lt. ... 154	——— J. H., Sub.-Lt. 145	Crockett, G. P., 2/Lt. ... 54
——— H. H. E. Q.,	Cooney, J. M., Lieut. ... 136	——— J. M., Capt. ... 53	Crockford, F. R., 2/Lt. 52
Lieut. ... 111	Coope, N. N., Lieut. ... 172	——— R. H., 2/Lt. ... 158	Croft, C.E., 2/Lt. ... 41
——— W. T., Lieut. 154	Cooper, A. O., Capt. ... 122	——— S. W., 2/Lt.... 69	——— J. C., Lieut.... 176
Colledge, G., 2/Lt. ... 155	——— E. J., Lieut. ... 176	——— W. E., Lieut. 162	——— J. W., 2/Lt. 29
Colles, T. O., 2/Lt. ... 78	——— E. J., Lieut. ... 188	Coward, G. B., Lieut. ... 164	——— W. A., 2/Lt.... 35
Collett, H. S., Lieut. ... 164	——— E. P., 2/Lt. ... 44	——— S. R., Lieut. ... 167	Crofts, E. C. J., 2/Lt. ... 58
Colley, A., Capt. ... 79	——— G. C., Capt. ... 116	Cowell, R. G., 2/Lt. ... 45	——— T. A., 2/Lt. ... 25
Collier, A. C., 2/Lt. ... 146	——— G. M., 2/Lt. ... 104	Cowgill, W. A. F., Lieut. 170	Croker, E., 2/Lt. ... 110
——— J. D. A., 2/Lt. 137	——— G. W., Lieut. 49	Cowie, T. McK., 2/Lt. ... 181	Croker, W., Capt. ... 131
Collinge, F. J., 2/Lt. ... 75	——— H., 2/Lt. ... 61	Cowley, A. T., Fl.-Lt. ... 176	Crole, G. B., Capt. ... 158
——— J. C., 2/Lt. ... 51	——— H. A., Lieut. 151	——— G. E., Capt.... 113	Croll, A. G., 2/Lt. ... 68
Collings, H. J., Sub-Lieut.144	Coops, F. C., 2/Lt. ... 150	——— R. L., 2/Lt. ... 81	Crompton, W., 2/Lt. ... 24
——— L., 2/Lt. ... 32	Coote, C. M., Lieut. ... 61	Cownley, J. J., 2/Lt. ... 48	Crone, A. C., Lieut. ... 118
Collingwood, P. H., Major 131	Cope, E. M., 2/Lt. ... 98	Cox, A. G., 2/Lt. ... 34	Crookell, S. E., 2/Lt. ... 169
——— T. F., 2/Lt. ... 88	——— H. A., 2/Lt.... 39	——— C. E. S., Major 183	Crook, H. W., 2/Lt. ... 38
Collins, C., Capt. ... 76	——— H. S., Lieut.... 76	——— D., 2/Lt. ... 37	——— W., 2/Lt. ... 29
——— E. R., Major 63	Copeland, A. H. M.,	——— E. J., Lieut.... 138	Crosbie, C. H., 2/Lt. ... 159
——— H. L., Lieut. 182	Lieut. 149	——— F. B., 2/Lt. ... 171	——— D. S., Capt. ... 146
——— I. T. M., 2/Lt. 45	——— George, 2/Lt. 26	——— George, Lieut. 138	——— J., 2/Lt. ... 53
——— J. C., 2/Lt. ... 174	Copestake, T. A. B.,	——— H. A., 2/Lt. ... 179	Cross, A. S., 2/Lt. ... 162
——— L. G., Lieut.... 50	Lieut. 11	——— P. H., Lieut. 17	——— H. L., 2/Lt. ... 166
——— L. M. C., 2/Lt. 99	Copley, A., Lieut. ... 176	——— S. H., Capt.... 36	——— J. G., Lieut. ... 49
——— N. B. F., Capt. 28	Corbett, Chas. H., 2/Lt. 68	——— W., 2/Lt. ... 167	——— R. W., Lieut. 150
——— W. G., Lieut. 34	——— D. M., Capt.... 131	——— W. C. C., 2/Lt. 35	——— W. T., 2/Lt. 36
Collis, D. P., 2/Lt. ... 155	——— P. B., Capt. ... 132	——— W. J., 2/Lt. ... 138	Crossland, E. A., 2/Lt. 102
——— G. D., 2/Lt. ... 98	——— R., Lieut. ... 150	——— W. R., 2/Lt.... 58	Crossley, F. S., Lieut.,
Collison, C. B. J., 2/Lt. 33	——— R. D., Capt.... 183	Coxon, A. C. M., Capt.... 178	The Hon. ... 9
Colquhoun, H. G., 2/Lt. 19	Corbett-Winder, F.,	Cozens, E. O., 2/Lt. ... 128	——— H., Lieut. ... 172
——— W. G., Lieut. 139	Lieut. 50	Crabb, R. B., 2/Lt. ... 65	Crossman, A. F., Capt. 140
Colville, F. M., Capt. ... 72	Corbey-Smith, M., Lt.... 183	Crabbie, W. M., 2/Lt. ... 146	——— R., Major ... 143
Colvill-Jones, T., Capt. 162	Corbould-Warren, E.,	Crabtree, C. P., 2/Lt. ... 56	Crosthwaite, J. D.,
Comerford, J. J., 2/Lt. 165	Major 185	Craddock, D. V. L., Lieut. 17	Lt.-Col. 84
Comley, R. H., 2/Lt. ... 26	Corcoran, J. P., 2/Lt. ... 47	——— P. E., 2/Lt. ... 75	Crow, Alex., 2/Lt. ... 19
Compton, F., 2/Lt. ... 82	Corfe, A. C., Lt.-Col. ... 84	Cragg, J. C., 2/Lt. ... 142	Crowder, G. E., Lieut.,
Condon, D., 2/Lt. ... 24	Cork, C. H., Capt., M.C. 92	Craig, C. C. Capt. ... 108	M.C. 118
——— J. E. S., Capt.,	Corlett, R. F., 2/Lt. ... 85	——— F. C., 2/Lt. ... 152	——— W. H., Lieut. 11
M.C. 109	Cornish, E. W., Capt. ... 174	——— J. L., 2/Lt. ... 15	Crowson, A. H. T., 2/Lt. 47
Conheeny, G., 2/Lt. ... 24	——— P. A., Lieut. ... 70	——— J.L.W., Lieut. 188	Crowther, C. R., Capt.... 134
Conlan, R. L. H., Capt. 113	Cornock, R. B., 2/Lt. ... 142	——— J. W. H., 2/Lt. 64	——— E., Lieut. ... 42
——— Tom, Lieut.:... 166	Cornwall, C. E., Major... 106	——— W. G., 2/Lt.... 102	Cruden, A., 2/Lt. ... 106
Connal Rowan, G. F.,	Cornwell, S. F., 2/Lt. ... 88	Craigie, B. E., Lieut. ... 86	Cruikshank, J. P., 2/Lt. 31
Lieut. 112	——— F., 2/Lt. ... 174	Crake, J. W., Lieut. ... 25	——— K. G., 2/Lt. ... 156
Connolly, S. D., Lieut.... 168	Corps, E. L., 2/Lt. ... 76	Cramer Roberts, W. E.,	Crummer, E. R., Sub-Lt. 145
——— S. M., 2/Lt. ... 164	Corrie, A. J., 2/Lt. ... 127	Major 186	Crump, A. G., 2/Lt. ... 51
Conolly, T. P., 2/Lt. ... 27	Cory, R. S., Capt. ... 139	Crammond, G. R., Lieut. 160	Crutchley, G. E. V., 2/Lt. 18
Connon, F. G. W., 2/Lt. 91	Costar, D. H., 2/Lt. ... 14	Crane, C. G., 2/Lt. ... 156	Cruttenden, C., 2/Lt. ... 17

Name	Page
Crymble, William	131
Cudmore, E. O., 2/Lt.	159
Cuffley, J. T., Lieut.	119
Cule, D. M., Capt.	120
Cull, W. A., Capt.	136
Cullen, A. A., Lt.	181
——— H. W., 2/Lt.	51
——— W. D., Lieut.	154
Cullings, E. C., Capt.	138
Culver, D. E., Lieut.	168
——— J. G., M.C., 2/Lt.	76
——— R., Capt.	93
Culverwell, F. N., 2/Lt.	137
Culy, L. V., Lieut.	122
Cumming, G., Lieut.	105
——— I., Capt.	106
——— J. R., Lieut.	107
——— N., Lieut.	138
——— R. H. O., Lieut.	136
——— R. F., 2/Lt.	105
——— S. C., 2/Lt.	20
Cummins, G., 2/Lt.	136
——— H. A. V., Lt.-Col.	183
Cunliffe, W. R., Major	11
Cunningham, E. W., 2/Lt.	127
——— G. J., 2/Lt.	52
——— J., Capt.	112
——— J. B., Capt.	102
——— J. C., 2/Lt.	75
——— K. E., Capt.	67
Cunnington, D. G. L., Lieut.	140
Curle, A. C., Lieut.	104
Curlewis, T., 2/Lt.	149
Curphey, E. J., 2/Lt.	14
Currie, J. D., Lieut.	160
Curry, H. D., 2/Lt.	124
Curtis, A. E., 2/Lt.	15
——— C. R., 2/Lt.	51
——— G., 2/Lt.	142
——— H. A., Capt.	82
——— M. K., Lieut.	169
Cushing, D., 2/Lt.	149
Cust, L. G. A., Lieut.	13
Cuthbert, J. P., Staff Capt.	7
Cutbill, A., Capt.	37
——— E. H., 2/Lt.	157
Cuthbertson, R. A., Lieut.	103
Cyr, A. J., Lieut.	166
Dabb, R. H., 2/Lt.	136
Dabbs, J. C., 2/Lt.	38
Dacombe, A. W., 2/Lt.	117
Dacre, G. D., Flt. Com.	180
Dagg, L. S., 2/Lt.	91
Dain, W. S., Sub.-Lt.	145
Dakin, E. L. V., Major	16
Dalby, A. A., Lieut.	124
Dale, G., Lieut.	75
——— P. E., Lieut.	76
——— W., 2/Lt.	52
Dalgarno, J. H., Capt.	89
Dalgety, G. H., 2/Lt.	20
Dallimore, F., Capt.	133
D'Alton, A. J., Lieut.	91
Dalton, N. D., 2/Lt.	117
Daltrey, F., Lieut.	164
Daly, A. P. V., Capt.	150
——— E., Capt., Rev.	135
——— McC., 2/Lt.	33
Dalzell, W., Lieut.	146
Dalziel, G. N. C., Capt.	130
Dams, F. D., Lieut.	41
Dana, H. F., 2/Lt.	23
Dandy, J. M., 2/Lt.	172
Daniel, E., 2/Lt.	112
Daniell, H. J., Capt.	143
——— H. J., Capt.	183
——— J. B., 2/Lt.	153
Daniels, T. H. R., 2/Lt.	181
Dann, D. G., 2/Lt.	44
Danson, F. A., 2/Lt.	24
Darby, E., 2/Lt.	173
——— R., Capt.	120
Darbyshire, J. F. R., 2/Lt.	60
D'Arcy, M. J., 2/Lt.	137
Darke, S. J., Capt.	133
Darley, C. B., 2/Lt.	10
——— C. C., Capt.	146
Darling, E., M.C., Capt.	14
Darnell, W. G., 2/Lt.	12
Darvell, S., Capt.	56
Darwent, G. T., 2/Lt.	67
Davenhill, R. E., Lieut.	118
Davenport, H., 2/Lt.	178
——— J. A., Capt.	50
Davern, F., Lt.	185
Davey, B. E., 2/Lt.	81
——— H. J., Lieut.	117
——— T. E., Lieut.	77
David, C. K., 2/Lt.	169
Davidson, C., Lieut.	57
——— D. A., Lieut.	143
——— F. A. J., 2/Lt.	108
——— F. W., Lieut.	60
——— G., Lieut.	116
——— H. J., Capt.	132
——— J., 2/Lt.	104
——— L. K., 2/Lt.	167
——— M. R., Lieut.	94
——— N., 2/Lt.	27
——— T., Capt.	154
Davie, J., Lt.-Col.	182
Davies, A. V., Lieut.	50
——— C. W., 2/Lt.	155
——— D. H., 2/Lt.	93
——— D. M., 2/Lt.	73
——— D. P., 2/Lt.	174
——— D. P., Major	116
——— E., Lieut.	131
——— E. A., Capt.	141
——— E. H., Capt.	52
——— E. O., 2/Lt.	58
——— F. T. H., Capt.	132
——— H., 2/Lt.	171
——— H., Lieut.	57
——— H., Rev.	135
——— H. D., 2/Lt.	151
——— H. E., 2/Lt.	159
——— H. G., Capt.	24
——— H. H., 2/Lt.	27
——— H. H. T., Lieut.	107
——— H. R., Lieut.	152
——— H. V., 2/Lt.	29
——— H. W., Major	185
——— H. W., Major	63
——— J. C., Capt., The Rev.	135
——— J. E., 2/Lt.	152
——— J. H., 2/Lt.	126
——— J. H., 2/Lt.	12
——— J. L., Major	76
——— L. A., Lieut.	39
——— R. D., Capt.	143
——— R. S., 2/Lt.	126
——— T., Lieut.	17
Davies, T. H., 2/Lt.	12
——— T. E. H., 2/Lt.	146
——— V. G., 2/Lt.	102
——— W. H., 2/Lt.	102
——— W. W., 2/Lt.	55
Davis, A. J., Lieut.	42
——— D. W., 2/Lt.	150
——— E. B., Lieut.	67
——— F. M., Capt.	128
——— F. P., Capt.	119
——— F. T., 2/Lt.	27
——— G., 2/Lt.	154
——— L. D. McN., Capt.	36
——— R. A., 2/Lt.	33
——— R. H. L., 2/Lt.	86
Davison, Alex., 2/Lt.	108
——— C., Capt.	48
——— D. J., 2/Lt.	22
——— R. M. R., Capt.	47
Davy, G. M. O., 2/Lt.	13
——— P., Capt.	131
——— W. H. C., Major	87
——— W. K., 2/Lt.	32
Dawbarn, J. S., Major	122
Dawes, A. J., Capt.	178
——— A. F., 2/Lt.	162
Dawkins, F. S. S., 2/Lt.	121
Dawney, C. S., 2/Lt.	12
Dawson, C. H. T., Lieut. Qtmr.	108
——— E., 2/Lt.	166
——— F. G., Capt.	126
——— F. S., Brig.-Gen., C.M.G.	141
——— J. H. T., Lieut.	178
——— L., Lieut.	66
——— W. R., Capt.	19
——— W. V., Capt.	11
Day, A. F., Lieut.	16
——— D. A. L., Major	28
——— G. A., 2/Lt.	110
——— G. W., Lieut.	55
——— H. M., 2/Lt.	90
——— J. E., 2/Lt.	21
——— O., 2/Lt.	42
Deacon, C. H., 2/Lt.	31
Dean, A. C., Lieut.	161
——— H., 2/Lt.	161
——— L. G. H., 2/Lt.	188
——— W., 2/Lt.	96
Deane, B., Capt.	112
——— G. A., Capt.	110
——— G. S., 2/Lt.	150
Dear, J. A., Lieut.	169
Dearman, C. S., Capt.	47
Deason, T. G., Lieut.	156
Deaton, F., 2/Lt.	144
De Carteret, H. J. T., Capt.	23
De Colagan, A. T. B., Capt.	128
Deedes, J., Capt.	86
de Grey, Capt. & Adj.	186
Dehn, H. G., 2/Lt.	93
Dekin, G., Major	30
Delamain, Major Gen.	182
Delaney, V., 2/Lt.	51
Del Court, S. Fitz-W., Capt.	88
De Lemo, C., 2/Lt.	188
Dell, R., 2/Lt.	119
Delmege, J. C. R., Capt.	113
De Lozey, L., 2/Lt.	52
De Mauny, L., 2/Lt.	77
Deming, R. M., Capt., M.O.	132
Denahy, P. A., 2/Lt.	113
Dendrino, S., 2/Lt.	149
Denham-Smith, H. F., 2/Lt.	10
Denholm, T. S., 2/Lt.	108
Denison, E. B., 2/Lt.	156
——— N. C., 2/Lt.	151
Denning, C. W., 2/Lt.	128
Dennis, B. W., 2/Lt.	114
——— E. E., 2/Lt.	179
——— R. T., 2/Lt.	25
Dennistoun, J. R., Lieut.	147
Denny, C. H., Lieut.	168
Dennys, K. G. G., 2/Lt.	38
Dee, D. M., 2/Lt.	175
Dent, A. E., Lieut.	136
Denton, J. S., Lieut.	81
——— W. H., Lieut.	81
De Paravicini, C. P. E., Lieut.	92
De Pass, D. H., 2/Lt.	116
De Pennington, D., 2/Lt.	72
De Quetteville, R. G., Capt., M.C.	50
Derbyshire, H., 2/Lt.	34
Derham, J. A. T., 2/Lt.	128
Derrett, J. H., 2/Lt.	49
Desbarats, E. W., Fl. Sub-Lt.	177
De Selincourt, A., Capt.	153
De Souza, S. A., Asst. Surg.	182
De St. Legier, G. W., 2/Lt., M.C.	82
De Trafford, O., Capt.	70
Devereux, W., Lieut.	185
Devlin, A. C., Lt., A/Capt.	72
De Voil, W. H., 2/Lt.	40
Dewey, J. H. J., 2/Lt.	127
Diamond, W. E. de B., 2/Lt.	155
Di Balme, L. T. B., Count, 2/Lt.	153
Dicey, G., 2/Lt.	54
Dick, W., 2/Lt.	180
Dick-Cunyngham, J. K., Brig.-Gen.	7
Dickey, R. F. L., Capt.	163
Dickie, T. H., Lieut.	103
Dickins, W. A., Lieut.	70
Dickinson, A. M., Capt.	63
——— C. F., Capt.	44
——— H. C., Lt.-Col.	189
——— H. W., 2/Lt.	26
——— J., 2/Lt.	32
——— T. M., Lieut.	153
——— W., 2/Lt.	72
——— W. C., 2/Lt.	26
Dickson, G. L., Lieut.	104
——— G. L., 2/Lt.	33
——— H. E. B., 2/Lt.	37
——— J. H., 2/Lt.	111
——— T. H., 2/Lt.	145
Digby, T. K., 2/Lt.	43
Dight, C. C., Lieut.	138
Dilliway, L. J., 2/Lt.	119
Dillon, M. A. M., Lieut.	144
Dillon-Kelly, C. F., Capt.	131
Dillnutt, E. J., Lieut.	152
Dimmock, W., 2/Lt.	30
Dingley, K. M., 2/Lt.	37
——— R. L., 2/Lt.	149
Dinwiddy, M. J., Capt.	187
Diplock, P. B., 2/Lt.	91

	PAGE		PAGE		PAGE		PAGE
Dixon, E. C., Lieut.	55	Dowson, S. T., 2/Lt.	93	Durlacher, H. W., 2/Lt.,		Ellenberger, G. F., Capt.	86
———— L. W., 2/Lt.	127	———— W. B., Capt.	33	M.C.	127	Ellerbeck, E. A. V., 2/Lt.	156
Dobeson, R. G., Lieut.	175	Dowty, G. D., Lieut.	88	Durnford, H. G. E., 2/Lt.	10	Ellinger, C., 2/Lt.	16
Dobbie, E. T., Major	11	Doyle, A. J., Lt.	40	Durrant, B. W., Sub.-Lt.	145	Elliot, G. A., Capt.	47
———— G. N., Lieut.	20	———— D. C., 2/Lt.	159	———— F. J., 2/Lt.	96	———— W., Lieut.	107
Dobbs, F., Lieut.	113	———— J. E., Capt.	170	Dusgate, R. E., Lieut.	158	———— W. T. W., 2/Lt.	109
Dobie, M. B., 2/Lt.	136	Drabble, A. S., 2/Lt.	116	Dutton, A. H. D., 2/Lt.	55	Elliott, A. H., 2/Lt.	30
———— P., 2/Lt.	53	Draffen, F. G. W., Lt.-		Duxbury, 2/Lt.	182	———— C., Lieut.	21
Dobson, Alan, 2/Lt.	100	Col.	59	Dyer, A. B. C., 2/Lt.	95	———— D. W., Lt.	139
———— D. F., Capt.	132	Drain, W. F., 2/Lt.	84	———— A. J. L., Major	54	———— G. L., Lieut.	176
Dodd, G. C., Lieut.	138	Drake, C. D., Capt.	113	Dyson, H., Capt.	178	———— J. E., 2/Lt.	14
———— A. A., 2/Lt.	118	———— R. G. C., Lieut.,		———— M. J. S., 2/Lt.	46	———— H., 2/Lt.	167
———— H. F., 2/Lt.	26	M.C.	39	———— W. E., 2/Lt.	36	———— H. E. D., Lieut.	76
———— W. R., 2/Lt.	25	———— W., Lieut.	16	Dyte, S. T., 2/Lt.	39	———— R. D., Capt.	178
Dodds, A., Lieut.	158	Drake-Brockman, F. T.,				———— W. G. R., Capt.	54
———— J., 2/Lt.	12	Lieut.	182	Eadie, W. E., 2/Lt.	64	Elliott-Cooper, N. B.,	
———— H. G., Capt.	25	Drew, G. A., 2/Lt.	37	Eagar, E. F., Major	60	Col., V.C., D.S.O., M.C.	30
———— W. M., Capt.	27	———— G. M., Lieut.	59	Earl, G., 2/Lt.	123	Ellis, A. H., 2/Lt.	34
Dodridge, B. J. S., 2/Lt.	46	Drew-Brook, T. G., 2/Lt.	163	Earle, M., Lt.-Col.	17	———— C., 2/Lt.	86
Dodson, I., Lieut.	151	Driver, H. S., 2/Lt.	19	Earp, K. S., 2/Lt.	142	———— F. G., 2/Lt.	78
Dodwell, C. G. S., 2/Lt.	63	Dronsfield, S. W., 2/Lt.	156	Eason, A. A., Lieut.	84	———— F. H., Lieut.	23
———— T. B., 2/Lt.	168	Druce, G. C., Lieut.	87	———— A. T., 2/Lt.	149	———— F. R., Capt.	186
Doe, J. E., Lieut.	164	Druitt, H. H. W., Lt.	45	Eastman, A. J., Lieut.	82	———— G., 2/Lt.	61
Doehler, H. H., 2/Lt.	169	Drummond, G. L. P.,		———— T. J. G., 2/Lt.	92	———— J., 2/Lt.	103
Dogherty, F. W., 2/Lt.	159	2/Lt.	175	Easton, J., 2/Lt.	31	———— J. C., 2/Lt.	125
———— J. W., 2/Lt.	107	———— P., 2/Lt.	108	Eastwood, E. H., Lieut.	146	———— J. L., 2/Lt.	12
Doig, A. T., Lieut.	137	———— W., Capt.	7	Eaton, C., Lieut.	165	———— J. W. H., Lieut.	139
———— W. H., Major	105	Drury, D. D., 2/Lt.	146	———— J. A., Lieut.	163	———— R. H., Lieut.	168
Doke, T. W., 2/Lt.	70	Drury-Lowe, W., Capt.	77	Ebden, W. S., 2/Lt.	188	———— S. A., 2/Lt.	55
Dolbey, R., Lieut.	131	Du Cane, R. E. M., 2/Lt.	180	Eberli, F. H., 2/Lt.	146	———— S. H., 2/Lt.	148
Dollingsmith, C., 2/Lt.	146	Duce, William	162	Eccles, C. E. S. S., Lieut.	90	———— S. R., Lieut.	95
Doman, G. H. R., 2/Lt.	26	Ducksbury, O. H., 2/Lt.	80	———— J. E., 2/Lt.	100	———— T. W. R., 2/Lt.	39
Domville, C. L., Capt.,		Duckworth, E., Asst.		Edbrooke, F., Capt.	39	———— W. B., 2/Lt.	148
M.C.	90	Surg.	182	Edelston, R. H., Lieut.	160	———— W. O. H., Lieut.	56
Don, F. P., Major	153	———— G. R. J., 2/Lt.	30	Edgar, A. P., 2/Lt.	62	Ellison, H., 2/Lt.	95
Donald, J. A., 2/Lt.	108	Ducray, M. J., Lieut.	165	———— J., Lieut.	122	———— J. H. E., 2/Lt.	31
Donaldson, E. J., Major	62	Duff, F. M., 2/Lt.	20	———— J., Capt.	51	Ellmann, J., Capt.	17
———— F. L. H., 2/Lt.	111	———— R. W., Lieut.	175	Edge, A. H., 2/Lt.	127	Ellwood, A. G. F., Lieut.	78
———— J., 2/Lt.	119	Duff-Taylor, S., Capt.	114	Edkins, R. A., 2/Lt.	123	———— D. E., 2/Lt.	102
———— M., Capt.	134	Dugan, H. G., Lieut.	161	Edmonds, E. J. L., 2/Lt.	137	———— E. S., Lieut.	51
———— R., Sub.-Lt.	144	Dugdale, J. G., 2/Lt.	169	———— E. P. P., 2/Lt.	160	Elmitt, J. G., Lieut.	121
Doncaster, A. E., 2/Lt.	167	Duggan, T. F., Capt.		———— G. M., Lieut.	81	Elphinston, C., 2/Lt.	149
Donell, F., 2/Lt.	35	Rev.	135	———— P., Lt.	185	Elston, A. J., 2/Lt.	35
Donnelly, J. A., Lieut.	10	Duggins, C. J., 2/Lt.	21	Edmunds, C., Capt.	131	———— W. E., Lieut.	178
———— W. J., Lieut.	103	Duggleby, R., 2/Lt.	43	Edmundson, S., 2/Lt.	119	Eltham, G., 2/Lt.	29
Donoghue, P. E., Lieut.	184	Dugmore, W. L. E.,		Edsted, F., Lieut.	173	Elton, G., Lieut.	187
Donovan, J. J., Lieut.	47	Capt.	54	Edward, E. J., Lieut.	15	Eltringham, A., 2/Lt.	129
Dooley, J. A., 2/Lt.	186	Duke, L. G., Lieut.	21	———— J. D., 2/Lt.	104	Elvin, A. J., 2/Lt.	164
Doorley, J., 2/Lt.	113	———— R. E., Lieut.	160	Edwards, Capt.	162	Elwes, R. P., Capt.	18
Dore, J. W., 2/Lt.	86	Dumaresq, R. G., Capt.	120	————	180	Elwig, H. J. C., 2/Lt.	172
Dorling, L. H. G., Capt.	185	Dunand, A. M., Lieut.	117	———— A. G., 2/Lt.	131	Elworthy, L., Lieut.	173
Dougall, A. R., 2/Lt.	54	Duncan, H. J., 2/Lt.	39	———— A. V., 2/Lt.	30	Ely, E. J. W., 2/Lt.	83
———— C. R., 2/Lt.	150	———— R. R., Capt.	132	———— E. H., 2/Lt.	52	Emberson, A. E., 2/Lt.	72
———— H. F., 2/Lt.	159	———— W., Lieut.	33	———— E. L., 2/Lt.	152	Emblem, E., Lieut.	73
Dougan, W. L., Lieut.	173	———— W. H., 2/Lt.	112	———— G., Lieut.	77	Emerson, J. M., 2/Lt.	118
Dougherty, B. H. L.,		Dunford, E. T., 2/Lt.	151	———— G. B., Capt.	32	Emmett, R. B., Lieut.	78
Capt.	142	Dunley, O. L., 2/Lt.	112	———— G. H., 2/Lt.	32	Emslie, A., 2/Lt.	68
Doughty, E. C., Major	37	Dunlop, G. B., Lieut.	172	———— G. R., 2/Lt.	157	Enderby, S. H., Lt.-Col.	24
Douglas, A. B., Capt.	60	———— H., Lieut.	187	———— H., 2/Lt.	176	Endsor, W., 2/Lt.	106
———— A. S. D., Baird,		———— J. M., 2/Lt.	168	———— H. J., 2/Lt.	57	England, R., Capt., M.C.	38
Lieut.	23	———— W. F., Capt.	134	———— J. E., Lieut.	136	English, C. V., Sub.-Lt.	144
———— Ed. M., Lieut.	72	Dunn, E. G., Major	182	———— J. L. A., Capt.,		———— J. W., 2/Lt.	16
———— J. H., Lieut.	140	———— E. J., 2/Lt.	52	Rev.	135	———— T. H., 2/Lt.	42
———— M. B., Major	122	———— C. P., 2/Lt.	121	———— J. R., 2/Lt.	12	———— W., 2/Lt.	156
———— S. C. M., Lieut.	105	———— M. A., Lieut.	170	———— L. D., Lieut.	36	Enright, J. E., Lieut.	119
———— W. L., 2/Lt.	19	———— M. W., 2/Lt.	174	———— R. H., 2/Lt.	94	———— T. N., 2/Lt.	176
Douglass, E. C., Lieut.	123	———— R. H., 2/Lt.	165	———— R. O., 2/Lt.	35	Entwisle, N., 2/Lt.	80
Dow, J. N., Lieut.	135	Dunnington, J. W., 2/Lt.	40	———— R. W., 2/Lt.	92	Entwistle, J. M. B.,	
Dowden, L. F., 2/Lt.	118	Dunscombe, G., Lieut.	96	———— W. E., 2/Lt.	71	Capt.	178
Dower, T., 2/Lt.	126	Dunster, C. H., Lieut.	163	Egan, S. F., 2/Lt.	27	Erskine, B. L., Capt.	94
Dowie, A. B. B., 2/Lt.	20	Dunsworth, D., Capt.	136	———— W., Capt.	131	Esler, M. S., Capt.	134
Down, R. T., 2/Lt.	172	Dunthorne, S. W., 2/Lt.	30	Eidmans, S., 2/Lt.	116	Estcourt, T. E. S., Capt.	8
Downes, A., 2/Lt.	71	Dupre, H. E., 2/Lt.	126	Elcock, R. R. E., 2/Lt.	61	Estridge, I. A., Lieut.	39
Downing, A., Lieut.	66	Dupree, V., Capt.	124	Elder, J. G., Capt.	132	Etherton, H., 2/Lt.	69
———— H. G. O., Lieut.	47	Durant, W. M., Lieut.	141	Ell, N. S., 2/Lt.	84	Evans, A. J., Major	181
Downman, T. F. C., 2/Lt.	77	Durkin, F. V., 2/Lt.	153	Ellam, H. J., Lieut.	155	———— A. J., Capt.	148

Name	PAGE
Evans, A. M. G., Lieut...	56
———— A. W. R., 2/Lt.	174
———— D.	86
———— D. C., 2/Lt. ...	21
———— E. V., Lieut.	73
———— F. M. St. H., Lieut. ...	73
———— H. B., Lieut.	164
———— H. F., 2/Lt. ...	149
———— H. G., 2/Lt.	55
———— H. W. D., 2/Lt.	86
———— J., 2/Lt. ...	73
———— N. W., Brig.-Gen. ...	182
———— R. B., Capt....	20
———— R. D., 2/Lt.	91
———— R. du Boulay, 2/Lt.	86
———— R. J., Lieut....	31
———— W., Lieut. ...	97
———— W. A., Capt.	46
———— W. D., 2/Lt.	171
———— W. G., 2/Lt.	37
Eveleigh, F. R., 2/Lt. ...	173
Everard, A. J., Capt. ...	180
Everitt, J. W., 2/Lt. ...	92
Evershed, A. P., Major, M.C.	13
Evitt, C. V., 2/Lt.	131
Ewart, G. D., Major	71
Ewen, L. McK....	59
Exley, J., 2/Lt. ...	39
Eyden, M. V., 2/Lt. ...	81
Eyre, B. J., Lieut. ...	110
———— F., Lieut. ...	52
Eyres, L. H., 2/Lt. ...	175
Faber, L. E., Major	120
Facer, G. S., 2/Lt. ...	65
Fairall, T. W. R., 2/Lt.	89
Fairbank, F. E., 2/Lt....	41
Fairbairn, J. V., 2/Lt....	150
Fairclough, P. H. E., 2/Lt.	87
Fairfax, H. H., Capt. ...	132
Fairhurst, A., 2/Lt. ...	172
Fairweather, I., Lieut.	54
Falconer, W., Lieut. ...	107
Falkenberg, G. D., Lieut.	160
Fane, H. W. N., 2/Lt. ...	12
Faraday, M. S., 2/Lt. ...	149
Farbon, S. E., 2/Lt., M.C.	81
Farbrother, E. S., Lieut.	182
Farmar, W. C. R., Major	185
Farmer, A., 2/Lt. ...	144
———— A. E., 2/Lt. ...	82
———— E. R., Lieut.	148
———— G. M. G., Lieut.	15
———— N. J. C., Capt.	16
———— S. A., 2/Lt. ...	43
Farnham, A. K., Lt.-Col. Lord	60
Farquhar, J., Lieut. ...	166
Farquharson, A. A., Lieut.	20
———— A. G., 2/Lt. ...	58
———— F. B., 2/Lt. ...	157
———— R. J., Lieut....	174
Farquharson-Hicks, V., Lieut.	48
Farr, L. C., 2/Lt. ...	62
Farrand, E. S., Lieut. ...	176
Farrar, G. R., 2/Lt. ...	74
Farrell, J., 2/Lt. ...	115
———— J. T., 2/Lt. ...	48
———— P., 2/Lt. ...	53
Farren, R. H., Major ...	11
Farrington, C. H., 2/Lt.	128
Farrow, G. H., 2/Lt. ...	123
Faulder, J. H., Lieut. ...	27
Faulds, W. F., V.C., 2/Lt.	142
Faulkner, B. B., Lieut.	9
Fawcett, E., Capt., M.C.	99
Fawkes, W. G. S., 2/Lt.	178
Fawsett, F. W., Capt. ...	131
Fearnside, F., Lieut. ...	137
Featherstone, L. W., 2/Lt.	26
Feetham, O. J., Capt. ...	68
Feez, C. M., Lieut. ...	138
Fehr, A. H., 2/Lt. ...	85
Fell, A. J., Lieut. ...	137
———— C. A., Lieut....	11
Fellowes, H. V., Lieut.	169
———— P. F. M., Lt.-Col.	163
Felton, C. T., 2/Lt. ...	154
Fenn, L. N., 2/Lt. ...	123
Fennell, A. H., 2/Lt. ...	17
Fenner, H. R., Capt. ...	83
Fenton, C. B., 2/Lt....	160
———— W. G., Lieut. ...	35
Fenwick, B., Capt. ...	65
———— C., 2/Lt. ...	44
———— T. B., 2/Lt. ...	156
———— W., 2/Lt. ...	22
Fereman, A. E., 2/Lt. ...	152
Ferguson, H. A., 2/Lt....	138
———— J. A., 2/Lt. ...	160
———— J. D., Lieut. ...	20
———— J. F., Capt. ...	179
———— J. G. W., 2/Lt.	125
———— J. J., Lieut. ...	107
———— R. G., Capt. ...	53
———— W., 2/Lt. ...	109
———— W. G., 2/Lt....	34
Fergusson, J. A., Capt.	36
Fernie, W. Y., 2/Lt. ...	68
Ferrand, J. P. B., Major	187
Ferte, J. de la, Lieut. ...	146
Fessenden, C. V., Lieut.	139
Ffrench, C. F. T. O'B., Lieut.	47
Field, C. A., 2/Lt. ...	127
———— F. L. A., 2/Lt. ...	125
———— G., 2/Lt. ...	23
———— G. B., Capt. ...	140
———— G. C., Capt. ...	29
———— H., 2/Lt. ...	120
Fielder, T. L., Lieut. ...	40
Fielding, H., 2/Lt. ...	114
Fielding-Clarke, A., 2/Lt.	159
Fife, N. B., 2/Lt. ...	54
Filby, T. C., Capt. ...	21
Fillery, T. C., 2/Lt. ...	22
Finch, A. W. B., 2/Lt....	116
———— F. E., 2/Lt. ...	171
———— L. H., Capt. ...	77
———— L. H. K., Lt.-Col. ...	70
———— W. G., 2/Lt. ...	121
Findlay, A. S., Lieut. ...	134
———— J., Lieut. ...	134
Findley, H. E., 2/Lt. ...	25
Fine, H., Capt. ...	22
Finlay, F. L., Lieut. ...	108
Finlayson, A., 2/Lt. ...	15
Finnerty, H. C., Lieut.	148
Firminger, F. W., 2/Lt.	32
Firstbrook, J. H., 2/Lt.	147
Firth, C. R., 2/Lt. ...	40
———— G., Lieut. ...	9
———— H. W., Lieut. ...	35
Fisher, C. C., 2/Lt. ...	171
———— E. L., Major...	95
Fisher, H. B., Lieut. ...	113
———— H. G., Major, A/Lt.-Col., D.S.O. ...	13
———— H. L. H., 2/Lt.	15
———— J., 2/Lt. ...	60
———— J. E., 2/Lt. ...	24
———— J. R., 2/Lt. ...	20
———— R. E., 2/Lt.	26
Fison, F. G., Capt. ...	91
Fitch, W. R., 2/Lt. ...	76
Fitzgerald, H. C., 2/Lt.	137
———— J., Capt. ...	47
———— J. J., 2/Lt. ...	156
———— M. R., Lieut. ...	18
———— R. J., Lieut., M.C. ...	62
Fitzgibbon, C. J., 2/Lt.	161
Fitzmaurice, W., Rev....	135
Fitzpatrick, H. A. C., Capt. ...	44
———— R. D., 2/Lt. ...	42
Fitzroy, R., Lieut. ...	18
Fitzwygram, F. L. F., Capt., Sir ...	18
Flanagan, J. T., 2/Lt.	60
Fleetwood, C. P., 2/Lt.	129
———— G. C., Capt. ...	53
Fleming, A., Lieut. ...	59
———— E. L., Lieut.	68
———— F., Lt.-Col. ...	13
———— F. N., 2/Lt. ...	15
———— J. A. M., 2/Lt.	157
———— P. J. A., 2/Lt.	171
Flere, C. H., 2/Lt. ...	160
Fletcher, A., 2/Lt. ...	173
———— A. D. S. A., Capt. ...	64
———— G., 2/Lt. ...	64
———— W. T., Lieut. ...	143
Flight, H. E., 2/Lt. ...	82
———— O. T., Lieut. ...	138
Flint, A. H., Lieut. ...	15
———— C., 2/Lt. ...	89
Flintoft, H. T., Lieut. ...	167
Florance, J. B., Capt. ...	28
Flower, N. L., Capt. ...	94
Floyd, A. B., Capt. ...	186
———— H., 2/Lt. ...	148
Floyer, E. A., Lieut. ...	179
Fluke, W. G., Lieut. ...	160
Flux, R. L., Lieut. ...	185
Flynn, G. E. C., 2/Lt. ...	182
———— J. A. A., 2/Lt. ...	49
Foggo, N. O. N., Lieut.	167
Foley, H. A., Capt. ...	39
Foljambe, E. W. S., Lieut.	114
Folkard, G. D'A., 2/Lt.	136
Fooks, E. L., 2/Lt. ...	188
Footman, D. J., Capt....	83
Footner, F. L., Major ...	187
Forbes, A. G., Lieut. ...	187
———— C. A., Lieut. ...	182
———— E. E., Major	185
———— G. W., 2/Lt....	157
———— H., 2/Lt. ...	102
———— J. N., Lt.-Col.	93
———— M. H. O., Capt.	106
———— S. Alex., Capt.	133
Ford, E. L., 2/Lt. ...	64
———— H. S., 2/Lt. ...	68
Forder, E. G., Lieut. ...	162
Fordham, R. S. W., Lieut.	139
Foreshew, C. E. P., Capt.	75
Forman, H., Lieut. ...	54
———— J. H., Capt. ...	170
Formilli, G. C., Lieut. ...	147
Forrest, L. H., Lieut. ...	167
———— N. V., 2/Lt. ...	114
———— W. A., 2/Lt. ...	74
Forrester, G. R., 2/Lt....	19
Forsdike, L., Lieut. ...	86
Forse, L. N., Rev. ...	135
Forshaw, J., Lieut. ...	80
Forster, E. S., Capt. ...	32
———— H. K., 2/Lt....	128
———— L. A., Capt. ...	54
———— L. P., 2/Lt. ...	117
Forsyth, A. F., Lieut. ...	167
———— D. M., Lieut. ...	105
———— D. S., 2/Lt. ...	91
———— W. A., Capt. ...	165
Forward, E. R., 2/Lt. ...	123
Foss, B. T., Capt and Adjt....	90
Fosse, E. L., 2/Lt. ...	157
Foster, A. E., 2/Lt. ...	102
———— E., Fl. Sub.-Lt. ...	177
———— F. P., Lieut....	78
———— G. E., Capt. ...	126
———— J. W., 2/Lt. ...	55
———— L. J., Lieut.	101
———— P. J., Major ...	28
———— P. La T., 2/Lt.	160
———— R. C. G., Capt.	21
———— W., Lieut. ...	70
———— W. E., Capt. ...	176
———— W. E., Sub.-Lt. ...	181
Foster-Sutton, S. W. P., Lieut.	167
Fothergill, R. A., 2/Lt.	61
Foulds, C. L., Capt. ...	41
———— D. T., 2/Lt. ...	87
Foulkes, K., Lieut. ...	47
———— R. W., 2/Lt. ...	32
Foulkes—Roberts, P. R., Capt.	56
Fowke, G. H. G., Capt.	106
Fowler, C. W., Capt. ...	134
Fowles, S., Lieut. ...	186
Fox, A. G., Capt. ...	136
———— A. R., 2/Lt. ...	127
———— C. V., Capt. ...	18
———— D. S., Lieut. ...	174
———— H., Capt. ...	130
———— J. R., 2/Lt. ...	168
———— L. H., Capt.	184
———— R. W., Lieut.	95
———— T. M., Lieut.	144
Foy, G., 2/Lt.	111
Frame, G. S., Lieut. ...	189
Frampton, H. L., 2/Lt.	38
Francis, C. E., 2/Lt. ...	170
———— F. H., 2/Lt. ...	72
———— F. W., Lieut.	54
———— L. E., Capt. ...	92
———— R. F., 2/Lt. ...	103
———— R. H., 2/Lt....	87
———— W. F., Lieut.	131
———— W. J., Lieut.	87
Frank, C. C., 2/Lt. ...	41
———— C. O., Lieut....	14
———— J. N., Capt. ...	68
Franklin, J. S., 2/Lt. ...	58
Fraser, A., 2/Lt. ...	152
———— Hon. A. A. ...	105
———— A. H., Capt....	137
———— A. S., Capt. ...	71

	PAGE		PAGE		PAGE		PAGE
Fraser, H. N., Capt.	140	Gallagher, J. R., 2/Lt.	137	George, T. L., Lieut.	37	Glover, R. E., 2/Lt.	110
Fraser-Lyn, Capt., M.C.	105	Gallie, A. H., Lieut.	76	Gerrity, W. B., 2/Lt.	40	Gluyas, O. S., Lieut.	136
Fraser-MacKenzie, 2/Lt	105	Galloway, W., Lieut.	184	Gerson, Louis M., 2/Lt.	161	Glynn, T. W., Lieut.	94
Frayne, E., Lieut.	87	Gallup, H. C., Lieut.	185	Gerstenberg, R.A., 2/Lt.	53	Goodhugh, P. H., Lieut.	169
Frazer, A., Lieut.	47	Galvin, B. St. J., Capt.,		Geyton, John A., 2/Lt.	71	Goad, C. R., Lieut.	180
——— A. E. G., Capt.	131	M.C.	110	Gibbon, R.N.R., Major	96	——— J.F.E., Lieut.	90
Frazier, R. W., Sub.-Lt.	188	Gamage, L. C., Capt.	130	Gibbons, F. R., 2/Lt.	35	Goddard, J. S., Lieut.	157
Free, J. A., 2/Lt., M.C.	33	Gamble, H., 2/Lt.	72	——— P. H., Lieut.	11	——— Samuel George,	
Freedman, E., 2/Lt.	131	——— P. A., Lieut.	28	——— S. W., Sub-Lt.	144	2/Lt. ...	24
Freeland, K. F., Capt.	185	Ganley S., Lieut.	125	———Wm., Lieut.	95	Goddin, P., 2/Lt.	100
——— J. H. K., 2/Lt.	110	Garbett, L. C., 2/Lt.	72	Gibbs, A. C. H., 2/Lt.	137	Godfrey, A. D., 2/Lt.	46
Freeman, F. P., 2/Lt.	95	Garbutt, D. G., 2/Lt.	40	——— G. M., 2/Lt.	31	——— E. N., Lieut.	11
——— J., 2/Lt.	176	Garden, Douglas, Lieut.	79	——— J. A., Lt.-Col.	67	——— F., Capt.	21
——— L. W., 2/Lt.	89	Gardiner, G. G., Capt.	136	——— J. D., 2/Lt.	142	Godly, A., Capt.	84
——— W., 2/Lt.	76	——— Noel, Lieut.	127	——— J. E., Capt.	18	Godman, F. T., Capt.	69
French, A. W., 2/Lt.	40	——— J. T., 2/Lt.	108	——— J. W., 2/Lt.	69	——— J., Capt.	9
——— C. E., Lieut.	153	——— W. C., Capt.	179	Gibson, A., 2/Lt.	27	Godsal, P., Capt.	75
——— E. F., 2/Lt.	12	Gardner, J.A.S., Lieut.	140	——— A. J. E., Lieut.	109	Godsall, S. A., Capt.	63
——— F. J., 2/Lt.	122	——— J. W., 2/Lt.	40	——— C. C. G., Capt.	133	Godson, R. G., Lieut.	17
——— G. S., Lieut.	152	——— R. D., Major	189	——— E. G., 2/Lt.	72	Goetz, C. E. G., Major	10
——— H. R., Capt.	15	——— W. F., 2/Lt.	17	——— E. M., 2/Lt.	55	Goffe, W., Lieut.	167
Fretz, W. L. E., Capt.	181	——— W.H.D., Sub-		——— Geo. M., 2/Lt.	27	Going, A. J., 2/Lt.	13
Frew, J. G. H., 2/Lt.	152	Lieut.	145	——— J., 2/Lt.	20	Gold, D. G., Lieut.	161
Fricker, A. J., Lieut.	165	Garewal, A. S., Lieut.	143	——— J. A., 2/Lt.	60	Goldfrap, H. W., Capt.	183
Frielinghaus, A., Lieut.	141	Garland, E. H., 2/Lt.	155	——— J. E., Lieut.,	91	Goldie, G. N., Lieut.	159
Friend, E. J., 2/Lt.	123	——— F. G., Capt.	131	——— J. G., 2/Lt.	107	Golding, C. B., Capt.,	
Frisby, E. R., 2/Lt.	124	——— F. J. R., 2/Lt.	61	——— J. H. S., 2/Lt.	32	M.C.	13
Frith, R. G., 2/Lt.	157	Garlies, Lord, 2/Lt.	18	——— Norman, Lieut	44	——— K. L., 2/Lt.	157
Frost, H. G., 2/Lt.	147	Garner, Robert K., 2/Lt	114	——— P., 2/Lt.	101	——— W., Major	13
——— J. W., 2/Lt.	156	——— W. P., 2/Lt.	73	——— P. D., 2/Lt.	127	Goldingham, G.R., Capt	117
Fry, C. W., Lieut.	128	Garnett, F., 2/Lt.	15	——— P. J., Lieut.	48	Goldsack, L. J., 2/Lt.	92
——— D. A. B., 2/Lt.	30	——— J. N., Lieut.	179	——— W.H.K., 2/Lt.	110	Goldsmith, R. L., Lieut.	16
——— H. E., 2/Lt.	83	Garnham, T. W. Scott		Gilbert, C. G., Lieut.	150	——— R. P., 2/Lt.	130
——— H. W., Lieut.	82	2/Lt.	129	——— F. C., 2/Lt.	159	Goldstein, L., Lieut.	10
——— R. H., 2/Lt.	39	Garrard, J.G., Capt., M.C.	25	——— L., Lt.-Col.	79	Gompertz, H. T. C. 2/Lt	176
——— W., Major	131	——— P., Major	189	——— R. S., 2/Lt.	157	Gondre, Jean, 2/Lt.	166
Fryar, M.S., Capt.	77	Garrett, A. L., Lieut.	165	Gilbertson, H. Marshall		Gonne, M. E., Capt.	167
Fryer, A. E., 2/Lt.	62	——— B. N., 2/Lt.	165	Lieut.	133	Gooch, H. C., Sub-Lt.	177
——— C., Capt.	139	——— J. C., 2/Lt.	157	Gilchrist, W., 2/Lt.	153	Goodall, J. H H., Lieut.	153
——— F. E., Capt.	176	Garrity, Wm. J., Lieut.	166	——— W.F.G., Major	183	Goodbehere, P., 2/Lt.	157
——— F. E., Capt.	15	Garrow, W., 2/Lt.	33	Gile, H. H., 1st Lieut.	164	Goodchap, A. F., 2/Lt.	158
——— H. G., 2/Lt.	107	Garstang, T., Lieut.	142	Gilfillan, J. A., Capt.	132	Goode, H. M., Lieut.	146
——— K. G., 2/Lt.	84	Gascoyne, B. B., Lieut.	119	Gill, A. W., 2/Lt.	103	——— R. J. E. P.	
——— P. S., Capt.	39	——— C., Capt.	78	——— C.E.G., Lieut.	169	Lieut.	157
Fulford, E., Lieut.	172	Gaskell, R. W., Capt.	143	Gillan, Chas. J., Lieut.	162	——— S. C., Lieut.	123
Fuller, O. L., 2/Lt.	130	Gasson, C. B., 2/Lt.	181	Gillespie, D., Capt.	134	Goodenough, K.M. 2/Lt.	14
Fullerton, A., Sub.-Lt.	144	——— C. G., Capt.	25	——— J. M., Lieut.	131	Gooderham, S.E., Lieut.	141
Fulton, E. J., 2/Lt.	180	——— N. E., 2/Lt.	43	——— J. W., 2/Lt.	155	Goodfellow, S. J., 2/Lt.	175
——— E. P., Lieut.	155	Gatacre, W. E., Capt.	85	——— R. D., 2/Lt.	106	Gooding, Jack A., 2/Lt.	142
——— J., 2/Lt.	165	Gates, C. E., 2/Lt.	15	Gillet, W. H. G., 2/Lt.	172	Goodison, F. B., 2/Lt.	181
Furbisher, J. W., 2/Lt.	110	——— Richard, Lieut	49	Gilliat, R. S., Lieut.	82	Goodman, E. V., Lieut.	11
Furlonger, C. A., Lieut.	153	Gateshill, H. V., 2/Lt.	26	Gillies, W. L., Lieut.	74	Goodrich, H, A., Lieut	133
Furmidge, P. W., Lieut	141	Gatherer, A., Capt.,	183	——— J., Capt.	103	Goodridge, T.W.W., 2/Lt	11
Furneaux, T. E., 2/Lt.	183	Gatheral, G. M., 2/Lt.	33	Gilliland, L. G., 2/Lt.	79	Goodsall, W., Lieut.	137
Furnell, G. O. E., Capt.	47	——— T. M., Lieut.	14	——— W. E., Lieut.	188	Goodship, G. R., Lieut.	83
——— M., Col.	110	Gaul, A., Lieut.,	140	Gillings, V. De F., 2/Lt.	127	Goodson, A. R. L., 2/Lt.	147
Furness J., Major	131	Gay, G., 2/Lt.	117	Gillitt, W., Lieut.	81	——— E. J., Lieut.	138
Furniss, A. S., Capt.	99	Gaye, A. D., Capt.	146	Gillmore, N. J., 2/Lt.	52	Goodwin, F. W., 2/Lt.	50
——— K. R., 2/Lt.	152	Gayer, J. H. C., Lieut.	186	Gilmer, E. H., 2/Lt.	111	——— S.T.W., 2/Lt.	178
Furrell, B., 2/Lt.	51	Gayford, D. B., 2/Lt.	147	Gilmour, L. C., Lieut.	166	Goolden, R. O., 2/Lt.	62
Furze, E. K. B., Lt.-Col.	93	Gaynor, H. F., 2/Lt.	188	——— S. G., Capt.	169	Gopsill, J. E., 2/Lt.	29
Fyfe, R.J.R. Duff, Lieut	164	Gaze, I. O., Lieut.,	175	Ginger, H. S., 2/Lt.	126	Gordon, Chas. A., Lieut.	163
		Gedge, G., 2/Lt.	173	Girling, F. A., Lieut.	45	——— E. G. S., Lieut	158
Gadd, C. B., Lieut.	141	Gee, F. W., 2/Lt.	65	Gladstone, C. A., Lieut.	146	——— G. N., Lieut.	139
——— H. R., Lt.-Col.		Geen, C., 2/Lt.	148	——— T. H., 2/Lt.	127	——— John, 2/Lt.	121
M.C.	77	Geggie, D., 2/Lt.	26	Glanville, A. E., 2/Lt.	25	——— J. A., Lieut.	133
——— W. G., 2/Lt.	175	Gell, E. A. S., Lt.-Col.	51	——— L. S. H., Capt.	132	——— J. R., Lieut.	74
Gade, F. W., Capt.	30	Gemmel, H. J., 2/Lt.	175	Glass, H. E. L., Capt.	87	——— Jas. S., Capt.	40
Gage, C. R., 2-Lt.	170	Gemmell, T., 2/Lt.	112	Glasspoole, G. H., 2/Lt.	164	——— Pat, 2/Lt.	11
Gage-Brown, C.J., Lieut	8	Genese, J. D., Hon.,		Gladding E., Lieut.	79	——— W., 2/Lt.	106
Galbraith, R. F., 2/Lt.,		Capt. and Qmr.	134	Glazebrook, R. F., Lieut.	169	——— W. E., Col., V.C.	105
M.C.	119	Gentry-Birch, C., Capt.	83	Gleave, P. N., 2/Lt.	15	Gordon-Ralph, P. L. N.	
Galer, H. E., 2/Lt.	159	George, H. D. K., Lieut.	151	Glenn, G. F., 2/Lt.	15	2/Lt.	111
Gall, W. S., Lieut.	14	——— J. B., Capt.	47	Glover, C., 2/Lt.	45	Gore, F. D. C., 2/Lt.	159
Gallagher, B. J., Lieut.	133	——— P. A. R., 2/Lt.	33	——— G. E., Capt.	67	——— M., Lieut.	136
——— E. G., Lieut.	171	——— T. E., 2/Lt.	34			Gore-Brown, R. F., 2/Lt.	10

	PAGE		PAGE		PAGE		PAGE
Goring, A. L., 2/Lt. A/Capt.	49	Gray, Frank, 2/Lt.	129	Grice, L. C., Capt., M.C.	98	Hacklett, L. A., Lieut.	163
Gorman, G. W., Lieut.	167	——— G., Capt.	50	Grier, H. D., Brig-Gen.	184	Hackman, T., Fl.-Com.	181
Gormley, A. J. C., 2/Lt.	169	——— G. A., 2/Lt.	100	Grierson, C. D., 2/Lt.	153	Hackney, J.S.G., Lieut.	73
Goschen, C. G., Lieut.	17	——— G. Morgan, Lt.	164	Grieve, L., 2/Lt.	136	Hadden, A. Barnes, 2/Lt.	48
Gosden, A. C., Lieut.	72	——— H., Lieut.	110	——— M. D., 2/Lt.	35	——— C. S., Lieut.	116
Gosling, H. M., Lt.-Ccl.	90	——— H. M., 2/Lt.	75	——— W. F., 2/Lt.	108	——— F. K., 2/Lt.	31
Gosmore, E., 2/Lt.	11	——— J., 2/Lt.	25	Griffin, E. H., Capt.	132	Haddock, R., Lieut.	104
Gotch, D. I., Lieut.	81	——— J. A., Capt.	164	——— G. B., 2/Lt.	94	Haddon, C. L., 2/Lt.	100
Gott, J. I., 2/Lt.	100	——— J. B., Capt.	92	——— H., 2/Lt.	81	——— J. B., Capt.	28
——— W. H. E., Lieut.	90	——— J. H., 2/Lt.	12	——— J.A.A., Lt.-Col	82	——— R. J., 2/Lt.	100
Gough, C., Lieut.	44	——— K. W., Lieut.	147	——— J. W., Capt.	29	Haddow, Robert B., 2/Lt.	82
——— G.V.H., Lieut.	90	——— R. A., Major	110	——— R. T., 2/Lt.	148	Hadley, G. H., Lieut.	29
——— R.G.H., 2/Lt.	75	——— R. H., Lieut.	165	Griffith, H. M., Capt.	91	Hadlow, Wm., 2/Lt.	142
——— T. A., 2/Lt.	71	——— R. G., Sub.-Lt.	144	——— J. C., 2/Lt.	154	Hadrill, G. C. T., 2/Lt.	153
Gould, K. W., 2/Lt.	108	——— T. A., 2/Lt.	103	——— J.F.U., Capt.	51	Hadwick, W., 2/Lt.	50
——— S., 2/Lt.	128	——— V. C., 2/Lt.	75	——— J. W., 2/Lt.	95	Haffield, C. C., 2/Lt.	63
——— W. T., 2/Lt.	30	——— William, Lieut.	48	——— T. C., Lieut.	79	Hagen, E. C., Capt.	10
Goulding, H. B., Capt.	61	——— Wm. A., Lieut.	141	——— W. H. E. N. Lieut.	95	Hagenbush, R. J., 2/Lt.	173
Gourlay, Wm. N., 2/Lt.	114	——— W. J., 2/Lt.	149	Griffith-Jones, Melville P., Capt.	99	Hague, W., 2/Lt.	77
Govan, H. F. C., 2/Lt.	74	——— W.M.R., 2/Lt.	160	Griffiths, C. D., 2/Lt.	148	Haig, A. B., Capt.	183
Gow, J. E., Lieut.	166	Grayston, A. V., Lieut.	101	——— E. C., 2/Lt.	92	——— A. E., Major	58
——— W.S.P., 2/Lt.	91	——— S. E., 2/Lt.	77	——— F. W., 2/Lt.	148	——— A L., Lieut.	21
Gower, O. C. D., Lieut.	136	Greaves, H. P., Capt.	78	——— H. E., 2/Lt.	57	——— F. W., Lieut.	179
——— E. W., Lieut.	113	——— J. A., 2/Lt.	63	——— T. E., Rev.	135	Haigh, G. D., 2/Lt.	127
Grace, H. C., Capt.	81	Green, A. G. N., Lieut.	101	Grigg, Raymond, Lieut.	85	——— J., Lieut.	99
——— W. A., 2/Lt.	141	——— E. G., Lieut.	159	Griggs, B. L., Lieut.	59	Haight, J. L., 2/Lt.	156
——— W. J., Capt.	128	——— E. M. L., 2/Lt.	45	Grimwade, F. N., 2/Lt.	147	——— W. L., Capt.	180
Gracey, R. V., 2/Lt.	109	——— G. A., 2/Lt.	49	Grimwood, F. R., Major A/Lt.-Col.	130	——— W.R.W., Capt.	140
Gracie, J. McA. C., 2/Lt.	54	——— G. W., 2/Lt.	82	——— H., Lieut.	97	Haighton, E. S., Lieut.	82
Graham, F., Lieut.	101	——— H. D., 2/Lt.	118	Grinling, F. W., Capt.	25	Haile, W. L., 2/Lt.	83
——— F. H. H., 2/Lt.	52	——— J. H., 2/Lt.	47	Grinnell-Milne, D. D. Capt.	147	Hair, N. B., 2/Lt.	153
——— G. L., Capt.	29	——— P. H., Capt.	133	——— D. W., Lieut.	147	Haldane, G. C., 2/Lt.	112
——— Henry, Capt.	25	——— R., Lieut., M.C.	100	Groner, R. E. A., Lieut.	77	Hale, L. E., Lieut.	84
——— H. A., 2/Lt.	127	——— R. R., 2/Lt.	12	Gross, C. R., Lieut.	172	Haley, H., 2/Lt.	33
——— H. P., 2/Lt.	115	——— W., Capt.	21	Grosset, W. E., Lieut.	154	Halford, A. E., 2/Lt.	147
——— J., Capt.	131	——— W. H., Lieut.	151	Grosvenor, Lord G., Lieut.	18	——— E. S., Capt.	182
——— J. R., Lieut.	122	——— W. E., 2/Lt.	13	Grout, E. J., Sub-Lt.	153	Halkyard, A., Lieut.	47
——— L. N., Capt.	148	Greenaway, G. K., 2/Lt.	58	Grover, C. W., Capt.	23	Hall, A. H., Major	109
——— M. A., Lieut.	141	Greene, G. E. D., Lieut.	139	——— F. C., Capt.	143	——— B., Lieut.	167
——— N., Lieut.	68	——— Wm. J., Capt.	114	Groves, J. O., Sub.-Lt.	146	——— C. C., 2/Lt.	75
——— Peter, Lieut.	25	Greenfield, C. R. M., 2/Lt.	26	Grundy, Percy, 2/Lt.	32	——— C. F., Capt.	84
——— R. P., Capt.	91	Greenhill, B. M., 2/Lt.	8	Guard, S. G., 2/Lt.	142	——— C. R., Capt.	113
——— W., 2/Lt.	14	Greenhow, H. M., 2/Lt.	99	Gubbins, J. R. F., 2/Lt.	188	——— C. R., Lieut.	164
Graham-Toler, L.J.,Capt.	87	——— M. W., 2/Lt.	146	Gudgeon, G.F.C., Lieut.	131	——— C. T. M., 2/Lt.	88
Graham-Watson, A. F., Capt.	19	Greenless, T., Capt.	112	——— R.E., Capt., M.C.	11	——— E. H., Lieut.	141
Granger, A. G., 2/Lt.	63	Greenslade, D. A., Capt.	61	Guest, J., Capt.	96	——— E. W., Capt.	89
——— T. E., Lt.	187	——— R. L., Lieut.	157	——— J.E.C., 2/Lt.	28	——— E.W.O., Lieut.	175
Grant, A., Rev., C. F.	135	Greensmith, E. B., Capt.	77	Guild C., 2/Lt.	171	——— G. W., Lieut.	40
——— A. E., Lieut.	22	——— W., 2/Lt.	77	Guildford, T.W.F., 2/Lt.	75	——— H. E., 2/Lt.	111
——— A. I., 2/Lt.	20	Greenstreet, T. W., 2/Lt.	188	Guise, V. R., Capt.	185	——— J. G., 2/Lt.	72
——— A. V. S., 2/Lt.	93	Greenwood, C. L. E., Lieut.	185	Gulich, J. D., 2/Lt.	33	——— J. N., Lieut.	26
——— D., Capt.	22	——— C. J. R., Capt.	16	Gulland, J. P., Lieut.	143	——— J. R., 2/Lt.	13
——— D. L., Capt.	147	——— G., 2/Lt.	11	Gummer, H. L., 2/Lt.	15	——— K.W.J., Lieut.	164
——— H. D., 2/Lt.	59	——— O., Lieut.	43	Gunn, A. A., 2/Lt.	105	——— L. C., Capt.	16
——— J. H., 2/Lt.	27	——— P.G., Lieut.	175	——— A. D., Capt.	184	——— L. G., 2/Lt.	171
——— Jack R., Capt. (A/Major), M.C.	17	Greer, S. P., 2/Lt.	123	——— J. C., 2/Lt.	172	——— M. A., Lieut.	36
——— R. A. P., Capt.	183	Gregg, C., 2/Lt.	59	——— J. D., Lieut.	139	——— M. E., 2/Lt.	156
Grant-Dalton, E. F., Capt.	39	Gregory, B. W., 2/Lt.	36	Gunner, F. H., Bde.-Maj	7	——— N. D., F.-Sub-Lt.	177
——— H., Lieut.	144	——— H. P., Lieut.	49	Gunston, F. J. D., 2/Lt.	62	——— R., Lieut.	173
——— L., Lieut.	71	——— H. W., 2/Lt.	71	Gurney, Henry, Capt.	8	——— Robert, 2/Lt.	11
Grantham, V. M., 2/Lt.	147	——— J. L., 2/Lt.	36	——— J., 2/Lt.	128	——— R. S., Agent	189
——— W., Capt.	67	——— M. C., 2/Lt.	119	——— K. G., 2/Lt.	61	——— T. F., 2/Lt.	110
Graves, Cecil, Lieut.	53	——— R. J., 2/Lt.	163	——— P. S., Lieut.	15	——— W. A., Lieut.	170
——— T. F., 2/Lt.	100	——— S. B., Lieut.	186	Gurtrell, W. H., Capt.	136	——— W. E., Lieut.	170
Gray, Archibald, 2/Lt.	115	Greig, C. W., 2/Lt.	188	Guthrie, H. S., 2/Lt.	74	Hallam, H. A., 2/Lt.	149
——— A. C. H., Lt.-Col.	134	——— D. S., Capt.	74	——— L. W., 2/Lt.	20	Hallenquist, J. E., Lieut.	175
——— B. W., Lieut.	33	——— G. G. F., 2/Lt.	115	Guy, C. G., 2/Lt.	155	Halley, G. S., 2/Lt.	82
——— Cyril, Lieut.	51	——— O., Capt.	150	Guyatt, T., 2/Lt.	117	Halliley, W. S., Lieut.	183
——— C. G. D., 2/Lt.	156	——— R., Lieut.	88	Gwyer, N. E., Lieut.	168	Hallinan, C., 2/Lt.	110
——— C. V., Lieut.	189	Grey, A. A. D., Lieut.	177	Gwynne, W. C., Lieut.	144	Halls, S., Lieut.	69
——— D. B., Capt.	149	——— J.P.B., Lieut.	101			Hallsmith, G., 2/Lt.	38
		——— R., Capt.	146	Hacking, E. J., 2/Lt.	93	Halstead, G. A., 2/Lt.	94
		Gribble, J. R., Capt., V.C.	29			Halvorsen, W. A., Lieut.	136
		——— R. H., 2/Lt.	10			Hambling, T. C., 2/Lt.	62

Name	Page	Name	Page	Name	Page	Name	Page
Hamer, R. B., Lieut.	96	Harman, A. J., Capt., M.C.	130	Harvey, Robt., Capt.	139	Heaton, R., 2/Lt.	98
Hamilton, G. S., Lieut.	112	——— C. E., Lieut.	89	——— R. G., Lieut.	37	Heaver, A. R., 2/Lt.	169
——— G., 2/Lt.	107	Harmer, J. M., 2/Lt.	38	——— S. A., 2/Lt.	23	Heawood, G. L., Lieut.	187
——— Gail, Lieut.	162	Harness, F. G., Lieut.	16	——— W. A., Lieut.	147	Hedges, A., 2/Lt.	30
——— G. C., Lieut.	139	Harnett, W. G., Capt.	134	Harvey-Samuel, G. D., Lieut.	88	Hedley, A. F., 2/Lt.	105
——— H. D., 2/Lt.	151	Harper, F., 2/Lt.	47	Haseler, G. F., 2/Lt.	150	——— J. H., Capt.	161
——— H. F. T., 2/Lt.	38	——— M. L., 2/Lt.	127	Haslam, Cyril, 2/Lt.	95	Heelis, H. L., 2/Lt.	52
——— I. B. M., Lieut.	106	——— S. A., Lieut.	155	——— C. G., 2/Lt.	78	Heggie, A. D., 2/Lt.	15
——— J. R., 2/Lt.	125	Harries, L. W., Capt.	188	Haslett, H. R., Major	43	Heine, R. W., Lieut.	171
——— W. N., Lieut.	152	Harrington, H., Capt.	39	Hastie, H. E., Lieut.	174	Hehir, P., Col.	184
Hamilton-Hamilton, Brig.-General	182	——— H.B.D., Lieut.	162	Hastings, E. W., Lieut.	45	Helder, L. B., Lieut.	149
Hamlet, F. A., Capt.	124	——— H. N., Lieut.	54	Hastings, H., Lieut.	51	Hele, G. Melvin, Capt.	62
——— H. A., 2/Lt.	175	——— T. F., 2/Ly.	22	Haswell, T. S., 2/Lt.	110	Hellier, Maurice J., Capt	87
Hammersley, F. J. B., 2/Lt.	158	Harris, A. C., 2/Lt.	77	Hatfield, A. C., Capt.	156	Helwig, N. W., Lieut.	172
Hammond, F., 2/Lt.	55	——— C. M., 2/Lt.	110	——— R. E., 2/Lt.	43	Hemmens, R. H., Lieut.	167
——— H. T., 2/Lt.	156	——— D. R., Lieut.	168	Hatherall, W. C., 2/Lt.	110	Hempel, A. E., 2/Lt.	157
——— John, Lieut.	144	——— E. E., 2/Lt.	110	Hatton, G. A. L., Capt.	83	Hemphill, H. H., Capt.	46
——— R. M., Lieut.	11	——— F. E., Lieut.	36	——— J., 2/Lt.	40	Hempsall, H. T., 2/Lt.	171
Hammonds, E. H., 2/Lt.	37	——— H., 2/Lt.	153	Haughton, J. W., Capt.	38	Hemstock, F., 2/Lt.	79
Hampton, J. D., 2/Lt.	123	——— H., Lieut.	145	——— S. Capt.	184	Henderson, A. B., 2/Lt.	172
——— P. R., Lieut.	162	——— H. R. Dale, Lieut.	11	——— S. P. O., Lieut	187	——— B. M., Capt.	107
Hancock, C., Lieut.	174	——— J. A., 2/Lt.	92	Havill, F., 2/Lt.	76	——— E. E. J., 2/Lt.	94
——— F. W., Lieut.	179	——— N. B., 2/Lt.	163	Haward, C. P., Capt.	21	——— G., 2/Lt.	89
——— H.L.N., Lieut.	180	——— J. H., Lieut.	187	Hawker, H., Sub-Lt.	145	——— G., 2/Lt.	106
——— W. H., 2/Lt.	120	——— R. T., 2/Lt.	28	Hawkins, F. A., Capt. and Adjt.	115	——— G. D., Capt. D.S.O., M.C.	22
Hand, E. McN., Lieut.	163	——— W., 2/Lt.	46	Hawkins, H. R., Capt.	152	——— G. H., 2/Lt.	20
Handfield-Jones, R. M., Major	134	——— W. H., 2/Lt.	115	——— T., 2/Lt.	38	——— G. R. B., 2/Lt.	74
Handford, W., 2/Lt.	47	——— W. N., 2/Lt.	127	Haworth, C., 2/Lt.	71	——— H. G., 2/Lt.	67
Handley, F. A. W., 2/Lt.	152	Harrison, Aidan, Capt., D.S.O.	79	——— T. T., 2/Lt.	29	——— H. Y. G., Capt.	104
——— J., Capt.	81	——— A. G., 2/Lt.	171	Hay, A. F. A., 2/Lt.	21	——— J., Capt.	19
——— J., Lieut.	162	——— A. H., Lieut.	165	——— E. S., Lieut.	123	——— Ian, Capt.	129
Hankin, H. M., Capt.	146	——— C. A., 2/Lt.	173	——— Hon. Ivan	9	——— J. E., 2/Lt.	27
Hanley, E. D., Capt.	47	——— C., Capt.	77	——— J., Lieut.	177	——— J. F., 2/Lt.	155
Hanna, A. S., 2/Lt.	161	——— F. A., 2/Lt.	28	——— J. B., Home Capt.	169	——— K.S.S., Capt.	39
Hannam, W. J., 2/Lt.	36	——— F. C. S., 2/Lt.	101	Hayden, W. A., 2/Lt.	109	——— M. J., 2/Lt.	53
Hannan, G., 2/Lt.	188	——— F. P., 2/Lt.	121	Haydon, J. S., 2/Lt.	70	——— R.W.M., 2/Lt.	48
——— L., Lieut.	11	——— F. V., 2/Lt.	96	Hayer, J., 2/Lt.	88	——— W., Lieut.	100
Hannay, J., 2/Lt., M.C.	92	——— H. H., Lieut.	25	Hayes, E. D. F., Capt.	131	——— Wilfred, Commodore	143
Hanney, W. C. A., 2/Lt.	83	——— L. J., 2/Lt.	110	——— Frank, Lieut.	80	——— W. I., 2/Lt.	116
Hanson, D. C., Capt.	132	——— M. C. C., Capt.	47	——— F., 2/Lt.	96	——— W. R., Lieut.	166
Harbord, E. R., Capt.	54	——— W., 2/Lt.	24	——— Fredk. Graham 2/Lt.	127	Hendry, S. J., Lieut.	32
Harbour, E. R., Lieut.	48	——— W. L., Lieut.	158	——— H. F., 2/Lt.	120	Hendrie, H. A., Capt.	97
Harbron, Frank, 2/Lt.	94	——— W.R.E., Capt.	171	——— J. Milton, 2/Lt	95	Hendry, John N., Lieut.	122
Harcourt, C. B., Capt.	143	Harrop, R. H., 2/Lt.	125	——— W. E., 2/Lt.	39	Henehan, M., Capt.	111
Harcourt-Vernon, A. A., Capt.	175	Harrower, A. P., Lieut.	26	Hayes-Newington, B. V. Lieut.	54	Henley, A. E., 2/Lt.	82
Harding, G. P., Lieut.	151	Harryman, S., Lieut.	150	Hayford, A. R., 2/Lt.	89	——— C. F., Major	187
Harding, W. D., Lieut.	140	Hart, A. L., 2/Lt.	84	Haygarth, C.H.S., Lieut	16	Henley-Mooney, W. Lieut.	173
Hardman, E. F., Lieut.	118	——— J. W., Lieut.	13	Hayley, J. P., 2/Lt.	64	Hennessy, J., Lt.-Col.	186
——— E. P., Capt.	167	——— N. N., 2/Lt.	23	Haylock, F. A., 2/Lt.	34	——— P., 2/Lt.	60
Hardy, E. H., 2/Lt.	43	——— Percy G., 2/Lt	94	Hayman, E.W.P., 2/Lt.	22	Henning, C. E., 2/Lt.	129
——— F., 2/Lt.	29	——— W. M., Capt.	140	——— Y. R., Lieut.	131	Henry, A. W., 2/Lt.	108
——— George, Lieut.	28	Hart-Davies, H. R., 2/Lt.	155	Haywood, C., Lieut.	45	——— F. R., Lieut.	151
——— G., 2/Lt.	111	Hartley, E. F., 2/Lt.	122	——— H., 2/Lt.	83	——— N. C., 2/Lt.	27
——— J. L., Lieut.	111	——— R. L., Capt.	117	Hazard, C. J., Major	70	——— R. Alex., Lieut	170
——— R. L., Lieut.	131	——— H., 2/Lt.	167	Hazeley, E., Lieut.	122	——— S. S., 2/Lt.	158
——— V. C., 2/Lt.	24	——— R. W., 2/Lt.	35	Hazell, A. N., 2/Lt.	72	——— W. D., Lieut.	141
——— W., Lieut.	118	Hartshorn, J. E., Lieut.	78	Hazlewood, Geo. H. E., Lieut.	107	Henshaw, J. E., Lieut.	16
Hargreaves, G. W., Lieut.	119	——— L. A., Lieut.	100	Heagerty, J. S., 2/Lt.	151	Henslow, E. L., Capt.	93
——— A., Capt.	38	Hartigan, M. M., Major	113	Heale, W. V., 2/Lt.	83	Hepburn, A. C., Major	132
——— B. F., Capt.	72	Harvard, A. J. N., Col.	183	Heanley, R. E. M., Capt.	25	Heppel, Philip F., 2/Lt.	149
——— C. F., Capt.	63	Harvey, A., Major	185	Heaphy, G. M., 2/Lt.	84	Hepper, T. E., Lieut.	131
Harker, B., 2/Lt.	157	——— A. M., 2/Lt.	36	Heard, A. P., Capt.	89	Heptinstall, P. M., 2/Lt.	16
——— G. T., 2/Lt.	154	——— A. W., Capt.	92	——— F. S., Lieut.	88	Hepton, A., Lieut.	49
——— M. J., 2/Lt.	12	——— C. M., Lieut.	14	Hearder, Stanley F. 2/Lt.	57	Hepworth, L., Capt.	37
——— R. H., Lieut.	66	——— E., 2/Lt.	130	Hearn, G. S., 2/Lt.	65	Herapath, C. B., Capt.	186
Harkin, F. W., 2/Lt.	32	——— F. W., 2/Lt.	61	Heath, E. E., Lieut.	160	——— J. N., Lieut.	188
Harland, Robert, 2/Lt.	16	——— F. W., Lieut.	55	Heathcote, F.G.P., Capt	134	——— P. W., Capt.	127
Harle, W., Lieut.	152	——— G. S., Lieut.	168	——— L. W., Lieut.	179	Herbage, P. F. W., 2/Lt.	57
Harley, N. F., 2/Lt.	94	——— H. C., Lieut.	69	Heather, C. L., Lieut.	140	Herbert, C. C., 2/Lt.	178
——— Vivian, 2/Lt.	170	——— J. B. B. de M. Lieut.	152			——— E., Rev.	135
		——— J. H. F., Lieut.	87			——— G. M., Major	187
						Herman, R. D., 2/Lt.	149
						Hermon, J. A., Lieut	104

	PAGE		PAGE		PAGE		PAGE
Herold, J. C., 2/Lt.	129	Hillman, E. C., Major, M.C.	17	Hollis, G. T., Lieut.	43	Houslop, W.A.S., Lieut.	129
Heron-Jones,C. V., Lieut.	184	Hills, F. E., Lieut.	150	——— H. R., 2/Lt.	44	Houston, T., Lieut.	110
Herring, A. C., 2/Lt.	81	——— H., Lieut.	131	——— J. A. Lieut.	150	Hovil, F. A., Lieut.	135
——— David,D., 2/Lt.	62	——— J., 2/Lt.	168	Holloway, C. P., 2/Lt.	83	Howard, B., 2/Lt.	121
——— Gordon, E., 2/Lt.	169	——— O.M.,2/Lt.,M.C.	157	——— G. W., Lieut.	41	——— C. E., Lieut.	92
Herriot, W. M., Lieut.	170	——— W. B. B.,2lLt.	150	Holman, H.G., 2/Lt.	162	——— De W., 2/Lt.	87
Hervey, H. E. 2/Lt.	151	Hillyard, Victor W.,2/Lt.	162	——— L., 2/Lt.	153	——— Douglas W., 2/Lt.	51
Hett, E. J. R., Capt.	35	Hilpern, W. H. T., 2/Lt.	63	——— S. A., Capt.	27	——— F. C., Lieut.	139
Hewat, H. B., 2/Lt.	173	Hilton, T. R., 2/Lt.	168	Holme, J. J., Lieut.	25	——— G. R., 2/Lt.	168
——— W. E., Lieut.	43	Hinchcliffe, G., Capt.	82	Holme-Barnett, K., 2/Lt.	13	——— P. L., 2/Lt.	83
Hewetson, R. J. P., Capt.	80	——— H. Edgar, 2/Lt.	165	Holmes, A., 2/Lt.	114	Howard-Bury, C. K., Lt.-Col.	91
Hewett, W. G., 2/Lt.	128	Hind, C., 2/Lt.	110	——— C. W. D., 2/Lt.	151	Howarth, A., Lieut.	42
Hewitt, F. B., 2/Lt.	80	Hinder, A., 2/Lt.	171	——— E. A., Lieut.	99	——— B., 2/Lt.	100
——— Harold, 2/Lt.	51	Hindson, R. E., Lieut.	56	——— E. G., 2/Lt.	15	——— G. H., 2/Lt.	64
——— H. A., 2/Lt.	159	Hine, J. B., 2/Lt.	154	——— J. D. V., 2/Lt.	153	——— H., 2/Lt.	87
——— N. M., Lieut.	176	Hirst, J., Capt., M.C.	44	——— R. G., Lieut.	112	——— J., 2/Lt.	52
Hewlett, R. F. L., 2/Lt.	128	——— W. S., Capt.	133	——— W., 2/Lt.	23	——— Wm. T., 2/Lt.	120
Hewson, F. A. A., 2/Lt.	149	Hirtzel, H., Lieut.	142	——— W. R., 2/Lt.	49	Howat, W. D., 2/Lt.	20
Heyes, A. C., 2/Lt.	172	Hiskens, G. A.,;Lieut.	118	Holms, J. F., 2/Lt.	103	Howe, G. R., Lieut.	22
Heywood, L. R., 2/Lt.	147	Hislop, J., 2/Lt.	74	Holroyde, R. E., Lieut.	143	——— L. A., 2/Lt.	102
——— P. H., A/Capt.	96	Hitchcock, C. G., 2/Lt.	169	Holt, A. T. S., 2/Lt.	96	——— R. G., 2/Lt.	188
Heyworth, E. L., Lieut.	151	——— C. H., 2/Lt.	38	——— G., 2/Lt.	80	——— S. G., 2/Lt.	98
Hibbard, S. R., Lieut.	176	Hixon, A. J. Asst. Surg.	182	——— J. G., 2/Lt.	120	Howell, E. A., 2/Lt.	128
Hibbert, H. B., Capt.	85	Hoad, F. J. S., Capt.	136	Holwill, W. B., 2/Lt.	123	——— H. C., 2/Lt.	100
——— J. E., 2/Lt.	48	Hoare, George, Lieut.	189	Holyoake, A. V., Lieut.	178	——— Reg., Lieut.	61
——— O. R., 2/Lt.	172	Hobbs, J., 2/Lt.	20	Hommert, L. A. E. E., Lieut.	36	Howes, R. M., Capt.	49
——— O. Y., Capt.	187	Hoblyn, S. E., Lieut.	177	Honeyman, W. M., 2/Lt.	58	——— W. H., Lieut.	155
Hibbett, H., 2/Lt.	83	Hobson, E. C., 2/Lt.	29	Honeysett, J. H., Lieut.	136	Howey, J. E. P., 2/Lt.	147
Hickman Sir A.	8	——— H. N., 2/Lt.	80	Hood, John, Capt.	183	Howie, J., Capt., M.C.	127
——— A., 2/Lt.	178	——— S., 2/Lt.	46	——— J. M., 2/Lt.	118	Howitt, N. J., 2/Lt.	64
——— H., 2/Lt.	78	Hodgins, C. W., 2/Lt.	106	——— M. G., 2/Lt.	103	——— W., 2/Lt.	46
——— J. H., 2/Lt.	71	Hockaday, F. W., 2/Lt.	118	Hooper, A. S., Capt.	93	Howl, R., 2/Lt.	11
Hicks, A. H., Lieut.	99	Hodder, F. J., 2/Lt.	14	——— C. W., Lieut.	137	Howlett, J. W., Capt.	35
——— A. L., Lieut.	47	Hodge, G. G. G., Fl. Lt.	176	——— E. T., 2/Lt.	89	Hoy, E. C., Capt.	173
——— C. M. H., 2/Lt.	12	Hodges, P., 2/Lt.	40	——— G. B., 2/Lt.	126	Hoyne-Fox, L. V., Capt.	182
——— G. E., Lieut.	152	——— F. A., 2/Lt.	11	——— Kenneth, Lieut.	63	Hubbs, F. S., Lieut.	141
——— V. W. F., Lieut.	47	Hodgkin, H. S., Col.	78	——— W.H.V., Capt.	138	Huddleston, G., Lieut.	183
——— W. B., Capt.	25	Hodgkinson, J. N., 2/Lt.	95	Hope, J. B. A., 2/Lt.	68	Hudson, A. R., Capt.	155
Hield, V., 2/Lt.	70	Hodgson, A. G., Lieut.	163	——— M. B., 2/Lt.	90	——— F. D., 2/Lt.	161
Higgins, J., 2/Lt.	35	——— A. M., 2/Lt.	119	——— Sydney, 2/Lt.	34	——— F. N., Lieut.	176
Higham, H. G., 2/Lt.	128	——— E. E., Lieut.	146	Hopegood, C. J. T. F., Lt. (A/Capt.)	76	——— F. N., Capt. M.C.	154
Highett, C. T., Capt.	187	Hodgson-Jones, R., Capt.	132	Hopewell, D. C., Lieut.	161	——— G. L., Capt.	85
Hight, P. H., Lieut.	122	Hodgson-Smith, W. B., Capt.	83	Hopgood, F. J., 2/Lt.	161	——— G. L., Capt.	85
Highton, R. D. C., Capt.	21	Hogan, G. S., 2/Lt.	92	Hopkins, G., Lieut.	38	——— J. H., Capt.	13
Higinson, G. S., Major	113	Hogg, H. A., 2/Lt.	116	——— G. M., 2/Lt.	152	——— S. P., 2/Lt.	98
Higson, J. T., 2/Lt.	81	——— H. J., Lieut.	17	——— G. W. S., Capt.	28	——— T., Lieut.	77
Hilder, P., 2/Lt.	109	——— R. M., Lieut.	99	——— J. A. S., Capt.	60	Huggard, J. C., 2/Lt.	155
Hildyard, B. V., 2/Lt.	43	Hoggarth, N. S., 2/Lt.	46	Hopper, M., Lieut.	101	Hughes, G. E., 2/Lt.	174
Hill, A. S., 2/Lt.	154	Holbrook, C., 2/Lt.	115	——— R. W., 2/Lt.	174	——— G. R., 2/Lt.	33
——— A. B., Capt.	100	——— C. M., Lieut.	172	Hopton, H. P., 2/Lt.	34	——— H. D., 2/Lt.	99
——— A. C. L., 2/Lt.	34	Holcroft, A. B., Fl.-Sub.-Lt.	177	Hopwood, W., 2/Lt.	76	——— H. L., Lieut.	76
——— C. H., Major	184	Holden, A., 2/Lt.	150	Hore, L. B., Lieut., M.C.	125	——— J. B. W., 2/Lt.	61
——— C. W., Lieut.	179	——— H. S., 2/Lt.	80	Horgan, E. P., 2/Lt.	115	——— John P., 2/Lt.	27
——— D., Lieut.	10	——— J. F., 2/Lt.	80	Horn, A. K., 2/Lt.	64	——— J. J., Major	136
——— E. St. C., Capt.	143	——— M. M., Lieut.	117	Hornby, J. H., 2/Lt.	130	——— N.A.A., Major	134
——— F. C. R., 2/Lt.	83	Holdsworth, J. A., Lieut.	51	——— R. D., Lieut.	88	——— P., 2/Lt.	103
——— Francis, Major	89	Hole, W. G., 2/Lt.	16	Horne, D. E. A., 2/Lt.	126	——— R. D., 2/Lt.	169
——— G. A. R., 2/Lt.	168	Hollamby, H. J., 2/Lt.	55	——— H. F., 2/Lt.	75	——— S. C., 2/Lt.	109
——— G.E.M., Lt.-Col.	64	Holland, A., Capt.	24	——— O. W., Capt.	76	Hulbert, H. J., 2/Lt.	94
——— J. O., 2/Lt.	73	——— C. B., 2/Lt.	151	——— W. G., Lieut.	9	Hull, G., Lieut.	13
——— J. B., 2/Lt.	117	——— E. V., Lieut.	170	Hornsby, H. R., Lieut.	14	Hullah, M. C., 2/Lt.	13
——— J. S., 2/Lt.	36	——— R. P., 2/Lt.	95	Horrocks, B. G., 2/Lt.	87	Hulls, A. R., 2/Lt.	89
——— N. J., 2/Lt.	137	Holleran, O. C., Capt.	170	Horseman, W. M., 2/Lt.	15	Hulme, J. B., Lieut.	176
——— R. F., Lieut.	156	Holley, T. G., Lieut.	150	Horsfall, R. W., Lieut.	41	Hulse, W., Lieut.	16
——— R. F. B., 2/Lt.	36	Holliday, C. E., 2/Lt.	14	Horsfield, Wm., Lieut.	11	Humberstone, J. E., Capt.	13
——— R. I. V., Lieut.	156	——— G. R., Lieut.	35	Horsley, P. H., 2/Lt.	28	Humble, A. D., 2/Lt.	112
——— S. J., 2/Lt.	167	——— J., 2/Lt.	21	Horwood, J. C., Lieut.	186	——— T., 2/Lt.	156
——— T. L., Lieut.	77	——— J., 2/Lt.	11	Hostler, A. C. V., 2/Lt.	39	Hume, Arthur J., 2/Lt.	124
——— T. R. V., 2/Lt.	161	Hollingsworth, R. L., Lieut.	166	Horton, John A., 2/Lt.	84	——— R. C., 2/Lt.	154
——— W., 2/Lt.	119	Hollins, E. T., Lieut.	96	Houghton, D. L., 2/Lt.	152	——— Ronald M. 2/Lt.	73
——— W. R., Lieut.	101	Hollis, A., Lieut.	160	Houldsworth, J. F. H., Lieut.	106	——— S. S., Lieut.	153
Hillam, A. W. M.,Sub-Lt.	144			Houlgrave, C., Lieut.	174		
Hillian, John, 2/Lt.	97			Houlton, S., Capt.	124		
Hillier, R. J., Capt.	65						

	PAGE		PAGE		PAGE		PAGE
Hume, W. M., Sub-Lt.	144	Ingham, C. R., 2/Lt.	43	James, C. P., Lt.-Col.,		Johnson, M. E. S., Major	183
Hummerston, H.S.,Capt	136	———— H., 2/Lt.	72	D.S.O.	72	———— P., 2/Lt.	91
Humphreys, A. W., 2/Lt	12	Ingle, A., 2/Lt.	26	———— E., 2/Lt.	31	———— R. F., 2/Lt.	98
———— G. N., Lieut.	146	Inglesby, S. G., Lieut.	189	———— F. E. S., 2/Lt.	15	———— S., Lieut.	127
———— L. B., Lieut.	96	Ingleson, W., Fl. Sub.-		———— G. C., Capt.	98	———— S. M., 2/Lt.	78
———— I. G., Lieut.	131	Lt.	177	———— H. P., 2/Lt.	37	———— W. D., Capt.	23
Humphries, E. A., Capt.,		Inglis, A. G., Capt.	174	———— L. E., Lieut.,		———— W., Lieut.	189
M.C.	62	———— D. A., Sub-Lt.	144	M.C.	92	———— W. C., Hon. Lt.	
Hungerford, S. A. H.		Ingram, J., 2/Lt.	137	———— L. R., Lieut.	173	and Qtmr.	144
Capt.	184	———— L. J. W., Obs.	164	———— M. A., Capt.,		———— W. J., 2/Lt.	173
Hunt, A. S., 2/Lt.	120	———— R. S. S., Capt.	168	M.C.	61	———— W. W., Capt.	140
———— B. P. G., Lieut	150	Inman, H.	161	———— O., 2/Lt.	50	Johnston, B., 2/Lt.	92
———— C. B., 2/Lt.	75	———— T. E., 2/Lt.	77	Jameson, M., 2/Lt.	73	———— B L., Lieut.	138
———— George, 2/Lt.	96	Insall, G. S. M., V.C.,		———— W. C., Sub.-Lt.	181	———— E. W., 2/Lt.	109
———— K., 2/Lt.	163	2/Lt.	147	Jamieson, J. W., 2/Lt.	102	———— G. B., 2/Lt.	179
———— K. F., 2/Lt.	149	Insoll, F. N., 2/Lt.	150	———— P., 2/Lt.	120	———— G. D., 2/Lt.	67
———— O. G., Capt.	24	Ireland, J. W., 2/Lt.	31	Jardine, S. H., Lieut.	189	———— G. I. O'F.,	
———— R. E. B., Capt	146	Ireland-Blackburne,		Jarvis, J. F., Lieut.	81	Lieut.	111
Hunter, G. D., 2/Lt.	152	G. M., Capt.	63	———— K., Lieut.	139	———— G. N. S., Lieut.	145
———— H. C., Lieut.	163	Irvine, A. C., 2/Lt.	98	Jasper, H., 2/Lt.	47	———— J. E., Capt.	158
———— J., 2/Lt.	91	———— C. G. S., Lieut.	23	Jay, T. W., 2/Lt.	150	———— L. J., Capt.	109
———— J., Lieut.	103	———— W. F., 2/Lt.	109	Jeff, R. N. W., 2/Lt.	155	———— M. A. B., Lieut.	185
———— Philip W.		Irwin, H. G. W., Lieut.	71	Jefferd, W. W., Capt.	148	———— T. P., 2/Lt.	112
Lieut.	133	———— H. J., 2/Lt.	144	Jefferson, G. R., 2/Lt.	27	———— V. H., 2/Lt.	64
———— R. G., 2/Lt.	114	———— N. F., 2/Lt.	110	Jeffkins, E. C., 2/Lt.	172	———— W., Sub.-Lt.	144
———— Stanley, 2/Lt.	108	———— R. B. W., 2/Lt.	60	Jeffreys, C. J. N., 2/Lt.	88	———— W., Major	184
———— Sam S., 2/Lt.	59	———— R. V., Lieut.	166	———— M. D. W.,		———— W. A., 2/Lt.	170
———— W. E., Lieut.	13	———— S. S., 2/Lt.	117	Lieut.	189	———— W. S., Lieut.	112
———— Wm. P., 2/Lt.	55	Isaacs, J. B., 2/Lt.	175	———— P. J., 2/Lt.	91	Johnstone, B. D., D.C.M.,	
———— W. T., Lieut.	122	———— K. E., Lieut.	189	Jeffs, C. H., Lieut.	156	M.M., 2/Lt.	66
Hunter-Blair, D. W.		Isbell, A. T., 2/Lt.	160	Jehu, W. J., 2/Lt.	41	———— G. R., 2/Lt.	107
Lieut.	106	Isbister, W. J., Capt.	133	Jenkins, A., Major	108	———— J., 2/Lt.	153
Hurley, Albert, 2/Lt.	62	Ivamy, W. J., 2/Lt.	160	———— T. M., Capt.	181	Joicey, E., Lieut.	9
Hurrell, J. N., Lieut.	37	Ivens, J., 2/Lt.	168	———— B. P., 2/Lt.	168	———— Edwin, 2/Lt.	102
Husband, A. L., 2/Lt.	16	———— J. P., 2/Lt.	29	———— E., Capt.	67	Jolliffe, B. G., Capt.	18
———— C.E.P., Capt.	132	Ives, E., 2/Lt.	80	Jenkinson, B. P., 2/Lt.	85	———— C. J., Capt.	54
Huss, Thos. C. S., Lieut.	73	———— F. J., Lieut.	25	———— T., Major	186	Jones, A. B., 2/Lt.	181
Hustwitt, S. A., Lieut.	162	Ivey, T., Capt.	187	Jenks, J. L., Lieut.	180	———— A. Basil, Lieut.	119
Hutcheon, Allen G. 2/Lt	15	Ivison, B. M., 2/Lt.	94	Jenner, P. C., Lieut.	173	———— Alex. D., Capt.	19
Hutcheson, W.B., Lieut.	155	Izod, F., 2/Lt.	89	Jennings, C., Capt.	7	———— A. D. R., Lieut.	164
Hutchings,V.R.L.,Lieut.	121			———— C. C., 2/Lt.	104	———— A. J., 2/Lt.	188
———— W. M. M.,		Jack, G. W., 2/Lt.	119	———— E. D., 2/Lt.	152	———— A. M., 2/Lt.	98
Sub-Lt.	145	Jackman, J. R., 2/Lt.	164	———— J. C. V., 2/Lt.	98	———— A. R., 2/Lt.	29
———— W. R., Capt.	61	Jackson, Lt.	166	———— J. E., 2/Lt.	173	———— A. R., Lieut.	166
Hutchins, A.J.A., 2/Lt.	69	———— A., Lieut.	120	———— J. L., 2/Lt.	81	———— A. V., 2/Lt.	162
Hutchinson,C.A.,Capt.	84	———— A. R., Capt.	22	———— L. H., 2/Lt.	66	———— C. C., Capt.	134
———— C. D., Lieut.	155	———— A. T., 2/Lt.	70	———— L. N., Lieut.	137	———— C. E. M., Capt.	186
———— J., Capt.	101	———— C. H., 2/Lt.	88	Jenyns, C. G., Lieut.	164	———— David, 2/Lt.	56
———— J. P., Lieut.	14	———— E. A., Capt.	54	Jerrard, A., V.C., Lieut.	161	———— D. O., Lt.	57
———— Miles, Lieut.	99	———— F. H., Lieut.	146	Jervis, B. A., 2/Lt.	178	———— Ernest, 2/Lt.	32
———— W.H.H.,Major	13	———— F. McN., 2/Lt.	13	———— H. S., Capt.	113	———— E., 2/Lt.	83
———— W. J., Lieut.	166	———— H. A., 2/Lt.	90	Jessop, H. T., Capt.	76	———— Evan, 2/Lt.	96
Hutchison, C. K., Capt.	18	———— G. G., Lieut.	159	Jewett, F. F., Lieut.	171	———— E. C., Lieut.	122
———— J., 2/Lt.	11	———— G. G., Capt.	75	Jimenez, A. J., Major	84	———— E. D., 2/Lt.	119
Hutson, H., 2/Lt.	86	———— H. B., Major	43	Joberns, E. J., 2/Lt.	118	———— E. H., 2/Lt.	181
Hutton, J. L., 2/Lt.	81	———— H. M., 2/Lt.	47	Jobson, M., Major	104	———— E. H., Capt.	134
———— T.W.M., 2/Lt.	67	———— J. A., 2/Lt.	80	John, D. M., 2/Lt.	173	———— E. H., Major	10
Huxley, H. W., Capt.	53	———— J. B., 2/Lt.	26	———— J. H., Capt.	45	———— E. H., 2/Lt.	81
Hyde, E. P., 2/Lt.	188	———— J. L., Lieut.	131	Johns, R. A. P., Lieut.	153	———— E. H., 2/Lt.	62
———— Herbert E.		———— J. V. R., Capt.	22	———— R. C., 2/Lt.	66	———— E. L., 2/Lt.	35
Lieut.	172	———— P. E., 2/Lt.	78	———— T. M., Lieut.	149	———— F. B., 2/Lt.	12
Hyslop, A. L., 2/Lt.	116	———— R. W., Lieut.	30	———— W. E., 2/Lt.	171	———— F. V., Lieut.	139
		———— S. C. F., Lt.		Johnson, A., 2/Lt.	163	———— G. A., Capt.,	
J'Anson, H., 2/Lt.	101	Col., D.S.O.	69	———— B., Capt.	131	M.C.	30
Ibbotson, H., 2/Lt.	156	———— S. A., 2/Lt.	97	———— C. S., Lieut.	43	———— G. Lewis,Capt.	133
Ibbott, W., 2/Lt.	85	———— S. S. I., 2/Lt.	40	———— E., Capt.	43	———— G. V., 2/Lt.	87
Icke, J., Lieut.	71	———— W. E., Lieut.	167	———— E. F., 2/Lt.	83	———— H., 2/Lt.	81
Iles, R. V., Lieut.	101	———— W. R., Lieut.	169	———— F. R., Lieut.	171	———— H. B., Capt.	133
Ilett, F. C., Lieut.	29	Jacob, F. W., Lieut.	120	———— F. W. B., Capt.	100	———— H. B., 2/Lt.	123
Illingworth, C. F. W.,		———— G. P. S., 2/Lt.	21	———— H., Col.	98	———— H. E., Lt.	185
2/Lt.	167	Jacobs, A. H., 2/Lt.	96	———— H., 2/Lt.	138	———— H. F., 2/Lt.	125
———— F. W., 2/Lt.	153	———— G. S., Lieut.	54	———— H. L., 2/Lt.	26	———— H. G., 2/Lt.	123
———— H. C. H., Capt.	94	———— T. C., 2/Lt.	67	———— J. H., Lieut.	163	———— H. J., 2/Lt.	48
———— O., Capt.	42	Jaggers, W. H., Lieut.	9	———— J. W., Lieut.	145	———— J. C., 2/Lt.	55
Ince, W. H., 2/Lt.	80	Jago, J. W., 2/Lt.	78	———— J. W. E., 2/Lt.	35	———— J. W., Lieut.	134
Inge, R., Lieut.	176	James, C. E. H., Capt.	72	———— K. L., 2/Lt.	137	———— Leonard, Lieut	97

	PAGE		PAGE		PAGE		PAGE
Jones, Llewellin, 2/Lt.,	56	Kelly, R., 2/Lt.	167	King, E. S., 2/Lt.	89	Labouchere, A. M., Major	75
——— L. E., Capt.	119	——— R. J., 2/Lt.	48	——— F. L., Capt.	31	Lacey, G. Wm., 2/Lt.	26
——— M. B., 2/Lt.	32	——— W., 2/Lt.	62	——— F. W., 2/Lt.	171	Lacy, J. B., Lieut.	171
——— Percy J., 2/Lt.	39	Kelsall, C. H., Lieut.	51	——— G. G., S/Lt.	125	——— R. S., Lieut.	187
——— R. G. M., 2/Lt.	12	——— J., Capt.	71	——— G. H., 2/Lt.	115	Ladler, J., Lieut.	139
——— R. H. H., Lieut.	8	Kemble, A. F., 2/Lt.	37	——— G. L., 2/Lt.	98	Lagden, F. C. W., 2/Lt.	88
——— R. L., Capt.	10	Kemp, Fred, Lieut.	165	——— G. P., 2/Lt.	34	Laing, J. D., 2/Lt.	157
——— S. E., Capt.	44	——— H. T., 2/Lt.	147	——— Harold, Capt.	184	——— S. Van B., Capt.	183
——— S. L., Major	139	——— J. E., 2/Lt.	170	——— John P., 2/Lt.	34	——— W. F., Capt.	101
——— S. T., 2/Lt.	57	——— N. H., 2/Lt.	157	——— J. T., 2/Lt.	91	Laird, D. A., Capt.	131
——— T. B., Lieut.	30	——— P., 2/Lt.	164	——— P., 2/Lt.	174	——— F. M., 2/Lt.	114
——— V. E., 2/Lt.	125	——— W. J., 2/Lt.	130	——— P. P., Lieut.	61	Lamb, F. O., 2/Lt.	41
——— W. G., 2/Lt.	63	Kempson, H. L., 2/Lt.	109	——— S., 2/Lt.	55	——— F.W.M., Lieut.	134
——— W. G. S., Capt	88	Kempton, F., 2/Lt.	99	——— Wm., 2/Lt.	67	——— G. W., Lieut.	34
——— W. H., 2/Lt.	157	Kendall, Sidney, 2/Lt.	158	King-Smith, P. E., 2/Lt.	94	——— H. L., Capt.	129
——— W. O., Lieut.	123	——— W. J., Lieut.	32	Kingdom, S. St. G. S., Capt.	29	——— J.M., 2/Lt.	44
——— W. R., 2/Lt.	55	Kennard, C., 2/Lt.	149	Kingham, R. L., 2/Lt.	172	Lambert, A., 2/Lt.	27
Jones-Lloyd, O. J. F., Lieut.	164	Kennedy, A. K., Capt.	136	Kingsland, W. R., 2/Lt.	158	——— C. J., Capt.	20
Jonsson, A. T., Capt.	108	——— C. A., 2/Lt.	17	Kininmonth, D., Capt., M.C.	19	——— F. W. M., 2/Lt.	70
Jordan, G. B., 2/Lt.	55	——— C. J., 2/Lt.	148	Kinloch, H. T., Capt.	103	——— R., 2/Lt.	36
——— Henry, Lieut.	47	——— F. E., 2/Lt.	114	Kinnes, J. R., Lieut.	20	——— S.C., 2/Lt.	31
——— S. R., Lieut.	178	——— J., Major	132	Kinniburgh, R. C., 2/Lt.	109	Lambie, J. B., Lieut.	46
——— T. C., 2/Lt.	57	——— J. A. C., 2/Lt.	109	Kippen, E. D., 2/Lt.	117	Lamble, A. B., Lieut.	145
——— W. A., Capt.	71	——— J. O. N., 2/Lt.	33	Kirby, F. B., Lieut.	15	Lamont, John C., 2/Lt.	121
Joseph, H. H., Capt.	101	——— P. A., 2/Lt.	118	Kirby, H., 2/Lt.	152	——— W., 2/Lt.	162
Josephs, L. H.O., Capt.	87	——— W. H., 2/Lt.	84	——— L. L., 2/Lt.	130	Lamport, A. J., Lieut.	121
Josland, L. A., 2/Lt.	81	Kennett, L. H., Lieut.	22	Kirk, K. L., Capt.	51	Lanagan, A., Capt.	136
Jotcham, W. E. S., 2/Lt.	130	Kent, A. L., 2/Lt.	113	Kirkcaldy, G. T., Lieut.	73	Lander, T. E., Lieut.	180
Joule, A., Lieut.	111	——— G.C.H., Capt.	94	Kirkby, J. W., 2/Lt.	99	——— T. E., Capt.	176
Jowett, E., 2/Lt.	40	——— J.A.V., Lieut. M.C.	111	Kirkham, F. J., 2/Lt.	152	Landers, J., 2/Lt.	125
——— H. E., 2/Lt.	41	——— R. Leslie, Sub-Lt.	177	Kirkland, F. A., Lieut.	119	Landreth, T. A., 2/Lt.	63
Joyce, W., Lieut.	147	——— T. J., 2/Lt.	158	——— G., Lieut.	138	Lane, C. W., 2/Lt.	153
Joyes, W., 2/Lt.	14	Kent-Jones, D.W., Lieut.	160	Kirkman, R. K., Capt.	161	——— E. D., 2/Lt.	123
Joynson, R., Capt.	58	Keppel, A. R., Capt.	85	Kirkpatrick, A.E., Major	138	——— F. O., 2/Lt.	119
Jubb, G. B., 2/Lt.	85	——— R. O. D., Capt. the Hon.	18	——— John, 2/Lt.	142	——— G. E. W., Capt.	114
Judkins, O. V., 2/Lt.	173	Ker, A. E., Lieut.	123	——— S., 2/Lt.	50	——— J. R. C., 2/Lt.	35
Judge F., Capt.	53	Kerr, A., 2/Lt.	74	——— T. R., 2/Lt.	69	——— L. C.,	162
Julius, S., Major	186	——— C., 2/Lt.	148	Kirkup, J. G., Capt.	28	——— T. W., 2/Lt.	89
Jump, H., Capt.	8	——— S. J., 2/Lt.	26	——— W. S., 2/Lt.	100	——— W. S., Lieut.	145
Juriss, M., 2/Lt.	128	Kert, L., Lieut.	158	Kirkwood, C. H., Capt.	182	Lane-Davies, J. G., Capt. Rev.	135
Justice, H. M., Lieut.	180	Kettle, W. R. B., 2/Lt.	128	——— H. S., 2/Lt.	111	Lane-Roberts, E.G., 2/Lt.	46
Kaizer, M. M., 2/Lt.	152	Kevill-Davies, H. S., Capt.	106	Kirwan, R. C.,2/Lt.	114	Lang, A., Lieut.	186
Kane, H. F., Capt.	134	Kewley, B. H., Lieut.	172	Kissack, A. H., Lieut.	55	Langford, S. J., 2/Lt.	16
——— M.H.K., Lieut	165	Keyes, Cleveland, Major	14	Kitch, A. W., 2/Lt.	80	Langley, L., 2/Lt.	27
Kantel, F. W., Lieut.	153	Keys, S., 2/Lt.	95	Kitchen, E., 2/Lt.	72	——— R., 2/Lt.	50
Karney, A. B. L., Rev.	135	Kidd, A. L., 2/Lt.	159	Kitching, G. C., Capt.	130	——— R. K., Lieut.	130
Kay, E. O., Capt.	70	Kidder, W. S. G., Lieut.	166	Klingenstein, G., Lieut.	149	Langner, D. A. J., 2/Lt.	12
——— H., Lieut.	123	Kier, J. N., 2/Lt.	172	Knapp, F. R., Lieut.	161	Langran, W. H., Lieut.	39
——— Harold Isherwood, 2/Lt.	117	Kiernander, O. G., 2/Lt.	183	Kneller, F. Kneller, 2/Lt.	160	Langston, N., Lieut.	83
——— J. R., 2/Lt.	59	Kilbourne, Watson H., Lieut.	168	Knight, C., Lieut.	174	Lanham, F. W., Lieut.	66
Kearney, P. W., 2/Lt.	186	Kilburn, Frank S., 2/Lt.	15	——— C. C., Lieut.	154	Lansdale, E. C., Lieut.	173
Keating, O. J. F., Major	98	Killick, C. H. P., 2/Lt.	170	——— C. G., Fl.-Sub-Lt.	176	——— H., 2/Lt.	175
——— W. F., 2/Lt.	13	Killin, J., 2/Lt.	179	——— G. F., Lieut.	149	Lansley, H., Lieut.	68
Keay, R. A., Capt.	136	Killingback, H. C., Capt.	87	——— H. W., Lieut.	49	Lanyon, T. S., 2/Lt., M.C.	86
Keeble, Francis John, 2/Lt.	168	Killingsworth, H. L., 2/Lt.	138	——— J. E. M., 2/Lt.	22	Lapworth, C., Capt.	69
Keeling, E. H., 2/Lt.	184	Kilpatrick, W. J., Lieut.	137	——— N. L., 2/Lt.	151	Larcombe, A. H., 2/Lt.	67
——— F. W., 2/Lt.	96	Kilsby, M. J., Lieut.	138	——— P. C., Capt.	104	Larder, F., 2/Lt.	47
——— John, 2/Lt.	79	Kinahan, J. H., 2/Lt.	117	Knight-Bruce, J. H. W., Capt.	28	Larkin, E. P., Lieut.	182
Keen, S. H., 2/Lt.	118	Kincaid-Smith, M. A., Capt.	103	Kniveton, F. M., 2/Lt.	32	Larrabee, E. P., Lieut.	172
Keene, H., Lyndon 2/Lt	29	Kinder, M. Fitzgerald, Capt.	121	Knott, H. W., 2/Lt.	J119	Lart, E. L. B., Lieut.	71
Keighley, E., 2/Lt.	42	King, A. E., 2/Lt.	129	Knowlden, W. E., 2/Lt.	149	Latham, Arthur S., Lieut.	23
Keightley, G. S., 2/Lt.	38	——— C. H., 2/Lt.	87	Knowles, B. M., Lieut.	94	——— C., 2/Lt.	62
Keiller, J. M. R., Capt.	74	——— C. L., 2/Lt.	49	——— M. B., Capt.	151	——— H., 2/Lt.	118
Kelk, C. Kingston, Lieut	49	——— C. L., Capt., M.C., D.F.C.	175	Knox, R. S., Lieut.	107	Latimer, D., Capt., M.C.	168
Keller, C. F., Lieut.	158	——— C. M., 2/Lt.	128	Knox Shaw, P., Lieut.	79	Latta, A. Stuart, 2/Lt.	72
Kellog, W. B., 2/Lt.	154	——— D. B., Capt.	158	Koop, C., 2/Lt.	89	Lattimer, J. E., Capt.	140
Kelly, A., Capt., M.C.	106	——— E. A., 2/Lt.	22	Koplik, G. W., 2/Lt.	44	Lauder, I. A., Lieut.	122
——— C. C., Lieut.	87			Krook, A. D. C., Capt.	73	——— J., Lieut.	131
——— C.Moore, 2/Lt.	149			Kruger, Max, 2/Lt.	45	Lauderdale, W. A., 2/Lt.	64
——— H., Major	131					Laughlin, N. A., 2/Lt.	74
——— H. B., Lt.-Col.	134			Labatt, W. H. E., 2/Lt.	166	Laurence, C., Fl.-Lt.	177
——— J. M., 2/Lt.	173			Labother, Lieut.	182	Laurenson, D. G., Lieut.	9
						Laurie, K. S., 2/Lt.	166

	PAGE		PAGE		PAGE		PAGE
Laverack, E., Capt.	43	Leigh, F. G., Lieut.	29	Liddell, A. R., Lieut.	27	Lodge, C. F., Lieut.	150
Law, B., 2/Lt.	57	——— J., Lieut.	100	——— H. H., 2/Lt.	90	——— H. J., 2/Lt.	36
——— C., Major	93	Leigh-Bennett, P. R.,		Lidiard, H. S., Capt.	127	Lofthouse, G., 2/Lt.	51
——— C. B., 2/Lt.	163	2/Lt.	183	Liefeldt, A. W., Capt.	141	Loftus, W., 2/Lt.	115
——— C. H., 2/Lt.	80	Leighton, A. A., Sub.-Lt.	144	Liggett, M., Lieut.	96	Logan, G. C., 2/Lt.	159
——— E. R., 2/Lt.	152	——— Gordon, Lieut.	142	Light, D. O., Lieut.	89	——— J., Lieut.	16
——— J. R., Lieut.	159	——— J., Lieut.	31	Lightbourne, A. H.,		——— R. A., Capt.	151
——— W. K., Capt.	67	——— K. A. W.,		Capt.	140	——— V. D. O., Capt.	131
Lawe, A. G., Lieut.	168	Lieut.	169	Lilley, W. D. N., Lieut.	33	Lomax, A. K., 2/Lt.	161
——— F. W., Capt.	44	——— R. T., Lieut.	155	Lilly, H. H., 2/Lt.	77	——— C. N. L., 2/Lt.	156
Lawes, J. H., Lieut.	44	——— T. W., Capt.	133	Lindley, A., Capt.	172	——— J. G., Lieut.	10
Lawrence, C. J., Lieut.	139	Leishman, W., Capt.	71	——— G. R. C. D., Lt.	81	London, F. J., Lieut.	94
——— C. W., 2/Lt.	63	Leith, P. Fredk., 2/Lt.	103	Lindop, V. S. E., Lieut.	146	Lonergan, C. J., Capt.	65
——— E. I., 2/Lt.	24	Leith-Hay-Clark, N., Lt.-		Lindsay, A. T. W., 2/Lt.	160	Lones, R. E., Lieut.	126
——— J., 2/Lt.	82	Col.	28	——— H. J., 2/Lt.	90	Long, B. E., 2/Lt.	84
——— S. C., Lieut.	45	Leithead, W. B., 2/Lt.	32	Line, W. W., 2/Lt.	30	——— F. W., 2/Lt.	10
Lawrie, W., 2//Lt., M.M.	20	Leivers, F. A., Lieut.	39	Lines, T. H., 2/Lt.	153	——— G. R., Lieut.	156
Lawson, A. N., 2/Lt.	25	Leman, L. L. L., Lieut.	81	Lingard, J. E., Lieut.	152	——— H., Major	131
——— F. G., Lieut.	140	Le Mesurier, H. F. A.,		Linge, C. E., Capt.	66	——— H. O., Lieut.	148
——— P., 2/Lt.	49	Major	56	Lingwood, C. R., Capt.	26	Longdon, W. F., 2/Lt.	12
——— R. G., 2/Lt.	161	Lemon, A. B., Capt.	45	Linnell, H. G. B., Fl.-		Longland, C. V., 2/Lt.	50
——— T. D., 2/Lt.	27	——— G. H., 2/Lt.	110	Sub.-Lt.	157	Longmuir, J. B., 2/Lt.	16
——— W. D., Lieut.	120	Lennard, R. G., 2/Lt.	28	Linsley, F., 2/Lt.	43	Longworth, T., 2/Lt.	97
——— G. R. W., 2/Lt.	120	Lennox, G. S., Lieut.	140	Lipp, G. R., Capt., M.C.	132	Lonsdale, V. O., 2/Lt.	150
Lawton, J. B., Lieut.	149	Le Patourel, E., Lieut.	184	Lipscomb, J. K., Lieut.	124	Lord, G., 2/Lt.	13
Lax, W. L., 2/Lt.	17	Lepper, A. W., 2/Lt.	86	Lipsett, R. S., 2/Lt.	171	——— T. V., 2/Lt.	157
Laycock, C., Capt.	16	Le Ray, Hugh G., Lieut.	11	Lister, B. S., 2/Lt.	153	Loudan, S. M., 2/Lt.	82
——— L. J. P., 2/Lt.	82	Leresche, G., Lieut.	97	——— C. H., 2/Lt.	102	Loudoun, L. G., Capt.	169
Lazarus-Barlow, A. J.,		Le Roy, H. L., Lieut.	163	——— E. A., Lieut.	49	Lough, J. W., Lieut.	25
2/Lt.	179	Lerwill, O., 2/Lt.	147	——— G. D., Capt.	83	Loughbridge, J. A.,	
Lea, R. H. M., 2/Lt.	92	Lescher, F. G., Major	134	——— J., Lieut.	176	Lieut.	133
Leach, A., 2/Lt.	72	Leslie, D., Capt.	137	Litt, C. E. R., Capt.	87	Loupinski, J., Lieut.	165
——— C. H., 2/Lt.	75	——— G., 2/Lt.	119	Little, A. H., Capt.	133	Lovatt, J. M., 2/Lt.	91
——— J. M., Lieut.	158	——— H. H., Lieut.	123	——— C. B., Capt.	65	Love, G. M., Sub.-Lt.	144
——— R., 2/Lt.	42	Leslie-Moore, A., 2/Lt.	188	——— E., 2/Lt.	75	——— H. K., Lieut.	138
——— Wilfred L. W.	118	Lesley, J. W., Capt.	90	——— J. C., Lieut.	140	——— J. H. A., Lieut.	45
Leadbitter, C. O., 2/Lt.	18	Lesmond, C., 2/Lt.	183	——— J. W., 2/Lt.	68	Lovejoy, H. R., Lieut.	136
Leader, Leonard, Capt.	60	Lester, G. E., 2/Lt.	128	——— O. H., Lieut.	179	Lovell, C. E. A., 2/Lt.	167
Leahy, M. B., Civil Surg.	131	Letchworth, H. M., Capt.	113	——— W. S., 2/Lt.	33	——— G. B., Lieut.	129
Leathard, L. F., 2/Lt.	27	Lethbridge, E., Lt.-Col.	187	Littledale, J. F., Lieut.	86	Low, W. T., 2/Lt.	20
Leather, V. S., 2/Lt.	83	——— H. W., 2/Lt.	115	Littlewood, J., 2/Lt.	40	Lowe, F. H., 2/Lt.	33
Leavitt, H. J., Lieut.	162	Leverton, H. S., Lieut.	66	——— S. C. T., Lieut.	147	——— G. P., 2/Lt.	92
Leckler, A. N., 2/Lt.	151	Leveson-Gower, J., Lieut.	170	Living, C. H., 2/Lt.	170	——— J. W., 2/Lt.	83
Lecky, R., Lieut.	184	Levett, E., 2/Lt.	69	Livingstone, W. E., 2/Lt.	58	——— P., Capt.	39
Leckyand, Lieut.	182	Levey, E., 2/Lt.	84	Llewelin, L., Lieut.	126	——— T. G., 2/Lt.	126
Ledgard, R., Capt.	48	Levy, J. M. D'Arcy,		Llewellin, M. C., Capt.	126	——— W. A., 2/Lt.	16
Ledger, H. G., 2/Lt.	75	Midshipman	176	Llewellyn, W E., 2/Lt.	144	——— W. J. M., Lieut.	9
Lee, A. C., Lieut.	153	Lewes, F. H. M., Capt.		Llewellyn-Davies, G.,		Lowes, E. J., 2/Lt.	100
——— E. B., Lieut.	160	& Adjt.	77	Lieut.	176	Lowndes, R. C., Capt.	185
——— E. G., Lieut.	47	Lewis, Archibald	166	Lloyd, A. C., Lieut.	168	Lowson, G. F., Lieut.	116
——— Joseph J., 2/Lt.	91	——— A. D. M., Sub.-		——— C. B. E., Lieut.	172	——— J. H., Lieut.	149
——— J. L., Capt.,		Lt.	177	——— E. A., Capt.	57	——— S. G., 2/Lt.	76
M.C.	51	——— C. J., 2/Lt.	50	——— E. A. L., 2/Lt.	153	Loyd, E. E. F., 2/Lt.	156
——— M. C., Lieut.	181	——— C. S., 2/Lt.	88	——— E. R., Capt.	60	Luard, R. B., Lieut.	169
——— R. A., Lieut.	15	——— D. F., Lieut.	177	——— G. C., 2/Lt.	38	Lucas, A. S., Capt.	116
Leech, A. C., 2/Lt.	76	——— D. G., 2/Lt.	161	——— G. P., Lieut.	86	——— J. M., Capt.	28
——— C. J. F., Capt.	10	——— D. R., 2/Lt.	124	——— H. W. C., Capt.	93	——— S., Lieut.	90
——— J. C., Capt.	146	——— F. S. J. McK.	73	——— J. P., Lieut.	170	——— W. J., 2/Lt.	45
Leembruggen, R.A., Capt.	133	——— F. W., 2/Lt.	12	——— J. W., Major	17	Luff, R. G. R., 2/Lt.	12
Lees, A., Capt.	150	——— G. T. M., 2/Lt.	84	——— O. S., Major	185	Luffingham, L. J., Lieut.	89
——— J. C., 2/Lt.	149	——— H. G., 2/Lt.	175	——— R. B., 2/Lt.	188	Lumley, A. F. C., 2/Lt.	126
——— P. R., 2/Lt.	26	——— H. M., 2/Lt.	154	Lloyd-Atkins, J. R., 2/Lt.	120	Lumsden, A. C., Lieut.	139
Leeson, D., Lieut.	146	——— H. S., Lieut.	139	Loch, A. C., 2/Lt.	184	Lunn, H. K., Sub.-Lt.	144
Leeson-Ball, T. Major	185	——— H. T., 2/Lt.	137	Lochhead, A. G., 2/Lt.	53	——— J. J., 2/Lt.	100
Le Fevre, F. E., 2/Lt.	159	——— John S., 2/Lt.	57	Locke, C. J., Lieut.	176	Luscombe, L. H., 2/Lt.	178
Lefroy, C. B. H., Lieut.	167	——— M., 2/Lt.	151	——— G. H., Lieut.	171	Lusty, R. A., 2/Lt.	69
Le Gallais, A., Capt.	53	——— N. A., Major	31	——— H. M., 2/Lt.	33	Luscombe. B. P., Lieut.	10
Legg, W., Capt.	16	——— R. G., 2/Lt.	164	——— P. J., Capt.	138	Luther, A. C. G., Capt.	85
Leggatt, E. W., Capt.	148	——— R. P., Asst.		Lockhart, F. R., Lieut.	118	——— H. G., 2/Lt.	175
——— C. W., Lieut.	159	Surg.	182	Lockhead, R. O., 2/Lt.	59	Luxmoore, F. L., Capt.	160
Legge, W., Capt.	105	——— P. S., Lieut.	181	Lockey, B., 2/Lt.	174	Lycett, N. L., Capt.	135
Le Grand, H.	7	——— T. C., 2/Lt.	114	Lockwood, G. F., 2/Lt.	48	Lyle, A. M. A., 2/Lt.	87
Le Hunte, J., Lieut.	69	——— W. T. S., 2/Lt.	169	Loder-Symmonds, W.,		Lymer, J. G., 2/Lt.	52
Le Huquet, G., Capt.	93	Leybourne, E. A., Capt.	101	Lieut.	93	Lynch, J. P., Capt.	131
Leicester, G. W. F.,		Leyson, B. W. de B.,		Lodge, F. C., Lt.-Col.	186	——— S. A., Lieut.	109
Lieut.	54	Lieut.	164			Lynch-Watson, H., 2/Lt.	84

	PAGE
Lynes, W. P., Capt.	90
——— W. S., Capt.	71
Lynn, F., Lieut.	175
Lyon, M. M., 2/Lt.	104
——— M. C. H. B., Capt. Hon.	20
——— P. H. B., Capt.	100
——— P. W., Lieut.	106
——— P. W., Lieut.	137
——— W. J. G., 2/Lt.	137
Lyons, F. J. W., 2/Lt.	99
Lyster, P., Capt.	10
MacAllan, P. R., Capt.	59
McAllister, A., 2/Lt.	115
MacAlpine, Ian F., Lieut.	135
McAnally, A. R., 2/Lt.	81
MacAndrew, P. M., Lieut.	20
McAndrew, W., 2/Lt.	23
McArthur, G. A. D., Capt.	132
MacArthur, R., Lieut.	11
MacArtney, W. F. R., Lieut.	19
MacAskie, D. S. C., 2/Lt.	148
MacAulay, A. C., Lieut.	175
——— G. J. R., 2/Lt.	12
McBain, J. M., Lieut.	78
McBeath, W. J., 2/Lt.	95
MacBryan, J. C. W., Lieut.	38
McBryde, K., 2/Lt.	12
McCaffrey, W. P., 2/Lt.	115
McCallum, A. H. K., Lieut.	151
McCallum, P., Lieut.	136
McCann, A. F., 2/Lt.	114
——— A. J., 2/Lt.	113
——— Cecil, Lieut.	161
McCarter, W. H., Capt.	133
McCarthy, J., 2/Lt.	16
——— P., 2/Lt.	114
McCaughey, F. H., Capt.	134
McChleary, D., 2/Lt.	112
McChlery, W. R., Sub.-Lt.	145
McColl, A., 2/Lt.	120
McCombie, J. M., Lieut.	187
MacConchie, T. Lloyd, Lieut.	165
McConnachie, J. S., Major	132
McConnell, R. B., 2/Lt.	59
——— S., Lieut.	59
——— S. B., 2/Lt.	60
McConnell-Wood, A., Lieut.	167
McConville, J., 2/Lt.	185
McCormick, A. M., Lieut.	134
——— H., Lieut.	118
McCovey, H. J., 2/Lt.	79
McCracken, E. C. J., Lieut	168
——— J., 2/Lt.	74
——— W., Major	112
MacCrea, P. C. S., 2/Lt.	174
McCreary, A. T. S., Capt.	186
McCrorie, A. W., 2/Lt.	115
McCuaig, D. R., Major	138
McCuish, A. C., 2/Lt.	108
McCulloch, A. F. G., 2/Lt.	138
——— I. M., 2/Lt.	170
McCullough, J. D., 2/Lt.	60
McDermott, C. H., 2/Lt.	186

	PAGE
MacDonald, Alex., Fl.-Sub.-Lt.	177
——— A. T. C., Capt.	132
——— D. A., Lieut.	163
——— D. C., 2/Lt.	175
——— D. P., 2/Lt.	151
——— E. W., Capt.	58
——— F. H. C., Lieut.	139
——— H. O., Lieut.	154
——— I. G., 2/Lt.	105
——— J., 2/Lt.	105
——— J., Lieut.	169
——— J. C., 2/Lt.	64
——— J. C. J., 2/Lt.	174
——— J. J., Lieut.	171
——— K. W., Lieut.	155
——— N., Lieut.	19
——— Roy, 2/Lt.	159
——— R., Capt.	129
——— R. A., 2/Lt.	16
——— R. T. A., Lieut.	178
——— R. M., Lieut.	173
McDonnell, C. J., 2/Lt.	79
——— H. W., Lieut.	139
——— R. de Courcy, Lieut.	82
McDougall, I., Major	142
McDowell, R., 2/Lt.	127
——— V. A. G.	139
McElligott, J., 2/Lt.	179
McElnea, H. J., 2/Lt.	113
McElroy, C. H., Lieut.	189
——— H. F., 2/Lt.	130
——— J. O., Capt.	97
McEntee, G. O., 2/Lt.	152
McErvel, J. E., Lieut.	117
McEwan, J. G., 2/Lt.	147
——— J. H. F., Capt.	148
McEwen, A. F., 2/Lt.	87
——— P. A., 2/Lt.	13
MacFayden, A., 2/Lt.	184
MacFarlane, A., 2/Lt.	117
——— J. L., Lieut.	155
——— W. K., Lieut.	169
McFie, J. A., Lieut.	130
——— J. D. A., 2/Lt.	148
McGeachy, E., 2/Lt.	13
McGeoch, W., 2/Lt.	116
McGeorge, W. B., 2/Lt.	104
Macghie, D. S., Lieut.	179
McGilton, D. J., 2/Lt.	109
McGown, A., 2/Lt.	136
——— J. C., Lieut.	154
McGregor, A. H., Major	53
——— D. A., Capt.	82
——— J. F., 2/Lt.	15
——— J. R., Lieut.	189
——— J. S., 2/Lt.	20
——— R. R., 2/Lt.	156
——— W. K., 2/Lt.	74
McGroarty, E. C., 2/Lt.	72
McGruer, A. G., 2/Lt.	107
McHugh, P., 2/Lt.	54
McIlwaine, H. L., Capt.	88
McIndoe, G. E. B., 2/Lt.	104
McInnes, John, Lieut.	107
MacIntosh, D. R., 2/Lt.	142
——— E. H. de M., 2/Lt.	142
——— F. G., 2/Lt.	148
——— R. R., 2/Lt.	153
MacIntyre, C. C., 2/Lt.	74
——— D. H., 2/Lt.	148
——— J. A., 2/Lt.	25
——— J. C., 2/Lt.	48
——— W., 2/Lt.	92

	PAGE
MacKay, Alex., Lieut.	103
——— A. R., 2/Lt.	36
——— D., Asst. Surg.	182
——— D. R., 2/Lt.	51
——— E. A., Capt., M.C., D.F.C.	169
——— G. G. W., Lieut.	49
——— J. E., 2/Lt.	59
——— J. R., 2/Lt.	107
——— J.W.M., Lieut.	105
——— N. D., Lieut.	17
——— P. W., 2/Lt.	73
——— W. B., Lieut.	154
Macky, F. C. S., Lieut.	113
McKeag, V. M., 2/Lt.	114
MacKechnie, W., 2/Lt.	115
McKechnie, W. L., 2/Lt.	116
McKegney, E. W., Lieut.	60
McKellen, F., Capt.	28
McKelvey, M. T., Lieut.	162
McKenna, H. P., Capt.	60
——— J., A.D.C. & Major	187
——— J. C., Major	183
McKenny, C. N., 2/Lt.	110
McKenzie, A., 2/Lt.	105
——— A., 2/Lt.	91
——— E. G., 2/Lt.	67
——— F. P., Lieut.	141
——— J. M., Capt.	134
McKeown, C. J. W., 2/Lt.	159
MacKereth, J., Capt.	169
McKerrell, A. D., 2/Lt.	58
McKerrow, W. A., Surg.	144
McKessock, R. R., Lieut.	139
McKie, J., 2/Lt.	103
——— L. G., 2/Lt.	91
——— R. C., 2/Lt.	11
MacKinnon, J., Capt.	26
MacKintosh, I. K., 2/Lt.	74
——— J. D. V., 2/Lt.	67
McKissock, R. R., 2/Lt.	152
McKnight, Leo M., 2/Lt.	98
McLachlan, A. E. W., 2/Lt.	19
McLare, W. M., Lieut.	25
McLaren, A. T., Lieut.	20
——— James, Lieut.	112
McLaurin, D., 2/Lt.	157
McLean, Alex. G., Lieut.	106
——— A. J. H., Capt.	112
——— A. P., Capt.	160
——— G. D., 2/Lt.	136
——— G. N., Capt.	106
——— I. C., Capt., D.S.O., M.C.	133
——— Murdo, 2/Lt.	175
——— N A., 2/Lt.	91
——— V. A., Lieut.	138
——— W. A., 2/Lt.	146
——— W. H., 2/Lt.	92
——— W. L., 2/Lt.	25
McLennan, J., Lieut.	74
——— J. E., 2/Lt.	150
——— J. McM., Lieut.	173
MacLeod, A., 2/Lt.	117
——— G. D., Lieut.	163
——— E. R., Capt.	72
——— F. G., 2/Lt.	104
——— J., Lieut	14
——— L., 2/Lt.	73
——— Lachlan, 2/Lt.	108
——— N., 2/Lt.	58
——— R. W., Lieut.	10
McLoughlin, J., 2/Lt.	47
McLurg, J. E., Lieut.	138

	PAGE
MacMahon, C. L., Capt.	43
——— L. S., Lieut.	137
MacManus, A.A.L., 2/Lt.	108
——— G. E., 2/Lt.	171
——— O. B., 2/Lt.	110
McMechan, J., Capt.	59
McMeeken, G. S. P., Capt.	19
McMichael, G. B., Lieut.	156
McMicking, H., Lt.-Col.	19
McMillan, A., Capt.	112
——— C. D., 2/Lt.	179
——— J. F., 2/Lt.	65
——— R. E., Fl. Sub-Lt.	177
McMinn, H. H., Capt.	137
——— W., 2/Lt.	53
McMullen, J. R., 2/Lt.	83
McMurtrie, G. D. J., Capt.	39
McNab, J. S., 2/Lt.	108
MacNair, D., Capt.	132
McNamara, J. F., 2/Lt.	175
McNally, Irwin, 2/Lt.	81
McNaughton, E. H. C., Sub-Lt.	143
——— J. L., 2/Lt.	65
McNeal, H. S. D., Lieut.	181
McNeile, J. H.	18
MacNeill, I. D., 2/Lt.	103
McNeill, K. D., 2/Lt.	103
McNicol, D., 2/Lt.	74
McNish, J. A., 2/Lt.	126
McPhail, A. G., 2/Lt.	106
——— G. R., Capt.	122
MacPhee, G. G., Lieut.	161
——— Roland, Lieut.	170
McPherson, B., 2/Lt.	161
——— D. B., 2/Lt.	115
——— J. M., 2/Lt.	168
——— R., Lieut.	81
——— R. C., 2/Lt.	146
McQuaid 2/Lt.	54
McQueen, J. F. F.	94
McQuiggan, A. J., Lieut.	136
McQuinn, W., 2/Lt.	96
McQuiston, T. E., 2/Lt.	101
MacRae, A., Lieut.	104
——— J. D. G., Lieut.	180
——— J. P., Lieut.	158
McSweeny, D. H., 2/Lt.	80
McTaggart, M. F., Lt. Col., D.S.O.	106
MacTavish, D., 2/Lt.	152
McVey, J. S., 2/Lt.	122
Mabbett, R. W., 2/Lt.	52
Maben, James, 2/Lt.	58
Mace, C. A., 2/Lt.	101
Mack, A. J., 2/Lt.	13
Mack, R., Capt.	177
Macky, J. B. B., Capt.	28
Maddison, E. J. C., Lieut.	120
Madeley, R., 2/Lt.	90
Madge, J. B. C., Lieut.	155
Magee, E. A., 2/Lt.	163
Magin, J., 2/Lt.	86
Maggs, D. O. C., 2/Lt.	85
Magrath, C. G., Lieut.	47
——— W. S., Fl.-Lt.	177
Mahaffy, W. G., 2/Lt.	48
Maguire, M. L., 2/Lt.	180
Mahon, B. E. S., Lieut.	24
Mahony, M. R., Lieut.	173
Main, R., 2/Lt.	158
Maitland-Heriot, A., Fl. Lt.	181
Major, F. C., 2/Lt.	101
——— W. E., Lieut.	46

Name	Page
Makeham, L. C., Capt.	94
Makepeace, I. W., Lieut.	26
Makin, K. K., 2/Lt.	40
Makins, H. E., Capt.	39
Makinson, H., Lieut.	95
Malby, R. C., 2/Lt.	129
Malcolm, R. M., 2/Lt.	102
Malcolmson, J. C., 2/Lt.	173
Malkin, F., 2/Lt.	36
Mallabar, W. L., 2/Lt.	131
Mallace, M., Capt.	59
Mallett, Donald, 2/Lt.	165
——— H. P., Lieut.	167
Mallinson, B. 2/Lt.	33
——— C. H., Capt.	65
——— R., Lieut.	137
Malloch, A. C., Lieut.	154
Mallous, C. G., 2/Lt.	155
Malone, J. G., 2/Lt.	109
Maloney, M., 2/Lt.	188
Malton, P. L., 2/Lt.	66
Mance, J. D., Lieut.	165
——— J. F., 2/Lt.	31
Mandel, Oscar, 2/Lt.	170
Mander, J. G. H., Lieut.	29
Manders, T. C., Capt.	88
Manley, G. A. C., 2/Lt.	159
——— P. S., Lieut.	173
Mann, F. A., 2/Lt.	150
——— J., 2/Lt.	24
——— J. J., Lieut.	19
Manners, C. M. S., Capt.	183
——— E. W., 2/Lt.	102
——— T. G., 2/Lt.	122
Manners-Smith, J. A., Lieut.	155
Manning, B. O'D., 2/Lt.	18
Mansbridge, C., Lieut.	52
Mansel Moullin, O., Lieut.	146
Mansell, R., 2/Lt.	97
Mantle, A., 2/Lt.	33
——— H. S., Lieut.	172
Manzer, R., Capt.	167
Mapleton, R. I., 2/Lt.	107
Mapp, C. H., 2/Lt.	15
Mapplebeck, T., Capt.	149
March, C. H., Lieut.	150
Marchand, E. F., 2/Lt.	158
Marchant, E. A., 2/Lt.	171
——— E. W., Lieut.	89
——— F. S., 2/Lt.	59
——— G. A., 2/Lt.	129
Marcus, G., Sub-Lt.	145
Mardock, F. W., Lieut.	176
Mardon, S. R., 2/Lt.	40
Mare-Montembault, M. J. J. G., 2/Lt.	150
Marfell, C., 2/Lt.	61
Margetts, C. F. M., Capt.	71
Mark, A. W. D., Capt.	27
Markham, W. H. J., 2/Lt.	25
Marks, J. H., 2/Lt.	88
——— J. S., Capt.	76
Marlow, O. L., 2/Lt.	90
——— W., 2/Lt.	12
Marple, G. W., 2/Lt.	30
Marrion, J. F., 2/Lt.	32
Marriott, Reginald, Lt.	53
Marris, E. N., Major	124
Mars, W. S., Lieut.	169
Marsden, C., Lieut.	163
——— F. A., 2/Lt.	86
——— F. G., 2/Lt.	41
——— J. W., 2/Lt.	40
——— J. W., 2/Lt.	25
Marsden, T. R., D.S.O., Lt.-Col.	138
——— W., 2/Lt.	80
Marseille, R. K. G., Capt.	80
Marsh, A. G. V., 2/Lt.	44
——— G. R. T., 2/Lt.	159
——— G. V., 2/Lt.	64
——— J., 2/Lt.	178
——— L., Sub.-Lt.	188
——— Lewis, Capt.	117
——— R. M., 2/Lt.	154
——— S. S., 2/Lt.	123
Marshall, A. F. W., 2/Lt.	44
——— A. M., 2/Lt.	137
——— C. C. B., 2/Lt.	130
——— C. C. N., 2/Lt.	76
——— C. O., Lieut.	25
——— C. T., 2/Lt.	97
——— D., 2/Lt.	51
——— G. E., 2/Lt.	142
——— H., Capt.	35
——— J., 2/Lt.	65
——— N. H., 2/Lt.	165
——— R., Capt.	169
——— R. C., Capt.	62
——— S., 2/Lt.	51
——— T., Capt.	72
——— T., Capt.	—
Marsland, T., Lieut.	17
Marson, H. W., Lieut.	137
Marthews, L. G., 2/Lt.	72
Martland, E. N. P., Lieut.	133
Marten, C. W., 2/Lt.	46
Martin, A. V. P., Lt.-Col.	14
——— A. W., Lieut.	152
——— D. A., Lieut.	169
——— E. C. de R., Lt. Col.	52
——— E. P., 2/Lt.	121
——— E. T., Capt.	185
——— G. C. R., Lieut.	98
——— G. M. K., Lieut.	60
——— J., Lieut.	176
——— H., Lieut.	7
——— J. D., Capt.	186
——— J. M. J., 2/Lt.	60
——— J. R., Lieut.	140
——— J. S. S., Capt.	182
——— L. W., 2/Lt.	23
——— P. C. C., 2/Lt.	159
——— R. E., 2/Lt.	70
——— R. V., Lieut.	184
——— S. A., 2/Lt.	21
——— S. T., 2/Lt.	64
——— T. G., Lieut.	62
——— W., 2/Lt.	93
——— W. J., 2/Lt.	88
Martineau, C., Capt.	29
Martinson, W. F., Capt.	76
Martyn, M. C., Lt.-Col.	46
Mase, H. F., Lt.	148
Maskell, G. N., Lieut.	118
Mason, A. E., Lieut.	187
——— C. G., 2/Lt.	142
——— H., Lieut.	164
Massey, G., 2/Lt.	52
——— H. H., 2/Lt.	64
Massey-Cooke, W. E., Lieut.	140
Masson, J. R., 2/Lt.	58
Massy, B. E., Capt.	54
Master, H. F. H., Capt.	21
Mather, A. S., Sub.-Lt.	177
——— E. E., Capt.	133
——— G. R., 2/Lt.	87
Matheson, A. M., Lieut.	173
Matheson, J., 2/Lt.	20
——— R. K., Lieut.	97
Mathew, C. G., Lieut.	154
——— H. C., M.C., Lieut.	38
Mathias, L., Lieut.	184
Mathieson, E. N., 2/Lt.	120
——— W. A., 2/Lt.	20
Matson, A. W., 2/Lt.	160
——— G., Lieut.	35
Matterson, C. A. K., Capt.	54
Matthews, A. B., Lieut.	185
——— A. H., 2/Lt.	31
——— E. V., 2/Lt.	62
——— F., 2/Lt.	151
——— G., 2/Lt.	41
——— J. S., Lieut.	48
——— J. A., 2/Lt.	171
——— J. H., Lieut.	136
——— R., 2/Lt.	130
——— S. E., 2/Lt.	79
——— S. H., M.C., Capt.	27
——— T. F. V., Capt.	62
Matthewson, R. W. B., 2/Lt.	157
Mattison, H., 2/Lt.	111
Maude, J., 2/Lt.	67
Maudslay, R. V., Major	11
Maughfling, T., 2/Lt.	98
Maule, H. S., Lt.-Col.	184
Maunder, W. C., 2/Lt.	36
Maunsell, Chas. F., Lieut.	28
Mawer, A. L., 2/Lt.	174
Maxfield, W. J., 2/Lt.	25
Maxson, C. W.,	135
Maxted, O. D., Lieut.	151
Maxwell, E. C., Lieut.	16
——— G. A., Capt.	49
——— G. E., 2/Lt.	147
——— K. G., Capt.	95
——— S. W., 2/Lt.	108
May, L. B., Lieut.	158
——— P. E., 2/Lt.	21
——— R. G. S., Lieut.	77
——— T. A., 2/Lt.	123
——— W. E., 2/Lt.	127
Mayhew, T. G., 2/Lt.	43
Maynard, C. E., Capt.	27
——— F. L., 2/Lt.	14
——— H., Lieut.	10
——— J. E., Lieut.	88
——— L. H., 2/Lt.	13
Mayne, H. G. L., Lieut.	146
——— H. T., Lieut.	146
——— R. A., 2/Lt.	160
Mayo, C. D., 2/Lt.	19
——— F., Lieut.	185
Mayor, A., 2/Lt.	55
Meade-King, W. T. P., Capt.	134
Meaden, C. A., Capt.	133
Meadon, A. A., Capt.	131
Meaking, G. E. R., 2/Lt.	146
Mearne, Colin, Capt.	132
Mears, H., Lt.	183
Mecey, E. J., Lieut.	83
Medlicott, H. W., 2/Lt.	147
——— R. F. C., Capt.	142
Meggitt, W. G., Lieut., M.C.	158
Meigham, S. S., Capt.	133
Meikle, T. J., Lieut.	11
Meiklejohn, R., Major	28
Mein, H. C., Lieut.	19
Mellis, C. G., Maj.-Gen., Sir, V.C., K.C.B.	182
Mellor, J. S. P., Lieut.	187
Mellowes, H. A., Capt.	64
Melvin, David L., Lieut.	173
Menzies, C. D., 2/Lt.	128
——— Daniel, Lieut.	122
——— J. F., Capt.	77
——— R., 2/Lt.	103
Meo, I., 2/Lt.	11
Mercer, G. A., Lieut.	16
——— H., 2/Lt.	17
——— W. T., 2/Lt.	14
Mercer-Smith, V., 2/Lt.	164
Mcredith, G. C., Capt.	55
——— H. T. D., Lieut.	72
——— J. J., 2/Lt.	161
——— L. A., Lieut.	105
Merrall, E., 2/Lt.	99
Merriman, G. V., 2/Lt.	142
——— R. D., Lieut.	184
Metcalf, R., 2/Lt.	117
Metcalfe, J., Lieut.	28
——— L. W., 2/Lt.	41
Metson, G. F., 2/Lt.	168
Metters, H. H., 2/Lt.	47
Meyer, C. B., Lieut.	136
——— J. V., 2/Lt.	126
——— O. F., Lieut.	168
Meyers, V. H. L., Lieut.	88
Michell, P. C., Lieut.	165
Michelmore, R. F., 2/Lt.	89
Middlebrook, N., 2/Lt.	149
Middleditch, R. H., Lieut.	48
Middlemas, G., Lieut.	19
Middlemass, R. W. H., Major	185
Middlemiss, G. A., 2/Lt.	78
Middleton, A. H., 2/Lt.	158
——— B. L., Lieut.	76
——— C. de C., Capt.	84
——— E., Capt.	131
——— G. V., 2/Lt.	78
——— J. R., Lieut.	150
——— J. S., Lieut.	33
——— L. N., Lieut.	53
——— R., Capt.	129
Midgley, C. W., 2/Lt.	125
Milani, R. S., 2/Lt.	163
Milburn, H. E., Capt.	47
——— O. L. F., Lieut.	133
Miles, A. A., 2/Lt.	160
——— B., 2/Lt.	83
——— C. S., 2/Lt.	96
Milford, E., Major	183
Millar, D., Lieut.	141
——— E. A., Capt.	36
——— John, 2/Lt.	19
——— J. W., 2/Lt.	70
——— T. S., 2/Lt.	153
——— W. A., 2/Lt.	18
Millard, B. A., Fl.-Sub.-Lt.	187
Miller, A. D., 2/Lt.	106
——— A. H., 2/Lt.	128
——— A. L., Lieut., M.C.	74
——— A. M., 2/Lt.	170
——— A. W., Lieut.	161
——— C. C., Capt.	60
——— David, 2/Lt.	158
——— D. H., 2/Lt.	115
——— F. K., Lieut.	132
——— I. R. F., Lieut.	60
——— R. M., Capt.	103
——— R. S., Lieut.	63

Miller, R. T., 2/Lt. ... 94	Monypeny, R. W., Lieut. 129	Morrison-Bell, A. C., Major ... 18	Murray, A. M., 2/Lt. ... 89
——— S., Lieut. ... 187	Montgomerie, F. D., Lieut. ... 23	Morritt, W. S., Lieut. ... 65	——— A. R., 2/Lt. ... 106
——— S., Lieut. ... 133	Montgomery, A. N., Lieut. ... 101	Morrogh, J. D., Major... 48	——— A. S., 2/Lt. ... 112
——— S. S., Lieut. ... 94	——— J., Capt. ... 8	Morse, T., Lieut. ... 158	——— C., Lieut. ... 189
——— W., Lieut. ... 180	——— K. B., Capt. ... 159	Mort, J., 2/Lt. ... 106	——— D. C. G., Lieut. 154
——— Z., 2/Lt. ... 169	——— R. N., 2/Lt. ... 16	Mortensen, W. M., 2/Lt. 138	——— H. R., 2/Lt. ... 57
Miller-Stirling, A. E. S., Lieut. ... 106	Monteith, R., 2/Lt. ... 109	Mortimer-Phelan, 2/Lt. 147	——— J. C. E., 2/Lt. ... 107
Millership, L. R., Lieut. 94	Moodie, A. M., Capt. ... 74	Morton, D. H., Capt. ... 60	——— J. G., Lieut. ... 139
Milligan, A. D., Lieut. ... 107	——— O., Capt. ... 74	——— J., 2/Lt. ... 109	——— P. S., Lieut. ... 43
Milling, H. B., Lieut. ... 152	——— B. C., 2/Lt. ... 153	——— J. D. M., Lieut. 99	——— R. V., 2/Lt. ... 175
Millman, F. H., Capt. ... 36	Moon, R. C., Major ... 122	——— J. G., 2/Lt. ... 87	Murton, H. S., Fl. Lt. ... 164
Mills, A. S., Lieut. ... 180	——— W. J., 2/Lt. ... 29	——— R. H., Lieut. ... 108	Musgrove, H. S., 2/Lt. ... 167
——— C., Capt. ... 136	Moore, A., Lt.-Col. ... 183	Moseley, G., Capt. ... 49	Mussared, W. J., 2/Lt. ... 154
——— D. W., Lieut. ... 56	——— A., Lieut. ... 165	——— R. A. D., Lieut. ... 113	Mutch, F. R., Lieut. ... 53
——— F. G., 2/Lt. ... 175	——— A. R., 2/Lt. ... 94	Moss, G. E., 2/Lt. ... 122	Myers, E., 2/Lt. ... 119
——— H. J. F., Lieut. 90	——— C. C., 2/Lt. ... 52	——— S. C., 2/Lt. ... 17	——— J. C., 2/Lt. ... 35
——— J., 2/Lt. ... 187	——— C. H. E., Capt. ... 93	Moss-Blundell, F. B., Lt.-Col. ... 13	——— F. C. A., Lieut. 138
——— J. F., 2/Lt. ... 80	——— C. R., Lieut. ... 173	Mossop, Wm. N., Capt. Adj. ... 41	
——— M., 2/Lt. ... 45	——— E. E. J., Capt. ... 59	Mott, J. E., Capt. ... 136	Nalder, R. F., Lieut. ... 125
——— W. B., 2/Lt. ... 118	——— E. S., 2/Lt. ... 153	Mottram, P., 2/Lt. ... 105	Nantes, G. J., Major ... 13
——— W. G., 2/Lt. ... 115	——— H. S., Capt. ... 132	Mouat-Biggs, J. A., Lieut. 47	Napier, H., Lt.-Col. Hon. 7
Miles, W. H., Capt. ... 187	——— H. W. H., 2/Lt. 31	Mould, W. J., Lieut. ... 73	——— J., 2/Lt., Sir 181
Millyard, T., Capt. ... 87	——— L., 2/Lt. ... 141	Moulton, T., Lieut. ... 55	——— L., Capt. ... 107
Milne, A., 2/Lt. ... 106	——— L. G., Lt.-Col. ... 92	Mount, W. J., Lieut. ... 114	——— W., 2/Lt. ... 72
——— C. G., 2/Lt. ... 172	——— M., Lieut. ... 154	Mousley, E. O., Lt. ... 185	Nash, C. P., Lt. ... 135
——— D. W., 2/Lt. ... 107	——— R. M., 2/Lt. ... 110	Moutrie, L., 2/Lt. ... 127	——— E. L. F., Capt. 132
——— S. B., 2/Lt. ... 27	——— R. S., Lieut. ... 9	Mowat, A., 2/Lt. ... 105	——— F. M., 2/Lt. ... 156
——— W., Capt. ... 20	——— T. S., 2/Lt. ... 89	——— M., 2/Lt. ... 105	——— G. E., Fl. Lt. ... 177
——— W., Major ... 121	Moorhead, W. B., Lieut. 31	Mowlam, H. J., Capt. ... 101	——— J. F., 2/Lt. ... 113
Milne-Thomson, A., Col. 134	Morant, N., 2/Lt. ... 48	Moxon, N. F., 2/Lt. ... 173	Nathan, G. S. M., 2/Lt. 28
Milner, J., Capt., M.C. ... 36	Morey, S. K., 2/Lt. ... 70	Moylan, F. E., Lieut. ... 128	Nattrass, F. J., Capt. ... 133
Milward, R., 2/Lt. ... 79	Morgan, D., Lieut. ... 10	Moyle, F. W., 2/Lt. ... 69	Naylor, C. B., Lieut. ... 171
——— W. E., Lieut. ... 64	——— F. N., 2/Lt. ... 46	Moysey, F., Capt. ... 37	——— F., 2/Lt. ... 102
Mingo, E. W., Lieut. ... 139	——— H. L., 2/Lt. ... 68	Mucklow, S. L., Lieut. ... 174	——— F. A., 2/Lt. ... 75
Minifie, R. P., Fl. Com. 160	——— H. L., Lieut. ... 57	Mudd, W. A., 2/Lt. ... 38	——— G., 2/Lt. ... 187
Miscampbell, A., Capt. ... 68	——— H. T., 2/Lt. ... 120	Mudie, K., Lieut. ... 51	Neal, A. F., Lieut. ... 16
Miskin, W. L., Capt. ... 184	——— J. B., Lieut. ... 31	Muff, W. R., 2/Lt. ... 99	Neale, A. W., 2/Lt. ... 69
Mitchel, G. W., Lieut. ... 172	——— R. J., Capt. ... 173	Muir, A., 2/Lt. ... 158	Neame, E. G., 2/Lt. ... 65
Missingham, W. S., 2/Lt. 137	——— T. E., 2/Lt. ... 16	——— J. C., Capt. ... 132	Needham, E., Capt. ... 123
Mitchell, A. D., 2/Lt. ... 142	——— T. P., 2/Lt. ... 158	——— J. C., Lieut. ... 34	——— Hayden, 2/Lt. ... 43
——— A. P., Lieut. ... 153	——— T. W. M., Capt. ... 146	Muirden, N. H., Lieut. ... 164	——— R. P., 2/Lt. ... 81
——— F. H., Lieut. ... 189	——— W. G., 2/Lt. ... 157	Muirhead, W. D., 2/Lt. ... 41	——— T. H., Capt. ... 122
——— H., 2/Lt. ... 163	Morland, W., Capt. ... 187	Mulcahy, M., 2/Lt. ... 48	Neil, R. W., Lieut. ... 139
——— H. B. O., 2/Lt. ... 149	Morison, R. B., 2/Lt. ... 120	Mulhall, H. F., Lieut. ... 175	Neild, Arthur, 2/Lt. ... 77
——— H. G., 2/Lt. ... 58	Morley, C., Capt. ... 94	Mullaly, J. C. D., Capt. 143	Neill, J. W. F., Lieut. ... 155
——— J. R. McC., 2/Lt. 122	——— R. S., Capt. ... 51	Mullan, P. J., Father ... 181	——— P., 2/Lt. ... 16
——— J. V. R., Lieut. ... 20	Morlidge, A., Capt. ... 27	——— H. P., 2/Lt. ... 24	Neilson, T. A., Lieut. ... 59
——— R. R., 2/Lt. ... 91	Morony, W. V., Lieut. ... 60	Mullis, F. L., 2/Lt. ... 33	——— W., Capt. ... 103
——— R. T. L., Lieut. 106	Morpeth, R. S., Lieut. ... 122	Mumford, G. W., Lieut. 156	Neish, F. H., Col. ... 105
——— Sam, 2/Lt. ... 33	——— S., Lieut. ... 25	Mummery, H. N. S., Capt. ... 104	——— W., Capt. ... 105
——— T., 2/Lt. ... 39	Morrell, H. G., Capt. ... 182	Munday, J., 2/Lt. ... 115	Nelson, G. W., 2/Lt. ... 106
——— W., Capt. ... 131	Morrill, T. J., Capt. ... 43	Mundey, C. B., Capt. ... 186	——— J. H., 2/Lt. ... 58
——— Wm., 2/Lt. ... 173	Morris, A. A., 2/Lt. ... 27	Mundy, J. E., 2/Lt. ... 127	——— J. W., Major ... 187
——— W. G., 2/Lt. ... 11	——— B. A., 2/Lt. ... 107	Munn, L. S., 2/Lt. ... 87	——— R. C., Lieut. ... 138
——— W. T., Capt. ... 104	——— C. A., 2/Lt. ... 102	Munro, A., Lieut. ... 19	Nesbitt, A. W., 2/Lt. ... 101
Mitchelson, J. K., Capt. Rev. ... 135	——— H. O., 2/Lt. ... 128	——— F. F., Lieut. ... 122	——— F. W. R., Lieut. 101
Mitchiner, H. G., 2/Lt. ... 127	——— L. B. F., 2/Lt. ... 149	——— J., 2/Lt. ... 168	Neumann, C. W., Major 182
Mitten, R. C., Lieut. ... 173	——— R., Lieut. ... 136	——— J. G., Lieut. ... 170	Nevard, J. S., 2/Lt. ... 23
Moberly, B. E., Lieut. ... 140	——— V. C., 2/Lt. ... 151	Munroe, C. H. C., Lt. ... 182	Neville, D. A., Lieut. ... 172
Moffatt, F. B., 2/Lt. ... 19	——— W. A., Lieut. ... 66	Murchison, R., 2/Lt. ... 19	——— W., Capt. ... 110
Mogridge, V., 2/Lt. ... 142	——— W. F., Rev. ... 135	Murdoch, H. H., 2/Lt. ... 60	Newbery, T. F., Lieut. ... 118
Moline, R. W. H., Capt. 123	——— W. H., Lieut. ... 86	——— W., 2/Lt. ... 136	Newbold, J. W., Lieut. 186
Molloy, T. P. L., 2/Lt. ... 149	——— W. P., 2/Lt. ... 92	Murphy, D. G. C., Lieut. 126	——— L. A., 2/Lt. ... 147
——— W. C., 2/Lt. ... 20	Morrish, D. R., Lieut. ... 44	——— E. M., Capt. ... 33	Newbury, G. G., 2/Lt. ... 160
Molony, J. G., Capt. ... 133	Morrison, H. C., Lieut. ... 137	——— G. G. D., Lieut. 139	Newcomb, C., Capt. ... 184
Molson, J. H., Lieut. ... 140	——— H. St. J., Capt. 109	——— J. P., Lieut. ... 174	——— M., 2/Lt. ... 157
Monaghan, H. B., Lieut. 172	——— J. B., Capt. ... 130	——— L., Capt. ... 181	Newcombe, L., Major ... 49
——— M. J., 2/Lt. ... 115	——— K. R. M., Lieut. ... 140	——— L. W. R., 2/Lt. 113	——— S. F., Lt.-Col., D.S.O. ... 179
——— P. J., Capt. ... 143	——— K. S., Lieut. ... 158	——— P. A., 2/Lt. ... 78	Newenham, G. A., Lieut. 152
Monday, T. E., 2/Lt. ... 61	——— L. S., Capt. ... 138	——— T. F., Lieut. ... 126	Newey, T., 2/Lt. ... 172
Money, H., Lieut., M.C. 75	——— R., 2/Lt. ... 117	——— W. S., Capt. ... 47	Newland, N. C., 2/Lt. ... 126
——— R. R. N., Capt. 149	——— S., Lieut. ... 120		Newman, C., Lieut. ... 176
Monkman, Eric, 2/Lt. ... 127			——— Cyril, 2/Lt. ... 32
Monks, C. A., 2/Lt. ... 42			——— C. M., Capt. ... 52
			——— L. C., Lieut. ... 57

Newman, W. A., 2/Lt. 121	Nutter, R. U., 2/Lt. ... 12	Ormerod, E., Lieut. ... 51	Palmer, G. H., 2/Lt. ... 154
Newsholme, W. S., 2/Lt. 83	Nye, A. C., 2/Lt. ... 21	Ormiston, Peter, 2/Lt. ... 58	——— Harold, 2/Lt. ... 51
Newson, H. A., Lieut. ... 113	——— G. J., 2/Lt. ... 41	——— T., Major ... 141	——— Jack M., Capt. 144
——— H. M., Lieut. 142		O'Rorke, Rev. 135	——— J. W. E., 2/Lt. 120
Newstead, C. W., Lieut. 175	**Oakes**, J., Lieut. ... 34	Orr, A. P., 2/Lt. ... 53	——— K. R., Lieut. ... 8
——— W. C., Capt.,	Oakley, R. S., 2/Lt. ... 171	——— R. R., Capt. ... 112	——— N. St. C., Capt. 98
M.C. 40	——— W. E. B., Fl.-	Orr-Ewing, A. J., 2/Lt. 156	Panchaud, L. A., Lieut. 84
Newton, E. A., 2/Lt. ... 179	Sub-Lt. ... 177	Ortweiler, F. J., 2/Lt. ... 157	Panting, F. Owen, 2/Lt. 41
——— G. E., Lieut. 129	O'Brian, W., Capt. ... 133	Osborn, C. C. F., Lieut. 153	Papenfus, M.T.S., Lieut. 166
——— H. M., 2/Lt. ... 52	O'Brien, C. R., Lieut. ... 152	Osborne, E. B., 2/Lt. ... 64	Papworth, A. S., 2/Lt. ... 169
——— H. W. G., Lieut. 38	——— J. F., 2/Lt. ... 60	——— F. W., 2/Lt. ... 178	Paramore, L., 2/Lt. ... 70
——— I. H., 2/Lt. ... 127	——— P. A., 2/Lt. ... 155	——— H. P., Lt.-Col. 86	Parfect, G. F., 2/Lt. ... 30
Niall, A. M., 2/Lt. ... 8	O'Bryne, A. J. O., 2/Lt. 148	——— J. E., Major 139	Parfitt, E., Capt. ... 89
Nichol, R. W., 2/Lt. ... 148	O'Callaghan, C. E., Lieut. 113	——— V. E., Lieut. ... 121	——— E. G., 2/Lt. ... 12
Nicholas, E. M., 2/Lt. ... 164	O'Carroll, A. D., Capt. ... 131	Osborough, A. H., 2/Lt. 109	Paris, A. E., Capt. ... 16
——— T. C., 2/Lt. ... 116	O'Connell, M. Wm., 2/Lt. 114	Osgerby, R. W., 2/Lt. ... 35	——— D. K., Lieut. 152
Nicholl, D. S. D., 2/Lt. 12	O'Connor, O., Lieut. ... 170	Osgood, Edwin D., 2/Lt. 23	Parish, J., Lieut. ... 39
Nicholls, C. B., Capt. ... 37	——— R. D., Lieut. 112	O'Shea, H. A., 2/Lt. ... 168	——— W. G., 2/Lt. ... 130
——— W. H., 2/Lt. 138	Oddlafson, August, 2/Lt. 128	Osmond, E. P., Lieut. ... 181	Park, C. A. R., 2/Lt. ... 130
Nichols, C. L., 2/Lt. ... 10	Oddy, E. A. H., 2/Lt. ... 115	——— T. E., Capt., ... 186	——— F. S., Capt. 140
——— F. C., Capt. ... 133	O'Dell, W. H., 2/Lt. ... 102	Ostler, R., Lieut. ... 75	——— S. M., Lieut. ... 157
——— F. G., Lieut. 44	Oddy, N., 2/Lt. ... 42	Oswald, G. A., Lieut. ... 25	Parke, J. E., 2/Lt. ... 168
——— W. H., Major 39	Odling, B. G., Lieut. ... 148	Oswell, S. H., 2/Lt. ... 82	Parker, F. V., Capt. ... 45
Nicholson, D. A., Major 107	Odom, G. C., Lieut. ... 122	Oswin, P., 2/Lt. ... 121	——— C., 2/Lt. ... 57
——— E. B., Capt.,	O'Donnell, A. B., Capt. 29	Otter, R., Col. 22	——— G. W., Lieut. 36
M.C. ... 20	——— T. F., 2/Lt. ... 113	Outran, J. L., Lieut. ... 7	——— J., 2/Lt. ... 28
——— G., Lieut. ... 50	O'Donoghue, J. H., 2/Lt. 184	Ovenstone, J. J., 2/Lt. 61	——— J. K., 2/Lt. ... 149
——— G. H., Lieut. 149	——— P. E., Lieut. ... 186	Overbury, G. E., 2/Lt. ... 62	——— M. J., Capt. ... 189
——— H. A., Capt. 31	O'Dowd, F. B., Lieut. ... 134	Overell, A. N., 2/Lt. ... 88	——— N., 2/Lt. ... 42
——— J. A., 2/Lt ... 32	O'Dwyer, J. E. A., Capt. 188	Owen, A. L., 2/Lt. ... 141	——— R. W. W., Capt. 101
——— J. H., Lieut. 27	Oehl, G., 2/Lt. 88	——— D., Capt. ... 157	——— S. J., 2/Lt. ... 93
——— T., Lieut. ... 47	Oerton, Thomas, Lieut. 36	——— D. C., Lieut. ... 13	——— W. B., 2/Lt. ... 117
——— S., Lieut. ... 187	O'Farrell, W. R., Capt. 178	——— G.C.F., Capt. 176	——— W. B., 2/Lt. ... 66
——— T., Lieut. ... 95	Ogden, A., 2/Lt. ... 21	——— H. E., Lloyd,	——— W. B. H.,
——— T. G., 2/Lt. ... 19	——— C. E., 2/Lt. ... 158	Lieut. ... 139	Lieut. ... 181
Nicol, I. S., 2/Lt. ... 13	Ogilvie, S. S., Lt.-Col. ... 93	——— H. H., 2/Lt. ... 55	——— W. G., 2/Lt. ... 129
Nightingale, A. J., Fl.	Ogilvy, W. F., Lieut. ... 170	——— H. W., Sub.-Lt. 151	Parkes, E. L., Lieut. ... 16
Lt. 181	O'Grady, W. de C., Lieut. 139	——— J. C. F., Lieut. 188	——— G. A. H., 2/Lt. 154
Nilen, F. P., Lieut. ... 86	O'Halloran-Giles, R.,	——— L. D., 2/Lt. ... 34	——— G. W., 2/Lt. ... 14
Nilson, A. C., 2/Lt. ... 66	Lieut. 9	——— L.V.D., Lieut. 75	——— P. R., 2/Lt. ... 129
Nisbet, R. I., 2/Lt. ... 27	O'Hanlon, L. T., Lieut. 58	——— O. A., Lieut. ... 112	Parkhouse, J. F., Lieut. 60
Nixon, G., 2/Lt. ... 101	O'Hara, D. H., 2/Lt. ... 60	——— R. J., 2/Lt. ... 161	Parkin, G., 2/Lt. ... 72
——— J. G., 2/Lt. ... 68	O'Hare, O. J., 2/Lt. ... 113	——— R. O., Lieut. ... 73	Parkinson, J. A., Lieut. 172
——— L. G., 2/Lt. ... 158	Ohrt, F. M., 2/Lt. ... 159	——— T., 2/Lt. ... 123	——— P., Lieut. ... 179
Nobbs, C. H. F., 2/Lt. 156	O'Keefe, E. C. K., 2/Lt. 141	Owens, G., 2/Lt. ... 73	——— V. J., Lieut. ... 181
——— H. G., Capt. 128	O'Keefe, L., 2/Lt. ... 48	——— James, 2/Lt. ... 114	——— V. J., 2/Lt. ... 138
Noel, J. B., 2/Lt. ... 85	O'Kelly, L. C., 2/Lt. ... 136	Oxlade, E. R., 2/Lt. ... 70	Parks, G. C., 2/Lt. ... 112
Noble, T. E., 2/Lt. ... 73	Old, R. M., Lieut. ... 84	Ozanne, H. W., Capt. ... 28	Parr, F. S., Capt. ... 146
——— W., 2/Lt. ... 105	Oldfield, G. P., 2/Lt. ... 93		——— H. O., Lt.-Col. 183
Nocton, V., 2/Lt. ... 35	O'Leary, D. A., Lieut. ... 173	**Pack**, D. H., Capt., M.C. 32	——— J. W., Lieut. 103
Nolan, J., Chap. ... 135	Olerenshaw, J., 2/Lt. ... 172	Paddison, R. M., Lieut. 66	——— V. H., Major 60
——— J. G., 2/Lt. ... 15	O'Lieff, P. H., Lieut. ... 161	Paeo, A., Lieut. ... 182	Parrish, E. P., 2/Lt. ... 82
Norcross, Bernard, Lieut. 171	Oliphant, G. W., Lieut. 67	Page, C. A. S., Major	——— F. W., Lieut. 92
Norden, W. G., Lieut. ... 167	——— K. J. P., Lieut. 93	(A/Lt.-Col.), D.S.O. ... 88	Parrott, A. E. H., 2/Lt. 40
Norman, A. L., 2/Lt. ... 99	Oliver, D. C. M., 2/Lt. ... 84	——— R. A., Lieut. 79	Parry, C. F., Lieut. ... 78
——— C. W., Lieut. 9	——— F. G., 2/Lt. ... 27	——— W. F., Lieut. 57	——— W., 2/Lt. ... 57
——— E. H., 2/Lt. ... 79	——— G., 2/Lt. ... 102	Paget, G., Lieut. ... 34	——— W. S., Sub.-Lt. 145
——— G. R., 2/Lt. 161	——— Henry, Lieut. ... 105	——— O. L., 2/Lt. ... 98	Parsons, A. F., 2/Lt. ... 91
Norris, A. R., 2/Lt. ... 69	——— J. C., 2/Lt. ... 87	Paine, E. H., Capt. ... 70	——— B. K., Capt. 29
——— Edwin J., 2/Lt. 171	——— R. C. D., 2/Lt. 161	——— L. P., Fl.-Sup.-	——— C. St. C., 2/Lt. 162
——— R. W., 2/Lt. 61	Olphert, A. V., Lieut. ... 110	Lt. 176	——— G., 2/Lt. ... 95
Norrish, R. G. W., 2/Lt. 12	——— W., Capt. ... 145	Pakenham-Walsh, L. H.,	——— J., 2/Lt. ... 27
North, E. A., 2/Lt. ... 52	O'Malley, J. F., Lieut. ... 113	Lieut. 179	——— J. C. L., 2/Lt. 12
——— F. R., 2/Lt. ... 66	O'Mally, Cusack, Capt. 133	Palin, A. H., 2/Lt. ... 87	——— R. G., Lieut. 185
Northey, H. G., 2/Lt. ... 85	O'Neill, J. G., 2/Lt. ... 60	——— G. W., Lieut.,	Partington, J. S., 2/Lt. 96
Northwood, G. W., Capt. 139	Onslow, E. M., Lieut. ... 28	M.C. ... 189	——— O. J., Lieut. ... 154
Norton, P. C., 2/Lt. ... 157	Openshaw, G. O., Capt. 36	Paling, W. E., Lieut. ... 69	Partridge, A. T., Lieut. 168
Norvill, V. A., Lieut. ... 154	Oram, H. W. H., 2/Lt. ... 95	Palk, C. E., 2/Lt. ... 52	——— E. G., 2/Lt. ... 81
Nottidge, P., Lieut. ... 189	Orchard, A. F., 2/Lt. ... 65	Palmer, A. E. P., Lieut. 140	Pascoe, P. J., 2/Lt. ... 26
Noxon, F. C., 2/Lt. ... 51	——— E. F. G., Lieut. 33	——— A. W., 2/Lt. 158	Pass, W. D., Lieut. ... 178
Nugent, T. C., Lieut. ... 79	——— W. D., 2/Lt. ... 115	——— C. B., 2/Lt. 179	Patch, H., Capt. ... 157
Nurse, F., 2/Lt. ... 79	Orde, M. A. J., 2/Lt. ... 147	——— C. W., 2/Lt. 147	Patenaude, A. J., 2/Lt. 163
Nutt, A. C. R., Major ... 10	Ordish, B. W. A., 2/Lt. 149	——— E. A., Capt. ... 13	Paterson, A., Lieut. ... 48
——— A. H., Capt. 70	Orford, E., Capt. ... 37	——— E. B., Capt. ... 20	——— C., 2/Lt. ... 30
Nuttall, H., 2/Lt. ... 78	Organ, A. F., 2/Lt. ... 148	——— F., 2/Lt. ... 34	——— J. R., Lieut. ... 103
——— J. C., Lieut. ... 167	Orgill, Philip, 2/Lt. ... 123	——— F., Major ... 141	Patey, H. A., Capt. ... 170

	PAGE		PAGE		PAGE		PAGE
Patman, A. C., Capt.	48	Peers, I. A., Lieut.	163	Phillips, P. A., Lieut.	64	Pond, Fredk., 2/Lt.	88
———— G. H., Lieut.	168	Pegg, J. S., 2/Lt.	120	———— P. L., 2/Lt.	174	Pont, E. S., 2/Lt.	12
Patmore, F. J., Lieut.	187	Pegge, E. E., Lieut.	94	———— R., Lieut.	64	Pontin, S. C. M., Lieut.	164
Paton, G. G. R., 2/Lt.	11	Peile, A. H., 2/Lt.	159	———— R. E. G., Lieut.	47	Poole, A. A., 2/Lt.	179
———— J. H., 2/Lt.	120	Peiler, M. F., 2/Lt.	161	———— T. P., 2/Lt.	107	———— B. C. H., Lieut.	56
Patrick, R. F. W., Lieut.	105	Peirson, G., Capt.	7	———— V. G. M., Lieut.	37	———— J. S., 2/Lt.	90
———— W. D., Capt.	161	Pemberton, A. L., 2/Lt.	161	———— W. A., Lieut.	183	———— S. B., Lieut.	32
———— J., Lieut.	74	———— J., 2/Lt.	57	Phillipson, E., 2/Lt.	51	Pooley, H. R., 2/Lt.	30
Patten, A. G. B., 2/Lt.	37	Pendleton, W., 2/Lt.	174	Philpott, J. R., Capt.	180	Pope, A. D., 2/Lt.	161
Patterson, A. F. A., 2/Lt.	149	Penfold, F. S., 2/Lt.	87	———— W. G., 2/Lt.	127	———— C., Lieut.	45
———— E. A., 2/Lt.	76	Pengilley, E. E., 2/Lt.	31	Phippard, F. H., 2/Lt.	126	———— E. E. E., Capt.	159
———— I. A., Lieut.	10	Penman, G., 2/Lt.	58	Phipps, W. G., 2/Lt.	21	———— R. A. B., Lieut.	170
———— K. S., 2/Lt.	10	Penney, C. M., 2/Lt.	91	Pickard, C. E., 2/Lt.	102	———— J., 2/Lt.	16
———— R. M., 2/Lt.	12	Penruddocke, N. F., Lieut.	162	Picken, J. C., 2/Lt.	104	———— P. M., Capt. and Adj.	90
———— W., Lieut.	49	Pentney, A. F., Rev.	135	Pickering, B. H., Lieut.	23	Porteous, J. D., 2/Lt.	41
Pattinson, J. F., Lieut.	163	Penwarden, H. G., 2/Lt.	181	———— E. G., 2/Lt.	44	———— J. S., 2/Lt.	92
———— J., H., Lieut.	102	Peppé, C. G. H., Lieut.	56	———— H. A., Capt.	99	———— W. F., Lieut. M.C.,	118
———— T. S., 2/Lt.	42	Pepper, A. C., 2/Lt.	151	———— W. J., 2/Lt.	9	Porter, A. C., 2/Lt.	168
Patton, G. E., Lieut.	14	———— C. N., 2/Lt.	41	Pickett, A. C., 2/Lt.	155	———— E. J., Lieut.	130
———— W. F., Lieut.	180	———— E., Lieut.	41	Pickford, E. W., Lieut.	161	———— G. T., Lieut.	147
Paul, R. F., Capt.	163	Percival, B., 2/Lt.	24	Pickthall, H. C., 2/Lt.	78	———— R. P., Capt.	95
———— Sir R. J., Lieut.	178	———— E., 2/Lt.	152	Picton-Warlow, I., Capt.	106	———— S. B., 2/Lt.	165
———— W. B., 2/Lt.	39	———— R. L., 2/Lt.	35	Pickup, H. J.	92	Porteus, J., 2/Lt.	52
Pawsey, C. R., Capt.	63	Percy, F., Lieut.	62	Pidduck, E. W., Lieut.	72	Portman, G. M. B., Capt.	128
———— J. S., 2/Lt.	62	Pereira, A. E. W., 2/Lt.	100	Piesse, C. L., 2/Lt.	21	Potter, A. T., Lieut.	68
Paxton, A. G., Capt.	98	———— F. V. C., Lieut.	37	Pighills, J. A., 2/Lt.	52	———— G. W. H., 2/Lt.	15
———— J., 2/Lt.	98	Perham, W., Fl. Lt.	177	Pike, A. B., Lieut.	140	———— H. W., 2/Lt.	52
Payne, A. C. J., 2/Lt.	173	Perkins, C. J. T., 2/Lt.	111	———— C.B., Capt. Rev.	135	———— K. R., Capt.	34
———— A. S., 2/Lt.	117	———— G., Capt.	189	———— E. A., Lieut.	101	———— L. R., Lieut.	183
———— H. E. A., 2/Lt.	34	Perks, G., Agent	189	———— P. R., Lieut.	129	———— S., 2/Lt.	30
———— H. S., 2/Lt.	22	———— H., Capt.	88	Pilcher, A. M., 2/Lt.	129	Potts, D., Lieut.	131
———— J. M., 2/Lt.	175	Perrett, F. C., 2/Lt.	63	Pill, S. V. P., Capt.	134	———— J. P., 2/Lt.	129
———— P., 2/Lt.	171	———— R. E., Capt. and Adjt.	130	Pilley, A. E., Capt.	85	———— W. J., 2/Lt.	175
Peacey, R., Lieut.	114	Perring, J. H., 2/Lt.	174	Pim, A. S., Capt.	47	Poulter, C. G., 2/Lt.	38
Peachey, B. W., Lieut.	80	Perry, A M., Sub-Lt.	144	Pinder, F. G., 2/Lt.	147	———— W. F., Lieut.	160
Peacock, B., 2/Lt.	27	———— B. B., Lieut.	157	———— L., 2/Lt.	64	Pouncey, J. R., 2/Lt.	70
———— F., 2/Lt.	142	———— H., Capt.	131	Pineau, C. F., Lieut.	174	Powell, D., Lieut.	189
———— N. L., Lt.	186	———— P. P., Lieut.	117	Pinkerton, A. L., 2/Lt.	149	———— D. G., Lieut.	156
———— J. W., 2/Lt.	138	———— S. T. J.	33	Pinkney, M. R., 2/Lt.	100	———— F. G., Capt.	167
———— M. A., 2/Lt.	156	Perryman, H. M., 2/Lt.	120	Pinnick, L. W., Lieut.	66	———— F. J., Major, M.C.	159
Peake, C. W. V., Lieut.	62	Peskett, R. F., Lieut.	35	Pinnington, E. A., 2/Lt.	181	———— G. E., 2/Lt.	51
Pearce, C., 2/Lt.	31	Petavel, Paul Major	66	Pinnock, A., Lieut.	90	———— J. F., 2/Lt.	79
———— E., Lieut.	117	Peters, J. F. J.	169	Piper, A. L., 2/Lt.	75	———— T., 2/Lt.	14
———— J. P., 2/Lt.	75	———— S. F., 2/Lt.	121	———— E. C., 2/Lt.	69	———— T. C. K., 2/Lt.	128
———— K., 2/Lt.	38	Peterson, G. G.W., 2/Lt.	158	———— Percy, 2/Lt.	31	———— W., 2/Lt.	64
———— L. W. C., Lieut.	166	Petley, R. E., Lieut.	130	———— H. T., Lieut.	181	———— W. B., Lt.-Col.	184
———— W. H., 2/Lt.	13	Petit, G., 2/Lt., M.C.	114	Pirouet, E. K. G., Lieut.	42	Power, H. E., 2/Lt.	174
Pearcy, G. S., Capt.	30	Petrie, W. R., Capt.	105	Pirie, D. A., Capt.	142	———— J. F., Lieut.	133
Pearse, L. H., 2/Lt.	65	Pettigrew, W., 2/Lt.	61	Pitblado, C. B., Lieut.	138	———— K. W., Lieut.	10
Pearson, B. C., 2/Lt.	167	Pettit, A. W. B., Lieut.	137	Pitman, R. C., Lieut.	171	Poweys, A. R., Capt.	49
———— D. H., Major	179	———— S. L., Capt.	181	Pitt, W H., 2/Lt.	62	Powl, S. R., 2/Lt.	128
———— E., Capt.	37	Peverell, T.H., Capt.-Adjr.	104	Pittar, G. P., 2/Lt.	12	Pownall, J. W., 2/Lt.	85
———— F. A., 2/Lt.	88	Phelan, R. S., 2/Lt.	155	Pittard, R. S. R., Lieut.	56	Pragnell, F., Capt.	78
———— H. F., Capt.	88	Phelps, A., Capt.	29	Pitts, F. B., 2/Lt.	46	Pratt, A. B., Capt., M.C.	62
———— J. M., Lieut.	174	———— H. J., 2/Lt.	34	Pitz, R. F., 2/Lt.	44	———— A. R., 2/Lt.	175
———— L. H., Lieut.	46	———— H. M. P., 2/Lt.	30	Place, C. O., Lt.-Col.	7	———— H., 2/Lt.	92
———— L. J., 2/Lt.	147	Philby, G. B., Lieut.	38	Plackett, C. H., Capt.	85	———— O. S., Major	89
———— M., Major	184	Philip, D., 2/Lt.	68	Plant, C. B., Lieut.	125	Preston, A., Lieut.	131
———— R. W., Capt.	134	———— G. H., 2/Lt.	12	Platt, Percy, 2/Lt.	50	———— A., 2/Lt.	170
———— W. G., Capt.	23	———— J. W., Capt.	186	Player, J. G., 2/Lt.	63	———— H., 2/Lt.	40
———— W. N., 2/Lt.	49	Philips, G. P., 2/Lt.	17	Pleasance, M. D., Lieut.	96	———— J. T., Capt.	35
———— W. O., 2/Lt.	88	Phillimore, G. W., Lieut.	57	Plews, J. C., Lieut.	85	Pretty, C. W., 2/Lt.	43
———— W. S. L. M., Lieut.	180	Phillips, A., 2/Lt.	127	Plimsoll, S. R. C., Capt.	14	———— H. J., 2/Lt.	172
Pease, D., 2/Lt.	19	———— A. W., Fl. Sub-Lt.	177	Plowman, Paul, Lieut.	72	———— R. C., 2/Lt.	172
Peat, R. W., Lieut.	163	———— C. W., 2/Lt.	76	Plumb, R. H., Lieut.	23	Price, H. W., Major	185
Peck, A. J., Capt.	28	———— E. C. M., Lt.-Col.	131	Plummer, J. E. B., Capt.	33	———— J. H., 2/Lt.	152
———— J. N., Lt.-Col.	34	———— E. S., Lieut.	133	Pocock, A. N. D., 2/Lt.	187	———— L., Capt.	89
Peckham, C. W., Lieut.	164	———— G. C., Capt.	130	———— J. A., Lieut.	185	———— O., Lieut.	67
Peddie, F., 2/Lt., M.C.	25	———— G. N., 2/Lt.	15	———— P. F., Major	184	———— P., 2/Lt.	180
Pedley, J. G., 2/Lt.	42	———— J. R., 2/Lt.	84	Pollack, J., Lieut.	110	———— R., Lieut.	143
Pedrick, F. B., Lieut.	133	———— J. S., Lieut.	118	Pollard, A. M., Capt.	131	———— R. T., 2/Lt.	113
Peebles, A., Major	37	———— K. McN., 2/Lt.	100	———— R. W., 2/Lt.	30	———— W., 2/Lt.	59
Peek, R. G., Lieut.	9			———— W. H., Lieut.	168	———— W. G., 2/Lt.	65
Peel, B. G., Major	182			Pollitt, G. P., Lt.-Col.	52		
Peeling, H. V., 2/Lt.	169			Pollock, J. B., 2/Lt.	74		
				———— J. J. McE., 2/Lt.	111		

	PAGE		PAGE		PAGE		PAGE
Price, W. N., 2/Lt.	98	Ramsay, R. W., 2/Lt.	73	Rees, C. B. R., Lieut.	49	Richardson, G.T., Lieut.	175
Prichard, F. H., Capt.	10	——— W. A., Lieut	75	——— D. Ivor, 2/Lt.	73	——— H. R., Capt.	141
——— O. T., Capt.	96	Ramwell, J., Sub-Lt.	145	——— E. C., 2/Lt.	125	——— John, 2/Lt.	26
Priday, H. E. L., 2/Lt.	68	Randall, C. H., Capt.	54	——— E. T., Lt.-Col.	34	——— J. B., 2/Lt.	171
——— N. H., 2/Lt.	42	Randell, W. B., 2/Lt.	159	——— H., Brig.-Gen.	7	——— J. P., Lieut. & Qmr.	186
Prideaux-Brune, F. K., Lieut.	8	Ranken, W. J. S., 2/Lt.	122	——— H. R., 2/Lt.	25	——— L. N., Lieut.	108
Prier, W. J., 2/Lt.	162	Rankin, C. D., Lt.-Col.	131	——— W., 2/Lt.	67	——— R. H., 2/Lt.	156
Priest, W. E. G., 2/Lt.	100	——— W. A., Lieut.	173	——— W. A., Capt.	134	——— W. J., 2/Lt.	101
Priestly, H. E., Capt.	131	Rankine, A. C., 2/Lt.	58	——— W. H., Lieut.	111	——— W. M., Lieut.	66
Prime, H. L., 2/Lt.	174	Ransome, J. E. G., T/Capt.	189	Reeve, A., Lieut.	34	Riches, J. E., 2/Lt.	92
Pring, W., 2/Lt.	106	Ranson, A., Lieut.	101	Reeves, C. H., 2/Lt.	118	Richey, R. A., 2/Lt.	111
Pringle, R. M., 2/Lt.	20	——— F. R., Capt.	136	——— R., Lieut.	12	Richmond, A. H. D., Lieut.	112
Prior, E. G., Lieut.	91	Rasmussen, F. G. J., 2/Lt.	11	——— W. A., 2/Lt.	150	Rick, J. H., Lieut.	52
——— W. H., 2/Lt.	30	Ratcliffe, B. Lieut.	39	Reid, A., 2/Lt.	74	Rickards, A. R. M., 2/Lt.	151
Pristo, W. E., 2/Lt.	91	——— T., Lieut.	162	——— A.McK., Capt.	121	Rickard, H., Lieut.	67
Pritchard, R. J., 2/Lt.	121	Rathbone, C. E. H., Lt.-Col.	151	——— C. W., Lieut.	159	——— J., Lieut.	131
Pritchett, W., Capt.	78	——— G. P., Lieut.	98	——— G. C. W., Lieut.	137	Rickett, G. F., Lieut.	129
Profit, G. S. W., 2/Lt.	77	——— H. J., 2/Lt.	90	——— H. G., Lieut.	176	——— W. H. A., 2/Lt.	164
Prothero, A. G., Major	72	——— Leonard, 2/Lt.	97	——— H. C., Lieut.	93	Riddell, L. H., Lieut.	167
Pruden, W. C., 2/Lt.	158	Rathborne, H. B., 2/Lt.	71	——— J. E., Lieut.	170	Riddle, A. B., Lieut.	188
Pryde, R. M., Capt.	109	Ratliff, P. G., 2/Lt.	162	——— J. F., Lieut.	164	Rideout, F. O., 2/Lt.	43
Pryce, F. M., 2/Lt.	179	Rattborne, C., Lieut.	177	——— Kenneth, 2/Lt.	104	Ridgard, B. H., 2/Lt.	64
Pryor, J. W., Lieut.	164	Raven, C. H., 2/Lt.	128	——— L. K., 2/Lt.	109	Ridgewell, L. P., 2/Lt.	137
Puckridge, H. V., Capt.	165	Ravenshaw, H. S. L., Brig.-Gen.	7	——— S. E., Capt.	51	——— S. C., 2/Lt.	179
Pugh, J., 2/Lt.	175	Rawden, C. H., Lieut.	85	——— W., 2/Lt.	146	Ridgway, F. J., 2/Lt.	68
——— J. A., Lieut.	165	Rawes, A. N., 2/Lt.	12	Reidy, F. J., Capt.	26	Ridley, C. A., 2/Lt.	148
Pughe-Evans, H., 2/Lt.	157	Rawlings, E. E., 2/Lt.	47	Reilly, H. L., Major	180	——— C. B., Lieut.	165
Pulfer, L. H., 2/Lt.	76	——— F. R., 2/Lt.	61	Rendle, G. A., 2/Lt.	30	——— H. M., 2/Lt.	102
Pullin, A. H., 2/Lt.	14	Rawlinson, C. R., Capt.	113	Rennells, F. C., 2/Lt.	84	——— P., 2/Lt.	125
Pulpher, L., 2/Lt.	95	——— G. E., Lieut.	126	Rennie, H. R., 2/Lt.	108	——— R. T., Capt.	91
Punchard, F. N., 2/Lt.	184	Rawson, Herbert, Sub-Lt.	145	——— W. K., Lieut.	120	Riecke, A. F. M., Major	11
Purcell, V. W. W. S., Lieut.	49	——— H. W., Capt.	20	Renshaw, H. W., 2/Lt.	70	Riffkin, R., 2/Lt	174
Puri, M. L., Capt.	182	Rawson-Shaw, K., Lieut.	146	Rethman, H. M.	142	Rigby, C., 2/Lt.	80
Purnell, A. W., 2/Lt.	15	Rayment, S. C., 2/Lt.	78	Reveley, P. T. A., 2/Lt.	167	——— H. A., Lieut.	138
Purry, R. O., Capt.	164	Rawstorne, R. A., Lieut.	178	Reynard, C. H., 2/Lt.	90	——— H. J., 2/Lt.	40
Purves, A. B., Capt. and Adjt.	54	Raymond, A. B., Lieut.	153	Reyne, G. R., Capt.	183	Rigden, B. L., Lieut.	17
——— G., Lieut.	115	——— L. B., 2/Lt.	169	Reynell, A. W., 2/Lt.	148	Riley, A. H., Lieut.	42
——— S. S. B., 2/Lt.	150	Raymond-Barker, A. B. Lieut.	149	Reynolds, B. W., Lt.	183	——— E. J., 2/Lt.	166
Purvis, W. B., Capt.	97	Rayner, A. E., 2/Lt.	47	——— E. R. B., 2/Lt.	12	——— F. B., Lieut.	93
Puryear, G., 2/Lt.	169	——— C., 2/Lt.	91	——— G. N., Capt.	9	——— H. A., Lieut.	64
Pye, B. W., 2/Lt.	35	——— L. S. P. H., 2/Lt.	121	——— J. W., Lieut.	36	——— R. R., Lieut.	70
Pym, F. G., Lieut.	173	Raynor, C. A., Capt.	183	——— L. G. S., Major	174	Rimington, H. P., 2/Lt.	84
Pye, S., Lieut.	93	Rea, W. G., 2/Lt.	18	——— T., Capt.	85	Ringer, E. C. S., 2/Lt.	157
Pyrke, L., 2/Lt.	83	——— W. Q., 2/Lt.	110	——— T. B., Lieut.	121	Ringham, H. T., 2/Lt.	96
Quaintrell, A. E., 2/Lt.	64	Read, B. R. C., 2/Lt.	116	——— W. J., Capt.	90	Rintoul, A., 2/Lt.	138
Quayle, M., Lieut.	63	——— J. A., Lieut.	189	Rhett, R. B., Lieut.	133	Risk, J. B., 2/Lt.	168
Quigley, J. E., Lieut.	133	——— J. F. W., Lieut.	186	Rhodes, C. W., Lieut.	138	Rissik, A. W. M., Capt.	115
Quill, M. J., 2/Lt.	70	——— L., 2/Lt.	155	——— F. O., Lieut.	120	Ritchie, F. K. St. M., 2/Lt.	142
Quilter, E. G. C., 2/Lt.	155	——— R. J., 2/Lt.	142	——— J. F., Lieut.	67	——— J. N., Major	13
Quine, A. H., 2/Lt.	181	Reader, R., 2/Lt.	92	——— Tom, 2/Lt.	124	——— T. M., 2/Lt.	166
——— R. H., 2/Lt.	25	Reakes, S. R. K., 2/Lt.	14	Riach, W. H., Capt.	107	——— W. H., 2/Lt.	31
Race, A., 2/Lt.	99	Reay, R. H., Lieut.	17	Ribbons, A., Lieut.	111	Ritson, J. R., Major	101
——— C., 2/Lt.	35	Record, J. A. C., 2/Lt.	22	Rice, J. A. T., Capt., M.C.	9	Ritzema, J. R., Lieut.	26
Rackett, A. R., Lieut.	138	Reddie, Robert, Capt.	34	Rich, H. H., Lieut.	184	Rivers, S., Lieut.	48
Radfield, J. J., 2/Lt.	169	Redfern, L., 2/Lt.	97	Richardes, R. A. W. P., Lieut.	188	Robb, A. G., Lieut., M.C.	59
Radford, W., 2/Lt.	63	Redgrave, W. T., Lieut.	118	Richards, A., 2/Lt.	33	——— A. W., 2/Lt.	58
Radley, J. E., Lieut.	175	Redhead, St. G., 2/Lt.	46	——— C. R., 2/Lt., M.C.	155	——— R. B., Lieut.	118
Rae, G. R., Capt.	183	Redington, F. H. C., Lieut.	120	——— C. S., 2/Lt.	129	Robbins, G., 2/Lt.	118
——— R. M., 2/Lt.	24	Redman, C. E., Capt.	132	——— F. W., 2/Lt.	115	——— W. A., 2/Lt.	115
Raggett, R. J., 2/Lt.	109	Redmond, M. Snowdon	133	——— H. U., Lieut.	62	Roberts, A. D., Lieut.	14
Raikes, J. F. C., Lieut.	126	Redpath, H. S., Lieut.	161	——— J., 2/Lt.	57	——— A. K., 2/Lt.	12
Railton, R., 2/Lt.	100	Reece, C., 2/Lt.	152	——— J., 2/Lt.	24	——— A. M., Lieut.	166
Raine, H. E., Lieut.	102	——— S. B., 2/Lt.	163	——— J. D. M., 2/Lt.	56	——— A. W., 2/Lt.	42
Rainier, G. A., 2/Lt.	163	Reed, F. H., 2/Lt.	174	——— J. Ivor, Lieut.	73	——— C. L., 2/Lt.	149
Rainsford-Hannay, A. G., Major	17	——— W., Lieut.	187	——— R., 2/Lt.	90	——— D. R. E., Capt.	132
Raleigh, A. G., 2/Lt.	46	——— W. J., 2/Lt.	37	——— R. H., 2/Lt.	32	——— E., Capt.	41
Ralston, K. B., 2/Lt.	55	Reeks, Neville, Capt.	187	——— R. J., 2/Lt.	75	——— E., 2/Lt	46
Rampling, H., Capt.	167	——— V. R., Capt.	185	——— R. J., Lieut.	141	——— E, Capt	85
Ramsay, A. FitzG., Major	8	Rees, B. E., Lieut.	17	Richardson, A. R., Lt.-Col.	127	——— E. D., 2/Lt.	70
——— H. S., Lieut.	137			——— D. D., Lieut.	161	——— F. W., Capt., M.C.	84
				——— D. H., 2/Lt.	101	——— G. D., Lieut.	100
				——— G., 2/Lt.	92		

Roberts, G. T., 2/Lt. ... 127	**Robson**, F., 2/Lt. ... 95	**Ross**, J. A., Lieut. ... 140	**St. Ledger**, A., 2/Lt. ... 70
——— H. E., 2/Lt. ... 64	——— G. B., 2/Lt. ... 66	——— L. J., 2/Lt. ... 108	Sabey, A. R., 2/Lt. ... 170
——— H. G., Lt.-Col. 51	——— H. T., 2/Lt. ... 49	——— P. B., 2/Lt. ... 98	Sadgrove, K. H. O'R., Capt. ... 72
——— H. J. W., Lieut. 169	——— J. W., 2/Lt. ... 68	——— P. M., Lieut. 58	Salisbury, O., Lieut. ... 73
——— N., 2/Lt. ... 117	——— L. S., Capt. ... 20	——— R. Y., 2/Lt. ... 127	Salley, A., 2/Lt. ... 13
——— P. A., Lieut. ... 57	——— N. K., 2/Lt. ... 107	——— W., Lieut. ... 159	Salmond, H. G., Capt. ... 148
——— R. E., Lieut. 83	——— T. A., Lieut. ... 49	——— W. A. N., 2/Lt. 106	Salmons, H., 2/Lt. ... 40
——— R. M., Lieut. 153	——— W., 2/Lt. ... 74	Rothery, W., Lieut. ... 156	Salter, H. P., Sub.-Lt. 177
——— T. H., 2/Lt. ... 83	Roche, S., 2/Lt. ... 151	Rought, C. J., 2/Lt. ... 21	——— Y. W., 2/Lt. ... 108
——— W. S., 2/Lt. 179	——— W. J., Lieut. 47	Rounds, R. W. ... 77	Salvidge, A. T., Capt. ... 33
Robertshaw, P. S., 2/Lt. 23	——— W. W., Capt. 111	Roussel, R., Capt. ... 111	Sampson, F. A., Lieut. 30
Robertson, A., Lieut. ... 19	Rochester, G., 2/Lt. ... 169	Routh, L., Lieut. ... 131	——— H. W., 2/Lt. ... 85
——— A. S., Capt. ... 136	Rochford, S. W., Lieut. 170	Routley, W. F., Capt. ... 97	——— H. V., Lieut. 64
——— A. W. M., 2/Lt. 106	Rockey, J., Lieut 176	Rowan, A., Lieut. ... 188	Samson, H. W., Capt. ... 58
——— Hon. B. F. R., Capt ... 9	Rodger, J. C., 2/Lt. ... 27	Rowbotham, G. V., Capt. 75	Sams, F. D. H., 2/Lt. ... 148
——— C A., 2/Lt ... 80	——— K. M., Lieut. 159	Rowbottom, J., 2/Lt. ... 64	Samuel, J. R., Lieut. ... 152
——— C G., Lieut. ... 139	——— W. H., 2/Lt. 116	Rowden, W. H., Lieut. 133	——— F. D., Capt. ... 89
——— C. T. A., Major 106	Rodman, F., Lieut. 62	Rowe, C. D., 2/Lt. ... 31	Samuels, F. A., 2/Lt. ... 66
——— C. W., 2/Lt. 96	Rodney, C. C. S., Lieut. 17	——— G. F., Lieut. 100	Sandbach, A. E. W., 2/Lt. ... 22
——— D., Lieut. ... 134	Rodwell, L. H., Capt. ... 38	Rowe-Evans, C. B., Lieut. 12	Sandeman, F. S., 2/Lt. 107
——— D. B., Lieut. 64	Roe, W. R., 2/Lt. ... 30	Rowland, T., 2/Lt. ... 56	——— H. B., Capt. ... 112
——— F., 2/Lt. ... 68	Roebuck, E. de L. W., Lieut. ... 36	Rowlerson, G. A., 2/Lt. 75	——— M. G., Capt. ... 112
——— G., Capt. ... 54	Rofe, H. H., 2/Lt. ... 174	Rowley, C. S., Lieut. ... 17	Sanders, C. E. 2/Lt. ... 119
——— G. J., 2/Lt. ... 107	Roffe, H. F., 2/Lt. ... 142	Rowsell, G. W. N., Lieut. 68	——— D. C. W., 2/Lt. 146
——— G. M., 2/Lt. 153	Rogers, C. W., Lieut. ... 182	——— V. N., Lieut. 18	——— G., Capt., V.C. 41
——— G. P., 2/Lt. ... 155	——— D. A., Lieut. 27	Royall, A. R., Lieut. ... 47	——— H. W., Lieut. 89
——— H G., Staff Surgeon ... 7	——— E. S., 2/Lt. ... 32	Roylance, C. K., 2/Lt. 16	——— J. W., Lieut. 149
——— J., 2/Lt. ... 123	——— Fred. I., Lieut. 167	Royle, A. H., 2/Lt. ... 25	——— R. E., Lieut. 136
——— J. A. M., 2/Lt. 158	——— G. F., 2/Lt. ... 49	——— J., 2/Lt. ... 46	——— W., 2/Lt. ... 175
——— J G., 2/Lt 148	——— G. N., 2/Lt. ... 183	Rubinstein, R. F., Capt. 61	——— W. L., Lieut. 90
——— J. S., 2/Lt. ... 104	——— G. W. H., 2/Lt. 30	Rudd, G. B. F., Capt. 46	——— W. T., 2/Lt. ... 37
——— N. C., Capt. ... 70	——— H. G., Lieut. 140	Ruddock, H. W., 2/Lt. 60	Sanderson, C. B., 2/Lt. 172
——— R., 2/Lt. ... 91	——— J. N., 2/Lt. ... 101	Rudge, G. P., Lieut. ... 100	——— H. E., Capt. ... 19
——— R. S., 2/Lt. ... 122	——— P. D., 2/Lt. ... 91	Rudman, Walter, Lieut. 162	——— J., 2/Lt. ... 87
——— T., 2/Lt. ... 30	——— R. P., Lieut. 93	Rumble, G. L., 2/Lt. ... 116	——— O., Capt. ... 8
——— W. C., Lieut. 142	——— S., 2/Lt. ... 15	Rundle, S., Lieut. ... 67	Sandes, E. W. C., Capt. 185
Robey, S., 2/Lt. ... 118	——— S. A., Capt. ... 78	——— W., 2/Lt. ... 63	Sandiford, H. A., Capt. 132
Robins, L. I. O., Major 72	——— S. E., Capt. ... 142	Runnels-Moss, E. C. A., 2/Lt. 12	Sandison, R. E. W., 2/Lt. 123
——— S. M., Lieut. 164	Rogerson, E. W., 2/Lt. 47	Rush, A. W., 2/Lt. ... 157	Sandys-Thomas, C. J., 2/Lt. 148
Robinson, A., 2/Lt. ... 64	——— H., Lieut. ... 154	Rushton, E. R., Lieut. 87	Sanford, S. A., Lieut. ... 146
——— A., 2/Lt. ... 20	——— J. C., Lieut. ... 9	——— P. C., 2/Lt. ... 63	Sankey, I., Capt. ... 52
——— A. C., 2/Lt. ... 128	Rolfe, B. R., Lieut. ... 173	Rushworth, H. M., Capt. 155	Sargent, E. F., Lieut. ... 92
——— A. D., 2/Lt. ... 43	——— C. F., 2/Lt. ... 69	Russel, C. H., Lieut. ... 66	Sarson, E. V., Col. ... 13
——— A. K., 2/Lt. ... 17	——— R. W. T., Lieut. 126	Russell, A. Scott, Capt. 16	Saunders, E. J., Lieut. ... 55
——— A. Q., 2/Lt. ... 54	Rollo, W., Lieut. ... 103	——— A. L., Lieut. 147	——— J. A., Capt. ... 115
——— A. S., Capt. ... 135	Rolls, J. A., 2/Lt. ... 89	——— D. J., 2/Lt. ... 163	——— J. T., Lieut. ... 121
——— B. W., 2/Lt. ... 161	Rolph, E. G., Lieut. ... 172	——— F. C., Lieut. 167	——— P. C., Major ... 185
——— C. R., 2/Lt. ... 142	——— J., Lieut. ... 118	——— G. C., Lieut. ... 171	——— T. W., Lieut. 32
——— D. E., Major ... 23	Rolston, G. R., 2/Lt. ... 123	——— H. B., Lieut. 147	——— W. J., 2/Lt. ... 165
——— E., Lieut. ... 180	Rooke, W. E., 2/Lt. ... 91	——— H. V., Lieut. 25	Savory, A. J., 2/Lt. ... 154
——— E., Lieut. ... 137	Root, H. W., Lieut. ... 121	——— H. W., Lieut. 176	Saward, N. C., Lieut. ... 155
——— E. B., Capt. ... 43	Roots, H. Sydney, 2/Lt. 70	——— J. E., 2/Lt. ... 21	Sawrey, K. W., 2/Lt. ... 15
——— E. M., 2/Lt. 128	Roper, D. A., 2/Lt. ... 64	——— J. J., 2/Lt. ... 69	Sawyer, E. V., 2/Lt. ... 84
——— F. B., 2/Lt. ... 169	Ropner, R., 2/Lt. ... 122	——— L. C., Lieut. ... 30	Saxon, H., Capt. ... 69
——— H. E., 2/Lt. 48	Rose, A. M., Capt. ... 131	——— L. W. E., 2/Lt. 45	Saxton, R. C., 2/Lt. ... 81
——— H. G., 2/Lt. ... 157	——— C. S., Capt. ... 135	——— Thos. R., Lieut. ... 17	Sayer, C., Lieut. ... 101
——— H. W., Lt. ... 41	——— Donald, 2/Lt. ... 170	——— W. O., Lieut. 152	Sayes, J., Lieut. ... 40
——— J., 2/Lt. ... 109	——— E. C., Lieut. 11	——— W. W., Lieut. 17	Scadding, Eric, Lieut. 166
——— J., 2/Lt. ... 27	——— F. C., Capt. ... 35	Ruston, R. M., 2/Lt. 7, 14	Scallen, W., Lieut. ... 142
——— J. B., 2/Lt. ... 147	——— F. L., 2/Lt. ... 35	——— A. F. G., Major 16	Sclater, V. C., 2/Lt. ... 179
——— J. C., Lieut. 164	——— Geoffrey, Lieut. 165	Rutherford, D. W., Capt. 180	Scanlen, W. A., Rev. ... 135
——— J. D, Lieut. ... 76	——— G. A., Lieut. ... 155	——— G., 2/Lt. ... 106	Scarborough, F., 2/Lt. 155
——— J. P., 2/Lt. ... 9	——— G. T., Lieut. 70	——— H., 2/Lt. ... 102	Scarfe, C. G., 2/Lt. ... 46
——— J. P., 2/Lt. ... 59	——— H. B., Lieut. 93	Rutledge, A. E., Lieut. ... 36	Scarisbrick, C., Lieut. ... 19
——— L. K., 2/Lt. ... 15	——— J. B., Lieut. ... 140	Ryall, A. G., 2/Lt. ... 150	Scarlett, J. C. D., 2/Lt. 14
——— L. M., Capt. ... 51	——— P., Capt. ... 7	Ryan, F. B., Capt. ... 132	Scharff, R. L., 2/Lt. ... 169
——— N., Lieut. ... 148	——— R. H., 2/Lt. ... 171	——— J. J., Lieut. 9	Schneider, C., Lieut. ... 77
——— R. W. G., Lieut. ... 100	Rose-Troup, J. M., 2/Lt. 21	——— T. F., Lieut. 132	Schofield, H., 2/Lt. ... 83
——— W. L., Capt., V.C. ... 151	Rosenbleet, A. M., Lieut. 176	Rybot, N. V. I., Major 183	——— J. A., 2/Lt. ... 129
Robison, H. J., Lieut. ... 59	Roser, W. C., 2/Lt. ... 65	Ryden, W., 2/Lt. ... 55	——— J. F., 2/Lt. ... 95
Robotham, J. A., Lieut. 117	Ross, H., 2/Lt. ... 51	Ryder, A. L. D., Lieut. 22	Scholefield, E. R. C., Lieut. 146
Robson, C. C., Lieut. ... 162	——— J., 2/Lt. ... 34	Rylands, F., 2/Lt. ... 93	——— R. S., Capt. ... 30
	——— J. A., 2/Lt. ... 65	Rylatt, A., 2/Lt. ... 85	
	——— , Capt., M.C. 133	Rymer, L., 2/Lt. ... 49	
	——— James, Capt. 112		

	PAGE		PAGE		PAGE		PAGE
Scholfield, J. A., Capt.	95	Sharpe, J. S., Lieut.	46	Silverwood, A. E., 2/Lt.	78	Sloan, J. W. J., 2/Lt.	121
Scholtz, E., 2/Lt.	157	——— S. A., 2/Lt.	151	Sime, A. W., Lieut.	139	Sloane, D., 2/Lt.	101
Schooling, G. R., 2/Lt.	167	——— T. S., Capt.	161	——— T., Lieut.	117	——— S. L. F., Capt.	87
Schoon, C. F., Lieut.	90	Shaw, C., 2/Lt.	126	Simmonds, W. A., Capt.	70	Sloggett, A. J. H., Lt.-Col.	115
Schorn, F. F., 2/Lt.	168	——— E. B. B., Lieut.	189	Simmons, D. A., Lieut.	187		
Schreiber, R. T. B., Lieut	151	——— E. H., Lieut.	95	——— J. A., 2/Lt.	38	Sloper, G. O., Capt.	24
Sclanders, A. R., 2/Lt.	104	——— F. S., 2/Lt.	96	——— W. R., 2/Lt.	48	Sly, F. C., Lieut.	186
Scoby, H. H., Lieut.	43	——— G. M., Lieut.	159	Simms, P. J., 2/Lt.	75	Smail, H. M., 2/Lt.	66
Scott, A., 2/Lt.	110	——— H. M., Lieut.	189	Simner, P. R. O. A., Lt.-Col.	41	Smailes, E. B., 2/Lt.	170
——— A. N., Capt.	63	——— J. de B., 2/Lt.	124			Small, F. G. H., 2/Lt.	117
——— C. A., Capt.	144	——— J. P., 2/Lt.	87	Simon, G. P., Lt.	154	Smart, A. H., Lieut.	69
——— C. E., 2/Lt.	86	——— J. W., Lieut.	154	Simonds, J. B., 2/Lt.	70	——— F. L., Lieut.	26
——— C. H., Lieut.	116	——— W., Lieut.	126	Simons, A. T., 2/Lt.	165	——— R. W., 2/Lt.	88
——— C. R., Lieut.	138	——— W. H., Lieut.	81	——— F. L. C., 2/Lt.	95	——— W. P., 2/Lt.	32
——— D. L., 2/Lt.	58	——— W. R., 2/Lt.	45	Simpson, A., 2/Lt.	90	Smedley, J. H., 2/Lt.	46
——— E. J. F., 2/Lt.	45	Shaw-MacLaren, T. D., Lieut.	74	——— A. A., 2/Lt.	52	Smillie, T., 2/Lt.	54
——— E. T., Lieut.	11			——— A. B., Capt.	134	Smith, Andrew, 2/Lt.	109
——— F., 2/Lt.	104	Shawcross, E. L., 2/Lt.	42	——— A. M., 2/Lt.	74	——— A., Lieut	165
——— F. G., Capt.	90	Sheard, F. M., Capt.	34	——— C. J., Major	105	——— A. E., Lieut.	124
——— F. N., 2/Lt.	80	Shearer, A., 2/Lt.	102	——— E. H., Lieut.	139	——— A. F., Lieut.	173
——— H. J. W., 2/Lt.	100	——— T., 2/Lt.	109	——— G., Capt.	76	——— Arthur J. 2/Lt	78
——— J., 2/Lt.	111	Sheather, R. W. E., 2/Lt.	21	——— J. B., Lieut.	105	——— A. McB., 2/Lt.	44
——— J. P., Lieut.	114	Shebbeare, F. W., 2/Lt.	117	——— L., Capt.	85	——— B., Lieut.	153
——— J. Y., Lieut.	22	Shedel, W. G., Capt.	169	——— R., Lieut.	70	——— C., 2/Lt.	148
——— R. A., 2/Lt.	19	Sheen, R. C., Capt.	89	——— W. J. S., Lieut.	88	——— C. F., Lieut.	153
——— T. R., 2/Lt., M.C.	13	Shell, W. H., Lieut.	166	——— R. W., 2/Lt.	72	——— C. H., Capt.	130
——— V. R., 2/Lt.	40	Shelley, G., 2/Lt.	75	——— W., 2/Lt.	122	——— C. H., 2/Lt.	48
——— W., Lieut.	112	——— V. B., Capt.	98	——— W. L., Capt.	37	——— C. R., 2/Lt.	21
——— W. A., Lt.	163	Shelton, F. E., Capt.	45	Simson, J. A., 2/Lt.	174	——— C. S., 2/Lt.	99
——— W. D., 2/Lt.	39	——— L. J., Lieut.	71	Sinclair, A. J., 2/Lt.	62	——— C. W., Capt.	98
Scott-Brown, N. A., 2/Lt.	147	Shepard, T., 2/Lt.	150	——— A. S., 2/Lt.	167	——— D. Muro, Capt.	134
Scott-Kerr, W. F, Lieut.	163	Shepheard, E. P. W., 2/Lt.	92	——— D. B., 2/Lt.	170	——— E., Lieut.	141
Scovil, M. A., Capt.	140			——— E. H., 2/Lt.	122	——— E. A. L. F., 2/Lt.	157
Scrivener, H. A., 2/Lt.	170	Shepherd, A. L. M., 2/Lt.	149	——— G. I., Lieut.	17	——— E. F. H., Capt.	116
——— H. K, 2/Lt.	165	——— A. S., 2/Lt.	154	——— L. R., 2/Lt.	162	——— E. Senior, 2/Lt.	40
Scrutton, H. U., Capt.	188	——— R. S., 2/Lt.	38	——— P., Lt.-Col., Rev.	135	——— F., Capt.	93
Scudamore, T. V. S, Capt.	139	——— W. E., Capt.	99			——— F., 2/Lt.	166
Sealy, H. G., Capt.	189	Sheppard, G. M., 2/Lt.	61	——— R. F., Capt.	105	——— F. G., Lieut.	139
Seaman, W., Lieut.	47	——— H. J., 2/Lt.	32	——— S. E., 2/Lt.	119	——— F. I., Lieut.	63
Searle, R. J., 2/Lt.	169	Sheridan, F. S., 2/Lt.	180	Singleton, E., 2/Lt.	166	——— F. J. K., Lieut.	87
Sears, H., 2/Lt.	27	——— T., 2/Lt.	64	——— H., 2/Lt.	99	——— F. L., 2/Lt.	156
——— R. L., 2/Lt.	89	Shewen, W. N., Lieut.	58	Sinkinson, F. G., 2/Lt.	124	——— F. P., Capt.	132
Seath, C. P., 2/Lt.	110	Shewin, H. M., Major	113	Sisson, G., Lieut.	15	——— F. S., 2/Lt.	62
Seaton, J. W. S., Lieut.	65	Shield, T. L., Lieut.	41	——— J. A., 2/Lt.	33	——— G., 2/Lt.	126
Sebright, J. H. K., Lieut.	89	Shields, P. R., Capt.	80	Sitch, J. E., Lieut.	174	——— G. B., Brig.-Gen.	184
Seccombe, G., Capt.	143	Shillington, T. C., Lieut.	147	Skaife, E., Capt.	56		
Seddon, A D., Capt.	23	Shipman, T. T., Lieut.	168	Skead, E. S., Lieut.	141	——— G. C., Capt., M.C.	104
Selby, C. W. P., 2/Lt.	147	Shipton, G. A., 2/Lt.	170	Skeet, C. H. L., 2/Lt.	31	——— G. C., 2/Lt.	137
Sellars, F. M., Lieut.	169	——— H. E., 2/Lt.	71	Skene, A., Lieut.	104	——— G. F., 2/Lt.	57
Sen, E. S. C., 2/Lt.	156	Shipway, W. G., Lieut.	61	——— I., 2/Lt.	51	——— G. H., Capt.	18
Senecal, C. H., 2/Lt.	171	Shipwright, A. T., 2/Lt.	155	Skerrett, W. C., Capt.	24	——— G. H., Lieut.	49
Senior, H. H., 2/Lt.	171	Shook, J. K., Lieut.	173	Skill, H. J., Capt.	89	——— G. H. B., Lieut.	169
——— T. W., 2/Lt.	31	Shore, J. L., Capt.	54	Skinner, A. H., 2/Lt.	156	——— G. Johnston, Lieut.	173
Sergeant, G., Lieut.	40	Shorman, L. E., 2/Lt.	31	——— F. G., Capt.	88		
Settle, M., Capt.	98	Short, J. R., Capt.	26	——— R. L. G., 2/Lt.	162	——— G. M., 2/Lt.	155
Settrington, C., Lord	18	——— O. J., 2/Lt.	63	——— R. T., 2/Lt.	79	——— G. Mackenzie, Capt.	63
Severn, FitzD., 2/Lt.	77	——— W. P., Lieut.	98	——— T. C., Lieut.	118	——— G. W., 2/Lt.	40
Sewell, J. H. B., Lieut.	95	Shorter, R. M., Capt.	58	——— W. H., 2/Lt.	118	——— H. B., Lt.-Col.	184
Seymour, L., Lieut.	163	Shott, V. B., 2/Lt.	45	——— W. R. K., 2/Lt.	155	——— H. E., Lieut.	141
Shackleton, W., Lieut.	175	Shreeve, F. D., 2/Lt.	161	Slack, C. M., Capt., M.C.	43	——— Hy. Edward, 2/Lt.	79
Shadbolt, G. G., 2/Lt.	127	Shubrook, A. W., 2/Lt.	61	——— J. N., Lieut.	100		
Shadwell, L. M., 2/Lt.	156	Shufflebotham, J., Capt.	72	Slade, R. J., 2/Lt.	146	——— H. M., Lt.-Col. D.S.O.	86
Shakesby, C. V., 2/Lt.	160	Shum, C. A. R., 2/Lt.	150	Slatem, S. S., 2/Lt.	142		
Shakeshaft, A. J., Capt.	186	Shurrock, F. A., Lieut.	41	Slater, G. B., Capt.	128	——— H. Nelson, Lieut.	29
Shanks, W. Y., 2/Lt.	114	Shutt, F. J., 2/Lt.	97	——— K., Lieut.	177		
Shanley, H. J., Lieut.	111	Shutte, L. A., 2/Lt.	103	Slatter, T., Capt.	111	——— H. T., 2/Lt.	65
Shannon, J. A., 2/Lt.	181	Sibley, S. J., Capt.	159	Slattery, F. J., Capt.	17	——— H. T., 2/Lt.	51
——— J. H., 2/Lt.	61	Siddons, J. T., 2/Lt.	77	Slaughter, G. H., 2/Lt.	54	——— Harold Worley, 2/Lt.	53
Shapton, H. W., 2/Lt	31	Siems, F. W. M., 2/Lt.	97	Slavitz, S., 2/Lt.	87		
Sharp, C. C., Capt.	155	Sieveking, L. de G., Fl. Lieut., D.S.O.	177	Sleath, W. F., Capt.	43	——— I. C., 2/Lt.	130
——— E. E., 2/Lt.	52			Slee, F. D., 2/Lt.	154	——— I. W., Lieut.	16
——— H. F., 2/Lt.	17	Sievers, R. F., Capt.	130	Sleigh, H., Capt.	68	——— J., 2/Lt.	70
——— S. R. C., 2/Lt.	91	Silburn, L., Lieut.	100	——— T. W., 2/Lt.	175	——— J. E., Lieut.	137
Sharpe, F., Lieut.	154	Silcock, F. H., 2/Lt.	130	Slipper, R. A., 2/Lt.	162	——— J. F., 2/Lt.	115
——— F., 2/Lt.	35	Silk, R. W., Lieut.	174	Sliter, E. D., Lieut.	154		
		Sills, F. C., 2/Lt.	128	Sloan, A. T., Major	10		

214

Name	Page
Smith, J. G., Rev.	135
——— J. H., 2/Lt.	52
——— J. L., 2/Lt.	165
——— J. R. Leslie, 2/Lt.	20
——— J. Sercombe, Sub-Lt.	177
——— L. A., Capt.	153
——— L. Coleman, Capt.	35
——— L. G., 2/Lt.	172
——— L. H., Lieut.	181
——— L. H., Lieut.	22
——— L. H., Lieut.	174
——— M. L. C., 2/Lt.	183
——— Norman, 2/Lt.	175
——— Noel A., Lieut	162
——— P. N., Capt.	48
——— R., Capt.	93
——— R. B., 2/Lt.	160
——— R. E., 2/Lt.	56
——— Reginald Gilbert, Lieut.	25
——— R.H., 2/Lt.	42
——— R. H. T., Capt.	42
——— R. L., 2/Lt.	111
——— R.M., 2/Lt.	157
——— Robert Wm., 2/Lt.	45
——— S., 2/Lt.	187
——— Sidney, Capt.	132
——— S. B., 2/Lt.	137
——— S. C., 2/Lt.	93
——— S. R., 2/Lt.	97
——— S. R., 2/Lt.	72
——— Vivian, Lieut.	153
——— V. H., Capt.	189
——— W., 2/Lt.	40
——— W. C., 2-Lt.	154
——— W. C. Lindsay, Lieut.	107
——— W. H., 2/Lt.	97
——— W. R., 2/Lt.	32
Smith-Masters, H. A., Rev.	135
Smithers, E., 2/Lt.	161
Smithwick, J. A., Capt.	47
Smitten, Peter, 2/Lt.	92
Smurthwaite, A. S. T., 2/Lt.	89
Smyth, D. M., Capt.	97
Smyth, E. C., 2/Lt.	112
Smythe, C., Lieut., M.C.	157
——— Ingoldsby Lister, Capt.	10
Smythe-Osborne, J. G., Capt.	56
Snadden, W. McN., Lieut.	112
Snape, J. A., Lieut.	55
Snell, W., Lieut.	186
Snodgrass, H., 2/Lt.	11
Snook, C. W., Capt.	148
Snow, S. R. E., Capt.	178
Snowdon, G. C., 2/Lt.	28
Snowden, Robt., Capt.	139
Soames, C. E., Capt.	21
——— J. A., 2/Lt.	56
——— R. M., Capt.	133
Sole, S. G., 2/Lt.	35
Somervell, W. E., 2/Lt.	147
Somerville, D. H. S., Major, M.C.	57
——— G. B., Lieut.	28
Somerfelt, Allister	166
Sopwith, G., Major	99
Sorel-Cameron, Major	107
Sorley, J. T., Lieut.	174
Sotham, E. G., Major. M.C.	96
Souden, S., 2/Lt.	104
Soutar, D. H., Lieut.	107
——— Geo. C., 2/Lt.	125
Souter, L. F., 2/Lt.	183
Southern, Frank J., 2/Lt	69
——— H., 2/Lt.	182
——— Norman, Major	13
Southon, H. G., Lieut.	150
Southorn, T. N., Lieut.	153
Sowerbutts, J. A., Lieut.	115
Sowerby, J., 2/Lt.	25
——— J. P., 2/Lt.	27
Spackman, W.O., Lieut.	184
Span, F. H., Capt.	66
Spargo, W. H., 2/Lt.	33
Sparkes, C. P., Lieut.	172
——— P. J., 2/Lt.	58
Sparks, H. J., 2/Lt., M.C.	160
Speagell, H.M.D., 2/Lt.	173
Spear, J. C., 2/Lt.	119
Spearpoint, H. D., Lieut	154
Speedy, N., 2/Lt.	43
Speer, L.A.T., 2/Lt.	86
Spence, C., 2/Lt.	68
——— H. F., Capt.	87
——— H. N., 2/Lt.	68
——— R., Lieut.	185
Spencelayh, V. C. H., 2/Lt.	63
Spencer, A., Lieut.	122
——— Cecil H., 2/Lt.	113
——— E. A., Lieut.	10
——— E. W., 2/Lt.	22
——— Fredk. J. E., 2/Lt.	94
——— John, 2/Lt.	32
——— J. H., Capt.	50
——— W.A.L., 2/Lt.	155
Spencer Smith, P., Lieut	129
Spensley, J. R., Lieut.	131
Spibey, F. W., 2/Lt.	71
Spicer, E. M., Lieut.	64
——— W. E. Hardy, Lieut.	39
Spikesman, W. R., 2/Lt.	30
Spink, H. M., Capt.	182
——— H. W., 2/Lt.	85
Spira, S., Capt.	188
Spiro, S. G., 2/Lt.	158
Spite, J. L., 2/Lt.	11
Spooner, H. Father, Capt.	186
——— F. P., Lieut.	120
Spratt, N. C., Lieut.	146
Spring, D. M., Capt.	132
Sprott, R., 2/Lt.	110
Sproule, E. R., Lieut.	170
Sprowell, B. W., 2/Lt.	94
Spurge, F. J. C., 2/Lt.	130
Squibb, H. M., 2/Lt.	39
Squire, E. A., 2/Lt.	61
Stack, T. J., 2/Lt.	60
Stace, R. E., Capt.	185
Staff, O. H., 2/Lt.	42
Stafford, A., 2/Lt.	39
——— F. W., 2/Lt.	88
——— Robt. H., 2/Lt.	35
Stainton, A. E., 2/Lt.	24
Stair, J. J., Earl of, Major	18
Stalker, D., Lieut.	103
Standage, A. K., 2/Lt.	75
Standen, A. O., 2/Lt.	14
Stanford, J., Lieut.	10
Stanier, F. A. H., Capt.	87
Stanley, G. K., 2/Lt.	11
——— J. B., 2/Lt.	93
Stansby, J., 2/Lt.	98
Staples, E. G., Capt.	181
Stapleton, H. E., Lieut.	183
Stark, Conrad, 2/Lt.	78
——— J. D., 2/Lt.	58
Starkey, F. E., Lieut.	116
Starnes, D. S. B., 2/Lt., M.C.	89
Start, B. J., Capt.	111
——— D. M., 2/Lt.	77
Startin, C. B., Capt.	97
——— J. S., Capt.	184
Statham, Richard L., 2/Lt.	71
Stead, G. C., 2/Lt.	154
——— M.W.B., 2/Lt.	158
Stealey, E. T., Lieut.	126
Stearne, G. F., 2/Lt.	30
Stearns, H. D., 2/Lt.	184
Stedman, A. R., Lieut.	168
——— F., 2/Lt.	152
Steel, A. K., Lieut.	121
——— G., 2/Lt.	24
Steele, N. L., 2/Lt.	181
——— T. Murray, Lieut.	173
——— W., Lieut.	179
Steer, C., Rev., M.C.	135
Steeves, D. T., 2/Lt.	153
——— Gordon T., Lieut.	160
——— R. P., Lieut.	139
Steggall, G. E. A., 2/Lt.	22
Stein, C. J., Capt.	142
——— Ian, Lieut.	9
Steinberg, Roy D., 2/Lt.	89
Stempt, L. F., Capt.	14
Stenhouse, J. A., Lieut.	131
Stenson, W., 2/Lt.	120
Stephen, A. M., Major	15
——— J. C., Lieut.	73
——— J. T., 2/Lt.	106
Stephens, C. H., Lieut.	169
——— D. E., Lieut.	168
——— H. T., 2/Lt.	43
Stephenson, C.M., Lt-Col	58
——— G. F., 2/Lt.	43
——— Geo H., Lieut	166
——— H., Lieut.	186
——— L., Sub-Lt.	144
——— M. M., 2/Lt.	79
——— W. S., Lieut.	166
Sterndale-Bennett, J. B. Capt.	57
Steuart-Menzies, R., Lieut.	18
Stevens, A. C., Lieut.	176
——— B., Lieut.	140
——— Charles F., Lt.-Col.	10
——— E. G., 2/Lt.	42
——— E. H., 2/Lt.	153
——— W. T., 2/Lt., M.C.	22
——— W. T., Lieut.	46
Stevenson, C. S., Lieut.	84
——— E. A., 2/Lt.	127
——— F., 2/Lt.	43
——— F. B., 2/Lt.	46
——— Gerald,	131
——— John F., Lieut.	43
——— J. G., 2/Lt.	156
——— Ralph C. S., Capt.	114
Stewardson, E. A., Lieut	153
Stewart, A.D.L., Lieut.	106
——— A. F., Major	185
——— A.W.F., Capt	59
——— C. W., 2/Lt.	105
——— Douglas, Lieut	148
——— D. J., Lieut.	151
——— G. A., 2/Lt.	20
——— H., Lieut.	54
——— H. F., 2/Lt.	32
——— H. S., Capt.	188
——— H. W., Asst. Surg.	182
——— John, Lieut.	140
——— I. A., 2/Lt.	33
——— J., 2/Lt.	104
——— John D., Lieut.	74
——— J.D.M., 2/Lt.	152
——— J. H., Capt.	109
——— P., 2/Lt.	188
——— P. D., 2/Lt.	40
——— R. J. G., 2/Lt.	159
——— R. R., Lieut.	32
——— W., Capt.	105
——— W., Lieut.	54
Stewart-Cox, A., Capt.	10
Stewart-Murray, J. T., Capt.	107
Stewart-Smith, Dudley C., Lieut.	73
Stickings, A. E., Capt.	93
Stiles, R. A., 2/Lt.	45
Still, J., Lieut.	178
Stillwell, J. G., Lieut.	180
Stirk, C. W., 2/Lt.	49
Stirland, H., 2/Lt.	77
——— A., Capt.	112
——— A. C., 2/Lt.	15
Stiven, R.W.S., Capt.	53
Stockley, C. H., Capt.	183
Stockman, E. J., Lieut.	171
Stockwell, Lionel Geo., 2/Lt.	175
Stogden, J., Lieut.	94
Stokeld, F. E., Lieut.	50
Stokes, H., Capt.	189
Stokes-Roberts, A. E., A/Lt.-Col.	51
Stokoe, J. S., 2/Lt.	25
Stone, H. R., 2/Lt.	128
——— John L., Lieut.	178
——— R., 2/Lt.	78
——— R. Harris	171
——— W. J.G., 2/Lt.	16
Stonehouse, David U.	37
Stoneman, J. W., 2/Lt.	13
Stones, J. E., Capt.	189
——— W., Lieut.	136
Stopher, A. C., 2/Lt.	187
Storer, Samuel, 2/Lt.	76
Stormouth, S. L., Lieut.	178
Storry, E. R., Lieut.	67
Story, D., Lieut.	24
——— J. C., Lieut.	49
Stotesbury J. M., 2/Lt.	127
Stott J. H., Lieut.	50
——— J. N. S. Capt.	146
——— J. W., Sub-Lt.	145
——— Leslie Hamilton, 2/Lt.	69
Strachan, A. H., 2/Lt.	113
Stradling, C., 2/Lt.	142
Strang, A. R., Lieut.	165
Strange, J. S., Capt.	73
——— L. A. T., 2/Lt.	151
——— M. H., 2/Lt.	148

	PAGE		PAGE		PAGE		PAGE
Stranger, Philip, 2/Lt.	135	Swallow, S. H., 2/Lt.	69	Taylor, R. A., 2/Lt.	23	Thompson, H. M., 2/Lt.	21
Strangham, C. F., 2/Lt.	189	Swann, J. H., 2/Lt.	12	——— R. C., Lieut.	158	——— H. S., 2/Lt.	13
Strangward, F. L., Lieut	173	——— T. H., Lieut.	172	——— R. E., Lieut.	167	——— H. T., 2/Lt.	68
Strathearne, Wm. Miller, Lieut.	170	Swart, O. B., 2/Lt.	159	——— R. R., Lieut.	189	——— H. W., 2/Lt.	73
Strauss, A., 2/Lt.	133	Swatman, C. M., 2/Lt.	33	——— S. H., 2/Lt.	156	——— J. C., 2/Lt.	64
Street, H., Capt.	63	Swaby, Geo. F., 2/Lt.	67	——— S. H., Lieut.	98	——— J. C., Lieut.	161
Streets, Arthur H., 2/Lt.	127	Swayne, H. D., 2/Lt.	109	——— T. H., Lieut.	23	——— J. C., 2/Lt.	24
Streight, J. E. L., Capt.	138	——— J. G., Lieut.	38	——— T. H., 2/Lt.	28	——— L. E., Lieut.	137
Strettell, E.F.D., 2/Lt.	22	Swayze, W. K., Lieut.	170	——— W., 2/Lt.	180	——— N. B., 2/Lt.	100
Stretton, A.L.de C., Capt	189	Sweet, R., Lieut.	184	——— W., 2/Lt.	24	——— P. E., 2/Lt.	63
Strickland, A. W., Lieut.	178	Swift, W. F., Lieut.	96	——— W.C., 2/Lt.	58	——— P. G., Capt.	180
——— D.de E., 2/Lt.	11	Swinburne, M., 2/Lt.	24	——— W. G. E., 2/Lt.	80	——— P. R., 2/Lt.	50
——— W. A., 2/Lt.	154	Sydenham, E. G., Capt.	28	——— W. H., 2/Lt.	160	——— Ralph, 2/Lt.	43
——— W. E., Lieut.	13	Sydie, J. Errol, Lieut.	165	——— W. H., 2/Lt.	92	——— R. C., 2/Lt.	128
Stringer, Ernest, Lieut.	189	Syer, H., Major	185	——— W. H., 2/Lt.	162	——— S., 2/Lt.	32
——— F. H., Lieut.	172	Sykes, H. A., 2/Lt.	116	——— W. J., 2/Lt.	119	——— Sidney, 2/Lt.	155
——— J. S., 2/Lt.	170	——— I., 2/Lt.	61	——— W. R., 2/Lt.	22	——— S. F., 2/Lt.	155
Strohm, E. C., 2/Lt.	108	——— J. A., 2/Lt.	14	——— W. U. C., 2/Lt.	84	——— S. J., 2/Lt.	30
Strong, A. H., 2/Lt.	49	Symes, C. H., Lieut.	100	Teager, W. E., 2/Lt.	38	——— W., 2/Lt.	131
——— C. C., Capt.	147			Teague, H. J. P., 2/Lt.	122	——— Wm. H., Lieut.	142
——— F. C., Lieut.	126	**Tadman**, R., 2/Lt.	36	Tebb, H. G., Lieut.	82	——— W. T., Capt.	131
——— P. J., 2/Lt.	46	Taggert, H. E., 2/Lt.	111	Teeling, T. F., Lieut.	58	Thomsen, C. J., Capt.	162
——— Robt., Sub-Lt.	145	Tahourdin, V., Capt.	54	Telfer, H. C., 2/Lt.	173	Thomson, A., 2/Lt.	106
——— W., 2/Lt.	42	Tailyour, G. H. F., Major	10	——— S., 2/Lt.	118	——— A. B., Lieut.	13
Stroud, Sidney Arthur 2/Lt.	129	Talbot, F. W., 2/Lt.	157	——— V. A., 2/Lt.	50	——— A. D., Capt.	85
Stroudley, A., Lieut.	12	——— H. E., Lieut.	9	Temperley, E., Lt.-Col.	25	——— A. R., Capt.	183
Strover, E. J., Lieut.	147	Tallent, G. H. L., 2/Lt.	179	Tempest, W. C., 2/Lt.	164	——— C. D., 2/Lt.	103
Struben, H. M., Lieut.	166	Tambling, H. G., 2/Lt.	155	Templer, C. F. L., Lieut.	61	——— D. A., 2/Lt.	173
Stuart, C. E., 2/Lt.	156	Tannenbaum, H., 2/Lt.	163	Templeton, W., 2/Lt.	54	——— G. F., Lieut.	164
——— J.A.G., Lieut.	15	Tansley, H. E., 2/Lt.	163	Tennant, P. S., 2/Lt.	175	——— H., 2/Lt.	38
——— J.E.A., 2/Lt.	137	——— V., Lieut.	41	Tenney, F., Lieut.	48	——— H. E., Lieut.	164
——— Thos., 2/Lt.	11	Taplin, L., Lieut.	138	Terry, J. M., 2/Lt.	48	——— H. G., Major	181
——— Wm., Lieut.	179	Tapping, A., 2/Lt.	171	Tetlow, A. R., 2/Lt.	33	——— J. W., Lieut.	164
——— W., 2/Lt.	91	Tarver, A. A., 2/Lt.	118	Tew, D. McL., 2/Lt.	70	——— R.W.L., Lieut.	174
——— W. G., 2/Lt.	144	Tasker, W. T. B., 2/Lt.	151	Thackrah, N. H., 2/Lt.	160	——— W. R., Capt.	122
Stuart-Kelso, E. St. Brandon, 2/Lt.	40	Tate, J., Capt.	132	Thamer, O., 2/Lt.	159	Thorn, J. C., Lieut.	139
Stubbs, H. B., 2/Lt.	146	——— R. S., 2/Lt.	42	Thatcher, A. R., 2/Lt.	170	——— P. E., 2/Lt.	21
——— W., 2/Lt.	46	Tatlow, A., 2/Lt.	43	——— W.A.N., Lieut.	39	Thorne, A. C., Major	183
——— W. H., Lieut.	164	Tatnall, E. W., Lieut.	165	Thierens, J. P., Capt.	133	——— D. S., Capt.	16
Sturgess, T. M., 2/Lt.	154	——— A. H., Capt.	124	——— V. T., Lieut.	72	Thornhill, N., Lieut.	31
Style, Oliver, 2/Lt.	18	Tattersall, H. V., 2/Lt.	97	Thin, J. A., 2/Lt.	7	Thornley, S. C., 2/Lt.	166
Styles, W. B., 2/Lt.	155	Tayler, A. G. E., 2/Lt.	92	Thomas, C., 2/Lt.	171	Thornton, C. P., 2/Lt.	151
Sugden, F., 2/Lt.	41	——— H. M., 2/Lt.	154	——— C. H., 2/Lt.	63	——— R. A., Lieut.	95
——— J.E.W., 2/Lt.	163	Taylor, A., Lieut.	184	——— C. H., 2/Lt.	176	——— T., Capt.	77
Sugden-Wilson, W., Lieut	146	——— A., 2/Lt.	55	——— C. H. G., A/Capt.	93	——— W., 2/Lt.	49
Sugrue, T., Capt.	73	——— A., Lieut.	156	——— C. S., 2/Lt.	73	——— W. R. Lieut.	172
Sullens, C. H., 2/Lt.	89	——— A. L. T., 2/Lt.	160	——— D. H., Capt.	73	——— W. T., 2/Lt.	68
Sullivan, J., Capt.	133	——— A. N., Lt./Col.	184	——— E. C., 2/Lt.	56	Thorp, A. F., Lieut.	72
——— W., 2/Lt.	92	——— A. O. D., 2/Lt.	23	——— E. H., Lieut.	13	Thorpe, A. H., 2/Lt.	29
Sulston, H. E., 2/Lt.	142	——— A. S., 2/Lt.	26	——— G., Lieut.	162	——— C. E., 2/Lt.	168
Summers, G. D., 2/Lt.	34	——— C. D., 2/Lt.	33	——— G. H. de B., Lieut.	142	——— G. L., 2/Lt.	78
——— I. K., Capt.	168	——— C. E., 2/Lt.	86	——— G. P. F., Lieut.	160	Threadgold, T. C., 2/Lt.	23
Summerskill, J. H., 2/Lt.	116	——— D., 2/Lt.	108	——— H., 2/Lt.	174	Threlfell, G. R., 2/Lt.	82
Sumner, M. G., Lieut.	94	——— D. B., Lieut.	109	——— H. W. M., 2/Lt.	104	Thresher, E. W., 2/Lt.	175
Surtees, W. M., 2/Lt.	112	——— D. H., 2/Lt.	90	——— J., 2/Lt.	61	Thrush, H., Capt.	52
Sutcliff, A., Capt.	131	——— E. E., Lieut.	171	——— J. T., 2/Lt.	141	Thrustle, A. V., 2/Lt.	44
Sutcliffe, A. H., 2/Lt.	120	——— E. H., Lieut.	121	——— M. D., Lieut.	17	Thuillier, D'A. F., 2/Lt.	114
——— A. L., 2/Lt.	156	——— E. N., 2/Lt.	79	——— R. W., Capt.	113	Thyne, T. P., Major	70
——— C. A., 2/Lt.	156	——— F. F., 2/Lt.	96	——— W., Major	186	Tibbitts, G. D., Lieut.	134
——— Geo., 2/Lt.	68	——— F. N. G., Capt.	179	——— W., Lieut.	54	Tibbetts, J. Lister, 2/Lt.	149
——— J.E.T., Lieut.	167	——— G., 2/Lt.	32	——— W. B., Lieut.	59	Tibbotts, A. H., 2/Lt.	17
Sutherland, A., Major	183	——— G. T., 2/Lt.	38	Thomason, W. L., 2/Lt.	137	Tickle, F. R., Capt.	132
——— A. M., 2/Lt.	153	——— H. G., 2/Lt.	188	Thompson, A., Major	131	Tidmarsh, D. W., Capt.	151
——— C. H., 2/Lt.	19	——— H. G., 2/Lt.	77	——— A., 2/Lt.	158	Tilbury, E. J., Capt., A/Major	134
——— F. H., Lieut.	77	——— J., Lieut.	38	——— Alex., Lieut.	25	Tildesley, T. E., Capt., M.C.	98
——— H. O., Lieut.	24	——— J. A., Lieut.	188	——— A. M., 2/Lt.	50	Tilley, H. W. V., 2/Lt.	38
——— J.L.C., Lieut.	168	——— J. C., 2/Lt.	148	——— A. N., 2/Lt.	27	Timmins, Leonard, 2/Lt.	174
Suthrien, G., Lieut.	44	——— Leofric, 2/Lt.	50	——— C. D., Lieut.	155	Timmis, A. W., Capt.	93
Sutters, A J., 2/Lt.	92	——— L. B., 2/Lt.	72	——— C.W.M., Lieut.	173	——— L. W., 2/Lt.	158
Sutton, M. F., 2/Lt.	162	——— L. G., 2/Lt.	169	——— D. H., 2/Lt.	14	Timpson, N. M., 2/Lt.	36
Swain, A. B., 2/Lt.	81	——— L. G., 2/Lt.	159	——— E. L., 2/Lt.	82	Tingle, R. L. A., 2/Lt.	41
Swales, M., 2/Lt.	16	——— L. W., Capt.	100	——— F. E., 2/Lt.	45	Tinney, H. G., 2/Lt.	155
Swallow, M.W.J., 2/Lt.	83	——— M. E., 2/Lt.	144	——— F. G., Lieut.	166	Tinniswood, J. N., 2/Lt.	16
		——— N. J., 2/Lt.	156	——— G., Capt., M.C.	49	Tipton, R. J., Capt.	179
		——— P. R., 2/Lt.	127				
		——— R., Capt.	139				

Name	Page	Name	Page	Name	Page	Name	Page
Tison, M., 2/Lt.	167	Tredwell, H. O., 2/Lt.	62	**Ubsdell**, A. R., 2/Lt.	183	Vines, C. H., 2/Lt.	51
Titterton, H. N., Lieut.	189	Tregear, F. C., Major	183	Udall, T. C. B., Capt.	119	Vipond, F. E., 2/Lt.	154
Tod, A. A., Major	115	Trembath, N. T., Lieut.	175	Underhill, E., Capt.	132	Voelcker, F. W., 2/Lt.	86
———— A. R., Lieut.	65	Tremlett, G. W., Capt.	88	Unett, W. H., Lieut.	85	Vorley, C. A., 2/Lt.	69
———— C. F., 2/Lt.	11	Trendell, C. J. W., 2/Lt.	35	Uniacke, D. P. F., 2/Lt.	156	Vosper, R. A., Lieut.	165
Todd, A., Lieut., M.C.	151	Treloar, W. N., Capt.	178	Upson, R. H., 2/Lt.	152	Vucovitch, T., 2/Lt.	142
———— A. E., 2/Lt.	110	Tresham, W. H., 2/Lt.	175	Upton, D. F., Lieut.	129		
———— D. L., Capt.	136	Tresilian, C. S., 2/Lt.	128	———— J. T., Lieut.	9	**Waddell**, D., 2/Lt.	12
———— J., Capt. Rev.	135	Trevor, A. C. H., Capt.	183	———— W. A., 2/Lt.	82	Wadden, G., Lieut.	149
———— J., 2/Lt.	12	Tricker, W. R., 2/Lt.	30	Ure, Colin M. G., Lieut.	16	Waddington, C., Capt.	63
———— James, 2/Lt.	19	Trigonna, A. S., Capt.	114	Uren, C. Trewhellan, 2/Lt.	93	———— W. C., 2/Lt.	44
———— J. A., Major	19	Triggs, H. T., Lieut.	69	Urie, W. A. E., Lieut.	95	Wadner, T., Lieut.	90
———— R. F., 2/Lt.	12	Trollope, J. L., Capt.	161	Urquhart, A. M., Lieut.	13	Wadsworth, F. A. R., Lieut.	119
Todhunter, W. H., 2/Lt.	62	Troops, A., Lieut.	77	Urry, A. C., 2/Lt.	82	Wadworth, W., 2/Lt.	80
Tolkien, C., 2/Lt.	26	Troughton, L. H. W., Lt.-Col.	116	———— R. T., 2/Lt.	116	Wagstaff, W., Lieut.	45
Tollemache, C. H., Lieut.	81	Trower, R. F., 2/Lt.	11	Urwin, T. A., 2/Lt.	159	Wahl, B., 2/Lt.	43
———— D. P., Lt.-Col. Hon.	81	Trulock, J. C., 2/Lt.	154	Usher, C. L., Lieut.	94	Waine, V. J., Major	136
———— E. A., Lieut.	79	Trusler, A., 2/Lt.	11	———— C. M., Lieut.	106	Wainwright, B.M., 2/Lt.	148
Toller, W. S. N., Lt.-Col.	78	Tucker, G. L., 2/Lt.	42	Usher-Somers, C.E., 2/Lt.	171	———— T., 2/Lt.	122
Tollett, G. W., Lieut.	80	———— J. C., 2/Lt.	73	Ussher, J.F.H., Lt.-Col.	140	Waite, C. W., Major	44
Tolley, C. I. H., 2/Lt., M.C.	124	———— N. O., Lieut.	40	Utley, Clarence	99	Wakefield Saunders, A., Lieut.	90
Tomley, W. P., 2/Lt.	21	———— R. J., 2/Lt.	39	Utterson, A. T. Le M., Lt.-Col.	46	Walcott, E. P. M., 2/Lt.	74
Tomlinson, F. W., Capt.	22	Tuckett, H. S., Lieut.	68			Walden, H. F., 2/Lt.	109
———— H., Capt., M.C.	151	Tudor-Hart, W.O., Lieut.	147	**Vacher**, W. E., Lieut.	63	Walding, T. W., Lieut.	122
———— H. W., Capt.	185	Tudhope, E. D., Lieut.	14	Vagg, E. G., 2/Lt.	144	Waldram, H. G., Lieut.	187
Tomson, W. J. M., Lieut.	148	Tudway, Lionel, Lieut., R.N., D.S.C.	187	Valentine, J., Lieut.	169	Walgate, W. C., 2/Lt.	43
Tonathy, H., 2/Lt.	20	Tuffs, E. W., Lieut.	99	Van Baerle, P. E. H., 2/Lt.	150	Walker, A. P., 2/Lt.	70
Tonks, W., Capt.	118	Tullett, J., 2/Lt.	82	Vance, E., Lieut.	108	———— A. W., 2/Lt.	108
Tongue, A. N., 2/Lt.	95	Tullis, J. N., 2/Lt.	148	———— J. D., Lieut.	165	———— E., Lieut.	146
Toogood, C., Major	35	Tulloch, Keith E., 2/Lt.	148	Van der Weyer, B. G., Major	18	———— E. A., Major	184
———— F. A., 2/Lt.	43	Tunbridge, G. C., 2/Lt.	188	Vane Tempest, C. S., Lieut.	150	———— E. A., Capt., M.C.	132
———— H. S., 2/Lt.	29	Tunnicliffe, E. C., Lieut.	56	Van Humbeeck, C., 2/Lt.	86	———— F. C., Capt.	129
———— J., 2/Lt.	153	———— F. R., 2/Lt.	98	Van Nostrand, C. T., 2/Lt.	147	———— E. G. S., Capt.	162
Toomer, J. C. J., 2/Lt.	51	Tupper, H., Capt.	23	Vans-Agnew, F., Capt.	124	———— F. M., Capt., M.C.	132
Tooke, B. C., Lieut.	176	Turk, G. D., 2/Lt.	75	Vansittart, E., Colonel	84	———— H. E., Lieut.	118
Toone, J. W., 2/Lt.	147	Turnbull, E., 2/Lt.	27	Van Someran, E. C., 2/Lt.	36	———— H. S., Capt.	107
Toothill, Joseph, 2/Lt.	104	———— G. I., Lieut.	73	Van Tilburg, J.A., Lieut.	166	———— J., Lieut.	141
Toovey, K. St. C. H. 2/Lt.	24	———— J. B., Lieut.	106	Varah, G. I., 2/Lt.	80	———— James, 2/Lt.	43
Topliss, R. H., Lieut.	160	———— J. S., Lieut.	68	Vasey, W., 2/Lt.	48	———— J. C., Lieut.	170
Torrance, G., Capt.	132	———— J. W. E., Capt.	101	Vass, F. C., 2/Lt.	84	———— J. E. M., Lieut.	77
———— P., 2/Lt.	53	———— M. R., McG., Major	179	Vaughan, B., 2/Lt.	84	———— J. G. B., Capt., M.C.	104
Torrens, D. F., Capt.	133	Turner, A., Major	82	———— D., 2/Lt.	161	———— J. R., 2/Lt.	13
Torrington, Viscount	188	———— C. A. C., Lieut.	111	———— H. W., 2/Lt.	21	———— J. W., 2/Lt.	48
Tottenham, R. C., Lieut.	16	———— E. G., Lieut.	165	———— R. M., Capt.	60	———— M., 2/Lt.	53
Touchstone, G. R., Lieut.	167	———— E. Lenten, 2/Lt.	38	———— Stanley, Lieut.	23	———— P., Lieut.	101
Tounsend, F. H., Major	40	———— E. S. F., Lieut.	119	———— W., 2/Lt.	82	———— P. L. E., Major	9
Towers, R., 2/Lt.	52	———— G. F., 2/Lt.	158	Vautin, C. E., 2/Lt.	181	———— P. S., Major	38
Towler, E. E., Lieut.	72	———— G. M., 2/Lt.	76	Vaux, H. C., Capt.	88	———— R. B., 2/Lt.	41
Towne, L. L. F., 2/Lt.	161	———— H. P., 2/Lt.	76	Velho, S. F., Lieut.	33	———— R. D., Lieut.	148
Townesend, E. J. D., Lieut.	151	———— J., 2/Lt.	124	Vellacott, P. C., Major	7	———— R. E., Capt.	188
Townley, D. C., Lieut.	166	———— J. C., Lieut.	148	Veness, V. G., 2/Lt.	138	———— R. H., Lieut.	99
———— E. J., 2/Lt.	50	———— K. K., 2/Lt.	148	Venter, J. C., Capt.	168	———— R. S., 2/Lt.	21
Townsend, A. A., Lieut.	188	———— L. J., 2/Lt.	35	Vereker, H. C., Capt.	176	———— S. H., Lieut.	108
———— E. N., Major	67	———— T. B., 2/Lt.	106	Vergette, R. G., 2/Lt.	125	———— W., Lieut.	176
———— H., 2/Lt.	10	———— W., 2/Lt.	164	Verity, G. H., 2/Lt.	55	———— W. J., 2/Lt.	44
———— H. E., Lieut.	163	Turrell, J. W., Lt.-Com.	144	Vernon, H. R., 2/Lt.	14	Wall, A. M., 2/Lt.	23
———— J. G., Lieut.	123	Turvey, A. E., 2/Lt.	157	———— J. E., Lieut.	113	———— H. R., Lieut.	55
———— J. W., 2/Lt.	41	Tussaud, H. C., Lieut.	166	Vessey, J. O., Lieut.	45	Wallace, A., 2/Lt.	50
Townshend, C. V. F., Maj.-General	182	Tuxford, G., 2/Lt.	91	Vetch, D. M., Lieut.	146	———— C. L'E., 2/Lt.	128
Tozer, W., Lieut.	185	Tweedale, G., Capt.	95	Veysey, G. C., 2/Lt.	15	———— D., 2/Lt.	19
Tracey, H. A., 2/Lt.	188	Tweedie, G. S., Major	19	Viccars, Harold W., 2/Lt.	64	———— J. F., Capt.	40
Trafford, E. B., Capt.	18	Twinberrow, J. S., 2/Lt.	178	Vick, C. W., 2/Lt.	33	———— J. R., 2/Lt.	17
———— W. E., 2/Lt.	185	Twiss, C. C. H., Lt.-Col.	42	———— D. W., 2/Lt.	61	———— P. M., Lieut.	173
Tragett, J. C. B., Capt.	57	Twist, T. F., 2/Lt.	39	———— Horace, Lieut.	164	———— W., Capt.	183
Tranchell, H. G., Lieut.	182	Tye, Harold, 2/Lt.	51	———— W. W., 2/Lt.	157	———— W. B., Colonel	37
Tratman, L. W. D. T., Lieut.	166	Tyer, Eric, 2/Lt.	65	Vickerman, F.H.D., Capt.	7	Wallace-Simpson, G., Lieut.	176
Trattles, R., 2/Lt.	154	Tylor, Cyril E., Lieut.	162	Vickers, E. R., Capt. & Adjt., D.C.M., M.C.	91	———— Sydney, Lieut.	67
Travers, Gordon, 2/Lt.	166	Tyndale-Biscoe, N. E., Lieut.	11	———— J. B., 2/Lt.	175	Waller, E. B., 2/Lt.	12
Treachman, B. A., Lieut.	180	Tysoe, C. G., Lieut.	162	Vidal, A. C., Capt.	131	Wallich, M. G. L., Lieut.	21
Trebilco, R. J., 2/Lt.	76	Tyson, G. D., Capt.	32	Villiers, A. H., 2/Lt.	92	Wallington, C. H., 2/Lt.	75
		———— J. D., Capt.	112				

	PAGE		PAGE		PAGE		PAGE
Wallis, C. E., 2/Lt.	79	Watkins, S., 2/Lt.	56	Welinker, S. C., Lieut.	164	Whitehead, Harry, 2/Lt.	80
——— H., Capt.	189	Watkinson, A. V., 2/Lt.	137	Wellard, J. H., 2/Lt.	95	——— H. H., Lieut.	148
——— J. D., 2/Lt.	188	——— W., 2/Lt.	46	Wellby, H. S., 2/Lt.	157	——— H. R., 2/Lt.	165
——— Percy, 2/Lt.	43	Watson, A., 2/Lt.	152	Wells, A. J., 2/Lt.	38	——— M. J., 2/Lt.	99
——— S. W., 2/Lt.	30	——— C. H., 2/Lt.	45	——— C., 2/Lt.	71	——— W.H.N., Lieut.	149
Walmisley, E. A., 2/Lt.	21	——— F. H. E., 2/Lt.	181	——— D. P., Capt.	136	Whitehouse, C. E. L., Capt.	71
Walmsley, H. D., 2/Lt.	65	——— F. W., Capt. & Adjt.	23	——— E. W., 2/Lt.	63	——— S. L., 2/Lt.	157
——— J. H., 2/Lt.	117	——— Guy, 2/Lt.	60	——— G. A., Capt.	170	Whitehurst, C. W., 2/Lt.	98
——— R. H., 2/Lt.	17	——— G. P. H., Lieut.	16	——— H. A. T., Asst. Surg.	182	Whiteley, R. F., Lieut.	67
Walpole, A., Sub.-Lt.	145	——— H. S., Lieut.	23	——— H. P., Lieut.	169	Whiteman, H. R., 2/Lt.	13
Walrond-Skinner, D. D., Capt.	156	——— H. St. J. B., 2/Lt.	98	——— N. B., 2/Lt.	160	Whiteside, H., 2/Lt.	33
Walsh, R. E., Lieut.	16	——— J., Lieut.	25	——— N. L., Lieut.	140	——— H. S., Lieut.	150
Walter, C. G., Capt.	69	——— J. F. J., Lieut.	106	——— R. C., Lieut.	16	Whitfeld, G.H.P., Capt.	167
——— J. S., Capt.	21	——— J. H., 2/Lt.	137	——— S. R., 2/Lt.	161	Whiting, Wm. C., 2/Lt.	41
Walthew, F. S., 2/Lt.	131	——— J. L., Capt.	67	——— Walter, Lieut.	89	Whitington, L. A., Lieut.	137
Walton, H. W., 2/Lt.	51	——— L. C., Lieut.	41	——— T. A., Capt.	186	Whitley, W. E., 2/Lt.	43
——— L. S., 2/Lt.	42	——— M. R., Lieut.	93	Welman, J. B., 2/Lt.	180	Whitlock, A. W., Lieut.	30
——— M. J., 2/Lt.	137	——— M. T., Fl.-Sub.-Lt.	157	Welsby, W. F., 2/Lt.	17	——— H. H., 2/Lt.	174
Walters, A. J. C., 2/Lt.	56	——— N. T., 2/Lt.	160	Welsh, W. A., Capt.	68	Whitney, R. T., 2/Lt.	150
Wand-Tetley, Lieut.	93	——— N. V., Lieut.	13	Wenn, J. L., 2/Lt., M.C.	87	Whitrow, P. B., Lieut.	84
Wanstall, L., 2/Lt. (A/Capt.), M.C.	88	——— S. H., Lt.	61	Wensley, J. H., Lieut.	160	Whittaker, B. K., 2/Lt.	95
Warbrick, H. J., 2/Lt.	24	——— T. W. N., 2/Lt.	127	Wesson, J. S., Lieut.	179	——— F. W., Capt.	40
Warburton, E., 2/Lt.	79	——— W., Lieut.	27	West, C. H. L., Lieut.	113	——— R., Capt.	82
——— E. D., 2/Lt.	151	Watt, A., 2/Lt.	104	——— W. G., Major	66	Whittall, F. K. B., Lieut.	62
——— P., 2/Lt.	65	——— A. G. M., 2/Lt.	103	Westby, F. H., Lieut.	99	Whittell, W. I., 2/Lt.	41
——— S. E., 2/Lt., M.C., M.M.	99	——— H. J., 2/Lt.	81	Westcott, G. F., Lieut.	156	Whittingham, H., Major	15
——— T., 2/Lt.	172	——— John A., Capt.	92	Westfield, F. J., Lieut.	161	Whittington, R. N., Capt.	31
——— W., Capt.	132	——— K. M., 2/Lt.	179	Westing, C. F., 2/Lt.	160	Whittle, O. L., Capt.	148
Warbutton, G., 2/Lt.	117	——— W. H., 2/Lt.	155	Weston, G. A., Rev.	135	Whitworth, H., Lieut.	158
Ward, A., Lieut.	180	Watts, C. V., 2/Lt.	32	——— P. O., Capt.	182	Whyte, A., Capt.	20
——— A. A., 2/Lt.	157	——— E., Capt.	84	Westwood, A. L., 2/Lt.	85	——— J. C., 2/Lt.	103
——— A. E., 2/Lt.	115	——— F. H., Capt.	15	Wetenhall, J. P., 2/Lt.	124	——— J. R., Lieut.	97
——— A. H., 2/Lt.	37	——— J. A., 2/Lt.	48	Whale, J., 2/Lt.	63	——— R. Paisley	165
——— A. O., 2/Lt.	32	——— P., Lieut.	144	Wharrier, R. H., Capt.	101	——— W.W., Lieut.	14
——— A. P., 2/Lt.	78	——— R., 2/Lt.	149	Wharton, C. E., 2/Lt.	164	Wickenden, H. J., 2/Lt.	79
——— E. S., Capt.	178	——— W. E., 2/Lt.	157	——— H. A., 2/Lt.	117	Wickett, T. H., Lieut.	153
——— H. E., Capt.	22	Waud, C. W. H. P., Lieut.	21	Wheatley, A. E., Capt.	21	Wickham, W. C., 2/Lt.	121
——— H. K., Capt.	131	Waugh, Alec., Lieut.	117	Wheeler, F., 2/Lt.	32	Wicks, W. E., 2/Lt.	123
——— H. S., 2/Lt.	147	——— F. F., Capt.	52	——— L. F., 2/Lt.	156	Widgery, H. J., 2/Lt.	76
——— K. H. W., 2/Lt.	90	Wavell-Paxton, R. J., Capt.	18	——— V., 2/Lt.	128	Wigan, A. P. C., 2/Lt.	160
——— L. N., Lieut.	158	Waydelin, F. W., Capt.	84	Whelan, H. G., Lieut.	113	Wiggans, D. E., Capt.	116
——— W. A., Lieut.	54	Weall, T. G., 2/Lt.	121	Wherry, J. H., Lieut.	60	——— J. T. V. Capt.	27
Ward-Davis, W. L., Lieut.	92	Wearne, A., 2/Lt.	138	Whincup, H., 2/Lt.	97	Wiggett, A. J., 2/Lt.	92
Warden, G. W., Major	23	Weaterton, S., 2/Lt.	25	Whistler, L. G., 2/Lt.	69	Wiggins, H., 2/Lt.	40
Wardlaw, J. M., Capt.	56	Weatherill, G., 2/Lt.	42	Whitaker, G. G., Lieut.	99	Wigley, L., 2/Lt.	155
Wardell, J. M., Capt.	48	Weaver, J., Capt.	164	——— H. G., Capt.	72	Wignall, G., 2/Lt.	167
Wardle, L. F., 2/Lt.	128	Webb, Charles, 2/Lt.	125	——— J. A. C., Capt.	18	Wike, W., Major	51
Ware, D. R., 2/Lt.	180	——— C. G., Capt.	92	——— J. W., Capt.	11	Wilce, W. J., 2/Lt.	39
——— G. R., 2/Lt.	43	——— G. H., 2/Lt.	56	——— S. G., 2/Lt.	70	Wilcox, C. H., 2/Lt.	173
——— H. E. A., 2/Lt.	155	——— G. W., 2/Lt.	77	Whitbourn, C. D., 2/Lt.	84	——— A. J., Chap.	180
Warne, H. F. M., Major	129	——— H. E., 2/Lt.	49	Whitbread, G. F., 2/Lt.	89	——— E. N., Capt.	127
Warner, C. T., Capt.	183	——— H. R., Capt.	70	White, A. J., 2/Lt.	24	——— G., 2/Lt.	31
——— W. E., 2/Lt.	41	——— R. R., 2/Lt.	66	——— A. M., 2/Lt.	19	——— H., 2/Lt.	40
Warnock, Lieut.	110	——— S. H., 2/Lt.	84	——— D. C., 2/Lt.	34	Wild, F. J., 2/Lt.	65
Warr, A. E., Major	20	Webber, Maurice, 2/Lt.	82	——— G., Capt.	186	——— O., Lieut.	82
Warre-Dymond, G. W., Capt.	66	——— N. V., Lieut.	86	——— George, Major	26	——— S. V., Sub.-Lt.	144
Warren, A. N., Lieut.	115	Webster, E. C., 2/Lt.	53	——— H., Sub.-Lt.	177	Wilford, J. R., Fl. Sub-Lt	177
——— A. P., 2/Lt.	151	——— John, Lieut.	164	——— H. E., 2/Lt.	87	Wilken, A. G., Capt. & Chap.	140
——— D. F., 2/Lt.	114	——— T. M., 2/Lt.	155	——— H. P., Capt.	126	——— W. A., 2/Lt.	17
——— D. D., Lieut.	45	Wedgwood, F.C.B., 2/Lt.	161	——— H. W., Capt.	37	Wilkes, A. H. P., 2/Lt.	14
——— F. S., Lieut.	126	Weeks, E. A., 2/Lt.	65	——— I. H., 2/Lt.	14	Wilkie, H. J., Capt.	58
——— M., 2/Lt.	20	Weighill, E. H., Capt.	49	——— P. J., 2/Lt.	91	——— J., 2/Lt.	13
Washington, J. N. C., 2/Lt.	146	——— E. N. O., 2/Lt.	80	——— P. R., Capt.	162	——— J. F. McL., 2/Lt.	74
Wasley, V. B., 2/Lt.	62	Weir, Archibald, 2/Lt.	54	——— R., 2/Lt.	102	——— R. C., 2/Lt.	19
Waterhouse, Herbert, Capt.	77	——— A. G., Lieut.	146	——— R. E., 2/Lt.	165	Wilkin, B. O., 2/Lt.	146
Waters, C. B., Lieut.	155	——— H. L., Lieut.	109	——— R. W., Lieut.	150	——— F. G. W., 2/Lt.	114
——— H. E., 2/Lt.	153	——— William, 2/Lt.	104	——— S., Lieut.	178	——— W. H., Capt.	77
Watkins, D., 2/Lt.	15	Welbourne, A. C., Lieut.	86	——— S. G., 2/Lt.	86	Wilkins, H. O. D., Capt.	154
——— H. Cyril, Lieut.	73	Welch, T. A. L., Capt.	102	——— T. G., Capt.	73	Wilkinson, B. L., 2/Lt.	12
		Welchman, P. E., Capt.	172	——— T. W., Capt.	181	——— D. F., 2/Lt.	128
		Weld, D. S., Lieut.	154	——— T. W., 2/Lt.	154	——— D. S., Lieut.	155
		Weldon, T., 2/Lt.	85	——— W. D., 2/Lt.	103	——— E., 2/Lt.	95
				——— W. E., 2/Lt.	14	——— F. D., Lieut.	23
				Whitehead, A. D., Lieut.	150		
				——— F., 2/Lt.	32		

	PAGE		PAGE		PAGE		PAGE
Wilkinson, H., Capt.	101	Wilson, D. C., Major, D.S.O.	13	Wischer, J. V., 2/Lt.	152	Wright, A. Y., Rev.	186
———— H. M., Capt.	55	———— D. W., Lieut.	166	Wisdon, A. L., 2/Lt.	129	———— C. M., 2/Lt.	78
———— J. R., Lieut	50	———— E. J., 2/Lt.	53	Wise, D., Capt.	113	———— D. C., Lieut.	159
Wilks, J. M., 2/Lc.	63	———— F. A., Lt.-Col.	185	Withers, H. G., 2/Lt.	179	———— D. H., 2/Lt.	111
Will, G. K., Lieut.	41	———— F. C., Lieut.	123	With, P. M., 2/Lt.	127	———— Ernest, 2/Lt.	44
———— W. B. J., Lieut.	62	———— H. B. B., Lieut.	162	Witherington, A. S., Lieut.	14	———— E. F., Lieut.	170
Willcox, C. E., 2/Lt.	35	———— F. H., Lieut.	150	Withers, K. G., Lieut.	187	———— G. B., 2/Lt.	178
———— W. T., 2/Lt.	149	———— F. H., Lieut.	141	Witts, Chas., Capt.	134	———— G. St. J., 2/Lt.	50
Wilies, A. H., 2/Lt.	28	———— F. J. C., Capt.	146	Witty, William, 2/Lt.	96	———— H. W., 2/Lt.	37
Willey, B., 2/Lt.	42	———— F. T., Major	37	Wodehouse, E., 2/Lt.	56	———— J. W., 2/Lt.	71
Williams, Lieut.	166	———— F. W. B., Lieut.	185	Wolfenden, F., Capt.	97	———— M. H., 2/Lt.	86
———— A G, 2/Lt.	83	———— G. E. H., Capt	143	Womersley, A. S., Lieut.	95	———— M. T., Lieut.	155
———— A. M., A/Capt., M.C.	81	———— H., Lieut.	117	Wood, A. M., Capt. (A/Major)	134	———— P. L., 2/Lt.	43
———— C. D., 2/Lt.	82	———— H. J., 2/Lt.	27	———— A. S., Capt.	49	———— S. G., Lieut.	83
———— E. Ll., 2/Lt.	121	———— J., 2/Lt.	41	———— A. W., Lieut.	152	Wrighton, E., Lieut.	78
———— E. G., Capt.	63	———— J. D., Lieut.	140	———— C. L., Lieut.	168	Wrigley, E., 2/Lt.	80
———— E. J., Lieut.	185	———— J. O., 2/Lt.	101	———— C. W., 2/Lt.	20	Wylde, B. J. F., 2/Lt.	81
———— F. C., 2/Lt.	60	———— J. R., Lieut.	86	———— F., Capt.	96	Wylie, J. K., 2/Lt.	110
———— F. P. G., Lieut.	185	———— L. G., 2/Lt.	53	———— F. H., Lieut.	141	———— Macleod, Capt.	143
———— F. T., 2/Lt.	57	———— L. W., Lieut.	100	———— H. H., Lieut.	168	Wyman, J. B. H., 2/Lt.	156
———— G., 2/Lt.	73	———— M., 2/Lt.	125	———— J. A. V., 2/Lt.	83	Wymer, G. P., Capt.	94
———— G. B., Capt., M.C.	46	———— M. G., 2/Lt.	168	———— J. C., 2/Lt.	162	Wyncoll, A. W., 2/Lt.	163
———— G. E., 2/Lt.	124	———— N., 2/Lt.	166	———— J. H. A., Lieut.	81	Wyndham, J. R., Major	93
———— G. E. E., 2/Lt.	98	———— N. M., Capt.	184	———— J. L., Lieut.	101	Wynne, Albert, Lieut.	56
———— G. G. R., Lieut.	189	———— R., 2/Lt.	80	———— J. O., 2/Lt.	172	———— A. F., 2/Lt.	159
———— G. J., Observer	180	———— R., Capt.	116	———— J. S., 2/Lt.	12	———— G. C., Capt.	85
———— H., 2/Lt.	97	———— R., 2/Lt.	116	———— P., Capt.	182	Wynne-Eyton, R. M., Capt.	160
———— H., 2/Lt.	31	———— R., 2/Lt.	16	———— Ronald, 2/Lt.	149		
———— J. R., Czpt.	33	———— R., Lieut.	123	———— S. C., 2/Lt.	118	Yacomeni, W. McE., 2/Lt.	24
———— J. R., Capt.	56	———— R. E., Capt.	148	———— T. W., 2/Lt.	46	Yapp, G. H., Lieut.	51
———— L. J., 2/Lt.	159	———— S. B., 2/Lt.	43	———— W. R., Capt.	130	Yardley, J. H., 2/Lt.	12
———— N. E., Lieut.	168	———— T., Lieut.	189	Woodacre, A., 2/Lt.	96	Yates, D., Lieut.	123
———— O. J., Lieut.	100	———— T. C., 2/Lt.	147	Woodcock, A. T., 2/Lt.	43	———— G. A., 2/Lt.	71
———— R. J., Capt.	144	———— T. H., Lieut.	109	———— H. F., 2/Lt.	24	———— J. A., Lieut.	167
———— S. G., 2/Lt.	159	———— T. S., 2/Lt.	160	Woodfield, F. W., 2/Lt.	181	———— L. W. P., Capt.	60
———— S. H., Lieut.	94	———— W., Major	10	Woodford, A. F., Lieut.	45	———— R. A., Lieut.	165
———— S. M., 2/Lt.	120	———— W., Lieut.	109	Woodhead, W., 2/Lt.	115	Yearsley, K. D., Capt.	185
———— S. W., Lieut.	155	———— W. A., 2/Lt.	171	Woodhouse, C. M., Lieut.	71	Yeate-Brown, F. C., Capt.	181
———— T. A., 2/Lt.	49	———— W. K., Lieut.	164	Wooding, James, 2/Lt.	168	Yelland, W., 2/Lt.	64
———— V., Maj.-Gen.	139	Wilson-Browne, R. M., Lieut.	148	———— P. H., 2/Lt.	17	Yellowlees, J., Capt.	39
———— W. A., Lieut.	55	Wimble, A. S., Capt.	7	Woodland, P., Lieut.	181	Yelverton, C. N., 2/Lt.	172
———— W. A., 2/Lt	12	Windebank, S., 2/Lt.	65	Woodman, K.C.B., 2/Lt.	165	Yendell, R. B., 2/Lt.	125
———— W. E., Lt. Col.	55	Winder, E., 2/Lt.	96	Woodrow, N. G., 2/Lt.	36	Yeo, H. A., 2/Lt.	158
———— W. M., 2/Lt.	73	———— H. J., Lieut.	10	———— W. H. V., 2/Lt.	78	Yeomans, F. L., 2/Lt.	157
Williams-Taylor, T., Lieut.	181	Windle, B. C., 2/Lt.	159	Woods, A., 2/Lt.	76	———— J. H. M., Lieut. M.C.	170
Williams-Thomas, F. S., Major	178	Windover, W. E., Capt.	174	———— Alex., Capt.	117	Yerex, Lowell, Lieut.	170
Williamson, A., 2/Lt.	26	Windrum, C. H., Lieut.	150	———— H. E., 2/Lt.	26	Youens, H. St. J. E., Fl.-Sub-Lt.	177
———— G. S., Lt.-Col.	131	Windsor, D. R., 2/Lt.	57	———— J., 2/Lt.	15	Young, A., 2/Lt.	116
———— J. C., 2/Lt.	162	———— J., 2/Lt.	179	———— M. E., 2/Lt.	150	———— A. M., 2/Lt.	19
———— T., Lieut.	79	Winfield-Smith, S. C., Capt.	186	Woodward, E. G., Capt.	96	———— G. W., Lieut.	93
———— W. M., Capt.	85	Wing, A., Lieut.	31	Woodyer, C. de Witte, Capt.	55	———— E. J., Lieut.	21
Willis, A., Capt.	25	———— W. R., Flt. Sub.-Lt.	177	Wookey, H. C., 2/Lt.	157	———— E. W., Lieut.	17
———— G. H., 2/Lt.	92	Wingate-Gray, A. G., Lieut.	161	Woolcott, R., 2/Lt.	44	———— F., Major	54
———— N. D., Lieut.	172	Wingfield, E. N., 2/Lt.	149	Woolley, C. L., Lieut.	181	———— F. C., 2/Lt.	76
Willison, E., Lieut.	43	———— L. A., 2/Lt.	147	———— D. B., Lieut.	150	———— G. E., 2/Lt.	57
Willmer, H. T., Capt.	34	Winkler, M. H., Lieut.	174	———— R. M., Capt.	45	———— G. W., Lieut.	74
Willmott, B. C. N., Capt.	76	———— W. O. B., 2/Lt.	153	Woolliams, F. H., 2/Lt.	152	———— Hugh, 2/Lt.	115
———— F. B., 2/Lt.	159	Winkworth, R. W., 2/Lt.	31	Woolnough, C. W. F., Lieut.	117	———— Harry, 2/Lt.	109
———— S. J., Lieut.	27	Winn, L. S., Lieut.	117	Wooster, H. T. L., 2/Lt.	82	———— J. G., 2/Lt.	155
Willock, G. W., Capt.	59	Wise, S., Lieut.	188	———— F. G. L., 2/Lt.	61	———— J. H., 2/Lt.	159
Willoughby, H., Lieut.	70	Winsloe, H. E., Major	185	Worrall, W. R., 2/Lt.	41	———— M. A., 2/Lt.	116
Wills, C. R., Capt.	132	Winston, J. H. E., Lieut.	49	Worsley, R. S. L., 2/Lt.	151	———— M. C. B. K., Lieut.	67
———— O. S. D., Lieut.	34	Winter, Lieut.	131	———— W., Capt.	48	———— N. E., Capt.	69
———— S. T., 2/Lt.	152	———— A. E., 2/Lt.	28	Wotherspoon, G. W., Lieut.	104	———— R., Lieut.	50
Wilmot, E. P., 2/Lt., M.C.	158	———— F. C., 2/Lt.	23	———— H.C.F., A/Capt.	36	———— S. H., Lieut.	30
Wilson, A. E., 2/Lt.	34	———— R. L. V., 2/Lt.	111	Wotton, H. S., 2/Lt.	22	———— T., 2/Lt.	56
———— A. I., Lieut.	101	———— W. H., 2/Lt.	157	Wray, C. B., 2/Lt.	80	———— V. C. H., 2/Lt.	76
———— C. B., Capt., M.C.	176	Winterbotham, F. W., Lieut.	154	———— W. S., 2/Lt.	100	———— W., 2/Lt.	24
———— C. B., Lieut.	147	Wisbey, George W., 2/Lt.	43	Wreford, C. B., 2/Lt.	36	———— W. P., Capt.	135
———— D. A., Capt.	132			Wren, H. L., Lieut.	175	———— W. W., Capt.	114
				Wrigglesworth, E. H., Lieut.	47	Younger, J. E., Capt.	10
						Zieman, J. R., Lieut.	163